Research Handbook on Services Management

Edited by

Mark M. Davis

Formerly of Bentley University, USA

EE **Edward Elgar**
PUBLISHING

Cheltenham, UK • Northampton, MA, USA

Published by
Edward Elgar Publishing Limited
The Lypiatts
15 Lansdown Road
Cheltenham
Glos GL50 2JA
UK

Edward Elgar Publishing, Inc.
William Pratt House
9 Dewey Court
Northampton
Massachusetts 01060
USA

Paperback edition 2024

A catalogue record for this book
is available from the British Library

Library of Congress Control Number: 202938798

This book is available electronically in the **Elgar**online
Business subject collection
http://dx.doi.org/10.4337/9781800375659

ISBN 978 1 80037 564 2 (Hardback)
ISBN 978 1 80037 565 9 (eBook)
ISBN 978 1 03533 426 1 (Paperback)

Printed and bound by CPI Group (UK) Ltd, Croydon, CR0 4YY

Contents

List of contributors   vii

A tribute to Mark M. Davis   ix
Joy M. Field

Introduction to the Research Handbook on Services Management   x
Ravi S. Behara and Gang Li

PART I   SERVICE STRATEGY

1   Strategy in information intensive services   2
Uday M. Apte, Uday S. Karmarkar and Hiranya K. Nath

2   Servitization and innovation strategy – the trade-off between product
R&D and service investments   23
Ornella Benedettini and Christian Kowalkowski

3   Understanding scarcity strategies in service firms   36
Huiling Huang, Stephanie Q. Liu and Jay Kandampully

4   Adopting a low-contact, high-focus healthcare service strategy in the
era of pandemics   54
Uzay Damali, Enrico Secchi, Stephen S. Tax and Jeff Kessler

PART II   SERVICE INNOVATION AND DESIGN

5   Service innovation process in creative-intensive business services organizations   71
Fengjie Pan and Rohit Verma

6   Service design: managing services as a way of designing   88
Birgit Mager and Tina Weisser

7   Service support systems for ecostructuring decision support   103
Ralph D. Badinelli

8   Perceived justice and control of priority lines   117
Michael Dixon, David Rea, Liana Victorino and Craig Froehle

9   Co-creating services at the Base of the Pyramid (BoP): the role of bricolage   128
Karla Cabrera and Javier Reynoso

10   Failsafing service quality   143
Richard B. Chase and Douglas M. Stewart

11   Customer-focused service design for faster and more efficient services   153
Gang Li, Joy M. Field and Mark M. Davis

PART III   UNDERSTANDING AND SERVING CUSTOMERS

12   Customer success management   166
      Vijay Mehrotra and Krishnamoorthy Subramanian

13   Culture and religion in service provision   180
      Richard Metters

14   Are tech-savvy users more likely to use technology? An examination of
      market entry and customer experience   194
      Xin Ding

PART IV   HEALTHCARE SERVICES

15   Implications of COVID-19 on operations in healthcare services   212
      Sanjeev Bordoloi

16   Applying Lean healthcare in a non-profit hospital in Brazil   231
      *Ana Carolina Honda, Raquel Mizuki Eguchi Yoshida, Mateus Cecílio
      Gerolamo, Jeanne Liliane Marlene Michel and Mark M. Davis*

PART V   SERVICE ANALYTICS

17   Service science in a world flooded with data   247
      *Jorge Grenha Teixeira, Vera Miguéis, Henriqueta Nóvoa and
      João Falcão e Cunha*

18   The evolution of business analytics and their impact on the service industry   263
      Ronald Klimberg

19   Text analytics of service customer reviews and feedback: understanding
      customers' emotions and cognition in the hospitality industry   275
      Jie J. Zhang, Spring H. Han and Rohit Verma

PART VI   AI IN SERVICES

20   The service robot revolution   296
      Stefanie Paluch, Jochen Wirtz and Werner H. Kunz

21   Companion robots for well-being: a review and relational framework   309
      *Andrea Ruggiero, Dominik Mahr, Gaby Odekerken-Schröder, Tiziana Russo
      Spena and Cristina Mele*

22   Rise of humanoid robots in hospitality services   331
      Lina Zhong and Rohit Verma

Epilogue: Service 4.0   346
Ravi S. Behara
Index   348

Contributors

Uday M. Apte, Naval Postgraduate School, USA

Ralph D. Badinelli, Virginia Tech, USA

Ravi S. Behara, Florida Atlantic University, USA

Ornella Benedettini, Politecnico di Bari, Italy

Sanjeev Bordoloi, University of St. Thomas – Minnesota, USA

Karla Cabrera, Tecnológico de Monterrey, Mexico

Richard B. Chase, University of Southern California, USA

João Falcão e Cunha, University of Porto, Portugal

Uzay Damali, University of Wisconsin–La Crosse, USA

Mark M. Davis, formerly of Bentley University, USA

Xin Ding, Rutgers University, USA

Michael Dixon, Utah State University, USA

Joy M. Field, Boston College, USA

Craig Froehle, University of Cincinnati, USA

Mateus Cecílio Gerolamo, University of São Paulo, Brazil

Spring H. Han, Kyoto University, Japan

Ana Carolina Honda, University of São Paulo, Brazil

Huiling Huang, The Ohio State University, USA

Jay Kandampully, The Ohio State University, USA

Uday S. Karmarkar, UCLA Anderson School of Management, USA

Jeff Kessler, Allergy Associates of La Crosse, USA

Ronald Klimberg, Saint Joseph's University, USA

Christian Kowalkowski, Linköping University, Sweden

Werner H. Kunz, University of Massachusetts Boston, USA

Gang Li, Bentley University, USA

Stephanie Q. Liu, The Ohio State University, USA

Birgit Mager, Köln International School of Design and Service Design Network, Germany

Dominik Mahr, Maastricht University, the Netherlands

Vijay Mehrotra, University of San Francisco, USA

Cristina Mele, University of Naples Federico II, Italy

Richard Metters, Texas A&M University, USA

Jeanne Liliane Marlene Michel, Federal University of São Carlos, Brazil

Vera Miguéis, University of Porto, Portugal

Hiranya K. Nath, Sam Houston State University, USA

Henriqueta Nóvoa, University of Porto, Portugal

Gaby Odekerken-Schröder, Maastricht University, the Netherlands

Stefanie Paluch, RWTH Aachen University, Germany

Fengjie Pan, University of Birmingham, UK

David Rea, University of Cincinnati, USA

Javier Reynoso, Tecnológico de Monterrey, Mexico

Andrea Ruggiero, University of Naples Federico II, Italy

Enrico Secchi, University College Dublin, Ireland

Tiziana Russo Spena, University of Naples Federico II, Italy

Douglas M. Stewart, The University of New Mexico, USA

Krishnamoorthy Subramanian, President, STIMS Institute, USA

Stephen S. Tax, University of Victoria, Canada

Jorge Grenha Teixeira, University of Porto, Portugal

Rohit Verma, Cornell University, USA

Liana Victorino, University of Victoria, Canada

Tina Weisser, Innovation and Organizational Change Consultant, Munich, Germany

Jochen Wirtz, National University of Singapore, Singapore

Raquel Mizuki Eguchi Yoshida, University of São Paulo, Brazil

Jie J. Zhang, University of Victoria, Canada

Lina Zhong, Beijing International Studies University, China, and Cornell University, USA

A tribute to Mark M. Davis
Joy M. Field

Mark M. Davis: Scholar, Teacher, and Friend

Mark M. Davis, Professor of Operations Management at Bentley University, and Decision Sciences Institute Fellow and Past President, was the inspiration behind this handbook. He worked tirelessly as its editor to harness the collective wisdom of top service management scholars and to make it available to the broader service management community. It is a tribute to Mark's stature in the service management field – as well as his tenacity – that he was able to assemble such a diverse and esteemed team of scholars as contributors to the handbook. However, Mark was not only our colleague, but also a dear friend to all of us involved with this handbook and to so many others. Sadly, he passed away on February 24, 2021, before the handbook was completed.

Mark was a foundational scholar in service operations; his most-cited research articles focus on the relationship between waiting times and customer satisfaction. He was also a co-author of both service operations and operations management textbooks. As a senior scholar, Mark felt it was his responsibility to give back and to mentor junior faculty. As his colleagues at Bentley University and other academic institutions can attest, Mark's early support was instrumental to their career progressions. In recognition of his scholarly impact, Bentley University awarded him its highest research honor, the 2017–2018 Mee Family Prize for "a lifetime of research excellence." Mark continued to be an active researcher until the end, with this handbook intended as the capstone to his storied career.

Mark's teaching skills and devotion to his students were legendary. He stayed in touch with many of his past students, offering advice as they began their careers and his continuing friendship long after they graduated from Bentley. Wherever he traveled in the world (and Mark loved to travel!), he would contact his vast network of former students, who were delighted to reconnect with their beloved professor. Many of Mark's travels included teaching at locations around the world. He especially loved his many times teaching at HEC Paris, where he could practice his questionable French language skills, much to the amusement of his students.

But more than the accomplishments in his professional life, Mark leaves a legacy of family, friends, and colleagues who love and respect him for the person he was. As news of Mark's passing spread, so many beautiful tributes to Mark poured in from colleagues, including stories of their personal connections to him. Let me add one of my own. I originally met Mark through one of the pancake breakfasts he hosted at Bentley University to bring together academics and practitioners in the Boston area. He and I went on to have a close professional relationship, co-authoring multiple research articles. We also became good friends. My husband and I had the honor of attending his 50th wedding anniversary party a few years ago, celebrating Mark and his wife, Carolyn (Cookie). After many loving tributes to Mark and Cookie, Mark stood up and spoke of his tremendous support system of family and friends during his cancer treatments. Well, Mark, what goes around comes around. He was always there for the people he cared about, and they were there for him when he needed them – truly a life well lived. Mark was one of a kind and will be sorely missed.

Joy M. Field

Introduction to the *Research Handbook on Services Management*
Ravi S. Behara and Gang Li

Professor Mark Davis brought together a global team of service researchers, and their collective expertise is reflected in the chapters of this book. It is truly a compendium of the wisdom of an expert crowd. It reflects the latest breakthroughs of researchers as well as best practices in services, providing a handbook for quick adoption and ready reference to both researchers and practitioners worldwide. The book's chapters can be naturally categorized into two schemes, each with three major parts, from a big-picture, strategic perspective, to more focused discussions on issues including analytics and service robots and their impact.

The first half of the book is focused on service strategy and operations management. Part I provides a strategic perspective that is informed and influenced by current and emerging forces impacting service organizations. In Chapter 1, Apte, Karmakar, and Nath lead with a comprehensive discussion of information intensive services whose growth has been driven by advances in information and communication technologies in recent decades. They guide us through several general service strategies that are technology induced, as well as strategies that are sector specific. Other specific approaches are explored in the remaining chapters of Part I. An increased focus on servitization as a strategy adopted by manufacturing companies has often led to significant changes of their innovation strategy to the detriment of product innovation. Benedettini and Kowalkowski examine the relationship and trade-offs between servitization and product innovation in Chapter 2, and highlight the notion of research and development (R&D) strength, a company's competency in their R&D activities. Huang, Liu, and Kandampully, in Chapter 3, alert us of the unintended consequences of scarcity strategies. They provide theoretical and managerial insights into how to effectively manage scarcity strategies. In Chapter 4, Damali, Secchi, Tax, and Kessler explore the challenges of shifting to a high-focus, low-contact strategy in healthcare coupled with a growth strategy, only to be further complicated by the COVID-19 pandemic. The rapid transition to low-contact services due to the pandemic has been seen not only in healthcare, with the rapid expansion of telemedicine, but in most other traditional high-contact services as well.

In Part II, a variety of important emerging and established challenges in service innovation and design are addressed. In Chapter 5, Pan and Verma study the new service development process in creative-intensive service organizations using the advertising industry as their context. They specifically identify a problem diagnosis phase as a precursor to the traditional first step of idea conceptualization, and an evaluation and learning phase that follows the traditional last phase of idea commercialization. Mager and Weisser begin Chapter 6 by highlighting the importance and impact of service design. They broaden this discussion to show how service design can be an integral part of service management, and they envision a future in which service organizations dedicate themselves to design as a long-term cultural commitment. Badinelli focuses on how successful design and innovation in services is predicated on the quality of decision-making by the multiple actors involved. In Chapter 7, he develops a detailed framework for a service support system to guide the ecostructuring decision-making that is at the core of enabling a successful service journey.

In Chapter 8, Dixon, Rea, Victorino, and Froehle tackle a long-standing issue that is integral to all service journeys, that of waiting in line. However, they focus on the increasingly pervasive priority lines, and address their design through the distinctly humanistic perspectives of fairness, perceived justice, perceived control, and social norms. They leave us with many questions that still need to be explored regarding prioritizing some customers, especially as we move into a future in which customers are acutely aware of the many societal inequities that exist. Cabrera and Reynoso tackle the other end of the societal spectrum in Chapter 9 by exploring micro services at the Base of the Pyramid (BoP). They specifically explore the role of bricolage, "making do with what is available," as a basis for co-creation in informal service micro-businesses at the BoP. Looking at a future where climate change could affect resource availability and distribution globally, a better understanding of services in resource-constrained settings would benefit the development of sustainable practices and innovation that are needed to adapt to such changes.

Chase and Stewart remind us that to err is human, but to failsafe is divine! In Chapter 10, they provide a framework to create and deploy failsafe devices or procedures to help ensure the delivery of quality services. In Chapter 11, Li, Field, and Davis continue in this spirit by proposing "a failsafe" for services so they may continue to deliver greater responsiveness at ever lower costs. They adopt a systems perspective and propose an end to the classic service design that decouples back-office and front-office operations. They propose constant staffing levels and shared employee resources as a means to develop integrated operations. After all, there is only one office that serves the customer.

Part III of the book leans into understanding and serving customers and goes beyond the traditional customer satisfaction perspective. Mehrotra introduces a growing organizational philosophy and functional area called customer success management in Chapter 12. This is a systemic customer-facing function whose outcome is the mutual success of the firm and its customers. In Chapter 13, Metters explores service provision and consumption from cultural and religious belief perspectives of both employees and customers. He provides various examples and highlights the paucity of research in the field of national culture and religion in service operations. Ding, in Chapter 14, discusses his research findings that show a strong relationship between customer technology readiness and service outcomes, including frequent usage of technology-based services. The discussion is derived from the results of a survey of customers of major online financial services.

The second half of the book is focused on specific domains that are at the forefront of services today. Part IV presents a timely discussion of healthcare services, as the world continues to deal with the pandemic. In Chapter 15, Bordoloi leads us through the impact of the pandemic on a variety of healthcare operations issues, as he helps us understand what "normal" post-pandemic operations could look like, from the traditional issues of demand–supply management to the adoption of emerging technologies. Honda, Yoshida, Gerolamo, Michel, and Davis, in Chapter 16, present a case study of applying lean principles at a large non-profit hospital in Brazil. The case highlights the successful implementation of lean principles resulting in not just process improvements, but also significant cost savings. This approach can be transferred to other developing economies to address inequities and improve healthcare services, as the world attempts to recover from a global disruption that has exposed the fragility of not just healthcare services, but all operations.

Parts V and VI address data analytics and artificial intelligence (AI), respectively. They are part of the toolkit that contemporary organizations are using to respond to an increasingly challenging environment by leveraging advanced technologies. Part V discusses the evolution of business analytics and its impact on service organizations. In Chapter 17, Teixeira, Miguéis, Nóvoa, and Falcão e Cunha highlight the impact of data science on services, especially in a sensor-driven, data-intensive, interconnected world. They systematically study the relationship between service science and data science and identify the recent emergence of research that integrates the two approaches. Klimberg traces the arc of history of business analytics and gives us a glimpse of its future in services in Chapter 18. He explores the transformation of service firms into analytically driven competitors and discusses the critical success factors that are essential for a successful transformation. Then, in Chapter 19, Zhang, Han, and Verma conclude Part V by demonstrating a data-driven business analytics study in the hospitality sector. They highlight the importance of unstructured data – customer comments, in this context – to explore customers' emotional and cognitive states as reflected in their textual feedback, and relate it to satisfaction ratings. In doing so, they provide an excellent use case of data-driven business analytics in services.

Part VI explores AI in services, specifically robotics, with an emphasis on service robots. The emergence of robots as companions and service providers makes the fantasy of *The Jetsons* (Hanna-Barbera's 1960s animation series about a utopian future) one step closer to reality. Paluch, Wirtz, and Kunz set the stage in Chapter 20 by developing a framework to help organizations deploy service robots on the front lines. They discuss a case in financial services and provide implications for managers who will certainly have to integrate robots into future operations in many services. In Chapter 21, Ruggiero, Mahr, Odekerken-Schröder, Spena, and Mele highlight the importance of social robots, and develop an integrated framework that provides a systematic understanding of this sub-domain in robotics. They introduce us to this realm through specific examples in wellness. Zhong and Verma evaluate hotel robots in Chapter 22. They find that, while service robots seem to be economically viable, the outcomes are mixed from a social perspective. Customers appear satisfied with robot-based service, while employees seem to be burdened with an increased workload associated with collaborating with robots. These chapters set the stage for future research into the development and deployment of service robots.

Together, the chapters of this book provide a collective peek into the future and epitomize Mark's insights and global perspective. The text represents an early foray into the new frontier of Service 4.0.

We thank all the contributors to this book for working with us to fulfill Mark's dream. We give special thanks to Joy Field for her memorable tribute to Mark. We also thank Ellen Pierce and Edward Elgar Publishing for their patience in guiding this effort to a successful completion.

PART I

SERVICE STRATEGY

1. Strategy in information intensive services

Uday M. Apte, Uday S. Karmarkar and Hiranya K. Nath

INTRODUCTION

There have been two major developments in the U.S. economy over the past half century. The first is the continuing shift from products to services. The service sector has become the dominant sector, generating most of the wealth and employment in the economy. The second development involves a shift of economic activities from the physical or material domain to the information domain of the economy. Machlup (1962) and Porat (1977) were among the first to identify and quantify this shift.

It is helpful to juxtapose the two broad trends mentioned above to create a conceptual framework for analyzing the structural changes in the U.S. economy (Apte et al., 2008, 2012, 2015). This "double dichotomy" divides the economy into four super sectors: material products, material services, information products, and information services (Figure 1.1a). In terms of value addition to the U.S. economy, the information services super sector has been the largest and fastest-growing segment of the economy over a period of three decades until the beginning of the 21st century. As shown by Nath et al. (2020), the contribution of information services to the U.S. gross national product (GNP) increased from about 36 percent in 1967 to more than 49 percent in 1992—the very beginning of the internet era—to about 57 percent in 2017. Figure 1.1b presents a snapshot of this evolution of the U.S. information services economy. There have been similar, yet somewhat modest, increases in employment and wage bill shares of information workers in the U.S. economy. The average annual wage of information workers has also been increasing faster than that of non-information workers in the past two decades; in 2017, it was about 56 percent higher. These trends in the U.S. economy have been driven by multiple factors, including productivity increases, globalization, demographics, and the creation of new products and services. New information and communications technologies (ICT) contribute to many of these underlying factors (though not demographics).

There have been substantial changes in the relative sizes of sectors and industries and in their structure and organization. As suggested by Chase and Apte (2007), in this paper we address the information intensive service (IIS) industries, which now constitute the largest part of the U.S. economy, and we focus on the emerging nature of management strategies for firms in those sectors. Major categories of IIS include transactional (financial, eCommerce), functional (search and information), content delivery (music, news), markets and exchanges (eBay), social networks (Facebook, Twitter), and asset sharing platforms (Airbnb, Uber), though that is not an exhaustive list. We also consider the information intensive components of physical services, such as transportation, health care, physical distribution, food services, and asset rentals, which in some cases are becoming significant portions of those industries. We also touch upon certain implications for products and the mechanism of "servitization," which is greatly expanded and supported by new technologies.

Delivery Form

		Product (Manufacturing)	**Service** (Process)
End Market	**Material (atoms)**	Chemicals Steel Automobiles Aerospace	Transportation Construction Maintenance & Repair Hospitality Retailing
	Information (bits)	Computers TV, Radio Books CDs, DVDs	Financial Services Professional Services Telecommunications Education

Source: Nath et al. (2020).

Figure 1.1a   *The structure and size of the U.S. information economy: 2 × 2 decomposition of the U.S. economy*

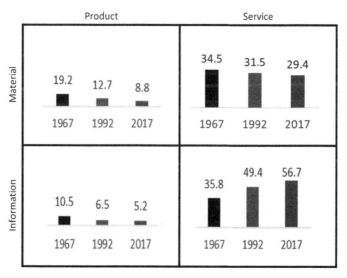

Source: Nath et al. (2020).

Figure 1.1b   *The structure and size of the U.S. information economy: evolution of the U.S. information economy (percent shares of GNP)*

CHARACTERISTICS OF IIS AND THE IMPLICATIONS FOR STRUCTURE AND STRATEGY

There is a well-known list of characteristics associated with "services," which are still to be found in most texts (Bordoloi et al., 2018; Johnston et al., 2012) and articles (Apte et al., 2008, 2012). A typical list of service characteristics usually includes:

● Intangible output, hard to quantify;
● No inventories;
● Lack of portability;
● Presence of customer;
● Simultaneous production and consumption;
● Customer may be a co-producer; and
● Valuation is subjective, experience matters.

It is easily seen that many of these do not always apply to IIS (Karmarkar & Apte, 2007). For example, on-demand music delivery has inventories, can be quantified to an extent, is portable, and is remotely provided. However, the customer is present in time and "online" even if not physically present, and valuation of the service is still subjective and experience based. On the other hand, there are some IIS industries to which most or all of the above characteristics apply. For education, especially for young children, all more or less still apply, though we are seeing changes. They also apply to business-to-business (B2B) services such as business consulting. However, increasingly with the application of technologies to the service delivery "chain," the economics and characteristics of information intensive processes are having a dramatic impact on many industry sectors.

The implications of the traditional characteristics listed for service strategies have been addressed by Bordoloi et al. (2018), Chase (1978), Fuchs (1968), Heskett (1986), and Karmarkar and Pitbladdo (1995). For example, the lack of portability of services has historically meant that access to the point of service delivery is a crucial issue, leading to the expansion of service delivery systems to provide easier access to customers. For IIS, the combination of some traditional characteristics, with the addition of the special features conferred by new technologies, can mean substantial shifts in strategic thinking. As an example, with respect to location decisions for service facilities, the mantra for retailing was "location, location, location." For retail banking, too, branch location was crucial for customer acquisition, service delivery, and retention. Subsequently, mini-branch and ATM networks became important features of the design of banking systems. Now, as retailing sales shift to eCommerce and online shopping, the importance of retail location is diminishing and that of home delivery is increasing. There is a similar effect at a faster rate with retail banking as transactions shift from branches to phones (smart or otherwise). As some aspects of service systems, such as location, decrease in importance, other aspects, such as the design of the online experience, become more crucial for competitive success.

The crucial new characteristics for IIS that derive from new digital technologies (Karmarkar, 2020, 2021) include:

● Convergence;
● Standardization of functions and interfaces;
● Reduction of logistics and processing costs;

- Speed of transportation, transactions, and processing;
- Real-time interactivity; and
- Capacity dispersion and miniaturization.

Convergence starts with the digitization of all kinds of information in all industries, in the form of bits. As an immediate consequence, storage, transportation, and processing all use essentially the same resources across all IIS sectors. Consumption and utilization of many services occur on screens, differing mainly in their portability and form factors. Not surprisingly, there is some convergence in the pattern of consumer use of and access to services so that traditional activity separation over time begins to blur. While it is less pronounced, there is a process of ongoing convergence in the design and structure of service processes as well. The convergence of service logistics and delivery systems across IIS sectors has led to a substantial standardization of functionality and interfaces. This, in turn, has led to a degree of commoditization and modularization of the end-to-end service chain. Convergence also means that the same technologies are available to all competitors and are common across all IIS sectors. Two consequences are an increased difficulty in differentiating services and easier entry for new firms—both leading to more intense competition.

The costs of all types of information processing and logistics have dropped precipitously over just a few decades. Combined with the speed of processing, convergence, and standardization, it has become feasible for third parties to provide much of the logistics and processing capacity required by companies and consumers as cloud, Web services, and "everything as a service" (XaaS). In a manner comparable to water and power systems, information logistics, storage, and processing have become utilities for industry and consumers. The costs of capacity and operations for many information intensive businesses have dropped, while fixed capital expenditures and period costs are being transformed to operating expenses. Again, these factors result in easier entry for new firms, low operating costs, and more intense price competition.

The high speed and low costs of information logistics expand geographic reach on the market side, and enable geographical dispersion of production, storage, and delivery systems across regional and global levels. At a macro level, the digitization of content, "convergence," the automation of on-demand delivery, and the ubiquity and speed of information logistics and personal devices have resulted in very different formats for IIS in terms of both service delivery processes and the larger structure of industries. In many cases, the changes have reached the point of extreme disruption already, with others likely to be affected in the near future.

Convergence, modularization, standard interfaces, and the commonality of underlying systems and technologies across sectors have led to functional decoupling of service stages, vertical de-integration, and lateral or horizontal expansion. These have in turn facilitated new entry in services, often at the level of just one operation or stage of the chain (Karmarkar, 2020). Other concomitant effects include the emergence of platforms and of bundling strategies.

Many of the strategic approaches that are effective for IIS sectors can be considered as being general in the sense that they apply to most sectors. However, there is a high level of heterogeneity across IIS, so that there are also strategies that are specific to certain industries and types of service. In the next section we outline important general strategies for IIS, some of which have been briefly mentioned above. In the subsequent section we present sector-specific strategic approaches for certain major IIS categories.

GENERAL IIS STRATEGIES

The broad characteristics of IIS that derive from the traditional properties of services in combination with the economics of information (Varian et al., 2014), and the functional characteristics of ICT, were outlined in the previous section. These give rise to the applicability of certain general—one might say generic—strategies that are relevant to most IIS sectors. It should be mentioned that some of the general strategies, such as industrialization and servitization, have been used in the past in manufacturing industries, while others are new. All are calibrated to serve the specific and emerging needs of IIS and take advantage of the capabilities of new ICT. Note also that some of these strategies overlap in scope but are separately listed here since they are often thought of conceptually under different labels and executed under different organizational jurisdictions—which are also in a concurrent process of change, albeit at a slower rate.

Service Industrialization

This is an umbrella term for the application of new technologies, designs, and configurations to service production and delivery processes at a more fine, granular level down to the individual operations (Apte et al., 2008, 2012; Karmarkar, 2004, 2010, 2014, 2020; Karmarkar & Apte, 2007; Levitt, 1970, 1972; Nath et al., 2020). While individual process changes can be very local, the overall effects are extensive and have significant strategic implications. The term correctly emphasizes the close analogy to the traditional notion of industrialization in manufacturing and logistics, though there are some key differences induced by the special features of information economics and information process characteristics. Service industrialization strategies include:

- Automation (software and hardware);
- Outsourcing and offshoring;
- Process re-engineering (internal and industry-wide);
- New service design and innovation;
- Web or communication enabling (of products), and the Internet of Things (IoT);
- Markets and exchanges;
- Social (many-to-many) and group (few-to-few) networks;
- Operations shifting;
- Self-service; and
- Mobile access and delivery.

Automation of information processes has rapidly progressed from the large-scale, backroom automation of the early days of computing to the extensive front-office automation, which is very much an ongoing phenomenon, with the pace partly depending on customer education and generational change effects. Outsourcing and offshoring are common terms for geographic dispersion of information processes and operations (Apte & Karmarkar, 2007). A fast-growing area driven by logistics convergence, which combines automation and outsourcing, is that of cloud and Web services for companies and consumers. Process re-engineering driven by the implementation of new technologies, possibly in the form of local substitution, can involve substantial changes in overall configuration. In classroom teaching, projecting slides does not completely change the lecture format; however, using online webcasts, recorded lectures, or interactive software is a highly disruptive change to the entire system. New service designs range from radical changes in logistics systems, as with music streaming, to completely new activities, such as online, multi-player games.

Web-enabling, in combination with IoT, is facilitating the automation and redesign of physical products and services in dramatic fashion.[1] One major arena of application is the home, where new services will proliferate, ranging from entertainment and security to self-managed and intelligent devices and systems, including environmental control, cleaning, and maintenance. Another is that of transportation, where automobiles and other vehicles are becoming networked, in addition to being automated and autonomous. Physical services, such as supply chains and distribution logistics, were early users of RFID (radio frequency identification) devices for tracking. Security and surveillance are other early applications for Web-enabling.

Markets and exchanges take many special forms, from simple search-and-match sites for low-volume specialized goods, to what are essentially transaction-less bartering and sharing mechanisms. Social and business networks can be passive posting sites or active group collaboration platforms. We have recently seen the huge implications of these networks for social and political activism. Examples of this phenomenon include the *Arab Spring* involving a series of anti-government protests, uprisings and armed rebellions that spread across much of the Arab worldin the early 2010s. The *#MeToo* movement that started in 2006 in the US is another example. It is a social movement against sexual abuse and harassment, in which people share their experience of sexual violence to empathize with and empower others who had endured similar experiences by letting them know that they are not alone.

Operations shifting refers to the relocation of tasks along information and service chains. For example, formatting of content used to be a specialized task undertaken by publishers and printers. Today much of text formatting happens at the creation stage, with the author using word processing and document formatting tools, to the point of following a template provided by the publisher. In some cases, operations shifting can lead to the elimination of jobs; secretarial employment is declining quite rapidly, as employees take on many administrative, scheduling, and interfacing activities formerly done by secretaries (Nath et al., 2020).

The rapid progress of ICT in the past several decades has made it increasingly feasible for employees to work remotely (also known as telecommuting or teleworking). In early 2020, employees in many companies were forced to self-isolate and work from home due to the novel coronavirus (COVID-19) pandemic. A survey showed that 17 percent of U.S. employees worked from home five days or more per week before the pandemic, and that share increased to 44 percent during the pandemic (Miltz, 2021). That experience has demonstrated that teleworking is not necessarily an impediment to productivity. For this reason, analysts have suggested that the pandemic could be a "tipping point" for teleworking and that different teleworking models are likely to persist.

Self-service is the special case of the shifting of operations to the end customer, which was already happening with physical services, such as gas stations and buffet restaurants. The recent and ongoing wave of front-office IIS automation in sectors like financial services, travel, content delivery, and eCommerce is complementary to self-service models, which again is having large effects on employment and therefore on human resources management and organizational structure. Finally, mobile access and delivery is complementary to geographic reach of services, dispersion of service creation and delivery, and process re-engineering and new service design. It is also affecting consumer and household appliance markets and creating new service models in a large spectrum of industries ranging from health care to security.

Servitization and Everything as a Service

The combination of convergence, low-cost logistics, rapid transport, and widespread logistics infrastructure (telecommunications) has made it feasible to substitute for many internal facilities and resources with outsourced services on a pay-as-you-go basis. Cloud and Web services are growing rapidly in both consumer and B2B markets. Modularization and interface standardization make it feasible to easily assemble custom systems as a combination of third-party outsourced services, together with local devices and apps, even at the level of individual consumers. While this shift is very much in progress, the result appears to be a situation where equipment and capacity need not be owned by the user. With adequate security of data and with specialized software, the resources are available as a utility. While we have mentioned the reductions in all the costs of equipment and processing in information chains, there are still economies of scale related to processing (servers) and logistics networks including communication networks that favor centralization. This model also provides more flexibility and lower costs of adopting new technologies and architectures. For servers, there is some shift toward parallel processing with low-cost chips and chips designed for graphics. For telecommunications, the major current change is to 5G with the next generation already on the horizon.

For companies, the strategic decisions here relate to considering how they wish to structure their position with respect to the use of information technology. This is not unlike a "buy or lease" decision, except that it has very substantial implications for organizational structure and internal function.[2] One of the major consequences is that the internal centralization of facilities and functions, typically induced by the traditional, large IT function, is now dissipating and disappearing. This has great advantages for flexibility and customization, but it can create huge security problems that are not acceptable in some areas. Hence, a brokerage firm or bank may be much less inclined to use outsourced Web services.

An analogous trend is that of "servitization," or the direct provision of end services substituting for the sale (and ownership) of products (Baines & Lightfoot, 2013; Vandermerwe & Rada, 1988). In part, this is simply a different business model where the equipment is leased and not sold. This was the approach used initially by Xerox for their large copiers, which were not sold but leased, and priced on the basis of usage measured by the number of copies made. On the one hand, this took away the risk of a large purchase and the headaches of machine maintenance from the user's domain. There was an incentive for controlling overuse, and a mechanism for tracking internal use across departments. On the other hand, Xerox enjoyed the benefits of a compelling sales proposition, and near-perfect price discrimination.

A recent version of servitization, or asset sharing, is the appearance of sharing platforms (Apte & Davis, 2019). Some of these match owners of assets with users. Others use their own asset pools, like fleets of scooters, and make them available as rentals. Again, neither of these models is completely new, but they have become feasible in areas such as "micro-mobility," enabled by the new infrastructure provided by Web-enabling, smartphones, and apps.

From a strategic perspective, one concern is the disruptive change faced by manufacturers due to the change in ownership patterns. It is clear that autonomous vehicles will greatly expand the market for car and ride sharing, with a reduction of individual car ownership and growth in fleets. This could also be an opportunity for car manufacturers to integrate forward into markets for car rental and even insurance. Both approaches are already visible.

Vertical De-Integration, Repositioning, and New Integration

Vertical de-integration in many information sectors is occurring as a consequence of competition, modularization, functional de-coupling, and new entry. It is becoming a strategic necessity as a response to changing conditions. Taking a positive view of this structural change means identifying the best new position to occupy in a chain. In content-based sectors, such as music and newspaper publishing, the largest firms historically occupied much of the chain, from recording music and capturing news events, to delivering content to customers on physical media. Those sectors have been heavily disrupted with de-integration and new entry. The most successful new entrants are positioned quite differently, with a changed focus and new business models driven by the changes in information economics. In music, the most successful new firms have assembled large libraries with subscription pricing and delivery for consumption on demand on mobile devices. Apple has been highly successful in integrating the library with consumption devices, which was not a feasible strategy in the older medium-based music content chain. Amazon has also attempted integration of content libraries with devices (Kindle and Fire), with somewhat less success. Vertical integration of service chains was historically based on media and the tie between information acquisition and distribution channels. That model no longer applies. Current forms of integration seem to be mostly about tying service production and delivery to personal devices and the consumption stage (i.e., forward rather than backward integration). As personal consumption devices become increasingly commoditized with standardization of delivery flows, files, and interfaces, this model may also decline. However, in general, it is essential for firms in IIS sectors to actively review structural changes in their industries and to consider how to reposition. Regrettably, in many cases, incumbents have failed to see the impending changes, and have lost ground, often irretrievably.

Bundling and Lateral Expansion

The phenomenon of convergence implies that very similar technologies and capacities are employed across a range of services. So unlike manufacturing and physical (material) services (like restaurants), the same technology providers expand laterally (horizontally) across IIS sectors. However, that does not necessarily lead to very high profits. Convergence also implies that the technologies are similar from the point of users. As a result, if there are multiple technology suppliers, price competition can be intense, and profits are curbed. This has been the situation with telecommunications, which in its basic form is an extreme commodity, dismissively labeled as a "bit pipe." This is also true to some extent of cloud and Web services where there have been recent drastic price cuts. However, there are some opportunities for differentiation by adding new services. The biggest opportunity for Web service differentiation is in Software as a Service (SaaS), and Web service providers are likely to be forced to go in that direction.

Bundling is a common consequence of the same factors that grow out of convergence. Firms in a particular sector that have strengths in one or more service stages have the ability to bundle multiple services, including those that are adjacent to their main offering, but also many that are not. Bundling additional services based on common underlying platforms and technical strengths can provide multiple benefits. An obvious one is revenue growth. Another is relative cost advantages resulting from economies of scale in the use of underlying resources and infrastructure, including server farms, communications costs, and software systems. A third benefit is the classic effect of increasing the appeal of the bundle to capture multiple heterogeneous customer segments. A fourth benefit is differentiation to escape the commoditization trap to mitigate the intensity of competition. Bundling is an important strategy for service sectors where competitors appear rather similar to customers due to commoditization of the service—retail banking is one example.

Business Models, Pricing, and Contracting

Services have always presented challenges for pricing and contracting with buyers and suppliers. The fundamental reasons include the intangibility of service outputs, difficulties of measuring outputs (in terms of both quantity and quality), the unobservability of efforts, and the difficulties of tying outputs to inputs and efforts (Karmarkar & Pitbladdo, 1995; Xue & Harker, 2002). Additionally, the application of new technologies in IIS has led to substantial restructuring in service chains and processes that often require a rethinking of pricing and contracting.

In many content delivery sectors, such as music and video distribution, there has been a convergence to a library model, priced on a subscription basis. That is to say, the customer pays an ongoing subscription fee for access to a large data store or library of content. For music, this is now the dominant format, with streamed delivery, and with a decline of pricing by the unit (based on physical media or unit downloads). For book publishing, unit pricing is still a dominant model, but it is entirely possible that it will also change to the library and subscription format. It is already the case that many intermediaries, such as public and institutional libraries, use the format.

For certain online services that involve a large number of small transactions or service contacts, and that face difficulties of quantifying the service "amount," the advertising-based revenue models have become common. The companies with the largest revenues today from digital advertising are Google and Facebook. Digital services have the advantage of a very high number of customer "touches" coupled with a high level of precision possible in terms of segmentation and customization. For Google, this comes down to the value of search terms for advertisers, with bidding and auction mechanisms used to give Google a high degree of price discrimination. In the case of Facebook, the company is able to compile a very rich description of its customers at an individual level, given the amount of information provided for free by those customers. The combination of touch volume and detailed data is leading to a shift of advertising money from the traditional media of print (news) and TV to online consumer services, to the point that the former services are being severely disrupted as their main source of revenue declines rapidly.

A complete review of business models for both revenue and cost management is not possible here. However, platform models for sharing of assets and XaaS are changing business models from asset sales and ownership to renting and leasing. Sharing platform models, such as Uber and Lyft, result in a rental model for cars where the platform owner does not own the fleet but is only an intermediary. However, the next wave of transition to autonomous vehicles will create a substantial new shift in the other direction, since it may be necessary for the rental platform to own a fleet of vehicles. There is also some likelihood that car manufacturers will consider integrating forward into the car rental business, in a form of "servitization." Web services are shifting capital expenditures for ICT assets to operating expenses. On the cost side, open sourcing and crowd sourcing can both reduce costs of acquisition, as well as improve the reach and availability of the markets for inputs.

The many massive structural shifts occurring in IIS, along with the creation of new IIS forms, will mean concomitant changes in terms of business models that will need to be addressed strategically.

Globalization and Geographic Dispersion

The low cost, high capacity (bandwidth), and speed of information transport over global distances has made it feasible to extend the reach of delivery systems to the most distant locations (Apte & Karmarkar, 2007; Apte & Mason, 1995; Apte et al., 2015; Mithas & Whitaker, 2007; Ramasubbu et al., 2008). As noted above, the importance of the location of service creation and delivery points has declined for transaction-based sectors, such as financial services, retail sales, content delivery, and many interactive consumer services like call centers and help desks. A similar shift has occurred on the supply and sourcing side for certain acquisition and processing activities, including many that occur interactively and in real time. Many backroom operations have already been dispersed to lower-cost locations, first regionally and then globally. However, there are still laggards. Many U.S. banks are still rather localized in both their supply and market-facing facilities. From a performance perspective, cost arbitrage and cost reduction is a major driver on the supply and production side, and revenues on the market side. In addition, temporal availability can be helped by global delivery systems that are always available, as with hotlines and call centers, and with internal processes, such as data management or accounting, and production processes like content management.

Platform Strategy

Platforms are a by-product of digital convergence (Karmarkar, 2020). A platform is a set of resources that provides the basis for the creation and delivery of multiple services streams. By that definition, platforms are not new. We could consider many consumer appliances, such as radios and televisions, to be platforms. Newspapers were very effective information platforms, carrying everything from news to cartoons and classified ads. However, the information platforms enabled by technology and the convergence of information chains have a huge impact and much wider domain (Parker & van Alstyne, 2018).

By examining the characteristics of an information service or information chain—including acquisition, processing, and capacity acquisition and delivery—it can be seen that there are not many points of differentiation. In fact, it appears that there are two major stages where differentiation or segmentation is substantial. One is that of service inputs or content creation and capture, including creative activities and performance. This stage appears to be highly fragmented, with individuals capturing a significant portion of revenues. The other is the service response and delivery stage, which for IIS is typically a software-based capacity located on a server. Despite convergence, this stage is usually quite distinct *across* service sectors. So, a server streaming music is very different from a search algorithm or a retail banking transaction server. However, the threat of commoditization and convergence still applies to platforms *within* service sectors, so that to customers, retail banking, music, or search sites do not look very different, as all use similar platform models. Once again, there are advantages from bundling services for differentiation and expansion.

On the market-facing side, platform strategies often involve bundling. Google is an excellent example. Though it began as a search engine, Google now provides hundreds of services. Many of these services are bundled in some form, though not all. Amazon's platform carries a range of services. Some services are bundled into Prime membership, which provides shipping and some special deals and discounts, includes streamed video at a discounted price, and continues to expand with other services.

Platforms are very visible in services that entail delivery to end consumers, but also in B2B markets as with Web and cloud services. In sourcing content, they also appear in social networks, and in many other applications.

Service Process Design and Experience Management

Most services historically involved customer presence at the service delivery site. So customer experience mattered, even for transaction-based services, such as banking and brokerage. Now on-site customer presence is decreasing or vanishing for many IIS, and this trend is likely to continue. As a result, customer experience is also less significant in such cases. But it would be a mistake to assume that it can be ignored completely. Because of the commoditization that goes along with digitization and convergence, experience can take on a disproportional significance as a differentiator. Of course, this is in the new form of "digital experience" which is perhaps not as well understood and is still evolving in terms of customer preferences as well as design choices. Initially, the design of online interfaces and processes was driven by functionality, mass provision, speed of response, and efficiency in a period of uncertain bandwidth. Over time there has been an evolution toward higher customer expectations regarding online experience, and competition driven by the experience quality enabled by higher bandwidth availability.

A good example of a basic and efficient website design is the look of a Google search page. There is nothing fancy about the design, which is simple with no pictures or complex formatting. Even the Google logo colors are the same primary colors (red, blue, yellow, and green) that seem most prevalent for kindergartens and sports cars. Apart from the high functional efficiency of Google's page rank search algorithm, the search has always returned results quickly and the Web page has loaded fast. This was especially important when bandwidth was lacking, so it was a noticeable differentiating factor. While efficiency, speed, and simplicity are still relevant for fast-loading pages, they may be less so as large bandwidths become more available. But there is still an issue as to whether a more complex or well-formatted page provides any positive experiential features, when all the user is going to do is to click on a few links to check what is on those sites. There is also the inertia inherent in a design and an existing strong brand's look and feel. Alphabet's logo, too, is a simple all-red logo. However, we do see some moves toward a more complex design with the Google title illustrations, doodles, animations, and games. It remains to be seen whether we will see some bigger design changes soon, though there doesn't seem to be a pressing need.

Digital experience management is naturally more important for sites where visitors spend much more time on a given visit and which they visit frequently. This includes eCommerce sites (Amazon, Etsy), sites for services such as financial (brokerage and banking), content delivery (music and video libraries, magazines, and education), and social networking or exchange (Facebook, Instagram, Pinterest). It is clear that such websites already pay much more attention to consumer experience, though there are many that still have a long way to go.

Special forms of experience management include approaches such as theatricalization and gamification. The former refers to the idea of adding "show" and story components to the service process. This can help to capture and engage customers. Examples include the use of videos, illustrations, and simulations to explain functionality, provide examples of application, or to convey references from other users. Gamification refers to the inclusion of interactive elements that involve the customer in a game that can help to improve engagement and possibly factors like learning. These kinds of entertaining designs can improve the customer's experience and act as differentiators or aids to memory and retention. Care must be taken to ensure that they do not create a backlash, or become tedious, if repeated too often.

Crowdsourcing, Open Sourcing, and the Gig Economy

Given the characteristics of IIS, the strategies of crowdsourcing, open sourcing, and making use of gig or freelance workers are particularly useful for accessing talented labor at reduced cost.

Crowdsourcing involves collecting information, opinions, or solutions for a task or project from a large number of knowledgeable people, typically via the internet. Crowdsourcing work allows companies to save time and money while tapping into people with different skills or thoughts from all over the world (Hossain & Kauranen, 2015). One of the most famous examples of a company that utilizes crowdsourcing is Waze. Its traffic and navigation app allows car drivers to share real-time traffic information with other drivers, saving them time and gas in their commute (kmuller, 2018). The other interesting, successful example is the grand prize offered by Netflix to a winning team of programmers for creating the best movie recommendation engine (Gerrish, 2018).

Wikipedia describes *open source* as a source code that is made freely available for possible modification and redistribution (Open source, 2020). Open-source software or other products are released under an open-source license as part of the open-source-software movement. Use of the term originated with software, but it has expanded beyond the software sector to cover other open content and forms of open collaboration. Open-source software projects are built and maintained by a network of volunteer programmers and are used in free as well as commercial products. Notable examples of open-source software include internet browsers Mozilla Firefox and Google Chromium, and the full office suite LibreOffice.

In the past two decades we have seen a shift to a new kind of work. The traditional "full-time job with benefits" is becoming less common, replaced by new "gig" or "freelance" work where individuals engage in supplemental, temporary, or project- or contract-based work. Recent surveys suggest that about 57 million Americans, or about 35 percent of the U.S. workforce, have some type of gig work arrangement (Upwork, 2019). Furthermore, presently, a roughly equal number of freelancers view freelancing as a long-term career choice as those who view it as a temporary way to make money.

SECTOR-SPECIFIC IIS STRATEGIES

Despite the phenomenon of convergence, IIS sectors are quite heterogeneous in terms of the markets they address, and the nature of their service delivery systems. While there are those strategic concepts that apply broadly across all IIS as described in the previous section, there are many strategies that are driven by sector-specific characteristics. We address a few leading examples in this section.

Transactional Services

Examples of transactional services include financial services (retail banking, brokerage), eCommerce (retailing, bill payment, subscriptions), and online consumer services (search, information). These sectors were very early to industrialize, and especially to automate back-room operations as well as the front-office operations and user interfaces. A service transaction may involve a single session or multiple contacts with the service provider. Providing capacity for executing these transactions online can cost far less than that under traditional formats, but the cost structure often involves a high initial fixed cost with low operating (variable) cost. These automated systems have the benefit of being highly accessible and available at all times. But they are also (still) somewhat inflexible in their operation. What is more, the large, fixed costs associated with the creation and change of automated systems mean that the initial launch and subsequent changes become sporadic or occasional events. The online presence becomes the new facade for the organization and is therefore a large component of the evolving brand. There can be a tendency to think of the service system in terms of efficiency, speed, and functionality. However, while these are all crucial, commoditization can be a continuing problem, and customer experience as well as differentiation are important.

Consider the example of retail banking. For the most part, service instances are brief and quite specific in terms of what the customer wishes to do, though there are exceptions with substantial and sometimes unpredictable variations. While the online service interface and service process can be well defined for basic transactions, exceptions pose a problem. Security is an important and occasionally tedious issue, but most customers are comfortable with that need. An issue with process design is that of commoditization, with a need to create some differentiation, while not losing on response time and efficiency. When a customer's requirement falls outside the basic and well-defined set, core automated processes may fail. The fallback processes, designed to handle those cases, are where many problems and failures are observed. Customers usually have online access to contact human resources, but the reality of those processes means that there is not a personal and familiar point of contact, especially if there are repeated problems. Furthermore, unlike a bank branch, when the initial online contact cannot solve an issue, a clumsy online handoff often follows. A possible solution is a response system where the initial responding person remains online to make the transfer, but this is rarely done, and the service instance usually devolves into the all-too-familiar online wait accompanied by assurances of the customer's importance. Banks have used backroom industrialization extensively, but they have been appropriately reluctant to consider outsourcing. However, they have formed partnerships and mergers to enable them to offer expanded and bundled services such as credit cards, investment services, and mortgages. Unfortunately, these bundles are often very poorly integrated with a lot of seams showing.

For insurance (home, car) the most important customer contact instance is when the customer has a severe problem. As above, the design of the response process, including personal contact and speed, are important. Apte et al. (2010) illustrate the value of quick response in an empirical study of insurance claims-handling operations. By conducting statistical analyses of a large sample of claims data from a property and casualty company, the researchers isolate key drivers of service performance and identify preemptive actions that can favorably impact the performance metrics. They find that timely interaction between a claims rep and the claimant can significantly reduce the probability of attorney involvement and thereby improve the company's performance in terms of customer satisfaction and retention, and reduced loss payout and the amount of time and work required to close a claim.

As online and physical automation use increases, self-service in conjunction with automation has become ubiquitous in online services ranging from banking to retailing, and in physical services such as supermarket checkouts and airline desks. In such settings there is a transition period during which customers are learning their way around the new service process. Initially, it is helpful to have a human backup to solve any problems that occur due to customer unfamiliarity. Such difficulties are likely to occur with infrequent users, and with those who are less comfortable with technology, which is often a generational phenomenon.

Content-Based Services

These include the acquisition and distribution of music, video, books, news (broadcast and print), commercial databases, and other information and data-based service sectors. Many of these sectors have already been severely disrupted by the changes induced by technology and industrialization.

In the case of music recording, there have been significant losses of revenue and in employment. New entrants now dominate the service distribution side, with the library and subscription models predominating. Commoditization is beginning to lead to price competition and some of the early entrants are struggling. Many of the new entrants are very large firms (Amazon, Apple, and Disney) who have the ability to bundle extensively. Those firms that cannot will have to look for other forms of differentiation, reconsider their processes and experiential design, and perhaps look for special niches where they can build some advantage—possibly with more customization. Apart from bundling and platform strategies, some entrants either have integrated content production and distribution channels (Disney did that in a forward direction) or are starting to integrate backward into production activities (Netflix, Amazon). While this affords more options for creative talent, competition between distributors increases their costs. Some firms (Apple, Amazon) have also integrated forward into consumer devices, such as smartphones and readers.

Newspaper publishing has seen substantial disruption. Revenue is being lost, as advertising money shifts to digital channels. The internal production model for news collection and processing is going away. Newspapers were early examples of bundled information, where the high costs of print meant that bundling was highly cost effective. This is no longer the case with online publishing. The library and subscription model does not yet appear to be entirely successful. Differentiation through niche occupation may be one way to go with news. Acquisition costs might be reduced by employing different sourcing strategies with more open and crowdsourcing, with captive bloggers adding to in-house staff. Some news channels (*Huffington Post, Forbes, WSJ*) have already done so. Platform models like medium.com are an extreme version of open sourcing.

Infrastructure Services

Telecommunications underlies most if not all information services, with a few very large players in core national infrastructure, and a larger number of smaller firms providing regional and local services.[3] Basic telecom service is an extreme commodity, with high levels of price competition and low returns on asset investments despite economies of scale. The fast-changing rate of technology (currently in the version labeled as 5G) means that continuing investments still have to be made. The sector has historically missed many opportunities to add proximate services such as hosting, Web services, and payment and bill pay. Many incumbents are now attempting to differentiate by adding services such as content distribution, but they may be too late as there is already considerable competition there. Globalization has been undertaken by some firms but it has not always been successful due to the combination of high investments and intense competition in many markets, leading to low returns. In many cases firms have had to pull back or exit (often through mergers and acquisitions). Vodafone still operates in over 20 markets, with partners in many other countries. Orange (France Telecom) also operates in many countries with their own services, partnerships, and joint ventures. Deutsche Telekom operates in about 20 countries primarily in Europe, with wholly owned subsidiaries, joint holdings, and partnerships. In the United States, T-Mobile has merged with Sprint under the former name. American, Chinese, and Japanese telecom companies, though very large, are much less global.

Web and cloud services are highly platform- and asset-centric, and the sector is occupied by very large players, including Apple, Google, Amazon, IBM, Microsoft, Alibaba, and Verizon. There are also many newer entrants like Rackspace and Kamatera. These services are much like utilities in that they are quite standardized, highly portable, remotely provided, and (unlike many services) are also quantifiable. The resulting level of commoditization and comparability means extreme price competition, and prices have been dropping rapidly in recent years. Given the large, fixed costs associated with equipment (as with processors and servers), scale and scope are important. Some firms now include their own provision of resources, like telecommunications (including global transport), server farms, and processors. Differentiation is happening through the addition and bundling of related services. However, this direction is largely open to other providers as well. One direction that is likely to be explored further in the future as a service bundling opportunity is SaaS, where there are indeed opportunities for differentiation both within and across sectors. This will also make it easier for some providers to integrate forward into those sectors. It is also likely that providers will consider mergers and acquisitions in that arena. Without some form of differentiation, many Web services providers—especially the smaller ones—are likely to fail or exit via acquisitions and mergers.

Markets and Exchanges

The creation of the Web and internet permitted the creation of new large online market and exchange platforms for both B2B and business-to-consumer (B2C) transactions (Apte & Nath, 2004). Both types proliferated rapidly. However, over time, the number of B2B markets has dropped, with many firms disappearing. One reason for that could be that B2B transactions tend to be narrower and more stable. It is possible that there were too many entrants who saw the market as attractive, but were then unable to distinguish themselves adequately. Figure 1.2 shows a simple 2x2 categorization of B2B transactions based on the frequency of purchases and the complexity or degree of specialization of the product or service. What is apparent is that new markets or exchange platforms are not necessary in all of these subcategories.

In the case of frequent recurring purchases with specific or specialized requirements, it is most efficient to undertake bilateral contracts that usually last over longer periods. Part and

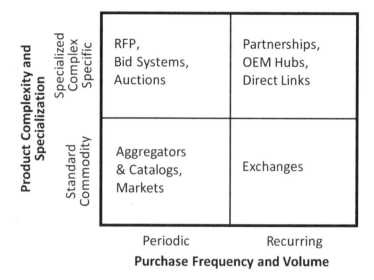

Figure 1.2   *B2B market types and platforms*

subassembly purchases in the auto industry are a leading example. These contracts may be operationally managed today through "hubs" or XML-based transactions. For specialized products, infrequent purchases, searching, and matching become more important, and mechanisms such as requests for proposals (RFP), bid, or auction systems work. Of course, these can also function over platforms. When products or services are standardized, aggregators, wholesalers, and market platforms work. If volumes and frequencies are high, with regular requirements, bilateral long-term supply contracts work well.

In most B2C cases, each purchase quantity is not likely to be large, even when total volumes are substantial. When products or services are standardized, online markets are common. However, when products or services are customized, when providers are fragmented, or when there are geographical niches with clusters of customers, direct bilateral relationships are quite common.

The largest online retailers for consumer goods are now Amazon and Walmart, with Amazon far ahead. Amazon started famously with books and has now expanded to many categories of consumer products. Amazon is also by far the largest Web-services provider with Amazon Web Services. It entered the B2B or industrial supply markets with Amazon Supply in 2012. This service was relaunched in 2015 as Amazon Business. The Amazon eCommerce model includes not only fulfillment from their own inventories, but also order taking and fulfillment for other retailers, as well as simply order taking. The immediate strategy for Amazon is pretty clear. Its strength in infrastructure and Web services gives it a huge advantage in bundling additional services, which it will continue to do. Amazon is also familiar with integrating forward into devices, and backward into content acquisition, as with video products.

Increasingly, due to the high granularity and resolution of online methods, intermediary online market platforms also work for infrequently purchased or infrequently available items for B2C markets. Some examples are eBay, Craigslist, Etsy, and homeadvisor.com. These platforms are substitutes for classified ads in newspapers and, of course, increase both reach and efficiency.

Asset Sharing

Asset sharing platforms are a subset of online markets that provide a channel for durable asset rentals (Apte & Davis, 2019). In some cases, the assets are not owned by the platform, as with Airbnb, Uber, or Lyft. In other cases of asset rental, as with Lime for electric scooters and bikes or Zipcar (acquired by Avis) for cars, the assets are owned by the company. Asset rental is not really a new model, and renting of cars, industrial equipment, and office equipment (as with Xerox copiers) has been around for a long time. Asset sharing for living space is also hardly new. However, online platforms have enabled an expansion in the accessibility of the services. For example, scooters for "micro-mobility" can be picked up at many sites, and returned anywhere with a fast transaction using an app. For ride- and car-sharing, the model is more novel since the company does not have to own or maintain the vehicle.[4]

Social Networks

Online social networks are an entirely new form of service, enabled by new technologies that permit many-to-many interactions including communications (Twitter), information sharing and relationship building (Facebook and Instagram), and barter-like exchange (YouTube).[5] The largest networks have among the largest audiences of any online platform—reaching into the billions for Facebook and YouTube. One of the reasons for the popularity of these sites is that they do not cost anything to users. Their revenue is derived from advertising. This was a historically successful model for many broadcast services like radio and television, and the underlying appeal of the new service sites for advertisers is much the same—eyeballs, stickiness, and repeat visits. The newer sites also have much higher levels of precision in segmenting, and in being able to track and quantify the movement of purchasers along the classic sales funnel, and therefore, the return on advertising expenditures.

Some of the largest social networking sites have apparently begun to falter in their growth rates as their markets saturate. Several have already expanded globally with high rates of penetration in every country in the world. In addition to that, advertising revenues (expenditures) have a limit—in the United States, they are usually 1–2 percent of gross domestic product (GDP). So all firms that earn revenues from advertising are not only competing in terms of audience time (eyeballs) but also for a limited advertising dollar. These sites are essentially competing with each other as well as with other functional services such as Google search and entertainment for both those limited and linked resources. The big winners for digital ad dollars are presently Google and Facebook, with the latter catching up and with a lead in mobile advertising, which is the only growing advertising channel today.

These firms have not as yet all been very active in considering bundling and horizontal expansion strategies to the extent of Google, Amazon, Apple, and Microsoft. However, Facebook appears to be moving rapidly down that path. Facebook acquired Instagram in 2012, which was clearly a very complementary addition. It acquired WhatsApp in 2014. Facebook is now building a digital wallet service combined with its own cryptocurrency (the Libra). These efforts will make Facebook a transactional platform, in part, which is a substantial departure from its initial model, from a technological and functional perspective.

Internet of Things and Smart Services

The technologies gathered under the label IoT involve intelligent automation, sensors, actuators, computational elements, data storage, and communication enabling of physical products.[6] These are sometimes called Micro-Electro-Mechanical Systems, or MEMS. These components have set off a wave of redesign and reconfiguration of products, leading to significant changes in existing services, further "servitization," and the creation of entirely new types of services. Many of these developments will have substantial economic impacts. A McKinsey Global Institute study estimated the cumulative effect at US$3.9 to $11.1 trillion per year in 2025 (Manyika et al., 2015). There are reasons to be cautious about that estimate in terms of both magnitude and timing, and its range is indicative of its uncertainty. Nevertheless, it is apparent that the impact will be both large and disruptive.

In the private sector, B2C services that will see large effects due to IoT include health care, home services, personal transportation (autonomous vehicles), physical service delivery, and utilities. The automotive sector is likely to be dramatically transformed at a global scale. Cars are already filled with new sensors, actuators, and driver assist systems. The shift to electric vehicles is firmly underway. The combination of asset sharing and autonomous electric vehicles will go beyond the automotive product sector, and affect multiple related service sectors ranging from rides and rentals, to insurance and post-sales repair. In general, the B2B logistics in the supply chains for many sectors are large and early users of devices such as RFID. Automation is taking hold in the warehousing, order fulfillment, freight, and delivery layers.

Public sector services are a major part of IoT-led digitization and transformation. The role of the public sector in the adoption of autonomous vehicles will be very large, since traffic flow, real-time flow control, parking, security, and policing will all fall under various jurisdictions across the town, county, state, and federal (interstate) levels. Public transportation is likely to undergo large changes, with better integrated multi-modal systems tying together trains, buses, shuttles, and local rides. The changed economics of autonomous vehicles means that the annual cost of shuttles and buses will drop, and it will be feasible to have more routes (with higher flexibility during days, weeks, and seasons) with higher frequencies. It will be interesting to see how the balance between rail and road public transport shifts; there are those who opine that rail could shrink and even disappear. Many other urban services, such as power, water, street lighting, security and policing, and emergency response, are already seeing implementation of "smart service" approaches.

SUMMARY, CONCLUSIONS, AND RESEARCH OPPORTUNITIES

ICT has had a large impact on all industries/sectors but especially IIS, which is the largest component of the U.S. economy (GDP share, wage bill share) today. These services will continue to grow in share due to a number of ICTs and ICT-enabled innovations that include IoT, automation, AI, and asset-sharing markets, which cause many product sectors to "servitize" and physical services to become more information intensive. IIS sectors are changing dramatically in terms of their structure, competition, and participants. These changes have macro-level implications for jobs, wages, and income distribution. However, because of their evolving nature, the net effects are not yet clear. Concurrently, the strategic landscape has also changed, with extreme examples in sectors like content delivery, financial services, and retailing, along with new services including markets, exchanges, and social networks. While IIS are quite diverse, there are some technology-induced general strategies that work well for many of them, including industrialization, servitization, service redesign, vertical de-integration, globalization, lateral expansion, mobile consumer access through apps, platform models, and service bundling. In addition, certain strategic approaches are more industry specific, including digital experience management, monetization methods, crowd sourcing, flexible contracting, and automation of physical services and servitization of products. Some old strategies—widely used in manufacturing in the past—have been recalibrated to serve the specific and emerging needs of IIS with new features and complications added. Some of the entirely new strategies are driven by production-side changes (e.g., platforms, global delivery), some by logistics (devices, the Web), and some by demand shifts (mobility, interactivity, social networks). Some strategies have been (and will be) transitional that accommodate staggered developments of component and complementary technologies. The complete arrival and implementation of new technologies, such as IoT and AI, will create another wave of structural changes and disruptions, with a new set of strategic imperatives. Firms need to frequently review their strategic approach, to shorten planning horizons, to look "end-to-end," and to keep abreast of new technology developments to assess how they might be affected.

There are several potent areas for future research. The most important areas are nascent but growing with increasing use of IoT, automation, and AI. There will be continuing changes in markets, consumer behavior, and demand patterns that will be of interest to researchers in a wide range of disciplines and their intersections. Organizational changes due to technology (telework, telecommuting, automation) in both backrooms and front-office consumer interfaces are an evolving area for those who are interested in business organization and efficiency. Future research should also focus on search for differentiation and segmentation to avoid commoditization. The use of these technologies has also facilitated provision of effective and efficient public goods and services often portrayed as the "smart city." With rapid urbanization, particularly in the emerging market economies, there is a need for appropriate strategies and policies to provide such goods and services to address certain long-standing issues with the growth of urban centers. Conversely, it is entirely possible that the increased ability to work and collaborate remotely will create a move to more dispersion, or perhaps just more "sprawl."

NOTES

1. Bell (2020) examines the relationship between artificial intelligence (AI), data-driven IoT systems, business process optimization, and sustainable industrial value creation.
2. Tronvoll et al. (2020) examine the strategic organizational shifts that underpin digital servitization.
3. Weill et al. (2002) emphasize the importance of building IT infrastructure for strategic flexibility.
4. Kumar et al. (2018) consider multigenerational aspects to propose a conceptual strategic framework for the development of service providers and customers in the sharing economy.
5. Benthaus et al. (2016) evaluate how the management tools using these social networks, as part of an overarching social media strategy, help companies to positively influence public perceptions among social media users.
6. Sestino et al. (2020) investigate the role of IoT and big data in terms of how businesses manage their digital transformation.

REFERENCES

Apte, U., Cavaliere, R., & Kulkarni, S. (2010). Analysis and improvement of information intensive services: Empirical evidence from the insurance claims operation. *Production and Operations Management, 19*(6), 665–678.

Apte, U., & Davis, M. (2019). Sharing economy services: Business model generation. *California Management Review, 61*(2), 104–131.

Apte, U., & Karmarkar, U. (2007). Business process outsourcing (BPO) and globalization of information intensive services. In U. Apte & U. Karmarkar (Eds.), *Managing in the information economy: Current research issues* (pp. 59–81). Springer Science + Business Media.

Apte, U., Karmarkar, U., & Nath, H. (2008). Information services in the U.S. economy: Value, jobs and management implications. *California Management Review, 50*(3), 12–30.

Apte, U., Karmarkar, U., & Nath, H. (2012). The U.S. information economy: Value, employment, industry structure, and trade. *Foundations and Trends in Technology, Information and Operations Management, 6*(1), 1–179.

Apte, U., Karmarkar, U., & Nath, H. (2015). The growth of information-intensive services in the U.S. economy. In J. Bryson & P. Daniels (Eds.), *Handbook of service business: Management, marketing, innovation and internationalization* (pp. 170–204). Edward Elgar Publishing.

Apte, U., & Mason, R. (1995). Global disaggregation of information-intensive services. *Management Science, 41*(7), 1250–1262.

Apte, U., & Nath, H. (2004). Assessing cross-industry effects of B2B e-commerce. *Journal of Strategic E-commerce, 2*(2), 51–80.

Baines, T., & Lightfoot, H. (2013). *Made to serve: How manufacturers can compete through servitization and product service systems.* Wiley.

Bell, E. (2020). Cognitive automation, business process optimization, and sustainable industrial value creation in artificial intelligence data-driven Internet of Things systems. *Journal of Self-Governance & Management Economics, 8*(3), 9–15.

Benthaus, J., Risius, M., & Beck, R. (2016). Social media management strategies for organizational impression management and their effect on public perception. *Journal of Strategic Information Systems, 25*(2), 127–139.

Bordoloi, S., Fitzsimmons, J., & Fitzsimmons, M. (2018). *Service management: Operations, strategy, and information technology* (9th ed.). McGraw-Hill.

Chase, R. (1978). Where does the customer fit in a service operation? *Harvard Business Review, 56*(6), 138–139.

Chase, R., & Apte, U. (2007). A history of research in service operations: What is the big idea? *Journal of Operations Management, 25*(2), 375–386.

Fuchs, V. (1968). *The service economy.* Columbia University Press.

Gerrish, S. (2018). *How smart machines think.* MIT Press.

Heskett, J. (1986). *Managing in the service economy.* Harvard University Press.

Hossain, M., & Kauranen, I. (2015). Crowdsourcing: A comprehensive literature review. *Strategic Outsourcing: An International Journal, 8*(1), 2–22.

Johnston, R., Clark, G., & Shulver, M. (2012). *Service operations management: Improving service delivery* (4th ed.). Pearson.

Karmarkar, U. (2004). Will you survive the services revolution? *Harvard Business Review* (June). https://hbr.org/2004/06/will-you-survive-the-services-revolution

Karmarkar, U. (2010). The industrialization of information services. In P. Maglio, C. Kieliszewski, & J. Spohrer (Eds.), *The handbook of services science.* Springer Science.

Karmarkar, U. (2014). Service industrialization. In E. Baglieri & U. Karmarkar (Eds.), *Managing consumer services: Factory or theater* (pp. 25–32). Springer.

Karmarkar, U. (2020). Service industrialization, convergence, and digital transformation—I. *Management and Business Review, 1*(1), 133–143.

Karmarkar, U. (2021). Service industrialization, convergence, and digital transformation—II. *Management and Business Review.* https://mbrjournal.com/2022/02/03/service-industrialization-convergence-and-digital-transformation-ii/

Karmarkar, U., & Apte, U. (2007). Operations management in the information economy: Information products, processes and chains. *Journal of Operations Management, 25*, 438–453.

Karmarkar, U., & Pitbladdo, R. (1995). Service markets and competition. *Journal of Operations Management, 12*(3–4), 397–411.

kmuller. (2018, November 12). How crowdsourcing is changing the Waze we drive. *Technology and Operations Management.* https://digital.hbs.edu/platform-rctom/submission/how-crowdsourcing-is -changing-the-waze-we-drive/

Kumar, V., Lahiri, A., & Dogan, O. (2018). A strategic framework for a profitable business model in the sharing economy. *Industrial Marketing Management, 68*, 147–160.

Levitt, T. (1970). The industrialization of service. *Harvard Business Review, 48*(5), 63–74.

Levitt, T. (1972). Production line approach to services. *Harvard Business Review, 50*(5), 32–43.

Machlup, F. (1962). *The production and distribution of knowledge in the United States.* Princeton University Press.

Manyika, J., Chui, M., Bisson, P., Woetzel, J., Dobbs, R., Bughin, J., & Aharon, D. (2015, June 1). *Unlocking the potential of the Internet of Things. McKinsey Digital.* https://www.mckinsey.com/ business-functions/mckinsey-digital/our-insights/the-internet-of-things-the-value-of-digitizing-the -physical-world

Miltz, A. (2021). *Remote work frequency before and after COVID-19 in the United States 2020.* Statista. https://www.statista.com/statistics/1122987/change-in-remote-work-trends-after-covid-in-usa/

Mithas, S., & Whitaker, J. (2007). Is the world flat or spiky? Information intensity, skills, and global service disaggregation. *Information Systems Research, 18*, 237–259.

Nath, H., Apte, U., & Karmarkar, U. (2020). Service industrialization, employment and wages in the U.S. information economy. *Foundations and Trends in Technology, Information and Operations Management, 13*(4), 250–343.

Open source. (2020, October 28). In *Wikipedia.* https://en.wikipedia.org/w/index.php?title=Open_source &oldid=985850550

Parker, G., & van Alstyne, M. (2018). Platform strategy. In M. Augier & D. Teece (Eds.), *The Palgrave encyclopedia of strategic management.* Palgrave Macmillan.

Porat, M. (1977). *The information economy.* Office of Telecommunications Special Publication, U.S. Department of Commerce.

Ramasubbu, N., Mithas, S., Krishnan, M., & Kemerer, C. (2008). Work dispersion, process-based learn-ing, and offshore software development performance. *MIS Quarterly, 32*(2), 437–458.

Sestino, A., Prete, M., Piper, L., & Guido, G. (2020). Internet of Things and big data as enablers for business digitalization strategies. *Technovation, 98*, 1–9.

Tronvoll, B., Sklyar, A., Sörhammar, D., & Kowalkowski, C. (2020). Transformational shifts through digital servitization. *Industrial Marketing Management, 89*, 293–305.

Upwork. (2019, October 3). *Sixth annual "Freelancing in America" study finds that more people than ever see freelancing as a long-term career path* [Press release]. https://www.upwork.com/press/ releases/freelancing-in-america-2019

Vandermerwe, S., and Rada, J. (1988). Servitization of business: Adding value by adding services. *European Management Journal, 6*(4), 314–324.

Varian, H., Farrell, J., & Shapiro, C. (2014). *The economics of information technology.* Cambridge University Press.

Weill, P., Subramani, M., & Broadbent, M. (2002). Building IT infrastructure for strategic agility. *Sloan Management Review* (Fall).

Xue, M., & Harker, P. (2002). Customer efficiency: Concept and its impact on e-business management. *Journal of Service Research, 4*(4), 253–267.

2.   Servitization and innovation strategy – the trade-off between product R&D and service investments

Ornella Benedettini and Christian Kowalkowski

INTRODUCTION

Rapid technological progress, growing product commoditisation, and market saturation challenge manufacturing companies in their efforts to stay competitive so that product innovation alone is no longer sufficient to ensure business success. In response, many such companies have progressively shifted the focus of their traditional product-centric offerings towards greater service orientation as a way to capture new revenue streams and increase profitability (Kowalkowski et al., 2017b; Raddats et al., 2019).

This transition from manufacturing to services, conventionally known as 'servitization', is a departure from the company's core identity (Neu and Brown, 2005; Josephson et al., 2016), often resulting in significant changes to the company's innovation strategy. Under servitization, value innovations achieved by combining product offerings with complementary service elements are regarded as a flagship for competition and are adopted as viable substitutes for research and development (R&D)-based product innovation (Eggert et al., 2011; Coreynen et al., 2017). The resulting innovation strategy implies that fewer resources are devoted to product innovation through R&D to the benefit of value innovation via services (Visnjic et al., 2016; Ambroise et al., 2018). While there are positives to this type of strategy, it is not without costs. These include the relative perils of decreasing the accumulation of expertise through product R&D which, in turn, affects the company's competence at R&D activity in the long run. Despite this, discussions of servitization seem more focused on exploring the role of services as a new value catalyst or driver, rather than understanding how to sustain the strategic use of such value over time.

As an organisational change process, servitization adheres to a diversification logic of expanding into service activity as a way to exploit the stock of knowledge from prior investment in product R&D and existing customer relationships (Fang et al., 2008; Benedettini et al., 2017). Unfortunately, emphasising the strategic content of services to the detriment of R&D-based product innovation pulls resources away that otherwise would have been used to maintain and increase the company's stock of R&D know-how and improve its ability to translate future R&D efforts into effective product innovations. Indeed, because of the cumulative nature of knowledge and as emphasised by organisational learning theory (Cyert and March, 1963) and the resource-based view of the firm (Barney, 1991), new product technology is generated using both accumulated knowledge capital and resources expended in the current period. Therefore, substituting R&D-based product innovation with service activity may erode the company's ability to leverage R&D outlays in future development of product innovations—that is, its *R&D strength* (Danneels, 2008). This chapter brings to the fore the notion of R&D strength to examine the relationship and trade-offs between servitization and a company's product innovation activity. This motivation emanates from evidence suggesting that diversifying into services does not always produce the returns that manufacturers expect (Gebauer et al., 2005; Spring and Araujo, 2013), and from our awareness that product-based knowledge is too often treated as a stable, unproblematic element in servitization discussions. Therefore, this chapter presents a conceptual discussion that addresses two questions: (1) How does servitization affect a company's ability to bring innovative products to the market? and (2) How may servitization be approached to enable valuable exploitation of services as a component of the company's long-term innovation strategy?

SERVITIZATION

Servitization can be defined as the transformational process whereby a company (or business unit) shifts from a product-centric to a service-centric business model and business logic (Kowalkowski et al., 2017a). Hence, the relative importance of service offers to a company increases, amplifying its service portfolio and augmenting its service business orientation. To various degrees, servitization also entails changes to the traditional business model, which is generally based on product sales, basic services, and spare parts. A service-centric business model and logic, on the other hand, mean that a company focuses on the utility provided to customers (Kindström, 2010). Thereby, it assumes greater responsibility for the customer's value-creating process (e.g. guaranteeing a level of availability of equipment or achieving an expected level of performance) through total offers—even if it may affect the sales of products negatively.

Successful examples of servitized companies include Caterpillar, the global leader in earth-moving products. The company, which operates through a global network of independent dealers, provides a broad range of services spanning from maintenance and repair, financing, and remanufacturing, to advanced service agreements and subscription-based connectivity services. In the aviation industry, Rolls-Royce pioneered service contracts with a revenue mechanism on a dollar-per-engine-flying hourly basis. With this 'power-by-the-hour' business model, risks are transferred back to the company, and predictability and reliability become a profit driver for both Rolls-Royce and its aviation customers. Such service-based business models oftentimes imply that the manufacturer (or a third party) retains ownership of the equipment. For example, rather than buying trucks, many of Toyota Material Handling's customers pay a fixed monthly fee for a rental solution, including trucks, financing, maintenance, spare parts, and driver training. In doing so, they have a stipulated cost for all their material-handling-related activities.

INNOVATION STRATEGY

From an innovation perspective, servitization deviates from traditional methods of value creation and often leads to significant changes in the innovation strategy of manufacturing companies (Table 2.1). Historically, manufacturing companies have centred most of their innovation efforts on technological innovation related to new and improved products (Carlborg et al., 2013; Eggert et al., 2015), attempting to gain competitive advantage through core competences

Table 2.1   Innovation within traditional companies and servitized companies

	Traditional approach	Servitization approach
Innovation strategy	Investing in technological R&D to gain competitive advantage through product innovation	Embedding products in a value proposition of product-service systems to enhance the ability to fulfil customer needs
Competitive drivers	Product excellence and technology leadership	Service-based value concepts connected to customer experience and functional needs
Sources of customer value	Technical product features that address customer needs	Utility provided to the customers through a total offer including combined products and services
Focus of innovation	Value-creating product technology	Specific modes of value proposition, value creation, and value capture (i.e. business model)

in value-creating product technologies. Traditional manufacturers typically conduct market research, analyse customer satisfaction, examine how the products are used, identify conscious or unconscious customer needs, and then focus on developing technical product features that address those needs (Shelton, 2009). The underlying strategy is to rely on R&D, technology, and product development to target opportunities such as creating barriers for potential new competitors and controlling premium market segments, opening new markets, defining industry standards and dominant product designs, and building solid market reputations (Tongur and Engwall, 2014).

In contrast, the servitization approach suggests that customer value can be created in other ways besides pure technological innovation (Salonen, 2011). Under servitization, value innovations achieved by combining product offerings with complementary service elements are regarded as a flagship for competition and are adopted as viable substitutes for R&D-based product innovation (Eggert et al., 2011; Coreynen et al., 2017). A servitized company extends the conventional boundaries of product manufacturing activities (Spring and Araujo, 2013) by integrating the value chain from product design to service provision, embedding the product in a value proposition of a seamless service experience for the customer and integrated product-service solution. The role of product technical features is diminished since the focus is on the utility provided to the customers, in line with the purpose of creating a total offer, including combined products and services. Consequently, by emphasising service-based value concepts connected to customer experiences and functional needs, servitized companies can move away from an innovation strategy with technological R&D and product development as main competitive drivers. Specifically, such companies adopt an innovation strategy of pursuing business model innovation instead of technological innovation (Matthyssens et al., 2006; Shelton, 2009; Kindström, 2010; Forkmann et al., 2017).

Within the business and management fields, the business model concept refers to the underlying logic of the company's go-to-market approach, including how the company converts the value potential embedded in its knowledge and resources into market outcomes (Chesbrough and Rosenbloom, 2002). Thus, the notion of the business model revolves around the company's value proposition to the market—that is, the value that the company promises to deliver to customers through its products and services. In addition, the business model outlines the mechanisms that the company employs to create such value (Zott et al., 2011), as well as how the company captures value (e.g. earns revenues) from delivering products and services to customers (Teece, 2010). In short, business model choices define the modes of value proposition, value creation, and value capture adopted by the company. While the notion of value is clearly central in the business model concept, companies may or may not use technological innovation and product R&D as a basis for the value that they offer to customers. That is, the business model—the discovery and adoption of specific modes of value proposition, value creation, and value capture—can be a source of competitive advantage that is distinct from the company's product market position (Christensen, 2001; Zott et al., 2011). Along these lines, servitized companies adopt value attributes and value-capture techniques that are based primarily on providing systems of combined products and services, rather than product development, to enhance their ability to match value propositions with customer demands (Tongur and Engwall, 2014; Story et al., 2017).

Manufacturing companies are moving into servitization because of both external factors tied to the environment and company-related motivations, as summarised by Kowalkowski and Ulaga (2017). First, a growing number of product markets are saturated or commoditised, leading to eroding profit margins and limited growth opportunities in the product domain. Second, as customers are becoming more professional, they often reduce their supplier base and expect their remaining suppliers to provide a more complete product-service portfolio. In addition, many customers seek to pay for achieved performance instead of product and service components. Third, proliferation of competition means that not only other industry incumbents but also competitors form emerging markets, pure-service companies, and software companies outside the traditional industry borders and challenge the position of product companies. An example is Amazon's cloud arm, AWS, which looks to boost its presence in the industrial sector through machine-learning-based services, including computer vision hardware. Fourth, servitization enables companies to capture more customer relationship value. Services such as long-term preventive maintenance contracts enable closer and potentially more strategic relationships throughout the life cycle of the product. Fifth, by exploiting their unique technology expertise, companies can provide novel services that enhance the functionality of the product. Finally, servitization provides opportunities for new anything-as-a-service business models with potentially disrupting effects. For example, Caterpillar hopes to transform the construction industry with smart machines and subscription-based connectivity services.

PRODUCT STRATEGY

As already noted, the servitization perspective sees services as a strategic alternative to product innovation. Servitized companies seek to differentiate themselves through a value proposition of functional sales and product-service combinations, rather than just via their ability to address customers' product requirements (Shelton, 2009; Tongur and Engwall, 2014; Story et al., 2017). The higher the level of servitization chosen by the company, the higher the share of total value creation that stems from service elements. Thus, with their service-based business model, servitized companies have less incentive to invest in product development and technological R&D. Products may even represent only a small part of the solution or wider function provided to the customers. Moreover, product innovation and service provision compete for limited company resources. Resources that are committed to service endeavours are at the same time unavailable to other uses and therefore limit the flexibility to assign resources to the pursuit of more traditional strategies. Therefore, when companies embrace servitization, they find it more difficult to assign resources to product innovation efforts (Eggert et al., 2011).

In line with this notion, the mainstream servitization research tends to assume that a company's core products or product technology would remain unchanged when it integrates forward into service business (Gebauer et al., 2005; Tongur and Engwall, 2014; Coreynen et al., 2017). Since the emphasis is placed on the opportunities for value creation stemming from service elements, R&D-based product innovation is ignored, or at least taken for granted. The product is treated as a stable platform against which the offer of various service elements can be configured.

In general terms, products appear to perform two main functions in servitized offerings. The first function is to provide a vehicle for the sale of services. Although manufacturers' service arrangements may include product-independent services (e.g. business consulting, general financing, professional training; Mathieu, 2001; Godlevskaja et al., 2011; Raddats and Kowalkowski, 2014), servitized offerings typically include services that support customer processes in the primary and complementary activity chains (Sawhney et al., 2004) associated with an installed base of products (e.g. product maintenance, operation, insurance, renewal and upgrade, take-back). The point is that installed products require a range of services during their life cycle, and a manufacturer, especially if it has already provided the product, is well placed to provide such services since it has an established relationship with the customer and experience concerning the product (Raddats and Easingwood, 2010). Moreover, in some forms of servitization where the manufacturer retains ownership of the product with the customer being charged for access or functional result (cf. the section on 'Servitization' above), product-based transactions ordinarily include services to support the product in the operational environment. The second function that servitization theory assigns to products is to carry competences and resources that can be leveraged for service provision. Certain service extensions (e.g. maintenance of capital equipment) draw on similar capabilities as the product business. To offer these services, manufacturers can take advantage of the capabilities conferred by product-based assets and intangible input such as knowledge of product technology (Benedettini et al., 2017). In this sense, products are implicit signifiers of potential spill-overs that may reduce the need for service-specific resources (Fang et al., 2008). Clearly, neither of these product functions point to R&D-based product innovation as the main source of customer value and competitive advantage. This further supports the argument that the servitization perspective is substantially based on the premise of a stable core product and product technology around which the services are created (Tongur and Engwall, 2014).

KNOWLEDGE ACCUMULATION THROUGH R&D-BASED PRODUCT INNOVATION

It resonates with the view of products discussed above that many servitized companies tend to underinvest in product innovation through R&D to the benefit of investments in value innovation via services (Visnjic et al., 2016; Ambroise et al., 2018). While there are positives to this type of strategy, it is not without costs. Drawing on organisational learning theory and the resource-based view, we suggest that reducing the investment in product R&D holds the prospect of important long-term effects on a company's knowledge assets and capabilities.

Organisational learning theory provides insights into how companies acquire, retain, update, and act upon knowledge (Bell et al., 2002). This theory emphasises the emergence and development of know-how as the result of experience (Cyert and March, 1963; Levitt and March, 1988). The notion of know-how refers to procedural knowledge—that is, knowing how to do something. Therefore, the know-how is a description of what defines current practices and routines within a company, including how to operate plants, manufacture products, structure processes, or conduct R&D activities (Kogut and Zander, 1992). In the terminology of organisational learning theory, 'know-how is the accumulated practical skill or expertise that allows someone to do something smoothly and effectively' (von Hippel, 1988: p. 6). The key word in this definition is 'accumulated', which implies that know-how must be learned and acquired over time (Kogut and Zander, 1992). In short, organisational learning theory holds that experience-based learning is essential in improving an organisation's competence at particular activities. This means that the productivity of R&D outlays is based on learning, which is itself the product of experience accumulated through past R&D activity.

Similarly, the resource-based view of the firm focuses on know-how as a strategic, company-specific asset that cannot be bought in factor markets but must necessarily be built or accumulated internally by following a consistent pattern of resource investments over some period of time (Barney, 1991). In particular, R&D or technological know-how is viewed as a 'stock' of knowledge that is accumulated over time through a history of R&D outlays or 'flows' (Dierickx and Cool, 1989). The 'bathtub' metaphor (Dierickx and Cool, 1989) illustrates the fundamental distinction between stocks and flows. At any moment, the stock of water in a bathtub is given by the level of water in the tub; it is the cumulative result of flows of water into the tub (through the tap) and out of it (through leaks). With respect to R&D, the level of water in the tub represents the stock of technological know-how at a particular moment. The flow of water into the tub represents current R&D spending, whereas the flow of water leaking out of the tub illustrates the fact that R&D know-how depreciates over time so that the contribution of older R&D investments becomes less valuable as time passes (Hall et al., 1986).[1] In essence, R&D know-how is a strategic asset that cannot be adjusted instantaneously. It takes a consistent pattern of R&D spending (resource flows) to build a required level of R&D know-how (asset stock) (DeCarolis and Deeds, 1999). Clearly, the level of R&D know-how determines a company's potential for successful R&D—that is, its *R&D strength* as defined by Danneels: 'the ability of the firm to build new technological competences' (Danneels, 2008: 521).

As just outlined, R&D know-how (referred to as R&D strength from now on) decays in the absence of adequate 'maintenance' expenditures. Moreover, as an asset stock, R&D strength is commonly related to time compression diseconomies (Dierickx and Cool, 1989), where maintaining a given rate of R&D spending over a particular time interval produces a larger increment to the stock of R&D know-how than maintaining a higher rate of R&D spending over a proportionally shorter time interval. This point in often backed up (e.g. Henderson, 1999) with the example of 'crash' R&D programmes, which are typically less effective at building R&D know-how than programmes in which annual R&D expenditures are lower but spread over longer periods. In short, R&D strength derives its value from long-term development (Oliver, 1997).

THE CASE OF SERVITIZED COMPANIES

As discussed, R&D strength is cumulative and depends on past R&D investments. New technological knowledge is generated using both accumulated knowledge capital and resources expended in the current period. Therefore, when servitized companies pull resources away from product R&D to expand into services, they turn down opportunities to increase their R&D strength and hence to improve their ability to translate R&D outlays into effective product innovations. In addition, since the value of R&D know-how depreciates over time, inadequate funding of product R&D activity may further result in erosion of the stock of R&D know-how (R&D strength) that was built incrementally across the company's R&D history. Finally, the challenges of path dependency and time compression diseconomies make it difficult and costly to offset periods of lower R&D spending and their effects on the company's R&D strength. In short, these issues imply that treating services as a substitute for product innovation results in a decline in R&D spending, which should be followed by a decline in R&D strength.

Figure 2.1 is drawn from Cummings and Knott (2018) and can be used to illustrate this concept. It shows the R&D intensity (R&D spending/sales) and R&D strength history for General Electric under Jack Welch's tenure (1981–2001). In those years, General Electric adopted a strategy of divesting businesses in which it was neither number one nor number two in the market (television, semiconductors, aerospace) and expanding into businesses that did not rely on R&D (Cummings and Knott, 2018). In this way, it pursued a comprehensive servitization business model, whose cornerstone was the growth of its financial arm, GE Capital. GE Capital grew from a small financing operation supporting the product business to an empowered source of sustained growth, which in 2002 accounted for 49 per cent of the company's total revenues (Davies, 2004). General Electric was among the first companies to offer financial services as a part of integrated solutions packages combining products, maintenance, services, and financing, as well as real estate and other loans unrelated to its manufacturing businesses. The company's R&D strength decayed dramatically because, to mine service opportunities, it depleted the stock of R&D know-how from previous R&D investments.

Premised on the idea that services can be a leading source of customer value, the strategy followed by servitized companies is to substitute service elements and integrated product-service products for superior product design. As a result of this substitution process, the existing stock of R&D know-how becomes partly obsolete since the value that technological excellence and product innovation create for the customers is sharply diminished (Salonen, 2011; Eggert et al., 2015). Hence, declines in R&D strength (as shown in Figure 2.1) would not weaken the company's competitive position because they are counterbalanced by rent-earning investments in service activities.

We submit – and this is our main point – that this traditional perspective of servitization neglects the strong connection between the products and the services typically offered by manufacturing companies. As previously outlined (cf. the 'Product Strategy' section above), manufacturers may servitize by extending their business into either one or both of two service categories: product services, which support customer processes in the primary and/or complementary activity chains related to the company's product(s); and product-independent services, which can be experienced by the customers without consuming the company's product(s) (Mathieu, 2001; Godlevskaja et al., 2011; Raddats and Kowalkowski, 2014; Benedettini et al., 2015).

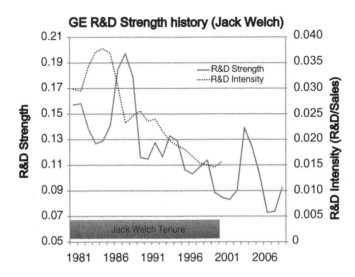

Note: R&D strength is measured using the 'Research Quotient' metric defined in Cummings and Knott (2018).
Source: Drawn from Cummings and Knott (2018).

Figure 2.1   *R&D intensity and R&D strength of General Electric under Jack Welch's tenure*

However, we maintain that, although servitized companies may use their product-based experience to also service other vendors' products (Raddats and Easingwood, 2010), in most cases the bulk of their sales of product services consists of services supporting use/functioning of their own products (e.g. maintenance, upgrade, and refurbishing) or perhaps services supporting customer processes related to such products (e.g. management of spare parts, rental services, management of product operations, 'vertical' financing; Antioco et al., 2008). Nevertheless, there are very few companies that, like General Electric, IBM, or Xerox, have engaged primarily with product-independent services, such as 'non-vertical' financing, technology consulting, and business process outsourcing. In addition to providing technology products and solutions, IBM has become one of the world's largest providers of services in the areas of management consulting (especially financial and technology consulting) and of IT outsourcing (Spohrer, 2017). After selling its personal computer group to China-based Lenovo, IBM changed its registration at the New York Stock Exchange (NYSE) from product to service company. Just like General Electric under Jack Welch, Xerox moved into product-independent services with the 2010 acquisition of ACS, the world's largest diversified business process outsourcing company. However, only six years later, the company decided to split into two—the more hardware-centric Xerox and the service-centric Conduent—due to lack of complementarities between the two types of business. In practice, manufacturers' service businesses are still very much anchored in product services complementing their own products. Further to contributing to the company's reputation and relationship to customers, the product offering therefore provides the cornerstone of the market demand for its services. That is, the market demand for the services offered by a servitized company importantly depends on the customer interest in its product(s) (Salonen, 2011). This is particularly the case for capital intensive products with long lifespans of several years or even decades (Kowalkowski and Ulaga, 2017). And this is true regardless of the share of revenues that services account for.

Accordingly, we conclude that when a manufacturing company loses competitiveness in product design and technology, service-based differentiation becomes ineffective. If the customers are no longer interested in the company's products, there will be no market for pre-sale and at-sale services; the company may still be able to sell some after-sales services (e.g. maintenance and spare parts) but only while the existing product installed base remains in use. An example provided by Dierickx and Cool (1989) appears interesting in this respect. It refers to the strategy followed by Canon to overstep Xerox in the low- to medium-volume copier market. Capitalising on its stock of R&D know-how, Canon was able to separate the product from the services and substitute its superior product design for Xerox's extensive service network. As the customers found Xerox products to lag behind competition, the value created by the company's services was sharply diminished.

Hence, servitized companies still need to be able to bring innovative products to the market—that is, compete through their R&D strength. This in turn implies that the decline in R&D strength caused by heavy investment in service activities at the cost of inadequate funding of R&D efforts is, so far, a neglected, long-term risk to which servitized manufacturing companies are exposed.

DISCUSSION AND CONCLUSION

Since most companies operate under resource constraints, exploration of novel competitive domains reduces the speed with which competences in existing ones can be enhanced (March, 1991). Hence, it is clear that heavy investment in service opportunities comes at the cost of underinvestment in product R&D, which in turn affects the extent to which a manufacturing company will be capable of improving and sustaining its competence at new product development (R&D strength).

The research discourse on servitization has so far ignored this trade-off. The theoretical view held by most prior works has indeed focused on services as key sources of customer value and competitive advantage, implicitly assuming that, while manufacturing companies integrate forward into services, their core products and product technology would remain unchanged. Following this line of thought, previous research has tended to neglect product innovation, or at least to take it for granted. One implication is that R&D strength has not been treated as a strategic asset for servitized companies.

We have defined R&D strength as the ability to come up with effective product innovations and relied upon organisational learning theory and the resource-based view of the firm (e.g. Dierickx and Cool, 1989; Kogut and Zander, 1992) to argue that R&D strength is experiential in nature and is developed incrementally through a history of R&D activity. Therefore, at any moment, the R&D strength possessed by a company is the cumulative result of the choices made by the company about R&D outlays over an appropriate period. This implies that, when servitized companies underinvest in product R&D to allocate more of their strategic resources to differentiate themselves through service elements and product-service products, they forsake the opportunity to improve their R&D strength. Further still, as a knowledge asset, R&D strength decays over time since the contribution of older R&D investments becomes less valuable as time passes. Thus, inadequate funding of product R&D efforts is most likely to result in the erosion of the company's R&D strength.

Our analysis reveals that R&D strength is necessary for servitized companies to avoid losing service revenues because their service-based value propositions are created around products that have become obsolete or because they adopt obsolete technology. Through its influence on product innovation capabilities, R&D strength sets the reference point for the development of functional offerings and product-service solutions that match the competitive context and technology landscape. The utility provided by product platforms remains essential for the soundness of servitized offerings, even though the competitive emphasis is on service attributes and service-based value concepts. Therefore, we submit that, although previous research into servitization seems to suggest otherwise, R&D strength remains a critical asset also for servitized companies.

The importance of investing in product R&D to ensure that the company can rely on an adequate R&D strength may not be evident at the time when servitization is embraced because the company can still mine the value of R&D strength from prior R&D investments. However, over time, heavy investment in services at the cost of inadequate funding of product R&D will result in the progressive erosion of the initial R&D strength, which in the long term will create the abovementioned risk that the company struggles to devise competitive value propositions. Additionally, the background theories upon which our analysis is based bring about the issue of time compression diseconomies, which make it difficult and costly for servitized companies to sustain their R&D strength through discontinuous investment in product R&D. Building up R&D strength is a time-consuming process and making up for declines in R&D strength after shifting the focus of innovation investments from product R&D to service initiatives is likely to involve crash R&D investments.

In sum, we argue that the view that servitized companies can simply substitute product innovation with value innovation and business model innovation is too simplistic. The opportunity cost associated with a service-based innovation strategy needs to be addressed from a long-term perspective and concerning its effects on the company's competence at product R&D. Such competence, which we label as R&D strength, remains an important knowledge asset to ensure that product-service offerings do not become quickly obsolete and that servitized companies can retain a competitive edge. Hence, while manufacturing companies should leverage service-based value concepts to create innovative market offerings, they should also be careful to maintain an adequate level of investment in product innovation to protect the core R&D-based competences that remain the foundation of their competitive advantage.

The real managerial issue then becomes not the total benefits or experiences the customers obtain in the use of the company's services, but the division of available resources and their allocation between product R&D and service endeavours. Such resource allocation decisions, we suggest, should importantly adopt a policy of integrating service market aspects into product innovation processes. Many manufacturing companies still pursue product R&D and launch new products without paying sufficient attention to service opportunities, which are often considered only later. Instead, servitized companies should design their products also with the service market in mind, for example, taking into account serviceability and durability. This is even more important today given that software has become an integral part of most products and servitization opportunities lie increasingly in the digital domain with remote control, automation, and subscription-based models (Tronvoll et al., 2020). While servitized companies should be aware of the continued importance of investing in product R&D, they should at the same time work to make their product innovation processes (along with their business models) more service-oriented.

NOTE

1. In addition, organisational learning theory makes the point that knowledge acquired through organisational learning decays or depreciates through time (e.g. Argote and Miron-Spektor, 2011).

REFERENCES

Ambroise, L., Prim-Allaz, I., & Teyssier, C. (2018). Financial performance of servitized manufacturing firms: A configuration issue between servitization strategies and customer-oriented organizational design. *Industrial Marketing Management*. 71. 54–68.

Antioco, M., Moenaert, R.K., Lindgreen, A., & Wetzel, M.G.M. (2008). Organizational antecedents to and consequences of service business orientations in manufacturing companies. *Journal of the Academy of Marketing Science*. 36, 3. 337–358.

Argote, L., & Miron-Spektor, E. (2011). Organization learning: From experience to knowledge. *Organization Science*. 22, 5. 1123–1137.

Barney, J.B. (1991). Firm resources and sustained competitive advantage. *Journal of Management*. 17, 1. 99–120.

Bell, S.J., Whitwell, G.J., & Lukas, B.A. (2002). Schools of thought in organizational learning. *Journal of the Academy of Marketing Science*. 30, 1. 70–86.

Benedettini, O., Neely, A., & Swink, M. (2015). Why do servitized firms fail? A risk-based explanation. *International Journal of Operations & Production Management*. 35, 6. 946–979.

Benedettini, O., Swink, M., & Neely, A. (2017). Examining the influence of service additions on manufacturing firms' bankruptcy likelihood. *Industrial Marketing Management*. 60. 112–125.

Carlborg, P., Kindström, D., & Kowalkowski, C. (2013). The evolution of service innovation research: A critical review and synthesis. *The Service Industries Journal*. 34, 5. 373–398.

Chesbrough, H., & Rosenbloom, R. (2002). The role of the business model in capturing value from innovation: Evidence from Xerox Corporation's technology spin-off companies. *Industrial and Corporate Change*. 11, 3. 529–555.

Christensen, C.M. (2001). The past and future of competitive advantage. *MIT Sloan Management Review*. 42, 2. 105–109.

Coreynen, W., Matthyssens, P., & van Bockhaven, W. (2017). Boosting servitization through digitization: Pathways and dynamic resource configurations for manufacturers. *Industrial Marketing Management*. 60. 42–53.

Cummings, T., & Knott, A.M. (2018). Outside CEOs and innovation. *Strategic Management Journal*. 39, 8. 2095–2119.

Cyert, R.M., & March, J.G. (1963). *A Behavioral Theory of the Firm*. Prentice-Hall.

Danneels, E. (2008). Organizational antecedents of second order competences. *Strategic Management Journal*. 29, 5. 519–543.

Davies, A. (2004). Moving base into high-value integrated solutions: A value stream approach. *Industrial and Corporate Change*. 13, 5. 727–756.

DeCarolis, D.M., & Deeds, D.L. (1999). The impact of stocks and flows of organizational knowledge on firm performance: An empirical investigation of the biotechnology industry. *Strategic Management Journal*. 20, 10. 953–968.

Dierickx, I., & Cool, K. (1989). Asset stock accumulation and sustainability of competitive advantage. *Management Science*. 35, 12. 1504–1512.

Eggert, A., Hogreve, J., Ulaga, W., & Muenkhoff, E. (2011). Industrial services, product innovations, and firm profitability: A multiple-group latent growth curve analysis. *Industrial Marketing Management*. 40, 5. 661–670.

Eggert, A., Thiesbrummel, C., & Deutscher, C. (2015). Heading for new shores: Do service and hybrid innovations outperform product innovations in industrial companies? *Industrial Marketing Management*. 45. 173–183.

Fang, E., Palmatier, R.W., & Steenkamp, J.E.M. (2008). Effect of service transition strategies on firm value. *Journal of Marketing*. 72, 5. 1–14.

Forkmann, S., Ramos, C., Henneberg, S.C., & Naudé, P. (2017). Understanding the service infusion process as a business model reconfiguration. *Industrial Marketing Management*. 60. 151–166.

Gebauer, H., Fleisch, E., & Friedli, T. (2005). Overcoming the service paradox in manufacturing companies. *European Management Journal*. 23, 1. 14–26.

Godlevskaja, O., Iwaarden, J., & Wiele, T. (2011). Moving from product-based to service-based business strategies: Services categorisation schemes for the automotive industry. *International Journal of Quality & Reliability Management*. 28. 62–94.

Hall, B.H., Griliches, Z., & Hausman, J.A. (1986). Patents and R&D: Is there a lag? *International Economic Review*. 27, 2. 265–283.

Henderson, A.D. (1999). Firm strategy and age dependence: A contingent view of the liabilities of newness, adolescence, and obsolescence. *Administrative Science Quarterly*. 44, 2. 281–314.

Josephson, B.W., Johnson, J.L., Mariadoss, B.J., & Cullen, J. (2016). Service transition strategies in manufacturing: Implications for firm risk. *Journal of Service Research*. 19, 2. 142–157.

Kindström, D. (2010). Towards a service-based business model—Key aspects for future competitive advantage. *European Management Journal*. 28, 6. 479–490.

Kogut, B., & Zander, U. (1992). Knowledge of the firm, combinative capabilities, and the replication of technology. *Organization Science*. 3, 3. 383–397.

Kowalkowski, C., Gebauer, H., Kamp, B., & Parry, G. (2017a). Servitization and deservitization: Overview, concepts, and definitions. *Industrial Marketing Management*. 60. 4–10.

Kowalkowski, C., Gebauer, H., & Oliva, R. (2017b). Service growth in product firms: Past, present, and future. *Industrial Marketing Management*. 60. 82–88.

Kowalkowski, C., & Ulaga, W. (2017). *Service Strategy in Action: A Practical Guide for Growing Your B2B Service and Solution Business*. Service Strategy Press.

Levitt, B., & March, J.G. (1988). Organizational learning. *Annual Review of Sociology*. 14. 319–340.

March, J.G. (1991). Exploration and exploitation in organizational learning. *Organization Science*. 2, 1. 71–88.

Mathieu, V. (2001). Service strategies within the manufacturing sector: Benefits, costs and partnership. *International Journal of Service Industry Management*. 12, 5. 451–475.

Matthyssens, P., Vandenbempt, K., & Berghman, L. (2006). Value innovation in business markets: Breaking the industry recipe. *Industrial Marketing Management*. 35, 6. 751–761.

Neu, W.A., & Brown, S.W. (2005). Forming successful business-to-business services in goods-dominant firms. *Journal of Service Research*. 8, 1. 3–17.

Oliver, C. (1997). Sustainable competitive advantage: Combining institutional and resource-based views. *Strategic Management Journal*. 18, 9. 697–713.

Raddats, C., & Easingwood, C. (2010). Services growth options for B2B product-centric businesses. *Industrial Marketing Management*. 39, 8. 1334–1345.

Raddats, C., & Kowalkowski, C. (2014). A reconceptualization of manufacturers' service strategies. *Journal of Business-to-Business Marketing*. 21. 19–34.

Raddats, C., Kowalkowski, C., Benedettini, O., Burton, J., & Gebauer, H. (2019). Servitization: A contemporary thematic review of four major research streams. *Industrial Marketing Management*. 83. 207–223.

Salonen, A. (2011). Service transition strategies of industrial manufacturers. *Industrial Marketing Management*. 40, 5. 683–690.

Sawhney, M., Balasubramanian, S., & Krishnan, V.V. (2004). Creating growth with services. *MIT Sloan Management Review*. 45, 2, 34–43.

Shelton, R. (2009). Integrating product and service innovation. *Research – Technology Management*. 52, 3. 38–44.

Spohrer, J. (2017). IBM's service journey: A summary sketch. *Industrial Marketing Management*. 60. 167–172.

Spring, M., & Araujo, L. (2013). Beyond the service factory: Service innovation in manufacturing supply networks. *Industrial Marketing Management*. 42, 1. 59–70.

Story, V.M., Raddats, C., Burton, J., Zolkiewski, J., & Baines, T. (2017). Capabilities for advanced services: A multi-actor perspective. *Industrial Marketing Management*. 60. 54–68.

Teece, D.J. (2010). Business models, business strategy and innovation. *Long Range Planning*. 43, 2. 172–194.

Tongur, S., & Engwall, M. (2014). The business model dilemma of technology shifts. *Technovation*. 34, 9. 525–535.

Tronvoll, B., Sklyar, A., Sörhammar, D., & Kowalkowski, C. (2020). Transformational shifts through digital servitization. *Industrial Marketing Management*. 89. 293–305.

Visnjic, I., Wiengarten, F., & Neely, A. (2016). Only the brave: Product innovation, service business model innovation, and their impact on performance. *Journal of Product Innovation Management*. 33, 1. 36–52.

Von Hippel, E. (1988). *The Sources of Innovation*. Oxford University Press.

Zott, C., Amit, R., & Massa, L. (2011). The business model: Recent developments and future research. *Journal of Management*. 37, 4. 1019–1042.

3. Understanding scarcity strategies in service firms

Huiling Huang, Stephanie Q. Liu and Jay Kandampully

INTRODUCTION

Have you ever received a coupon stating that "This coupon will expire xx/xx/xxxx"? Have you ever encountered a message like "In high demand, only xx rooms left!" when searching for a hotel room on online booking platforms? Have you ever seen a similar restaurant advertisement highlighting that the venue is "Serving only xx dinners at a time"? Scarcity strategies are ubiquitous across a wide range of service domains, including the hospitality and tourism industries (e.g., Booking.com, Airbnb, Homestay, OpenTable, and Viator.com), car rental services (e.g., Avis, Turo, and Drivy), shared-ride services (e.g., Uber and BlablaCar), and airline ticket booking (e.g., Hotwire.com and easyJet; Teubner & Graul, 2020). Why have scarcity strategies become so popular in the service industry? Services are intangible performances that generally cannot be previewed before consumption. As a result, customers often find it difficult to evaluate service quality and become unsure about their purchases. Due to the intangible nature of services, it is also challenging for marketers to communicate their essence and benefits to customers. Scarcity strategies can convey the value of the service and reduce the perceived risk involving these purchases. When a service becomes scarce, customers tend to believe that the service is high in quality and, as a result, exhibit more purchase behaviors.

However, prior research on scarcity has three crucial gaps. First, previous research on scarcity has predominantly focused on its roles in the retail industry (Gierl et al., 2008; van Herpen et al., 2005, 2009), and little work on the service industry has systematically analyzed different types of scarcity strategies. Therefore, service companies lack systematic guidance regarding effective ways to apply such strategies. Due to the popularity of scarcity strategies in the service industry, it is necessary to fill this research gap. Second, previous research has mainly highlighted the positive effects of scarcity strategies (van Herpen et al., 2005, 2009); however, the backfiring effects have received far less attention. This research gap needs to be addressed since scarcity strategies are not always silver bullets. Indeed, some companies may convey false scarcity information to attract consumers; for example, a customer who was told that the available tables are scarce arrives at the restaurant and finds that the restaurant is actually not busy. Moreover, it is not uncommon to find that some companies frequently send scarcity messages to customers, intending to push them to make a quick purchase. However, these inappropriate uses of scarcity strategies might lose consumers' trust or create too much pressure for customers, which subsequently scares customers away.

The third research gap is that scarcity strategies might create two challenges for the service industry that have been largely neglected to date. The first challenge is that scarcity strategies can enhance customer expectations of the services prior to consumption. Customer gap—differences between expected service and perceived service—appears when service companies fail to meet the customer's increased expectations, leading to greater dissatisfaction. For example, suppose you see a marketing communication emphasizing that most of the tables have been reserved; you are very likely to set high expectations for the restaurant and then use these expectations as reference points to judge the service quality. When you actually go to the restaurant and are served good (but not excellent) food, you probably feel disappointed. Therefore, it is critical for service companies to coordinate improvements in service quality with scarcity strategies. Another potential challenge is the overuse of services induced by scarcity strategies. Service capacity is relatively constrained when facilities and the number of staff are fixed. Overuse of service refers to a situation in which demand for a service exceeds its capacity. Scarcity strategies can increase the demand for services, bringing more revenue in the short term to service companies. However, the overuse of services may push facilities and staff to work beyond their abilities to offer consistent quality, resulting in a drop in service quality. For example, the available number of tables and waiters in a restaurant is fixed. When there are too many customers, the dishes might be delayed, and the tables might not be adequately cleaned due to the overloading of employees; as a result, service quality declines. Moreover, some customers may not be able to enjoy the services; for example, a customer arrives at the restaurant and finds that there is no available table due to the high demand. In these cases, customers tend to be dissatisfied with the services, or even angry. Worse still, these unhappy customers may never come back again, leading to long-term business losses. By closing this research gap, service companies using scarcity strategies can better understand these two potential challenges and develop strategies to avoid them.

To fill these three gaps, we first classify different types of scarcity strategies by thoroughly reviewing the extant literature on scarcity. Next, based on the types of scarcity strategies, we dive into the psychological processes behind the positive and negative scarcity effects. We then summarize individual differences and contextual boundary factors that affect the effectiveness of scarcity strategies and offer a discussion on managerial implications for the service industry. Finally, we identify and discuss two potential challenges of scarcity strategies and, more importantly, provide strategies for quality improvement and demand and capacity management to overcome these challenges.

In doing so, this chapter makes important theoretical contributions. While scarcity strategies have been widely used in the service industry, prior research on scarcity has mostly examined its role in marketing tangible goods rather than intangible services. This book chapter contributes to the service marketing literature by deepening our understanding of the applications of scarcity strategies in the service industry. Moreover, by discussing the two potential challenges of scarcity strategies and their corresponding solutions, this chapter also adds to the service quality improvement literature and service management literature. Furthermore, we offer a comprehensive overview of scarcity based on different types of scarcity strategies, contributing to the scarcity literature as well.

THE CLASSIFICATION OF SCARCITY

Different types of scarcity strategies are frequently used to emphasize the limited availability of services (Figure 3.1). Generally, scarcity can be classified into limited time and limited quantity (Gierl et al., 2008). Limited-time scarcity indicates that services are available to customers for a restricted period of time. The degree of scarcity increases when the expiration dates are closer. For example, many restaurants utilize scarcity strategies in their promotions, with announcements such as "Valid [date]" or "Expire [date]." Similarly, online hotel booking websites (e.g., Hotels.com and Expedia.com) often include phrases such as "Only available until [date]" and "Today 20 percent off." Time scarcity is a marketer-driven circumstance as it is the marketer who determines the time restriction available for customers to buy the service.

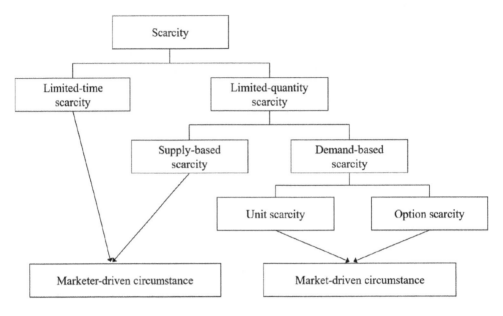

Figure 3.1   Types of scarcity

On the other hand, limited-quantity scarcity communicates that the number of available services is scarce. Quantitative scarcity can be driven either by "high demand" from the customer side or "limited supply" from the service-provider side. The former refers to demand-based scarcity and the latter is supply-based scarcity. Demand-based scarcity highlights that the service is in high demand, and many customers have already bought this service. For example, online booking platforms (e.g., Booking.com, Expedia.com, and OpenTable) commonly utilize demand-based scarcity strategies such as "In high demand, 95 percent of rooms have been booked," and "Only [number] left." Recently, demand-based scarcity has been further divided into unit scarcity (i.e., brand-specific scarcity) and option scarcity (i.e., alternative brands' scarcity; Song et al., 2019). Specifically, unit scarcity, such as "95 percent of the rooms *in this hotel* have been booked for your dates," implies the unavailability of a specific brand (Song et al., 2019). In contrast, option scarcity, such as "95 percent of the hotels similar to this hotel *in this city* have been booked for your dates," suggests that the availability of substitute brands is scarce (Song et al., 2019). Demand-based scarcity arises during the selling process and is caused by customers' high demand; therefore, it is considered a market-driven circumstance outside marketers' control. However, supply-based scarcity is caused by the actions of service companies that restrict the service to a predefined quantity. For example, the successful Denny's Grand Slam breakfast was available for up to 2 million customers nationwide (Aguirre-Rodriguez, 2013). Ultraviolet, a famous restaurant in China, declares: "Only serving ten dinners at a time" (Huang et al., 2020). Supply-based scarcity is a marketer-driven circumstance because marketers have control over the availability of the service distributed to customers at the outset of the offer.

Importantly, not all scarcity strategies are equally effective, and the underlying mechanism might also be different. To better employ scarcity strategies, service companies need to have a clear understanding of the positive and negative scarcity effects along with the science explaining these effects.

THE SCIENCE BEHIND SCARCITY EFFECTS

The Science Underlying Positive Scarcity Effects

The power of scarcity strategies in enhancing the customer's value perceptions, service desirability, and purchase behaviors has been widely acknowledged. The value-enhancing function of scarcity is based on the commodity theory, which posits that "any commodity will be valued to the extent it is unavailable" (Brock, 1968, p. 246). Anything that is useful, transferable, and has the potential to be possessed can be a commodity, such as a service, a product, and a message (Lynn, 1991). For example, Worchel et al. (1975) find that people believed that cookies were tastier when there were only a few cookies left than when there were abundant cookies in the jar. While different types of scarcity strategies can increase service value, the psychological mechanisms behind the positive scarcity effects sometimes vary from one to another, as illustrated in Figure 3.2. Yet, the positive effects of different scarcity strategies can sometimes be explained by the same psychological mechanism. For example, as shown in Figure 3.2, both limited-time and limited-quantity (i.e., supply-based and demand-based) scarcity strategies can activate a sense of urgency and fear of missing out (FOMO), influence customers' price perceptions, and, in turn, positively shape consumer responses. In this section, we discuss these psychological mechanisms in detail.

Triggering a sense of urgency and FOMO

The presence of scarcity can trigger a sense of urgency and FOMO on the promoted services, which subsequently motivates customers to make purchase decisions before the opportunities are gone. Both limited-time and limited-quantity scarcity strategies can induce such effects. In the case of limited-time scarcity, a timer or countdown is typically added to the advertised services, reminding customers that the service will disappear if they do not act quickly. For example, when promoting a new beverage called "Unicorn Frappuccino," Starbucks placed a timer on this offer and informed customers that this beverage would only be available for seven days (Bernazzani, 2017). This limited-time scarcity strategy attracted thousands of customers to flock to Starbucks stores. Ultimately, this beverage was sold out in one day and became an Instagrammable beverage garnering almost 160 000 user-generated shares (Bernazzani, 2017). Moreover, limited-time scarcity might induce a last-minute surge since the degree of scarcity is stronger when the deadline is approaching. For example, Marcus Taylor, a musician who promoted certain music packages online (e.g., iTunes distribution and recording time), launched a campaign by stating that the promotion would expire in only 100 hours, and a countdown timer was included on the website (Riska, 2017). Such a ticking countdown timer created a sense of urgency and triggered FOMO, promoting customers to

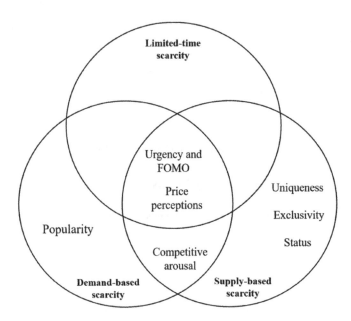

Figure 3.2   The science of positive scarcity effects induced by different types of scarcity

make a purchase. In the end, Marcus increased his sales by 332 percent with this limited-time scarcity strategy (Riska, 2017).

Limited-quantity scarcity implies that customers will miss out on scarce good deals if they do not catch them before other customers. The degree of urgency and FOMO induced by limited-quantity scarcity is enhanced with each unit sold. For example, OpenTable, an online restaurant-reservation service company, always displays the number of booking times and available time slots on their website. Similarly, tourism-related online booking platforms (e.g., Hotels.com, Booking.com, and Expedia.com) often highlight the limited available hotel rooms, flight tickets, or tourism packages with the intention of triggering a sense of urgency and to stimulate customers to make a reservation quickly.

Shaping price perceptions
Positive scarcity effects can arise by shaping the customer's price perceptions in two ways. First, scarcity can enhance customers' perceptions of the expense of services, which subsequently elevates their perceived service quality. Indeed, economic theory posits that people tend to associate scarce products or services with a relatively high price (Mittone & Savadori, 2009). Similarly, customers tend to require a higher price to give up their chosen products when the products are scarce rather than abundant (Mittone & Savadori, 2009). Higher prices offer customers the perception of quality because services with high quality often cost more to offer than do those with low quality (Chen et al., 1994). Therefore, the expensiveness perceptions of services, which are induced by scarcity, can lead customers to believe that the service has a high quality. Starbucks provides a good example since they place higher prices on limited-time drinks. To illustrate, Starbucks only sells pumpkin spice lattes in the fall and sets a timer for customers (Moore, 2019). More importantly, compared to a non-seasonal drink that is priced at $6.67, the price for a seasonal pumpkin spice latte is $7.81 (Moore, 2019).

Although the price is higher, customers still rush to the stores and scramble to get a pumpkin spice latte, creating more revenue for Starbucks.

Second, scarcity intensifies the customer's price uncertainty, or a customer's doubts regarding their ability to secure a price as good as the current price promotion (Noone & Lin, 2020). High price uncertainty suggests that customers are uncertain about their ability to receive a price similar to the promotional price after the offer is over. When employing a price promotion, service companies commonly tie scarcity to the discounted price. Such a practice generally creates pressure on customers and strengthens the price uncertainty, encouraging buyers to take advantage of the current promotional price.

Inducing competitive arousal

Scarcity can stimulate service purchases by triggering competitive arousal, which refers to "feelings and thoughts regarding the competitive nature of a purchase situation, and the belief that one would need to compete with other buyers to achieve a goal in a particular buying situation" (Nichols, 2012, p. 193). Importantly, it is limited-quantity scarcity not limited-time scarcity that induces such competitive arousal among customers. For limited-time scarcity, marketers provide as many services as customers want in a predefined period, and there is no competition among customers as all of them can secure their services as long as they arrive within the specified deadline. However, limited-quantity scarcity restricts services to a limited number of units. Every time a customer makes a purchase, the remaining number of available services reduces. Therefore, in the limited-quantity scarcity condition, customers need to compete against other customers for the focal service. In this case, obtaining the limited-quantity service signifies a victory in the competition (Knowles & Linn, 2004); thus, customers can enjoy more utilitarian (e.g., monetary value) and hedonic contentment (e.g., joy-of-winning; Aggarwal et al., 2011). These values are added to the scarce service, driving customers to desire the service even more.

Though two types of quantitative (demand-based and supply-based) scarcity can activate a sense of competition, demand-based scarcity tends to trigger a more salient competitive arousal than supply-based scarcity. Specifically, for supply-based scarcity, the cause of scarcity lies in the company's supply restriction of the service, which is a marketer-driven circumstance that is outside the customer's control. However, demand-based scarcity ascribes the service scarcity to the excess demand of other customers, aiming to encourage customers to fight with others for the same service (Huang et al., 2020). Therefore, customers who are exposed to demand-based scarcity are likely to experience a more intense level of competitive arousal and become more aggressive in grasping the scarce service before other customers do.

Signaling uniqueness, exclusivity, and status

Supply-based scarcity, a type of limited-quantity scarcity, can enhance perceived service value through signaling the uniqueness and exclusivity of the service. Uniqueness theory posits that people have a need to differentiate themselves from others for the purpose of boosting their social and self-image (Snyder, 1992). As people often define their sense of self by consumption patterns, they tend to seek unusual products/services to differentiate themselves from others (Gierl & Huettl, 2010). Supply-based scarcity implies that only a limited number of customers can enjoy the service, and therefore the consumption of a limited-supply service can signal one's uniqueness. For example, customers can express their distinctiveness to others when they go to a concert where only a limited number of tickets is available (Gierl & Huettl, 2010).

Moreover, service scarcity due to supply can signal exclusivity and serve as a status symbol (van Herpen et al., 2005, 2009). As supply-based scarcity restricts the total number of services in the marketplace, customers who can enjoy the service with limited supply tend to perceive themselves to be superior in social status (van Herpen et al., 2005, 2009). Therefore, customers sometimes desire the service more when it is only available to certain customers rather than to a majority. For example, when promoting a new program called Google+ in 2011, Google did not sell it directly to all customers. Instead, Google+ was sold only to users who had been invited by Google or by friends who shared an invitation with them (Bernazzani, 2017). By conveying a sense of exclusivity and status, 10 million users were motivated to join Google's social network within two weeks. By September 2011, Google+ was available to all Google account users and ended up with 400 million customers signing up in its first year (Bernazzani, 2017). Conversely, demand-based scarcity suggests that the majority of people have already bought the service, and limited-time scarcity implies that every customer can secure the service as long as they make the order within the predefined time limit. In both of these cases, the service can no longer fulfill the customer's need for uniqueness and provide a sense of exclusivity or status.

Signaling popularity

To boost sales, service companies often utilize demand-based scarcity to emphasize that the advertised service is popular and will be unavailable soon because of its high demand. A common situation that arises in a purchase context is that a customer's desire for the service increases when they know that others are purchasing the same service (Amaldoss, 2005; Fromkin & Snyder, 1980). For example, customers are likely to choose a hotel or a restaurant that has been booked by many other customers. The popularity signal has been used to explain the positive scarcity effects that are induced by demand-based scarcity. For one thing, signaling popularity can provide customers with the social proof of service quality. Put differently, customers tend to believe that services that have been purchased by a majority of people must be of good quality (Surowiecki, 2004). Service is intangible, making it challenging for customers to evaluate its quality prior to consumption. By providing information about other customers' purchase behaviors, demand-based scarcity can boost customers' confidence in service quality and value. Furthermore, while people have a need to differentiate themselves, they also have a need to belong to a social group. Purchasing a popular service can help them to "fit in" with the majority of customers.

The Backfire Effects of Scarcity

Despite the power of scarcity strategies, its magic does not always work. The inappropriate use of scarcity strategies can backfire, leading to the loss of customer trust, reduced perceived service value, and decreased sales. However, negative scarcity effects have received little attention to date, and there is little guidance available for service companies to avoid these negative influences. In this section, we broaden our understanding of negative scarcity effects by discussing the underlying psychological mechanisms.

Triggering falsity inferences

The incorrect use of scarcity strategies might trigger falsity inferences, which are defined as the customer's belief that companies are using false scarcity information to entice them to purchase. Such falsity inferences can be activated when customers notice that service companies fail to convey accurate scarcity information. For example, when promoting a new service, some companies use demand forecasting to inform customers that the advertised service will be in high demand, aiming to stimulate purchase behaviors (Aguirre-Rodriguez, 2013). Given that such scarcity information is a prediction, not a fact, customers tend to be suspicious of the companies' motives and consider these types of companies as deceptive or distrustful (Aguirre-Rodriguez, 2013). Another inappropriate use of scarcity that induces falsity inferences is to communicate "artificial" scarcity messages. It is not uncommon to find that some companies utilize computer programs to randomly generate false scarcity messages on their websites, hoping customers will quickly make a purchase. However, today's customers have gradually learned how to identify false scarcity claims. When they catch a lie, customers will no longer trust the company. Therefore, when applying scarcity strategies, service companies should be honest and convey accurate scarcity information. Otherwise, an inauthentic scarcity message can reduce a company's reputation in an instant.

However, even when companies convey accurate scarcity information, the inappropriate use of limited-quantity scarcity strategies could sometimes induce falsity inferences. For example, when the predefined service quantity is unreasonably low and/or customers' demand for the service promoted by a limited-quantity scarcity strategy is extremely high, it is very likely that the service quantity will run out quickly. However, from some customers' perspectives, they might feel scammed and think it is too popular to be real, even though the scarcity information is correct. To avoid this problem, service companies should chart customers' demand for the promoted service before determining the total service quantity. To better predict service demand, service companies could track previous demand patterns from customer information systems or conduct marketing research. If the promoted service is expected to be very popular, companies should increase the total service quantity when using limited-quantity scarcity strategies. In this way, companies may avoid inducing falsity inferences among customers and enjoy more revenue as well.

Posing too much pressure
Scarcity strategies may trigger, to a different level, anxiety-producing urgency, motivating customers to react quickly before the scarce deal disappears. However, putting too much pressure on customers may dilute the power of scarcity strategies or even scare customers away. For example, Groupon often "shouted" between four and six emails daily to subscribers and included scarcity messaging to promote services, whether it was an airline ticket or a facial massage package. However, the high frequency of scarcity messages may induce a perception that the scarce services are not really scarce, tarnishing the positive scarcity effects. Moreover, scarcity messaging might make customers feel stressed and consider that the company is forcing them into action. Suppose that you are intending to purchase an airline ticket on a booking website. At the top of each page, there is always a countdown timer telling you that the ticket is going to shortly disappear. How would you feel? Clearly, too much pressure might induce anxiety and ultimately frighten customers away. For example, limited-quantity scarcity strategies put customers in situations where they need to fight with other customers for the same service. Moreover, compared to supply-based scarcity, demand-based scarcity tends to activate a more salient sense of competition. However, some customers might have a tendency to avoid competition. These customers may instead turn to other available options when

they know they need to compete with other customers for the service (Huang et al., 2020). Altogether, it would be wise for service companies to utilize scarcity strategies in moderation.

THE CONTEXTUAL BOUNDARY FACTORS OF SCARCITY EFFECTS

Even if the scarcity information is accurate and moderately distributed, scarcity strategies do not work for every customer and every brand. Recent marketing literature has offered insights into boundary factors, such as individual differences, other self-related factors, and brand concepts, to understand which customers or brands are more susceptible to a certain type of scarcity strategy. In this section, we introduce these boundary factors and discuss important managerial implications regarding how to maximize the positive scarcity effects by applying the right scarcity strategy to the right customer and the right brand. Table 3.1 displays boundary factors that influence scarcity effects.

Table 3.1   *Contextual boundary factors that influence scarcity effects*

Boundary factor	Scarcity effect
Individual differences	Need for uniqueness (NFU)
	Regulatory focus
	Power
	Need for cognitive closure (NFCC)
Other self-related factors	Expectations of scarcity
	Familiarity with the service
Brand concepts	Functional and symbolic brands

Individual Differences

Need for uniqueness
An individual's need for uniqueness (NFU) has been considered an important factor that sways the effectiveness of scarcity strategies. NFU refers to an individual's motivation for pursuing differences relative to others in an attempt to boost social and self-image (Tian et al., 2001). People often differentiate themselves through the acquisition and consumption of products or services. For example, when selecting a hotel, some customers might prefer traditional hotels while others might favor special ones (e.g., treehouse and capsule hotels) that offer unique experiences. Individual differences in NFU lead customers to respond differently to different types of scarcity strategies. Specifically, for customers with a high NFU, supply-based scarcity is considered more effective than demand-based or limited-time scarcity. This is because supply-based scarcity signals the buyer's special tastes by restricting the number of customers who can enjoy the service. However, demand-based scarcity suggests that many other customers have already purchased the same service and, as a result, fails to satisfy the consumer's NFU. Similarly, in the limited-time scarcity condition, all customers can receive the same service as long as they purchase it within the allotted time. As a result, for customers with a high NFU, the attractiveness of the service will be diminished when it is marketed by demand-based or limited-time scarcity strategies.

In terms of service marketing, when managers want to target customers with a high NFU, it is a good idea to utilize supply-based scarcity. Meanwhile, when the services are relatively unique, highlighting supply-based scarcity can be an effective way to strengthen the distinctiveness of the service. For example, many tourism companies—such as Wild Frontiers, which was voted the second-best tour operator in the UK in 2014—are famous for providing unique and innovative travel experiences (Yellow Place, n.d.). These types of companies may consider employing supply-based scarcity strategies to enhance the uniqueness of the experience and drive up downstream sales.

Regulatory focus

Individual differences in regulatory focus (promotion vs. prevention) have been shown to affect customers' susceptibility to both demand-based and supply-based scarcity. Customers can be broadly classified as promotion-focused or prevention-focused individuals on the basis of the differences in motivational orientations that are used to pursue goals (Aaker & Lee, 2001; Higgins, 2002). Specifically, promotion-focused customers are concerned with advancement and achievement, and they strive to maximize the positive outcomes eagerly, whereas prevention-focused customers are concerned with safety and responsibilities, and they are motivated to minimize the negative consequences with enhanced vigilance (Aaker & Lee, 2001; Higgins, 2002). Given that demand-based scarcity can signal service popularity and offer a sense of security by avoiding choosing a service with low quality, prevention-focused customers who favor safer options tend to respond more favorably toward demand-based scarcity (Ku et al., 2012). However, as supply-based scarcity signals uniqueness and confers consumers with enhanced status, the consumption of services with a limited supply can create a sense of achievement. Hence, promotion-focused customers tend to exhibit more favorable responses toward supply-based scarcity due to their focus on achievement (Ku et al., 2012).

To maximize the persuasion effects of scarcity, service managers can utilize personalized scarcity strategies that align with consumers' regulatory focus. Promotion-focused customers tend to engage in impulse buying and report greater hedonic shopping values (e.g., shopping for fun, excitement, and adventure), whereas prevention-focused customers tend to be conservative in making purchase decisions and report greater utilitarian shopping values (e.g., fair prices, convenience). With the help of consumer data from customer relationship management (e.g., loyalty memberships), marketers may segment their customers as promotion-focused or prevention-focused and distribute tailored scarcity advertisements to the "right" person. Moreover, an individual's regulatory focus can be situationally activated through messaging. For example, customers are prone to adopt a promotion focus when they are exposed to a Thai massage advertisement highlighting health-promotion benefits (e.g., boosting energy and improving muscle flexibility; Liu et al., 2018). Conversely, their prevention focus is stimulated when the advertisement emphasizes illness-prevention benefits (e.g., relieving fatigue and decreasing muscle stiffness; Liu et al., 2018). Following this logic, marketers that employ supply-based scarcity strategies may consider stressing the promotion benefits of the service, whereas underscoring the service's prevention benefits is a good idea when utilizing demand-based scarcity strategies.

Power

The effectiveness of scarcity strategies can also be shaped by an individual's sense of power. Power refers to "an individual's relative capacity to modify others' states by providing or withholding resources or administering punishments" (Keltner et al., 2003, p. 265). As a universal factor in social interaction, power can influence customers' information searching behavior, spending propensities, brand choices, and feelings about themselves and others (Rucker et al., 2012). Importantly, compared to their powerless counterparts, powerful customers are more proactive in competitive situations in order to grasp opportunities and rewards. While limited-quantity scarcity stimulates competitive arousal, demand-based scarcity can trigger a more salient sense of competition than can supply-based scarcity. Due to their approach tendency to competition, powerful customers react more favorably toward demand-based scarcity than supply-based scarcity (Huang et al., 2020). However, powerless customers would respond indifferently toward these two types of limited-quantity scarcity strategies as they are not particularly motivated by demand-based scarcity that highlights competition among customers (Huang et al., 2020). Based on these findings, marketers are recommended to utilize demand-based scarcity strategies when targeting powerful customers. A critical question that needs to be answered here is: How can service companies identify powerful customers?

To this end, service companies can program algorithms to assess customer power states through their socioeconomic status, education levels, and job positions. Generally, customers who have higher incomes and education levels (e.g., doctors and lawyers) or have more autonomy at work (e.g., managers) tend to feel powerful. Moreover, an individual's socioeconomic status can be forecasted through their previous travel experiences and homeownership, which are accessible through customer loyalty programs or with the help of big data. With these methods, service managers are able to distribute demand-based scarcity advertisements to powerful customers. Alternatively, service managers can situationally manipulate an individual's power state through messages. For example, an advertisement featuring a slogan, "We all feel powerful in the morning: Treat yourself to free bagels," can help consumers feel powerful (Dubois et al., 2011). Therefore, when applying demand-based scarcity strategies, service managers may consider including a similar power-activated message in the advertisement, such as "You are more powerful than you think! A luxurious getaway is only a click away," to temporally enhance the sense of power and to subsequently intensify the positive scarcity effects (Huang et al., 2020).

Need for cognitive closure
It has been shown that scarcity effects can be more influential among customers with a relatively high rather than low need for cognitive closure (NFCC). NFCC refers to an individual's desire for a definitive answer to a question as opposed to ambiguity (Houghton & Grewal, 2000). Compared to those with low NFCC, customers with high NFCC are more motivated to make quick decisions and rely more on heuristic cues in their decision-making process. Limited-quantity scarcity strategies can help to simplify information processing by providing heuristic cues that signal service quality and value. For example, demand-based scarcity offers social validation for service quality. Similarly, supply-based scarcity communicates the value of the service by conveying a sense of uniqueness or high status. Therefore, customers with high NFCC are more susceptible to limited-quantity scarcity strategies.

Importantly, a customer's NFCC increases with age. As a result, service managers should consider the average age of their target customers when choosing a marketing strategy. For example, tourism companies often design certain tour packages that target older travelers. Similarly, healthcare centers commonly develop programs that are designed for older people. In these cases, employing limited-quantity scarcity strategies could be a good idea to boost sales. Moreover, a customer's NFCC can be situationally activated by increasing the time pressure. Along with this logic, customers who want to grab a quick bite due to their busy schedules might be more prone to limited-quantity scarcity effects. Given that the target customers of quick-service restaurants (e.g., McDonald's and Subway) tend to experience time pressure, employing limited-quantity scarcity strategies in marketing might be particularly effective for these restaurants. For example, when promoting a burger, McDonald's might utilize the demand-based scarcity strategy by informing customers that there is only a limited number of burgers available at this price due to the high demand. Accordingly, customers might generate inferences that the burger is popular and tasty and become more willing to buy it. Similarly, when advertising a new chicken wrap, Subway may use the supply-based scarcity strategy by telling customers that only the customers who join the MyWay Rewards program can enjoy a certain discount. This practice might induce a sense of high status, which subsequently stimulates targeted customers to make a purchase.

Other Self-Related Factors

Expectations of scarcity

Customer expectations of scarcity are another important factor that shapes the effectiveness of scarcity strategies. Expectations of scarcity describe the customer's previous anticipation about a service that is likely to be in short supply, before exposure to advertising (Mukherjee & Lee, 2016). In other words, customers with high expectations of scarcity consider in advance of advertising that the service is likely to become unavailable, whereas customers with low expectations of scarcity believe beforehand that the service is unlikely to be scarce. Importantly, customer expectations of scarcity can be driven by perceptions of other customers' high demand for services or by a company's restriction of supply (Mukherjee & Lee, 2016). For example, customers' demand for airline tickets and hotel rooms tend to be higher during peak travel days (e.g., Thanksgiving and Christmas) compared to regular travel days in September or October. In the case of higher demand, customers tend to consider that the supply of services might not be able to meet demand, leading to higher expectations of scarcity. However, during winter, customers tend to generate low expectations of scarcity toward the maintenance services of air conditioning firms due to the low demand for such services at this time. Apart from the demand-side elements, customer expectations of scarcity can be affected by the supply-side elements (Mukherjee & Lee, 2016). For example, customers are likely to have high expectations of scarcity when they know that service companies have suffered from supply disruption. During the COVID-19 pandemic, airline companies had to limit the number of certain flights in response to changes in government policies. In many restaurants, such as Red Lobster, the supply of some menu offerings were restricted due to supply disruptions during the pandemic. In these cases, customers previously had high expectations of scarcity toward the services.

Notably, inconsistencies occur when customers are exposed to a scarcity claim while they do not expect the advertised service to be scarce. Such an inconsistency can lead customers to believe that the company is using false scarcity information to push them over the purchasing fence (Mukherjee & Lee, 2016). Therefore, service companies are not recommended to apply demand-based or supply-based scarcity strategies when the services are not previously expected by their customers to be scarce. For example, tourism companies promoting tour packages should be prudent in utilizing demand-based scarcity in the off-season for travel. On the other hand, companies should take advantage of scarcity strategies when customers have high expectations of scarcity for the services. For example, in the time of COVID-19, companies that suffer from supply shortages can utilize a supply-based scarcity strategy to enhance the service value and subsequently increase sales. For example, because of the COVID-19 pandemic, Red Lobster may have to increase the prices of seafood offerings to compensate for the higher costs in supply and transportation. Red Lobster might inform customers that the number of seafood offerings for each day is restricted (i.e., supply-based scarcity) due to the impact of the COVID-19 pandemic. Since customers initially have a high expectation of scarcity for the seafood offerings, this strategy might enhance the offerings' value and motivate customers to buy them even though they are more expensive than usual.

Familiarity with the service
Scarcity strategies are more persuasive among customers who are relatively unfamiliar with the service. When customers are unfamiliar with the service, they tend to find it difficult to evaluate service quality, and therefore become uncertain about making a purchase. To reduce such uncertainty, they often rely on peripheral cues, such as scarcity messages, to make purchase decisions. For example, when exposing a demand-based scarcity message, customers with low familiarity with the service might follow other customers' purchase behaviors as they believe "hot" services must have a higher quality. Similarly, a supply-based scarcity message can enhance the perceived service value so that customers might actively embrace the "high-value" service even though they are not familiar with it. Such beneficial effects of demand-based and supply-based scarcity might be discounted among customers with high familiarity since they tend to utilize personal knowledge in their decision-making process (Jung & Kellaris, 2004).

Therefore, scarcity strategies are particularly beneficial for newly opened companies, brands with a relatively low business awareness, or companies that are promoting new services. For example, Snap Inc., a famous social media company, is a beneficiary of scarcity strategies. For the initial launch in 2016 of Snapchat Spectacles, which were sunglasses dedicated to recording short videos from the perspective of the wearer, Snap Inc. did not sell them online or at their store (Bernazzani, 2017). Instead, this new gadget was only sold by Snapchat-themed vending machines (i.e., Snapbots) that were randomly dropped in several cities. More importantly, these spectacles were only available on the day that the Snapbot was in the city, and the supply was also limited on that day. While no official announcements were made before the arrival of the Snapbots, hundreds of people queued in long lines hoping to receive a pair of these scarce spectacles (Bernazzani, 2017).

Brand Concepts

It is worth noting that certain scarcity strategies are particularly effective for specific brand concepts. Brand concepts can be broadly classified into two main categories: functional and symbolic. Functional brands focus on the utilitarian aspects of services and mainly satisfy the consumer's practical needs. For example, limited-service hotels (e.g., Holiday Inn Express, Super 8, and Comfort Inn) that emphasize budget-friendly accommodation create a functional brand concept. However, symbolic brands stress the social and hedonic aspects of services and mostly fulfill the customer's needs for self-expression and status. For instance, luxury hotels (e.g., The Ritz-Carlton, Four Seasons Resort Hualalai, and Montage Palmetto Bluff) can project a symbolic brand concept because staying in these hotels can elevate one's social image. Moreover, services from symbolic brands are typically characterized as unique and exclusive, offering customers an opportunity to differentiate themselves through their service consumption. Therefore, customers who seek symbolic values should respond favorably to messages that do not damage the uniqueness or exclusivity of these services.

By offering symbolic benefits, such as uniqueness, exclusivity, and status, supply-based scarcity has been considered to be congruent with the symbolic brand concept. Therefore, supply-based scarcity is more effective when marketing symbolic brands (Aggarwal et al., 2011). Following this logic, symbolic brands, such as luxury hotels, upscale restaurants, salon and spa services, and first-class airlines, should employ supply-based scarcity to maximize their marketing efforts. However, demand-based scarcity and limited-time scarcity may destroy the benefits provided by symbolic brands, leading to a backfire effect. As functional brands are purchased mostly for practical reasons, the differences in effectiveness among different types of scarcity strategies tend to be mitigated when marketing functional brands (Aggarwal et al., 2011).

POTENTIAL CHALLENGES FROM SCARCITY

While the power of scarcity strategies has been extensively documented, scarcity strategies might bring two challenges to the service industry that have been largely neglected by previous research. First, scarcity strategies can enhance customer expectations, and unmet expectations can result in a wider customer gap in service performance, thus leading to greater dissatisfaction. Second, scarcity strategies can enhance service demand. This has to be well-thought-out since maintaining quality is not always easy when demand increases. Additionally, given that the capacity in service companies is relatively fixed, the mismatch of demand and capacity can cause undesirable customer responses and a loss of revenue. In this section, we fill this research gap by discussing how the two potential challenges occur and suggesting important strategies to help overcome these challenges.

Quality Improvement Strategies to Meet Enhanced Expectations

When employing scarcity strategies, service companies should also implement quality improvement tactics to meet the enhanced customer expectations induced by the scarcity effects. Generally, the presence of scarcity tends to lead customers to expect that the services are of a high quality, and such expectations can become the standard or reference point that is used to compare actual service quality. If customer perceptions of the actual service experience fall short of their expectations, a wider customer gap might appear, leading to further dissatisfaction with the service. To avoid or minimize the customer gap, it is crucial for managers to employ quality improvement strategies that are discussed below.

First, service companies can develop strategies that are intended to help employees deliver higher-quality services during the high-demand period. Employees often represent the service and serve as brand ambassadors; therefore, they are the key to reducing or avoiding customers' negative perceptions. Indeed, in many personal services, such as counseling services, child care, and hairdressing, employees single-handedly provide the entire services. In such cases, customer evaluations of the service providers directly shape their perceptions of the brand.

For example, customers might consider Edward Jones as a competent and reliable financial advising company since their employees provide personalized and memorable services. Therefore, to ensure that employees are able to deliver improved services, service companies should invest in their employees, such as by providing ongoing training and promoting team-work. Meanwhile, service companies can empower employees so that they are able to provide personalized services to their customers. For example, employees at The Ritz-Carlton are required to complete at least 250 hours of training each year, and they are directed to a service value stating that "I am empowered to create unique, memorable, and personal experiences for our guests" (Morin, 2019).

Second, service companies should consider offering support systems, such as technology and equipment, to assist their employees to improve service quality. For example, to provide more tailor-made services, Starbucks employs reinforcement learning technology. This is a machine learning system that helps Starbucks offer personalized order recommendations based on the time of day, weather, popularity, and customers' previous purchase history (Sokolowsky, 2019). Meanwhile, cloud-connected devices were implemented in Starbucks to ensure that the machines would work properly (Sokolowsky, 2019). With the help of these technologies, service employees spend less time on machine maintenance and more time on providing better services.

Demand and Capacity Management to Avoid Overuse of Services

Scarcity strategies can also boost service demand, which might cause the overuse of a service, leading to a drop in service quality or a loss of business. Service companies are constrained in their ability to increase or decrease their capacity. For example, a hairdresser, a lawyer, or a doctor are able to serve only one customer at a time; therefore, they can serve only a limited number of customers. Similarly, the available number of hotel rooms for sale on any given day is fixed. Therefore, when the demand for hotel rooms is too high, the rooms might not be properly cleaned before being turned over to new guests due to the overtaxing of employees, resulting in a decline in service quality. What is worse, if demand surpasses capacity, the hotel will not be able to offer additional rooms for customers. While there are no clear strategies to increase the capacity, an available option is to manage demand. For example, airline com-panies and hoteliers often use yield management and dynamic pricing strategies to combat this challenge. This means they increase the price of hotel rooms and airline seats during high-demand days and times. Moreover, utilizing supply-based scarcity should be supported with dynamic pricing strategies; if this is not the case, limited sales of services might affect a company's revenue. Therefore, when employing scarcity strategies, a critical question for service companies is to identify a strategy that is able to wisely match capacity and demand.

As scarcity strategies can boost customer demand, managers can add new resources, such as using part-time employees, renting, and sharing facilities and equipment, to meet the increased demand. For example, restaurants and tourist resorts can hire part-time employees to cope with the increased demand to ensure that quality is maintained during a period when scarcity marketing is used. Moreover, if possible, modifying or adjusting existing resources is another way to enlarge the capacity. For example, many hotels (e.g., Marriott, Hyatt, and Best Western Hotels & Resorts) use this method by reconfiguring connecting rooms (i.e., two rooms connected with a locked door), such that they will sell these rooms as a family suite in slow-demand times, and then turn them into two separate rooms during the high-demand period.

Furthermore, service companies might enhance the service rate—the speed that employees use to complete a service—so that they can serve more customers at a certain time. For example, service providers in restaurants, banks, and plumbing companies are often requested to serve more customers when promotions are employed to attract more customers than usual. But as discussed earlier, serving too many customers at a time might exceed employees' capacity and cause a drop in service quality. To avoid this, companies need to better train their employees in advance and enhance their abilities and efficiencies in delivering consistent quality. In this way, companies can increase their service rate without experiencing a drop in service quality. However, for customer-intensive services, an increase in service rate often inevitably reduces service quality (Anand et al., 2011). Customer-intensive services, such as spas and beauty care, refer to services where quality is often determined by the length of service time and an employee's attention (Anand et al., 2011). Hence, increasing the service rate to serve more customers might not be a wise idea for companies that specialize in customer-intensive services. Taken together, when using scarcity strategies, managers should take service type into consideration before enhancing the service rate to meet increased customers.

Given that there is a relatively limited possibility to fluctuate capacity in many service companies, managers should also consider coordinating demand patterns of services with the implementation of scarcity strategies. A customer's demand for services often fluctuates, and these fluctuations could be seasonal, weekdays to weekends, or during different times of the day. For example, the Phoenician Hotel in Scottsdale, Arizona, often experiences high demand for hotel rooms between November to mid-April. However, the demand for rooms drops considerably from mid-May to September when temperatures are extremely high. This means that service companies can utilize scarcity strategies to increase demand during low-demand periods. For example, air-conditioning service companies utilize scarcity strategies to promote preventive maintenance services in early spring when it is a low-demand period. These companies set a time frame for the promotion and remind customers by stating, "Make sure your home is ready for the upcoming season with these special offers! Offers expire in 30 days with this card" (PostcardMania, 2020). Similarly, a customer's enthusiasm for traveling to South Florida during July and August may also be influenced by the hot weather and insects, causing slow demand. To attract consumers during such off-seasons, online booking platforms (e.g., Hotels.com, Expedia.com) can incorporate scarcity strategies to signal the popularity of tour packages with simple scarcity messages (e.g., "In high demand, we only have four packages left") to reduce customers' concerns and to enhance the desirability of their services. However, employing scarcity strategies during a period when demand is already high is very likely to cause excess demand and reduce service quality. Therefore, if the predictable pattern is for high demand, service companies should be cautious in deciding whether they need to implement scarcity strategies or not.

SUMMARY

Scarcity strategies are prevalent in the service industry and have been proven effective in enhancing the perceived quality and value of services. However, using inaccurate scarcity information and inappropriate scarcity marketing can put a damper on customers' trust and scare them away. In addition, not all scarcity strategies are equally effective for customers or brands. It is also worth noting that scarcity strategies create two challenges for service companies. First, scarcity strategies can raise customer expectations, which can result in customer gaps and service dissatisfaction if the company fails to meet these increased expectations. Second, scarcity strategies can elevate service demand, which may cause the overuse of services if the company's existing capacity fails to meet this enhanced demand. Taken together, service companies need to be honest when implementing scarcity strategies and use them in moderation. Moreover, it would be wiser for marketers to consider such boundary factors as different psychological traits, other self-related factors, and brand concepts so that they can leverage the power scarcity strategies. Finally, when employing scarcity strategies, service companies should implement quality-improvement strategies to satisfy the increased customer expectations and try to balance demand with its capacity. This chapter also offers avenues for future research. Specifically, the existing literature, including this chapter, has not examined whether and how different types of scarcity strategies can interact with each other to influence consumer responses. Will marketing effectiveness be strengthened when simultaneously using both limited-time and limited-quantity scarcity strategies? What is the corresponding psychological process? These questions might be of interest for future research.

REFERENCES

Aaker, J. L., & Lee, A. Y. (2001). "I" seek pleasures and "we" avoid pains: The role of self-regulatory goals in information processing and persuasion. *Journal of Consumer Research, 28*(1), 33–49.

Aggarwal, P., Jun, S. Y., & Huh, J. H. (2011). Scarcity messages. *Journal of Advertising, 40*(3), 19–30.

Aguirre-Rodriguez, A. (2013). The effect of consumer persuasion knowledge on scarcity appeal persuasiveness. *Journal of Advertising, 42*(4), 371–379.

Amaldoss, W., & Jain, S. (2005). Pricing of conspicuous goods: A competitive analysis of social effects. *Journal of Marketing Research, 42*(1), 30–42.

Anand, K. S., Paç, M. F., & Veeraraghavan, S. (2011). Quality–speed conundrum: Trade-offs in customer-intensive services. *Management Science, 57*(1), 40–56.

Bernazzani, S. (2017). *The scarcity principle: How eight brands created high demand.* Hubspot. https://blog.hubspot.com/marketing/the-scarcity-principle

Brock, T. C. (1968). Implications of commodity theory for value change. In A. G. Greenwald, T. C. Brock, & T.M. Ostrom (Eds.), *Psychological foundations of attitudes* (pp. 243–275). Academic.

Chen, I. J., Gupta, A., & Rom, W. (1994). A study of price and quality in service operations. *International Journal of Service Industry Management, 5*(2), 23–33.

Dubois, D., Rucker, D. D., & Galinsky, A. D. (2011). Super size me: Product size as a signal of status. *Journal of Consumer Research, 38*(6), 1047–1062.

Fromkin, H. L., & Snyder, C. R. (1980). *The search for uniqueness and valuation of scarcity.* Springer.

Gierl, H., & Huettl, V. (2010). Are scarce products always more attractive? The interaction of different types of scarcity signals with products' suitability for conspicuous consumption. *International Journal of Research in Marketing, 27*(3), 225–235.

Gierl, H., Plantsch, M., & Schweidler, J. (2008). Scarcity effects on sales volume in retail. *International Review of Retail, Distribution and Consumer Research, 18*(1), 45–61.

Higgins, E. T. (2002). How self-regulation creates distinct values: The case of promotion and prevention decision making. *Journal of Consumer Psychology, 12*(3), 177–191.

Houghton, D. C., & Grewal, R. (2000). Please, let's get an answer—any answer: Need for consumer cognitive closure. *Psychology & Marketing, 17*(11), 911–934.

Huang, H., Liu, S. Q., Kandampully, J., & Bujisic, M. (2020). Consumer responses to scarcity appeals in online booking. *Annals of Tourism Research, 80*, 102800.

Jung, J. M., & Kellaris, J. J. (2004). Cross-national differences in proneness to scarcity effects: The moderating roles of familiarity, uncertainty avoidance, and need for cognitive closure. *Psychology & Marketing, 21*(9), 739–753.

Keltner, D., Gruenfeld, D. H., & Anderson, C. (2003). Power, approach, and inhibition. *Psychological Review, 110*(2), 265.

Knowles, E. S., & Linn, J. A. (2004). *Resistance and persuasion*. Lawrence Erlbaum Associates.

Ku, H. H., Kuo, C. C., & Kuo, T. W. (2012). The effect of scarcity on the purchase intentions of prevention and promotion motivated consumers. *Psychology & Marketing, 29*(8), 541–548.

Liu, S. Q., Mattila, A. S., & Bolton, L. E. (2018). Selling painful yet pleasurable service offerings: An examination of hedonic appeals. *Journal of Service Research, 21*(3), 336–352.

Lynn, M. (1991). Scarcity effects on value: A quantitative review of the commodity theory literature. *Psychology & Marketing, 8*(1), 43–57.

Mittone, L., & Savadori, L. (2009). The scarcity bias. *Applied Psychology, 58*(3), 453–468.

Moore, K. (2019). *9 scarcity marketing tactics*. Sumo. https://sumo.com/stories/scarcity-marketing

Morin, C. (2019). *How the Ritz-Carlton creates a five-star customer experience*. CRM.org. https://crm.org/articles/ritz-carlton-gold-standards

Mukherjee, A., & Lee, S. Y. (2016). Scarcity appeals in advertising: The moderating role of expectation of scarcity. *Journal of Advertising, 45*(2), 256–268.

Nichols, B. S. (2012). The development, validation, and implications of a measure of consumer competitive arousal (CCAr). *Journal of Economic Psychology, 33*(1), 192–205.

Noone, B. M., & Lin, M. S. (2020). Scarcity-based price promotions: How effective are they in a revenue management environment? *Journal of Hospitality & Tourism Research, 44*(6), 883–907.

PostcardMania. (2020). *Your heating and air conditioning experts!* https://www.postcardmania.com/designs/heating-air-conditioning-marketing/#heating-air-conditioning-marketing-7

Riska, S. (2017). *How a musician increased sales by 322% using scarcity marketing*. Daily Deals for Massive Profits. http://dailydealsformassiveprofits.com/2017/03/how-a-musician-increased-sales-by-322-using-scarcity-marketing/

Rucker, D. D., Galinsky, A. D., & Dubois, D. (2012). Power and consumer behavior: How power shapes who and what consumers value. *Journal of Consumer Psychology, 22*(3), 352–368.

Snyder, C. R. (1992). Product scarcity by need for uniqueness interaction: A consumer catch-22 carousel? *Basic and Applied Social Psychology, 13*(1), 9–24.

Sokolowsky, J. (2019). *Starbucks turns to technology to brew up a more personal connection with its customers*. Microsoft. https://news.microsoft.com/transform/starbucks-turns-to-technology-to-brew-up-a-more-personal-connection-with-its-customers/

Song, M., Noone, B. M., & Han, R. J. (2019). An examination of the role of booking lead time in consumers' reactions to online scarcity messages. *International Journal of Hospitality Management, 77*, 483–491.

Surowiecki, J. (2004). *The wisdom of crowds: Why the many are smarter than the few and how collective wisdom shapes business, economies, societies, and nations*. Doubleday & Co.

Teubner, T., & Graul, A. (2020). Only one room left! How scarcity cues affect booking intentions on hospitality platforms. *Electronic Commerce Research and Applications, 39*, 100910.

Tian, K. T., Bearden, W. O., & Hunter, G. L. (2001). Consumers' need for uniqueness: Scale development and validation. *Journal of Consumer Research, 28*(1), 50–66.

Van Herpen, E., Pieters, R., & Zeelenberg, M. (2005). How product scarcity impacts on choice: Snob and bandwagon effects. *Advances in Consumer Research, 32*, 623–624.

Van Herpen, E., Pieters, R., & Zeelenberg, M. (2009). When demand accelerates demand: Trailing the bandwagon. *Journal of Consumer Psychology, 19*(3), 302–312.

Worchel, S., Lee, J., & Adewole, A. (1975). Effects of supply and demand on ratings of object value. *Journal of Personality and Social Psychology, 32*(5), 906.

Yellow Place, (n.d.). Wild Frontiers Travel. https://yellow.place/de/wild-frontiers-adventure-travel-london-britain

4. Adopting a low-contact, high-focus healthcare service strategy in the era of pandemics

Uzay Damali, Enrico Secchi, Stephen S. Tax and Jeff Kessler

INTRODUCTION

As the COVID-19 pandemic hit the world in 2020, many healthcare providers were forced to rapidly shift their service delivery to a low-contact, at-a-distance model. This chapter presents a case study of Allergy Associates of La Crosse (AAOL), a clinic based in Wisconsin (USA) which was in the process of moving from a low-focus, high-contact general allergy clinic model to a high-focus, low-contact specialty clinic model when the pandemic unfolded. While the intent of the clinic's strategic evolution was to achieve productivity increases and to deliver superior patient value, the arrival of COVID-19 added to the importance of being able to deliver healthcare remotely in times of a pandemic or another disruptive event. In this chapter, we pay particular attention to how COVID-19 suddenly eliminated some of the barriers that had obstructed the clinic's strategic shift (e.g., insurance payment for remote visits, and patient and physicians' willingness to embrace new technologies) and what it meant for AAOL's strategic transition. Further, our case study provides a set of research questions to promote future research aimed at understanding the long-term impacts of major disruptions on strategic service design.

First, this chapter contributes to our understanding of healthcare service strategy and design, in particular, the challenges of replacing a traditional high-contact, low-focus service with a low-contact, high-focus strategy. Service strategy and design research has expounded the value of high-focus (Heskett, 1983; Hyer et al., 2009) and low-contact operations (Chase & Tansik, 1983; Froehle & Roth, 2004; Kellogg & Chase, 1995) in increasing service productivity. Specifically, the service focus literature posits that as a service reduces the number of offerings, productivity increases through promoting swift, even flow (Schmenner, 1986) and economies of scale (Hyer et al., 2009). The customer contact model argues that as the amount of interaction between customer and service provider decreases, service productivity increases as activities are pushed to the back-office and are executed in a more "industrial" fashion (Levitt, 1976; Schmenner, 2012; Tsikriktsis, 2007). In mapping the strategic journey of AAOL through the classical dimensions of contact and focus, we highlight trade-offs and challenges of the transition, centering on their implications for healthcare services in the current environment.

Second, this chapter contributes to our understanding of service innovation. Our case study revealed the opportunities and the barriers experienced by AAOL in shifting their strategy from a traditional clinic to a loosely coupled referral network of practitioners and patients. We examine this shift through the lens of the diffusion of innovation literature. Our case analysis pushes the conversation forward by moving beyond the traditional product-focused discussions (Rogers, 2003) and their extension to considering a single, salient aspect of innovation (e.g., co-creation; Damali et al., 2016, 2021). Developing a deeper understanding of service innovation requires the simultaneous consideration of multiple factors (such as technologies, human behaviors, and service characteristics; Menor & Roth, 2008; Spohrer & Maglio, 2008). Moreover, in services, the configuration of those factors is often more important than the influence of individual factors (Ordanini et al., 2014). The network (or, as it is often referred to, ecosystem) approach to understanding the different actors involved in service delivery has been at the center of service research in the past decade (Lusch & Nambisan, 2015; Tax et al., 2013). Specifically, the complex interrelationships between co-creation practices and service networks have been shown to affect service outcomes (Beirão et al., 2017).

This chapter responds to two research priorities in service innovation highlighted by Ostrom et al. (2015), namely, "managing customers' and partners' collaboration throughout the service innovation process" (p. 131) and "understanding the interrelationships among service-product, service-process, and business-model innovation" (p. 131). These priorities reflect the strategic moves made by AAOL, who are trying to innovate their business model by changing their technologies and processes and developing a network approach to service delivery. Specifically, our case analysis is aimed at answering the following exploratory research questions, with the goal of generating insights to guide future research:

RQ1. What barriers did AAOL face in moving to a low-contact, focused business model?

RQ2. How did the COVID-19 pandemic affect the strategic journey of AAOL?

This paper proceeds as follows. In the second section, we present the methodology and the rationale for the single case study of AAOL. In the third section, we present the background of allergy treatment and AAOL, and analyze the strategic changes adopted by AAOL. Next, we explain the barriers related to patients, physicians, and insurance companies that slow adoption. Finally, we assess the pandemic's effect on reducing these barriers and state three research questions that are of central interest.

METHODOLOGY

This paper presents a single case study of an allergy clinic in Wisconsin. Data were collected through a series of semi-structured interviews with the operations executive who participated as a member of the research team. We conducted four interviews lasting about one hour and a half each, with topics ranging from strategy and market characteristics to operational issues. The questions asked in the first interview are listed in Appendix A. We supplemented the information obtained through the interviews by looking at Web resources connected to the case. Some of these Web resources are: the clinic website (www.lacrosseallergy.com) and testimonials on social media platforms such as Facebook, Birdeye, and Healthgrades. We followed up with the informant whenever we needed clarifications or feedback.

A single case study approach is most appropriate when the research questions are broad and in need of refinement. This methodology has been effectively used to gain a deeper understanding of service design and to gather the rich insights that are necessary for theory development (Edvardsson et al., 1995; Eisenhardt, 1989; Meredith, 1998; Toomer et al., 1993). Case research trades detail (internal validity) for generalizability (external validity).

We recognize the limitations of a single case study, which is why this research should be considered exploratory with the purpose of stimulating further research on service strategy and innovation processes.

ALLERGY ASSOCIATES OF LA CROSSE CASE ANALYSIS

This section presents an analysis of the strategic changes adopted by AAOL throughout the years and the obstacles they faced. To better understand the context of the case, we first provide an overview of the treatment of allergies and the history of the clinic, as well as a description of their current operating model. We then describe the strategic progression of the clinic from a traditional low-focus, high-contact service to the current multi-channel, network-based, high-focus, low-contact service.

Background: Allergy Treatment and AAOL

Worldwide, the rise in prevalence of allergic diseases has continued in the industrialized world for more than 50 years. Roughly 7.8 percent of people 18 and over in the U.S. have hay fever, and 8 percent of children have a food allergy (Centers for Disease Control and Prevention, 2020). The operations executive of AAOL estimated that there are roughly 60 million allergy patients in the U.S., one-third of which are considered to have severe symptoms, such as anaphylaxis or comorbidities.

The treatment of allergies has a long medical history and has taken many forms. Allergies are reactions of the immune system to substances that are normally tolerated and are often mild but could lead to significant impacts on daily life as well as serious medical complications (MedlinePlus, 2020). The condition is usually reported by the patient after an initial episode of discomfort, and then it is conclusively diagnosed by an allergy specialist through one or more of a variety of tests (skin tests, intradermal tests, challenge tests, blood tests; American Academy of Allergy, Asthma & Immunology, 2020).

AAOL focuses on providing sublingual immunotherapy, an emerging alternative to traditional treatments which are focused on managing the immune system reaction (Nadeau & Barnett, 2020). Immunotherapy aims at treating the underlying cause of allergies to "re-train," or desensitize, the immune system. Sublingual immunotherapy consists of a once-a-day tablet or drop that dissolves very quickly under the tongue. The patient is given a small dose of the allergen, which gradually increases tolerance and can result in fewer or less severe symptoms.

AAOL currently operates according to the model illustrated in Figure 4.1, whereby patients access their services through four entry paths. The first path entails patients experiencing allergies and related problems and directly contacting AAOL. The marketing strategy for this path relies entirely on positive word of mouth. When the clinic was established in 1970, this was the primary entry point of the service.

The second access path is through family practitioners' referrals. To increase referrals, AAOL formalized their method by creating a treatment protocol called the "La Crosse Method." Since 2001, the clinic has put significant effort into developing a referral network to increase their reach. As the clinic's reputation grew, some allergy specialists also started to refer patients (third path). This mostly happened when the standard treatment did not work.

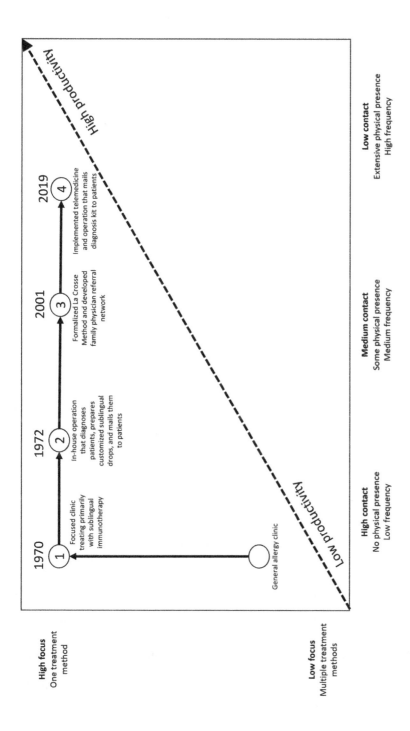

Figure 4.1   Patients' entry paths to AAOL service

Finally, the formalized treatment protocol of the La Crosse Method allowed family physicians and some allergy specialists to deliver the AAOL treatment without patients traveling to Wisconsin. This fourth path relies on AAOL providing testing kits and treatments to physicians. This significantly increased the potential patient base. While this path is usually reserved for simple cases, AAOL implemented the use of telemedicine in 2019 to allow clinic physicians to help patients, referring physicians, and specialists in virtual environments.

AAOL Strategic Progression

The strategic progression of AAOL to fulfill its intended value proposition of delivering the most effective allergy treatment using the most efficient means can be viewed by mapping it using the concepts of service focus and customer contact (Chase, 1981; Heskett, 1983; Skinner, 1974; Tsikriktsis, 2007). In Verma and Young's (2000) taxonomy of low-contact service strategies, AAOL would be classified in the "High Product–Service Quality Seekers" group, focusing on quality and innovation followed by cost reductions, and with financial gain only a secondary objective. Figure 4.2 illustrates the progression using a two-dimensional matrix with the level of service focus on the vertical axis and the level of customer contact on the horizontal axis. We evaluated the service focus by the number of treatment methods, and the customer contact by the extent of physical presence of the patient in the clinic.

AAOL's strategic progression from low focus/high contact to high focus/low contact was achieved in four strategic moves, from 1970 to the present, which correspond to the progressive addition of patient access options depicted in Figure 4.1. These moves are: (1) established a focused clinic, treating primarily with sublingual immunotherapy; (2) established an in-house operation that diagnoses patients, prepares customized sublingual drops, and mails them to patients; (3) formalized the La Crosse Method and developed a family physician referral network; and (4) implemented telemedicine and an operation that mails diagnosis kits to patients. As seen in Figure 4.2, the first strategy moved the clinic vertically to become a focused service, while the other moves shifted the clinic horizontally to become a low-customer-contact service. In the following subsections, we provide a detailed explanation of these moves.

Establishment of a focused clinic (Strategic Move 1)
The clinic founder, Dr. David Morris, had been searching for an effective way to treat patients with mold allergy; in particular, mold exposure was an occupational hazard to dairy farmers in Wisconsin. While many were non-smokers, they often suffered from chronic obstructive pulmonary disease. Damp hay stacked in small bales warmed as it composted, creating ideal conditions for mold growth that released billions of mold spores when the bales were opened and used for animal feed. Often these patients would feel so sick after receiving allergy shots that it was hard for them to work. In addition, busy farming schedules made it difficult for farmers to come to Dr. Morris's office frequently for injections. When Dr. Morris first started his Wednesday-night allergy clinic, he began offering patients a choice: shots or drops.

In 1970, Dr. Morris opened AAOL, a focused immunotherapy clinic, to treat food and environmental allergies and related diseases (e.g., asthma and sinusitis) using sublingual immunotherapy. At this point, the clinic mostly relied on one channel for patients, denoted as Path 1 in Figure 4.1, with occasional physicians' referrals (Path 2).

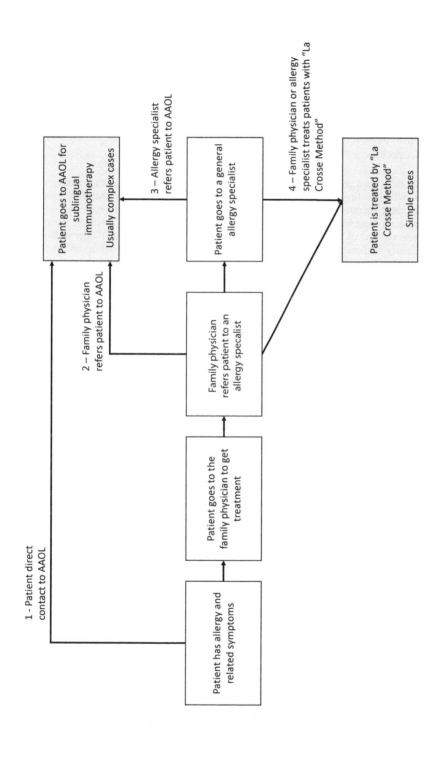

Figure 4.2   The strategic progression of AAOL

The clinic experienced three benefits of being a focused operation. First, the focused service strategy allowed AAOL to increase productivity. Specifically, AAOL significantly reduced and managed the uncertainty and complexity of the processes by focusing on one treatment method. This allowed for more streamlined processes and more efficient use of resources.

Second, the focused service provided for a superior patient experience. While their process is designed for one treatment, it can be highly customized for a particular case. Further, as the clinic significantly reduced uncertainty, they used this extra buffer capacity to provide superior service in terms of shorter wait times and clear guidance. The patient journey became more predictable, adding to patient satisfaction. An extensive number of patients posted positive testimonials online, such as:

> My daughter and I have been going there for 10 years. She has severe allergies, asthma, and an autoimmune disorder. When we first came, her lungs were working at 30 percent; now they're working at 80 percent. I think there's a good chance she could have died if we hadn't come there.
>
> I could not have been more impressed with Allergy Associates of La Crosse yesterday. We drove nearly 800 miles to see one of the best, brightest, most thoughtful and thorough allergy doctors in the nation. Our family was met with the most caring, kind, unassuming and humble staff at every turn of a nearly four hour visit. At no point did any person in their office assume anything about our knowledge, needs, or situation. I can't say enough times that every single person in their office acted patiently and selflessly to honor the needs of my child and our family. It's clear to me that every member of their staff is well taken care of, and are therefore able to focus their energy on the patients they treat. It's so refreshing and relieving to find a safe place that truly prioritizes people—theirs and ours—above all else.

Third, the strategy helped them to become the largest allergy clinic in the country. Gaining economies of scale increased the efficiency and productivity of the clinic. By becoming the destination of choice in the area for allergy treatment, the clinic was able to grow into one of the largest specialized allergy treatment facilities in the country and to promote the use of sublingual immunotherapy. This was accomplished by marketing based on word of mouth and patients' testimonials.

In-house diagnosis and production of sublingual drops (Strategic Move 2)
While the first move shifted the company on the vertical focus axis in Figure 4.2, the next three strategic moves shifted the clinic horizontally, from left to right, reducing customer contact. As the clinic became successful and expanded their staff by hiring more doctors, their capacity to increase the number of patients was limited by the geographical dispersion of the population (the average driving distance for many patients was about three hours). To reduce the number of visits, the clinic decided to develop a laboratory to diagnose patients and prepare the sublingual immunotherapy drops in-house. These were then mailed to patients. This strategic move reduced the number of visits to twice per year, while a general allergy clinic may require patients to visit twice a month.

This operational shift was aimed at accomplishing two goals. First, insourcing of the diagnosis and the preparation of the therapy reduced the lead times and increased efficiency. Second, it spearheaded the move toward a reduction of customer contact by allowing the patient to self-administer a custom-made treatment without the need to travel to the clinic. This reduction of customer contact was important both for the patients and for the clinic. The patients only needed to travel to the clinic once, for the diagnosis, therefore greatly reducing their time commitment. At the same time, the clinic's capacity was expanded, as the time physicians spend with a patient is the main driver of capacity utilization. In sum, this operational shift greatly increased the clinic's capacity.

The La Crosse Method and the physician referral network (Strategic Move 3)
Building on the work done to develop diagnostic and treatment protocols at the clinic, AAOL developed a protocol, the La Crosse Method, that could be implemented by referring physicians. Specifically, AAOL established a separate company, Allergy Choices (AC), with the goal of creating a network of physicians who could effectively use the La Crosse Method in their practice. These physicians were not normally allergists, but general practitioners who could use AC services to expand their offer range without substantial investment (Paths 2 and 4 in Figure 4.1). The outside physicians would be able to use the protocol to treat simpler cases, while complex cases would be expected to visit AAOL. AC also worked on diffusing awareness and interest in the La Crosse Method among allergy specialists (Path 3 in Figure 4.1).

Telemedicine and mailing diagnosis kits to patients (Strategic Move 4)
The most recent strategic move of AAOL was the implementation of telemedicine. Telemedicine has been implemented to significantly reduce the need for face-to-face patient contact. Given the limited capacity of the clinic and the geographical constraints, the high-contact nature of the service had been a significant obstacle to growth. In other words, the reliance on face-to-face interaction created both a demand and a capacity constraint for the service. Before the restrictions imposed by the COVID-19 pandemic, both patients and physicians were reluctant to shift toward telemedicine because of the engrained traditional way of providing care. Patients were unfamiliar with the method, physicians were not excited to learn the details of telemedicine, and insurance companies' reimbursements were significantly lower for telemedicine visits.

Further, the creation of a laboratory and of standardized blood test kits to send to external parties (patients or other physicians) was instrumental in fully realizing the move to a low-contact service environment. For patients who would have normally traveled to the clinic, the kit created the opportunity to choose their own local service to draw the blood and still use the services of the clinic to receive their personalized sublingual drops. Without this innovation, operational shifts 3 and 4 would not have been possible, as the kits provided the foundation for distributed testing of patients.

Barriers to Change

AAOL's value proposition has several relative advantages (e.g., lower price, limited side-effects, and a higher likelihood of full recovery). This value proposition requires them to pursue a low-focus/high-contact service strategy. However, barriers related to patients, physicians, and insurance companies slowed the strategic moves and the adoption of the treatment at a large scale (Table 4.1). We describe these barriers in the following sections.

Patient-related barriers
AAOL experienced a number of barriers on the road to becoming a high-focus clinic. While the productivity achieved by the focused strategy is significant, patients did not necessarily understand the value proposition, which includes reduced overall cost. Our interviews

Table 4.1   *AAOL barriers to strategic progression*

Strategic moves	Patients	Physicians/allergy specialists	Insurance companies
1. Established a focused clinic treating primarily with sublingual immunotherapy	Patients do not understand the value proposition of AAOL Patients do not want to drive to receive the service (the average driving distance is three hours) The treatment might take three to five years, depending on the complexity Patients can be price sensitive when insurance companies do not pay for the service	Physicians/specialists are not informed about the treatment and its effectiveness[a] Physicians/specialists are comfortable with their current high-contact/ low-focus model[a] Less patient physical presence in the clinic reduces the revenue for the allergy specialist	Some insurance companies are not informed about the effectiveness of the treatment, so they are not willing to reimburse the expenses
2. Established an in-house operation that diagnoses patients, prepares customized sublingual drops, and mails them to patients	Many potential patients believe that having allergy shots delivered at physicians' offices is more effective than sublingual immunotherapy drops sent to their home[a]		
3. Formalized the La Crosse Method and developed a family physician referral network	Many potential patients may not be part of the family physician referral network		
4. Implemented telemedicine and an operation that mails diagnosis kits to patients	Many potential patients do not feel comfortable with online visits[a]	Physicians/specialists do not feel comfortable with online visits[a]	Some insurance companies do not want to reimburse online visits[a]

Note: [a] COVID-19 significantly relaxed the barrier.

highlighted that many patients were unsure of the potential benefits of the treatment when they were making their initial decision to try it. Compounded with the perceived hurdles to receive the treatment, this constituted a significant barrier to adoption for the patients. Before the implementation of telemedicine and referral networks, obtaining the treatment at the clinic required patients to drive, on average, three hours. Even after the implementation of the telemedicine option, patients often resisted the change from in-person to remote visits, a well-known phenomenon in the study of telemedicine adoption and technology-mediated services (Kruse et al., 2018; Wünderlich et al., 2013).

Another problem related to patients is compliance with the prescribed treatment. The treatment may take, on average, three to five years, and as soon as patients feel better, they tend to prematurely stop taking the immunotherapy. This problem persists even when the physical barriers to receiving the treatment are removed. AC is working on creating analytic tools to better understand this issue.

Finally, there is a barrier to adoption linked to the insurance market. Not all insurance companies reimburse the treatment as it is not yet recognized as mainstream. Therefore, some patients might have to pay out of pocket.

Physician-related barriers
Throughout their strategic evolution, AAOL and AC faced several barriers related to physicians unwillingness to change. First and foremost, the treatment is not well known in the United States, and it has yet to gain widespread acceptance as a legitimate treatment, although it has been promoted by experts in the field (Nadeau & Barnett, 2020). The method is not generally taught in medical schools. AC creates opportunities to inform external physicians on the La Crosse Method through organizing conferences and training seminars.

The moves to increase focus and reduce contact also faced resistance from the clinic's own physicians. Many physicians were satisfied with the early high-contact/low-focus model, and focused clinics have a history of struggling to find doctors who are willing to narrow their practice (Heskett, 1983). A similar set of issues arises for the reduction in contact. Patient contact constitutes an important part of physicians' training and a potential source of work satisfaction. Finally, revenues for remote treatment were usually lower than those for in-person visits.

Insurance-related barriers
Both moves toward focus and reduced patient contact were significantly obstructed by the reliance of the U.S. medical system on private insurance. The higher costs associated with traditional allergy treatments usually result in higher margins in insurance payments for the clinics. Moreover, as mentioned before, some insurance companies do not reimburse allergy immunotherapy sublingual drops, making the treatment more expensive for the patient. Similarly, insurance companies either pay less or do not reimburse remote visits compared to in-person appointments. To address these issues, AAOL tried to bypass the insurance market and negotiate directly with large employers, who could offer allergy treatment at the clinic as a valuable benefit to their employees.

Impact of the COVID-19 Pandemic

After the formal declaration of the COVID-19 pandemic in March 2020, research has assessed the pandemic's effect on reducing barriers to telemedicine adoption in a variety of settings. This research found a strong correlation between the rate of increase in COVID-19 cases and telemedicine adoption (Wosik et al., 2020). While AAOL's product and service offerings are innovative, their service delivery system has been traditional, until COVID-19 hit. AAOL data show that before the pandemic, 99 percent of services were provided face-to-face, even though the clinic had the telemedicine capability. After the declaration of the COVID-19 pandemic, the clinic moved all patients to telemedicine. Gradually, the percentage of face-to-face appointments increased as the pandemic continued. As of October 2020, 40 percent of appointments were held through telemedicine.

Consistent with the literature on the adoption of innovations (Rogers, 2003), shifting to higher co-creation entails a set of perceived and actual risks for all parties involved in service delivery (Damali et al., 2021). Patients usually feel that the quality of care is better when they see the doctor in person, and physicians face a loss of potential revenue (as insurance reimbursements are lower for remote visits) as well as, most importantly, a loss of control (a different physician, chosen by the patient, will perform the skin or blood test). This explains why, even as AAOL invested in developing and implementing a telemedicine system that was completely integrated with electronic medical records and the clinic's appointment system, telemedicine was not widely adopted in the clinic. The pandemic suddenly eliminated the many barriers to adoption, and clinic operations completely shifted to telemedicine during the first lockdown.

Seven barriers to the adoption of telemedicine have been identified related to the parties involved in the complex healthcare system. These parties are software providers, government and insurance companies, healthcare providers, and patients (Kruse et al., 2018). Some research compared various countries with the level of governmental barriers and rate of telemedicine adoption (Bali, 2018). Other work explained how COVID-19 significantly speeded up the slow adoption rate of telemedicine, particularly healthcare services having organizational readiness (Blue et al., 2020; Serper et al., 2020). In general, the following aspects have been shown to ease the burden of telemedicine adoption during the pandemic:

1. Telemedicine software privacy, security, and performance has been increased;
2. Telemedicine software has been integrated with other software systems, making it easier to use;
3. Public and private insurance companies changed their reimbursement policies and are now willing to reimburse for telemedicine;
4. Legal requirements on privacy and security have been relaxed;
5. Patients are more skilled and motivated to use electronic channels;
6. Providers are more skilled and motivated to use telemedicine; and
7. Organizations integrated telemedicine use with other internal processes and policies.

Based on our previous discussion of AAOL, it is easy to see how these seven factors influenced their rate of adoption of telemedicine. The clinic was in a privileged position, considering that the preliminary work on developing and implementing the required IT systems had already been done. A substantial amount of training had already been imparted to doctors and other staff. Interestingly, even in this ideal situation, the clinic saw a substantial uptick in face-to-face visits at the beginning of the fall of 2020. The strategic question for management of the clinic is whether the strategic shift to a low-contact operation can be maintained beyond the pandemic.

Further, with telemedicine, AAOL put into practice another move to reduce customer contact: sending allergy test kits to patients and their physicians. This strategy served patients with less severe conditions particularly well. The clinic still expects patients with severe allergies to be tested at the clinic. The ultimate goal of the organization is to become a remote contact operation and a hub for physicians all over the U.S. who want to administer sublingual drops. This strategic move was in the works as the COVID-19 pandemic hit North America, which significantly altered some of the barriers that were preventing the move from coming to fruition. This move has two fronts, one concerning the operations of the clinic itself and one concerning the diffusion of the protocols outside the clinic. The ultimate goal of this strategic move was to reduce customer contact in the clinic itself, while at the same time developing a network that would adopt the clinic protocols and rely on AAOL's laboratories for diagnostic equipment and tests as well as for the development of the treatment.

The COVID-19 pandemic provided fertile ground for this type of remote service to become more mainstream. Standard allergy services have reported severe difficulties with the restrictions imposed by the pandemic because they require giving medication through shots. The main barriers to the adoption of the AAOL method that persisted were that insurance usually paid less if a test was not performed at a clinic, and the reduced revenue streams for physicians, as patients who visit the clinic usually avail themselves of additional services and exams. Consistent with service operations strategy theory, the move to a low-contact, high-focus operation relies on a significant increase in the number of patients served, which made operational shift 4 of pivotal importance. The availability of multiple paths for patient access (Figure 4.1) was the factor that allowed the clinic to swiftly accommodate the required changes in the patients' journeys.

In summary, while high-focus low-contact operations could provide higher productivity and a better patient experience, this strategy is still not common in the healthcare industry. There are multiple barriers slowing its adoption, in the form of resistance to change coming from physicians, patients, and insurance providers. However, the emergence of COVID-19 relaxed some of these barriers and created opportunities for experimenting with new healthcare delivery models.

FUTURE RESEARCH

The emergence of the pandemic reduced many of the existing barriers to the adoption of telemedicine. In some cases, it proved to be the only viable option. While the topic of the future of telemedicine could generate scores of research questions, we next develop three sets of questions that are of central interest. One overarching theme across all future research directions concerns the permanence of the behavioral changes after the current crisis is over. In the AAOL case, the question will be how many patients will want to continue being treated remotely rather than reverting to in-person visits? Similarly, will insurance companies and government regulations make the current relaxations permanent? AAOL and many other healthcare providers will have to find ways to make the efficiency gains of new delivery options permanent. The analysis of factors influencing future choices of patients and providers constitutes a ripe area of future research.

Research Theme 1: Healthcare Service Design during the Pandemic

There appears to be a consensus in the expert community that pandemics will be more frequent in the future due to extensive population growth and global activity. Beyond that, from a healthcare perspective, many patients like the convenience and the access to care, particularly in rural areas, that telemedicine provides. Some doctors have found that talking to patients in their home on a platform like Zoom offers a reasonable level of care. It also allows them to talk directly to caregivers who might not be available during traditional clinic visits. In the case of AAOL, while COVID-19 initially led to a total shift to telemedicine, three months after the initial shutdown it leveled at around 30 to 40 percent usage in consultations. While this is a significant drop, it is a dramatic increase compared to the pre-pandemic world. Thus, low-contact healthcare has momentum even without the immediate threat posed by the pandemic.

It is critical to address questions related to how service design can meet these challenges. In particular, understanding how traditional high-contact services can design and deliver the experience through low-contact channels is at the forefront of trying to make AAOL's operation pandemic proof. Marrying convenience and efficacy requires designs that re-think the entire service systems of many providers. Integrating information and experience across multiple delivery channels poses challenges that require additional research. Medical issues are particularly sensitive to privacy, so understanding how to operate in that environment is important.

Research Theme 2: Building a Healthcare Delivery Network

The case study also presented an interesting take on the challenges and opportunities of growth. The shift to a low-contact approach allows for geographic expansion but may require building a physician network to support the execution of the service, as the cost of other forms of growth could be prohibitive (Tax et al., 2013). Questions related to the design and membership of the network are critical, as is the challenge of maintaining quality when the number of participants expands. Ensuring potential patients are correctly informed about services becomes more challenging as touchpoints increase. Understanding the roles of network members is critical to these questions. Further, a challenge of developing a network is that network members may become competitors, so there are some strategic risks. How healthcare providers can manage this risk is an important issue.

Research Theme 3: Customer Participation Adoption in Healthcare Technology

The topic of customer participation and performance is central to understanding service design and delivery (Damali et al., 2021). Changing the medium from face-to-face to video contact requires further research to understand how this might affect the patient and physician experience (Ishii et al., 2019). The shift not only influences the communication of information but also may require patients to take on tasks previously performed by healthcare professionals. Research into understanding the types of tasks that are suited to patient performance and how those can be supported is an important area of inquiry. Further, the risks associated with patient performance in terms of whether they choose to adopt the new channel and their performance in the new channel impact both physician financial outcomes and patient health outcomes. Therefore, research aimed at understanding barriers to patient adoption and successful performance of telemedicine is fundamental.

REFERENCES

American Academy of Allergy, Asthma & Immunology. (2020). *Allergy testing.* https://www.aaaai.org/conditions-and-treatments/library/allergy-library/allergy-testing

Bali, S. (2018). Barriers to development of telemedicine in developing countries. In T. F. Heston (Ed.), *Telehealth.* IntechOpen.

Beirão, G., Patrício, L., & Fisk, R. P. (2017). Value cocreation in service ecosystems: Investigating health care at the micro, meso, and macro levels. *Journal of Service Management.* 28, 2. 227–249.

Blue, R., Yang, A. I., Zhou, C., De Ravin, E., Teng, C. W., Arguelles, G. R., & Lee, J. Y. (2020). Telemedicine in the era of COVID-19: A neurosurgical perspective. *World Neurosurgery.* 139. 549–557.

Centers for Disease Control and Prevention, National Centre for Health Statistics. (2020). *Allergies and Hay Fever.* https://www.cdc.gov/nchs/fastats/allergies.htm

Chase, R. B. (1981). The customer contact approach to services: Theoretical bases and practical extensions. *Operations Research.* 29, 4. 698–706.

Chase, R. B., & Tansik, D. A. (1983). The customer contact model for organization design. *Management Science.* 29, 9. 1037–1050.

Damali, U., Miller, J. L., Fredendall, L. D., Moore, D., & Dye, C. J. (2016). Co-creating value using customer training and education in a healthcare service design. *Journal of Operations Management*. 47–48, 1. 80–97.

Damali, U., Secchi, E., Tax, S. S., & McCutcheon, D. (2021). Customer participation risk management: Conceptual model and managerial assessment tool. *Journal of Service Management*. 32, 1. 27–51.

Donelan, K., Barreto, E. A., Sossong, S., Michael, C., Estrada, J. J., Cohen,A. B. & Schwamm, L. H. (2019). Patient and clinician experiences with telehealth for patient follow-up care. *Am J Manag Care*, 25, 1., 40–44.

Edvardsson, B., Haglund, L., & Mattsson, J. (1995). Analysis, planning, improvisation and control in the development of new services. *International Journal of Service Industry Management*. 6, 2. 24–35.

Eisenhardt, K. M. (1989). Building theories from case study research. *Academy of Management Review*. 14, 4. 532–550.

Froehle, C. M., & Roth, A. V. (2004). New measurement scales for evaluating perceptions of the technology-mediated customer service experience. *Journal of Operations Management*. 22, 1. 1–21.

Heskett, J. L. (1983). Shouldice Hospital Limited. *Harvard Business School Case*. 9–683.

Hyer, N. L., Wemmerlöv, U., & Morris, J. A. (2009). Performance analysis of a focused hospital unit: the case of an integrated trauma center. *Journal of Operations Management*. 27, 3. 203–219.

Kellogg, D. L., & Chase, R. B. (1995). Constructing an empirically derived measure for customer contact. *Management Science*. 41, 11. 1734–1749.

Kruse, C. S., Karem, P., Shifflett, K., Vegi, L., Ravi, K., & Brooks, M. (2018). Evaluating barriers to adopting telemedicine worldwide: A systematic review. *Journal of Telemedicine and Telecare*. 24, 1. 4–12.

Levitt, T. (1976). The industrialization of service. *Harvard Business Review*. 54, 5. 63–74.

Lusch, R. F., & Nambisan, S. (2015). Service innovation: A service-dominant logic perspective. *MIS Quarterly*. 39, 1. 155–175.

MedlinePlus. (2020). *Allergy*. https://medlineplus.gov/allergy.html

Menor, L. J., & Roth, A. V. (2008). New service development competence and performance: An empirical investigation in retail banking. *Production and Operations Management*. 17, 3. 267–284.

Meredith, J. (1998). Building operations management theory through case and field research. *Journal of Operations Management*. 16, 4. 441–454.

Nadeau, K., & Barnett, S. (2020). *The end of food allergy: The first program to prevent and reverse a 21st century epidemic*. Penguin.

Ordanini, A., Parasuraman, A., & Rubera, G. (2014). When the recipe is more important than the ingredients: A qualitative comparative analysis (QCA) of service innovation configurations. *Journal of Service Research*. 17, 2. 134–149.

Ostrom, A. L., Parasuraman, A., Bowen, D. E., Patrício, L., Voss, C. A., & Lemon, K. (2015). Service research priorities in a rapidly changing context. *Journal of Service Research*. 18, 2. 127–159.

Rogers, E. M. (2003). *The diffusion of innovation* (5th ed.). The Free Press.

Schmenner, R. (1986). How can service businesses survive and prosper? *Sloan Management Review*. 27, 3. 21–32.

Schmenner, R. (2012, July 23). The case study: Treating patients faster. *FT.com*. https://www.ft.com/content/17637170-d4b4-11e1-9444-00144feabdc0

Serper, M., Cubell, A. W., Deleener, M. E., Casher, T. K., Rosenberg, D. J., Whitebloom, D., & Rosin, R. M. (2020). Telemedicine in liver disease and beyond: Can the COVID-19 crisis lead to action? *Hepatology*. 72, 2. 723–728.

Skinner, W. (1974). The focused factory. *Harvard Business Review*. 52, 3. 113–121.

Spohrer, J., & Maglio, P. P. (2008). The emergence of service science: Toward systematic service innovations to accelerate co-creation of value. *Production and Operations Management*. 17, 3. 238–246.

Tax, S. S., McCutcheon, D., & Wilkinson, I. F. (2013). The Service Delivery Network (SDN): A customer-centric perspective of the customer journey. *Journal of Service Research*. 16, 4. 454–470.

Toomer, E., Bowen, K., & Gummesson, E. (1993). Qualitative methods in management research. *Journal of the Operational Research Society*. 44, 7. 735–736.

Tsikriktsis, N. (2007). The effect of operational performance and focus on profitability: A longitudinal study of the U.S. airline industry. *Manufacturing & Service Operations Management*. 9, 4. 506–517.

Verma, R., & Young, S.T. (2000). Configurations of low-contact services. *Journal of Operations Management*. 18, 6. 643–661.

Wosik, J., Ferranti, J., Katz, J. N., & Tcheng, J. (2020). Telehealth transformation: COVID-19 and the rise of virtual care. *Journal of the American Medical Informatics Association*. 27, 6. 957–962.

Wünderlich, N. V., Wangenheim, F. V., & Bitner, M. J. (2013). High tech and high touch: A framework for understanding user attitudes and behaviors related to smart interactive services. *Journal of Service Research*. 16, 1. 3–20.

APPENDIX A: SAMPLE QUESTIONS

Process-Related Questions:

How did allergy associates deliver the service to patients before and after the pandemic? The pandemic required health organizations to reduce physical contact. What type of practices did your organization implement to reduce physical contact? Do you think these new practices compromised your high quality and efficient service?

People-Related Questions:

Can you explain the different roles for patients and service providers in the face-to-face versus online services? What do you expect the providers to do in the various stages (diagnosis and treatment) of the service delivery? What types of knowledge and skills are needed for successful delivery?

Patient-Experience-Related Questions:

How did the pandemic affect the patient experience, service quality, and patient satisfaction? What types of practices did your organization implement to improve patient experiences?

Technology-Related Questions:

What are some technological competencies your organization has developed (utilized more) since the pandemic began? What types of technologies do you require your patients to use? What types of technologies do you require your providers to use?

Capacity-Related Questions:

What was the capacity and demand of AAOL before and after the pandemic?

Network-Related Questions:

Do you think your organization has improved collaboration with the doctors outside your clinic since the pandemic began?

PART II

SERVICE INNOVATION AND DESIGN

5. Service innovation process in creative-intensive business services organizations

Fengjie Pan and Rohit Verma

INTRODUCTION

In the last two decades, research focusing on services, service innovation, or new service development has seen significant growth (Biemans et al., 2015; Papastathopoulou and Hultink, 2012), but there is still little knowledge concerned with the innovation process of new service development (Adams et al., 2006; Drejer, 2004; Droege et al., 2009; Nijssen et al., 2006). Additionally, among the studies concerning new service development, the findings lack consensus, as many are based on the concepts, methods, and frameworks used to understand new product development (Biemans et al., 2015). With this in mind, the current research fails to provide consistent suggestions to managers on the question: How can we most effectively and efficiently manage the new service development processes (Biemans et al., 2015)? According to the description from Menor and Roth (2007), the extant theory and understanding of the strategies, processes, and tactics for new service development are inadequate.

Over the last several decades of economic development, professional services or knowledge-intensive business services (KIBS) have experienced substantial development and growth. In Europe, KIBS are regarded as a key driver of innovation and competitiveness (Rowley, 2007). This view is consistent with the study of Empson et al. (2015), who point out that in the global economy, the professional service sector has become one of the most profitable and strongest-growing service sectors. Miles (2012) argues that most of the KIBS activities are customized to specific clients, which indicates that the innovation process is difficult to organize in a linear way or exactly the same across projects. Although it cannot be organized in a linear way, the innovation process in service sectors tends to be more systematic and is often based on certain trajectories, particularly those of service professional firms (Sundbo and Gallouj, 2000). Although a large number of studies focuses on new service development, most of these works are based on the financial service industries (de Jong and Vermeulen, 2003; Droege et al., 2009). In the classification of KIBS, the concept includes a wide range of industries that have similarities and differences (Table 5.1). Surprisingly, other service sectors have not received much attention, such as the creative industries, which are famous for their originality and creativity. In terms of their differences, one is concerned with the characteristics of their clients and their service end-users; this means that in some industries, clients (customers) are also service end-users. In other industries, clients (customers) differ from service end-users.

The service industry contains a wide range of services and each type of service has some special characteristics. This indicates that applying the results generalized from one industry to all service industry categories is too straightforward (Kuester et al., 2013). As suggested by

Table 5.1   *The creative industries vs KIBS*

	KIBS	Creative industries
Similarities	Knowledge-intensive	Knowledge-intensive
Differences	Including different types of KIBS	Focusing on creative-intensive services

Atuahene-Gima (1996), future research should focus more on the differences within a variety of service industries instead of the differences between new service development and new product development. In addition, Lovelock and Gummesson (2004) point out that research should explore specific service categories rather than taking all the service industries as a whole. In this respect, investigating the new service development process in other service industries can contribute to our understanding of service innovation.

Based on this background, this study chooses the advertising industry to study the new service development process of creative-intensive service development, as it is situated in the intersection of the creative industries and KIBS. In the advertising industry, the main reason that clients end up in a relationship with their agencies is their desire for more creative ideas (Dowling, 1994). With relationship development, clients tend to increase their expectations of their agencies' creativity, or agencies lose their creativity. This demonstrates the importance of creativity and innovation in the advertising industry. However, the research concerning innovation in the advertising industry is relatively rare (Miles and Green, 2008). Focusing on creative services is highly likely to have implications in the aspects of how to design and develop new services for other industries. This is because of the interconnections among service sectors. Therefore, the research questions addressed in this chapter are:

RQ1: What is the new service development process in creative-intensive business services firms?

RQ2: How is the process similar to or distinct from the established new service development process?

This chapter is based on 25 case studies of creative (advertising) service providers. It investigates how they develop innovative services for their clients, and it identifies the main activities performed in each stage. As creative services represent an extreme end of the services spectrum, this research advances knowledge not only on the new service development in creative-intensive services, but also on the wider area of KIBS.

CREATIVE INDUSTRIES VS KIBS

KIBS refers to services that rely heavily on professional knowledge, which can be regarded as primary sources of information and knowledge for their users; their main clients are other businesses (Miles et al., 1995). In the European economy, KIBS occupy an important role and contribute much to the innovation development of other industries. Regarding innovations in KIBS, most are classified as ad hoc innovations (Gadrey and Gallouj, 1998), which refers to a 'solution to a particular problem by a given client' (Gallouj and Weinstein, 1997). Many scholars demonstrate the importance of clients/customers in KIBS firms' innovation processes (Alam and Perry, 2002; Slater and Narver, 1994; Sundbo and Toivonen, 2011), which manifests the interactive attributes of the innovation process in KIBS firms. In particular, KIBS firms can be categorized into different industries and different types of KIBS – for example, the 'traditional' professional services (P-KIBS), the 'new' technology-based service firms (T-KIBS; Miles et al., 1995), and C-KIBS, which refers to services dealing with the knowledge of social affairs, cultural trends, and aesthetics (Miles, 2012), such as market research, advertising, architecture, and others. The more creative advertising agencies are, the more successful they are in retaining clients, account portfolios, and individual accounts (Michell et al., 1996). The creative industries are characterized by their creative capability.

Given the growing importance of the creative industries, there is little knowledge and understanding of innovation within this sector (Miles and Green, 2008). Therefore, investigating the differences and similarities between the creative industries and other KIBS industries sheds light on the differences among services.

Creative industries constitute a large portion of our economies, yet the definition of the creative industries is unclear. According to a report by Bakhshi et al. (2013), in 1998, the creative industries were defined by the UK Department for Culture, Media and Sport (DCMS) as 'those industries which have their origin in individual creativity, skill and talent and which have the potential for wealth and job creation through the generation and exploitation of intellectual property'. Based on this definition, DCMS proposed 13 service sectors belonging to the category of the creative industries: advertising, architecture, art and antiques, design, crafts, designer fashion, film, music, computer games, performing arts, publishing, software, and television and radio. The UK's creative economy takes the leadership position in the world (Bakhshi et al., 2013). In the UK, there are 2.5 million people working in the creative economy (many more than those who work in the financial, advanced manufacturing, and construction industries), which constitutes at least 9.7 per cent of the UK's Gross Value Added (Bakhshi et al., 2013). This reflects the talent of Britain's creative people and entrepreneurs (Bakhshi et al., 2013). However, the success of the UK creative economy is in danger, as digital communications technologies become more pervasive. Although the creative economy in the UK has retained its leadership position in the world, it faces innovation problems (Bakhshi et al., 2013).

Although the advertising industry is only one of many industries categorized as a 'creative industry', given the importance of this industry in the UK and its close relationship with other creative industries, we suggest that an analysis of the new service development process may develop some frameworks or provide some insights that could be tested across the creative industries. In addition, we chose the advertising industry as the focus of our research for three reasons. First, the UK's creative industries depend on the advertising industry, which indicates that many firms in creative industries would disappear without the support of advertising (DCMS, 2011). Therefore, the advertising industry is critical to the development of the UK's economy. Second, the advertising industry is characterized by a high level of innovation activity (Miles and Green, 2008) and its members are renowned for their creativity. Although the level of innovation activity in the advertising industry is higher than that of many other high-innovation sectors (Chapain et al., 2010), research concerning innovation in the advertising industry is very rare (Miles and Green, 2008). Third, advertising services are situated at the intersection between the creative industries and KIBS. Studying the advertising industry will advance our knowledge of both the creative industries and KIBS. Moreover, creativity acts as the heart and soul of advertising services and plays a crucial role in business relationship development (Halinen, 1997). Therefore, investigating the advertising industry can contribute a lot to the research development of KIBS, particularly for the innovation research development of C-KIBS.

In the extant literature, some scholars attempt to unravel the new advertisement process. For example, according to Nov and Jones (2003), the new advertisement process can be divided into three main transformations: the transformation of the client's brief into insights and strategy by planners; the transformation of the insights and strategy into creative ideas by creative professionals; and the transformation of the creative ideas into advertisements to be published in media channels by a graphic or TV production company or some other relevant companies. From these three transformations, we can identify the important transition points in the innovation process and the important employees in every transformation phase.

When comparing the creative industries with other KIBS, companies in the creative industries place more emphasis on creativity development, and the services developed focus on the artistic and aesthetic dimension (Bakhshi et al., 2013), which is different from the development of financial services. Therefore, the research based on financial services cannot apply to the creative industries.

As the creative industries are characterized by their ability to develop creative output, whether using a systematic development process is conductive to or limits their creativity remains unclear. Therefore, exploring the new service development process should be helpful to reveal the mysteries in this area.

NEW SERVICE DEVELOPMENT PROCESS AND MODEL

The new service development process refers to 'a set of activities, actions, tasks, and evaluations (project screening, market research, product development, test marketing) that move the project from the idea stage through to launch' (Cooper et al., 1994). It is regarded as a systematic approach to develop new services (Singh et al., 2012). The typical stages of the new service development process are the creation of a concept, business analysis, idea development, and launch (Froehle et al., 2000; Johnson et al., 2000). Such development process involves activities aimed to improve the effectiveness and efficiency of developing new services and is often concerned with a stage-gate system (Cooper, 1990; de Brentani, 1991). The importance of having a formal new service development process or a stage-gate system has already been demonstrated in many studies (Cooper and Edgett, 1996; de Brentani, 1991; Edgett and Parkinson, 1994; Menor and Roth, 2007; Singh et al., 2012; Storey and Easingwood, 1996; Zomerdijk and Voss, 2011). Nevertheless, when compared with manufacturing companies, there are fewer service companies leveraging formal stage-gate systems to develop new services (Griffin, 1997; Griffin and Belliveau, 1997). Therefore, more research exploring the new service development process should be developed to shape our understanding of the relevant issues of the process (de Jong and Vermeulen, 2003; Droege et al., 2009; Johne and Storey, 1998).

INNOVATION PROCESS AND MODEL

Through reviewing the literature, we can simplify the innovation process as having three main components: idea emergence, idea development, and idea implementation (Heusinkveld and

Benders, 2002). In the service sector, most firms find it difficult to formalize and organize the innovation process in a systematic way (Sundbo and Gallouj, 2000). They argue that innovation is not a linear process, especially in services industries (Voss et al., 1992). In practice, innovation is often an iterative process and the innovation process in services firms is more likely to be seen as a search-and-learning process (Sundbo, 1997). Some researchers are studying the new service development process and conceptualizing the innovation process (Gadrey and Gallouj, 1998; Sundbo, 1997). For example, Sundbo (1997) divides the innovation process in service firms into four main phases: idea generation, transformation into an innovation project, development, and implementation. After his conceptualization, Gadrey and Gallouj (1998), based on the study of the consultancy industry, segment the innovation process into four main steps: identification of problems (the preliminary study stage), studying the problem (the stage of collecting information), providing advice about the problem (making recommendations), and implementation (Figure 5.1).

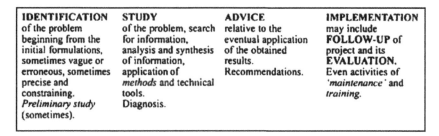

Source: Gadrey and Gallouj (1998).

Figure 5.1   The innovation stages in the consultancy industry

Then, Aarikka-Stenroos and Jaakkola (2012) developed a value co-creation process based on some KIBS firms. Instead of developing the co-creation process into detailed stages, they organized the process into five main steps: diagnosing needs, designing and producing the solution, implementing the solution, managing value conflicts, and organizing the process and resources (Figure 5.2).

Although the innovation process delineates a general picture of how new services are innovated, it is too abstract to let us understand the details of the process. Therefore, identifying the details of the innovation process will shed light on how to operationalize the innovation process more efficiently and effectively.

NEW SERVICE DEVELOPMENT MODEL

As for the concrete new service development model, some researchers are dividing the innovation process into detailed stages (Alam and Perry, 2002; Bowers, 1989; Scheuing and Johnson, 1989). Bowers (1989) was the first scholar to recognize the importance of breaking down the innovation process into stages. The model developed by Bowers (1989) for products includes eight steps: developing a business strategy, developing a new product strategy, idea generation, concept development and evaluation, business analysis, product development and testing, market testing, and commercialization. This model highlights the importance of strategy, which is neglected by many existing new service development processes. However,

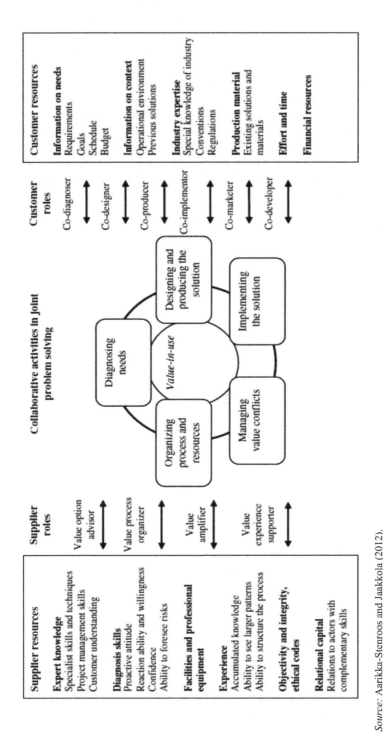

Source: Aarikka-Stenroos and Jaakkola (2012).

Figure 5.2   Joint problem solving as value co-creation in knowledge-intensive services

this model is quite similar to the one proposed by Booz Allen Hamilton (1982) for new product development. Therefore, to consider service uniqueness, Scheuing and Johnson (1989) proposed a more comprehensive new service development model for financial services, which had 15 stages. These stages are: formulating new service objectives, idea generation, idea selection, the development of concept, concept testing, business analysis, project authorization, service design and testing, process and system design and testing, market program design and testing, personnel training, service testing and pilot study, marketing test, launching the service, and post-launch evaluation. The importance of a well-designed strategy for new service development is also recognized by Scheuing and Johnson (1989). Based on these two models, Alam and Perry (2002) developed a new service development process incorporating customer–producer interactions into their model, which included ten stages: strategic planning, idea generation, idea screening, business analysis, formation of a cross-functional team, service design and process system design, personnel training, service testing and pilot run, test marketing, and commercialization.

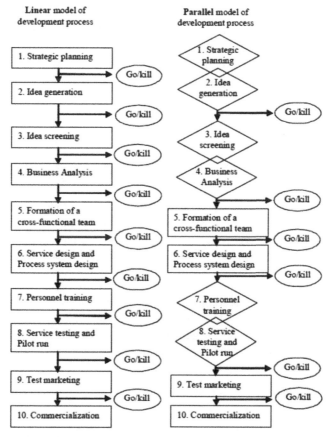

Source: Alam and Perry (2002).

Figure 5.3   The linear model and parallel model of service development stages

This development stage is almost the same as that developed by Bowers (1989), while Alam and Perry (2002) develop two models based on the same ten development stages: the linear model of development process and the parallel model of development process. In the parallel model, service providers can conduct different development tasks at the same time. Table 5.2 lists the existing new service development models.

In short, based on the review of the new service development literature, we summarize that the new service development process/service innovation process plays a significant role in influencing new service success; however, questions concerning how to conceptualize the new service development process in creative industries and its differences with other KIBS remain unexplored. Therefore, to gain a deeper understanding of this question, an exploratory investigation of the new service development process in the creative industries is required.

SERVICE INNOVATION STAGES IN ADVERTISING FIRMS

Table 5.3 shows the main stages of the new service development process and the main activities involved in each stage that were identified from 45 interviews with advertising firms. These interviewed companies were highly similar in reporting their new service development stages, which varied from 10 to 14 steps.

Stage 1: Client Brief

The first stage of the new service development process begins with the client brief, which is about the client requirements for the advertising campaign. Usually in this stage clients indicate their expectations for the campaign. In a sense, this stage is the formal starting point to determine how creative the advertising campaign must be. In KIBS, service innovation is driven by client needs. Drawing on the empirical evidence, four stages are needed before beginning to generate creative ideas: understanding the client's business, diagnosing the problem, shaping the strategy, and formulating the creative brief.

Although the respondents agreed on the role of the client brief, how the client brief plays its role was less consistent. Sometimes, a client's desire to have innovative advertising is straightforward, while in other cases, a client's desire is much more obscure. In the latter scenario, these cases require more discussion between the agency and the client. In addition, in some cases, the innovating element is clear-cut at the beginning of the process, while in others, it is worked out as the project develops. In general, the new service development process is shaped by both the advertising firm and the client – that is, the creative capacity of the advertising firm and the client's desire to develop innovative advertising.

Table 5.2   *The existing new service development models*

Authors	Bowers (1989)	Scheuing and Johnson (1989)	Alam and Perry (2002)
Stages	Developing a business strategy	Formulating new service objectives	Strategic planning
	Developing a new product strategy	Idea generation	Idea generation
		Idea selection	Idea selection
	Idea generation	Development of concept	Business analysis
	Concept development and evaluation	Concept testing	Formation of cross-functional team
	Business analysis	Business analysis	
		Project authorization	Service design and process system design
	Product development and testing	Service design and testing	Personnel training
		Process and system design and testing	Service testing and pilot run
	Market testing	Market program design and testing	Test marketing
	Commercialization	Personnel training	Commercialization
		Service testing and pilot study	
		Marketing test	
		Launching the service	
		Post-launch evaluation	
Research objects	Financial service industries	Financial service firms	Australian financial service firms

Table 5.3   *The identified stages and their activities*

New service development (NSD) stages	Activities
Client brief	The starting point – ask clients to write a brief about their project, their problem
Information collection	Obtain as much information as possible from clients
Problem diagnosis	Discuss the project problems with the client
Strategy planning	Propose the appropriate strategy
Creative brief	Shape the creative brief and deliver it to creative teams
Idea generation	Generate creative ideas
Idea testing	Test the ideas generated by creative teams to select several creative ideas
Idea selection	Select the best idea
Idea amplification	Amplify the core idea and apply it to different channels
Production	Work with product companies to bring the idea to life
Marketing test	Test the advertisement
Launch	Launch the advertisement
Evaluation	Evaluate the advertisement and check whether it satisfies the client
Learning	Learn from the advertisement and plan to revise it
Re-launch?	Re-launch the revised advertisement

Stage 2: Collecting Information

The stage following the client brief is collecting information. The goal of this stage is to under-stand the business and the client's requirements and expectations. Therefore, agencies will try to gain as much information as they can from their clients, such as the requirements, objec-tives, what worked before, what the problem is, what they need to do, and so on. If agencies cannot obtain all the required information from their clients, they will seek help from external partners, such as research organizations, consultants, and others. All the information required is used to further understand the client brief, to dip inside the client business, and to find out the advertising problem. Without gleaning adequate information from the client or from external organizations, it would be difficult for agencies to gain deep insights into the client's business, which implies that agencies cannot fulfil their potential to produce the best solution possible. All the best work is based on the deep understanding of the client's business and the client brief. Gleaning the required necessary information is the prerequisite of shaping a strong strategy and developing an idea to produce a creative and effective campaign. Therefore, collecting information plays a paramount role in influencing the results of the process.

Stage 3: Problem Diagnosis

The next stage involves diagnosing the advertising problem. Agencies need to find out what the real problem is, what the real need of the client is, what they need to do, what they can do, and so on. Sometimes the client may have the wrong perception of their advertising problem. Therefore, the responsibility of advertising agencies is to help the client diagnose their real problem.

Stage 4: Strategy Planning

After finding out the real problem, the next step is to shape the strategy of developing the creative idea. In the process of developing advertisements, strategy acts as the direction for the creative idea and plays a crucial role. In a sense, strategy is used to regulate the route for developing the advertisement.

Stage 5: Developing the Creative Brief

Strategists next need to transform the strategy into a creative brief, which guides the creative process and gives some instructions to the creative people to develop more appropriate ideas. Until this point, the information included in the creative brief is the most important information. The strategists have already screened out useless information to aid in the generation of creative ideas.

Stage 6: Idea Generation

At this stage, the main project participants transfer from the strategy department to the creative department. At first, the creative brief is delivered to creative teams who are responsible for generating creative ideas. Before settling on the most creative idea, the actors move back and forth between the generation and selection stages.

Stage 7: Idea Testing

The empirical evidence shows that there are two types of approaches for reaching the final creative idea. In the first approach, creative teams may generate some ideas first; then, they may conduct tests among consumers; third, they generate some new ideas or revise their existing ideas; finally, they conduct additional tests. Thereafter, the agency selects some ideas that they think are creative to present to the client. During the presentation, they explain every idea in detail to help their client understand it as thoroughly as possible. At this point, the client must decide which proposal will be used for their campaign, or whether the agency needs to regenerate ideas, make revisions, or conduct more tests. In the second approach, before giving a formal presentation to the clients, agencies tend to have a 'tissue session' with clients to better understand their requirements or preferences for the creative idea. Tissue sessions are informal discussions with clients in which draft or incomplete ideas are presented. These ideas represent how the agency plans to develop the campaign and show different routes for generating the final creative concept. What the agency wants to gain from the tissue session is to determine whether their clients have any preferences for the project and to help them narrow the possible range of ideas to avoid wasting time on proposing options that are not suitable. The tissue session implies the importance of communication between the creative teams and the client. Therefore, before having the tissue session with the client's marketing team, the copywriter and art designer brainstorm routes for designing the creative idea. Then, they discuss these routes with their clients to select one or some for further development. After this, to obtain some quantitative or qualitative evidence, the agency may conduct tests to demonstrate the effectiveness of their creative ideas.

Stage 8: Idea Selection

Based on the results of their research, the agency selects one or two ideas to present to their client. During the presentation, the agency does not present only the ideas that they think are the best. Because people have different thinking styles and personalities, during the idea presentation, the agency may give some other backup options to the client. Based on the agency's recommendation and presentation, the client decides which option they prefer. The proposal the client chooses becomes the core idea of the advertising solution.

Stage 9: Idea Amplification

The result of the creative process is that the agency and the client select a core idea together. The core idea needs to be further amplified to apply to different media channels. Therefore, once the core idea is selected, the next stage is to select the media channels. Because the core idea developed in the creative process can be used in different media channels, once the media channels are confirmed, the creative teams must revise the proposal to make it suitable for use in different channels.

However, not all campaigns follow the sequence of choosing the idea and then the media channel. Ideally, the process should work in this sequence, yet in some campaigns, the medium is confirmed before the creative idea is generated. That is, the campaign is guided by the confirmed media rather than the idea. Therefore, the creative teams need to generate some ideas that match the confirmed media channels. In terms of the right sequence of idea generation and media selection, opinions vary. Some interviewees thought that the right approach is to let the idea guide the media. The reverse tends to stifle the creativity of the creative staff. In short, the participants believed that letting the media guide the idea is not the right sequence for developing the best advertising campaign. In contrast, some other interviewees argued that this question mimics that of 'the chicken and the egg'. In their opinion, there is no rule here, and both sequences can work. What is important is how the agency and the client make the best match between the idea and the media. In other words, this is a problem for the industry, and they do not know which is the right approach, as illustrated by the following:

> Therefore, unlike the innovation process in manufacturing, sometimes in the advertising industry, before generating the idea, how to implement the idea has already been confirmed. In manufacturing, generally, the idea is generated first, then they decide how to produce it. Indeed, with advanced technology development, the media industry has experienced a transformation. There are many new and innovative media channels that have emerged in the last decade. On one hand, with the innovation in the media industry, advertising agencies get more approaches to amplify their creative ideas, which give more space to advertising agencies to create innovative campaigns. However, on the other hand, it has some negative effects on the creativity of generated ideas. This is because the power or the newness of the media technology makes people neglect the essence of advertising and the importance of ideas.

Stage 10: Idea Production

After identifying the media channels, the next stage involves producing the idea into a real advertisement. It is evident that the idea-generation stage is far more important than any other stage, but the value of the creative idea depends on how the agency produces it. Without having the right partners involved in the production phase, a creative idea can end up as a boring advertisement.

Stage 11: Marketing Test

After the production stage, some campaigns may need conduct tests before launching the advertisement into markets. The tests ensure the effectiveness of the campaign. Particularly in campaigns with large budgets, clients tend to require testing before releasing the advertisement.

Stage 12: Launch

Next, it is the time to launch the advertisement into the market. However, launching does not mean that all the work is finished.

Stages 13 and 14: Evaluation and Learning

Both agencies and clients need to observe how consumers respond to the advertisement and whether the advertisement produces the intended effects; if not, they must consider whether the agency needs to revise the advertisement and re-launch it. Moreover, as most agencies rely on retaining clients, the contracted agency has the responsibility to oversee the effectiveness of the advertisement and to learn from it. For retained clients, what the agency learned in previous projects can be quickly put into practice in future work. In addition, evaluation and learning enable agencies to be consistent across projects. Indeed, in KIBS firms, learning by doing is the approach that is used to improve skills, thus, evaluating and learning from each project are necessary stages.

Ultimately, the new service development process begins with the client brief and continues with the stages discussed here. Based on these stages, the author developed the following process (Figure 5.4). This model is idealized. In practise, the working process does not proceed in such a linear order, but rather moves back and forth between the phases or stages.

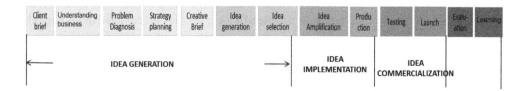

Figure 5.4   The detailed stages of the advertising service innovation process

THE SERVICE INNOVATION PROCESS

The above delineation of the new service development stages is the detailed version of the new service development process. Based on the above discussion and literature review, the new service development process in the advertising industry is constituted by the problem-diagnosis phase, the creative process (idea conceptualization), the idea-production phase, the idea-commercialization phase, and the evaluation and learning phase.

Unlike the product innovation process in manufacturing, the first phase of the new service development process focuses on diagnosing the problem for clients. The client is always the driving force of new service development in KIBS firms. Before generating the new service development concept, diagnosing the real problem of the client business acts as the guideline. In addition, different from the product-innovation and service-innovation processes for other industries, our process includes the phase of evaluation and learning. By adding this phase, we can see the connection points across projects.

In sum, although the creative services are characterized by their creativity and originality, they use a systematic approach to produce innovative services. A closer examination of the processes and stages described by respondents reveals that most of the companies put a great deal of effort into and emphasize the beginning of the process. The most important stage often was problem diagnosis or information collection. This is consistent with some scholars' findings (Zomerdijk and Voss, 2011). Every firm gathered as much information as possible at the beginning of the process to gain a thorough understanding of the client's business and the project. Typically, this involved interaction with the client's organization, the targeted consumer, and market research organizations.

DISCUSSION

The aim of this chapter is to conceptualize the new service development process. To do this, we address the research question: How do creative-intensive business services firms develop new services?

The analysis of 45 interviews reveals a detailed picture of how to develop new services for clients. It finds that the new service development process in advertising companies is composed of five phases: problem diagnosis, idea conceptualization, idea production, com-mercialization, and evaluation and learning. Each of these phases is broken down into several detailed stages that illuminate the new service development process in more detail. Although the new service development model looks like a linear process, it is not linear. Instead, the new service development model is rather complex and tough. Most of the time, the involved companies need to go through the stages described above, yet they do not need to go through them one by one. Therefore, in practice, the working process does not proceed in such a linear order, but rather moves back and forth between the phases or stages.

The innovation process has long been recognized as first involving idea generation, then idea development, and then the commercialization of the idea. This gives us a preconception that service innovation all begins with an idea. When compared with the new product innovation process in manufacturing, there are some differences. The first is the trigger of the new service development. In KIBS firms, the trigger is always the requirements or the ambitions of clients. Therefore, the first phase of the new service development is problem diagnosis, while that of the new product development is idea generation.

When compared with the extant literature on the new service development based on other industries, our process is quite similar. However, there are some differences. In the extant literature, most of the innovation processes end at the stage of commercialization, whereas in our cases, the process ends with evaluation and learning, which is facilitated by the development of technology and the digital economy. In addition, by adding the evaluation and learning innovation phase, the importance of how professionals in KIBS firms develop their skills is highlighted. For example, most professional service firms (PSFs) develop their human capital through recruitment, learning, and accumulating experience from the recursive practice of crafting skills in different situations; this is particularly true for the PSFs concentrating on creativity and innovation (Constant, 2000; Cook and Brown, 1999; Salter and Tether, 2014)

In sum, our findings have revealed the detailed stages of the new service development process and how creativity works in these stages. This study makes a series of contributions to the literature. First, a new service development process with detailed stages is developed in the service innovation area. The applicability of the process is not limited to the advertising industry, but also illuminates other creative industries or KIBS. The findings have identified the main activities performed in each stage of the process and reveal the complicated nature of the process, which is non-linear. Second, the study further investigates the service innovation process by incorporating changes occurring now in the advertising industry. The findings of this study highlight the importance of the evaluation and learning phase in the current new service development process.

MANAGERIAL IMPLICATIONS, LIMITATIONS, AND FUTURE RESEARCH DIRECTIONS

This research has several implications for service providers. The new service development process is not a linear process and is rather complicated. The findings suggest that the innovativeness of the new service development is triggered by the ambitions of clients; thus, to stimulate clients to accept more innovative service ideas, involving the clients early would be ideal. As different clients may have different types of working styles, the new service development process tends to vary across clients. This indicates that there is much flexibility in the new service development stages, and the process is characterized by trial and error. Service providers learn from each client and apply what they learn to the client's future projects and the relevant new service development process. Since the innovativeness of an idea is guided by the strategy developed in the problem diagnosis innovation phase, and the success of an idea is also partly decided by whether the service firm identifies the right project problem, managers need to focus much of their attention on the first new service development phase to ascertain whether or not it is progressing in the right direction.

This research points out the differences in the starting stage between new product development and new service development. Therefore, it is conducive to letting companies that are changing from pure service firms to include product development, or those that are changing from pure product firms to include service provision, better adapt to their new business development. Owing to the environment turbulence, more companies are beginning to provide both products and services. Under such conditions, having an awareness of the differences between how to develop new products and new services (business services) is conducive to achieving success.

Limitations and Directions for Future Research

The limitations of investigating only one industry are acknowledged. However, as the advertising industry is situated at the intersection between the creative industries and KIBS, the research findings can be applied to other industries to some extent. The limits of our study, including only interviewing the advertising managers rather than managers from both the client and agency sides, are also noted.

This study has emphasized the importance of breaking down the new service development process into more detailed stages and the significance of having an interactive process with clients. Further research can investigate how clients get involved in the process. In particular, it would be worthy to investigate the influence of project innovativeness on the details of the new service development process. This would allow service firms to better understand how to manage different types of projects.

In addition, future research could examine the importance and effects of different idea sources on service performance. Although our study found that employees in the advertising company are the main source of creativity, the importance of external sources needs more systematic investigation. How external sources influence the internal sources also needs to be discussed.

REFERENCES

Aarikka-Stenroos, L. & Jaakkola, E. (2012). Value co-creation in knowledge intensive business services: a dyadic perspective on the joint problem solving process. *Industrial MarketingManagement*, 41(1), 15–26.

Adams, R., Bessant, J., & Phelps, R. 2006. Innovation management measurement: A review. *International Journal of Management Reviews*, 8, 21–47.

Alam, I., & Perry, C. 2002. A customer-oriented new service development process. *Journal of Services Marketing*, 16, 515–534.

Atuahene-Gima, K. 1996. Differential potency of factors affecting innovation performance in manufacturing and services firms in Australia. *Journal of Product Innovation Management*, 13, 35–52.

Bakhshi, H., Hargreaves, I., & Mateos-Garcia, J. 2013. *A manifesto for the creative economy*. NESTA Innovation Fund UK.

Biemans, W. G., Griffin, A., & Moenaert, R. K. 2015. New service development: How the field developed, its current status and recommendations for moving the field forward. *Journal of Product Innovation Management*, 33, 382–397.

Booz Allen & Hamilton. 1982. *New products management for the 1980s*. Booz, Allen & Hamilton.

Bowers, M. R. 1989. Developing new services: Improving the process makes it better. *Journal of Services Marketing*, 3, 15–20.

Chapain, C., Cooke, P., de Propris, L., Macneill, S., & Mateos-Garcia, J. 2010. Creative clusters and innovation. *Putting creativity on the map.* NESTA.

Constant, E. 2000. Recursive practice and the evolution of technological knowledge. In *Technological innovation as an evolutionary process*, edited by John Ziman. Cambridge University Press, 219–233.

Cook, S. D., & Brown, J. S. 1999. Bridging epistemologies: The generative dance between organizational knowledge and organizational knowing. *Organization Science*, 10, 381–400.

Cooper, R. G. 1990. Stage-gate systems: A new tool for managing new products. *Business Horizons*, 33, 44–54.

Cooper, R. G., Easingwood, C. J., Edgett, S., Kleinschmidt, E. J., & Storey, C. 1994. What distinguishes the top performing new products in financial services. *Journal of Product Innovation Management*, 11, 281–299.

Cooper, R. G., & Edgett, S. J. 1996. Critical success factors for new financial services. *Marketing Management*, 5, 26.

De Brentani, U. 1991. Success factors in developing new business services. *European Journal of Marketing*, 25, 33–59.

De Jong, J. P., & Vermeulen, P. A. 2003. Organizing successful new service development: A literature review. *Management Decision*, 41, 844–858.

Department for Culture, Media and Sport (DCMS). 2011. *Creative industries economic estimates.* https://www.gov.uk/government/statistics/creative-industries-economic-estimates-december-2011.

Dowling, G. R. 1994. Searching for a new advertising agency: a client perspective. *International Journal of Advertising*, 13(3), 229–242.

Drejer, I. 2004. Identifying innovation in surveys of services: A Schumpeterian perspective. *Research Policy*, 33, 551–562.

Droege, H., Hildebrand, D., & Heras Forcada, M. A. 2009. Innovation in services: Present findings, and future pathways. *Journal of Service Management*, 20, 131–155.

Edgett, S., & Parkinson, S. 1994. The development of new financial services: Identifying determinants of success and failure. *International Journal of Service Industry Management*, 5, 24–38.

Empson, L., Hinings, R., Muzio, D., & Broschak, J. 2015. *The Oxford handbook of professional service firms.* Oxford University Press.

Froehle, C. M., Roth, A. V., Chase, R. B., & Voss, C. A. 2000. Antecedents of new service development effectiveness: An exploratory examination of strategic operations choices. *Journal of Service Research*, 3, 3–17.

Gadrey, J., & Gallouj, F. 1998. The provider–customer interface in business and professional services. *Service Industries Journal*, 18, 1–15.

Gallouj, F., & Weinstein, O. 1997. Innovation in services. *Research Policy*, 26, 537–556.

Griffin, A. 1997. PDMA research on new product development practices: Updating trends and benchmarking best practices. *Journal of Product Innovation Management*, 14, 429–458.

Griffin, A., & Belliveau, P. 1997. *Drivers of NPD success: The 1997 PDMA report.* PDMA.

Halinen, A. 1997. *Relationship marketing in professional services: A study of agency–client dynamics in the advertising sector.* Psychology Press.

Heusinkveld, S., & Benders, J. 2002. Between professional dedication and corporate design: Exploring forms of new concept development in consultancies. *International Studies of Management & Organization*, 32, 104–122.

Johne, A. & Storey, C. 1998. New service development: A review of the literature and annotated bibliography. *European Journal of Marketing*, 32, 184–251.

Johnson, S. P., Menor, L. J., Roth, A. V., & Chase, R. B. 2000. A critical evaluation of the new service development process. *New Service Development.* https://doi.org/10.4135/9781452205564.N1

Kuester, S., Schuhmacher, M. C., Gast, B., & Worgul, A. 2013. Sectoral heterogeneity in new service development: An exploratory study of service types and success factors. *Journal of Product Innovation Management*, 30, 533–544.

Lovelock, C., & Gummesson, E. 2004. Whither services marketing? In search of a new paradigm and fresh perspectives. *Journal of Service Research*, 7, 20–41.

Menor, L. J., & Roth, A. V. 2007. New service development competence in retail banking: Construct development and measurement validation. *Journal of Operations Management*, 25, 825–846.

Michell, P. C., Cataquet, H., & Mandry, G. D. 1996. Advertising agency creative reputation and account loyalty. *Creativity and Innovation Management*, 5, 38–47.

Miles, I. 2012. KIBS and knowledge dynamics in client–supplier interaction. In *Exploring knowledge-intensive business service: Knowledge management strategies*, edited by Di Maria, E., Grandinetti, R., and Di Bernardo, B. Palgrave Macmillan, 13–34.

Miles, I., & Green, L. 2008. *Hidden innovation in the creative industries*. NESTA.

Miles, I., Kastrinos, N., Flanagan, K., Bilderbeek, R., Den Hertog, P., Huntink, W., & Bouman, M. 1995. *Knowledge-intensive business services*. EIMS.

Nijssen, E. J., Hillebrand, B., Vermeulen, P. A., & Kemp, R. G. 2006. Exploring product and service innovation similarities and differences. *International Journal of Research in Marketing*, 23, 241–251.

Nov, O., & Jones, M. 2003. *Ordering creativity? Knowledge, creativity, and social interaction in the advertising industry*. European Conference on Organizational Knowledge, Learning, and Capabilities.

Papastathopoulou, P., & Hultink, E. J. 2012. New service development: An analysis of 27 years of research. *Journal of Product Innovation Management*, 29, 705–714.

Rowley, J. E. 2007. The wisdom hierarchy: Representations of the DIKW hierarchy. *Journal of Information Science*, 33, 163–180.

Salter, A., & Tether, B. S. 2014. Innovation in services: An overview. In *Managing services: Challenges and innovation*, edited by K. Haynes and I. Grugulis. Oxford University Press, 134–153

Scheuing, E. E., & Johnson, E. M. 1989. A proposed model for new service development. *Journal of Services Marketing*, 3, 25–34.

Singh, R., Seshadri, D., & Alam, I. 2012. New service development in India's business-to-business financial services sector. *Journal of Business & Industrial Marketing*, 27, 228–241.

Slater, S. F., & Narver, J. C. 1994. Does competitive environment moderate the market orientation-performance relationship? *Journal of Marketing*, 58, 46–55.

Storey, C. D., & Easingwood, C. J. 1996. Determinants of new product performance: A study in the financial services sector. *International Journal of Service Industry Management*, 7, 32–55.

Sundbo, J. 1997. Management of innovation in services. *Service Industries Journal*, 17, 432–455.

Sundbo, J., & Gallouj, F. 2000. Innovation as a loosely coupled system in services. *International Jounral of Services Technology and Management*, 1(1), 15–36.

Sundbo, J., & Toivonen, M. 2011. *User-based innovation in services*. Edward Elgar Publishing.

Voss, C., Tsikriktsis, N., & Frohlich, M. 2002. Case research in operations management. *International Journal of Operations & Production Management*, 22, 195–219.

Zomerdijk, L. G., & Voss, C. A. 2011. NSD processes and practices in experiential services. *Journal of Product Innovation Management*, 28, 63–80.

6. Service design: managing services as a way of designing

Birgit Mager and Tina Weisser

INTRODUCTION TO SERVICE DESIGN

A Short History of Service Design

Reflecting on services in *The Wealth of Nations*, Adam Smith (1776) wrote that "The labor of some of the most respectable orders … churchmen, lawyers, physicians … is unproductive of any value." Two hundred years later, in most organizations there was still no explicit idea of service management, marketing, or engineering, nor would an approach such as service design have been conceivable in the context of services. Services were classified as a tertiary sector and were often considered a cost-generating but necessary evil. There was no explicit science on these services and no systematic research investment had been made by either the private or government sector.

Design was commonly associated with "the good form" of physical artifacts. Since the industrial revolution, design often had a connotation of artistic or museum-like characteristics and was not always aligned with functionality. It had influenced the shaping of products and their packaging and communication in words and images. In an increasingly holistic sense, design involved the comprehensive orchestration of all sensually perceptible elements of the brand within "corporate identity" and "corporate design." This development was largely shaped by Dieter Rams at the German consumer products company Braun, who had the influence and resources to make design influential in the company's success to an extent that we did not see again until decades later with Apple (and Jonathan Ive has never made a secret of how much he was influenced by Dieter Rams).

In 2014, Rams stated that "design is in a constant flux, just like culture and technologies." So it came as no surprise to him that innovative design approaches in the '80s (such as interface and experience design) were able to respond to the new challenges of the human–machine interfaces created by digital technologies and that design should approach these new digital interfaces from the user's point of view. Again, it was no surprise to him that services should become the focus of design in the early '90s. The service sector was steadily gaining in importance—not least because many products could provide relevant benefit to customers only by being systematically embedded in service systems. Another reason for this development was the fact that customers were increasingly asking for precisely those solutions that would enable them to focus on their core businesses and the needs of their end users. This economic development, combined with the first signs of a societal transformation from "owning" to "using" (Erlhoff, 1998) and to "experiencing," combined with the emergence of new technological opportunities, led design to turn to intangible products, to services.

In the '80s, Lucius Burckhardt had already pointed the way to a time when design would be dedicated to the creation of useful systems within which material artifacts would be one component among others. "Design is invisible," he claimed. It is not the train that makes traveling a pleasant experience, it is the schedule (Fezer and Schmitz, 2012). In the early '90s, this design approach was formalized for the first time under the term "service design."

Service Design Basics

Based on a contemporary understanding of design in which design operates at the intersections of user needs, organizational interests, and technological capabilities, service design stands for the choreography of interactions, processes, and technologies in complex systems in order to co-creatively develop innovations that deliver benefits and values to relevant stakeholders within the system. In other words, service design uses co-creative processes to design scenarios of futures that do not yet exist in order to make them feasible through prototypical and iterative processes. In this sense, service design is deeply rooted in the tradition of human-centered design, but extends its values, approaches, and methods into the realm of processes, interactions, and systems. The well-established "design thinking" approach is very similar in the sense that it also focuses on the customer. However, design thinking tends to concentrate more on products, whereas service design focuses on services, processes, and entire service systems. The service design process can be described in four successive and, at the same time, iteratively interwoven phases, as shown in Figure 6.1.

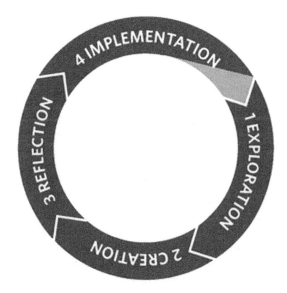

Figure 6.1   The service design process

Exploration
"If I had one hour to solve a problem, I would spend 55 minutes on understanding it," Albert Einstein is supposed to have said. A solution can only be as good as the question it is based on. A deep understanding of the problem is needed in order to ask the right questions. In service industries we are working with complex living systems, and the problems we are trying to solve are often "wicked" from the perspectives of the different actors involved. These prob-

lems involve relevant experts and building on existing knowledge; they are concerned with reframing views and questions so that new things can be sought and found. Service design, therefore, is an advocate of interdisciplinarity and user focus.

The more open the starting point of a service design project, the more potential there is for innovative approaches. Thus, in service design, tasks are reformulated in the exploration phase to ensure that solutions are not anticipated without having understood the problem in sufficient depth. Relevant stakeholders and actors are identified. Qualitative and quantitative research approaches are triangulated to arrive at core findings from different perspectives.

Creation

As important as it is not to solve problems until they are understood in depth and from different perspectives, it is equally important not to jump to the first solution right away. This is a central premise in service design. Thus, based on the core findings from the exploration phase, a dedicated creation process begins by first expanding the spectrum of possible solutions, focusing on quantity, diversity, and on extremes. This is done in interdisciplinary teams with the involvement of end users. Service design structures, choreographs, and moderates these processes, and methodically lays out inspiration and confrontation. Ideas are evaluated, prioritized, combined, and developed into concepts. Service design ensures a consistent visualization of scenarios of currently non-existent futures and the early development of low-fidelity prototypes, which are tested, iterated, and continuously developed into high-fidelity prototypes. Piece by piece—possibly alternative—concepts are formed, which are backed up with a business model canvas from frontstage, backstage, and business perspectives.

Reflection

In the reflection phase, the remaining concepts are tested in a setting that is as close to reality as possible with the end users, employees, and other relevant stakeholders. Fine-tuning takes place, feasibility studies are finalized, and decisions are made. Based on this, communication and training plans are prepared and implemented, and all further steps necessary for implementation are taken. All this is done with the involvement of the relevant stakeholders.

Implementation

In the implementation phase, the transition from service design to service management takes place. We see strong interweaving here: basic knowledge of service design and a service design mindset should be a matter of course for forward-looking service management. In addition, the service design process does not stop with implementation; continuous evaluation and iterative development are integral parts of any service. Service design thus becomes an integral part of corporate processes and corporate culture.

CASE STUDY: LUFTHANSA

In October 2013, Lufthansa engaged global design and innovation consultancy IDEO to analyze, redesign, and rethink its business-class service on long-haul flights from the ground up over the course of 15 weeks.

IDEO defined the signature moments during a business-class flight: boarding, the first meal service; the transition from eating, sleeping, working, and relaxing; and the final transition from sleeping to waking up to saying goodbye. The focus was primarily on the transitions from, for example, a meal to sleep. "Our common goal was to improve the service in these very private moments in such a way that the guest is offered a completely new flight experience with significantly more 'Quality Time'. Time he can use to work, relax or be pampered," says Anja Hübner, of Lufthansa Customer Experience. Outdated service processes, changing customer needs, and increasingly fierce competition in the business customer segment were the motivation for this. But getting there didn't just require weeks of research on the ground and in the air. It quickly became clear that a rethink among Lufthansa personnel was also essential.

Exploration was the foundation of the project. During the first weeks, numerous interviews were conducted and, of course, a lot of flying was done all over the world—with Lufthansa and also with competitors, as a passenger and, once, in the role of a flight attendant in order to get a feel for the complexity of the challenges on board. In addition, the team gained versatile service experiences in the airline context and also internationally in analog areas that are characterized by particularly good service, such as hotels or butler services, payment platforms, and other digital offerings.

In the creation phase, an interdisciplinary team ideated, prototyped, and tested. In the reflection phase, Lufthansa provided IDEO with a scale model of the business class of the Airbus A380 with 92 seats at the Lufthansa test center in Raunheim, Germany, to test the two final concepts for feasibility and attractiveness for the guest and crew.

This enormous effort was also new for the designers and thus a special incentive. At the test center, Lufthansa's team of experts and IDEO's designers were able to run through and evaluate various ideas and minute details with real passengers in choreographed scenarios. The findings from these days flowed directly into the fine-tuned design until the end result, the implementation of the vision of a new, holistic, and user-centric service, was practicable and satisfactory for everyone.

Source: Franz, Barbara (2015).

Basic Principles and Values

Service design is in the tradition of human-centered design. In recent decades, this has made a significant contribution to a new orientation toward the needs and experiences of people in contrast to a product- and technology-loving economy and a public sector oriented toward administrative regulations and hierarchical and silo-like structures. Today, however, pure people-centeredness is obsolete. Too much damage has been done by human-centrism in the system "world." It is not that human orientation should be abolished, but it is necessary for all projects to consider the system more holistically, including all living beings and plants, all raw materials, and of course the technologies, which have developed an increasing momentum of their own. This value orientation, which should include diversity and inclusion in equal measure, is brought in through the service design. In addition, there are some essential basic principles that we outline below:

- Understand the system and its actors.
  Services are complex systems that consist of mutually influenced subsystems. They have their own dynamics and cannot be controlled. To influence them in a goal-oriented way, it

is important to identify the relevant actors, to understand the dynamics in the system, and to identify the most important core problems and influencing factors. This includes not only human actors but also the entire ecosystem.

● Reframe problems.
Questions and tasks formulated in service design by the client often already contain a very precise idea of the solution and often also an idea of the problem that is to be solved, without sufficient exploration having taken place or appropriate critical reflection. One of the core competencies of service design is to critically question and reformulate problems. After all, the quality of the answer lies in the quality of the question.

● Working co-creatively.
Throughout the service design process, the systematic involvement of relevant stakeholders is of utmost importance. Service designers are experts in processes and methods. They have the ability to question things, read between the lines, creatively think the unthinkable, and thus open up new scope. However, they are not necessarily the experts or the stakeholders in the service process.

● Open up scope for new scenarios.
It is important not to jump to the first solution right away. Creating space to break out of familiar paths and develop divergent potential solutions is an important prerequisite to move beyond incremental improvements.

● Thinking with your hands.
Service design makes complexity comprehensible, creates images on which actors with different interests can agree, makes ideas tangible and thus quickly verifiable, and does all this with the hands! Visualizations and low-fidelity prototypes help to design change processes vividly.

● Develop and test prototypes.
The further the process of concept development progresses, the more precise and realistic the prototypes, which are continuously tested with users and other stakeholders. This makes it possible to make continuous improvements in iterative steps and avoid the high costs of later failure or substantial rework.

● Zoom in and zoom out.
The entire service design process is characterized by attention to detail without losing sight of the big picture. Services cross departmental boundaries, user needs are identified well before the actual service experience, and the success of a service is often not realized until well after service delivery is complete. In addition, service delivery is distributed across multiple channels, often involving external partners who are not necessarily perceived by the user as third-party service providers. During the process, it is important to keep an eye on this big picture and still work precisely on a small scale.

INTEGRATING SERVICE DESIGN WITHIN ORGANIZATIONS

In the following section, we explore when service design is the right approach for innovating or optimizing a service, suggest areas of application, and explore how to assess the expected complexity of the service. The advantages and disadvantages of an in-house department in cooperation with external partners are also highlighted. With regard to the implementation of service design in the organization, we discuss the advantages of a co-creative approach and look at how service design can be measured. We show that the three dimensions of capacity, culture, and commitment are indispensable for successful customer centricity in organizations.

The Application of Service Design

The use of service design is always promising when an existing service needs to be optimized or a completely new service is to be developed. This applies equally to services in the business-to-business and business-to-customer sectors, and to services offered to the end customer and to internal services. Service design deeply integrates the various users involved in all phases of the process. In service design, the term "user" refers to both a possible external customer and the internal stakeholders who will be involved in the future service experience. By assessing and evaluating user perspectives, existing services can be analyzed and optimized, and future service experiences can be developed. Both qualitative and quantitative methods are used to obtain user feedback. The objective of service design is to develop useful, usable, and desirable services from the user's point of view. For the service provider, on the other hand, it is essential that the service is both effective and efficient, that it adds financial value, and that it offers a clear differentiation from competitors. A user experience (UX) can be a commercial transaction, such as buying a car or an insurance policy, but it can also be a non-commercial transaction, such as a visit to the doctor. Another example would be public administrations wanting to introduce a new citizen service, such as ordering a new identity card. In this case, the result is called a new "user/citizen experience."

However, it can also be an internal service for the employees of one's own organization, for example, when generating a travel expense report. This is called the "employee experience" (EX). The ultimate goal of service design is to design and orchestrate an integrated process, the "user journey" from beginning to end ("end to end"), with the aim of deriving an integrated solution across all phases and touchpoints. A UX consists of both tangible and intangible elements and can include any form of media or interaction. It can be a combination of human-to-human, human-to-machine, and machine-to-machine interactions. The boundaries between physical product and intangible service dissolve; they are joined into a single entity and a complex system. Those who want to offer such UXs must understand user needs and user problems because only then will they be able to solve them.

Employee experience
Applying service design to internal processes that solely affect employees has only been practiced by organizations in recent years and is still rarely in the scope of service management in Germany, for example. This is somewhat surprising, as the correlation between customer satisfaction and employee satisfaction has been proven by many studies. Whitter (2019), for example, emphasizes that every customer interaction of an employee provides information about the quality and status of the EX. According to Bersin (2019), the term "employee experience" was used for the first time in association with Airbnb in 2017 when they started using design thinking to design and optimize internal employee services. EX can be defined as the sum of all contact points that an employee has with their employer, from the moment of a job application (active or passive) to the moment of leaving the company. EX and employee commitment are also linked. Where employees work in a work culture and atmosphere that is perceived as positive for them, this can have an impact on their commitment and work motivation (Morgan, 2015). The components of EX are manifold: in addition to the physical

environment of the office, all analog and digital processes (including software applications) can be designed, as well as interactions between managers, with human resources, or between colleagues. Striking events in the employee life cycle can be addressed (i.e., the employee journey within a company, including the job application, the first weeks in the new job, promotions, retraining, changes in private life situations due to marriage or the birth of a child, or finally leaving the company). All these moments that employees experience in the course of their work in an organization can be seen as employee journeys that can be shaped with service design in such a way that employees are more motivated and satisfied, stay longer, or even come back again after they have left. Considering that organizations with a well-designed onboarding process improve new employee retention by 82 percent and enhance their productivity by over 70 percent (Laurano, 2015), there is great potential here. As a response to this potential, Microsoft, among others, launched its first Employee Experience Platform at the beginning of 2021. Tackling EX using the service design approach could be a beneficial field for service management efforts.

Levels of complexity

When planning a new service, it is important to assess both technical feasibility and social complexity. Technical feasibility includes the use of new technologies, the recognition of new trends, as well as the internal skills available, and any external partners that may be required. Technical feasibility is generally the lesser challenge for most organizations (Weisser, 2018). It is rather the social complexity within an organization that requires significant barriers to be overcome. To assess the social complexity of a service, the following aspects need to be reviewed and, depending on the expected complexity (Figure 6.2), addressed:

● How many stakeholders and departments will be involved?
● How many touchpoints does the UX consist of?
● What are the stakeholders' explicit and implicit expectations of the service?
● How can the organization assess the stakeholders' willingness to cooperate with one another?
● Will several departments be involved, or just one? In the case of an existing service, it is possible to check how many contact persons the user currently has.
● Who has the internal decision-making authority and responsibility for the end-to-end service?

Implementing Service Design

Based on the social complexity described in the previous paragraph, it is a significant challenge to implement service design concepts and UXs, especially when they affect more than one department within an organization. Undoubtedly, implementing these concepts involves organizational and cultural change for the companies involved. Frequently mentioned barriers (Weisser, 2018) include, for example:

● The absence or overlooking of relevant stakeholders or internal knowledge carriers;
● Lack of targets/metrics for the product being developed;
● Low quality or lack of user integration;
● Insufficient qualification of staff;
● Unclear or obstructive power relations;

- Lack of clarity of expectations and goals;
- Lack of equipment and/or space; and
- Capacity bottlenecks due to day-to-day business.

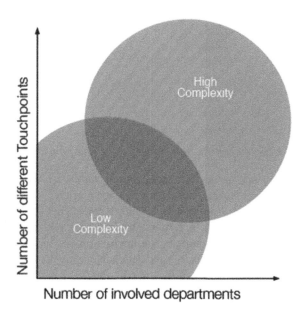

Note: Complexity can change during the course of a project and is not static.

Figure 6.2   *Simplified complexity assessment of service design projects/UXs*

When implementing user-centered products in a company, it is not only the service design process itself that has to be designed and planned; the specific context of the organization must also be considered and dealt with in a holistic way. The implementation model KUER (Figure 6.3) complements the classic service design development process (see Figure 6.1) with an additional Phase 1, "Key Prerequisites," at the beginning and Phase 4, "Reinforce & Deliver," at the end. For implementation to be possible at a later stage, it must be considered from day one. This starts with preparation and, for example, top management support, and ensuring sufficient staff capacity. The service development in Phases 2 and 3 is accompanied by adequate actions, for example, aimed at empowering staff. The last very decisive phase is characterized by the reduction of uncertainties and risks for the decision-makers. It is all about setting the internal agenda and considering and evaluating the consequences in the areas of compensation, skills development, new hires, and so on (see also p. 97).

To offer users an entirely integrated solution, a UX or the internal process required for it must be viewed and designed horizontally or end to end. This means that the responsibility has to be bundled in a central place and cannot be divided among the internal departments involved, as has often been the case in the past. Otherwise, the user is confronted with gaps in the service process consisting of media and interaction breaks and changes of contact persons ("One moment, I'll connect you further.").

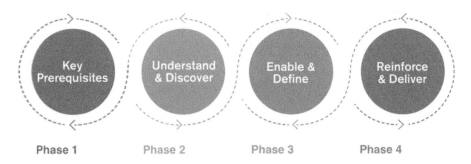

Phase 1   Phase 2   Phase 3   Phase 4

Source: Weisser (2018).

Figure 6.3   The KUER implementation model and its four phases

As an example, a Swedish service design agency redesigned the service "Becoming a Parent" with a Scandinavian public authority. The typical "citizen journey," with its numerous touch-points, was analyzed (i.e., at what point does the future parent contact whom, how, and why; what information do they need; etc.). A central contact person was then designated for each citizen who bundles all citizens' enquiries. The internal process behind this, called "back-stage," and the structures were made visible and actionable using the Blueprint method.

To implement service design successfully, specific internal capabilities and competences need to be in place or should be developed over time. These include staff with appropriate skills, sufficient human and financial resources, spaces for co-creative work, and the necessary technical equipment (Figure 6.4). Commitment and trust in the new approach is crucial at management level, which can be seen, for example, when interdepartmental work is allowed. Likewise, during the course of the first user-centered projects, suitable structures and condi-tions are needed to enable working and decision-making across departmental boundaries and to allow for an exploratory, iterative, and open-solution approach.

It also requires the establishment of an innovation culture and a "human-centered" mindset that allows user integration at every stage of the service design process to ensure that solu-tions can be tested and optimized rapidly and iteratively. Service design is often employed by organizations precisely in order to change their own innovation culture toward being human-centered or to develop this culture in the first place. It is important to understand service design not as a one-off project intervention, but to integrate it as part of organizational learning so that service systems can react to changing user needs and market conditions. Complex service systems, in particular, cannot be planned and controlled in the long term; they must be flexible and able to adapt based on user feedback. Rigid internal processes and rules are a major obstacle here.

One possible approach is to analyze the current state of the internal organization using a service design maturity model. There is, for example, a model based on the empirical KUER model (Weisser, 2018), which uses 24 factors to measure whether the necessary framework conditions, skills, and resources are already available in a company, and where possible levers for preparation and optimization for successful implementation can be found.

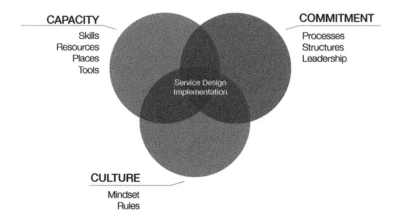

Figure 6.4   Culture, commitment, capacity: human-centered framework conditions within organizations

In-house capacity

Design-driven innovation labs are being set up using the most diverse names and focusing on different key issues. In organizations all over the world, these labs are a driving force for in-house innovation. However, the need for their existence can be disputed by management due to high costs and little profit (Bhan Ahuja, 2019). They strengthen a company's competitiveness by developing new ideas and opening up new business areas. Pioneers from 20 companies operating in six fields and located in eight countries have been analyzed. Based on this study, a typology of types of design-driven innovation labs has been developed (Mager et al., 2016).

If the goal is to establish service design sustainably in an organization, internal experts who know the process, the methods, and the potentials are indispensable. If an organization wants to implement service design, this not only affects the UX visible from the outside, but also the backstage processes of a company. Therefore, internal employees are needed who are in key positions; who know the corporate culture, processes, and decision-making principles; and who are politically well networked within the company. Due to size, it is not possible for every organization to set up a dedicated organizational unit for service design. However, internal competence development at all levels is a sensible and necessary measure to ensure the long-term anchoring of the thinking and working methods of service design.

Organizations often take a dual approach; in other words, they have well-trained internal service designers, but also work with external partners to gain new impulses and ideas, other skills, and greater delivery capacity. Especially in the development of new services, an unbiased view and perspectives from outside are always needed. Bold new approaches are important so that innovative solutions emerge, and solutions are also developed that have not worked in the past, often due to technical inadequacies (feasibility). As digitalization and technological development are advancing rapidly, it is vital to keep reviewing known problems with newly available technological possibilities. Service design, on the other hand, must not become a new, isolated department; rather, it needs open and co-creative collaboration and intensive exchange with experts from various departments and disciplines.

Co-creative working

Designing UXs in such a way that they are both of high quality and "valuable" for the user as well as for the offering company is not possible without an interdisciplinary and interdepartmental way of working. All relevant stakeholders should be identified at the beginning of the process and involved according to how they are or will be affected. Stakeholders' knowledge of internal processes is crucial for a successful UX. To ensure that a new service does not come to a standstill at a later stage as a result of resistance, for example, due to a lack of buy-in ("not invented here"), the broad participation of many employees from diverse hierarchical levels is advisable. It has been proven that the installation of suitable spaces, so-called innovation or service design labs, that enable co-creative work and intensive exchange are essential. After all, innovations only emerge through focused work in a safe environment. Additional virtual platforms that enable easy collaboration are just as important for cross-location work.

Measuring the impact of service design

Many innovation leaders do not yet have a formalized process and set of criteria to review and measure the results that is tailored to the various phases of their innovation projects. When deciding which services to design and initiate, there are, among others, four dimensions that need to be evaluated:

- What is the user value?
- What is the technical feasibility?
- What is the business value?
- What are the organizational consequences?

Depending on the strategic objective, measurable criteria may also include cultural, ethical, or sustainable values. Within each of these dimensions, leaders should consider different metrics, both qualitative and quantitative. The evaluation can be done at the beginning of the service design process (e.g., how many service ideas have been developed, how many employees need to be trained), as well as at an early stage shortly after launch in the market (e.g., how many times the app has been installed), and at a later stage when the service is well established (e.g., net promoter score, voice of the customer). To distinguish between short- and long-term metrics and between the process and the end results is a beneficial approach. One possible way is to differentiate between lead and lag measures, as it makes sense to evaluate the development process with different metrics than the established service or long-term customer value. The distinction is important because the choice of metric influences the process to be optimized (O'Brien et al., 2019).

Lead measures can be used as key figures to measure the process and its output, as they can be influenced and evaluated as an indicator of progress toward the goal. Lag measures, on the other hand, can be classic key performance indicators, such as net promoter scores, customer retention, profit, and revenue, but they can only be measured with a time lag. Whereas a lag measure tells whether the goal has been achieved, a lead measure tells whether the goal is likely to be achieved. Lead measures are drivers that track significant activities that drive or lead to the lag measure. They predict the future success of the lag measure and can be directly influenced by the service design team.

Creating a movement

To establish service design as a long-term practice, it is important to anchor it in multiple places within the company. An emergent approach can have a big impact. This means initiating many small initiatives and measures in different departments, staggered over time, so that momentum is created from within the organization and the employees. There are successful examples of how enterprises have managed to build up an internal "community of practice" that multiplies and anchors service design in the organization beyond individual drivers and promoters. A broad anchoring across many hierarchical levels is made possible by targeted training and the deployment of "evangelists," so-called change agents or UX ambassadors.

An international company with 50 000 employees realized that it would not be enough to set up an internal service design or UX department that acted as a self-contained unit. The aim was to prevent a new silo "department" from being created and the methodology kept entirely among specialists. Thus, ten years ago, this company started to train internal UX ambassadors who saw themselves as advocates of the users and advised company-wide projects. Every new project has to undergo a UX check at the beginning, which proves that user feedback has been gathered. The UX or service design ambassadors are not part of the internal UX department, whose job is to implement projects; instead, they act as advisors throughout the organization. To keep the community alive, innovation events are held regularly. These events are designed to build knowledge (e.g., through presentations and case studies from other successful companies) and skills to motivate employees, to learn from one another, and to network.

All these individual activities pay tribute to the growth of a suitable culture of innovation and a movement that is only established in the long term and primarily through the creation of suitable formal structures and processes.

PERSPECTIVES FOR SERVICE DESIGN

The "new normal" is today, a time in which service design no longer necessarily causes surprise, in which service designers lead projects inside and outside of organizations, organize and facilitate workshops, enable co-creation, build and test prototypes, organize and carry out further training for employees and managers of the organizations, and, above all, gain more and more influence at the strategic level in structural and cultural change processes.

So what are the big issues for "The Future of Service Design" (Mager, 2020)?

Wear Your Tie!

Service design will become increasingly important in organizations at the strategic level. It is no longer confined to selective projects that prove the usefulness of the discipline; instead, it is a comprehensive approach in which user orientation, explorative and creative approaches, visualization, prototyping, and co-creative development play a central role. Service design is, on the one hand, a process and, on the other hand, a systematic and methodically supported approach. But above all, it is an attitude that can have a profound influence on the cultures and structures in companies.

Go Public!

This development affects not only the private sector but also, and most importantly, the public sector. In the past decade, the public sector has increasingly used service design to initiate and implement innovations due to the great challenges it faces. Again, the importance of service design is growing not only on the operational level but also on the strategic level. Accompanying the public sector as a service designer means understanding and considering the special requirements that lie in developing services that have monopoly positions, which are often not really wanted by customers, but which are at the same time formative points of contact between the state and its citizens. These services therefore have to meet the challenges of digitization with regard to a holistic understanding of living environments in collaboration with citizens.

Keep Learning!

To expand the opportunities associated with these developments in the public and private sectors, however, changes in education are required. The training of service designers, for whom much more complex demands are made today, needs to incorporate an understanding of entrepreneurial thinking and acting, of the working methods and processes in the business world, and, above all, of the needs and the language of clients as well as the needs of users, and then respond to them.

It is also about training people within organizations. Thus, the thinking and working methods of service design become a natural part of the organization. Professional service designers are therefore no longer just designers; they are consultants, facilitators, trainers, and much more.

Humanize Technology!

The use of technology will become increasingly important. Not only will most services be offered on digital platforms, but the methodological approaches in service design, both in exploration and in creation, prototyping and testing, will be enriched by technology. While in the past it was primarily small research panels that were explored using qualitative methods, in the future these will be supported by additional procedures in dealing with big data and by digital research and development platforms. Not only through the recent pandemic, but certainly accelerated by it, the work of the service designer has established itself in a virtual space with an explorative and creative approach. Most important—embrace technology and humanize it!

Build on Ethics!

Ethical issues will play a major role in this process. Service designers intervene in people's lives, in their explorative research, in co-creative work with participants and affected persons, in the integration of technologies in services, and in the creation of working environments in which people provide services for others. These are just some of the dimensions in which ethical questions play an important role. Service design must have a clear attitude and a reflected code of conduct to deal with such ethical issues. Racial injustice and social discrimination are topics that will gain relevance for the service design field in its structures and in its practice.

Protect the Earth!

Sustainability issues are of particular importance in this context. The three pillars of sustainability and UNESCO's requirements for sustainable development must be a self-evident guideline in service design in the future, systematically accompanying the work in all phases. Our natural ecosystem deserves a seat at the stakeholder table—just as much as business and social aspects. We need to shift from human-centered design toward life-centered design, as Bruce Mau (2020) claims.

Stay Competitive!

The growing importance of service design will, in the future, also lead to areas of tension between different organizational structures and the integration structures of service design. While, on the one hand, the big management consultancies buy up service design agencies, on the other hand, companies and public organizations integrate service departments in their structures as a matter of course. Those service design agencies remaining on the market will, going forward, network internationally in order to be able to develop and implement qualified offers for big international customers in competition with the big management consultancies.

Embrace the Future!

Work in service design is always aimed at creating a future that does not yet exist. In the future, the integration of future forecasting will play an important role. Service design as an interface discipline has always integrated concepts and methods from other areas into its work. Future forecasting is an interface discipline that deserves special attention for the future.

Therefore, there are eight fields that have a special significance for the future of service design and for which we can prepare ourselves. By encouraging reflection and systematic examination of these topics in our network structures, we can naturally keep our eyes open for signals, including early warning indicators, and retain the openness and flexibility needed to deal with unforeseen situations. There will certainly be enough of those in the future.

CONCLUSION

Service design is a natural component of innovative service management. It is an attitude and mindset; it is the knowledge of a process. It is the competence to use a variety of methods within this process. It is the ability to initiate change processes and to network with other actors driving change within the organization. Hand in hand with professional service designers, service management will shape economic, ecological, and human service innovations.

REFERENCES

Bersin, J. (2019). *Which parts of employee experience matter most?* https://joshbersin.com/2019/11/which-parts-of-employee-experience-really-matter-most/

Bhan Ahuja, S. (2019). *Why innovation labs fail, and how to ensure yours doesn't. Harvard Business Review.* https://hbr.org/2019/07/why-innovation-labs-fail-and-how-to-ensure-yours-doesnt#:~:text=Lack%20of%20Metrics%20to%20Track%20Success&text=Many%20never%20have%20metrics%20to,%2C%20evolve%2C%20and%20incubate%20ideas

Erlhoff, M. (1998). *Nutzen statt besitzen.* Steidl Verlag.

Fezer, J. &, Schmitz, M. (2012). Design is invisible. In Fezer J. and Schmitz, M. (eds) *Lucius Burckhardt writings. Rethinking man-made environments* (pp. 153–165). Springer.

Franz, B., (2015). *Eine Fluglinie denkt Dienstleistung neu.* Touchpoint, Special German Edition 2015

Laurano, M. (2015). *The true cost of a bad hire. Study for Glassdoor.* Glassdoor. https://b2b-assets.glassdoor.com/the-true-cost-of-a-bad-hire.pdf

Mager, B. (Ed.) (2020). *The future of service design.* TH-Köln.

Mager, B., Evenson, S., & Longerich, L. (2016). The evolution of innovation labs. *Touchpoint, 8*(2), 50–53.

Mau, B. (2020). *MC24: Bruce Mau's 24 Principles for Designing Massive Change in your Life and Work.* Phaidon.

Morgan, J. (2015). *The three environments that create every employee experience.* Forbes. https://www.forbes.com/sites/jacobmorgan/2015/12/15/the-three-environments-that-create-every-employee-experience/?sh=2f6fba9c66c6

O'Brien, G., Xiao, G., & Mason, M. (2019). *Digital transformation game plan: 34 tenets for masterfully merging technology and business.* O'Reilly Media.

Rams, D. (2014). *Less but better.* Die Gestalten Verlag.

Weisser, T. (2018). *Systemische Betrachtung der Einflussfaktoren bei der Implementierung von Produkt und Service Design-Systemen.* HBK Braunschweig.

Whitter, B. (2019). *Employee experience: Develop a happy, productive and supported workforce for exceptional individual and business performance.* Kogan Page.

7. Service support systems for ecostructuring decision support

Ralph D. Badinelli

INTRODUCTION

This chapter defines the critical role of actor decision-making in service and derives prescriptions for service system design in accordance with this role. Although service science research has revealed decision-making as a feature of service, the essential and precise role of engagement decisions in service journeys has escaped all but the operational-level models of service (Calabrese et al. 2018). A consequence of this oversight has been a lack of coherent principles for service system design and vagueness in determining the viability of service systems as defined by the Viable Systems Approach (VSA; Badinelli et al. 2012; Barile and Savaiano 2011; Golinelli 2010). By analyzing actor decision-making, this chapter achieves several purposes:

- Defines the service ecostructure and decomposes the engagement decision into a two-step process of reconfiguring the service ecostructure and then engaging a selected ecostructure.
- Exposes the nature of a particular kind of service-journey decision called the ecostructuring decision.
- Establishes the essential role of ecostructuring decisions in determining the service journey.
- Provides a model of a complete decision support system for ecostructuring decisions and the integration of all forms of analytics in decision support.
- Clarifies the definition of smartness in service systems and identifies the features of a service support system that imbue the system with smartness.
- Defines the distinction between service support systems and resource providers in service systems.
- Establishes service support systems as a natural and essential infrastructure for viable service systems.

We posit some fundamental model constructs of service and service support systems on which the thesis of this chapter is built. This foundation is necessary, as readers may have many different perspectives of service. Over the last two decades, service science has broached the subject of service from a philosophical view, a macro view (Chandler and Vargo 2011; Echeverri and Skålén 2011; Edvardsson et al. 2011; Vargo and Lusch 2008, 2011, 2016, 2017), a meso view (Fujita et al. 2018; Jonas et al. 2018; Payne et al. 2008), and a micro view (Badinelli 2015; Jaakkola et al. 2015; Polese et al. 2017; Storbacka et al. 2016; Yi and Gong 2013;). The current chapter is motivated by the need for theories and models that enable operational (micro) design, management, and control of service systems in ways that are consistent with the overarching concepts of Service Dominant Logic (Lusch and Vargo 2014). For the purpose of this chapter, we adopt the following definition of service:

- *Service:* A sequence of resource-integrating activities initiated and mediated by two or more actors through which value can be co-created for these actors.

This definition is a little more precise than some more familiar versions from the literature. Overcoming some of the deficiencies in extant definitions of service, this description avoids distinguishing providers from consumers, admits any number of actors in each activity, and puts no constraints on the types of resources that are involved. The added specifications are significant and relevant to the model of service systems that we develop below.

To begin, we define the context of decision-making in service through a model of service systems at an operational level. Ironically, the explosive growth in the applications of big data analytics (BDA) and artificial intelligence (AI) has often led to misunderstanding by data analysts and corporate managers about the proper role of decision modeling in the design of service platforms and service systems (Badinelli and Sarno 2017). Consider the definition of a service ecosystem from Vargo and Lusch (2011).

- *Service ecosystem:* "A relatively self-contained, self-adjusting system of resource-integrating actors connected by shared institutional logics and mutual value creation through service exchange."

In this chapter we expand this definition by drawing it down from a macro view to a micro view. Our purpose in doing this is to develop principles for the design of operational service platforms that can create and manipulate institutional logics and assist actors in updating their engagements in resource-integrating activities (Koskela-Huotari and Vargo 2016).

For a working vocabulary for the remainder of the chapter, we construct a core ontology for service that is consistent with our definition of service and service ecosystem. The service ecosystem, like any system, has two aspects: ecostructure and dynamics (Barile et al. 2016). The service ecostructure includes the following components (see Badinelli, 2015, for more details):

- *Actor:* Actors are human. Actors are the people who engage in service activities to extract value from the service system (Brodie et al. 2011).
- *Agent:* An agent works on behalf of an actor. An agent can be human or a machine, website, computer application, and so on.
- *Resource:* A resource is a necessary capability, capacity, or physical stock that is a required input to a service activity or an output that is generated by a service activity. Resources can be tangible or intangible. Value is derived from resources (Barile et al. 2013).
- *Access:* Ownership of a resource is not always necessary for authorizing commitment. Data, information, advice from acquaintances, websites, equipment rentals, and other resources can be invoked by an actor or agent to configure an ecostructure.
- *Activity:* Irene Ng (2014) makes the point that service is a verb. Service activities transform input resources into output resources from which value is derived.
- *Engagement:* The integration of resources from two or more actors/agents in a service activity that produces output resources (Peters 2016). Figure 7.1 illustrates the elements of a service engagement.

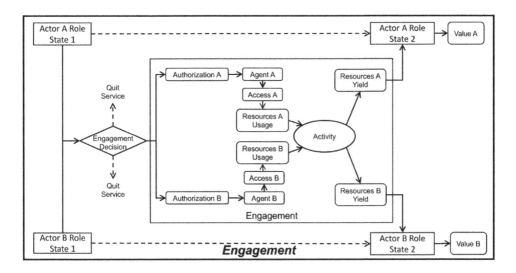

Figure 7.1   The service engagement

Service activities are the mechanisms that drive the dynamics of the service ecosystem. A service journey of an actor is a sequence of engagements in service activities. For example, a patient who experiences lower back pain begins a service journey through healthcare service. This journey might begin with several engagements with websites that provide information about treating lower back pain. The next engagement of the patient actor could be a visit to a physician who recommends pharmaceutical therapy and physical therapy. However, the patient might decide to ignore the doctor's advice about physical therapy and instead pursue a course of treatment recommended by a friend or relative. Each stage of the journey engages the actor in a service activity. This activity is selected by the actor from an ecostructure of activity propositions. The service journey continues through a sequence of actor-instigated engagements with various service systems. Figure 7.2 illustrates a service journey through a network of networks or a system of systems.

Prior to making a decision to engage in a particular activity, the actor must consider all of the activity propositions that are accessible. Hence, we can define the service ecostructure as a hypernetwork of activity propositions. Note that we distinguish an activity proposition from a value proposition. The term "value proposition" in the service science literature generally connotes an overall macro view of value exchange for an entire service. However, at an operational level, we can see that value is co-created in stages by a journey through multiple service activities executed by engagements with different service systems. Value for the actors involved in these activities is extracted from the resource outputs of the activities. The actor also represents a service system and can propose resource integration to other service systems or resource owners. In most service cases, as in our example of healthcare, the service eco-structure offers multiple activity propositions. Furthermore, the digitalization of service has and will continue to expand the offerings available to an actor.

We must pause here to highlight the significance of this view of activity and value propositions. The value proposition of a service is co-created through the engagements of an actor rather than predefined by a so-called service provider. Hence, a value proposition is

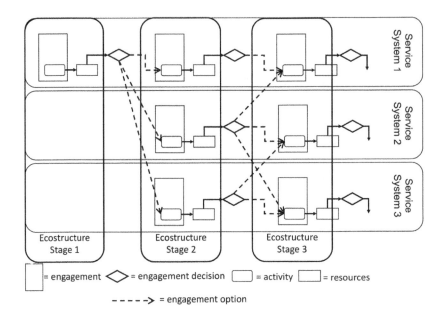

Figure 7.2   The service journey

co-created through operational-level engagements and not through the preconceived notions of a so-called service provider. This fact has strong implications for the design of service support systems, which we introduce later in this chapter. Furthermore, this view of the value proposition questions the validity of the common belief that service is "provided" by service providers as opposed to service being co-created by an actor in a journey through multiple activities. A value proposition, then, is an outcome of a service journey based on an individual actor's desires as opposed to a contractual agreement with another actor who adopts the role of service-journey guide. For business entities that currently position themselves as service providers, the reality of service journeys advocates their positioning as activity provider with concomitant revisions to key performance indicators and operating doctrines. For example, educational institutions committed to student success and institutionalized standards for holistic, long-term student outcomes could revise their strategies to position themselves as resource-integrating activity providers with the ultimate value creation the responsibility of the student.

An actor's engagement decisions determine the service journey of the actor and the actor's success in deriving value from the journey. This fact is an essential realization to unlock the operational modeling of service. Engagement decisions are the driving force of service system dynamics. Unfortunately, the literature has paid scant attention to this fact. It is through engagement decisions that the entire co-creative effort of a service is executed. Therefore, a central theme of this argument is that the core determinant of service system performance is the sequence of engagement decisions. In what follows, we focus on service engagement decisions and map their characteristics to the viability or failure of the service system.

THE NATURE OF ENGAGEMENT DECISIONS

Having established engagement decisions as the determinants of an actor's trajectory through a service ecosystem, we should investigate the distinctive features of the engagement decision. In general, framing any decision begins with identifying the options available to the decision-maker. In decision-modeling parlance, we identify this step as defining the decision variables. In the case of the engagement decision, this critical, initial, decision-framing step amounts to defining the ecostructure of resource-integrating activities that are accessible to the actor. From all the activity propositions accessible to the actor, the actor must select and, in some cases, co-create the resource integration of the activity. Hence, the engagement decision essentially specifies the structure of the next engagement. Consequently, from here on, we will refer to engagement decisions as ecostructuring decisions. From this understanding of the nature of an engagement decision, we define the following hierarchy of ecostructure (Breidbach et al. 2014; Golinelli 2010):

- *Extended Ecostructure:* The universe of ecostructures that are related to the service being pursued by the actor.
- *Accessible Ecostructure:* The subset of the extended ecostructure that is accessible to the actor due to access rights and resource requirements that are feasible to the actor's capabilities or capacities.
- *Relevant Ecostructure:* The subset of the accessible ecostructure that is amenable to the actor's journey history and the actor's particular value pursuit.
- *Engaged Ecostructure:* The ecostructure selected by the engagement decision.

Note that the extended, accessible, and relevant ecostructure may change during the service journey as the actor discovers and requires new activity propositions and attains a clearer understanding of the effectiveness of proposed service activities in pursuing the value that the actor desires. Consequently, the relevant ecostructure reflects the changing awareness and knowledge of the actor during the service journey. Furthermore, in the ever-changing environment of activity offerings, even the extended and accessible ecostructure can change during a service journey.

We must accentuate the fact that the initial step is building a decision model of the engagement decision by identifying the ecostructure hierarchy prior to selecting an ecostructure for a particular stage of the service journey. Discovering available options is often the most significant step in making a sound decision. When it comes to identifying the ecostructure hierarchy, actors are known to take advantage of several unconventional and co-creative approaches:

- *Emersion:* (Not emergence), an existing ecostructure that is revealed to the actor during the service journey.
- *Stigmergy:* Serendipitous discovery of a relevant ecostructure.
- *Vicariance:* The construction of a new relevant ecostructure through the application of an existing ecostructure in a new context.
- *Bricolage:* Creative construction of a selected ecostructure from diverse and sometimes seemingly irrelevant ecostructure components.
- *Exaptation:* Creative construction of a selected ecostructure by repurposing a seemingly irrelevant ecostructure.

The research literature, taking a macro view, has tended to define these methodologies for ecostructuring as emergent phenomena of complex systems (Barile et al. 2018). Our purpose in this chapter is to suggest approaches to service system platforms that demystify these processes and make them available to an actor through a decision support system.

The view of an actor's journey as a tour through evolving ecostructures imbues the service journey with a process of learning and adaptation. With each ecostructuring decision, the actor has the opportunity to explore directions for innovating the path to value co-creation or to exploit proven beneficial contexts for value-creating service activities (Polese 2018). This journey of learning, adaptation, and value co-creation can take many different paths for different actors with varying degrees of success (Wieland et al. 2012). Therefore, our goal in studying engagement decisions is to design service platforms that can assist the actor in discovering the personalized journey that leads to successful value co-creation. Such a journey can be expected to manifest fundamental principles of the VSA (Barile 2009; Barile et al. 2012; Golinelli et al. 2011).

A typical service journey, if it is successful, transports the actor through ecostructuring decisions that reflect conditions of dissonance, consonance, and resonance, depending on the status of the actor's learning process (Barile 2009).

- *Dissonance:* A condition of alienation, ambiguity, vagueness in trying to identify the relevant ecostructure due to the actor's lack of experience with the subject domain of the service activities. Inconsistencies in institutional norms of the actor and the ecostructure are often the source of dissonance. Abductive reasoning is typically applied during the dissonance stage of the journey (Siltaloppi et al. 2016).
- *Consonance:* A condition of comfort, accommodation, coherence between the actor and the selected ecostructure. Inductive reasoning is characteristic of the consonant stage of the journey.
- *Resonance:* A condition of synergy between the actor and the selected ecostructure. In the resonant stage, the actor is most likely applying deductive reasoning.

As the success or failure of a service journey depends on the transition to a condition of resonance, the effectiveness of an actor's restructuring decisions becomes the focal point of any attempt to design activity propositions, provide relevant resources, and implement decision support. Therefore, we turn our attention to modeling ecostructuring decisions.

DECISION SUPPORT SYSTEMS

The analysis of ecostructuring decisions places higher demands on a decision support system (DSS) than do more routine kinds of decisions. A DSS for service engagement must be smart.

What makes a service smart? This question has plagued the community of researchers in service science, data analytics, and AI (Barile and Polese 2010). One does not have to delve far into the blogs and opinion posts to discover that there is neither a consensus on the answer to this question nor a common understanding of what defines smartness. Unfortunately, the trendiness of the term "smart system" has motivated many creators of software applications to pin the "smart" label on their offerings with little regard for the elements of the system that earn this designation. For example, if an existing unsmart application is provided a front-end natural language processor or an AI-based pattern-recognition processor for the purpose of data input, the application is typically labeled smart. However, a more rigorous definition of intelligence might compare this application of the word smart to an assessment that a person's intelligence resides in their eyesight. Clearly, the locus of intelligence occurs in multiple stages of cognition directed toward learning, and we need to entertain the perspective of multiple types of smartness in a DSS. In what follows, we map out these dimensions of smartness in the construction of a holistic DSS.

What is the learning process? At the outset of a new experience, the system must contextualize the real-world application. This step in the learning process can be called abductive reasoning. Once a workable ontology of the application is developed, the learning system must validate hypotheses through inductive reasoning. Finally, with a validated understanding of the real system, deductive reasoning can apply the model to practical results.

Intelligence is manifested by the possession of applicable models of relevant phenomena. When we notice higher-level thinking in people, we can discern a knowledge base of abstract representations of a real phenomenon that allow the thinker to make deductive conclusions. For example, the patient suffering from lower back pain might reason from a model of pain that pain is caused by inflammation and inflammation can be caused by muscle exertion, leading to a decision to rest and take an anti-inflammatory medication as the engagement of the first step in the service journey. Model creation, in turn, requires some form of induction from an underling science. Creating scientific theories, in turn, begins with some form of abductive reasoning. Ideally, a robust DSS for engagement decisions provides support for all these levels of knowledge and reasoning. We can correlate this tiered understanding of cognition to components of a DSS, as shown in Figure 7.3.

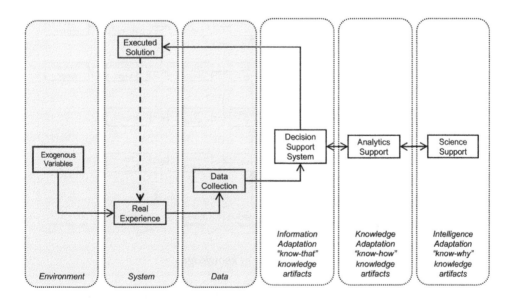

Figure 7.3   Hierarchy knowledge

Clearly, the inductive and abductive processes that engender scientific principles and models represent learning processes. We can conclude that smartness must be associated with the ability of a DSS to learn. However, there are several stages of learning and deduction in a comprehensive DSS. The question of smartness still requires further investigation. What are the differences among smartness in natural language processing, smartness in predictive modeling, smartness in robotics, or smartness in decision modeling? Does smartness reside in one of these components of a DSS, or are there different kinds of smartness? We assert here the latter.

A comprehensive description of a DSS requires an integrated hierarchy of models. This DSS framework clarifies the notion of smartness and the design of a complete DSS by defining the different types of intelligence that the system requires. Each model type is supported by its own form of analysis and its own science, as Figure 7.4 shows. Therefore, there is a form of smartness for each level of the hierarchy. There is data smartness, predictive smartness, decision smartness, value smartness (wisdom), prescriptive smartness, and so on. Therefore, the model of a DSS is two-dimensional: the stages of modeling are each supported by their own knowledge and intelligence.

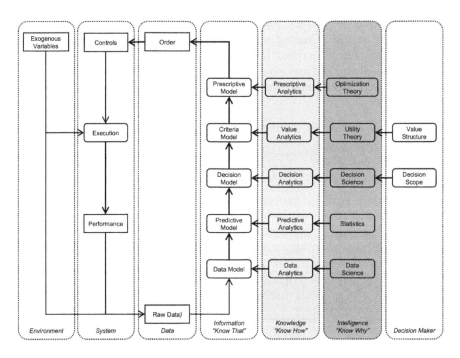

Figure 7.4   Stages of models and hierarchy of knowledge

A most important point to make about the framework in Figure 7.4 is that the decision model forms the core of the DSS. Every decision model is a representation of the cause–effect relationship from decision options to decision outcomes based on parameters that are beyond the decision-maker's control. The purpose of predictive modeling is to generate estimates of these parameters from other structured data. The purpose of data modeling is to source raw—perhaps unstructured—data, cleanse the data, and convert it to structured data for use by predictive models. Consequently, the decision model drives the processes of data collection and analytics. In other words, without a clear specification of the decision frame, relevant predictive analytics and data analytics cannot be applied. Therefore, the DSS cannot be built from the bottom stage in Figure 7.4 upward. This point is often lost on the army of data scientists who now dominate the IT departments of many organizations and who tend to begin the construction of a DSS by finding and analyzing data, and then assume that the decision-maker can make use of the data. Similarly, relevant prescriptive analytics must wait for a precise specification of an optimization problem in terms of criteria for performance measures, which are expressed in terms of functions of decision variables and parameters. Therefore, the DSS cannot be built from the top stage in Figure 7.4 downward (Badinelli 2015). A useful DSS can be built only by starting in the middle with a precise and complete specification of the decision model and the value function that the decision-maker places on the performance measures. Given the personalized nature of service, the ecostructure DSS must be capable of enabling the actor to formulate the decision frame and express the actor's value structure as a prerequisite to any applications of other forms of analytics.

DECISION MODELS

Now that we have a clear view of the structure of a DSS and the central role of the decision model, we can focus our attention to the nature of this model. Reprising our view of the ecostructure decisions as ecostructure identification and selection, we can identify specific characteristics of these kinds of decisions.

Indeterminacy is the hallmark of these decisions. Many parameters of the decision can only be estimated from data, making the decision model stochastic and introducing risk into the performance measures of the decision. Furthermore, given the abductive phase of a service journey, many parameters and relationships are vague and ambiguous, making the decision model fuzzy (Badinelli 2012). These indeterminacies of typical ecostructure decisions have led to a wealth of literature about the complexity of service systems and the phenomenon of emergence as endemic to service ecosystems (Ashby 1958; Bedau 2003, 2008; Chalmers 2006; Corning 2002; Goldstein 1999; Johnson 2001; Minati et al. 2006; Pessa 2002; Sawyer 2005).

Pursuing the goal of developing operational DSS for the ecostructuring decisions, we should not surrender the actor's decisions to phenomenological inscrutabilities. What can be done to make the service journey more manageable and reliable in terms of successful value co-creation? The indeterminacies of the engagement/ecostructure decisions naturally require learning and adaptation within the service journey. Hence, the service journey is both a journey of exploitation for value co-creation and an exploration of new ecostructures.

An example of the uncontrollability of service journeys when ecostructure decisions are fuzzy was performed by Badinelli (2013) in the form of a simulation study of actors who make the ecostructuring decision with only a fuzzy knowledge of the meaning of decision parameters and relationships. The results of the simulation studies showed actor trajectories that varied widely in terms of the amount of value achieved. These simulation studies illustrate how complex the ecostructuring decision process can be in the absence of a DSS.

A well-known model has been found applicable to describing this process: the multi-armed bandit problem. Applying the conventional multi-armed bandit model to service journeys introduces a number of special challenges. First, the available arms of the bandit can change with each stage of the service journey, as the accessible ecostructure can evolve. The actor's learning and adaptation is likely to be nonlinear and discrete. The value structure of the actor is likely to be multidimensional and fuzzy (Badinelli 2012). Therefore, the application of some variation of the multi-armed bandit problem to the ecostructuring decision seems to be a potentially fruitful subject for future research, but with limited applicability.

However, another more general approach is more promising. Constructing a DSS for each stage of a personalized actor's service journey should not be constrained by assumptions and limitations of a specific form of decision model, such as the multi-armed bandit problem. Instead, the DSS should incorporate interactive, model-framing support for the actor as well as more traditional model building tools. The mechanism for this kind of support comes in the form of cognitive assistants, such as IBM Watson. Such technology has been proven effective in decision framing and can become the backbone of platforms for service-journey management.

SERVICE SUPPORT SYSTEM

A service system must support the exploration and exploitation decisions of each actor. As exploration in service ecostructures requires access to multiple resource providers, the natural evolution of service systems is destined to result in two-tiered systems of platforms for exploration and resource providers for exploitation. We define the service support systems (SSS) as a new kind of business entity as follows:

- *Service Support System:* A platform that enables personalized, adaptable, comprehensive DSS for an actor's ecostructuring decisions throughout a service journey.

Such platforms already exist in various degrees of sophistication. For example, Amazon reinvented retailing as a service by providing its users with advice and recommendations for product purchases based on analyses of big data related to the user's values and budget. The manufacturing, distribution, and shipping of the product is performed by individual resource providers who are affiliated with Amazon. Other service platforms, such as those for travel reservations, are similarly configured and are well established. However, the awareness of the distinction between platform provider and resource provider has not yet permeated all forms of service. Healthcare and higher education are examples of industries that cling to an outdated notion of closed service systems that are designed to captivate the actor.

These two examples highlight key deficiencies in the approaches to an SSS to date. At one extreme (higher education and healthcare) we see institutions of provider-defined journeys that combine journey management with predefined resource-integrating activities (Barile et al. 2014; Beirão et al. 2017; Taillard et al. 2016). In these cases, the ecostructure decisions are commandeered by the actor known as the service "provider." However, conventional provider–customer viewpoints of service are not conducive to the increasing demands of actors for flexibility and personalization, and these industries have already experienced significant disaggregation of resource providers to fulfill the demands of students and patients. Ultimately, such service systems that are designed to be comprehensive in terms of resource provision and journey management will fail to support the needs of actors. The more modern approach, exemplified by companies like Amazon, is still hindered by DSS driven by big data analytics, which generally attempt to recommend a one-step engagement decision based on predictive models. In these cases, the ecostructuring decision of the actor is assisted with information gleaned from data, but the service system falls far short of interactively guiding the decision modeling process.

How should an SSS be designed? First and most essentially, a service platform must provide decision support for ecostructuring decisions. Several kinds of roles for platforms have been identified: Tool, Assistant, Collaborator, Coach, and Mediator (Maglio and Spohrer 2008). However, with a clear focus on the decision support function of the platform and the structure of DSS, we can refine the conceptual design of a platform to the structure shown in Figure 7.4. Accordingly, we can precisely define the roles of Big Data Analytics (BDA) and Artificial Intelligence (AI) and clearly identify the sources of smartness in the SSS.

The platform must be designed around decision *modeling*, not just decision-making. This point is a key to SSS design. The SSS's decision modeling function must be initiated with framing the decision, followed by construction of the decision model and the value model. The decision model is the prerequisite to predictive modeling, data modeling, optimization, and execution. The DSS structure in Figure 7.4 must be built from the middle outward.

The adaptability of the SSS to variation across actors and variability in the accessible ecostructures during a service journey requires the application of normalized systems theory (NST) to the platform design. NST is a conceptual approach to system design that is particularly relevant to platform design (Mannaert and Verelst 2009). NST began as a normative structure for information systems and for the process of systems design (Mannaert and Verelst 2009). De Bruyn (2014), in his Ph.D. dissertation, extends the theory to systems in general with interesting implications for service systems. NST considers adaptation in the form of updating the structure of a system, which is called system design, and in the form of responding to service requests through applying existing structure and processes, which is called system function (dynamics).

The application of NST principles creates a system with two key characteristics: evolvability and observability. System design adaptability is labeled evolvability, and system function transparency is labeled observability. The key feature of NST designs is modularity. It is well known that modularity can enable mass customization through configuration management of interchangeable (uncoupled) modules. Evolvability is the scalable capability of a system to be modified or redesigned to adapt to new requirements. Certainly, a viable service support system must be evolvable, except for the periods of dissonance.

Through the distinction of SSS versus resource-integrating providers we can clarify the mechanisms of viable SSS. Given the ever-changing technologies and innovations in tools, methods, and collaborations, it is not possible to consider an individual resource integrator capable of supporting the key features of a viable system: homeostasis, autopoiesis, and equifinality. However, SSS can achieve these performance standards through designs that are evolvable and observable. A DSS for ecostructuring decisions that is modular in terms of its ability to gain access to variability over time in the resource providers gains the property of autopoiesis. A DSS for restructuring decisions that is modular in the form of being adaptive to the variety in user preferences, backgrounds, and demographics gains the property of equifinality. A DSS for ecostructuring that is modular in terms of accommodating variations in the sequence of decisions in service journeys gains the property of homeostasis. Hence, the viability of an SSS derives from the application of NST to the design of DSS within an SSS.

CONCLUSION

After introducing basic concepts and definitions of service and service systems, this chapter focuses on decision-making in service journeys and the need for an SSS for a viable service system. Specifically, this chapter describes and advocates the following points:

* Ecostructuring decisions are essential steps in each stage of a service journey;
* Learning and adaptation are endemic to ecostructuring decision-making;
* SSS provide adaptable guidance for an actor throughout a service journey; and
* An SSS enables reframing and rebuilding the decision model at each stage of the journey and builds the rest of the DSS after the decision model and value model have been built.

REFERENCES

Ashby, W.R. (1958). Requisite variety and its implications for the control of complex systems, *Cybernetica*, 1, 2.83–99.
Badinelli, R. (2012). Fuzzy modeling of service system engagements, *Service Science*, summer, 4.135–146.
Bardinelli, R. (2013). Trajectories of viable and non-viable service systems, Naples Forum on Service, June, 2013.
Badinelli, R. (2015). *Modeling service systems*, Business Expert Press.
Badinelli, R., Barile, S., Ng, I., Polese, F., Saviano, M., and Di Nauta, P. (2012). Viable service systems and decision-making in service management, *Journal of Service Management*, 23, 4.498–526.
Badinelli, R.D., and Sarno, D. (2017). Integrating the internet of things and big data analytics into decision support models for healthcare management, in Gummesson, E., Mele, C., and Polese, F. (Eds.), *Service dominant logic, network & systems theory and service science: integrating three perspectives for a new service agenda*, 5.101, Youcanprint Self-Publishing.
Barile, S. (2009). *Management sistemico vitale*, G. Giappichelli.
Barile, S., Lusch, R., Reynoso, J., Saviano, M., and Spohrer, J. (2016). Systems, networks, and ecosystems in service research, *Journal of Service Management*, 27,4.652–674.
Barile, S., Pels, J., Polese, F., and Saviano, M. (2012). An introduction to the Viable Systems Approach and its contribution to marketing, *Journal of Business Market Management*, 5,2.54–78.
Barile, S., and Polese, F. (2010). Smart service systems and viable service systems: applying systems theory to service science, *Service Science*, 2,1.21–40.
Barile, S., Polese, F., Calabrese, M., Carrubbo, L., and Iandolo, F. (2013). A theoretical framework for measuring value creation based on the Viable Systems Approach (vSa), in Barile, S. (Ed.), *Contributions to theoretical and practical advances in management, a Viable Systems Approach (vSa)*, Aracne, 61–94.
Barile, S., Polese, F., Pels, J., and Sarno, D. (2018). Complexity and governance, in Farazmand, A. (Ed.), *Global Encyclopedia of Public Administration, Public Policy, and Governance*, Springer, Section C, 1–4..
Barile, S., Polese, F., and Saviano, M. (2014). Information asymmetry and co-creation in health care services, *Australasian Marketing Journal*, 22.205–217.
Barile, S., and Saviano, M. (2011). Foundations of systems thinking: the structure-system paradigm, in Barile, S. (Ed.), *Contributions to theoretical and practical advances in management. A Viable Systems Approach (vSa)*, 1–25, International Printing.

Bedau, M.A. (2003). Downward causation and autonomy in weak emergence, *Principia Revista Internacional de Epistemologica*, 6.5–50. (Reprinted in Bedau, M.A., and Humphreys, P. (Eds.) (2008). *Emergence: contemporary readings in philosophy and science*, MIT Press.)

Bedau, M.A. (2008). Is weak emergence just in the mind?, *Minds & Machines*, 18.443–459.

Beirão, G., Patrício, L., and Fisk, R.P. (2017). Value co-creation in service ecosystems: investigating health care at the micro, meso, and macro levels, *Journal of Service Management*, 28, 2.227–249.

Breidback, C., Brodie, R., and Hllebeek, L. (2014). Beyond virtuality: From engagement platforms to engagement ecosystems, *Managing Service Quality*, 24, 6. 592–631.

Brodie, R.J., Hollebeek, L.D., Juric, B., and Ilic, A. (2011). Customer engagement: conceptual domain, fundamental propositions and implications for research, *Journal of Service Research*, 14, 3.252–271.

Calabrese, M., Iandolo, F., Caputo, F., and Sarno, D. (2018). From mechanical to cognitive view: the changes of decision making in business environment, in Barile, S., Pellicano, M., and Polese, F. (Eds.), *Social dynamics in a systems perspective, new economic windows*, 223–240, Springer.

Chalmers, D.J. (2006). Strong and weak emergence, in Davies, P., and Clayton, P. (Eds.), *The re-emergence of emergence: the emergentist hypothesis from science to religion*, Chapter 11, Oxford University Press.

Chandler, J.D., and Vargo, S.L. (2011). Contextualization: network intersections, value-in-context, and the co-creation of markets, *Marketing Theory*, 11, 1.35–49.

Corning, P.A. (2002). The re-emergence of "emergence": A venerable concept in search of a theory, *Complexity*, 7, 6.18–30.

De Bruyn, P. (2014). Generalizing normalized systems theory: towards a foundational theory for enterprise engineering, Ph.D. dissertation, University of Antwerp.

Echeverri, P., and Skålén, P. (2011). Co-creation and co-destruction: a practice-theory based study of interactive value formation, *Marketing Theory*, 11, 3.351–373.

Edvardsson, B., Tronvoll, B., and Gruber, T. (2011). Expanding understanding of service exchange and value co-creation: a social construction approach, *Journal of the Academy of Marketing Science*, 39, 2.327–339.

Fujita, S., Vaughan, C., and Vargo, S.L. (2018). Service Ecosystem emergence from primitive actors in service dominant logic: an exploratory simulation study, in *Proceedings of the 51st Hawaii International Conference on System Sciences*, 1601–1610.

Goldstein, J. (1999). Emergence as a construct: history and issues, *Emergence*, 1, 1.49–72.

Golinelli, G.M. (2010). *Viable Systems Approach (VSA) governing business dynamics*, Wolters Kluwer Italia Srl.

Golinelli, G.M., Pastore, A., Gatti, M., Massaroni, E., and Vagnani, G. (2011). The firm as a viable system: managing inter-organisational relationships, *Sinergie Italian Journal of Management*, 58, 2.65–98.

Jaakkola, E., Helkkula, A., and Aarikka-Stenroos, L. (2015). Service experience co-creation: conceptualization, implications, and future research directions, *Journal of Service Management*, 26, 2.182–205.

Johnson, S. (2001). *Emergence: the connected lives of ants, brains, cities, and software*, Scribner.

Jonas, J.M., Boha, J., Sörhammar, D., and Moeslein, K.M. (2018). Stakeholder engagement in intra- and inter-organizational innovation: exploring antecedents of engagement in service ecosystems, *Journal of Service Management*, 29, 3. 399–421.

Koskela-Huotari, K., and Vargo, S.L. (2016). Institutions as resource context, *Journal of Service Theory and Practice*, 26, 2.163–178.

Lusch, R.F., and Vargo, S.L. (2014). *Service-dominant logic: premises, perspectives, possibilities*, Cambridge University Press.

Maglio, P.P., and Spohrer, J. (2008). Fundamentals of service science, *Journal of the Academy of Marketing Science*, 36, 18–20.

Mannaert, H., and Verelst, J. (2009). *Normalized systems: re-creating information technology based on laws for software evolvability*, Koppa.

Minati, G., Pessa, E., and Abhram, M. (2006). *Systemics of emergence: research and development*, Springer.

Ng, I. (2014). Creating new markets in the digital economy: value and worth, Cambridge University Press.

Payne, A.F., Storbacka, K., and Frow, P. (2008). Managing the co-creation of value, *Journal of the Academy of Marketing Science*, 36,1.83–96.

Pessa, E. (2002). What is emergence?, in Minati, G., and Pessa, E. (Eds.), *Emergence in complex cognitive, social and biological systems*, Kluwer, 379–382.

Peters, L. (2016). Heteropathic versus homeopathic resource integration and value co-creation in service ecosystems, *Journal of Business Research*, 69, 2999–3007.

Polese, F. (2018). Successful value co-creation exchanges: a VSA contribution, in Barile, S., Pellicano, M., and Polese, F. (Eds.), *Social dynamics in a systems perspective, new economic windows*, 19–37, Springer.

Polese, F., Pels, J., Tronvoll, B., Bruni, R., and Carrubbo, L. (2017). A4A relationships, *Journal of Service Theory and Practice*, 27, 5.1040–1056.

Sawyer, R.K. (2005). *Social emergence: societies as complex systems*, Cambridge University Press.

Siltaloppi, J., Koskela-Huotari, K., and Vargo, S.L. (2016). Institutional complexity as a driver for innovation in service ecosystems, *Service Science*, 8, 3.333–343.

Storbacka, K., Brodie, R.J., Böhmann, T., Maglio, P.P., and Nenonen, S. (2016). Actor engagement as a microfoundation for value co-creation, *Journal of Business Research*, 69, 8, 3008–3017.

Taillard, M., Peters, L.D., Pels, J., and Mele, C. (2016). The role of shared institutions in the emergence of service ecosystems, *Journal of Business Research*, 69, 8.2972–2980.

Vargo, S.L., and Lusch, R.F. (2008). Service-dominant logic: continuing the evolution, *Journal of the Academy of Marketing Science*, 36, 1.1–10.

Vargo, S.L., and Lusch, R.F. (2011). It's all B2B…and beyond: toward a systems perspective of the market, *Industrial Marketing Management*, 40, 2.181–187.

Vargo, S.L., and Lusch, R.F. (2016). Institutions and axioms: an extension and update of service-dominant logic, *Journal of the Academy of Marketing Science*, 44, 1.5–23.

Vargo, S.L., and Lusch, R.F. (2017). Service-dominant logic 2025, *International Journal of Research in Marketing*, 34, 46–67.

Wieland, H., Polese, F., Vargo, S.L., and Lusch, R.F. (2012). Toward a service (eco)systems perspective on value creation, *International Journal of Service Science, Management Engineering, and Technology*, 3, 3.12–25.

Yi, Y., and Gong, T. (2013). Customer value co-creation behaviour: scale development and validation, *Journal of Business Research*, 66, 9. 1279–1284.

8. Perceived justice and control of priority lines

Michael Dixon, David Rea, Liana Victorino and Craig Froehle

INTRODUCTION

Service providers make many process decisions when managing waiting lines. Two key choices are the queue configuration (e.g., single- versus multi-channel) and the queue discipline used when selecting which customer to serve next (e.g., first-come-first-served [FCFS], shortest processing time, or preemptive priority). These decisions affect not only objective process measures, such as the wait time, but, more importantly, they can substantially influence how customers perceive their waits (Maister, 1984; Larson, 1987; Rafaeli et al., 2002; Seawright & Sampson, 2007). When setting waiting-line policies and practices, service providers have an opportunity to fortify—or destroy—customers' perceptions of justice and control, which can influence their satisfaction.

To better understand how customers perceive justice and, relatedly, fairness in waiting lines, service providers can look to social norms (Fagundes, 2017). Norms help explain why and when groups of people queue, the unwritten rules they expect (and are expected) to follow when doing so (Larson, 1987; Schmitt et al., 1992; Fagundes, 2017), and how customers will react to certain waiting-line policies. Deviating from waiting-line norms, such as violating FCFS, can lead to perceptions of unfairness. In addition, their sense of control may diminish if it is no longer clear what order is being followed. Perceived control has been identified as an important service-design factor (Bateson, 1985; Dasu & Chase, 2013) and can help explain customers' responses to waiting-line policies and practices.

This chapter starts by summarizing issues related to social norms, perceived justice, and perceived control when considering priority-based waiting lines. Then, we describe a practical example of a priority-line application to highlight some of the many challenges associated with understanding customers' perceptions of these waiting contexts. Afterward, we demonstrate how principles of perceived justice and control might be useful in interpreting the insights gained from this practical example. The chapter concludes by reviewing practical issues related to priority lines and future research avenues.

BACKGROUND

Priority Lines

Priority lines are becoming more pervasive across multiple services that have traditional queues, including security lines, airline check-in and boarding, airport baggage claims, museum and sporting event entrances, highway lane usage, and college class selection (Walker, 2012). One particularly successful example is Disney's FastPass. Introduced in 1999, and used until 2021, the FastPass system was a virtual queue intended to allow guests to save a place in line without having to physically wait. Guests requested a spot in a virtual queue and were then told to return when that spot would be near the front. The standby, or regular, line was used to fill capacity due to the uncertain arrival times of the virtual queue members. The two-line system stayed in equilibrium as long as the virtual wait was slightly longer than the standby wait. Standby lines, therefore, included people who were waiting for their FastPass time for another ride. This system granted customers more control over their park experience by offering them a choice to use the FastPass option for certain rides throughout the day. In addition, it allowed customers to participate in more activities with less physical waiting and increased supplemental revenue by freeing customers' time; instead of waiting in line for an attraction, customers could spend money at retail and other revenue-generating parts of the park.

Since the initial inception of the FastPass system at Disney parks, allowing customers an opportunity to bypass physical waiting times has become popular in a myriad of contexts. For example, Cedar Fair Amusement Parks, managing 13 amusement parks across the US, offers a limited number of daily Fast Lane and Fast Lane Plus wristbands as paid add-ons that allow customers immediate access to the front of the line for rides. Different from Disney's FastPass, Fast Lane is not a reservation system, but a queue bypassing system available only to those who can afford to purchase it.

A similar queue structure is provided by the Transportation Security Administration's (TSA) security-check system within United States airports. To enter the boarding area of a US airport, passengers and staff must pass through the TSA security check. In most major airports, the TSA offers expedited security processes for passengers who have prequalified as lower risk (e.g., a membership fee of $85 or more for TSA PreCheck), fly often enough to earn elite status with an airline, or hold a first-class ticket. Furthermore, for $15 a month, passengers can bypass queues entirely through membership with Clear, a private company that has contracted with TSA to allow its customers front-of-the-line access to expedited security checks.

Increased revenue is one reason service providers may determine that using a priority line is right for their operations. If a priority line is adopted, then providers must also decide how it will be designed and managed. Insights related to social norms, perceived justice, and perceived control can help inform these important waiting-line policy and practice decisions.

Social Norms

Social norms have been studied for decades by scholars in many disciplines, including sociology, law, and economics. The study of norms considers how and why individuals within groups behave. Norms dictate whether a specific behavior is deemed appropriate by a social group and hold people accountable to principles that the group (e.g., society, an organization, or a team) deems important and appropriate (Brennan et al., 2013). Indicating their power, norms are often given precedence when they conflict with laws (Acemoglu & Jackson, 2017). Hence, norms become an efficient alternative to laws in many cases because they internalize negative externalities (Ellickson, 1994). To avoid problems stemming from violating norms, service providers must understand the norms of the society in which they operate.

The key norms governing queueing in many societies are: (a) *form a line*; (b) *no cutting*; (c) *FCFS*; and (d) *wait your turn*. Others include: (e) *limited acceptability for holding lines for others*, and (f) *no line holding for multiple other people* (please refer to Fagundes, 2017, for a comprehensive overview of queueing norms). FCFS, in particular, is often considered a default norm from which purposeful deviations must be justified.

These norms have been integrated into queueing theory since its inception, with models typically assuming norm-based behavior like no jockeying and the FCFS queue discipline (Wierman, 2011). Increasingly, however, some service providers are designing and implementing queues that violate well-established norms and, as a result, may not be perceived as justified in the mind of some customers. For example, priority access, when granted to valuable customers, such as high-rollers or repeat customers (Alexander et al., 2012; Malady, 2013), can be upsetting to those aware they're not receiving it.

While perhaps financially efficient in the near-term, norm-breaking waiting-line policies can negatively influence customers' perceptions of service providers. When customers see the violation of norms permitted by, or even benefiting, the service organization, the retaliation may be directed toward the organization in the form of poor reviews or abusive employee treatment (Milgram et al., 1986; Schmitt et al., 1992). Further, by converting a cooperative exercise into a competitive one, organizations can motivate customers to question the need for maintaining other social norms, potentially leading to mob-type behaviors (Fagundes, 2017). When customers perceive their treatment by the service provider to be within the bounds of established social norms, they are more likely to perceive their treatment to be fair and just. The use of priority queues has the potential to defy queue norms in the eyes of customers and result in perceptions of injustice.

Perceived Justice: Procedural, Distributive, and Interactional

When customers perceive that an *injustice* has occurred, or even merely that it *can* occur, it can result in perceptions of *unfairness* (Seiders & Berry, 1998; Rafaeli et al., 2002). Describing the normative standards for employee treatment, *organizational justice* provides a framework that is relevant to the fair management of waiting lines (e.g., Larson, 1987; Rafaeli et al., 2002). The relevance is due to the parallelism that exists between the organization–employee relationship and the service provider–customer relationship; both are managing the process and outcomes for a group of people (e.g., Seiders & Berry, 1998; Tax et al., 1998; McColl-Kennedy & Sparks, 2003). Dimensions of organizational justice include *procedural*, *distributive*, and *interactional* justice. Each has implications that can help to explain how the use of priority lines can influence customers' perceptions of justice.

Procedural justice refers to the fairness of the process by which decisions about the distribution of outcomes are made (Leventhal, 1980). When specific processes match generalizable norms and rules, the processes tend to be deemed more fair. Priority lines, for example, can violate some of the core aspects of procedural justice, including the consistent application of policies and conformance with moral standards. Because they permit violations of FCFS, multi-queue structures have been found to be perceived as less fair. Surprisingly, this perception of unfairness can result even when no FCFS violations have actually occurred (Rafaeli et al., 2002). However, FCFS violations are not universally perceived as unfair, particularly when individuals are prioritized based on *need* (Deutsch, 1975). When seating customers at a restaurant, for example, participants in one study (McGuire & Kimes, 2006) reported that seating customers based on party size (i.e., need for large or small tables) was an acceptable reason to violate FCFS. In contrast, prioritization of VIPs ahead of other guests was perceived as unfair. As a more drastic scenario, prioritization of severely ill or injured (i.e., higher-need) patients is broadly deemed a just practice in emergency medical services (Lauridsen, 2020). While processes that prioritize groups based on need are sometimes deemed palatable, there are also cases where the *need* to participate in the service becomes more difficult to justify. In these instances, some of the feelings of unfairness could be explained by customers perceiving that procedural justice is not being upheld.

While procedural justice implicates process decisions, *distributive justice*—the fairness in how goods and resources are distributed among group members (Deutsch, 1975)—provides another potential explanation for differing perceptions of fairness of queue practices. One reason FCFS queues are widely used as the baseline for fairness is that they result in lower variance (more equal) waiting times across customers (Kingman, 1962; Wierman, 2011). Indeed, research suggests that the equality of wait times across customers may contribute more to their satisfaction than the wait times themselves (Zhou & Soman, 2003). According to distributive justice, however, customer expectations for equal outcomes are not universal (Martínez-Tur et al., 2006). Equitable treatment, where individuals' outcomes reflect their inputs (such as money, time, expertise, or effort; Sampson & Froehle, 2006), can enhance individual perceptions of fairness. For example, in the case of priority lines, monetarily equitable treatment—rewarding those who paid for priority access with shorter waiting times—may result in higher perceptions of fairness for those who paid compared to those who did not. On the other hand, monetarily inequitable outcomes for those in the priority line can also result in feelings of injustice. For example, if the priority line is not sufficiently shorter than the main line, priority customers may not feel they received appropriate value for their additional expense (Alexander et al., 2012). Regular-line customers, on the other hand, would likely be happy to see more equality in waiting times.

Interactional justice refers to the fairness of the interpersonal treatment of people during an encounter (Bies & Moag, 1986), and has been found to impact repatronage and negative word-of-mouth intentions of complaining customers (Blodgett et al., 1997). For example, strategies such as offering an explanation, being honest, and displaying politeness, effort, and empathy have been noted as factors of interactional justice that lead to increased satisfaction when handling a complaint (Tax et al., 1998). The form and manner of communication about the outcomes and procedures may alter reactions; proper interactions can help people feel better about an unfavorable or seemingly unfair outcome (Greenberg, 1993). Applied to waiting lines, interactional justice refers to the treatment of customers in line and the way waiting-line policies are communicated to customers. In priority-line systems, for example, it could be the manner in which differences in waiting times for the priority and regular lines are explained to customers. Overall, implications of perceived justice (i.e., procedural, distributive, and interactional) can help to understand customer responses to priority lines.

Perceived Control

Perceived control is another factor that can offer understanding of customer attitudes toward priority lines. Control has been a topic widely studied in the psychology literature (e.g., Averill, 1973; Thompson, 1981) and has been defined as "the belief that one has at one's disposal a response that can influence the aversiveness of an event" (Thompson, 1981, p. 89). Applied to services, perceived control has been defined as "the degree to which customers or service providers perceived that they are able to influence the service process and outcome" (van Raaij & Pruyn, 1998, p. 818). In waiting lines, customers may perceive varying degrees of control over their wait experiences (duration, location, pleasantness, etc.).

There are two primary forms of control—behavioral and cognitive (Dasu & Chase, 2013); both have relevance to waiting-line management. *Behavioral control* refers to the level of influence the customer has on the process (Chase & Dasu, 2014)—for example, a customer's decision to join or leave a line. Often, behavioral control is related to giving the customer the opportunity of choice, such as choosing from among multiple lines or even a priority line (Rafaeli et al., 2002). *Cognitive control* refers to the customer's ability to create in their mind a sense of control that guides their behavior. Cognitive control mechanisms can happen even though a customer may have no direct influence on the process (Chase & Dasu, 2014). Often this type of control happens when customers have more information about processes in order to create mental pictures of their future behavior. In queueing contexts, cognitive control can be heightened by providing information about expected wait times, allowing customers to feel less anxious about unknown waits (Maister, 1984). In contexts where physical queues are not present, the take-a-number approach helps ensure FCFS and provides a level of transparency for waiting procedures (Maister, 1984; Chase & Dasu, 2014). Transparency and information allow greater predictability about the progress and process of waits. For example, a customer seeing a consistent application of FCFS queue discipline will sense greater levels of cognitive control given they know that everyone will be served based on their order of arrival (Dasu & Chase, 2013). When customers can better predict aspects of the process, their perceptions of cognitive control are enhanced.

Applied to priority lines, having information available to make customers aware of the priority line should enhance cognitive control and the opportunity to choose (i.e., choosing either the priority line or regular line should lead to greater behavioral control). Having a greater sense of perceived control has been shown to improve customers' evaluative perceptions (e.g., Hui & Bateson, 1991; Namasivayam & Hinkin, 2003; Namasivayam & Mount, 2006; Bolkan et al., 2010; Dasu & Chase, 2010).

Norms, perceived justice, and perceived control can all influence customers' perceptions of a waiting experience, and priority lines create complex environments where one or more of these subjective factors can modify a customer's satisfaction. In the next section, we explore an illustrative example where these factors might help us interpret the service customers' survey responses about the queueing context.

PRIORITY-LINE EXAMPLE

To examine how the aforementioned concepts might exist in a practical context, we present a priority-line example of a homecoming-night event that is based on a university tradition. At this university, tradition says that, to become a "True Aggie" (the school mascot is an "Aggie"), students have to kiss someone on a platform in the campus quad at midnight on homecoming night. Thousands of students usually participate in the tradition, often waiting for hours in a line that forms long before the event begins and typically wraps around the campus quad. Acting as a norm, the event was traditionally free for all participants.

In 2017, the student-body association began selling priority-line access to the True Aggie Night experience at a cost of $20 per couple. Line managers alternate between the priority and regular lines to decide who will go next on the platform. As long as the priority line is shorter than the regular line, the wait between the two lines could differ significantly. Money raised from the priority-line tickets goes toward scholarship funds, and the $20 ticket was priced to ensure line-size disparity. There were no costs (except for potentially embarrassing public displays of affection) associated with the tradition for participants in the regular line.

The use of a priority line in this manner, even if operated within the queueing norms participants expected, has the potential to incite perceptions of injustice. For example, the price for the priority line may be outside the budget for some students, leaving the option of the shorter wait available to only those who can afford it. Furthermore, the long, cold wait is a fundamental part of the tradition, and paying to shorten the wait may harm the reputation of the "True Aggie" designation, leaving students to question if there is any honor in the title when it can simply be purchased. Therefore, the introduction of the priority line may cheapen the importance of the tradition to the student body.

In 2018, under the direction of one of the authors, student researchers collected survey and observational data from the True Aggie Night event. Members of the research team approached students in both lines and invited them to scan a QR code from their phones and participate in a survey while they waited in line. In total, 141 participants completed the survey: 78 from the priority line and 63 from the regular line. Of those in the regular line, 24 were unaware of the priority line; this tradition draws thousands of people and it is reasonable that some students would not notice the priority line option when they arrive. Therefore, we identified three customer segments based on their waiting-line experience: (1) those who were *aware* of the priority line and chose the priority line, (2) those who were *aware* of the priority line and chose the regular line, and (3) those who were *unaware* of the priority line and joined the regular line.

Among other things, the survey asked participants about their perceptions of fairness for True Aggie Night and other priority-line scenarios (i.e., security checkpoints, amusement parks, and toll lanes). Participants were also asked to rate how satisfied they were with their True Aggie Night experience. Perceived fairness was rated on a five-point Likert scale, and satisfaction was rated on a seven-point Likert scale. The results are shown in Figure 8.1 and the statistical comparisons between the perceived fairness for the three customer segments are shown in Table 8.1.

For the two customer segments in the regular line—those who were aware of the True Aggie Night priority line compared to those who were unaware—the results indicate no significant difference in perceived fairness for any of the priority-line scenarios (i.e., True Aggie Night, security check points, amusement parks, and toll lanes). However, a significant difference was observed in the level of perceived fairness between regular-line and priority-line participants in some of the scenarios, including the True Aggie Night priority line. Those in the priority line at True Aggie Night rated it as being fairer than did those who were in the regular line. In addition, those who were originally unaware of the priority line at True Aggie Night rated their satisfaction lower than those in the priority line ($t = 1.74$, $p < 0.10$). The findings suggest that these three True Aggie Night customer segments had unique waiting experiences and, as a result, had differing perceptions of fairness and satisfaction based on these experiences.

The difference found in perceptions of fairness between those who paid for priority access at True Aggie Night and those in the regular line, regardless of their awareness of the priority line, could be interpreted through the lens of perceived justice. Regarding procedural justice, it seems difficult to argue that anyone *needs* to participate in the True Aggie Night tradition, which could explain some of the feelings of unfairness perceived by those in the regular line.

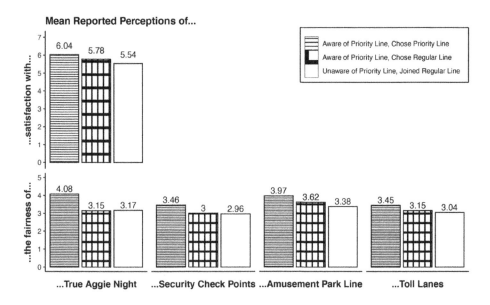

Figure 8.1   True Aggie Night survey results

Table 8.1   Independent two-sample t-test results for fairness perceptions

Comparisons			Toll Lanes	Amusement Parks	Security Checkpoints	True Aggie Night
Regular Line, Aware	vs.	Regular Line, Unaware	0.39	0.85	0.13	0.04
Regular Line, Aware	vs.	Priority Line, Aware	1.38	1.91*	1.95*	4.26***
Regular Line, Aware	vs.	Priority Line, Aware	1.41	2.40**	1.54	3.22***

Notes:
* $p < 0.10$, ** $p < 0.05$, *** $p < 0.01$.

Distributive justice implications may also be at play in this example. Those who paid for priority access may have found that the price was equitable to the reduction in their waiting time, which resulted in higher perceptions of fairness for this customer segment compared to those in the regular line. Interpreted from the view of those in the regular line, the lengthened wait times they experienced compared to those in the priority line could result in feelings of inequality, as customers are known to compare their own inputs and outcomes against those of others when assessing fairness (Oliver & DeSarbo, 1988). In addition, those in the regular line may have also felt they received inequitable treatment because their outcomes did not reflect their temporal contributions (i.e., time spent in line).

Providing a distinct perspective, the higher levels of satisfaction for those in the priority line versus the segments in the regular line may be due to perceptions of control. In the True Aggie Night example, those who were *unaware* of the priority line option had lower levels of satisfaction compared to those in the priority line, but those who were *aware* of the priority line were not significantly different. Unaware customers were lacking information about the process and may have perceived they were not given the choice to select which line they would join. Therefore, those who were aware of the priority line option likely had a greater sense of control than those who were unaware they had a choice in lines. This finding provides preliminary evidence that the perceived control afforded from awareness about a priority line option and the opportunity to choose which line to join may influence customer perceptions of satisfaction.

In summary, the True Aggie Night example demonstrates the potential implications that a priority line could have on perceived justice and control and how this can influence perceived fairness and satisfaction. More research is needed that examines different applications of priority lines in various service contexts to better understand the nuances of perceived justice and control and the corresponding impact on customer responses.

CONCLUSION

Our premise for this chapter was that service providers make choices about policy and practices for priority lines that can influence customers' perceptions of justice and control, which, in turn, can shape customers' satisfaction with the service experience. The True Aggie Night scenario provided an example for discussion of how aspects of perceived justice and control might explain differing perceptions of fairness and satisfaction with priority-line practices. To conclude, we return to considering the practice of priority-line queues and describe how managers and academics might pursue further research in this area.

Priority-line access has become common in some service industries and seems unlikely to disappear. Because some customers desire priority access and have the resources to acquire it, this approach can offer an additional source of revenue for companies. It also provides a means for customer segmentation and expansion into profitable higher-end markets. In some cases, it may even allow waiting lines to become a profit center or provide a *de facto* subsidy, allowing less-wealthy customers access to otherwise unaffordable services. The additional revenue generated from priority access could offset lower-cost alternatives, allowing service providers to better utilize expensive and/or perishable capacity. On the other hand, selling priority access could be seen by waiting customers as little more than a "money grab," putting profits before people.

All told, allowing a subset of customers to purchase their way out of the pain associated with waiting seems likely to engender feelings of injustice. In describing the problem, however, there exists hope for mitigating it; procedural, distributive, and interactional justice have all been shown to improve satisfaction when handling complaints or during service recoveries (Goodwin & Ross, 1992; Greenberg, 1993; Tax et al., 1998; Siu et al., 2013). Still, managers and researchers need to consider the context when making these decisions. Priority access may be broadly acceptable for paid services, particularly when such a "class" system has been historically established (e.g., airline seating). However, the same queue structure could introduce extreme feelings of injustice for traditionally/typically free services (e.g., True Aggie Night) or those considered a public good.

The contextual difference may stem from the connection of the service to underlying societal norms governing expectations of equality for individuals regardless of class or means. While unpaid priority access based on need or severity (e.g., emergency room priority for severe

Table 8.2   *Categorization of priority access and examples*

	Public Services	Commercial Services
Sell priority access based on ability or willingness to pay	Expedited US passport processing	Amusement park skip-the-line access
Assign priority access based on need or capacity-matching	Emergency room priority based on case severity	Restaurant seating priority based on party size

patients) fits within societal norms, permitting a patient faster emergency room priority simply because they have more means to pay for access likely does not. However, the societal norms around paying for priority access for commercial services seem to allow for different treatment based on levels of payment. Payment for priority access resembles that long-standing practice of payment for red-carpet treatment in many service contexts (e.g., first-class passengers on airlines). Table 8.2 organizes these priority-access scenarios with some examples.

The distinction between public and commercial services is not always clear-cut. For example, while airlines and air travel are clearly a commercial service, the security checkpoints in which queues develop are typically run by public entities (e.g., TSA). Customers pay for air travel, not for security checks, so while the primary service is commercial, a necessary secondary service of security screening is (largely) public. Should those who pay for priority servicing in the primary commercial service (e.g., first-class passengers) receive preferential treatment in the secondary public service? And should public services be restricted from generating revenue by selling priority access, even if the funds generated are used for the greater good? If the wealthy will pay for the privilege of not waiting, should the public welcome the additional revenue? The answers seem to be in the nature of the service and how connected it is to social equality norms. If the queue is for something that all members of the society have equal access to, then priority access is likely to be seen as more unjust.

The decisions of whether and how to incorporate a priority line are clearly complicated and, as described in this chapter, have implications for perceived justice and control. Keeping this in mind, service providers should consider questions like the following before deciding to pursue priority-line practices: Should all customers be treated equally with regards to the wait for the service? Are there exceptions that would make an individual a priority? What constitutes a "need" that might justify priority access? Will priority access lead to significant perceived or real lengthening of other customers' wait times? Will priority access require more investment in capacity, or will it shift capacity away from regular waiting customers? How is the investment in capacity justified? Would the investment be better spent to shorten the wait for all customers, or is there perhaps a business case that leads to improved service for all via the additional revenue from selling priority access? Can customers see or perceive service improvements or decrements based on priority waiting practices? Will customers feel they have control over their queueing situation? What norms, if any, might a priority line violate in this context? Can the reasons for norm violating policies be clearly communicated to customers? Does the communication process inhibit staff from performing tasks critical to the service process or expose them to customer abuse?

To aid service providers in answering such questions, a more complete understanding of the societal norms around perceived justice and control is needed. For example, examining the different forms of perceived justice (i.e., procedural, distributive, and interactional) and dimensions of control (i.e., behavioral and cognitive) for various service contexts is a rich area for future study. As shown in the True Aggie Night example, there appear to be compelling connections between *perceptions of justice and control* and *perceptions of fairness and satisfaction*. Moreover, research is needed to examine contextual factors that may affect the connections between these constructs. Such contextual factors could include important criteria, such as whether the service is pleasant (e.g., dinner at a nice restaurant) or not (e.g., a trip to the emergency department), the degree to which the service requires customer choice inputs, and whether the customer is aware of how their presence or decisions affect other customers. Research in this area would benefit from a multi-disciplinary approach, as scholarship from psychology, sociology, economics, marketing, and organizational behavior could all improve the ability to design and manage priority lines for maximum operational effectiveness.

REFERENCES

Acemoglu, D., & Jackson, M. O. (2017). Social norms and the enforcement of laws. *Journal of the European Economic Association, 15*(2), 245–295.

Alexander, M., MacLaren, A., O'Gorman, K., & White, C. (2012). Priority queues: Where social justice and equity collide. *Tourism Management, 33*(4), 875–884.

Averill, J. R. (1973). Personal control over aversive stimuli and its relationship to stress. *Psychological Bulletin, 80*(4), 286–303.

Bateson, J. E. G. (1985). Perceived control and the service encounter. In J. A. Czepiel, M. R. Solomon, and C. F. Surprenant (Eds.), *The service encounter* (pp. 67–82). New York University Institute of Retail Management.

Bies, R. J., & Moag, J. S. (1986). Interactional justice: Communication criteria of fairness. In R. J. Lewicki, B. H. Sheppard, and M. H. Bazerman (Eds.), *Research on negotiation in organizations* (pp. 43–55). JAI Press.

Blodgett, J. G., Hill, D. J., & Tax, S. S. (1997). The effects of distributive, procedural, and interactional justice on postcomplaint behavior. *Journal of Retailing, 73*(2), 185–210.

Bolkan, S., Goodboy, A. K., & Daly, J. A. (2010). Consumer satisfaction and repatronage intentions following a business failure: The importance of perceived control with an organizational complaint. *Communication Reports, 23*(1), 14–25.

Brennan, G., Eriksson, L., Goodin, R. E., & Southwood, N. (2013). *Explaining norms*. Oxford University Press.

Chase, R. B., & Dasu, S. (2014). Experience psychology – A proposed new subfield of service management. *Journal of Service Management, 25*(5), 574–577.

Dasu, S., & Chase, R. B. (2010). Designing the soft side of customer service. *MIT Sloan Management Review, 52*(1), 1–7.

Dasu, S., & Chase, R. B. (2013). *The customer service solution: Managing emotions, trust, and control to win your customer's business*. McGraw Hill Professional.

Deutsch, M. (1975). Equity, equality, and need: What determines which value will be used as the basis of distributive justice? *Journal of Social Issues, 31*(3), 137–149.

Ellickson, R. C. (1994). *Order without law*. Harvard University Press.

Fagundes, D. (2017). The social norms of waiting in line. *Law & Social Inquiry, 42*(4), 1179–1207.

Goodwin, C., & Ross, I. (1992). Consumer responses to service failures: Influence of procedural and interactional fairness perceptions. *Journal of Business Research, 25*(2), 149–163.

Greenberg, J. (1993). *The social side of fairness: Interpersonal and informational classes of organizational justice*. In R. Cropanzano (Ed.), *Series in applied psychology. Justice in the workplace: Approaching fairness in human resource management* (pp. 79–103). Lawrence Erlbaum Associates, Inc.

Hui, M. K., & Bateson, J. E. (1991). Perceived control and the effects of crowding and consumer choice on the service experience. *Journal of Consumer Research, 18*(2), 174–184.

Kingman, J. F. (1962). The effect of queue discipline on waiting time variance. *Mathematical Proceedings of the Cambridge Philosophical Society, 58*(1), 163–164.

Larson, R. C. (1987). Perspectives on queues: Social justice and the psychology of queueing. *Operations Research*, *35*(6), 895–905.

Lauridsen, S. (2020). Emergency care, triage, and fairness. *Bioethics*, *34*(5), 450–458.

Leventhal, G. S. (1980). What should be done with equity theory? New approaches to the study of fairness in social relationships. In K. J. Gergen, M. S. Greenberg, & R. H. Willis (Eds.), *Social exchange: Advances in theory and research* (pp. 27–55). Springer.

Maister, D. H. (1984). *The psychology of waiting lines*. Harvard Business School.

Malady, M. (2013, June 2). Want to save civilization? Get in line. *New York Times*. https://www.nytimes.com/2013/06/02/magazine/want-to-save-civilization-get-in-line.html

Martínez-Tur, V., Peiró, J. M., Ramos, J., & Moliner, C. (2006). Justice perceptions as predictors of customer satisfaction: The impact of distributive, procedural, and interactional justice. *Journal of Applied Social Psychology*, *36*(1), 100–119.

McColl-Kennedy, J. R., & Sparks, B. A. (2003). Application of fairness theory to service failures and service recovery. *Journal of Service Research*, *5*(3), 251–266.

McGuire, K. A., & Kimes, S. E. (2006). The perceived fairness of waitlist-management techniques for restaurants. *Cornell Hotel and Restaurant Administration Quarterly*, *47*(2), 121–134.

Milgram, S., Liberty, H. J., Toledo, R., & Wackenhut, J. (1986). Response to intrusion into waiting lines. *Journal of Personality and Social Psychology*, *51*(4), 683.

Namasivayam, K., & Hinkin, T. R. (2003). The customer's role in the service encounter: The effects of control and fairness. *Cornell Hotel and Restaurant Administration Quarterly*, *44*(3), 26–36.

Namasivayam, K., & Mount, D. J. (2006). A field investigation of the mediating effects of perceived fairness on the relationship between perceived control and consumer satisfaction. *Journal of Hospitality and Tourism Research*, *30*(4), 494–506.

Oliver, R. L., & DeSarbo, W. S. (1988). Response determinants in satisfaction judgments. *Journal of Consumer Research*, *14*(4), 495–507.

Rafaeli, A., Barron, G., & Haber, K. (2002). The effects of queue structure on attitudes. *Journal of Service Research*, *5*(2), 125–139.

Sampson, S. E., & Froehle, C. M. (2006). Foundations and Implications of a proposed unified services theory. *Production and Operations Management*, *15*(2), 329–343.

Schmitt, B. H., Dubé, L., & Leclerc, F. (1992). Intrusions into waiting lines: Does the queue constitute a social system? *Journal of Personality and Social Psychology*, *63*(5), 806–815.

Seawright, K. K., & Sampson, S. E. (2007). A video method for empirically studying wait-perception bias. *Journal of Operations Management*, *25*(5), 1055–1066.

Seiders, K., & Berry, L. L. (1998). Service fairness: What it is and why it matters. *Academy of Management Perspectives*, *12*(2), 8–20.

Siu, N. Y. M., Zhang, T. J. F., & Yau, C. Y. J. (2013). The roles of justice and customer satisfaction in customer retention: A lesson from service recovery. *Journal of Business Ethics*, *114*(4), 675–686.

Tax, S. S., Brown, S. W., & Chandrashekaran, M. (1998). Customer evaluations of service complaint experiences: Implications for relationship marketing. *Journal of Marketing*, *62*(2), 60–76.

Thompson, S. C. (1981). Will it hurt less if I can control it? A complex answer to a simple question. *Psychological Bulletin*, *90*(1), 89–101.

Van Raaij, W. F., & Pruyn, A. T. H. (1998). Customer control and evaluation of service validity and reliability. *Psychology & Marketing*, *15*(8), 811–832.

Walker, B. (2012, October 10). The rise of the priority queue. *BBC News*. https://www.bbc.com/news/magazine-19712847

Wierman, A. (2011). Fairness and scheduling in single server queues. *Surveys in Operations Research and Management Science*, *16*(1), 39–48.

Zhou, R., & Soman, D. (2003). Looking back: Exploring the psychology of queuing and the effect of the number of people behind. *Journal of Consumer Research*, *29*(4), 517–530.

9. Co-creating services at the Base of the Pyramid (BoP): the role of bricolage

Karla Cabrera and Javier Reynoso

INTRODUCTION

Co-creation has gained relevance in many business research fields, including strategy, innovation, and marketing (Nahi, 2016). In service management research, co-creation has become a central topic due to the interactive nature of service processes in which multiple actors actively participate integrating resources and capabilities to create value (Grönroos, 2012; Oertzen et al., 2018; Prahalad & Ramaswamy, 2004; Vargo & Lusch, 2008). However, the predominant service management approach mainly focuses on organizations and contexts with a relatively stable resource base. As a response to this research gap, some authors have started to conduct studies in non-traditional settings, such as the Base of the Pyramid (BoP), where different forms of resource constraints are prevalent (Cunha et al., 2014; Fuglsang & Sörensen, 2011; Linna, 2013b).

In the complex resource-constrained BoP setting, informal service micro-businesses emerge as a subsistence mechanism that relies on the co-creation of services involving three main actors: micro-business owners, employees, and customers (Reynoso & Cabrera, 2019). Informal service businesses are present in all economies. However, they are particularly relevant in BoP contexts due to extreme resource scarcity, high illiteracy levels, and under-developed formal institutions that threaten their survival (Chliova & Ringov, 2017; Reynoso & Cabrera, 2019; Webb et al., 2013). Such informal service businesses have distinctive characteristics and face diverse challenges resulting from the resource-constrained environments in four main aspects: service concept (e.g., limited offering), operations (e.g., low literacy levels), marketing and positioning (e.g., lack of investment to attract new customers), and service delivery (e.g., limited servicescape). For informal service micro-businesses, scarcity is a persistent condition they have to address to survive and grow.

Although some environments are objectively more penurious than others, different organizations may react distinctly to scarcity. Considering this scenario, the concept of bricolage, understood as the "construction ... achieved by using whatever comes to hand" (Merriam-Webster, n.d.), provides a useful framework to comprehend how businesses navigate the challenges of such complex environments. According to different authors, in management, bricolage refers to the set of behaviors to creatively combine available resources to exploit market opportunities (Baker & Nelson, 2005; Sarkar & Pansera, 2017; Senyard et al., 2014). Bricolage occurs when people explore and find value in existing resources in novel ways (Cunha et al., 2014; Senyard et al., 2014)—that is, when they identify "new potential services waiting to be extracted" (Cunha et al., 2014).

This chapter explores the distinctive challenges informal service micro-businesses face and how they find novel ways to overcome resource constraints. We argue that informal service businesses at the BoP can break through some resource constraints through bricolage, leading them to integrate resources and capabilities, thus enabling co-creation. This in turn can be seen as a way to empower BoP people and communities to overcome their structural restrictions and contribute to poverty reduction (Ansari et al., 2012; Kolk et al., 2010; Simanis & Hart, 2009).

The theoretical contribution is twofold. First, we extend co-creation research by shifting the attention from resource-rich to resource-constrained settings, identifying the relevance of bricolage in such contexts, particularly for informal service micro-businesses. Second, we explore how bricolage impacts the challenges faced by informal service micro-businesses, extending current knowledge on managerial practices of informal services at the BoP.

The chapter is structured as follows. First, we present the theoretical framework exploring management in resource-constrained environments, bricolage, and co-creation. Then, we discuss how bricolage helps informal service micro-businesses overcome those resource constraints they face and how it plays a key role as an enabler of service co-creation. Finally, the chapter concludes by discussing contributions and managerial implications, and proposes future research directions.

INFORMALITY IN RESOURCE-CONSTRAINED ENVIRONMENTS

Scarcity, the quality of something unavailable, insufficient, or not plentiful, is a central concept in social sciences affecting different facets of human life. In management, scarcity and resource constraints are commonplace (Cunha et al., 2014). There is an ongoing discussion focusing on how organizations use limited resources and creative problem solving to design innovative solutions in resource-constrained environments (Lampel et al., 2014; Radjou et al., 2012).

Resource scarcity can be considered a problem for organizations. However, studies suggest that resource abundance is not a source of competitive advantage (Cunha et al., 2014). Resource abundance or scarcity are not by themselves sources of competitive advantage or disadvantage; the way they are deployed makes the difference. In some cases, new products or services result from familiarity with resources, including those perceived as non-valuable or useless. Familiarity with resources combined with ingenuity may lead to organizational responses that will potentially satisfy some needs (Cunha et al., 2014).

Thus, scarcity can create preparedness and ingenuity for action, even in the face of resource constraints. Entrepreneurs can extract valuable services "out of nothing"—that is, from dormant resources or materials viewed as useless by the majority (Baker & Nelson, 2005). One of the major lessons from entrepreneurial initiatives is that innovation pursued under scarcity conditions requires new ways of thinking about innovation and resources. It is not only about improving the efficiency of existing models, but rather the reinvention of innovation models for penurious environments. As Cunha et al. (2014) mentioned, "mindsets and models that were developed for contexts of relative resource abundance are not necessarily adequate for contexts of scarcity" (p. 41).

In resource-constrained settings, the informal sector provides essential products and services (Chen, 2006). Most informal service businesses are small or micro-businesses, depending on the owner's ability to manage those limited resources to provide valuable solutions and address customer needs (Reynoso & Cabrera, 2019). Firms operating in the informal sector have distinctive characteristics (Darbi et al., 2018), atypical resources, and management practices (Godfrey, 2011) that help them overcome the challenges of such a complex setting. Therefore, organizational performance and survival of informal micro-businesses operating in resource-constrained environments depend on the ability to integrate and configure business resources in a unique way (Kelliher & Reinl, 2009). In this sense, we discuss the framework proposed by Heskett (1987) using those insights identified by Darbi et al. (2018) and Reynoso and Cabrera (2019) to classify the main challenges faced by informal service businesses into four main categories: service concept, operations, marketing and positioning, and service delivery. These are the basis for discussing the role of bricolage in the co-creation of services at the BoP later on.

BRICOLAGE

To successfully operate in resource-constrained environments, organizations need to deploy capabilities to combine and leverage their limited available resources to co-create ingenious solutions with their customers (Getnet et al., 2018). To understand how businesses navigate the challenges of resource constraints, the concept of bricolage has provided a useful framework in various contexts (Baker & Nelson, 2005; Desa & Basu, 2013; Senyard et al., 2014; Witell et al., 2017). The concept of bricolage was first proposed by Lévi-Strauss (1967) to explain how organizations embrace the challenges under resource-constrained environments. Some decades later, Baker and Nelson (2005) expanded Lévi-Strauss's work and defined bricolage as "making do by applying a combination of the resources at hand to new problems and opportunities" (p. 333).

Bricolage relies on a social constructionist perspective of the nature of resources under three main considerations. First, what is and is not a resource is not absolute but instead depends on the individuals' cognitions and actions who employ it as a resource. It is an informal process that requires recognizing and realizing the latent potential of some possible resources (Stinchfield et al., 2013). Second, bricolage involves substituting some conventional resource mobilization, referring to the processes by which businesses assemble the resources used to execute on an opportunity (Clough et al., 2019), with a cost-free, informal alternative that achieves the same ends. For example, instead of hiring employees to fill skills gaps, bricoleurs would learn those skills themselves (Baker & Nelson, 2005) or find volunteers to work for free. Sometimes, instead of buying new physical assets, bricoleurs repurpose artifacts ignored or discarded by others (Baker & Nelson, 2005). Third, bricolage embodies resourcefulness and adaptiveness in response to resource scarcity (Baker & Nelson, 2005; Desa, 2012). As such, it has been studied in diverse contexts, such as rural tourism (Yachin & Ioannides, 2020), social venturing (Desa, 2012), and BoP settings (Sarkar, 2018). The BoP's informal nature, disparities in social norms, institutional contexts, and educational backgrounds pose severe challenges for firms that often lack the skills and capabilities needed to create viable and valuable solutions in low-income markets (Hart et al., 2016). Thus, bricolage might represent a critical capability for informal service organizations at the BoP to create valuable solutions for their customers. Bricolage implies that entrepreneurs and firms find value in assets and resources that others can view as worthless, a behavior that can be particularly useful when operating under substantial resource constraints (Senyard et al., 2014). The direct consequence of this is a stream of low-cost, effective, and resource-efficient solutions hardly achievable under conditions of resource affluence (Sarkar & Pansera, 2017).

Bricolage has been used extensively to explore how resources are mobilized in different business settings. Some authors have studied the initiatives in the formal sector (An et al., 2018; Baker & Nelson, 2005; Salunke et al., 2013), while emerging literature has given attention to bricolage in the field of social entrepreneurship (Desa & Basu, 2013; Di Domenico et al., 2010; Langevang & Namatovu, 2019). However, little attention has been paid to bricolage processes among informal-economy businesses operating within resource-constrained environments.

To better understand how some entrepreneurs and organizations create value in resource-constrained settings and how bricolage can enhance the chances of survival of entrepreneurial firms, different frameworks have been proposed (e.g., Baker & Nelson, 2005; Cunha et al., 2014; Linna, 2013a; Sarkar, 2018; Witell et al., 2017; Yachin & Ioannides, 2020). Thus, we explore how bricolage helps informal service micro-businesses to overcome resource limitations and empower them to co-create valuable services with and for customers. For that purpose, we adopted the framework proposed by Witell et al. (2017), which considers that bricolage is built in four main behaviors: (i) actively addressing resource scarcity, (ii) making do with what is available, (iii) improvising when recombining resources, and (iv) networking with external partners.

Actively addressing resource scarcity means looking for alternatives to overcome resource limitations. Owners and employees of informal service micro-businesses are fully aware of their limitations and deal with them as an everyday condition in creative ways. This awareness implies that they know their resources well and can identify new resource uses and opportunities where others see only obstacles. For example, informal street food vendors that serve customers who lack the time and income to eat in formal establishments continually find ways to overcome the limitations of not having a fixed space. In some cases, they must make deals with established merchants to access electricity or find practical ways to carry out food preparation operations with only essential resources.

Making do with what resources are available is about applying a combination of resources at hand to new problems and opportunities (Baker & Nelson, 2005; Witell et al., 2017), creating solutions that are not perfect but good enough to help organizations to face market uncertainties and, in some cases, trigger innovations (Witell et al., 2017). Making do with what is available also implies using external resources, such as customers' skills, to enhance or complement existing resources (Witell et al., 2017). For example, due to the COVID-19 pandemic, some street vendors in Mexico saw their subsistence threatened for not having mechanisms to protect themselves and their customers from contagion. In response, they designed a structure made of PVC tubes (polyvinyl chloride) and transparent plastic to create an improvised, portable screen that helps them serve their customers while reducing physical contact. This good-enough alternative allows informal small businesses to continue their operations.

Improvising when recombining resources refers to the combination of available resources in novel ways. Improvisation can be seen as a business tactic that requires experience, intuition, and creativity to solve problems. It is strongly based on trial and error to create novel combinations of resources (Witell et al., 2017). For example, it is a common practice when demand surpasses capacity of informal service businesses that employees perform multiple tasks or family members become temporary employees.

Networking with external parties deals with getting access to external resources and coping with resource constraints. Given resource limitations, collaboration and partnering with external actors, such as other organizations or customers, might provide access to external resources (Witell et al., 2017). In this sense, collaborating with customers efficiently using the existing resources lies at the core of service co-creation. For example, those informal service businesses working in street markets usually collaborate with other informal micro-businesses to access shared resources that would not be accessible otherwise. Sometimes, they also use customer resources (e.g., skills and knowledge) to adapt the service offering to address specific demands or needs.

In sum, bricolage helps informal service micro-businesses to face the challenges of a resource-constrained environment. It allows them to better deal with scarcity and consequently improve their chances of survival. Furthermore, for informal businesses, bricolage implies, in many cases, collaboration and interaction among actors, mainly the owner, the employee, and the customer, developing basic co-creation mechanisms.

CO-CREATION OF SERVICES AT THE BOP

In this chapter, we use the term co-creation to describe the "activity, practice or process of jointly creating services in specific business contexts" (Oertzen et al., 2018, p. 642). The co-creation of services focuses on the mutual creation of services during service processes and service innovation activities. In the service context, it refers to the process in which service providers, customers, and other actors work together to create distinctive services, reduce costs, or improve service performance (Oertzen et al., 2018).

Co-creation has become an essential element of BoP strategies to create fortune with the BoP (London et al., 2010; Nahi, 2016). In research conducted by Nahi (2016), the author identified that co-creation in BoP literature also refers to interaction but differs from the traditional literature in the purpose of co-creation. She argues that "co-creation is not always necessary to bring affordable and necessary products and services to the poor, but it is crucial for BoP initiatives to address the structural drivers of poverty" (Nahi, 2016, p. 428). Many authors emphasize that people at the BoP can be active contributors to solve some infrastructural problems as they know their needs and capabilities and are experts on maneuvering in their complex operating environment (Halme et al., 2016; Simanis & Hart, 2009; Viswanathan & Sridharan, 2012).

After the publication of the seminal work by Prahalad and Hart (2002) identifying a "fortune at the Base of the Pyramid," multiple approaches have been developed to understand the complex nature and dynamics of this context. The initial approach, namely BoP 1.0, considered the poor as a passive recipient of those BoP strategies focusing on selling goods and services adapted from developed markets. After recognizing that this perspective was insufficient, BoP 2.0 emerged, stressing the importance of considering BoP people as active participants and including them in the co-creation of products, services, and business ventures (Casado Cañeque & Hart, 2015). Thus, co-creation is considered a central aspect of this second generation of BoP strategies aiming to create fortune *with* the BoP (Desa, 2012).

Actors come from varied contexts, literacy levels, and material circumstances at the BoP. Therefore, the type of resources involved in the co-creation of services are also diverse, more ordinary, and sometimes atypical (Ausrød, 2018). Like in other contexts, interaction is an essential element for co-creation; however, interaction becomes particularly relevant at the BoP because markets are frequently built through an iterative process (London et al., 2010; Nahi, 2016). Furthermore, few scholars suggest that co-creation is at the core of poverty reduction because co-creation empowers BoP people to develop their skills, agency, and voice (e.g., Ansari et al., 2012; Simanis & Hart, 2009; Yunus, 2007). In this sense, co-creation among diverse partners is a means to address many challenges that businesses face in low-income contexts (Prahalad & Hart, 2002), as in informal service businesses.

Traditionally, BoP initiatives have faced multiple challenges to succeed in this complex setting (Casado Cañeque & Hart, 2015; London & Jager, 2019). However, according to London and Jager (2019), co-creation within the BoP is key to develop novel solutions and achieve success. For informal service businesses, co-creation of services provides access to different types of valuable resources (e.g., insights, informal credits, skills, networks) to increase their opportunities to survive. In this sense, bricolage plays a critical role, as described in the following section.

THE ROLE OF BRICOLAGE IN THE CO-CREATION OF SERVICES AT THE BOP

This section illustrates how informal service businesses use bricolage to overcome the challenges that resource-constrained settings entail and how this impacts the co-creation of services (Figure 9.1). For this purpose, we consider the four main categories previously identified: service concept, marketing and positioning, operations, and service delivery. These categories help us draw an overall picture of the informal service business, showing how key business elements are most typically constituted and interrelated to co-create services among owners, employees, and customers at the BoP. The ability to integrate and configure business resources in a unique way becomes critical. Thus, the concept of bricolage is relevant to understand how informal service businesses deal with resource scarcity.

Service Concept

Starting an informal service micro-business is, in most cases, a "do-it-or-perish" decision that emerges as an alternative to provide financial support to the business's owner when facing difficulties getting formal jobs or unemployment. The business concept is concentrated in a core service with minimal additional elements, and decisions are influenced by economic, social, ethnic, and religious factors. In BoP contexts, business owners play different roles as buyers, sellers, and customers (London et al., 2010), making them aware of the market needs and dynamics; they are experts in surviving in scarce contexts. Thus, they can offer products and services aligned to the market needs. Through bricolage, owners of informal service micro-businesses integrate their customers' resources, mainly knowledge, to expand or modify their offering. This knowledge allows informal service micro-businesses to identify new opportunities, potential competitors, purchasing trends, and external threats. This permanent interaction between customers and business owners and the multiple roles played by entrepreneurs enables the co-creation of new services addressing evolving needs of BoP customers, thus improving business survival opportunities (see Table 9.1).

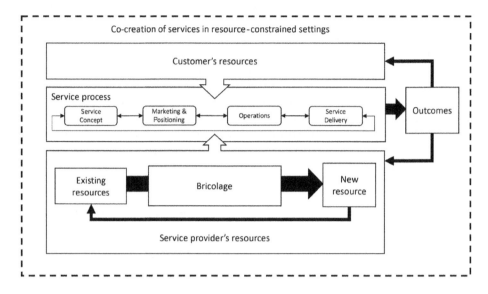

Source: Adapted from Oertzen et al. (2018).

Figure 9.1   *The role of bricolage in resource-constrained settings*

Operations

Business owners intuitively run informal service businesses as they usually do not have explicitly defined managerial processes. The decision-making process is highly centralized, and the "business culture" is strongly based on family organization. Supply is based on business owners' experience and intuition, and purchase decisions are made based on existing conditions. Financially, informal entrepreneurs have limited access to credit; thus, they rely on personal savings, family members' loans, informal credits, and microfinance. Transactions are cash based, and barter is also a mechanism sometimes used to enable exchange. There is no financial planning, so business owners reinvest the cash left after paying expenses and salaries. Frequently, employees have low literacy levels and lack formal training. Recruiting and hiring are based on personal referrals without written contracts. Operational challenges mainly involve interactions between employees and owners. However, sometimes suppliers and other institutions, such as family or the community, facilitate business-like exchanges. The interaction among these actors shapes operational and managerial practices, allowing informal micro-businesses to configure their resources to provide services.

Through bricolage, informal service businesses use different sources, such as competitors, suppliers, friends, and family, for resources to respond to operational deficiencies, uncertainty, or demand changes. Business owners and managers frequently get advice from suppliers to determine sale prices, reorder quantities, or define the store's layout. Business owners also build relationships with suppliers, creating mutual obligations that influence future actions of both parties. To overcome the lack of written contracts, business owners make oral agreements with both employees and suppliers based on trust and personal referrals. The formal

Table 9.1   *Bricolage in the co-creation of services at the BoP: service concept and operations*

Resource-constrained service business challenges		Bricolage[a] application	Impact on service co-creation outcomes
Service concept	Limited offering, focused on the core service with few additional elements	*Improvising*. Bricolage allows owners to make "as-we-go" adjustments to the service offering based on customers' suggestions and requests	Creation of new services, improvements to existing services
		Making do. Through bricolage, entrepreneurs use tacit knowledge, expertise, intuition, and embeddedness to create services aligned with BoP customer needs	Business survival
Operations	Lack of formal planning (inventories, capacity)	*Improvising*. Through bricolage, service micro-business can respond to operational deficiencies using different materials or unexpected resource sources (such as competitors)	Expansion of the business resource base Learning
	Lack of funding sources	*Making do:* By identifying less traditional funding sources (e.g., cooperatives, barter, or microfinance), entrepreneurs use bricolage to get financial support	Support for starting the business
	Lack of highly skilled labor	*Networking with external parties*. "By involving customers, suppliers, and hangers-on in providing work on projects, bricolage sometimes creates labor inputs" (Sarkar, 2018)	Creation of support networks Knowledge exchange
	Lack of formal contracts	*Making do*. Through bricolage, employees can be hired based on trust, using oral contracts and personal referrals	Creation of job opportunities Time and cost savings
	Basic or no formal training	*Improvising*. "By permitting and encouraging the use of amateur and self-taught skills that would otherwise go unapplied, bricolage creates useful services" (Sarkar, 2018)	Creation/improvement of services Creativity and ideas

Note: [a] In resource-constrained settings, scarcity is a permanent condition. Therefore, all actions taken to respond to these adverse conditions are considered to actively address resource scarcity.

training for employees is also substituted with "learn by doing" approaches and apprenticeship schemes. When work exceeds the owner's capacity, family members and close friends become part of the organization as temporary employees.

Due to the chronic resource constraints faced by the BoP, bricolage implies a "mindset of resourcefulness" (Halme et al., 2012; Linna, 2013b). Then, we argue that bricolage helps informal service micro-businesses deal with uncertainty, face changes in demand, and expand their resource base to be better prepared for co-creating services with customers. This expansion of the resource base might result in different outcomes, such as the creation and reinforcement of support networks, creation of job opportunities, and time and cost savings, to name just a few (Table 9.1).

Marketing and Positioning

Informal service micro-businesses do not have precise customer segmentation or a marketing plan to create business awareness and attract new customers. Often, buyers and sellers come from similar economic backgrounds and face similar adversities; therefore, considerable empathy characterizes marketplace dealings (Viswanathan et al., 2014). Thus, offerings are regularly customized considering both the customer and the service provider's circumstances. Also, word-of-mouth is a heavily used source of information for buyers and sellers alike. New customers are acquired by positive comments and personal selling, while business awareness is created mainly by recommendations from satisfied customers.

Economic exchange is considered an extension of everyday personal interaction. Therefore, social relationships are considered a community-owned resource that might be harnessed to add value for the community (Viswanathan et al., 2014). Due to customer-provider solid relationships, service business owners and employees can identify customer needs and, through bricolage, find distinctive ways to enhance the relationship with customers. For instance, since segmentation is instinctive and intuitive, bricolage allows business owners to quickly adapt their offerings to different customer types. Some examples are food street vendors, informal markets, or handypersons that offer their services to BoP customers and other segments. Trust-based relationships with frequent customers often derive extra benefits for customers, such as credit extension, adjustments to commercial terms, or some free services as courtesy. These practices are especially appreciated when consumers find themselves in times of need and create a form of customer lock-in that is not easily disregarded. Therefore, customers see advantages in buying from their usual service provider, even if prices are higher, because it builds goodwill with an individual who can offer them credit during the next crisis (Viswanathan et al., 2014). Then, bricolage allows informal service micro-businesses to use trust-based solid relationships and word-of-mouth as resources to foster customer engagement in the co-creation of services. This way, informal service micro-businesses might create a relatively stable customer base and increase customer loyalty and access to new markets (Table 9.2).

Service Delivery

Informal service businesses give limited attention to servicescape, layout, and tangible elements. The service is commonly located at the owner's premises, in a place nearby, or in street markets. Due to the lack of planning, unexpected demand variations are faced. The workforce is limited, so employees are multitasking, performing several activities as needed, and customers usually participate in the service delivery process, either by request or voluntarily. During the interaction, bargaining is a common practice in which price, quality, and exchange conditions are set in a discretionary way, considering the customer's circumstances. Over time, customers and service providers develop strong personal bonds that bring additional benefits, such as informal credits or ad hoc guarantees for the customer.

As previously described, in resource-constrained environments, individuals rely on others in times of need to find affordable solutions to everyday needs. Through bricolage, both employees and owners of micro-businesses find novel ways to use their available resources to solve the problems occurring in the service encounter. During service delivery, scarcity could lead to a series of setbacks, such as excessive delays due to lack of personnel or variations in delivering service quality. Thus, frequently, employees have to perform roles originally not planned, or redesign their activities to accommodate extraordinary customer requests. It is also common that external actors, commonly relatives or volunteers, are asked to perform some activities as a form of "temporary employees." Sometimes, business owners ask some competitors to "borrow" the necessary resources to meet customers' demands or, in exceptional cases, even

Table 9.2   *Bricolage in the co-creation of services at the BoP: marketing/positioning and service delivery*

Resource-constrained service business challenges		Bricolage[a] application	Impact on service co-creation outcomes
Marketing/ positioning	Lack of formal mechanisms to target new segments	*Improvising.* Bricolage allows service businesses to attend to different customer profiles inside and out of the BoP to satisfy their specific needs	Access to new segments
	Lack of positioning mechanisms	*Making do.* Through bricolage, BoP service micro-businesses build on their positioning on the strong customer-provider ties based on empathy and trust	Customer loyalty
Service delivery	Unexpected petitions	*Networking with external parties.* Through bricolage, service providers might ask for resources from some other nearby micro-businesses or even with competitors. "Co-opetition" happens	Service quality Customer satisfaction Service performance
		Improvising. Through bricolage, employees perform roles that were originally not planned, or redesign activities to accommodate extraordinary customer requests	
		Making do. Bricolage allows informal service businesses to ask external actors, commonly relatives or friends, to perform some activities as "temporary employees"	

Note: [a] In resource-constrained settings, scarcity is a permanent condition. Therefore, all actions taken to respond to these adverse conditions are considered to actively address resource scarcity.

direct customers to some competitor to solve a customer need. Even though this might sound counterintuitive, this phenomenon occurs because solving a customer need is prioritized over gaining economic benefits. During service delivery, the role of bricolage in the co-creation of services is more evident because of the higher levels of customization and the number of exceptions needed in this setting (see Table 9.2). The permanence of micro-businesses has a high impact on the subsistence of its owners and employees; thus, there is a high orientation to find multiple ways to meet customer requests to increase the chances of business survival.

In sum, bricolage allows informal service businesses to better cope with those challenges the resource-constrained setting entails. Through interactions between business owners, employees and customers, bricolage helps these businesses expand their resource base, impacting co-creation outcomes.

We argue that informal service micro-businesses integrate resources in novel ways to address business and customer needs by actively addressing resource scarcity, making do with what is available, improvising when recombining resources, and networking with external parties. This way, they co-create affordable solutions to everyday problems. In Tables 9.1 and 9.2, we illustrate how bricolage impacts the co-creation of services in different ways.

Bricolage may have multiple impacts on the co-creation of services in resource-constrained environments; we highlight four main aspects in this chapter. First, by recognizing atypical sources and finding novel resource recombination alternatives, bricolage enables informal service micro-businesses to expand the available resource base to engage in the co-creation of services. It also helps to respond to the higher levels of customization and exceptions required in this setting. Second, given the relevance of trust-based social relationships in resource-constrained settings and the key role of institutions such as family, bricolage allows informal service micro-businesses to integrate multiple actors in support networks, co-creating value for all: the business, the customer, and the community. Third, informal service micro-businesses consider resource scarcity as a fact that has to be actively addressed. Therefore, they are continuously strengthening their ability to make do with what is available, improvise the reconfiguration of resources, and network with external partners. These behaviors lead to the co-creation of new services that solve customer needs and improve business opportunities to survive and grow. Finally, bricolage allows informal service micro-businesses to recognize the benefits of the co-creating services to integrate financial and non-financial outcomes. In this sense, these non-financial outcomes, such as increased customer satisfaction, improved service performance and quality, new job opportunities, and the development of new service solutions, are essential for business survival. Most importantly, they are fundamental for community development, empowerment, and thus, poverty reduction.

MANAGERIAL IMPLICATIONS

The role of bricolage in the co-creation of services in resource-constrained settings has diverse managerial implications. First, bricolage in resource-constrained settings is a matter of developing a mindset of resourcefulness. Entrepreneurs operating businesses at the BoP face scarcity as a permanent condition; thus, they must be familiar with the available resources and employ them effectively to face all the challenges threatening their business survival. It also implies creating supporting networks and collaborating with them in difficult times. Within these networks, entrepreneurs must identify the potential resources that other actors (family, customers, suppliers, competitors) might provide to the co-creation of services.

Second, managers outside the BoP must recognize the existence and relevance of atypical resources, including relationships, traditions, and capabilities, within the business dynamics at the BoP. To improve their chances of success, they must make strategic decisions about the alternatives to access these resources and integrate them into their offering. Alternatives such as creating alliances with key actors who are familiar with these atypical resources might be considered. Additionally, managers should be aware that bricolage influences service innovation but differs from traditional innovation approaches (Witell et al., 2017). It means that integrating atypical resources into a traditional innovations process might create some setbacks. The BoP requires high levels of flexibility, exceptions, and customizations that might be challenging for companies. Therefore, managers must evaluate their existing bricolage capabilities to identify potential shortcomings and learn how to integrate their available resources to address the BoP's unmet needs.

Third, in resource-constrained settings, relationships are the basis of the economic exchange. Thus, relationships are considered more important than transactions; therefore, empathy, trust and fairness become relevant business attributes. For practitioners, this entails investing in building and strengthening trustworthy relationships with customers, providers, and other actors, even competitors. Sometimes, it also implies putting immediate customer well-being ahead of business benefits to privilege the long-term relationship. However, practitioners must be aware that this high reliance on relationships might be a double-edged sword; it can bring multiple beneficial outcomes but also hold the potential for abuse and exploitation.

FUTURE RESEARCH

The study of bricolage in the co-creation of services at the BoP opens a wide range of future research perspectives. First, we explore bricolage as an enabler of co-creation of services in resource-constrained settings. Further research should explore the dynamics of co-creating services at the BoP. In this sense, some research questions might be identified. For example, what are the drivers that stimulate different actors at the BoP to participate in the co-creation of services? What are the possible counterproductive outcomes of co-creation in this context? What possible adverse effects could bricolage have?

Second, we argue that bricolage fosters the integration of multiple actors within the BoP to co-create value. More research is required to explore the implications of bricolage in resource integration from a systemic perspective involving multiple actors from different contexts, sectors, and sizes. In this regard, some research questions are worth exploring. For example, what role does bricolage play in cross-sectorial partnerships aiming to co-create sustainable solutions to customers' unmet needs? How are resources mobilized and integrated among formal and informal organizations? Here, research on collaboration and competition could provide valuable insights into the social, economic, and managerial implications of integrating multiple actors into service ecosystems.

Third, we argue that bricolage capabilities leading to the co-creation of services improve opportunities for informal micro-businesses to survive and grow. Different research opportunities are relevant here. For example, how does bricolage influence the resilience of informal service micro-businesses? How do bricolage capabilities change when informal micro-businesses become formal or scale-up?

Finally, effective resource utilization and sustainable innovation is a growing concern. Thus, what can we learn from small groups, families, villages, micro-companies, networks, and cooperatives about how their services are designed, operated, and managed within resource-constrained settings? How should the notion of resource availability be reimagined to foster more sustainable business practices?

CONCLUSION

In resource-constrained settings, such as the BoP, informal service businesses emerge to respond to a survival need. However, despite resource limitations, these subsistence businesses actively address scarcity to find ways to solve the challenges they face on a daily basis. Although they may not have sophisticated operational or financial support, they have a high customer orientation and a strong sense to go beyond their limitations to focus on what they have at hand. This approach lets them see opportunities where others do not and work hard to overcome any obstacle they face to survive and grow. Through bricolage, informal service businesses can break through some resource constraints, recognize the potential of some previously ignored resources, integrate resources and capabilities, and enable service co-creation among business owners, employees, and customers. Running an informal service business at the BoP is a highly collaborative process that relies on creating solid relationships among actors and support from a cohesive social network that includes family and close friends. Through bricolage, the co-creation of services at the BoP is enabled and helps businesses to overcome structural constraints that threaten their survival.

REFERENCES

An, W., Zhao, X., Cao, Z., Zhang, J., & Liu, H. (2018). How bricolage drives corporate entrepreneurship: The roles of opportunity identification and learning orientation. *Journal of Product Innovation Management, 35*(1), 49–65. https://doi.org/10.1111/jpim.12377

Ansari, S., Munir, K., & Gregg, T. (2012). Impact at the "Bottom of the Pyramid": The role of social capital in capability development and community empowerment. *Journal of Management Studies, 49*(4), 813–842. https://doi.org/10.1111/j.1467-6486.2012.01042.x

Ausrød, V. L. (2018). It takes two to tango: Mobilizing strategic, ordinary, and weak resources at the Base of the Pyramid. *Journal of Strategic Marketing, 26*(8), 665–687. https://doi.org/10.1080/0965254X.2017.1344290

Baker, T., & Nelson, R. E. (2005). Creating something from nothing: Resource construction through entrepreneurial bricolage. *Administrative Science Quarterly, 50*(3), 329–366. https://doi.org/10.2189/asqu.2005.50.3.329

Casado Cañeque, F., & Hart, S. L. (2015). *Base of the Pyramid 3.0: Sustainable development through innovation and entrepreneurship* (1st ed.). Greenleaf Publishing Limited.

Chen, M. A. (2006). Rethinking the informal economy: Linkages with the formal economy and the formal regulatory environment. In B. Guha-Khansnobis, R. Kanbur, & E. Ostrom (Eds.), *Linking the formal and the informal economy* (pp. 93–120). Oxford University Press.

Chliova, M., & Ringov, D. (2017). Scaling impact: Template development and replication at the Base of the Pyramid. *Academy of Management Perspectives, 31*(1), 44–62.

Clough, D. R., Fang, T. P., Bala Vissa, B., & Wu, A. (2019). Turning lead into gold: How do entrepreneurs mobilize resources to exploit opportunities? *Academy of Management Annals, 13*(1), 240–271. https://doi.org/10.5465/annals.2016.0132

Cunha, M. P. e, Rego, A., Clegg, S., Neves, P., & Oliveira, P. (2014). Unpacking the concept of organizational ingenuity: Learning from scarcity. In B. Honig, J. Lampel, & I. Drori (Eds.), *Handbook of organizational and entrepreneurial ingenuity* (pp. 34–56). Edward Elgar Publishing. https://doi.org/10.4337/9781782549048.00009

Darbi, W. P. K., Hall, C. M., & Knott, P. (2018). The informal sector: A review and agenda for management research. *International Journal of Management Reviews, 20*(2), 301–324. https://doi.org/10.1111/ijmr.12131

Desa, G. (2012). Resource mobilization in international social entrepreneurship: Bricolage as a mechanism of institutional transformation. *Entrepreneurship: Theory and Practice, 36*(4), 727–751. https://doi.org/10.1111/j.1540-6520.2010.00430.x

Desa, G., & Basu, S. (2013). Optimization or bricolage? Overcoming resource constraints in global social entrepreneurship. *Strategic Entrepreneurship Journal, 7*(1), 26–49. https://doi.org/10.1002/sej

Di Domenico, M. L., Haugh, H., & Tracey, P. (2010). Social bricolage: Theorizing social value creation in social enterprises. *Entrepreneurship: Theory and Practice, 34*(4), 681–703. https://doi.org/10.1111/j.1540-6520.2010.00370.x

Fuglsang, L., & Sörensen, F. (2011). The balance between bricolage and innovation: Management dilemmas in sustainable public innovation. *Service Industries Journal, 31*(4), 581–595. https://doi.org/10.1080/02642069.2010.504302

Getnet, H., O'Cass, A., Ahmadi, H., & Siahtiri, V. (2018). Supporting product innovativeness and customer value at the bottom of the pyramid through context-specific capabilities and social ties. *Industrial Marketing Management, 83*, 70–80. https://doi.org/10.1016/j.indmarman.2018.11.002

Godfrey, P. C. (2011). Toward a theory of the informal economy. *Academy of Management Annals, 5*(1), 231–277. https://doi.org/10.1080/19416520.2011.585818

Grönroos, C. (2012). Conceptualising value co-creation: A journey to the 1970s and back to the future. *Journal of Marketing Management, 28*(December), 1520–1534.

Halme, M., Kourula, A., Lindeman, S., Kallio, G., Lima-Toivanen, M., & Korsunova, A. (2016). Sustainability innovation at the Base of the Pyramid through multi-sited rapid ethnography. *Corporate Social Responsibility and Environmental Management, 23*(2), 113–128. https://doi.org/10.1002/csr.1385

Halme, M., Lindeman, S., & Linna, P. (2012). Innovation for inclusive business: Intrapreneurial brico-lage in multinational corporations. *Journal of Management Studies*, *49*(4), 743–784. https://doi.org/10.1111/j.1467-6486.2012.01045.x

Hart, S., Sharma, S., & Halme, M. (2016). Poverty, business strategy, and sustainable development. *Organization and Environment*, *29*(4), 401–415. https://doi.org/10.1177/1086026616677170

Heskett, J. (1987). Lessons in the service sector. *Harvard Business Review*, *65*(2), 118–126.

Kelliher, F., & Reinl, L. (2009). A resource-based view of micro-firm management practice. *Journal of Small Business and Enterprise Development*, *16*(3), 521–532. https://doi.org/10.1108/14626000910977206

Kolk, A., van Dolen, W., & Vock, M. (2010). Trickle effects of cross-sector social partnerships. *Journal of Business Ethics*, *94*(Suppl. 1), 123–137. https://doi.org/10.1007/s10551-011-0783-3

Lampel, J., Honig, B., & Drori, I. (2014). Organizational ingenuity: Concept, processes and strategies. *Organization Studies*, *35*(4), 465–482. https://doi.org/10.1177/0170840614525321

Langevang, T., & Namatovu, R. (2019). Social bricolage in the aftermath of war. *Entrepreneurship and Regional Development*, *31*(9–10), 785–805. https://doi.org/10.1080/08985626.2019.1595743

Lévi-Strauss, C. (1967). *The savage mind*. University of Chicago Press.

Linna, P. (2013a). Base of the Pyramid (BOP) as a source of innovation: Experiences of companies in the Kenyan mobile sector. *International Journal of Technology Management & Sustainable Development*, *11*(2), 113–137. https://doi.org/10.1386/tmsd.11.2.113_1

Linna, P. (2013b). Bricolage as a means of innovating in a resource-scarce environment: A study of innovator-entrepreneurs at the BoP. *Journal of Developmental Entrepreneurship*, *18*(3), 1350015. https://doi.org/10.1142/S1084946713500155

London, T., Anupindi, R., & Sheth, S. (2010). Creating mutual value: Lessons learned from ventures serving Base of the Pyramid producers. *Journal of Business Research*, *63*(6), 582–594. https://doi.org/10.1016/j.jbusres.2009.04.025

London, T., & Jager, U. (2019). Cocreating with the Base of the Pyramid. *Stanford Social Innovation Review*, Summer, 40–47. http://doi.org/10.48558/f00w-ed89

Merriam-Webster (n.d.). Bricolage. In *Merriam-Webster.com Dictionary*. https://www.merriam-webster.com/dictionary/bricolage

Nahi, T. (2016). Co-creation at the Base of the Pyramid: Reviewing and organizing the diverse conceptual-izations. *Organization and Environment*, *29*(4), 416–437. https://doi.org/10.1177/1086026616652666

Oertzen, A. S., Odekerken-Schröder, G., Brax, S. A., & Mager, B. (2018). Co-creating services—Conceptual clarification, forms and outcomes. *Journal of Service Management*, *29*(4), 641–679. https://doi.org/10.1108/JOSM-03-2017-0067

Prahalad, C. K., & Hart, S. L. (2002). Fortune at the Bottom of the Pyramid. *Strategy + Business*, *26*, 54–67.

Prahalad, C. K., & Ramaswamy, V. (2004). Co-creation experiences: The next practice in value creation. *Journal of Interactive Marketing*, *18*(3), 5–14. https://doi.org/10.1002/dir.20015

Radjou, N., Prabhu, J., & Ahuja, S. (2012). *Jugaad innovation: Think frugal, be flexible, generate break-through growth* (1st ed.). Jossey-Bass, Wiley.

Reynoso, J., & Cabrera, K. (2019). Managing informal service organizations at the base of the Pyramid (BoP). *Journal of Services Marketing*, *33*(1), 112–124. https://doi.org/10.1108/JSM-10-2018-0298

Salunke, S., Weerawardena, J., & McColl-Kennedy, J. R. (2013). Competing through service innovation: The role of bricolage and entrepreneurship in project-oriented firms. *Journal of Business Research*, *66*(8), 1085–1097. https://doi.org/10.1016/j.jbusres.2012.03.005

Sarkar, S. (2018). Grassroots entrepreneurs and social change at the bottom of the pyramid: The role of bricolage. *Entrepreneurship and Regional Development*, *30*(3–4), 421–449. https://doi.org/10.1080/08985626.2017.1413773

Sarkar, S., & Pansera, M. (2017). Sustainability-driven innovation at the bottom: Insights from grass-roots ecopreneurs. *Technological Forecasting and Social Change*, *114*, 327–338. https://doi.org/10.1016/j.techfore.2016.08.029

Senyard, J., Baker, T., Steffens, P., & Davidsson, P. (2014). Bricolage as a path to innovativeness for resource-constrained new firms. *Journal of Product Innovation Management*, *31*(2), 211–230. https://doi.org/10.1111/jpim.12091

Simanis, E., & Hart, S. (2009). Innovation from the inside out. *MIT Sloan Management Review, 50*(4), 77–86.

Stinchfield, B. T., Nelson, R. E., & Wood, M. S. (2013). Learning from Lévi-Strauss' legacy: Art, craft, engineering, bricolage, and brokerage in entrepreneurship. *Entrepreneurship: Theory and Practice, 37*(4), 889–921. https://doi.org/10.1111/j.1540-6520.2012.00523.x

Vargo, S. L., & Lusch, R. F. (2008). Service-dominant logic: Continuing the evolution. *Journal of the Academy of Marketing Science, 36*(1), 1–10. https://doi.org/10.1007/s11747-007-0069-6

Viswanathan, M., Echambadi, R., Venugopal, S., & Sridharan, S. (2014). Subsistence entrepreneurship, value creation, and community exchange systems: A social capital explanation. *Journal of Macromarketing, 34*(2), 213–226. https://doi.org/10.1177/0276146714521635

Viswanathan, M., & Sridharan, S. (2012). Product development for the BoP: Insights on concept and prototype development from university-based student projects in India. *Journal of Product Innovation Management, 29*(1), 52–69. https://doi.org/10.1111/j.1540-5885.2011.00878.x

Webb, J. W., Bruton, G. D., Tihanyi, L., & Ireland, R. D. (2013). Research on entrepreneurship in the informal economy: Framing a research agenda. *Journal of Business Venturing, 28*(5), 598–614. https://doi.org/10.1016/j.jbusvent.2012.05.003

Witell, L., Gebauer, H., Jaakkola, E., Hammedi, W., Patricio, L., & Perks, H. (2017). A bricolage perspective on service innovation. *Journal of Business Research, 79*, 290–298. https://doi.org/10.1016/j.jbusres.2017.03.021

Yachin, J. M., & Ioannides, D. (2020). "Making do" in rural tourism: The resourcing behaviour of tourism micro-firms. *Journal of Sustainable Tourism, 28*(7), 1003–1021. https://doi.org/10.1080/09669582.2020.1715993

Yunus, M. (2007). *Creating a world without poverty: Social business and the future of capitalism*. Public Affairs.

10. Failsafing service quality

Richard B. Chase and Douglas M. Stewart

SERVICE QUALITY CONTROL IS DIFFERENT

Service quality matters. It has a demonstrated impact on customer satisfaction, repeat purchase intentions, market share, and value. A significant portion of service quality is created by consistent delivery of the service in accordance with the service design, while the remaining portion is associated with the alignment of the service design with the needs and values of the customer.

There is an established body of theory and practice associated with quality control systems that originated in manufacturing practices and was subsequently extended to other business areas. The underlying paradigm and most of the associated quality control tools are based on the measurement, control, and reduction of Gaussian variation, which assumes distributions that are typically normal, binomial or Poisson, and stable over time.

Such variation-based methods are of limited use in services. They are effective when appropriate, but most of the time they are not. First, there are just not that many key variables being measured in most services; predominantly we are restricted to various measures of time and satisfaction. Time measures are problematic because queue durations do not follow any common Gaussian distribution even for simple queues; more importantly, they are not statistically stable since the process means move continuously throughout the day as demand and resources shift. Satisfaction measures are additionally problematic as they are not process control variables, but rather measures of system results. Shifts in satisfaction may indicate the existence of a problem, but provide little insight into controlling the process.

Most importantly, however, is that human error is one of the most frequent causes of service delivery failures, and variation-based quality control methods do not work well for human error (Stewart and Grout, 2001). Human errors differ in significant ways from the assumptions underlying the variation-based paradigm. First, human errors are discrete events not continuous variables. Although we do have some variation-based tools that deal with discrete failures, for instance p-charts, we don't know anything about the shape of the underlying distribution of human error frequency, which is based on psychological not physical processes. Moreover, we cannot easily identify the cause of a particular human error, as most common errors are due to failures in largely unconscious processes. Therefore, people are usually not aware of why an error was made. This means we cannot easily use an out-of-control signal to direct corrective actions. Finally, it is highly unlikely that the distribution of human errors is stable, as the base rate of error changes throughout the day due to factors such as fatigue, cognitive load, speed, and volume of work, along with undoubtedly many other unknown causes. Therefore, we can't even calculate reasonable control limits on human error.

There are fortunately more appropriate methods to control and decrease the likelihood and impact of human error, first among which is failsafing. Failsafing goes by many names, such as poka-yoke, mistake-proofing, and error-proofing, but we prefer failsafing. It is derived from a psychology-based paradigm, and when controlling service quality, failsafing is the best place to start. It is a direct, first-order solution to control the impact of human error on the customer experience. It is easy to understand and easy to apply; no secret initiation into the mysteries of Gaussian mathematics is required. It is fast to implement and widely applicable in most routine services that have consistent processes that are repeated for each customer.

MAJOR STEPS IN FAILSAFING A SERVICE

There are three major steps to failsafing your service. First, we need to identify the important errors that are being made. This can be errors that occur frequently, those that have a large negative impact, or both. Next, we need to locate potential control points where the error can be best detected and corrected. Then, we must create a failsafe device or procedure at the control point that prevents the adverse effect of the error from impacting the customer or disrupting the system.

It can be helpful to think of failsafing as a type of Hazard Analysis Critical Control Point (HACCP) quality control system. We begin with a hazard analysis, and then work through the process to identify the critical control points, putting in place controls at those points. If you have a service that has already widely implemented failsafing, new failsafes can be effectively added in an ad hoc fashion as new errors are encountered. A service new to failsafing will benefit from a more structured approach.

Begin by identifying the important errors that need to be controlled. This is the hazard analysis. We need to answer two related questions: (1) what potential errors could be made? and (2) how frequent or severe are they likely to be? The challenge, especially for a service new to failsafing, is that it can be overwhelming to simultaneously consider all of the potential errors that could be made. We can break the problem down into more manageable pieces using a tree structure.

Tree structures prevent getting lost in the forest. It is common in quality control and business problem solving to break a larger problem down into more manageable parts using some form of logical tree structure. Familiar tree structures include decision trees, process decision program charts, and the DuPont model from finance. When breaking the problem down, each branch should be distinct, with nothing assigned to more than one branch (mutually exclusive), and all aspects of the problem should be represented across the branches (collectively exhaustive). If the individual branches are still unwieldy, then each branch can be divided into twigs, and so on, until the individual endpoints are manageable.

3T/PER FAMEWORK FOR ANALYZING AND SOLVING SERVICE PROBLEMS

The 3T/PER framework is a good starting point for breaking down the service failsafing problem (Chase and Stewart, 1993, 1994). The 3Ts are the Task to be done, the Treatment accorded the customer, and the Tangibles – the physical and sensory elements of the service environment – and represent the broad types of errors that the service provider can make. PER (Preparation, Encounter, and Resolution) represents the types of errors the customer can make in failing to prepare for the service properly, failing to properly perform their role during the service encounter, and failing to perform appropriate resolution activities after the service concludes. This gives us an initial problem tree structure, as seen in Figure 10.1. This level of detail should be sufficient for most services. However, additional branching could be done if, for instance, the total scope of potential task errors remained overwhelming.

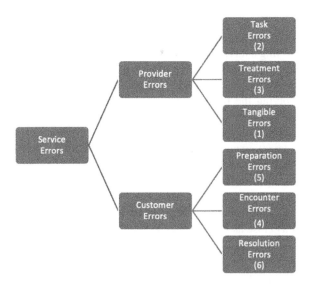

Figure 10.1   *Tree of service errors (prioritized)*

The benefit of creating a tree structure is that we can prioritize the most fruitful branches first. Unless we have strong reason to conclude that certain categories effectively dominate the error problems in our service, we prefer starting with the low-hanging fruit before climbing up to more challenging branches. Working on easier types of errors will allow us to build confidence and knowledge in developing failsafe devices and procedures before progressing on to more challenging ones.

Begin with the service provider branches, as these are under more direct control than those of the customer. The ease of addressing each of the 3Ts is based on the duration of each in the context of an active service (Stewart, 2003). Tangibles are enduring, existing prior to the service encounter and after it has ended, providing significant time and opportunity to control the error. The task is finite and time dependent, transpiring along the duration of the encounter. Control of the error must be established in a finite and often short time period. The treatment is transient, happening as fleeting psycho-social interactions between the provider and customer. Control of these errors must be nearly instantaneous or preemptive. Work first on the tangible errors, then the task errors, and lastly on the treatment errors.

Once we have a handle on failsafing the provider, we should move on to the customer errors. Since we will be attempting to modify the behavior of the customer, prioritization is based on the level of control and incentive that can be exerted. Begin with encounter errors, as the customer is present during the encounter and can be most easily controlled or influenced. Next, focus on the preparation errors. Although the customer is not present during the preparation, they have a shared interest in the upcoming service encounter progressing flawlessly. This creates an innate motivation to comply with preparation failsafing. The resolution errors will be most problematic because the customer is not only absent, but they will often lack the innate motivation to engage in resolution activities at all. This creates the additional burden of creating some form of extrinsic motivation to engage in the resolution process as well.

We should use data to identify the most problematic errors within the branch we are working on. Data can be known errors, but could also include near misses or even self-reports of most common errors. Don't, however, overlook the severity of the consequences of the error when collecting data. Controlling a rarer major error may be more important than controlling several more common trivial ones. Consider scaling the errors in much the same manner as one would in Failure Mode Effects Analysis (FMEA) with a scale of one to ten on both severity and frequency, and multiplying the resulting scores together. Prioritize errors with the highest combined score. (FMEA also scales detection, but that is less useful for our purposes as the whole point of failsafing is to make detection automatic.) As we work each branch, push forward through implementing controls on the errors within that branch rather than attempting to fully elaborate all of the errors the service is prone to.

Once an error has been identified as an important hazard to our service, we next need to determine the best control point for that particular error. Failsafing works by detecting and correcting errors. The control point is where we will detect the error. In general, we would like the control point as close as possible to the error. The error must be detected prior to the "point of no return." The further the control point is from the generation of the error, the less likely the error can be corrected, even if it has been successfully detected. The approach to identifying good control points will differ depending on the type of error we are working on.

Tangibles have an enduring nature, therefore much of our focus will be on ensuring that they are in good order prior to the next encounter. Typically this will be addressed during the time between encounters. Because of this, control points are typically the departure of the previous customer, or as a pre-condition of admitting a subsequent customer. This later form of control point can be seen with bussing tables, readying exam rooms, or with washroom attendants.

Services with a more sustained customer presence and services where the tangibles degrade during the encounter are a bit more challenging. Control points can be located at natural breaks in the process or at predictable low points in customer presence. For instance, in dining, the time between courses creates a natural break in the process, or in a train station, customer presence changes with the arrivals and departures of the trains. In the absence of such breaks or low points, we must monitor the tangibles directly to initiate a response when some threshold of degradation or time has passed.

The task unfolds over time, so to locate a control point we must use process analysis to trace the observed effect of the error back to its source. Our control point will be at the closest feasible point to the actual error. It is important to identify the source, even if we subsequently choose a later point in the process for control. The source bounds our analysis, marking one endpoint with the awareness of the customer of the error being the other endpoint. Our search for feasible control points must only then consider that portion of the process. The source also represents the ideal control point. Shingo's Zero Quality Control approach centers on catching an error at the source before it creates a defect that then must be fixed (Shingo, 1986, p. 50).

Treatment, with its fleeting, nearly instantaneous nature, poses particular challenges in identifying control points. Control must be established when and where the error occurs. Acknowledging the presence of the customer 5 minutes after they enter or otherwise signal a need for some assistance is very different from acknowledging them immediately, even if the actual assistance is delayed. The difficulty comes from the fact that in many cases there is little consistency when and where treatment exchanges occur. Moreover, because the interpretation of treatment is only partially consciously made, there may be insufficient purchase to attach a failsafe to the error, even if the control point can be identified. We should prioritize our efforts on those treatment errors that are amenable to failsafing because of consistent timing and location of the error, and because they are more behavioral than perceptual.

Identifying control points for customer encounter errors is very similar to identifying task errors. The customer's actions during the encounter are bounded and directed by the process, so we can again use process analysis to trace back to the source of the customer's error from the point where its effect is observed. The slight twist with customer encounter errors is that we need to then ask why the customer made that error. Was it truly a mistake on their part? If so, that will be the proper source of the error, and the first location for a potential control point. If not, we should look further for the actual source of the error. This could have been an earlier provider error, such as being given incorrect or incomplete instructions. Alternately, a different error by another customer could be the cause, as customers often take their cues from the actions of other customers, especially when they lack sufficient familiarity with the service process. The search for the best control point should then begin at this earlier source.

With customer preparation errors, is it not as much an issue of locating the control point as creating one. Because the customer "process" during preparation is inherently external to the service, we must create some external control point. Any natural contact with the customer that occurs a reasonable amount of time prior to the encounter provides an opportunity to create a control point – for instance, calls for appointments or reservations. In the absence of a natural contact point, a control point can be created by initiating contact with the customer for that purpose. For example, reminder cards or confirmation phone calls can be generated, not so much for reminding or confirming their future presence, but to ensure that they bring necessary materials and perform necessary pre-service activities. The last opportunity for a control point would be during the pre-process waiting, such as reminding people in the security line to have their boarding passes and IDs ready.

Customer resolution errors, like preparation errors, share the difficulty of being largely external to the service. The first and most obvious place to introduce a control point is as part of the final-process step of the encounter, for instance, providing a comment card at the time of settling the bill for services. There may also be some opportunity to create a control point after the service but while the customer is still present in your facility, such as the use of highly visible shopping cart return corrals. Finally, as with most customer preparation errors, you may need to create a control point by initiating some follow-up contact with the customer.

Once a potential control point has been identified, it is time to create a failsafe device or procedure to establish control at that point. When creating such failsafes, it helps to understand how they actually work. As humans, we detect errors by monitoring our actions and the environment for deviations from what we expect (Sellen, 1994). The self-monitoring of action is largely internal and thus cannot be directly influenced, but the cues from environmental deviations can be manipulated. Failsafing seeks to amplify or create environmental cues that provide clear and obvious signals when an error has been made (Stewart and Grout, 2001). To create a failsafe we need to identify something in the environment that is different when an error has been made, which we can then highlight to make the error obvious. In essence, we need a hook for our failsafe.

The taxonomy of (1) Physical Detection and Control; (2) Sequencing; (3) Grouping and Counting; and (4) Information Enhancement is a taxonomy of common hooks upon which to hang service failsafe devices and procedures (Chase and Stewart, 1995, p. 32). We refer to this taxonomy using the mnemonic aid PSGI. Physical detection and control failsafes rely on the elaboration or creation of physical cues in the environment, such as shape, orientation, or presence of an object or person. An example of a failsafe that relies on physical detection and control is the blind-spot sensors on newer cars that provide both audio and visual alerts if another vehicle is in our blind spot when the turn signal is activated. Sequencing failsafes highlight cues from the deviation, repetition, or omission of steps from the expected sequence. An example of a failsafe relying on sequencing is the ATM that will not dispense our money until we perform the often-missed step of retrieving our card. Grouping and counting failsafes amplify cues based on insufficient or excess items in sets or groups. A commonly encountered failsafe based on grouping and counting is having our daily medication doses pre-packaged in blister packs for each day. Information enhancement failsafes rely on cues from the unavailability of information necessary to make choices or take action. A basic example of a failsafe relying on information enhancement is the light that is visible from our seat on the plane that indicates the lavatories are occupied. A more advanced example is the geofencing ability of online ordering apps that can cue the restaurant to begin our order when we are 10 minutes away.

We can use the PSGI framework to evaluate potential control points. We ask the following questions about the control point we are currently evaluating. If this error has been made:

- Will something or someone be out of place, improperly oriented, too big or small, on or off, open or closed, missing or present?
- Has a step been omitted, repeated, or done out of order?
- Are there missing components or the wrong number of pieces or people?
- Was necessary information unavailable because it was elsewhere, had not been stored, had not been processed, or was lost in the background clutter?

Any affirmative answer identifies a potential hook for a failsafe device or procedure to control the error at this point. If we cannot identify a decent hook at our best control point, we move on to the next most promising control point until we can identify a hook that might work. Don't move too fast! It is better to be at or as close to the source as possible, so don't give up too easily on a particular control point simply because the hook is not obvious.

Once we have found a hook, we consider how it can be made so obvious that it would be hard to overlook. Making an obvious cue can be as simple as making the hook visually or physically more prominent, with a contrasting color, focused lighting, or inconsistent size or shape. Often, however, it involves detecting the actual hook with some form of mechanical system or sensor that is used to generate a more noticeable cue of a different form. There are two broad approaches to this. The first is to amplify the cue so that it stands out clearly against the background sensory input (i.e., contrasting colors or lighting, warning lights and sounds, or obviously empty spaces). The second is to turn the cue into an impediment to further action until the error has been resolved (i.e., blocked pathways, doors locked until power is off, or already full spaces). These correspond to Shingo's (1986) warning and control devices, and Sellen's (1994) outcome-based and limiting functions for error detection.

When amplifying a cue to make it stand out, consider the overall sensory environment. Don't try to make a cue compete for the attention of an already highly activated sense if it can be avoided. Instead, seek out senses that have low saturation. If the environment is quiet, consider an audio cue. If the environment is dark, consider a lighting cue. If the visual space is monochrome or bland, consider a color or bold marking. If the individual is stationary, consider a haptic cue. Coordinated cues across multiple senses (e.g., light with sound) can increase the likelihood of detection, especially if the sensory environmental load is variable.

One leverage point for enhancing visual cues comes from pre-attentive visual processing. We have a complex visual processing system, and certain visual cues are detected with little conscious processing. This is called pre-attentive visual processing, which appears hardwired to direct our attention to particular aspects of our visual field. Some common pre-attentive visual attributes include differences in: orientation, shape, color, intensity, spatial position, size, and motion (Knaflic, 2015, p. 234). Against a uniform background, such cues tend to be quickly and automatically detected.

We also appear to have similar pre-attentive audio capabilities – responding far more readily to our names, hearing a child in distress, nails on a blackboard, and so on. We are not currently aware of neurologic research similar to that on the visual system to guide us here. We can only suggest that although increased volume will make an audio cue more detectable, businesses should also be willing to experiment with different types and tones of audio cues if the initial cue is not consistently detected.

It is possible that the remaining primary senses of smell and taste could be used as cues. Although taste and smell are important aspects of food services, we are not aware of any instances of these senses being used for service failsafing. Perhaps this is because creating and administering taste and smell cues is more challenging; perhaps it is because these senses appear to be tied more directly to unconscious emotional processing; or perhaps it is because the most consciously noticeable tastes and smells tend to be strongly offensive. Parenthetically, with such strong direct connections to the basic emotional systems of the midbrain, there remains the intriguing possibility that smell and taste may ultimately be useful in influencing treatment perceptions.

If there is a high overall level of sensory saturation, it is probably better to opt for an impediment cue rather than an amplified sensory cue. Impediment cues have the benefit of being virtually impossible to ignore, but may be frustrating if it is unclear how to remove the impediment and resume progress. This is especially true for customers, who generally have less familiarity with the service process than the providers do.

At the most fundamental level, impediments prevent further progress toward a goal. In services, the goal is usually pretty clear to both customer and provider, and progress toward the goal follows the service process and the movement of individuals and items within the service facility. Commonly we will be impeding access, process, information, or duration.

Access can be impeded for both people and items in a service. Typically we are limiting entry to or exit from an area, but occasionally we may focus on directing flow between two areas. Entry to an area can be prevented by some form of lockout that is released by correction of the error, but entry can also be prevented because the area is full and there is no more space available. Similarly, exit from an area can be prevented by some form of lock-in, or items may not be released until a full set is in the area. Directional routing can be established with one-way access gates and constraints on the ability to deviate from a route once commenced.

Process impediments typically limit the conclusion of the current step or commencement of the next step until the error has been resolved. Behaviorally, we can prevent a more memorable or desirable step until a less memorable or desirable step has been completed. This is how the aforementioned ATM failsafe works. Occasionally, we may constrain alternatives or force alternate process steps in the presence of an error. This is particularly useful if corrective action is more complicated and requires a corrective process.

Information impediments are typically used to limit information to a form that can be efficiently processed by the service. Such impediments include not allowing invalid inputs, limited option choices, and limits to the input size of formats.

Time impediments can be particularly useful when customers become stuck, but can also be useful when workers must break away from the process and fail to resume it. Common time constraints are timeouts when the process has been idle for too long. Usually they are coupled with the automatic instigation of some recovery process, higher-level intervention by the service provider, or resumption of the process with default information assumptions.

When creating the failsafe device, we like to brainstorm and sleep on it. The design of the failsafe device or procedure that turns our hook into an obvious cue cannot be ultimately reduced to a mechanical operation. There remains a creative aspect to it. Often a solution is obvious, perhaps because the hook is easy to work with, or because we have experience with failsafing a similar hook in the past. Other times it is not so apparent. Active methods to facilitate creativity, such as team brainstorming and rapid prototyping, can help us identify possible solutions, but we shouldn't overlook the benefit of stepping away from the problem for a bit to allow time for our subconscious to chew on it. Often the solution will suddenly come to us in the shower the following morning.

Become attuned to the failsafes that are all around us. Sometimes these will appear as a particularly clever and intuitive design, other times as an obvious "fix" or "add-on," and sometimes even as a strangely located piece of commercial art. One of our local bank branches permanently closed several teller positions by erecting corporate art that hides them from view. Take a picture of the failsafe (just not in the bank lobby!). Keep a file of good ideas. The more solutions that we have seen in different contexts, the easier it is to come up with adaptations for our specific problems.

If we are unable to create an effective failsafe with a particular hook, the first option is to consider other hooks at the same control point that could be used instead. If we cannot identify any other hooks, we will be forced to move on to the next best control point in our search for a better hook.

Despite our best efforts, failsafing may just not work for some of the errors we have identified and we will need to use second-order methods. In particular, treatment problems are often too ephemeral to failsafe. There tends to be an absence of environmental cues to act as a hook for a failsafe device, the error itself often has a highly individual interpretation, and because the impact on the customer is immediate, there is often only one feasible control point to work with. Complex decision-making and diagnostic errors are also not as amenable to failsafing. Because the outcome of a decision process is not known ahead of time, there are no clear intentions for us to detect deviation from the expected result. In essence, the problem is that we cannot put in place a fixed device or procedure to detect deviation from a future unknown and variable outcome. This does not mean that failsafing cannot be used with decision-making and diagnostic processes at all; rather, it means that we should focus on failsafing the decision-making process rather than the decisions themselves. Failsafing can be applied to ensure that a rigorous decision process is properly followed, and that particular key data necessary for good decisions are not overlooked.

Second-order methods for error control focus primarily on ways to decrease the likelihood of errors being made in the first place, or to make the system otherwise robust to the adverse effects of the error (Stewart and Grout, 2001). Methods to decrease the likelihood of an error focus on reducing environmental complexity through visible system dynamics, ecological interface design, workload balance, simplified task structures, and so on. Making the system robust to the influence of mistakes tends to involve approaches that de-couple the system to reduce the propagation of errors, and tools to facilitate correction. There is also the potential to generate a robustness to service errors by exploiting interrelationships among the 3Ts (Stewart, 2003) or by making the errors themselves benign (Grout, 2003).

Failsafing is more of a bailing wire and bubblegum approach to quality (WD-40 and duct tape, for the younger generation). We are not trying to create a comprehensively designed and integrated ideal quality system. The idea is that we need a highly responsive quality system that can adapt as quickly as the service process changes and creates new failure points.

The necessary attitude is hit fast and move on, building our skills as we go. We start with the soft targets, the easier errors, so that we build the skills and knowledge to address more difficult ones later. We don't lay siege to our errors with a lengthy design planning process that validates that our failsafe has a high likelihood of working. Instead, we use probing attacks to learn the best approach. Shingo (1986) advocates a 50/50 rule whereby if we are 50 percent sure something will work, we try it. Typically, even if it fails we learn enough from the failure to succeed the next time. Avoid analysis paralysis. Prioritize and get to work. We don't want to get caught up trying to fully analyze all the branches prior to implementing any controls. Instead, we will analyze one branch of our 3T/PER tree, find a shortlist of the most problematic errors, pick one, and move forward with the process of identifying the best control point and maybe a couple of alternate ones. We use our PSGI framework to help identify a good hook, and then create a failsafe to establish control at that point. We repeat this process until the important errors in that branch have been addressed. Then we move on to the next branch. In the words of Bear Grills, "Adapt, Improvise, Overcome," and above all keep moving.

We conclude with some examples of low-tech service failsafe methods:

1. Error: Wrong medical dosage for children.
   Failsafe: The Broselow Pediatric Resuscitation System for Emergency Medical Services (EMS) workers uses a color-coded measuring tape to quickly determine the height of the patient. All of the medication in the matching color-coded bag is pre-dosed for that size patient.
2. Error: Surgical instruments left in the patient.
   Failsafe: Surgical instrument trays with indentations shaped for each instrument to ensure that all have been replaced after the procedure.
3. Error: Spotting date-rape drugs.
   Failsafe: DrinkSafe makes inexpensive drink coasters with test spots that change color when exposed to Gamma Hydroxybutyrate (GHB) and ketamine, the two most common date-rape drugs.
4. Error: Lost ski lift ticket.
   Failsafe: Lift tickets are often torn off jackets on lifts, during falls, and by tree branches for the more adventurous. New lift tickets with embedded Radio Frequency Identification (RFID) chips can be left securely in your pocket and scanned right through your clothes.
5. Error: Contamination of food during preparation.
   Failsafe: Some kitchens use color-coded cutting boards and utensils to insure preparers don't risk cross-contamination of ingredients.

6. Error: Forgetting to replace a credit card in a wallet or purse.
    Failsafe: A manufacturer has rigged wallets to sound an audible beep when a card is absent from the wallet.
7. Error: Allowing oversized bags to go as carry-on.
    Failsafe: Delta's "Size-Wise" devices are tubular metal frames used to check your carry-on bag. If your bag fits in the size-wise unit, it will fit in the overhead compartment.
8. Error: Variation in portions of fries at fast-food restaurants.
    Failsafe: The French fry scooper made famous at McDonald's effortlessly delivers remarkably low variation among servings of fries at fast-food restaurants the world over.
9. Error: Driving away from the gas station without removing the pump hose.
    Failsafe: Equipping gas station pumps with hose couplings that break away and quickly shut off the flow of gasoline.
10. Error: Theme park workers slouching with their hands in their pockets rather than appearing attentive to guests.
    Failsafe: A Korean theme park found a fix for this several years ago – sewing trouser pockets closed. (This might call for a revision in service training programs for the workers!)

REFERENCES

Chase, R.B., and D.M. Stewart, (1993) "Fail-Safing Services," in Scheuing, E., and W.F. Christopher (Eds)., *The Service Quality Handbook*, AMACOM, New York, pp. 347–357.

Chase, R.B., and D.M. Stewart, (1994) "Make Your Service Fail-Safe," *Sloan Management Review*, 35:3, 35–44.

Chase, R.B., and D.M. Stewart, (1995) *Mistake-Proofing: Designing Errors Out*, Productivity Press, Portland, OR.

Grout, J.R., (2003) "Preventing Medical Errors by Designing Benign Failures," *The Joint Commission Journal on Quality and Safety*, 29:7, 354–362.

Knaflic, C.N., (2015) *Storytelling with Data: A Data Visualization Guide for Business Professionals*, John Wiley & Sons, Hoboken.

Sellen, A., (1994) "Detection of Everyday Errors," *Applied Psychology: An International Review*, 43:4, 475–498.

Shingo, S., (1986) *Zero Quality Control: Source Inspection and the Poka-Yoke System*, Productivity Press, Cambridge.

Stewart, D.M., (2003) "Piecing Together Service Quality," *Production and Operations Management Journal*, 12:2, 246.

Stewart, D.M., and J.R. Grout, (2001) "The Human Side of Mistake-Proofing," *Production and Operations Management Journal*, 10:4, 440–459.

11. Customer-focused service design for faster and more efficient services

Gang Li, Joy M. Field and Mark M. Davis

INTRODUCTION

The customer's direct interaction with the service delivery process creates the well-recognized trade-off between providing services that are fast but expensive because they require additional capacity and services that are low cost but typically slower. However, in today's hyper-competitive business environment, which will likely continue for the foreseeable future, the power has clearly shifted to the customers (Cooperstein 2013), with the customer wanting and demanding both—that is, services that are not only fast but also reasonably priced.

Previously, accepted theory for designing processes in both manufacturing and services contexts isolated the technical core of the value creation process to maximize its efficiency (Chase and Tansik 1983). From a service perspective, this means that the back-office operations are decoupled from front-office operations. Service examples include banks with separate facilities and employees, in which front-office workers interact with customers in the bank's branches, while back-office workers in a central location perform standardized processes such as check processing. Another example is supermarkets where front-office activities include cashiers and baggers at checkouts, while back-office operations include restocking shelves, which is often done both while the store is open as well as at night when there are no customers in the aisles. A third example is the modern customer service center that handles myriad customer inquiries that require various response times, from immediate (e.g., telephone calls and online chats)—as in front-office—operations to those with longer, more flexible response times (e.g., emails and traditional postal mail)—as in back-office operations.

While isolating the technical core may make back-office operations more efficient, the variability and time-sensitivity of customer demand in the front office make it difficult to provide services that are both fast and efficient (i.e., low cost). Additionally, the literature on customer perceptions of waiting times suggests that the unexpectedly high costs associated with long perceived waits for front-office activities necessitate a process with higher service levels (Allon et al. 2011; Davis and Vollmann 1990; Lu et al. 2013). To address this trade-off, time-varying staffing models have been proposed to achieve high worker utilization over the planning horizon while at the same time providing a high level of customer service for front-office operations (Hall 1991; Whitt 2007). However, these models often rely on part-time employees and face numerous practical challenges, not only in their computational complexity but also in their practical applicability (e.g., managerial and legal difficulties with frequently fluctuating workforce levels; Gans et al. 2003; Silva et al. 2000). Silva et al. (2000) specifically identify the negative impacts of a fluctuating workforce on employee motivation due to the lack of job security, legal restrictions on firing of employees, legal and union constraints pertaining to the mandated minimum number of hours an employee must work, and the costs of frequent firing and hiring. They develop a constant workforce model in a manufacturing context and demonstrate that a constant workforce reduces the total relevant cost to the company.

We refer to the separation of front-office from back-office operations as the "classic design." Due to this separation, the classic design faces the challenge of efficiently planning the front-office operations. As a result, stochastic and complex planning models featured by time-varying staffing levels are often inevitably used in determining worker schedules in the classic design. We propose instead an integrated service process design that adopts a constant but mixed workforce strategy to perform both time-sensitive front-office and less-time-sensitive back-office activities, thereby creating a faster and simultaneously less expensive service. In our design, the back-office work can be viewed as a buffer that can quickly react to the volatile characteristics of the front-office demands. Thus, the workforce planning in the new design will be much less sensitive to the front-office demand patterns and uncertainties, resulting in a simple planning model featuring a constant staffing level that is now possible and very attractive. We define employees who perform both front-office and back-office activities as "versatile" employees who can easily transition between time-sensitive front-office activities and less-time-sensitive back-office activities as the situation dictates, while allocating a large portion of the work to dedicated and less expensive front-office and back-office employees. A successful service delivery process design that integrates both types of work and adopts a constant staffing level not only mitigates the disadvantages of the classic design, but is also applicable to virtually all types of services where individuals participate in providing the service.

As Li et al. (2017) demonstrated in their example in financial services, compared with the classic design, our new service process design achieves both a higher service level and lower cost over a wide range of worker wages, efficiencies, average-to-maximum demand ratios, and service level requirements. However, the one underlying assumption, which is critical, is that there is sufficient back-office work available when there are no immediate customers to be served. In fact, our new design can be better than the classic design even when the versatile workers are paid more but are also less efficient (which is often the situation in practice). Important advantages of our new approach, as suggested by Li et al. (2017), are that the results and insights tend to be robust for various demand patterns and only require a fairly accurate forecast of the maximum demand over the planning horizon. This is in sharp contrast to time-varying staffing models that require accurate forecasts of all demand periods over the planning horizon.

We begin by reviewing the relevant literature, including capacity planning with time-varying staffing and with flexible and dedicated workers. We then introduce our design concept and discuss how it differs from the classic design. We further discuss a few practical considerations and introduce extensions to our design to address them. In the end, we discuss the managerial implications that are followed by recognizing the limitations of the new design.

LITERATURE REVIEW

Staff Planning and Scheduling

Customer demand in service systems usually varies significantly over time, with two sources of variability, as shown in Figure 11.1: stochastic variability (uncertainty in demand within a given time period) and predictable variability (change in demand from time period to time period; Hall 1991).

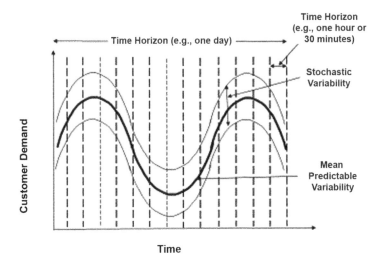

Figure 11.1   *Types of variability in customer demand*

When demand exhibits only stochastic variability—that is, average demand remains constant over the time horizon—the customer arrival process can often be modeled as a stationary Poisson process (Kolesar and Green 1998). With predictable variability, however, the customer arrival process is no longer stationary or constant across time. In this situation, the arrival process is typically divided into smaller time intervals with each interval having a separate arrival rate (Cachon and Terwiesch 2009). Green et al. (2007) and Whitt (2007) provided a review of staffing methods that address time-varying demand and applications of these methods in service systems. All these staffing methods maintain a constant staffing level within each time interval but vary these levels over time. Bear (1980) proposed a busy-hour engineering method to maintain a constant staffing level over an entire planning horizon, but this method has received little attention in practice since it results in over-staffing when the demand is less than peak.

Other limitations of time-varying staffing levels include: (a) they are technically challenging to derive, (b) their effectiveness relies heavily on accurate forecasting of demand distributions over the entire planning horizon (Taylor 2012), and (c) they make subsequent workforce scheduling very difficult (Gans et al. 2003). Consequently, part-time or temporary employees are frequently employed in practice (Bhatnagar et al. 2007). However, recognizing the strong relationship between employee satisfaction and customer loyalty (Kamikura et al. 2002), there appears to be a growing preference among service providers in many industries to employ as many full-time workers as practical, even when customer demand is highly variable over the time horizon (often a one-day time horizon).

Resource Flexibility

We position our proposed service design in the research stream of the "flexibility design problem" that determines the appropriate mix of flexible and dedicated employees in a service system (Akşin et al. 2007). A number of researchers have addressed the question of how to determine the amount and type of resources required to satisfy uncertain demand through the use of flexible resources. Typically, they find that there is an optimal combination of dedicated and flexible resources (e.g., equipment, employees) in terms of performance outcomes, such as minimizing cost or maximizing the service level. For example, McDonald et al. (2009) modeled the benefits and costs of increasing human resource flexibility through additional cross-training in the context of a lean manufacturing cell. They show that the net present cost (NPC) is minimized with a mix of low and high flexibility employees and that any further increase in cross-training reduces NPC. Although much of this type of research has been conducted in a manufacturing context (Attia et al. 2014; Deng and Shen 2013; Jordan and Graves 1995), researchers are increasingly focusing on the use of flexible capacity in service processes, particularly in call centers (Akşin et al. 2007; Gurvich et al. 2008; Mehrotra et al. 2012).

In a service context, especially call centers, much of the research assumes that all the activities employees perform are in the front office, where customer demand is completely time sensitive and the need for flexibility is driven by differing classes of real-time demand (Gurvich and Whitt 2010; Mehrotra et al. 2012). However, research on call centers with "blended operations" does consider how to allocate time-sensitive inbound calls and less time-sensitive outbound callbacks to agents (Akşin et al. 2007; Gans and Zhou 2003). Differing from the blended operations case, our research question focuses on a higher-level planning problem that derives the optimal mix of different types of workers rather than the detailed scheduling decisions for identical workers.

A NEW DESIGN PARADIGM FOR A FAST AND EFFICIENT SERVICE DELIVERY SYSTEM

A critical element that is necessary for designing fast and efficient customer service is the ability to keep front-office workers productive when there are no customers to be served. This can be accomplished by having at least some of the workforce be sufficiently flexible so they can easily shift from front-office activities to back-office activities as the situation dictates. In contrast, traditional queuing models assume that customer-facing workers are idle when there are no customers to serve. Thus, to provide faster service, more workers need to be scheduled, resulting in increased capacity and higher worker wages, which in turn translates into lower worker utilization and higher labor costs.

Another critical piece to our proposed service design is that there will always be sufficient back-office activities that need to be done when there are no customers to be served. Of course, there can be more than this minimum amount of back-office work to be performed, in which case this additional work would be performed by dedicated back-office workers. These back-office activities can vary significantly depending on the type of service. In addition to the more usual activities, such as updating client information (i.e., change of address), back-office activities can also include updating technical manuals for high-tech firms (Figure 11.2).

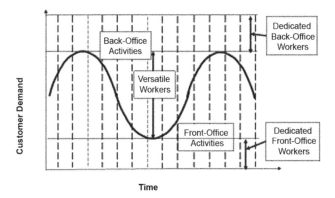

Figure 11.2   Allocation of flexible and dedicated workers across the planning horizon

The minimum amount of back-office work needed is determined by the ratio of the peak demand period to the smallest off-peak demand period. The greater this ratio, the more back-office activities that need to be available so that workers can be productive during off-peak periods. Another factor in determining the minimum amount of back-office activities is the relative breadth of the peaks to the breadth of the "valleys" caused by the off-peaks. The greater this ratio (i.e., the breadth of peaks to the breadth of off-peaks), the lower the minimum amount of back-office activities needed.

Integrating Front-Office and Back-Office Operations through a Constant but Mixed Workforce

To better serve customers, as defined by providing faster service, while simultaneously keeping the service as efficient as possible, we propose adopting a constant staffing approach where the maximum number of workers to be scheduled is based on the peak time period demand over a planning horizon. Using peak demand to determine the number of workers ensures excellent customer responsiveness; however, this will typically lead to excess capacity when demand is off-peak and is associated with higher labor costs. Our approach utilizes workers with excess capacities (when there are no customers) to perform the less-time-sensitive back-office activities. (As noted above, in the classical approach, these workers would otherwise remain idle, resulting in the higher costs associated with faster service.) In short, our new service design is based on three fundamental assumptions: 1) satisfying time-sensitive customer needs in the front office is a top priority; 2) front-office operations are more time sensitive than back-office operations; and 3) versatile workers can be employed who are capable of performing both front-office and back-office activities.

Assumption 1 establishes the action priority when a worker faces both front-office and back-office needs simultaneously. Under this assumption, the worker will always choose to perform the front-office activities whenever a new customer arrives and perform the back-office activities only when not serving front-office customers. Assumptions 2 and 3 make such actions feasible in terms of time sensitivity and workforce capability. Meanwhile, although less time sensitive, all back-office activities must be performed in the given planning

Table 11.1   *Comparison between classic service design and new service design*

Features	Classic Design	New Design
Focus	Protect the technical core to maximize efficiency	Customer-centered design to maximize effectiveness
Approach	Decouple back-office from front-office operations	Integrate back-office and front-office operations
Workforce Types	Specialists	Mix of versatile workers and specialists
Workforce Tenure	Full-time and part-time workers	All full-time workers
Workforce Size	Time-variable	Constant
Data Requirements	High: accurate demand forecasts for every time period	Low: forecast only for peak demand and average demand over all periods
Computational Requirements	High: complex stochastic models	Low: simple integer programming models
Implementation Requirements	High: various managerial, legal, and labor issues	Low: only permanent workers at a constant level

horizon. In addition to the versatile workers, dedicated workers for both front-office and back-office activities could also be used, as the situation requires, to form a mixed workforce.

Using the peak demand to determine the minimum worker capacity in combination with a constant staffing level also provides significant computational and managerial advantages over the classic design. (Of course, worker capacity could always be increased if there are additional back-office activities to be performed.) Because our approach does not require an accurate estimate of the customer demand pattern over the planning horizon, the computational burden is dramatically reduced. Consequently, simple models can work very well to provide a good estimate of the desired capacity. In addition, a constant staffing level also avoids the computational, managerial, and legal difficulties of the time-varying staffing level approaches, as explained earlier. Table 11.1 summarizes the key differences between the classic design and the new design we propose.

An Introduction to the Analytics behind the New Design

Given an estimate of the peak demand in the front office and the desired service level (e.g., 90 percent of the customers must be served in one minute or less) to meet the peak demand period, one can adopt a staffing model, such as the Square-Root-Staffing formula, the Erlang-C model, or more advanced models (e.g., Garnett et al. 2002), to determine a desired staffing level for the peak demand period. We denote such a desired level for the front-office operations with peak demand as DL. Let p be the average service time of a dedicated front-office worker, and DC be the *Desired Capacity* level; $DC = DL/p$. It is important to note that our design maintains DC for all the time periods for the front-office operations over the planning horizon, even when the demand is off-peak. Thus, a front-office worker will have time-varying utilizations during the planning horizon, which would increase when the demand is high but decrease when the demand is low. We further assume that the entire planning horizon can be divided into T time periods; within each time period, the customer arrivals can be approximately viewed as a stationary process, and the average service time is insignificant compared to the time period. Such an assumption is popularly used in multi-period staffing planning (Cachon and Terwiesch 2009) and is proper for many situations, such as when the average service time is counted in minutes and a time period is counted in hours. We use t to present the index of time periods and denote the utilization of a front-office worker in time t as ρ_t. Then $\rho_t = D_t/DC$, where D_t is the expected demand in time t. Because customers arrive stochastically at any time, ρ_t also represents the probability of the worker in time t being "busy," and $1-\rho_t$ is the probability of being idle with no customers to serve in the classic design. In the new design, however, we assign a portion of the back-office activities to a versatile worker whenever they become idle. Thus, $1-\rho_t$ is now a busy probability for performing back-office activities. Defining ρ as the average utilization over the entire planning horizon, we have:

$$\rho = \frac{\sum_{t=1}^{T} \rho_t}{T} = \frac{\sum_{t=1}^{T} D_t}{T*DC} = \frac{\bar{D}}{DC} \tag{11.1}$$

where $\bar{D}$ is the average demand over the planning horizon. Thus, $(1-\rho)T$ represents the total time that the versatile worker can contribute to the back-office operations.

Let TB be the total capacity requirement for all back-office operations in the planning horizon, and $BC = TB/T$ be the average back-office capacity level. Because we assume back-office demand is much less time sensitive and also less stochastic than the front-office operations, one can model the back-office operations as a single stochastic or deterministic process and use the classic staffing models (such as the Square-Root-Staffing formula mentioned earlier) to determine TB. As long as we ensure the available average back-office capacity is no smaller than BC, all back-office activities can be completed in the planning horizon. As a result of the above, the dynamic, multi-period capacity decision problem typically found in the existing literature is reduced to a much simpler static decision problem in our design. This static decision problem requires only that the available capacity in the front office *in any time period* is no smaller than DC and the available capacity in the back-office *on average* is no smaller than BC. We develop a simple decision model next to find the optimal workforce mix.

Decision Model for Optimal Workforce Mix

We define three types of workers in the decision model: A *Back-Office Worker* is able to perform only back-office activities, a *Front-Office Worker* is able to perform only front-office activities, and a *Versatile Worker* is able to perform both front-office and back-office activities. These workers are represented by B, F, and V, respectively.

The workers are paid an hourly rate for the time they are on the job. Let s_b, s_f, and s_v be the total wages paid to each type of worker over the planning horizon. Generally, $s_v \geq \max\{s_b, s_f\}$. $s_v \geq \max\{s_b, s_f\}$. In addition, let c_b and c_f be the efficiencies of a *Back-Office Worker* and a *Front-Office Worker*, respectively, and c_{vb} and c_{vf} be the efficiencies of a *Versatile Worker* if they work in the back-office or front-office, respectively. Let x_b, x_f, and x_v be the decision variables for the number of workers employed. We have the following decision model:

Minimize $s_b x_b + s_f x_f + s_v x_v$ $\tag{11.2}$

subject to:

sufficient capacity for front-office activities at the level desired:

$$c_f x_f + c_{vf} x_v \geq DC \tag{11.3}$$

sufficient capacity for back-office activities at the level required:

$$c_b x_b + c_{vb}(1-\rho)x_v \geq BC \tag{11.4}$$

non-negativity, integrality:

x_b, x_f, and x_v are non-negative integers. (11.5)

The objective (11.2) is to minimize the total cost by determining the number of workers for each of the three worker types. Constraints (11.3) and (11.4) ensure that sufficient capacity is available to achieve both desired front-office customer services and required back-office operations. Constraint (11.5) specifies that all decision variables are integers.

Another element that needs to be addressed is switching costs—that is, the cost of a versatile worker switching from either front-office activities to back-office activities or vice versa. We assume that in designing such a service process, workstations are combined or adjusted so that they can be used to perform both types of activities and the switching costs have been reduced to near zero. For example, a customer contact center for a financial services firm has designed workstations so, with just a flip of a switch, a versatile worker can change activities immediately from answering customer calls (i.e., front-office activities) to updating a customer's request for a change in address that was received by either email or traditional postal mail (i.e., back-office activities), and again switch back to answer a customer call when it comes in. In addition, the efficiency loss due to switching is also modeled by parameters c_{vb} and c_{vf}.

Service Design in a Complex and Uncertain Environment

We extend the simple model outlined above to incorporate more practical considerations via three directions: time sensitivity, worker type and cross-training, and real-time decision-making.

Time sensitivity of various activities
As stated on p. 157, we set a top priority for versatile workers to serve customers in the front office because front-office activities are more time sensitive. But when two unexpected front-office demands arrive simultaneously, which one should be served first? The same happens to the back-office activities, which cannot always wait a long time. Figure 11.3 shows time sensitivities of various back-office activities.

Based on the expected response time of an activity, we define its time sensitivity index, *alpha*, which varies from zero to one. An alpha of zero means the activity must be responded to without waiting, while an alpha of one suggests the lowest priority. The new design will determine the priority of an activity based on its time sensitivity index. (In the front-office demand case, the index is generated based on customer answers to some pre-recorded screening questions.) Note that the alpha value might change even for the same type of activity, depending on the time an activity arrives and its content. A meal order arriving during peak time has a smaller alpha than one arriving during non-peak time, for instance.

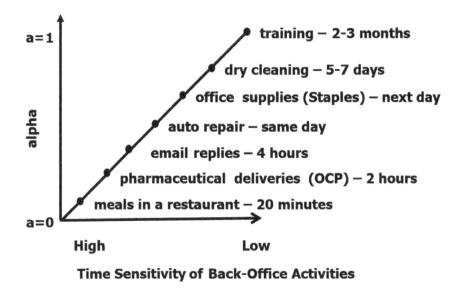

Figure 11.3   Time sensitivity of back-office activities

Worker type and cross-training
Versatile workers and specialists are special cases of a more general workforce framework built on worker skills, in which a specialist holds only one skill set but a versatile worker has two or more skills. Moreover, by cross-training, a specialist can learn another skill set, and a versatile worker can be more versatile by learning new skills. Therefore, our design allows a large variety of workers in the process. Meanwhile, training is both time consuming and costly, so the determination of when and how to train the existing workforce is critical. Li et al. (2015) introduced effective decision models that explicitly capture the development of the workforce through a training network. In the study, they investigate the impact of strategically aligning technology and workforce decisions through the comparison of joint and integrated models to each other and to a baseline hierarchical model. Their results show that an integrated model has the lowest cost across all conditions. This is because the integrated approach maintains a small but skilled workforce that can operate new and more advanced technology with higher capacity. The work of Li et al. (2015) provides a practical tool for the implementation of our new design in a technology-oriented and knowledge-intensive environment.

Real-time decision-making
The simple model on pp. 159–160 suggests an optimal mixture of workforce for service process. Based on it, we can develop a scheduling model that supports real-time decisions of deploying these workers to various demands. In this lower-level decision model, the arrivals of customer demands cannot be predicted accurately, and each demand requires workers of matched skill sets. Meanwhile, due to the time sensitivity index assigned to each demand, some can wait while some require immediate attention. Facing these challenges, a carefully designed mathematical model can help achieve lowest cost and maximum effectiveness. On the other hand, applying just simple rules, such as assigning an available worker to an activity

with a smaller time sensitivity index, and reserving capacity via back-office assignments in case of surging front-office demands, can obtain most of the benefits that a complex model would achieve but requires much less effort.

COMPARISON BETWEEN THE NEW DESIGN AND THE CLASSIC DESIGN

We now compare the performance differences between the classic design and our proposed design. To simplify the comparison, we assume that the scheduling/routing models that are often applied in the classic design can find the perfect match between the required staffing levels and the actual scheduled capacity required, although this is often not true in reality. More often, the scheduled capacity must be larger than the required staffing levels due to various labor and legal constraints (Gans et al. 2003; Silva et al. 2000). For instance, union regulations and/or government regulations may state that there is a minimum number of hours a part-time employee must work even when the scheduled capacity requirement is less. Consider this example: a part-time worker may only be needed for two hours, but state laws may require a minimum of four hours of work whenever a worker is called in. Thus, the cost savings from our new design represents the minimum savings; the actual savings after implementation would most likely be much higher. In addition, because of the perfect match assumption between capacity and demand, we are indifferent as to which particular staffing model is chosen for the classic design because all will result in the same lowest cost that such a design can possibly achieve. As far as our new design is concerned, since we use a staffing model primarily to determine the desired capacity level based on the peak demand, the selection of the staffing model has a minimal impact on its performance.

Application of the New Service Design Concept

We now relate two examples of how service providers are implementing our new service design approach and benefiting from it. In the first example, a relatively small customer contact center (50 customer support representatives) in Atlanta, GA, that provides technical support for medical equipment employs all full-time workers even though they speak with customers only about 35 percent of their time. The other 65 percent of their time, when there are no customers to serve, is spent performing less-time-sensitive back-office activities, such as: (a) training in new products; (b) performing activities with extended deadlines, such as sending out new product notices and writing adjustments to contracts; and (c) writing knowledge book articles. A major benefit of employing only full-time workers is a significant reduction in employee turnover, which is critical in knowledge-based services such as technical support. In addition, the customer contact center manager has improved the forecasts for customer demand during the day so he can now assign workers to do back-office activities of longer duration during those periods when he knows customer demand will be very low.

In the second example, a small community bank in the greater Boston area is trying to move more back-office work out to its branch locations because management knows that there are periods during the day when the workers at these branches are often idle with few customers to serve. In addition, they want to employ more full-time workers who are sufficiently trained to both interact directly with customers and also perform back-office activities when front-office demand is low. To allow workers to switch more readily from front-office activities to back-office activities during the day as the situation dictates, the newer branch designs allow both tellers and platform personnel to wait on customers, regardless of the type of customer transactions.

LIMITATIONS AND CONCLUSIONS

There are a number of limitations to our new service design that suggest potential research directions. First, the new service process design requires integration of front-office and back-office operations. However, certain back-office activities may be difficult or impossible to perform as part of an integrated service process. Also, certain back-office activities, such as demand forecasting or new product research and development, require special equipment and training and, thus, are poor candidates for integration. Nevertheless, this study will hopefully provide managers with additional insights for thinking outside the box in terms of possibilities for redesigning their service processes to be more integrated. Second, our model is most applicable in settings of minimal or relatively short switching times. While this is not always true in practice, innovations in workplace design and employee technologies have significantly reduced switching times. For example, the community bank mentioned previously has created a new banking specialist position that is a hybrid of a teller and platform employee. The workspace specifically redesigned for the specialist enables employees to switch easily between customer-facing and back-office tasks. Similarly, as noted previously, in customer contact center operations, the same computer terminal that the customer service representative uses to interact with customers can quickly be switched to working on email responses and other non-time-dependent activities.

Despite these limitations, our new service design has many advantages over the classic design approach of isolating the technical core from the customer-facing operations and time-varying staffing in terms of achieving higher service levels and lower costs to implement. Eliminating the boundary between front-office and back-office work allows the service to be viewed as a fully integrated process that can improve overall system performance. To take full advantage of the benefits from this approach to designing the service process requires companies to not only invest in multi-skilled employees but also to support a seamless working environment that allows employees to easily switch between these activities with minimal switching time and cost. As our customer contact center and bank examples demonstrate, managers are increasingly recognizing the advantages of an integrated constant staffing approach to service processes and making the design changes necessary to realize these benefits.

REFERENCES

Akşin, Z., M. Armony, and V. Mehrotra. 2007. "The Modern Call Center: A Multi-Disciplinary Perspective on Operations Management Research." *Production and Operations Management* 16 (6): 665–688.

Allon, G., A. Federgruen, and M. Pierson. 2011. "How Much is a Reduction of Your Customers' Wait Worth? An Empirical Study of the Fast-Food Drive-Thru Industry Based on Structural Estimation Methods." *Manufacturing & Service Operations Management* 13 (4): 489–507.

Attia, E.-A., P. Duquenne, and J.-M. Le-Lann. 2014. "Considering Skills Evolutions in Multi-Skilled Workforce Allocation with Flexible Working Hours." *International Journal of Production Research* 52 (15): 4548–4573.

Bear, D. 1980. *Principles of Telecommunication-Traffic Engineering. Institute of Electrical Engineers.* London: Peter Peregrinus.

Bhatnagar, R., V. Saddikutti, and A. Rajgopalan. 2007. "Contingent Manpower Planning in a High Clock Speed Industry." *International Journal of Production Research* 45 (9): 2051–2072.

Cachon, G., and C. Terwiesch. 2009. *Matching Supply with Demand: An Introduction to Operations Management.* 2nd ed. Boston: McGraw-Hill/Irwin.

Chase, R.B., and D.A. Tansik. 1983. "The Customer Contact Model for Organization Design." *Management Science* 29 (9): 1037–1050.

Cooperstein, D. 2013. *Competitive Strategy in the Age of the Customer.* Cambridge, MA: Forrester Research, Inc.

Davis, M.M., and T.E. Vollmann. 1990. "A Framework for Relating Waiting Time and Customer Satisfaction in a Service Operation." *Journal of Services Marketing* 4 (1): 61–69.

Deng, T., and Z.-J. Shen. 2013. "Process Flexibility Design in Unbalanced Networks." *Manufacturing & Service Operations Management* 15 (1): 24–32.

Gans, N., G. Koole, and A. Mandelbaum. 2003. "Telephone Call Centers: Tutorial, Review, and Research Prospects." *Manufacturing & Service Operations Management* 5 (2): 79–141.

Gans, N., and Y.-P. Zhou. 2003. "A Call-Routing Problem with Service-Level Constraints." *Operations Research* 51 (2): 255–271.

Garnett, O., A. Mandelbaum, and M.I. Reiman. 2002. "Designing a Call Center with Impatient Customers." *Manufacturing & Service Operations Management* 4 (3): 208–227.

Green, L.V., P.J. Kolesar, and W. Whitt. 2007. "Coping with Time-Varying Demand when Setting Staffing Requirements for a Service System." *Production and Operations Management* 16 (1): 13–39.

Gurvich, I., M. Armony, and A. Mandelbaum. 2008. "Service-Level Differentiation in Call Centers with Fully Flexible Servers." *Management Science* 54 (2): 279–294.

Gurvich, I., and W. Whitt. 2010. "Service-Level Differentiation in Many-Server Service Systems via Queue-Ratio Routing." *Operations Research* 58 (2): 316–328.

Hall, R.W. 1991. *Queuing Methods: For Services and Manufacturing.* Englewood Cliffs, NJ: Prentice Hall.

Jordan, W.C., and S.C. Graves. 1995. "Principles on the Benefits of Manufacturing Process Flexibility." *Management Science* 41 (4): 577–594.

Kamikura, W.A., V. Mittal, F. de Rosa, and J.A. Mazzon. 2002. "Assessing the Service-Profit Chain." *Marketing Science* 21 (3): 294–317.

Kolesar, P. J., and L.V. Green. 1998. "Insights on Service System Design from a Normal Approximation to Erlang's Delay Formula." *Production and Operations Management* 7 (3): 282–293.

Li, G., J. Field, and M. M. Davis. 2017. "Designing Lean Processes with Improved Service Quality: An Application in Financial Services." *Quality Management Journal* 24 (1): 6–20.

Li, G., J. Field, H. Jiang, T. He, and Y. Pang. 2015. "Decision Models for Workforce and Technology Planning in Services." *Service Science* 7 (1): 29–47.

Lu, Y., A. Musalem, M. Olivares, and A. Schilkrut. 2013. "Measuring the Effect of Queues on Customer Purchases." *Management Science* 59 (8): 1742–1763.

McDonald, T., K.P. Ellis, E.M. Van Aken, and C.P. Koelling. 2009. "Development and Application of a Worker Assignment Model to Evaluate a Lean Manufacturing Cell." *International Journal of Production Research* 47 (9): 2427–2447.

Mehrotra, V., K. Ross, G. Ryder, and Y.-P. Zhou. 2012. "Routing to Manage Resolution and Waiting Time in Call Centers with Heterogeneous Servers." *Manufacturing & Service Operations Management* 14 (1): 66–81.

Silva, J.P., J. Lisboa, and P. Huang. 2000. "A Labour-Constrained Model for Aggregate Production Planning." *International Journal of Production Research* 38 (9): 2143–2152.

Taylor, J.W. 2012. "Density Forecasting of Intraday Call Center Arrivals using Models Based on Exponential Smoothing." *Management Science* 58 (3): 534–549.

Whitt, W. 2007. "What You Should Know about Queuing Models to Set Staffing Requirements in Service Systems." *Naval Research Logistics* 54 (5): 476–484.

PART III

UNDERSTANDING AND SERVING CUSTOMERS

12. Customer success management
Vijay Mehrotra and Krishnamoorthy Subramanian

INTRODUCTION

Customer Success Management (CSM) is a relatively new functional area within many companies, an increasingly vital operational role, a rapidly growing profession, and an underlying systems management philosophy that is growing in importance, especially – but not exclusively – within the technology industry. One leading industry organization (Customer Success Association 2021) defines CSM as "a long-term, scientifically engineered, and professionally directed business strategy for maximizing customer and company sustained business value," while Hochstein et al. (2020b) describe the role of the Customer Success Manager as "a customer-facing, non-direct sales role that embodies the mindset of a counselor to proactively partner with customers to help them achieve their goals and promote long-term customer health that ultimately leads to relationship growth" (for other definitions, see Adams 2020, Mehta et al. 2016, and Vaidyanathan and Rabago 2020).

The CSM role has emerged from the software industry of the 21st century. In particular, the rise of cloud computing and open-source software has fundamentally shifted the software industry toward hosted "Software-as-a-Service" (SaaS) solutions, which are typically provided on a "subscription" basis. According to research by Gartner (Pettey 2018), 80 percent of existing software vendors – and 100 percent of new market entrants – were projected to offer subscription-based solutions to prospective customers by 2020. The implications of this shift are very significant for both software vendors and their customers.

When selling their software through a subscription, vendors are essentially leasing their software to their customers – typically on an annual, quarterly, or monthly basis – rather than through the traditional "perpetual license" model in which they would be receiving payment in full at the outset in exchange for providing customers with a license to use the software in perpetuity. In addition, such subscription-based software applications are typically provided as cloud-based services, meaning that the customer accesses the software via an internet connection. As such, the customer is no longer responsible for acquiring and monitoring computer hardware to run the vendor's software, or for managing software installation, integration, and maintenance.

In contrast to perpetual license contracts, subscription-based contracts for cloud-based software enable vendors to provide better entry-level pricing for acquiring new customers, a potentially much faster path to deployment, and a far less cumbersome process of providing software upgrades and new software components. For customers, there are also other tangible benefits associated with subscription-based solutions, including lower initial capital investment, faster time to deployment, and reduced risk.

Taken together, these shifts have fundamentally altered the dynamics between software vendors and their customers. In particular, under a subscription-based contract, the customer now holds far more power over the software vendor than ever before. This is in large part because the vendor's Customer Acquisition Cost is often greater than the revenue received from a customer's initial contract, meaning that the software vendor incurs a net financial loss when a customer chooses not to continue their relationship when this first contract expires. Conversely, a customer who renews their subscription on an ongoing basis produces a very lucrative revenue stream for the software vendor. However, this potential revenue stream (often referred to as Annual Recurring Revenue, or ARR, a key financial metric for subscription-based businesses) depends largely on customers' willingness to continue making ongoing payments – and this willingness to pay is largely based on the actual business value that they are able to accrue as a result of using the software, rather than on promises made during the initial sales process. We discuss this phenomenon from a systems perspective in more detail in "A Systems View of Customer Success" below.

These changes have in turn led to a fundamental operational shift for software vendors. Prior to the introduction of subscription-based models, software vendors had clear incentives to focus on the acquisition of new customers, as the bulk of the lifetime revenue was captured at the time when a customer made their initial purchase. However, since the advent of subscription-based pricing, the economic need to retain and expand revenues from their existing customers has forced software vendors to pay far more attention to their existing customers on an ongoing basis. This has led directly to the emergence of a new functional area, Customer Success Management (CSM), along with a dedicated group of employees directly engaged in this functional area (Customer Success Management Professionals, or CSMPs).

In simple terms, the role of the CSMP is to be the supplier's primary post-sales point of contact with a customer organization. The objective of the CSM function is to enable the customer to capture quantifiable value from the vendor's product in order to nurture, sustain, and ideally expand the customer's economic relationship with the vendor. In a very real sense, CSMPs are tasked with a great variety of activities (discussed in detail in "The Role of the Customer Success Management Professional" below) that historically have involved marketing, sales, professional services, training, product management, operations, and support. However, as we discuss below, the processes, metrics, and mindset associated with CSM are all fundamentally different from traditional task-oriented, customer-facing functions.

While initially developed to help software vendors address the challenges associated with retaining subscription-based customers, the CSM function has expanded significantly beyond these roots over the past decade. For example, a growing number of software vendors have begun to establish service contracts in which the payments that they receive are based on customers' usage levels; as a result, CSM is arguably even more important for these suppliers. In addition, as more businesses outside the technology industry move toward revenue models that explicitly depend on service-driven subscriptions and/or usage, these non-technology businesses are increasingly establishing CSM groups as an important functional area. According to a recent study (Gainsight 2019), nearly 25 percent of CSMPs work in industries other than technology. In particular, companies as diverse as Caterpillar, Philips, John Deere, GE, and Michelin having begun transforming many traditional product offerings into subscription-based services, creating additional demand for CSMPs. There are also rapidly growing numbers of CSMPs in industries such as consumer goods, agriculture, travel, and recreation.

As a result of all of this, the number of CSMPs has grown rapidly over the past decade, both in the United States and elsewhere. For the past several years, LinkedIn has rated the role of Customer Success Management, (or CSM) as one of its top ten "hottest" jobs. A more detailed study (Gainsight 2019) showed that from 2015 to 2018, the annual growth rate for

CSM jobs was 168 percent in the US, 234 percent in Europe, 180 percent in Asia, and 175 percent globally.

There are a handful of recent examples in the practitioner literature about the emerging importance of the CSM function (Atkins et al. 2018; Zoltners et al. 2019). But with only a few recent exceptions (Eggert et al. 2020; Hilton et al. 2020; Hochstein et al. 2020a), as yet there has been little research investigation into CSM. In particular, beyond one brief article (Mehrotra 2018), to date there has been little examination of CSM-related questions from a service operations management perspective. Thus, one primary purpose of this paper is to identify several important areas for future research with regard to CSM.

The remainder of this paper is organized as follows. In "The Role of the Customer Success Management Professional," we examine the role of the CSMPs in more detail, focusing on the types of activities in which CSMPs are engaged, the metrics that are typically used to measure and manage their performance, and how this role compares with traditional customer-facing positions. In "Organizing and Managing Customer Success Teams," we discuss the CSM function from an operations management perspective, identifying key business questions and challenges. In "A Systems View of Customer Success," we consider the CSM function from a systems perspective, focusing on the key inputs, transformations, outputs, and challenges. Finally, in "Summary and Conclusion," we conclude with a brief summary of the paper and our suggestions for future research.

THE ROLE OF THE CUSTOMER SUCCESS MANAGEMENT PROFESSIONAL

What CSMPs Do

The responsibilities associated with CSM roles will inevitably vary somewhat from company to company. In general, larger companies and/or companies with larger customers with more extensive needs will tend to have more specialized resources responsible for a smaller set of tasks. However, there are several core responsibilities for Customer Success Management Professionals that are quite consistent across organizations. To examine this role in more detail, it will be useful to examine the way that CSMPs typically engage with customers over the course of the Customer Journey, as shown in Figure 12.1.

Within some organizations, CSMPs may engage with prospective customers during the later stages of the sales process to (a) set customer expectations and demonstrate the supplier's commitment to continuity of engagement, and (b) capture information about the customer's needs that will be relevant once the sale has been completed. Similarly, within the software industry, some vendors will have technical specialists who are responsible for some or all implementation-related activities (e.g., software configuration, data integration), while at other companies these tasks are part of the work of CSMPs.

Within the context of subscription-based models, the remaining phases of the Customer Journey (Onboarding, Ongoing, and Customer Relationship Decision) are central to the work of virtually all CSMPs. For any given customer, Onboarding is generally defined as the period of time between the implementation of the technology and the time at which the customer successfully realizes some tangible component of the promised business value. This may include – but is not limited to – training on the usage of the product, which is often handled

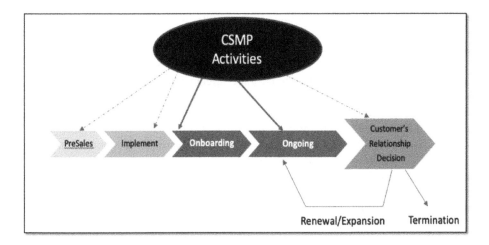

Figure 12.1   CSMP engagement in the Customer Journey

by CSMPs. It is during the Onboarding phase of the journey that the CSMP typically becomes the customer's primary point of contact within the software vendor's organization. In addition to training, other CSM activities during this phase of the journey may include articulating the value of the product in more detail, tracking initial product usage, providing information about industry best practices and/or other customers' experiences, informal leadership or coordination of change management initiatives within the customer organization, holding initial review meetings with stakeholders, gathering product feedback from customers, and setting expectations by building a "success plan" for the customer that includes goals, metrics, and timelines.

While Onboarding is a critical part of CSM, the work of the CSMPs is by no means complete at the end of this phase of the journey. In fact, the Ongoing phase of the Customer Journey often requires more effort and curiosity. In addition to much of what was described above, CSMP activities during this phase include managing and improving the relationship with the customer organization (which may feature many stakeholders with different perspectives and agendas), providing information about additional product features, advising the customer organization about best practices and additional ways to capture value from the product, understanding and advocating customer requests for additional product capability, leading periodic reviews of progress toward the goals articulated in the success plan (and helping the customer to quantify its progress toward those goals), and internal escalation of technical and/or commerical issues (especially those that are directly related to the achievement of the customer's goals).

Another important part of the work of the CSMPs is monitoring the customer's overall experience, which may include examining data about product usage, technical support issues, financial status, and customer surveys. This information is often used by CSMPs to set priorities, identify issues and opportunities, and drive escalations within their own organization. These types of measures are often synthesized in some manner to create a composite metric that is commonly referred to as "Customer Health Scores," which we discuss in more detail on p. 176.

From the perspective of the supplier who employs the CSMP, the Ongoing phase of the Customer Journey would ideally continue in perpetuity, as this would make this customer relationship as profitable as possible for the supplier. Within the context of a vendor's subscription-based revenue model, however, the end of the customer's contract with the supplier is a clear and critical step in the Customer Journey, which we refer to as the Customer Relationship Decision. At this point, the customer organization must decide (a) to renew or expand its contractual relationship, or (b) to terminate its use of the product and its business relationship with the supplier.

Indeed, at the highest level, the primary purpose of CSMPs is to drive customer retention and expansion, and in that process CSMPs are engaged with providing support to customers in a variety of ways. However, to achieve these goals, CSMPs seek to serve as trusted advisors to their customers, establishing and nurturing proactive, long-term relationships. In this way, the emerging role of the CSMP is distinctly different than – though clearly overlapping with – traditional customer-facing roles.

How the CSMP Role Compares to Sales and Account Management

Given that CSMPs regularly engage with customers and pay careful attention to contract renewals, there is clearly some overlap in their responsibilities with that of salespeople (especially those who play the role of "farmers," as described in DeCarlo and Lam 2016) and Account Managers (Homburg et al. 2002. Like salespeople and account managers, CSMPs are engaged with customers on an ongoing basis with an eye toward the financial interests of their own company. However, there are several significant differences as well.

First, as described above, CSMPs engage with customers in a wider variety of roles and contexts. This requires them to understand both their own company's product capabilities and their customers' business use cases far more thoroughly than salespeople or account managers. In addition, the metrics used to measure and reward CSMPs – which typically include customer engagement measures, product adoption metrics, and customer survey results, such as Net Promotor Scores, in addition to customer churn and retention rates – are far broader than those used for salespeople or account managers. Finally, compared to salespeople or account managers, the financial compensation for CSMPs is typically far less directly tied to specific financial outcomes.

Nevertheless, CSMPs are inherently interested in the commercial outcomes associated with Customer Relationship Decisions. This is in part because customer renewal and churn rates are key performance metrics (as discussed in more detail on p. 173) for CSMPs, with some part of their compensation typically tied to these metrics. Also, at a higher level, the commercial success of the supplier has a direct impact on its need for CSMPs (and the financial resources available to pay them!). As a result, while not nearly as commercially oriented as salespeople or account managers, CSMPs must nevertheless be constantly mindful of such considerations.

How the CSMP Role Compares to Customer Service and Technical Support

Given that CSMPs are engaged in transmitting information to customers to answer questions, help solve problems, and improve their effectiveness in deriving value from the supplier's products, there are also some clear similarities with traditional Customer Service and Technical Support (CS/TS) roles. However, there are several significant differences as well.

Most notably, CSMPs strive to engage with customers in a proactive manner with a long-term focus on customer value creation, while those in CS/TS roles are typically operating in a reactive mode with a focus on short-term issue resolution. As a result, the metrics that are used to evaluate the performance of CS/TS, at both the individual and team levels, are typically task oriented and focused on how successfully and how quickly specific customer issues are resolved. By contrast, CSM metrics are often based on integrated outcomes associated with several tasks that take place over time, and are viewed as "System Outputs," as discussed on p. 175. Hochstein et al. (2020b) provide additional information and examples of how the work of CSMPs is distinctly different from that of other existing customer-facing roles.

Research Questions

This initial description of the CSMP role presented above immediately points to many open questions that are of interest to both researchers and practitioners.

Research Question (RQ1): Given the variety of skills and aptitudes required for CSMPs to be effective, what are the most important characteristics and competencies for the individuals that are to be hired for these roles?

Given the cost associated with hiring and training CSMPs and the essential role that they play in interacting with their firm's customers, selecting individuals for these roles is clearly an important operational question. While there has been considerable research done on competency models and hiring criteria for other customer-facing roles (e.g., Cron et al. 2005), to date there has been no similar investigation for the rapidly emerging CSMP role.

Research Question (RQ2): After a customer has made an initial purchase, who should have responsibility and ownership for future sales (contract renewals, expansions, and upsells) to that customer? Should this be the CSMP associated with that customer or someone in a traditional sales or account management role?

There are strong arguments for the CSMP (in-depth knowledge of the customer environment, stronger customer relationships) as well as for salesperson or account manager (expertise in commercial matters, training and compensation more strongly tied to financial results, not wanting to compromise the CSMP's trusted advisor relationship with the customer). This is a hotly debated topic in industry, but to date there has been no objective research on this subject.

Research Question (RQ3): What is the economic value of a CSMP?

Given that CSMPs are relatively expensive customer-facing resources, CSM leaders are often asked to justify these investments. To date, there have been no rigorous objective studies on this topic, despite a great deal of interest from the practitioner community. This is also related to the System Outputs discussed on p. 175.

ORGANIZING AND MANAGING CUSTOMER SUCCESS TEAMS

In the previous section, our focus was on the CSMP role. In this section, we address the challenges and activities associated with organizing and managing teams of CSMPs.

Challenges

In addition to the fact that CSM is a relatively new functional area, there are several factors that make managing teams of CSMPs challenging. Many companies do not have standard post-sales processes for CSM activities, leaving both CSMPs and their management to determine the best course of action for each customer, and making operational efficiency difficult to measure. In addition, as a result of their close relationship with customers, CSMPs are often pulled into tactical support activities, reducing the time and attention that they are able to give to proactive customer engagement. Also, in many organizations, the Customer Success group has initially been created in reaction to a growing volume and variety of customer retention challenges and issues, leading managers and executives from other departments to route all sorts of unwanted problems to the CSMPs, further distracting them from their primary focus on building long-term relationships to enable customer value creation. Finally, the most critical metrics for Customer Success operations – customer churn and retention statistics – are lagging indicators, making it harder to identify and correct operational problems in a timely manner.

Customer Engagement Models and Segmentation Strategies

From the perspective of the supplier, different customers may be viewed as having significantly different levels of value (due to a variety of factors, including contract value, financial growth potential, industry visibility, and strategic significance). This assessment of value will often have a direct impact on the amount of post-sales attention received from the supplier's Customer Success resources. A common model for Customer Success engagement levels (Mehta et al. 2016) is to classify customers into high-touch (receiving a high level of personal attention from CSMPs due to a high perceived level of importance), medium-touch (a lower level of individualized attention), and tech-touch (predominantly automated, one-to-many Customer Success communications).

Beyond this, there are many other factors that may come into play when segmenting customers, including industry, product, organizational size, organizational maturity, geography, and revenue level (for more details, see Vaidyanathan and Rabago 2020, p. 107).

Designing CSMP Activities for Customers and Creating Account Portfolios for CSMPs

From the perspective of managing a Customer Success group, choices associated with customer engagement levels and customer segmentation have two primary purposes. First, these choices serve as a basis for developing the steps in the Customer Journey that CSMPs will engage in over time, which provide guidance for CSMPs in planning and organizing their work (and for CSM leaders to manage their teams). Second, these choices may play a significant role in assigning CSMPs to account portfolios. As these are both key responsibilities for CSM managers and executives, we discuss each in more detail here.

One important task for CSM leaders is to define the activities in which CSMPs engage. This set of activities will typically vary based on the level of engagement and the specific requirements of and strategies for different customer segments. The process of formally defining these customer segments and the associated CSMP activities – and tracking progress toward accomplishing these goals – is an important step in the maturing process for a CSM group. For each customer segment, the underlying assumption is that the activities that the CSMPs endeavor to undertake with those customers are strongly correlated with the System Outputs discussed on p. 175.

In addition to assigning activities to customers, CSM leaders are also challenged to assign specific customers to specific CSMPs. There are many factors to be considered, including attributes associated with each customer (including engagement model, customer segment, prescribed CSMP activities, contract renewal schedule, level of complexity, and strategic importance), attributes of each CSMP (including level of experience, domain expertise, existing relationships, and temperament), forecasts for new customers acquisition, and objectives for workload balancing.

Research Questions

We note that many of the decisions about customer engagement models, segments, and health scores described below are specific to a particular supplier's organization, resources, products, and priorities. With that said, it is also clear that the effective management of CSM teams has, to date, received almost no research attention. This is in part because CSM is still an emerging operational function and in part because the questions below are difficult to address in practice without access to detailed customer and operational data. However, over the past few years we have observed rapid advances in measurement methods as well as data capture and storage, creating both increased interest in these research questions and more data to help address them.

Research Question (RQ4): Given a portfolio of customers and a forecast for new customers, what is the best approach to establishing CSM engagement models and customer segments? Alternately, what models for customer engagement and segmentation produce better System Outputs for both suppliers and customers?

Research Question (RQ5): Given a set of existing customers, a forecast of new customers, and a strategy for customer engagement and segmentation, what is the optimal number of CSMPs to be hired?

From an operational perspective, answering these questions is a perpetual challenge for CSM leaders, in part because CSMPs are still sometimes viewed as a cost center rather than creators of value for the supplier organization (see RQ3). Part of the challenge is the fact that the key CSMP metrics (customer churn, retention, and growth) are lagging measures and it is often difficult to accurately estimate how different CSMP assignments might impact these future results.

Research Question (RQ6): For a given a set of CSMPs, customer engagement models, segments, and prescribed CSMP activities associated with each customer segment, what is the optimal assignment of CSMPs to customers?

As discussed above, there are many factors to consider when creating these assignments. It is our belief that these assignments can have a significant impact on the supplier's overall customer outcomes, including retention, account growth, and advocacy. The importance of these decisions is further enhanced by the fact that most CSM teams have a relatively limited number of CSMPs, meaning that this assignment process is often a de facto exercise in determining which customers receive what level of attention from CSMPs.

It is worth noting that RQ4, RQ5, and RQ6 are inextricably linked from an operations management perspective, and that it would be ideal to develop a set of jointly optimal solutions to all three of these questions simultaneously. We have presented them separately above for clarity of exposition and to illustrate the questions associated with smaller and potentially more tractable sub-problems.

A SYSTEMS VIEW OF CUSTOMER SUCCESS

In the previous two sections, we first examined the activities and skills associated with CSMP roles and then examined some of the main challenges associated with effectively managing CSM teams from a service operations management perspective. In this section, we consider the CSM function from a systems perspective, with a special focus on the key inputs and outputs associated with the ongoing interactions between CSMPs and their customers.

A Systems View of the CSM Function

Vaidyanathan and Rabago (2020) describe CSM as the intersection of two spheres of activities: Sales/Relationship and Services/Technical, as shown in Figure 12.2. Suppliers utilize their internal processes to address potential customers' needs by creating "Products" that are presented and sold to customers, first through the initial marketing and sales processes and then through activities undertaken by the supplier organization ("Sales/Relationship") after the initial sale. In addition, it is assumed that customer needs are better satisfied through training, information, and other forms of support provided by the supplier organization ("Services/Technical").

While it is generally presumed that selling a product directly generates revenue and profit for the supplier organization, the initial sale of the product is only a part of the story. Rather, in the context of subscription- and usage-based models, recurring revenue and sustained profitability are largely dependent on customers' perceptions of the value that they have received as a result of the use of the supplier's product. In addition, customers' experiences in trying to realize value sometimes also reveal unmet needs and identifies the gaps in product capabilities, which in turn points the supplier toward needs for new products and/or features.

From a systems perspective, the CSM function serves as a bridge, enabling suppliers to develop deep and sustainable connections with their customers. As discussed in Subramanian and Rangan (2013, Figures 5.1 and 5.2), the CSM function plays a role that is analogous to Applications Technology (AT) in other industries. Like CSM, AT pertains to the understanding of the performance of the product within the context of customers' needs and wants. AT helps an enterprise to develop a customer-centered viewpoint, which is essential and yet very difficult to achieve in day-to-day operations. It connects various business functions within the supplier and customer companies, as well as with other related suppliers. For many, the role

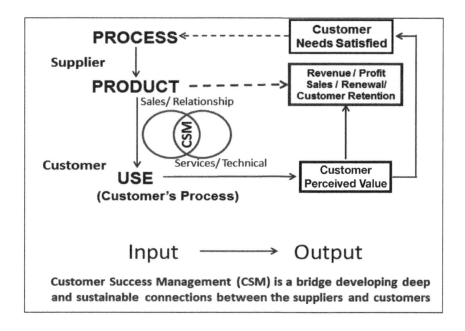

Figure 12.2   The role of the CSM function in connecting suppliers with customers

of AT – and CSM – may not be easily defined or readily visible, but it plays a critical role in creating positive outcomes. Like AT, CSM's purpose is to create value by enabling better use of the product to create realized value in the customer's environment.

In addition, it is important to note that another key responsibility of the CSM function is to capture information from the customer about the supplier's product. Given their direct and often intimate engagement with customers, CSMPs are often able to capture insights about product usability, features, and overall functionality that can lead directly to product improvements and new capabilities.

Next, we revisit the relationship between CSM and an individual customer. As described in the preceding sections, the CSMP engages with the customer to perform a broad and diverse set of activities over time. However, viewing the CSM function as an "Input/Transformation/ Output" system (Figure 12.3) provides a clearer and more comprehensive framework for management. Some of the tools or core capabilities accessible to the CSM are listed under "Transformation." The results are listed as the "Technical Outputs" (tangible outputs of CSM activity) and "System Outputs" (the value/benefit realized by the customer as well as the supplier).

Viewed through this lens, the CSM function can be seen as bridging the gap between the potential value embedded in the supplier's product and the customer's goals and expectations for how this product will deliver value. At the most fundamental level, a CSM's purpose is to enable the customer to utilize the product to meet or exceed their expectations in order to produce System Outputs that are positive for both the customer and the supplier. However, given that the CSM is part of a broader system, it is important to recognize that there are factors outside the control of the CSM that can influence these System Outputs.

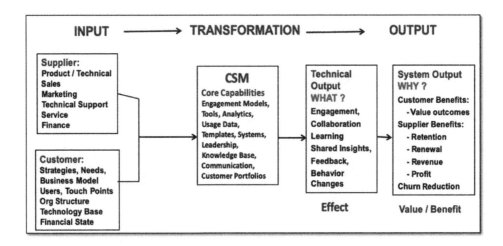

Figure 12.3   The CSM function as an "Input/Transformation/Output" system

Tracking System Inputs

Supplier's product and customer's expectations and capabilities

Even before a prospect becomes a customer, the supplier organization has provided significant inputs into this system. Specifically, as shown in Figure 12.3, the supplier's product team has made specific decisions about the capabilities of its product, the supplier's marketing team messages have established expectations for prospective customers, and the supplier's sales process has made promises (either implicitly or explicitly) to those prospects that have helped to influence the customer's decision to make an initial purchase.

Similarly, another set of inputs is provided by the customer. For example, within a Business-to-Business context, the customer's inputs may include its organizational structure, operational processes, technical infrastructure, personnel (including both product users and managers) and business strategies, goals, and priorities. Notably, from the perspective of the supplier organization, these customer inputs are only partially observable prior to deciding whether or not to engage in a commercial relationship with a given customer.

From the perspective of customer acquisition and near-term revenue, it may be tempting for a supplier to acquire as many customers as possible. However, as discussed in "The Role of the Customer Success Management Professional," Customer Acquisition Costs often exceed the revenue from an initial contract, which means that losing a customer at the end of an initial contract yields a net financial loss for the supplier. Moreover, because considerable costs and efforts typically go into supporting all customers (most notably through CSMPs and CS/TS/ Account Management), there are typically further negative financial consequences associated with acquiring customers for whom the supplier's product turns out to be a poor fit.

Customer Health Scoring

From the supplier's perspective, most of the Technical Outputs and System Outputs described above are often not directly observable or quantifiable, while the customer's decisions regarding its ongoing relationship with the supplier are lagging indicators. In addition, we note that relationships between suppliers and their customers are inherently dynamic, evolving on a regular basis and only partially as a result of the work of CSMPs.

All of this means that these supplier–customer relationships must be tracked and managed carefully. From a system perspective, this requires creating and monitoring metrics that (a) can be observed and (b) are believed to be strongly correlated with and predictive of key future customer decisions about its commercial relationship with the supplier. The process of quantifying the state of this relationship is known as "Customer Health Scoring." These types of metrics are utilized to make a variety of types of decisions, including prioritization and scheduling of previously planned CSM activities as well as specific responses to particular conditions, often referred to as "playbooks" (Vaidyanathan and Rabago 2020).

Customer Health Scores are typically a composite of several observable metrics. These scores are commonly based on both quantitative data (e.g., product usage, customer surveys, volume and types of interactions with the supplier organization) and qualitative observations by CSMPs and others within the supplier organization. From a systems perspective, these Customer Health Scores are an important input into the types of relationship management decisions that CSMPs and CSM leaders must frequently make.

Research Questions

Research Question (RQ7): Is it possible to develop a common language and systems-level understanding of CSM that brings all parties together, as illustrated in Figure 12.3, and what is the value of establishing this shared understanding?

This awareness of CSM as a system is the starting point for methodical development and deployment of its collaborative use in creating value for both the customer and the supplier. Adams (2020) refers to this collaborative and interdependent relationship directly, suggesting that suppliers treat their customers as "business partners."

While it is decidedly challenging to establish a common perspective for an ongoing supplier–customer relationship, we note here that key components of this shared understanding must include the desired System Outputs (often codified in a jointly developed "Success Plan," as described on p. 169), the data that will be shared between the parties, a shared set of assumptions about the system's Technical Outputs (and how these are believed to be connected to the System Outputs), and the areas of ownership and responsibility for each of the parties.

Research Question (RQ8): From the perspective of the supplier, what are the long-term consequences of acquiring customers for whom its product is not a good fit (because of a mismatch between the product's capabilities and the customer's needs, because of the customer's lack of readiness to effectively utilize the product, or because of other factors)?

Research into this question would likely be helpful for suppliers who are often wrestling with whether or not to capture the short-term benefits of acquiring a new customer while also considering the costs and risks associated with failing to successfully retain that customer.

Research Question (RQ9): What are the most effective data-driven models for Customer Health Scoring, and how should these models be used to manage the work of CSMPs?

The primary purpose of Customer Health Scoring is to serve as an early warning system to alert CSM leaders and CSMPs about potential customer risks so that problems can be identified and solved to prevent a customer deciding to terminate its relationship with a supplier. Current Customer Health Scoring models are typically driven by variables and weightings that are based on hypotheses and assumptions made primarily based on ad hoc historical observations and gut instinct. However, as more detailed longitudinal data continue to become available, the opportunities to build and validate models with demonstrably more predictive accuracy will continue to increase.

SUMMARY AND CONCLUSION

In this paper, we have sought to shine a light on the rapidly emerging new role and operational discipline of CSM. In particular, we have described the role of CSMPs, some of the challenges associated with effectively managing CSM teams, and a framework for creating successful customer outcomes that reflects the role of CSM functions within a broader system. We have also identified several research questions for service management scholars that are of great practical interest to those who are charged with leading and managing CSM teams.

The breadth and depth of these research questions reflects the fact that CSM is a relatively new functional area for which management practices are still evolving. As such, there is a clear need for objective research to help practitioners develop methodologies and standards that will guide and improve CSM and firm performance. Looking forward, the CSM domain provides many great opportunities for service operations researchers to make innovative and valuable contributions.

REFERENCES

Adams, R. (2020), *Practical Customer Success Management*, New York: Routledge.
Atkins, C., Gupta, S., and Roche, P. (2018), "Introducing Customer Success 2.0: The New Growth Engine," *McKinsey & Company Whitepaper*, https://www.mckinsey.com/industries/technology -media-and-telecommunications/our-insights/introducing-customer-success-2-0-the-new-growth -engine# (accessed January 4, 2021).
Cron, W.L., Marshall, G.W., Singh, J., Spiro, R.L., and Sujan, H. (2005), "Salesperson Selection, Training, and Development: Trends, Implications, and Research Opportunities," *Journal of Personal Selling and Sales Management*, 25(2), 123–136.
Customer Success Association (2021), "The Definition of Customer Success," https://www.custom ersuccessassociation.com/library/the-definition-of-customer-success/ (accessed January 4, 2021).
DeCarlo, T.E., and Lam, S.K. (2016), "Identifying Effective Hunters and Farmers in the Salesforce: A Dispositional–Situational Framework," *Journal of the Academy of Marketing Science*, 44, 415–439.
Eggert, A., Ulaga, W., and Gehring, A. (2020), "Managing Customer Success in Business Markets: Conceptual Foundation and Practical Application," *Journal of Service Management Research*, 4(2–3), 121–132.
Gainsight (2019), "The State of the Customer Success Profession 2019," https://info.gainsight.com/2019 -state-cs-profession-whitepaper.html (accessed January 4, 2021).

Hilton, B., Hajihashemi, B., Henderson, C.M., and Palmatier, R.W. (2020), "Customer Success Management: The Next Evolution in Customer Management Practice?" *Industrial Marketing Management*, 90, 360–369.

Hochstein, B., Rangarajan, D., Mehta, N., & Kocher, D. (2020a), "An Industry/Academic Perspective on Customer Success Management," *Journal of Service Research*, 23(1), 3–7.

Hochstein, B., Rangarajan, D., Nagel, D., Voorhees, C., Pratt, A., and Mehrotra, V. (2020b), "Delivering on the Promise of a New Marketing Function: The Role of Customer Success Management in Ensuring Customer Health and Firm Performance," Working Paper.

Homburg, C., Workman, Jr., J.P., and Jensen, O. (2002), "A Configurational Perspective on Key Account Management," *Journal of Marketing*, 66 (April), 38–60.

Mehrotra, V. (2018), "Customer Success Management," *Analytics*, March–April, https://pubsonline. informs.org/do/10.1287/LYTX.2018.02.07/full/ (accessed January 14, 2021).

Mehta, N., Steinman, D., and Murphy, L. (2016), *Customer Success*, Hoboken, NJ: John Wiley & Sons.

Pettey, C. (2018), "Moving to a Software Subscription Model," *Smarter with Gartner*, https://www. gartner.com/smarterwithgartner/moving-to-a-software-subscription-model/ (accessed January 4, 2021).

Subramanian, K., and Rangan, U.S. (2013), *Thriving in the 21st Century Economy*, New York: American Society of Mechanical Engineering Press (also available at https://stimsinstitute.com/ 20151207books/, accessed January 12, 2021).

Vaidyanathan, A., and Rabago, R. (2020), *The Customer Success Professionals Handbook*, Hoboken, NJ: John Wiley & Sons.

Zoltners, A.A., Sinha, P., & Lorimer, S.E. (2019), "What is a Customer Success Manager?" *Harvard Business Review*, 96(2), 1–5.

13. Culture and religion in service provision
Richard Metters

INTRODUCTION

A Korean Airlines pilot misjudged altitude while landing in Guam and ran his 747 into a mountain, killing 229. The cockpit voice recorder notes the First Officer telling the Captain that their landing equipment that helps determine altitude (the "glide slope") was malfunctioning long before landing. Yet, 30 seconds before the crash, the Captain asked, "Isn't the glide slope working?" As they were nearing their death, the First Officer, who likely realized they were about to crash, made the suggestion, "Let's make a missed approach" (abort the landing and try again). The third crew member in the cockpit, the Flight Engineer, concurred, saying the landing area was "not in sight." Time was running short. The First Officer again suggested a "missed approach." The Captain agreed to "go around," but he was too late (all quotes and descriptions from National Transportation Safety Board [NTSB] 2000).

Unfortunately, this was not an isolated incident. While Korean Air is now a safe airline, there was a time when it had problems. The "hull losses" (plane crashes resulting in destruction beyond repair) for Korean Air from 1989 to 1998 were 4.8 per 1 million departures. Comparatively, the hull losses of Delta, Northwest, United, and American Airlines totaled 0.2 per 1 million departures (NTSB 2000, p. 69). What made Korean Air 24 times worse than the other listed airlines combined? All pilots make mistakes. First Officers and Flight Engineers are supposed to correct those mistakes – but at Korean Air they didn't. The NTSB (2000) concluded that "the First Officer and Flight Engineer failed to properly monitor and/or challenge the Captain's performance, which was causal to the accident" (p. 175). A root cause is that "problems associated with subordinate officers challenging a Captain are well known … a challenge to a decision may be perceived as a direct challenge to the Captain's authority" (NTSB 2000, pp. 147–148). Why didn't the First Officer forcefully tell the Captain he was mistaken, or better yet, take control of the plane? National culture.

This cultural issue was noted in the Operations Management literature in Metters et al. (2010, p. 178):

> The primary reason attributed to the high loss rate was that subordinates to the Captain would not contradict the Captain at Korean Air, even though they believed the Captain's actions were dangerous. As one former Korean Air pilot puts it, "the Captain is in charge and does what he wants, when he likes, how he likes, and everyone else sits quietly and does nothing".

This is not peculiar to Korea. Helmreich and Merritt (1998) studied 9400 airline pilots in 19 countries. Some cultures have an extreme deference to authority: the captain is to be obeyed, not challenged. Accordingly, a worldwide training program termed Crew Resource Management (CRM) was instituted. CRM's goal was to help cockpit members appropriately challenge captains' actions. But culture can trump training. During a CRM training session, a Chinese pilot lost his temper and stated, "There are no circumstances when a first officer should challenge or disagree with the captain" (Helmreich and Merritt 1998, p. 187). Notably, China Airlines' plane loss rate from 1989 to 1998 was 11.7 – 2.5 times higher than that of Korean Air (NTBS 2000, p. 69).

This attitude of subservience to authority occurs in many cultures, over all industries, and is called "power distance" by cultural researchers (Hofstede 1984; House et al. 2004). Power distance is the extent to which the lower-ranking individuals of a society accept and expect that power is distributed unequally. It is extremely low in Nordic countries, high in China and many developing countries, and mid-range in the US. A high power distance is useful in making quick decisions, as a time-consuming consensus does not need to be sought, but it can be deadly in the service industry of transportation.

Let us now be equally alarmist about the effects of religion in services.

Consider the service sectors of journalism and education. In Christian nations, laws mandating torture or death for blasphemy (generally, insulting God) are now passé. The last execution for blasphemy in Great Britain was in 1697 (Graham 2008). The spirit now is "freedom of speech." In some Muslim countries, the spirit is "freedom of speech – except for religion." In these contexts, the penalty for blasphemy remains death (Uddin 2011). In France, for printing cartoons offensive to Islam, which was legal, 23 staff of the newspaper *Charlie Hebdo* were killed or injured by terrorists in 2015. In 2020, French schoolteacher Samuel Paty was beheaded for legally showing his students cartoons of the Prophet. These are not isolated experiences. In the workplace, religious clashes are far more likely to happen in services than non-services.

All service industry collisions with national culture and religion do not end in death; these cases are extreme. The point is that services are particularly prone to problems with national culture and religion. Most international trade in goods does not involve much person-to-person contact. There might be a negotiation between buyer/seller, but employee–employee or employee–customer contact between those of different cultures is rare. However, in hotels, restaurants, airlines, call centers, and other venues, inter-cultural/religious contact is common. For example, the average Christian living in Iowa may not speak to a Muslim for weeks. The percentage of Iowans adhering to "non-Christian faiths" is approximately 1 percent (Pew Research Center 2020). But if that Iowan calls an 800 number, the chance of speaking to a Hindu or Muslim increases sharply. If that Iowan travels internationally and utilizes hotels, restaurants, retail stores, and other businesses, the chances of inter-cultural/religious contact – and therefore the chances of misunderstandings – is far larger.

The potential problem of inter-cultural/religious issues in Service Operations is far higher now than at any point in history. In 1960, the international trade in services in the US was $6 billion, in 1990 it was $147 billion, and in 2019 it was $876 billion (Organisation for Economic Co-operation and Development 2020). There were 25 million international tourist arrivals worldwide in 1950 and 439 million in 1990; but in 2018 there were 1.4 billion (United Nations World Tourism Organization 2020). Many services today are still protected from international competition due to the need for customer contact – but that list of protected services was far larger in 1990. Services that are "electronically transmissible" are now open for foreign competition. The worldwide capacity for services now possibly coming from another culture tracks communications equipment capacity. In the mid-1960s, capacity limited telephone use between Europe and the US to 138 simultaneous calls (Metters et al. 2010). Fiberoptic cable technology revolutionized this. There was 1 GBPS (gigabyte per second) of cable capacity across the Atlantic Ocean in 1992; by 2014, Atlantic capacity was 16 000

GBPS (VisualCapitalist 2017). As a consequence of this, call centers for US customers are often in India or the Philippines. French customers are frequently handled in North Africa. These changes have increased the potential for inter-cultural/religious contact in electronically transmitted services.

While a deadly service encounter is rare, national culture and religion routinely ruin business plans and "kill" academic research. A quote from Voss et al. (2004) concerning their own Service Operations study says it well: "studies conducted in one country may not be generalizable to others because of national culture effects" (p. 214).

One point of this work is to change the notion of "generalizability" in Operations Management research. In theorem-proof, business-related research a business problem is reduced to mathematical expressions. Once the problem is translated mathematically, we agree that any solution to that mathematical expression will be a general one – but it is a "general" solution that has ignored "details" like culture and religion that may fundamentally undermine applicability. Speaking mathematically, ignoring culture and religion can lead to inappropriate objective functions and missing constraints. For survey research, "generalization" means that the results can be applied beyond the sample. There are a large number of statistical metrics to determine the probability of the sample representing the population. Our contention is that – sometimes – the notion of there being a single "population" is inappropriate. There do exist population means, but there are several distinct populations (cultures, religions), each with their own mean values, and mixing them is akin to stating the average color of paint is purple when one has five buckets each of red and blue paint. Consequently, false generalizations for Service Operations studies may occur.

In some cases, what is appropriate and leads to more predictive power is "generalizability of context." The argument is that context can be essential to external validity. Generalizability of context is a foundational premise of cultural anthropology as a field. At its core, generalizability refers to applying findings made in one case to others. The central idea is that cultural and religious knowledge confers predictive power across topic areas, rather than there being an inherent generalizability within a topic. The examples provided throughout this chapter are "obvious" to those steeped in the particular culture/religion – but unknown to the business executives that made corporate decisions without context knowledge.

National culture and religion are intertwined, but ultimately different. Where one religion dominates a country it may be difficult to parse them. But consider Nigeria: the population is roughly 50 percent Muslim, 50 percent Christian. India is the world's second largest Muslim nation in addition to being the world's largest Hindu nation. As will be discussed, even the Service Operations in Tel Aviv and Jerusalem, Israel, differ, given that the percentage of Ultra-Orthodox Jews is far different in those two locales.

From this point forward, the focus of this chapter is on specific cases that demonstrate the effect culture and religion have on Service Operations. The small extant literature is also reviewed. We divide the remaining pages in two sections: one dedicated to national culture, the subsequent to religion. The overall reasoning is inductive. That is, the many specific cases lead to a general point: culture and religion intertwine with Service Operations.

Lastly, please note that the author is a US citizen who was raised in the Christian tradition. This article cannot be free from author bias, and is written with a Western-centric viewpoint.

NATIONAL CULTURE AND SERVICE OPERATIONS

Two surveys point to the importance of national culture in Service Operations, both conducted in the heady days when it was thought that all electronically transmissible services not only could but should be offshored to exploit differential labor rates. Lewin and Peeters (2006) surveyed executives about the offshoring of Service Operations. The highest mentioned "risk of offshoring" was "quality of service," followed by "lack of cultural fit" in second place. In the Crane et al. (2007) survey, "culture problems" was the most cited "major problem" in Service Operations that were offshored.

In the next sub-section, we present specific examples of Service Operations having difficulty adapting to new cultures. Subsequently, the literature is reviewed. The remaining sub-sections are devoted to exploring topics that have not been researched widely, but may have great potential.

Examples of Culture and Operations Mismatches

Walmart long ago expanded internationally – but generally tried to keep the same processes as they had in the US. This caused them to abandon South Korea and Germany. In China, they faced interesting international differences. The CEO of Walmart China informed me during an interview that they first started by copying the US model. They wanted to "educate the customer." That failed. For example, in the US, "fresh meat" means meat wrapped in plastic under refrigeration. In China, "fresh" means "alive." Walmart faced an enormous number of differences in Service Operations that they were not expecting (e.g., Farhoomand 2006). The company claims its China operations finally became profitable after 12 years.

Home Depot tried to expand into China. Two Home Depot China CEOs stated in author interviews that the "do it yourself" mantra works with the individualist culture of the US, but Chinese customers wanted "do it for me." The cultural differences called for a complete revamp of the US-centric corporate strategy. Instead of stocking items for customer pickup, typical in US stores, only sample items were stocked, as Chinese customers tend to hire consultants to fit out the entire apartment at one time, rather than picking up individual items. Home Depot still failed, exiting the market after a decade of losses.

Ritz-Carlton is famous for empowering its lowest level of employees to solve customer problems immediately, even if it costs the hotel money. The expatriate GM of a China Ritz-Carlton told the author that his Chinese employees simply would not do that. This was consistent with interviews of restaurant and hotel executives throughout China: employee empowerment, and actively engaging Chinese employees in quality improvement, did not compare to US operations. It was claimed that the same Service Operation required more employees in China, as Chinese employees would do only what they were explicitly told. One hotel executive stated that there is a "kingdom" mentality: workers look to the boss for answers.

This aspect of the "too deferential" attitude also was prevalent in author interviews of expatriate American Airlines executives in a Barbados Business Process Offshoring initiative. Unlike their American counterparts, the Bajan employees simply refused to provide suggestions for improvements, thereby rendering moot their quality training. In the Bajan business culture, the boss is expected to fix processes. Suggestions by workers are viewed as rude and impertinent behavior.

An American expatriate working as a casino operator in Macau told the author that the dining table mix had to be changed for Chinese customers – fewer two- and four-tops, due to a higher percentage of communal dining. Therefore fewer restaurants/tables were needed. Customers came to gamble, not eat. As a result, the layout also had to be changed to incorporate more space between gaming tables, as large groups rush between tables when they find one that is "lucky." This made the casino's revenue management system unworkable. In the US, a pit boss notes the play of a customer who sits at the same table for some time. But Chinese customers dart from lucky table to lucky table – the pit bosses can't keep up. Chinese customers preferred table games to slot machines far more than Americans. Card dealers in the US need to engage customers, and customers like to drink alcohol while gambling. In Macau, the "friendly dealer" and omnipresent alcohol are simply not desired by the customer.

An important driving force for international trade in Service Operations is cost. The labor rate differentials remain substantial 30 years after the internet revolution allowed for electronically transmitted services to move across borders. In 2020 Indian call center employees are paid roughly $3600/year (Quora 2020), but US call center employees make an average of $28 000/year (Glassdoor 2020). This indicates that cultural interchange will only grow larger.

Prior Literature

The literature does not lack for research that documents the differences in Operations Management practices across the world. The Global Manufacturing Research Group (GMRG.org) lists 76 publications, and the International Manufacturing Strategy Survey (Manufacturingstrategy.net) lists 69 journal publications documenting differences. However, these groups are concerned with manufacturing, not services, and largely are not concerned with culture – just specific operational practices. Nonetheless, they provide abundant evidence of different operational practices across cultures.

A comprehensive review found 83 articles that are mainly concerned with national culture and Operations Management (Metters et al. 2019). Unfortunately, only eight of those 83 papers focused on Service Operations. Of the 83 articles, all but a few found that national culture makes a substantial difference in which Operations Management practices are used or a difference in the results gained from the same practices.

The eight manuscripts identified by Metters et al. (2019) as pertaining to national culture and focused on Service Operations are listed in Table 13.1. These eight should not be taken to be the only manuscripts in the literature on these topics. Whether a manuscript is classified as "Service Operations," "Service Marketing," or "Service Human Resources" is frequently in the eye of the beholder. Also, what rises to the level of being about national culture, versus simply mentioning national culture, is also open for disagreement.

The most common topic, encompassing over half the articles in Table 13.1, is one with great relevance to practice: the offshoring of services. The meta-conclusion from the five articles tackling this topic is that a Service Operation cannot be moved across national cultures without some processes not working as well, with some cultures being better adapted to offshoring than others. Most of these articles compared cultures, but Venkatesh et al. (2010) and Metters (2008) were studies of a single culture. Youngdahl et al. (2003) is the sole study found that claims national culture does not matter. However, it should be noted that their sample was 245 international graduate students from 40 countries, but who were all enrolled in two US univer-

Table 13.1 Articles focused on Service Operations and national culture

Authors	Journal*	Focus
Caniato et al. (2015)	IJPE	Service activities offshoring is investigated to understand what drives offshoring location choices, including cultural proximity
Hahn and Bunyaratavej (2010)	JOM	Countries with low uncertainty avoidance and high individualism (with partial support for high power distance) would attract more services offshoring projects. This was true for both Asian and Western firms
Metters (2008)	IJOPM	Study of the role of national culture on the decisions made during offshoring Service Operations. Local culture issues affect location: that is, which country and local site, total quality management (TQM) implementation, and use of night shifts. The paper emphasizes a "particularism" focus when it comes to cultural issues and concludes our bias toward "universalism" (trying to implement the same thing irrespective of context) that leads to failure
Pullman et al. (2001)	JOM	A single service unit simultaneously serving customers from multiple cultures is explored (a food court at an airport terminal that handles only international flights). Customers from different cultures arrived at different times (e.g., if the plane to Tokyo leaves at 10, Japanese customers are the major market from 8:30 to 9:30) Cultural differences in food choice and wait times were implemented in a time-sensitive adaptive service design that changed throughout the day depending on the customers present
Stringfellow et al. (2008)	JOM	Explored the "invisible costs" of offshoring service work. Theory only, no data
Venkatesh et al. (2010)	POM	Study of the effect of Information Technology (IT) implementation in one Indian bank. Implementation of IT, although enriching job characteristics, has an adverse effect on employee satisfaction and job performance. One of the reasons for this adverse effect is culture shock, especially the imposition of perceived Western cultural attributes through the IT system, with concurrent differences in the way people work together
Voss et al. (2004)	JSR	UK vs. US service quality. Executives interviewed in 130 firms primarily in financial services, retail, and hotels. Findings are that US and UK customers are equally responsive to good service, but UK customers are more tolerant of poor service. No specific service design changes proposed
Youngdahl et al. (2003)	JOM	Culture does not impact service satisfaction-seeking behaviors that include preparation, relationship building, exchange, and intervention. Relationship building needs the least effort and leads to highest satisfaction. Preparation and information exchange need more effort and result in lower levels of satisfaction. Intervention needs the most effort and has the lowest level of satisfaction. These findings were not different across cultures

Notes: *IJOPM: *International Journal of Operations and Production Management*; IJPE: *International Journal of Production Economics*; JOM: *Journal of Operations Management*; JSR: *Journal of Service Research*; POM: *Production and Operations Management*.

sities. The numerical findings were that, as customers, their behaviors did not correspond to Hofstede's (1984) cultural dimensions of the country they departed from.

Different service quality expectations between cultures are the subject of two studies in Table 13.1: Pullman et al. (2001) and Voss et al. (2004). There are several articles on the relationship between national culture and service quality that are not in Table 13.1, as they were considered more Marketing or Human Resources oriented, or did not investigate a specific operational change. Two examples demonstrate this point. Lee and Ulgado (1997) examined the differences in service expectations between Korean and US customers of McDonald's restaurants. But the respondents were students in their classes who happened to have gone to McDonald's, so no operational design changes were studied for that restaurant. Espinoza (1999) studied the cultural differences in response to service quality for supermarket customers in Quebec and Lima, Peru – but had no corresponding relationships with the supermarkets, and no actual operational aspects of the supermarkets were assessed. In sum, there is substantial work on national culture and service quality, far more than is cited here, but the relationship to Service *Operations* is tenuous.

Governmental Service and Corruption

Governmental service provision and national culture has not seen any attention in the Service Operations literature, though government spending is over 50 percent of gross domestic product (GDP) in many Western European countries and is 38 percent of GDP in the US (Trading Economics 2020). An element of government services that appears strongly related to national culture is corruption.

Governmental corruption is a massive problem worldwide. It is estimated that $120 billion in bribes were garnered by roughly 18 000 Chinese governmental officials who "took the money and ran," and fled the country from 1990 to 2010 (Haiguang 2011). It is possible that the single largest case of corruption was the $2.8 billion stolen by Zhang Shugang, Deputy Chief of the Minister of Railways in China. Mr. Zhang's crime was discovered when a bridge carrying a train collapsed, killing 40 and injuring 192. Bribes allowed the use of substandard materials (Beach 2012).

As a group, the governing body of Russia has been described as a "kleptocracy." That term has been applied to the governments of several countries. The main mission of the kleptocratic government is personal wealth accumulation, with actual governing an afterthought (Dawisha 2014). President Putin's net worth is estimated at $200 billion (Seun 2020).

Although bribes can certainly be paid through electronic means, cash is preferred. Corruption in India was so pervasive that in 2016 the government declared the two largest bills no longer legal tender, wiping out 80 percent of the physical monetary supply (Doshi 2016).

Several entities measure governmental corruption. We will focus on the "Corruption Index" of Transparency International (2020). Based on surveys of business people, a numerical score, called the Corruption Index, is given for each country for the overall expected amount of corruption.

Some national cultures are more accepting of corruption – or even encouraging of it – than others. There are two main measures of culture that have a high correlation with corruption: Individualism/Collectivism (e.g. Hofstede 1984, House et al. 2004) and Universalism/Particularism (Trompenaars and Hampden-Turner 1997). The raw correlations

Table 13.2   Comparison of corruption to cultural measures in selected countries

Country	Corruption Index (Lower = more corrupt)	Individualism/Collectivism (Lower = Collectivist)	Universalism/Particularism (Lower = Particularist)
United States	74	91	93
China	40	20	47
India	40	48	54
Russia	29	39	44
Venezuela	17	12	32
Overall correlation with corruption		0.67	0.72

of Individualism/Collectivism and Universalism/Particularism to the Corruption Index are 0.67 and 0.72, respectively. Some country examples are shown in Table 13.2.

Universalism/Particularism is a measure of the relative importance of rules versus relationships. A Universalist world view sees rules as sacrosanct. A Particularist sees rules as flexible, and relationships trump rules. To elucidate this spectrum, consider the following scenario from Trompenaars and Hampden-Turner (1997, pp. 33–34):

> You are riding in a car driven by a close friend. He hits a pedestrian. You know he was going at least 35 miles per hour in an area of the city where the maximum allowed speed is 20 miles per hour. There are no witnesses. His lawyer says that if you testify under oath that he was only driving 20 miles per hour it may save him from serious consequences. What right has your friend to expect you to protect him?
>
> 1a. My friend has a definite right as a friend to expect me to testify to the lower figure.
> 1b. He has some right as a friend to expect me to testify to the lower figure.
> 1c. He has no right as a friend to expect me to testify to the lower figure.
>
> What do you think you would do in view of the obligations of a sworn witness and the obligation to your friend?
>
> 1d. Testify that he was going 20 miles an hour.
> 1e. Not testify that he was going 20 miles an hour.

According to the researchers, a Particularist would answer A and D; a Universalist would answer C and E. The numbers in Table 13.2 are the percentages of respondents answering C and E. The response of a Particularist to this scenario is, why should some arbitrary speed limit set by some unknown person for unknown reasons ruin my friend's life? Each side believes the other to be acting immorally. In the paraphrased words of Trompenaars and Hampden-Turner (1997), an Individualist disparages a Collectivist by saying "you can't trust him, he only helps his friends." A Collectivist disparages an Individualist by saying "you can't trust him, he won't even help a friend."

A cultural scale named by both Hofstede (1984) and House et al. (2004) is called "Individualism/Collectivism." Individualism stands for a society in which the ties between individuals are loose: everyone is expected to look after themselves and their immediate family only. Collectivism stands for a society in which people from birth onward are integrated into strong, cohesive in-groups, which throughout people's lifetime continue to protect them in exchange for unquestioning loyalty (Hofstede, 1984, p. 197).

The link to corruption is, again, rules versus relationships. Collectivist societal relationships are more important than rules or laws, whereas in Individualist societies the "rule of law" takes precedence over relationships. Collectivist societies look more favorably upon in-group behavior such as nepotism and favoritism. Famously, "guanxi" – having influential relationships – is ubiquitously cited as highly important to business in China, and China (not coincidentally) has a major corruption problem.

The linkage of governmental corruption to these cultural metrics is merely a beginning. Detailed study of the relationship between national culture and corruption would be extremely practically helpful to firms, letting them know where to look for corruption and what form it might take.

Culture and Waiting Lines

The field of operations research has done an excellent job of calculating how long wait times will be. But a major difference between many (though not all) Manufacturing and Service Operations is that the actual wait time is not relevant: it is the perception of the wait that is important. This point has been clear to Operations Management researchers for decades. The "psychology of waiting" articles by Maister (1984) and Larson (1987) are staples in the Service Operations curriculum. Academic work on the differences between cultures and how they view and respond to time stretches as far back as Hall (1959).

Anyone who has traveled the world understands that the behavior in queues and the value attached to the time in queues varies tremendously by culture. The single-file, snaking lines seen in the UK are a stark contrast to the amorphous surge of tightly packed humanity that occurs in China. A running joke among Indian nationals is "Indian Standard Time," meaning that Indians will always arrive late to an event. As Gillam et al. (2014) write, "it is foolish to believe that all cultures perceive lines and waiting through the same lens" (p. 536).

Despite this cultural awareness, cross-cultural service design to address the differences in felt experience is lacking. Gillam et al. (2014) discuss cultural waiting line differences, but in very broad strokes, such as "Asians ... may be less concerned with duration of a wait than by their place/position in line," or for waiting customers in Asia "shade is more important than air conditioning" (p. 537). "Asia" is quite a large and diverse continent. A tad more specificity is given by a qualitative study of 19 expatriates living in Spain, ruminating on how the waiting experience in Spain is different than in their home countries (del Mar Pàmies et al. 2016). More quantitatively, Rose et al. (2003) studied the comparative effect of Web download times in the US, Finland, Egypt, and Peru. However, the range of waiting was only 15–90 seconds, and the test subjects were students in a lab.

Anderson and Brodowsky (2001) mailed surveys to consumers in the US, Mexico, and Thailand and asked the respondents to recall waiting in grocery stores, banks, and medical offices. They found minor differences in expectations about what a reasonable wait is.

In summary, as del Mar Pàmies et al. (2016) note, "despite three decades of academic research on waiting in services, we know little about how consumers wait across cultures or the potential services marketing implications of such differences" (p. 429). We intrinsically understand that there are differences in cultures and their acceptance of waiting. We know that these differences make a service design that works well in one culture inappropriate or destructive in another culture. However, the literature currently has little advice to provide practitioners who want to expand their business operations internationally.

RELIGION AND SERVICE OPERATIONS

The religious beliefs of either customers or employees can severely alter Service Operations. This is plainly obvious in many contexts that surprise no one: retailers in the US need extra employees and extensive overtime during the Christmas season. Not so much in Saudi Arabia. However, this difference is irrelevant, as no firm would make the mistake of not knowing there is a Christmas season when setting up US retail operations. Here, the focus is on religious differences that are not as apparent.

Home Depot offshored its call center to India. English-speaking employees were needed to field US calls. In India, fluent English speakers with acceptable accents for call centers tend to be from the Brahmin caste due to their educational opportunities. While officially outlawed, "hundreds of millions are held back by a deeply entrenched caste system that refuses to go away" (Friary 2020) and is often associated with Hindu religious traditions. However, Brahmins generally do not use or have any knowledge of Home Depot's products. If such work is to be done, they hire it out. From a caste point of view, that is not appropriate work for a Brahmin. As a Brahmin student of the author once put it, that work "would be beneath me." So, the call center workers had no product knowledge nor the desire to acquire it. The call center was quickly recalled (Metters 2019).

Other business disciplines have journals dedicated to religious differences, such as the *Journal of Islamic Finance*, the *Journal of Islamic Marketing*, and the *Journal of Islamic Accounting and Business Research*. In Service Operations, however, religion is ignored. A literature review has generated only one article, Metters (2019), and that article explores both manufacturing and Service Operations, rather than focusing on the latter.

While there are many examples of Service Operations differences due to religion, for the sake of brevity the focus hereafter is on two: gender segregation and healthcare.

Gender Segregation and Service Operations

The religious difference with perhaps the widest application in Service Operations is gender segregation and the highly related practice of social prohibitions on women. A tourist in Jerusalem would easily note the "women only" and "men only" sections of the world-famous "wailing wall" (or Western Wall). Reformed Jews do not require gender segregation, but Ultra-Orthodox Jews do. In areas with strong Ultra-Orthodox populations, there are many gender-segregated areas. Historically, Service Operations such as grocery stores, banks, and so on had either separate operating times for women and men or separate entrances and waiting lines (Shapira-Rosenberg 2010).

Transportation systems are sometimes affected by gender segregation as well. As late as the 1990s there were separate public bus lines in two Israeli cities – one for women and children, one for men. On commercial airline flights it is not uncommon for Ultra-Orthodox Jewish men to refuse to take their seat if they are seated next to a woman (e.g., Sherwood 2020).

Similarly, gender segregation is practiced in certain Muslim countries. For example, in some areas the rules of gender segregation mean that there is a small area in the front of public buses reserved for women. If that area is full, women cannot board the bus. This has the effect of rendering public bus transportation to employment difficult. In some areas, this causes women to seek out only positions that they are able to walk to.

The religious rules of gender segregation can effectively prohibit women from working in places where they might mix with men. Consider the following Islamic fatwa:

> It is permissible for a woman to go out of her house for work, but that is subject to certain conditions. If they are met, it is permissible for her to go out … The work should be suited to the nature of women, such as medicine, nursing, teaching, sewing, and so on. The work should be in a place that is only for women, and there should be no mixing with non-mahram men [note: "non-mahram men" are usually close relatives who must escort a woman when she is outside the home]. Her work should not lead to her travelling without a mahram. Her going out to work should not involve committing any haram [prohibited] action, such as being alone with the driver. (Al-Munajjid 2018)

While it is possible to have an all-women workforce in a factory to avoid this, this is very difficult to obey in the service sector where there is customer contact. Essentially, obeying this dictum would prohibit women from being employed in retail, banking, and other sectors. For example, in a study of 333 small retail stores in Morocco, not a single female employee, manager, or owner was found (Boulaksil et al. 2014).

Some societies have historically made it difficult for women to work at night. This is a mixture of culture and religion (Metters 2017). In short, female night work is against the law or, if legal, still socially inappropriate in several countries. Operational accommodations are expensive. In India, call centers catering to US and UK customers are, by nature, busy at night. It is socially inappropriate for women employees to drive themselves to work or take a taxi by themselves. To be out at night, they must be picked up by company vans. If a woman is the first to be picked up or last to be dropped off, this adds considerable time to her shift. Of course, operating a fleet of vans is also expensive for the firm.

Religion and Medical Services

Medical protocols can differ depending on the religious beliefs of the patient. An important case in point: there are nearly 9 million Jehovah's Witnesses globally (JW.org 2020). This particular religious sect does not allow blood transfusions. Service Operations are, of course, very different when blood transfusions cannot take place. There are many differences, but these few provide a flavor. Starting a month or more before an operation, "blood doping" is employed – taking blood from the patient, rather than relying on the transfused blood of others. The operating room is different: the patient is warmed and may wear a thermal suit, and the operating room temperature is recommended to be 81 degrees. The patient does not lay flat on the table. The body part operated on is physically elevated. The surgical team is larger, as minimizing time is a goal (Nalla et al. 2012; Rosengart et al. 1997). Despite this rather large change in procedures, outcomes appear to be similar to when transfusions are used (Marinakis et al. 2016; Vasques et al. 2016).

The list of specialized issues for different groups is not short. Amish generally will not allow heart surgery. Many pills have gelatin-based capsules so that they dissolve in the stomach, not the mouth. Unfortunately, gelatin contains the ingredient stearic acid from pork, so it is prohibited by Muslims. Gender segregation plays a role. Another Islamic fatwa: "a female doctor treats women and a male doctor treats men, and similarly in education. However, that a man treats a woman or vice versa, this is by no means allowed by shari'ah [Islamic law]" (Baz 2018). Consequently, staffing at hospitals is affected. Further, there are rules to follow if that fatwa cannot be observed for which a medical facility must be prepared.

For in-patients, hospitals and psychiatric facilities face religiously oriented diet problems. Meals must be kosher or halal for certain customers. Sikhs eat only certain types of meat (*jhatka*). Jains are lactovegetarians. If improper food is provided, patients will sometimes simply not eat and will not complain, so medical care suffers (Dawson 2011).

The subject of medicine and religion is the *raison d'être* of the academic journals *Journal of Religion and Health* and *Journal of Spirituality in Health Care*. The goal is to practice medicine that will be accepted by the patient. There are clearly different Service Operations practices and contingencies that could be investigated, and research that could provide practical guidance.

CONCLUSION

Earlier, the anecdote about Home Depot offshoring their call center was provided as an example of cultural clash. At the time the offshoring occurred, fellow business school faculty who were from India simply laughed. To them, the offshoring was so inappropriate and obviously doomed to fail that they thought it was a joke. Anyone with context knowledge could have helped Home Depot avoid this expensive mistake. That is, generalizability of context, rather than subject (e.g., location, quality) was more important.

The field of national culture and religion in Service Operations is wide open for research, as so little has been done. The specific areas highlighted here are merely the tip of the iceberg. However, I believe it is particularly worthwhile to pursue them. The offshoring of services is frequently done incorrectly and costs firms tens of billions of dollars per year. Unfortunately, government corruption is also valued at tens of billions per year, and research might guide businesses into better methods of minimizing it. The topics of culturally dependent waiting time and religiously dependent healthcare services also call out for further study.

REFERENCES

Al-Munajjid, A. (2018). *Islam question and answer.* https://islamqa.info/en/106815 (accessed October 5, 2018).

Anderson, B. B., & Brodowsky, G. (2001). A cross-cultural study of waiting as a satisfaction driver in selected service encounters. *Journal of East-West Business*, 7(1), 11–36.

Baz, I. (2018). *Fatwas of Ibn Baz.* https://abdurrahman.org/tag/fatwas-of-ibn-baz/ (accessed December 11, 2020).

Beach, S. (2012, October 15). Boss rail: How the Wenzhou crash exposed corruption in China. *China Digital Times.* https://chinadigitaltimes.net/2012/10/boss-rail-how-the-wenzhou-crash-exposed -corruption-in-china/

Boulaksil, Y., Fransoo, J., Blanco, E., & Koubida, S. (2014). *Small traditional retailers in emerging markets* (Beta Working Paper series 460).

Caniato, F., Elia, S., Luzzini, D., Piscitello, L., & Ronchi, S. (2015). Location drivers, governance model and performance in service offshoring. *International Journal of Production Economics*, 163, 189–199.

Crane, D., Stachura, J., Dalmat, S., King-Metters, K., & Metters, R. (2007). International sourcing of services: The "Homeshoring" alternative. *Service Business*, 1(1), 79–91.

Dawisha, K. (2014). *Putin's kleptocracy: Who owns Russia?* Simon & Schuster.

Dawson, J. (2011). *Religion in medicine.* Xlibris Corporation.

del Mar Pàmies, M., Ryan, G., & Valverde, M. (2016). Uncovering the silent language of waiting. *Journal of Services Marketing*, 30(4), 427–436.

Doshi, V. (2016, November 8). India withdraws 500 and 1000 rupee notes in effort to fight corruption. *The Guardian.* https://www.theguardian.com/world/2016/nov/08/india-withdraws-500-1000-rupee -notes-fight-corruption

Espinoza, M. M. (1999). Assessing the cross-cultural applicability of a service quality measure: A comparative study between Quebec and Peru. *International Journal of Service Industry Management, 10*(5), 449–468.

Farhoomand, A. (2006). *Wal-Mart Stores: "Every Day Low Prices" in China.* Asia Case Research Centre, University of Hong Kong.

Friary, H. (2020, March 22). English language impact on the Indian caste system. https://sites.psu.edu/ global/2020/03/22/english-language-impacts-on-the-indian-caste-system/

Gillam, G., Simmons, K., Stevenson, D., & Weiss, E. (2014). Line, line, everywhere a line: Cultural considerations for waiting-line managers. *Business Horizons, 57*(4), 533–539.

Glassdoor. (2020). https://www.glassdoor.com/Salaries/call-center-representative-salary-SRCH_KO0 .26.htm (accessed November 18, 2020).

Graham, M. F. (2008). *Blasphemies of Thomas Aikenhead: Boundaries of belief on the eve of the Enlightenment.* Edinburgh University Press.

Hahn, E. D., & Bunyaratavej, K. (2010). Services cultural alignment in offshoring: The impact of cultural dimensions on offshoring location choices. *Journal of Operations Management, 28*(3), 186–193.

Haiguang, X. (2011, June 23). Corruption in China: How public officials took $120 billion, and ran. *Worldcrunch.* https://worldcrunch.com/world-affairs/corruption-in-china-how-public-officials-took -120-billion-and-ran/c1s3355

Hall, E. (1959). *The silent language.* Anchor Books.

Helmreich, R. L., & Merritt, A. C. (1998). *Culture at work: National, organizational, and professional influences.* Ashgate.

Hofstede, G. (1984). *Culture's consequences: International differences in work-related values.* SAGE.

House, R. J., Hanges, P. J., Javidan, M., Dorfman, P. W., & Gupta, V. (Eds.) (2004). *Culture, leadership, and organizations: The GLOBE study of 62 societies.* SAGE.

JW.org. (2020). *Jehovah's Witnesses.* https://www.jw.org/en/ (accessed December 3, 2020).

Larson, R. C. (1987). OR forum—perspectives on queues: Social justice and the psychology of queueing. *Operations Research, 35*(6), 895–905.

Lee, M., & Ulgado, F. M. (1997). Consumer evaluations of fast-food services: a cross-national comparison. *Journal of Services Marketing.*

Lewin, A., & Peeters, C. (2006). The top-line allure of offshoring. *Harvard Business Review, 84*(3), 22–23.

Maister, D. H. (1984). *The psychology of waiting lines.* Harvard Business School.

Marinakis, S., van der Linden, P., Tortora, R., Massaut, J., Pierrakos, C., & Wauthy, P. (2016). Outcomes from cardiac surgery in Jehovah's Witness patients: Experience over twenty-one years. *Journal of Cardiothoracic Surgery, 11*(1), 67.

Metters, R. (2008). A case study of national culture and offshoring services. *International Journal of Operations and Production Management, 28*(8), 727–747.

Metters, R. (2017). Gender and Operations Management. *Cross Cultural & Strategic Management, 24*(2), 350–364.

Metters, R. (2019). The effect of employee and customer religious beliefs on business operating decisions. *Religions, 10*(8), 479.

Metters, R., Marshall, D., & Pagell, M. (2019). *Cultural research in the production and operations management field.* Now Foundations and Trends.

Metters, R., Zhao, X., Bendoly, E., Jiang, B., & Young, S. (2010). "The way that can be told of is not an unvarying way": Cultural impacts on Operations Management in Asia. *Journal of Operations Management, 28*(3), 177–185.

Nalla, B. P., Freedman, J., Hare, G. M. T., & Mazer, C. D. (2012). Update on blood conservation for cardiac surgery. *Journal of Cardiothoracic and Vascular Anesthesia, 26*(1), 117–133.

National Transportation Safety Board. (2000). *Aircraft incident report, controlled flight into terrain, Korean Air Flight 801.* https://www.ntsb.gov/investigations/AccidentReports/Reports/AAR0001.pdf

Organisation for Economic Co-operation and Development. (2020). Trade in services. https://data.oecd .org/trade/trade-in-services.htm

Pew Research Center. (2020). *Religious Landscape Study: Adults in Iowa.* https://www.pewforum.org/ religious-landscape-study/state/iowa/

Pullman, M. E., Verma, R., & Goodale, J. (2001). Service design and operations strategy formulation in multicultural markets. *Journal of Operations Management, 19*(2), 239–254.

Quora. (2020). *How much do call centre employees in India earn on an average?* https://www.quora .com/How-much-do-call-centre-employees-in-India-earn-on-an-average (accessed November 18, 2020).

Rose, G. M., Evaristo, R., & Straub, D. (2003). Culture and consumer responses to Web download time: a four-continent study of mono and polychronism. *IEEE Transactions on Engineering Management, 50*(1), 31–44.

Rosengart, T. K., Helm, R. E., DeBois, W. J., Garcia, N., Krieger, K. H., & Isom, O. W. (1997). Open heart operations without transfusion using a multimodality blood conservation strategy in 50 Jehovah's Witness patients: Implications for a "bloodless" surgical technique. *Journal of the American College of Surgeons, 184*(6), 618–629.

Seun, A. (2020, June 18). How Vladimir Putin achieved a net worth of about $200 billion. *Just Richest.* https://justrichest.com/vladimir-putin-net-worth-billion/ (accessed November 25, 2020).

Shapira-Rosenberg, R. (2010). *Excluded, for God's sake: Gender segregation and the exclusion of women in public space in Israel.* Israel Religious Action Center.

Sherwood, H. (2020, August 27). Passenger sues EasyJet after crew told her to move seats to satisfy ultra-Orthodox Jews. *The Guardian.* https://www.theguardian.com/business/2020/aug/27/woman -sues-easyjet-after-being-told-to-move-seats-due-to-ultra-orthodox-jewish-men

Stringfellow, A., Teagarden, M. B., & Nie, W. (2008). Invisible costs in offshoring services work. *Journal of Operations Management, 26*(2), 164–179.

Trading Economics. (2020). *Government spending to GDP by country.* https://tradingeconomics.com/ country-list/government-spending-to-gdp (accessed November 23, 2020).

Transparency International. (2020). *Corruption Perceptions Index.* https://www.transparency.org/en/cpi (accessed December 11, 2020).

Trompenaars, F., & Hampden-Turner, C. (1997). *Riding the waves of culture.* Nicholas Brealey Publishing.

Uddin, A. T. (2011). Blasphemy laws in Muslim-majority countries. *Review of Faith & International Affairs, 9*(2), 47–55.

United Nations World Tourism Organization. (2020). *Tourism.* https://ourworldindata.org/tourism (accessed 18 November 18, 2020).

Vasques, F., Kinnunen, E. M., Pol, M., Mariscalco, G., Onorati, F., & Biancari, F. (2016). Outcome of Jehovah's Witnesses after adult cardiac surgery: Systematic review and meta-analysis of comparative studies. *Transfusion, 56*(8), 2146–2153.

Venkatesh, V., Bala, H., & Sykes, T. A. (2010). Impacts of information and communication technology implementations on employees' jobs in service organizations in India: A multi-method longitudinal field study. *Production and Operations Management, 19*(5), 591–613.

VisualCapitalist. (2017). *Submarine cable network, 2015.* https://www.visualcapitalist.com/wp-content/ uploads/2017/08/submarine-cables-full.html (accessed February 26, 2019).

Voss, C. A., Roth, A., Rosenzweig, E., Blackmon, K., & Chase, R. (2004). A tale of two countries' conservatism, service quality, and feedback on customer satisfaction. *Journal of Service Research, 6*(3), 212–230.

Youngdahl, W. E., Kellogg, D. L., Nie, W., & Bowen, D. E. (2003). Revisiting customer participation in service encounters: Does culture matter? *Journal of Operations Management, 21*(1), 109–120.

14. Are tech-savvy users more likely to use technology? An examination of market entry and customer experience

Xin Ding

THEORETICAL BACKGROUND

Intention to Use

Intention to use derives from the theory of reasoned action (TRA) literature (Fishbein and Ajzen, 1975), which was further linked to actual behavior in the theory of planned behavior (TPB; Ajzen, 1991). TRA suggests that external variables, such as personal values or beliefs about the broader work environment, should directly affect beliefs that lead to specific intentions. TPB posits that individual behavior is driven by behavioral intentions where behavioral intentions are a function of an individual's attitude toward the behavior, the subjective norms surrounding the performance of the behavior, and the individual's perception of the ease with which the behavior can be performed (behavioral control). As suggested by Nicolaou and McKnight (2006), much of the work in TRA has focused on two key beliefs—perceived usefulness and ease of use—and their antecedents. However, other variables, such as personal beliefs in technology and actual elicited experience of the technology, may also predict intention to use (Ding et al., 2007; Sussman and Gifford, 2019; Tsikriktsis, 2004).

The notion of technology readiness (TR) captures people's propensity to embrace and use new technologies for accomplishing goals in home life and work (Hoyer et al., 2020; Parasuraman, 2000; Parasuraman and Colby, 2001). Through telephone interviews with a UK sample, Tsikriktsis (2004) found that TR-based segments differ in terms of their current use and intention to use technology-based services, including mobile phones, text messages, automated teller machines, phone banking, and online purchases. An early study by Curran et al. (2003) also found that overall attitudes toward self-service technologies are related to intentions to use technology-based services, such as automated telephone banking and online banking. The above findings suggest that scholars need to expand their research scope pertaining to intention to use by examining other personal values and beliefs, such as technology beliefs.

The literature on service dominant logic considers services as the application of various competences to serve another entity. During the service process, the creation of the services involves not only the "producer" or service providers, but also the "consumer." Specifically, consumers announce their preferences and actively engage in service activities to co-deliver service outcomes. As a result, the focus should shift from output-oriented models to a process-oriented logic by emphasizing value-in-use. As suggested by Merz et al. (2009), delivering value-in-use requires a thorough understanding of the complex networks in dynamic service ecosystems. Furthermore, understanding how consumers interact with the service systems and encounter various technical challenges and information flows could cast new light on potential ways to improve service design.

Technology Readiness

TR refers to people's propensity to embrace and use new technologies for accomplishing goals in home life and at work. As a multidimensional psychological construct, TR consists of four major components measuring various technology beliefs. The first two components of optimism and innovativeness are contributors that increase an individual's TR. The other two components of discomfort and insecurity are inhibitors that suppress an individual's TR. Briefly, optimism is a positive view of technology and a belief that it offers people increased control, flexibility, and efficiency in their lives. Innovativeness is a tendency to be a technology pioneer and thought leader, which measures the extent to which an individual believes that they are at the forefront of trying out new technology-based products/services. Next, discomfort refers to a perceived lack of control over technology and a feeling of being overwhelmed by it, which captures the extent to which people have a general paranoia toward technology-based products and services. Finally, insecurity is a distrust of technology and skepticism about its ability to work correctly. This facet focuses on specific aspects of comfort with technology-based transactions rather than on a lack of comfort with technology in general (Parasuraman and Colby, 2001).

These four facets of TR measure different aspects of people's beliefs in technology and are independent of each other, such that an individual can possess any combination of motivations or inhibitions. Based on the various combinations of positive and negative beliefs regarding technology, customers can be segmented into five distinct groups: Explorers, Pioneers, Skeptics, Paranoids, and Laggards (Parasuraman and Colby, 2001). These five customer segments are distinct not only in their beliefs about technology but also in their perspectives on life and their demographic composition. Each segment plays a distinct role in moving a new technology-based product to maturity, and enters the market at various stages with different agendas.

First, Explorers are highly motivated and fearless. They are extremely high in TR, ranking higher on drivers and lower on inhibitors of adoption. They are an easy group to attract when a new technology is introduced. Consequently, they will comprise the first wave of customers. The next to arrive are Pioneers, who desire the benefits of the new frontier but are more practical about the difficulties and dangers. They share the optimism and innovative tendencies of the Explorers, but they have a certain degree of discomfort and insecurity. The next wave consists of two groups: Skeptics, who need to be convinced of the benefits of settling the frontier, and Paranoids, who are convinced of the fruits but unusually concerned about the risks. Skeptics are dispassionate and do not believe strongly in technology; they also lack any desire for pure innovation. However, they do not loathe technology; rather, their level of optimism is slightly below the market average. Further, Skeptics lack inhibition, ranking low in discomfort and insecurity. Paranoids are optimistic about technology but lack a tendency to innovate. In addition, they exhibit a high degree of discomfort and insecurity. The last group, Laggards, is the opposite of Explorers, ranking lower in motivation and higher in inhibition than the market as a whole. Laggards are the last group to adopt new technology. Indeed, they may do so only because they have no choice.

The TR typology provides a useful way to segment customers into distinct groups based on their technology beliefs, which can be further extended to access usability evaluations (Massey et al., 2007) and final usage (Tsikriktsis, 2004). According to Massey et al. (2007), beliefs in technology form the foundations for expectations of how things should work out and how specific online service interfaces are evaluated. However, their empirical study with 160 participants suggested that TR customer segments do not have a significant main effect on usability evaluations. On the contrary, Tsikriktsis (2004) tested and extended the taxonomy of TR (Parasuraman and Colby, 2001) with a UK sample and claimed that the current usage and future intention to use technology-based services differ across TR segments. The sample statistics and relevant analysis from both studies implied that technology beliefs might or might not affect usability assessment, and actual usage depends on the site type and access method.

Although the TR typology and relevant research cast light on customizing service offerings based on technology beliefs and market needs, very few attempts have been made to resolve the inconsistency between technology belief and usability assessment or usage. The marketing literature suggests that new product/service adoption is highly correlated with consumer innovativeness (Im et al., 2007). However, the focus on innovativeness does not consider other technology beliefs. Assuming the site type (e.g., hedonic vs. utilitarian) mainly affects usability evaluations (Massey et al., 2007), what might contribute to our understanding of the usage patterns across TR customer segments on the same type of websites? Specifically, should we expect the motivated and fearless customers (e.g., Explorers) to rate technology favorably and tend to use it more, while unmotivated and inhibited customers (e.g., Laggards) are likely to rate technology unfavorably and tend to use it less? With these considerations in mind, our first two hypotheses are:

H1: TR segments differ in their intention to use a technology-based service.

H2: TR segments with higher technology beliefs demonstrate stronger future intention to use a technology-based service.

Market Entry

Similar to customer typology, companies can also be segmented into different clusters based on their entry into the market, namely, first entrant, Pioneer, early follower, and late entrant. To differentiate terminologies in market entry and TR, we use lowercase letters to present groups of companies based on their market entries. Traditionally, scholars have agreed that first-movers or Pioneers in the industry gain a competitive advantage over followers, which is based on the assumption that they possess an appropriate set of resources and a strategy that aligns those resources effectively (Gomez et al., 2019; Kerin et al., 1992; Lieberman and Montgomery, 1988).

However, the first-mover advantage is not guaranteed (White, 1983). As the entrant resources (e.g., goodwill and shared marketing) for the first entrant and the Pioneer are generally scarce compared to those of the early follower and the late entrant (Robinson and Fornell, 1985; Robinson et al., 1992), half of the pioneering efforts end in failure (Golder and Tellis, 1993). Instead, research and theory suggest that followers may achieve superior performance when there are significant shifts in technology or customer needs, the cost of imitations are low, Pioneers are slow to change, or scope economies are high (Carpenter and Nakamoto, 1990; Kerin et al., 1992; Lieberman and Montgomery, 1988).

From a new product/service design perspective, high-tech markets are highly volatile due to the rapidly changing technological conditions, shorter life cycle, increasing competition, and continually evolving expectations of customers (Davidow, 1986; Doyle and Saunders, 1985). In addition, high-tech companies frequently rely on a product focus (Dugal and Schroeder, 1995; Marcus and Segal, 1989) driven by innovations in technology rather than by the needs of the customer, which also leads to possible failure in launching new products/services. Rosen et al. (1998) presented three case studies (Philips's CD-I, Apple's Newton, Sony's NetaMax) to explain the failure of high-tech companies to successfully adopt a customer focus. Their study concluded that the nature of high-tech markets makes it essential to provide a "complete product" by identifying the "voice of the customer" and exploiting the innovators and early adopters (e.g., Pioneers and Explorers). Both the limited access to resources and the product-focus strategy might lead the first entrant and the Pioneer into a dilemma where the company can barely secure the necessary resources to sustain its own growth and it fails to reach the right customers with the right product/service (Rosen et al., 1998). Consequently, the very early customers (Explorers), who are extremely sophisticated and product/service savvy, might experience frustration and are likely to discontinue their interaction with the first entrant, regardless of the level of motivation toward new technology. Instead, the early follower and the late entrant can adapt to changes in customer tastes and purchasing patterns and dominate the market with equivalent or countervailing resources (Castro and Chrisman, 1995).

The volatility in the high-tech market may expose both the first entrant and Explorers to a higher level of risks. The product-focus design and first-to-market strategy might undermine customer expectations, miss the target market, and fail to fulfill promises made in promotion (Rosen et al., 1998). Consequently, Explorers, though highly motivated with the new technology, might turn down the offerings from the first entrant and/or the Pioneer and turn to other alternatives. In this case, it is unlikely for Explorers to rate the usability favorably or continue to use the product/service. In contrast, when Laggards enter the market with low motivation and high inhibition, they are likely to experience a variety of well-designed, easy-to-use, and valuable products/services, and end up being satisfied and loyal customers. Under such a condition, the studies by Massey et al. (2007) and Tsikriktsis (2004) are insufficient to explain the disruption between technology belief and usability evaluation and usage. Based on the above discussion, we propose that:

H3: Market entry directly affects intention to use.

H4: Market entry moderates the relationship between TR segments and intention to use.

Flow Experience

Technology, especially the technology embedded in human–computer interaction, can be viewed as a type of experience (McCarthy and Wright, 2005), which generally consists of interactions with emotional, intellectual, and sensual aspects. Major technology breakthroughs like the personal computer and the Internet enhanced efficiencies and productivity and changed individuals' lifestyles. For instance, technology advancement in the financial service industry led to over 65% of US citizens switching from brick-and-mortar to online banking and online stock trading. In this way, we don't just use technology—we experience it and live with it (McCarthy and Wright, 2005). As our economy is evolving from a predominant service orientation to one that focuses more on experience (Pine and Gilmore, 1999), it is critical to integrate experience into the service design process and provide services by appealing to customers with different technology beliefs. Relevant research and reports suggest that experience design effectively attracts customers using new technology. Customers enjoy a series of memorable events, engage themselves personally, leave with compelling experience, and return again and again. Studies in online financial services have suggested that customer experience is the major antecedent of attitude and satisfaction in online stock trading services (Ding et al., 2007). Online experience management is also gaining greater attention from marketing decision-makers and was ranked among the top priorities by marketing executives.[1]

In the service economy, when a customer pays for a service, they are purchasing a set of service activities carried out on their behalf. On the other hand, when a customer pays for an experience, they pay to spend time enjoying a series of memorable events that a provider stages—as in a theoretical play—to engage them in a personal way. This transition has created a paradigm shift that demands effective customer experience design and management from firms. Highly celebrated examples include value creation through enjoyment and memorability by Walt Disney, the Hard Rock Cafe, and casinos on the Strip in Las Vegas. Technology can also be experienced in an online environment, including virtual societies on SecondLife.com, Webkinz.com, and Barbie.com. Because experience design originated and has been studied almost exclusively in entertainment and hospitality businesses, investigations of how technology beliefs elicit actual experience and customer satisfaction in online financial services have been sparse.

In this study, we examine how flow experience varies across technology users and how the variation affects satisfaction and further usage in online stock trading services. The construct of flow experience has been studied in a wide range of service contexts, including sports, work, education, shopping, and information systems. Csikszentmihalyi (1991) reported that flow experiences exist in various service contexts and that an optimum state of flow or "autotelic experience" is engaged when there is a clear set of goals requiring an appropriate response, when feedback is immediate, and when a person's skills are fully involved in overcoming a high but manageable challenge. Only when these three conditions are satisfied does a customer's attention become ordered and fully engaged. Autotelic experience is also analyzed by Ghani and Deshpande (1994), who explored important task characteristics and optimal flow experiences in human–computer interaction. According to their analysis and empirical findings, flow can be determined by a customer's sense of being in control and the level of challenges perceived in using a system or the services it supports.

A review of prior studies suggests a focus on flow channel segmentation models or segment flow channels on the basis of desirable congruence of skills and challenges (LeFevre, 1988). Past studies applied the flow structure (Csikszentmihalyi, 1991) to describe human–computer interaction (Ghani and Deshpande, 1994; Huffman et al., 1996). Novak et al. (2000) further extended the construct of flow by conceptualizing flow on the Web as a cognitive state experienced during navigation that is jointly determined by skills, control, challenge and arousal, focused attention, interactivity, and telepresence. They found that online experiences are significantly associated with consumers' assessments and behaviors. Korzaan (2003) combined the flow construct and the TRA (Ajzen, 1991) and showed the psychological state of flow to be an important independent variable that influences Web exploratory behaviors and attitudes toward online purchases.

We adopt the flow construct conceptualized by Novak et al. (2000) and postulate that flow experiences in online stock trading are captured by essential cognitive states that include skills, control, challenge, focused attention, and interactivity. Our study responds to the call by Roth and Menor (2003) to examine customer experience on the basis of experience design, delivery, and performance measurement. This chapter fills the research void of few empirical examinations of design choices and contingencies, which affect customer experiences created by different servicescapes (Bitner, 1992), by investigating flow experience in online stock trading services and how they affect customer satisfaction and loyalty across customer segments. Therefore, we hypothesize:

H5: Customer experience directly affects intention to use.

H6: Customer experience moderates the relationship between TR segments and intention to use.

RESEARCH METHODOLOGY

We operationalized each investigated construct using five-point Likert scales (from "1" strongly disagree to "5" strongly agree). To examine the relationship between each investigated construct and intention to use, we collected relevant customer Web usage variables and appropriate scales commonly used by prior research. Specifically, items measuring flow experience were adopted from Novak et al. (2000) and Korzaan (2003). The TR measurements were adopted from Parasuraman and Colby (2001). The market entry construct was obtained through examining the entry time of each individual financial service company. The preliminary instrument was first pilot-tested for comprehensiveness and clarity, following the recommendation by Churchill (1979). Second, the face validity was assessed by an expert panel of 15 experienced business researchers and ten experienced online investors. Third, after a small-scale pretest with 35 students, the survey instruments were also pretested with a large-scale study of 230 financial service users to check the psychometric properties of the measurement scales. Following these pretests, we refined and validated the measurement instrument based on its statistical properties.

Sample

In this study, we chose to use online stock trading as the study context. Online stock trading is considered a technology-based service as it usually involves various technologies and technical analyses and requires certain levels of familiarity with financial products and specialized technologies.

We recruited subjects using the database of a leading US-based marketing research firm that specializes in online product/service design surveys. We randomly selected samples from the database consisting of registered participants with prior online financial service experiences. We emailed each subject an invitation to voluntarily participate in our online survey for a cash reward and a raffle for a $25 000 prize. After logging into a secure website, each subject was asked for their involvement in online financial services in the past year (i.e., 2016–2017). We screened out inactive investors and included only active investors in the analysis. Subjects that passed the screening questions were directed to the next section of questions concerned with their demographic characteristics of age, gender, education, household income, and trading history. In the remaining survey, subjects were asked to report their trading experience and satisfaction with their primary trading account provider.

Of the 8500 potential respondents, less than 10 percent chose not to participate in the study. Thus, gross non-response bias is not a factor (Flynna et al., 1990). As discussed previously, we also screened respondents based on their response to online financial service frequency (the number of online investments they made in the past year). After screening for involvement and incomplete responses, our final sample size was 905, leading to a qualified response rate of 10.65 percent. The characteristics of the sample are in conformance with published studies on online behavior that demonstrate similar sample statistics (Emmanouilides and Hammond, 2000).

The convenient and low-cost online survey approach greatly enhanced the opportunity to reach end-users and emerged as an appealing approach for conducting research in product and service design. However, there are several issues relating to coverage bias or selection error that are raised with the sampling approach to online panel surveys: first, of course, such surveys can reach only those who are online; second, they can reach only those who agree to become part of the panel; and, third, not all those who are invited respond (Terhanian, 2003). To address these issues, Duffy et al. (2005) compared data from online and face-to-face surveys and noticed that the online approach appears to attract a more knowledgeable, opinionated sample than do face-to-face surveys. Besides, electronic surveys can be coded in a flexible manner and offer researchers more capabilities with fewer missing responses (Boyer et al., 2002).

Even though the online approach appears to attract a more knowledgeable, opinionated sample, we suspect a portion of respondents were simply taking the survey for the rewards and did not pay enough attention to the survey itself. To screen out those respondents, we first examined survey duration, which was measured with a time window from the starting time to the completion time. Based on the survey company's length of the survey and trial tests, we believed that it should take at least four minutes for a subject to complete the survey. We suspected that those subjects who completed the survey in less than four minutes neither read the questions nor thought about how to answer those questions. We also examined the pattern of each respondent and made sure that their responses to the reversely worded questions were consistent with their responses to other questions. We scrutinized the survey responses and deleted the subjects who failed to meet the above two criteria. The process retained 734 subjects whose responses were used in the following analysis and model testing.

Descriptive Statistics

All respondents traded online in 2016–2017, with 57 percent making more than six trades. Furthermore, 59 percent of the sample was male, and about 50 percent of the subjects were 40–60 years old. In addition, 80 percent of the participants had at least some college education, 55 percent reported a household income of over $75 000, and 78 percent reported having traded online for more than three years. Among all subjects, 15.7 percent had their primary online trading account with Ameritrade, followed by Fidelity (14.9 percent), Scottrade (14.6

Table 14.1   *Summary statistics for the technology readiness index and its components*

TR components	Mean	SD	Skewness	Kurtosis	Correlation coefficients[a]			
					OPT	INN	DIS	INS
Optimism (OPT)	4.07	0.62	−0.30	−0.29	1.00			
Innovativeness (INN)	3.36	0.83	−0.05	−0.27	0.47	1.00		
Discomfort (DIS)	2.50	0.85	0.45	0.12	0.32	0.32	1.00	
Insecurity (INS)	2.65	0.78	0.39	0.10	0.25	0.13	0.49	1.00
Overall TRI	3.57	0.54	0.06	−0.02	0.68	0.69	−0.78	−0.67

Notes:
All mean values are on a five-point scale.
The overall technology readiness index (TRI) score for each respondent was obtained by averaging the scores on the four components (after reverse-coding the scores on the discomfort and insecurity components).
[a] All correlations are significant at $p \leq 0.001$.

percent), ShareBuilder (12.7 percent), E*Trade (11.4 percent), Charles Schwab (9.7 percent), TD Waterhouse (4.0 percent), American Express (1.0 percent), and others (15.8 percent). When asked to rate their satisfaction level with certain online brokers, 91.5 percent of participants reported high satisfaction (values of four or five on a five-point scale). Only 1.4 percent said that they did not feel satisfied (values of one or two on a five-point scale). Overall, the subjects rated high on optimism (4.07) and innovativeness (3.36) and showed less stress in discomfort (2.50) and insecurity (2.65) in online stock trading. All four dimensions of TR are strongly correlated with each other at $p < 0.001$ (Table 14.1).

Measurement Model Analysis

According to the approach suggested by Gerbing and Anderson (1988), we conducted both principal component analysis with direct oblimin rotation and confirmatory factor analysis (CFA) to analyze our scales. Without imposing orthogonal assumptions among relevant factors, principal component analysis with direct oblimin is superior for its greater simplicity and the wider range of possible oblique solutions (Harman, 1976). We also adopted a two-step approach to model construction and testing (Anderson and Gerbing, 1988). We first "purified" the measurement model by eliminating measured variables and latent factors that were not well fit by the initial CFA model. We performed separate CFAs on TR and intention to use to assess whether any structural model exists that has an acceptable goodness-of-fit. Two measures were excluded from the system construct for not loading strongly on any construct. One measure was excluded from the service construct for not loading strongly on any construct. One measure was excluded from the satisfaction construct for loading on two constructs. Second, we fit the structural model to the measured variables retained in the first step.

Table 14.1 reports the estimates of item loadings and cross-loadings for the nine constructs of challenge, control, focused attention, interactivity, product offerings, skill, service, system, and satisfaction from an unconstrained analysis. To confirm the psychometric properties of the measurement model, we further examined the indicators and constructs for their reliability, convergent validity, and discriminant validity. Internal consistency reliability was examined in two ways: Cronbach's alpha (Nunnally, 1978) and composite reliability (Fornell and Larker, 1981). In all cases, the construct reliabilities are greater than 0.70 and confirm the reliability of the scales (Fornell and Larker 1981; Nunnally 1978).

Table 14.2   Goodness-of-fit for 1–5 latent class clusters

# of Latent Clusters	L^2	BIC	AIC	CAIC	Entropy R^2	R^2
1	9,570.11	4,990.75	8,182.11	4,296.75	1.00	1.00
2	8,112.98	3,804.15	6,806.98	3,151.15	0.86	0.88
3	7,583.32	3,545.03	6,359.32	2,933.03	0.81	0.81
4	7,269.72	3,501.97	6,127.72	2,930.97	0.83	0.82
5	7,070.02	3,574.55	6,011.76	3,044.55	0.84	0.82

Notes:
L^2: The likelihood-ratio goodness-of-fit value for the current model.
BIC: Bayesianinformation criterion, AIC: Akaikeinformation criterion, CAIC: Conditionsl Akaike information criterion.
R^2 : The percentage of variance explained by the specific cluster model.

Convergent validity was assessed at both the item and construct levels by examining item loadings and the average variance extracted (AVE; Fornell and Larker, 1981). Individual item loadings of 0.7 or greater imply that the indicator shares more variance with its construct than error variance (Gefen et al., 2000). Meanwhile, AVEs of 0.50 or greater demonstrate that the construct shares more variance with its indicators than error variance (Fornell and Larker, 1981). The loadings of the measurement items on their corresponding constructs are 0.7 or greater, indicating that individual items converged appropriately on their intended constructs. The items also demonstrate good convergent validity, with AVEs for each construct greater than 0.50.

Finally, we examined the discriminant validity by comparing the correlations among constructs and AVE values (Fornell and Larker, 1981). To claim discriminant validity, the square root of AVE for construct X needs to be larger than the correlations between X and all other constructs. As shown in Table 14.2, the square roots of AVE on the diagonal are greater than the corresponding off-diagonal correlations. Hence, discriminant validity is established, and each construct is different from the other constructs. We also found support for discriminant validity by comparing item loadings and cross-loadings in Table 14.1. Because all items load higher on their intended construct than other constructs, we conclude that the indicators display solid discriminant validity (Fornell, 1992).

Common Method Bias

One potential issue in having a single respondent assess both independent and dependent variables is common method bias. Although specificity of the items and use of different scale anchors reduced such bias considerably, it probably would not eliminate it. As suggested by Podsakoff et al. (2003), we assessed the extent of common method bias with two tests. First, Harmon's single-factor test was conducted using exploratory factor analysis. The basic assumption of this technique is that if a substantial amount of common method variance is present, either (a) a single factor will emerge from the factor analysis, or (b) one general factor will account for the majority of the covariance among the measures. Results from this test suggested the presence of nine factors. As none of these factors account for the majority of the variance, the data do not indicate evidence of common method bias. Second, we applied a test of common method bias suggested by Podsakoff et al. (2003, p. 898; the specific source of common method bias cannot be identified). The results revealed that when adding a latent

Table 14.3   Segment variable profiles

| | Segment Variable Mean Scores (Standard Deviation) | | | | |
| | Contributors | | Inhibitors | | |
Segment	Optimism	Innovativeness	Discomfort	Insecurity	Segment Size
1. *Explorers*	4.58[h]	4.24[h]	1.70[l]	2.08[l]	75
	(0.44)	(0.49)	(0.54)	(0.61)	
2. *Pioneers*	4.27[h]	3.95[h]	3.62[h]	3.84[h]	169
	(0.52)	(0.60)	(0.77)	(0.60)	
3. *Skeptics*	4.06[l]	3.11[l]	2.30[l]	2.47[l]	304
	(0.44)	(0.51)	(0.46)	(0.54)	
4. *Laggards*	3.43[l]	2.57[l]	3.22[h]	3.09[h]	186
	(0.52)	(0.60)	(0.54)	(0.57)	

Notes:
The subscripts *h* and *l* refer to the differing technology beliefs across segments (high and low, respectively; Parasuraman and Colby, 2001). For example, Explorers are high on contributors of "Optimism" and "Innovativeness," but low on inhibitors of "Discomfort" and "Insecurity."

variable reflecting the common method, model fit was improved (χ^2 difference = 672.48, df = 97, p < .01), but the variance accounted for by the common method latent variable was only 6.5 percent of the total variance. Thus, using results from comparable investigations (Carlson and Perrewe, 1999; Williams et al., 1989), we concluded that common method bias was not a serious threat to our analysis.

TR-Based Segments

To decide whether or not the given model fits the observed data within acceptable limits, we applied measures of relative fit based on information criteria to evaluate the model's performance (Dayton, 1998). The information criteria assess the degree of improvement in explanatory power adjusted for the number of degrees of freedom required for the estimation of additional parameters. The most common information criteria include AIC (Akaike information criterion), BIC (Bayesian information criterion), and CAIC (Consistent AIC, which penalizes for sample size as well as model complexity). These are goodness-of-fit measures that take into account model parsimony and penalize for the number of parameters in relation to the maximum possible number of parameters. A good model generally has low AIC, BIC, or CAIC values.

The TR segment membership was identified by applying latent class cluster analysis using Latent Gold software. Table 14.2 shows the goodness-of-fit statistics for one to five class structures. Among all the structures, the four-class solution has the lowest BIC (3510.97) and CAIC (2930.97) values, and the second-lowest AIC (6127.72) value. The entropy R^2 (0.83) and R^2 (0.82) also suggest an acceptable fit of the latent class cluster structure to the data.

Combining the latent class cluster solution developed in Latent Gold and the differing belief of technology adoption segments developed by Parasuraman and Colby (2001), we found four distinct segments in our data set: 186 Explorers (25.34 percent), 75 Pioneers (10.22 percent), 304 Skeptics (41.42 percent), and 169 Laggards (23.02 percent). Table 14.3 and Figure 14.1 present the segment variable profile for the four TR segments. We reconfirmed the four-cluster solution by performing analysis of variance (ANOVA) tests to check the distinction among four clusters in terms of the TR dimensions. Table 14.4 summarizes the results of the pairwise

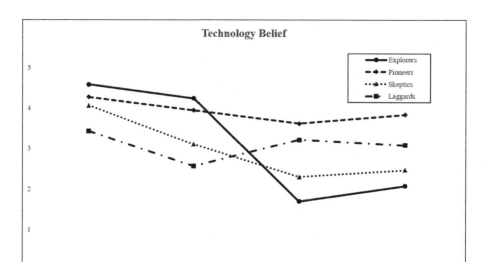

Figure 14.1   Technology beliefs of TR segments

Table 14.4   Significant segment mean (between-subject) differences on technology beliefs

Belief	Segment pairs		
Innovativeness	[1,2] ***	[2,3] ***	[3,4] ***
	[1,3] ***	[2,4] ***	
	[1,4] ***		
Discomfort	[1,2] ***	[2,3] **	[3,4] ***
	[1,3] ***	[2,4] ***	
	[1,4] ***		
Optimism	[1,2] ***	[2,3] ***	[3,4] ***
	[1,3] ***	[2,4] ***	
	[1,4] **		
Insecurity	[1,2] **	[2,3] ***	[3,4] **
	[1,3] ***	[2,4] ***	
	[1,4] ***		

Notes:
*** p ≤ 0.001
** p ≤ 0.01.

mean comparisons of between-subject differences across the four segments, with the number in brackets indicating which segment pairs were significant differences. As shown in Table 14.4, the four technology beliefs among the four TR segments are distinct at *p* ≤ 0.001 levels.

Table 14.5   Segment demographics and significant differences

	1. Explorers	2. Pioneers	3. Skeptics	4. Laggards	
Gender (M/F)	105/81	49/26	181/123	101/68	χ^2 : 1.77
Age	< 30: 7	< 30: 4	< 30: 7	< 30: 5	χ^2 : 31.79
	31–40: 34	31–40: 10	31–40: 39	31–40: 20	*p*: 0.007
	41–50: 58	41–50: 19	41–50: 70	41–50: 35	
	51–60: 59	51–60: 21	51–60: 106	51–60: 47	
	> 60: 28	> 60: 21	> 60: 82	> 60: 62	
Trading history	< 1 year: 4	< 1 year: 6	< 1 year: 16	< 1 year: 16	χ^2 : 16.48
	1–3 years: 32	1–3 years:10	1–3 years: 54	1–3 years: 29	*p*: 0.06
	3–5 years: 33	3–5 years: 17	3–5 years: 66	3–5 years: 44	
	> 5 years: 117	> 5 years: 42	> 5 years: 168	> 5 years: 80	
Education	High school: 17	High school: 4	High school: 40	High school: 23	
	College: 114	College: 46	College: 185	College: 103	χ^2 : 26.05
	Master's: 50	Master's: 24	Master's: 61	Master's: 35	*p*: 0.04
	Other: 5	Other: 1	Other: 18	Other: 8	
Income	< $25k: 4	< $25k: 3	< $25k: 14	< $25k: 10	
	$25k–50k: 29	$25k–50k: 13	$25k–50k: 53	$25k–50k: 43	χ^2 : 75.81
	$50k–100k: 67	$50k–100k: 35	$50k–100k: 141	$50k–100k: 75	*p*: 0.001
	$100k–150k: 50	$100k–150k: 12	$100k–150k: 59	$100k–150k: 31	
	> $150k: 32	> $150k: 10	> $150k: 30	> $150k: 6	
	Other: 4	Other: 2	Other: 7	Other: 4	

Notes:
This table summarizes the segment demographics, including gender, age, trading history, education, and income. The chi-squared test indicates significant differences between TR segments in terms of age (*p* < 0.01), income (*p* < 0.005), education (*p* < 0.10), and trading history (*p* < 0.05), but no significant difference in gender (*p* > 0.5).

TR and Usage: Testing H1 and H2

To test the first hypothesis (*H1*) that TR segments differ in their future intention to use online stock trading services, we conducted an ANOVA. Table 14.6 summarizes the ANOVA analysis results: means, standard deviations, and test statistics among the number of online trades, intention to use, flow experience, and technology readiness across the four TR segments. The tests indicate that TR segments differ in their further intention to use online stock trading services (*F* = 6.83, *p* ≤ 0.001). As shown in Table 14.6, TR segments also differ in their flow experience (*F* = 32.32, *p* ≤ 0.001) and TR (*F* = 893.60, *p* ≤ 0.001). However, there is no difference with regard to current usage across TR segments (*F* = 1.65, *p* > 0.10). To test the second hypothesis (*H2*) that TR segments with higher technology readiness index (TRI) demonstrate stronger intention to use online stock trading services, we conducted a correlation analysis and found that the TRI is strongly correlated with intention to use, at *p* ≤ 0.01 (Table 14.7). Thus, both *H1* and *H2* are supported.

Table 14.6   *ANOVA analysis of TR segments*

	Mean (standard deviation)				F
	1. Explorer	2. Pioneer	3. Skeptics	4. Laggards	
# of online trades[a]	3.94	4.13	3.64	3.72	1.65
	(2.10)	(2.15)	(1.95)	(2.02)	
Intention to use[b]	4.37	4.39	4.30	4.00	11.22***
	(0.71)	(0.68)	(0.66)	(0.65)	
Flow experience[c]	2.69	2.52	2.50	2.25	32.32***
	(0.38)	(0.45)	(0.44)	(0.41)	
Technology	3.01	1.35	2.13	1.01	893.60***
Readiness Index[d]	(0.15)	(0.56)	(0.52)	(0.11)	

Notes:
[a] The number of trades is based on the following scale: 1 (1–5 trades per year); 2 (6–10 trades per year); 3 (11–20 trades per year); 4 (21–30 trades per year); 5 (31–40 trades per year); 6 (41–50 trades per year); and 7 (> 50 trades per year).
[b] The rating for intention to use is based on the following scale: 1 (very unlikely); 2 (unlikely); 3 (not sure); 4 (likely); and 5 (very likely).
[c] Flow experience is calculated as (Control + Focused attention + Interactivity + Skill − Challenge) / 6.
[d] The TRI is calculated as (Optimism + Innovativeness + [6 − Discomfort] + [6 − Insecurity]) / 4.
*** $p \leq 0.001$.

Table 14.7   *Correlation analysis (2-tailed)*

	TRI	# of trades	Intention to use
TRI	1.00		
# of trades	0.04	1.00	
Intention to use	0.18**	0.06	1.00

Notes:
*** $p \leq 0.001$.

TR/Market Entry/Experience and Intention to Use: Testing H3–H6

Table 14.8 summarizes the market entry segmentation for surveyed online financial service vendors. Among all nine vendors, E*Trade (then TradePlus) first provided online stock trading services in the early 1980s (1985) to a growing number of discount brokerage houses and therefore constituted the first entrant. By the summer of 1987, TradePlus reported that its servers were in use nearly every minute, often by several people at once, 24 hours per day, including a large number of international customers as well as domestic customers.[2] Ameriprise and Ameritrade both started providing the service in 1994 and are classified as the Explorer. Compared with the average market entry year of 1995, the majority of the vendors started offering online trades in 1996 and therefore are categorized as followers (Charles Schwab, Scottrade, ShareBuilder, and TD Waterhouse). Fidelity is the last entrant to online trading service in 1997 and therefore is classified as a late entrant. The table also shows the percentage of each TR segment for each market entry cluster. For example, the percentage of TR segments for the first entrant is 30 percent (Explorer), 18 percent (Pioneer), 22 percent (Skeptics), and 30 percent (Laggards).

Table 14.8   *Market entry and TR segment*

	Explorer	Pioneer	Skeptics	Laggards	Company[a]	Total
First entrant	30%	18%	22%	30%	E*Trade (1985)	90
Explorer	28%	25%	24%	23%	Ameriprise (1994), Ameritrade (1994)	126
Follower	20%	27%	24%	30%	Charles Schwab (1996), Scottrade (1996), ShareBuilder (1996), TD Waterhouse (1996)	297
Late entrant	25%	17%	33%	25%	Fidelity (1997)	106
Average	24%	23%	25%	28%	1995	619

Note:
[a] The number in parentheses refers to the year when the company started providing online stock trading services.

Table 14.9   *Future intention to use online stock trading services: MANCOVA analysis*

	Hotelling's T^2	F	p-value
Main Effects:			
TR membership	0.08	3.52	< 0.001
Experience	0.19	13.18	< 0.001
Market entry	0.05	2.42	< 0.050
Interaction Effects:			
Market entry × TR membership	0.16	2.50	< 0.000
Market entry × Experience	0.08	1.74	< 0.050
Experience × TR membership	0.05	1.16	0.269
Experience × Market entry × TR membership	0.17	1.29	< 0.050
Covariates:			
Age	0.01	1.32	0.262
Education	0.01	0.82	0.511
Gender	0.02	2.63	< 0.050
Household income	0.01	1.21	0.305

To test *H3–H6*, we conducted a multiple analysis of variance (MANCOVA) with estimated TR segment, market entry, and flow experience as the main factors and intention to use as the dependent variable. We also included covariates including age, education, gender, and household income as suggested in past research (Ding et al., 2007). The results in Table 14.9 indicate that experience (Hotelling's $T^2 = 0.19$, $F = 13.18$, $p \leq 0.001$), TR membership (Hotelling's $T^2 = 0.08$, $F = 3.52$, $p \leq 0.001$), and market entry (Hotelling's $T^2 = 0.05$, $F = 2.42$, $p \leq 0.05$) all have significant main effects on intention to use. Also, market entry × TR membership (Hotelling's $T^2 = 0.16$, $F = 2.50$, $p \leq 0.001$), market entry × experience (Hotelling's $T^2 = 0.08$, $F = 1.74$, $p \leq 0.05$), and market entry × experience × TR membership (Hotelling's $T^2 = 0.17$, $F = 1.29$, $p \leq 0.05$) have significant interaction effects. Thus, we conclude that *H3*, *H4*, and *H5* are supported. However, *H6* is not supported because the interaction between experience and TR membership does not have any significant effect (Hotelling's $T^2 = 0.05$, $F = 1.16$, $p > 0.10$). The results also reveal that gender is a significant covariate (Hotelling's $T^2 = 0.02$, $F = 2.63$, $p \leq 0.50$).

DISCUSSION AND MANAGERIAL IMPLICATIONS

This chapter empirically investigated the relationship between customers' beliefs about technology and their intention to use online stock trading services. Drawing on service research and marketing theory, we argued that technology beliefs affect intention to use, which is contingent on market entry and flow experience. We adopted a psychographic scale of TR to capture the underlying technology belief across customer segments to facilitate the investigation. The analysis results support the proposed relationship between technology beliefs and intention to use, and the role of market entry and flow experience on intention to use online stock trading services. In the next section, we discuss our results and offer managerial implications.

Built on prior studies on TR and usability, we examined how the variation in technology beliefs affects future intention to use specific services—online stock trading services. Instead of evaluating usability, we looked at intention to use because only final usage generates profit from brokers' perspectives. Using online stock trading as the study context, we established the link between TR membership and intention to use and further examined the moderating effects of market entry and flow experience. As suggested by prior studies, we confirmed that intention to use online financial stock trading services differs across TR segments (*H1*). We also confirmed that segments with higher technology beliefs (e.g., Explorers) tend to demonstrate a stronger intention to use online stock trading services than segments holding lower technology beliefs (e.g., Laggards; *H2*).

The conflicting results from prior studies of TR segments and usability indicate that TR membership alone might be insufficient to predict intention to use. Instead, customers' actual experience with the service and vendors' entry into the market both directly and indirectly affect intention to use. The MANCOVA results (Table 14.9) show that both market entry and experience affect intention to use (*H3, H5*). Yet, only market entry moderates the relationship between TR membership and intention to use (*H4*). Overall, we found that intention to use is driven by a complicated interaction between TR membership, market entry, and flow experience.

This study contributes to current service research in two ways. First, we confirmed TR membership to be a useful tool to segment customers in online financial services (e.g., online stock trading service). The psychographic profiles pertaining to technology beliefs are comparably more accurate in predicting customers' future usage than are demographic characteristics. We also found a positive relationship between the TRI index and future intention to use, which further extends the application of TR and sheds light on promising strategies for effective direct marketing. Second, the paper explores the relationships among TR membership, market entry, and flow experience in predicting intention to use. The research model and final statistical analysis suggest that flow experience explains the majority of the variance in intention to use, followed by the three-way interaction.

As an empirical study, our research is subject to the limitation of generalizability. The study was conducted in the context of online stock trading services. As a result, it is challenging to generalize the results to other contexts. Future research might apply the same theoretical framework to other technology-based service platforms, such as telehealth, artificial intelligence-based virtual shopping, simulation, and so on. Although each technology-based service requires different sets of technical skills, we believe that general TR could largely explain individual consumers' overall experience and hence their intention to use such services. We also expect that the order of market entry for technology-based service providers could also be a good indicator of TR vs. resistance from consumers in the market.

Lastly, we acknowledge that the five consumer segments based on the TR scale only reflect an individual's technology belief at a single point. It is likely that the individual might develop different beliefs over time, either due to increasing confidence with technology applications or decreasing confidence associated with technology failures. Hence, it would be interesting to study how each individual holds different beliefs toward technology over time and how such changes further drive their intentions to use technology.

NOTES

1. Stucki, B., 2020, New study finds 3 top priorities for CX leaders. Availabile at https://www.forbes .com/sites/sap/2020/09/21/new-study-finds-3-top-priorities-for-cx-leaders/?sh=373e94f04c68 (accessed April 2022).
2. For more information, see the E*Trade Financial Corporation–Company Profile, available at http:// www.referenceforbusiness.com/history2/55/E-Trade-Financial-Corporation.html (accessed March 23, 2020).

REFERENCES

Ajzen, I. 1991. The theory of planned behavior. *Organizational Behavior and Human Decision Processes*, 50(2), 179–211.
Anderson, J. C., Gerbing, D. W. 1988. Structural equation modeling in practice: A review and recommended two step approach. *Psychological Bulletin*, 103(3), 411–423.
Bitner, M. J. 1992. Servicespaces: The impact of physical surroundings on customers and employees. *Journal of Marketing*, 56(2), 57–71.
Boyer, K., Hallowell, R., Roth, A. 2002. E-services: operating strategy – a case study and a method for analyzing operational benefits. *Journal of Operations Management*, 20(2), 175–188.
Carlson, D. S., Perrewe, P. L. 1999. The role of social support in the stressor-strain relationship: An examination of work-family conflict. *Journal of Management*, 25, 513–540.
Carpenter, G. S., & Nakamoto,K. 1990. Competitive strategies for late entry into a market with a dominant brand. *Management Science*, 36, 1268–1278.
Castro, J. O., Chrisman, J. J. 1995. Order of market entry, competitive strategy, and financial performance. *Journal of Business Research*, 33(2), 165–177.
Churchill, G. 1979. A paradigm or developing better measures of marketing constructs. *Journal of Marketing Research*, 16(1), 64–73.
Csikszentmihalyi, M. 1991. *Flow: The psychology of optimal experience*. Harper and Row.
Curran, J. M., Meuter, M. L., Surprenant, C. F. 2003. Intentions to use self-service technologies: A confluence of multiple attitudes. *Journal of Service Research*, 5(3), 209–224.
Davidow, W. H. 1986. *Marketing high technology: An insider's view*. The Free Press.
Dayton, C. M. 1998. Information criteria for the paired-comparisons problem. *The American Statistician*, 52, 144–151.
Ding, X., Verma, R., Iqbal, Z. 2007. Self-service technology and online financial service choice, *International Journal of Service Industry Management*, 18(3), 246–268.
Doyle, P., Saunders, J. 1985. The lead effect of marketing decisions. *Journal of Marketing Research*, 22(1), 54–65.
Duffy, B., Smith, K., Terhanian, G., Bremer, J. 2005. Comparing data from online and face-to-face surveys. *International Journal of Market Research*, 47(6), 615–639.
Dugal, S. S., Schroeder, J. E. 1995. Strategic positioning for market entry in different technological environments. *Journal of Marketing Theory and Practice*, 11, 23–27.
Emmanouilides, C., Hammond, K. 2000. Internet usage: Predictors of active users and frequency of use. *Journal of Interactive Marketing*, 14(2), 17–32.
Fishbein, M., Ajzen, I. 1975. *Belief, attitude, intention, and behavior: An introduction to theory and research*. Addison-Wesley.
Flynna, B. B., Sakakibarab, S., Schroederb, R. G., Batesb, K. A., Flynna, E. J. 1990. Empirical research methods in operations management. *Journal of Operations Management*, 9(2), 250–284.
Fornell, C. 1992. A national customer satisfaction barometer: The Swedish experience. *Journal of Marketing*, 56(1), 6–21.
Fornell, C., Larcker, D. F. 1981. Evaluating structural equation models with unobservable variables and measurement error. *Journal of Marketing Research*, 18(1), 39–50.

Gefen, D., Straub, D. W., Boudreau, M.-C. 2000. Structural equation modeling and regression guidelines for research practice. *Communications of the Association for Information Systems*, 4(7), 2–77.

Gerbing, D.W., Anderson, J. C. 1988. An updated paradigm for scale development incorporating unidimensionality and its assessment. *Journal of Marketing Research*, 25, 186–192.

Ghani, J. A., Deshpande, S. D. 1994. Task characteristics and the experience of optimal flow in human–computer interaction. *Journal of Psychology*, 128(4), 381–391.

Golder, P. N., Tellis, G.J. 1993. Pioneer advantage: Marketing logic or marketing legend? *Journal of Marketing Research*, 30(2), 158–170.

Gomez, J., Pérez-Aradros, B., & Salazar, I. 2019. Does order of entry shape competitive strategies? An analysis of European mobile operators. *Long Range Planning*, 54(2), 101874.

Harman, H. H. 1976. *Modern factor analysis*. University of Chicago Press.

Huffman, D. L., Kalsbeek, W. D., Novak, T. P. 1996. Internet and Web use in the United States: Baselines for commercial development. *Communications of the ACM*, 39, 36–46.

Hoyer, W.D., Kroschke, M., Schmitt, B., Kraume, K., Shankar, V. 2020. Transforming the Customer Experience through new technologies. *Journal of Interactive Maketing*, 51(1), 57–71.

Im, S., Mason, C. H., Houston, M. B. 2007. Does innate consumer innovativeness relate to new product/ service adoption behavior? The intervening role of social learning via vicarious innovativeness. *Journal of the Academy of Marketing Science*, 35, 63–75.

Kerin, R. A., Varadarajan, P. R., Peterson, R. A. 1992. First-mover advantage: A synthesis, conceptual framework, and research propositions. *Journal of Marketing*, 56(4), 33–52.

Korzaan, M. L. 2003. Going with the flow: Predicting online purchase intentions. *Journal of Computer Information Systems*, 43(4), 25–31.

LeFevre, J. 1988. Flow and the quality of experience during work and leisure. In M. Csikszentmihalyi and I. S. Csikszentmihalyi (Eds.), Optimal experience: Psychological studies of flow in consciousness, (pp. 307–318). Cambridge University Press.

Lieberman, M. B., Montgomery, D. C. 1988. First-mover advantages. *Strategic Management Journal*, 9(Summer), 41–58.

Marcus, A. I., Segal, H. P. 1989. *Technology in America: A brief history*. Harcourt Brace Jovanovich.

Massey, A. P., Khatri, V., Montoya-Weiss, M. M. 2007. Usability of online services: The role of technology readiness and context. *Decision Sciences*, 38(2), 277–308.

McCarthy, J., Wright, P. 2004. *Technology as experience*. MIT Press.

McCarthy, J., Wright, P. 2005. Putting "felt-life" at the center of human-computer interaction (HCI). *Cognition, Technology & Work*, 7, 262–271.

Merz, M. A., He, Y., Vargo, S. L. 2009. The evolving brand logic: A service-dominant logic perspective. *Journal of the Academy of Marketing Science*, 37, 328–344.

Nicolaou, A. I., McKnight, H. D. 2006. Perceived information quality in data exchanges: Effects on risk, trust, and intention to use. *Information Systems Research*, 17(4), 332–351.

Novak, T. P., Hoffman, D. L., Yung, Y. 2000. Measuring the customer experience in online environments: A structural modeling approach. *Marketing Science*, 19(1), 22–42.

Nunnally, J. C. 1978. Psychometric theory (2nd ed.). New York: McGraw-Hill.

Parasuraman, A. 2000. Technology readiness index (TRI): A multiple-item scale to measure readiness to embrace new technologies. *Journal of Service Research*, 2(4), 307–320.

Parasuraman, A., Colby, C. L. 2001. *Techno-ready marketing—How and why your customers adopt technology*. The Free Press.

Pine, B. J., Gilmore, J. H. 1999. The experience economy. Harvard Business School Press.

Podsakoff, P. M., MacKenzie, S.B., Lee, J.Y., Podsakoff, N. P. 2003. Common method biases in behavioral research: a critical review of the literature and recommended remedies. *Journal of Applied Psychology*, 88(5), 879–903.

Robinson, W. T., Fornell, C. 1985. Sources of market pioneer advantages in consumer goods industries. Journal of Marketing Research, 22(3), 305–317.

Robinson, W. T., Fornell, C., Sullivan, M. 1992. Are market pioneers intrinsically stronger than later entrants? *Strategic Management Journal*, 13(8), 609–624.

Rosen, D. E., Schroeder, J. E., Purinton, E. F. 1998. Marketing high-tech products: Lessons in customer focus from the marketplace. *Academy of Marketing Science Review*, 98(6), 1–17.

Roth, A. V., Menor, L. J. 2003. Insights into service operations management: A research agenda. *Production and Operations Management*, 12(2), 145–164.

Sussman, R., Gifford, R. 2019. Causality in the Theory of Planned Behavior. *Personality and Social Psychology Bulletin*, 45(6), 920–933.

Terhanian, G. 2003. The unfulfilled promise of internet research. In MRS Conference Paper, 37.

Tsikriktsis, N. 2004. A technology readiness-based taxonomy of customers: A replication and extension. *Journal of Service Research*, 7(1), 42–52.

White, A. P. 1983. *The dominant firm: A study of market power*. UMI Research Press.

Williams, L. J., Cote, J.A., Buckley, M. R. 1989. Lack of method variance in self-reported affect and perceptions at work: Reality or artifact? *Journal of Applied Psychology*, 74, 462–468.

PART IV

HEALTHCARE SERVICES

15. Implications of COVID-19 on operations in healthcare services

Sanjeev Bordoloi

INTRODUCTION

The first pandemic in over 100 years, COVID-19 spread across the world at an unprecedented speed. Populations in more than 120 countries have been subjected to lockdowns to control the virus and prevent health systems from being overwhelmed. This triggered an economic crisis with dire societal consequences, affecting the lives and livelihoods of most of the global population: 500 million people are at risk of falling into poverty (Bettinger, 2020). The crisis has exposed fundamental shortcomings in pandemic preparedness, socio-economic safety nets, and global cooperation. Governments, healthcare institutions, and businesses have struggled to address compounding repercussions in the form of workforce challenges, disruptions in essential supplies, and social instability. As the original strain of SARS-CoV-2 mutated, different variants affected different parts of the world in different phases. Originating in China, the early variant spread through Europe and North America in the spring of 2020. Subsequent variants affected South Africa, Brazil, and other Latin American countries in the fall of 2020; then the Delta variant devastated India in spring of 2021, and moved on to other parts of the world in the summer of 2021. Just when the world considered that COVID-19 was under control with the vaccine and other protections, another variant, Omicron, swept through the globe starting late 2021 through winter and spring of 2022. Omicron was less lethal but spread much more rapidly.

COVID-19 has not only challenged healthcare systems and government systems but also introduced several challenges in business management. This chapter addresses how COVID-19 impacted the traditional Operations Management policies in healthcare management, especially the service supply–demand relationship. Some of our discussions will be on the core aspects of Operations Management, such as capacity and demand management, inventory management, supply chain management, safety stock, service level, and queue management, as applied to the healthcare industry. Then, we will discuss how emerging technologies and business analytics will continue to expand their applications in future healthcare systems, especially because of the COVID-19 outbreak. Finally, we will also extend the discussion into economic, social, and governmental (ESG) aspects of healthcare management.

HEALTHCARE ECOSYSTEMS

An ecosystem is a set of capabilities and services that integrate value chain participants (customers, suppliers, and platform and service providers) through a common commercial model and virtual data backbone (enabled by seamless data capture, management, and exchange) to create improved and efficient consumer and stakeholder experiences and to solve significant pain points or inefficiencies. In healthcare, they have the potential to deliver a personalized and integrated experience to consumers, enhance provider productivity, engage formal and informal caregivers, and improve outcomes and affordability (Singhal et al., 2020).

Healthcare has shifted away from its post-World War II focus on contagious disease and workplace accidents, which necessitated episodic interventions. Today, the primary goal is preventing and effectively managing chronic conditions. New technologies promise care that is available near or at home, supports continuous self and autonomous care, and improves relationships between supporting stakeholders.

The healthcare ecosystems of the future, like other ecosystems, will be centered on the consumer, in this case, the patient. The capabilities and services that form the healthcare ecosystems of the future will include:

- Modalities of traditional care: direct care and pharmaceuticals administered by providers across traditional sites of care.
- Home and self-care: patient engagement, self- and virtual care, remote monitoring, retail clinics, provided monitoring tools.
- Social care: social and community networks related to a patient's holistic health focused on community elements, such as transportation services, faith institutions, and state assistance.
- Daily life activities: patient actions and habits enabling wellness and health, including fitness and nutrition.
- Financing support: payment and financing solutions, digital and automatic payments, benefits/insurance coverage, and so on.

Each of these capabilities and services contributes to the underlying data backbone and advanced analytics technologies. The consumer-oriented nature of these ecosystems also will increase the number of healthcare touchpoints to modify patient behavior and improve outcomes.

Big Tech firms are investing heavily in capabilities in the healthcare ecosystem. Singhal et al. (2020) offer three layers of the healthcare ecosystem: (1) Engagement layer (systems of consumer and patient engagement, e.g., search, wearables, e-commerce, behavioral health apps, Internet of Things [IoT]); (2) Intelligence layer (systems to convert data elements into insights and intelligence to inform or drive actions); and (3) Infrastructure layer (systems to convert data capture, curation management, and interoperability). Companies like Apple, Microsoft, Android, and Amazon are moving from the Engagement layer to the Intelligence layer, while companies like Microsoft Azure, Google, and Amazon Web Services are moving from the Infrastructure layer to the Intelligence layer. Therefore, there seems to be a convergence toward the Intelligence layer of the healthcare ecosystem by major technological firms, which will play an important role as we discuss the impact of COVID-19 in healthcare systems.

Overall, ecosystems have proven to be a powerful force in reshaping and disrupting industries. Healthcare ecosystems have tremendous potential to do the same and could lead to improved health outcomes and affordability by delivering a personalized, intuitive, and integrated experience to patients.

COVID-19 RISKS AND IMPLICATIONS

Bettinger (2020) balances health security imperatives against the economic fallout and rising societal anxieties while relying on digital infrastructure in unprecedented ways. In the economic shifts that include emerging risks from structural change, the healthcare industry could face increasingly adverse consumption, production, and competition patterns. COVID-19 diminished economic activity, which required trillions of dollars in response packages, testing kits, safety equipment, and medical personnel, and is likely to cause structural shifts. Sustainability setbacks are also possible as COVID-19 could have severe post-crisis effects on the planet and its species. Omitting sustainability criteria in recovery efforts risks hampering the climate-resilient, low-carbon transition, stalling years of progress in the healthcare industry. This would give way to a vicious cycle of continued environmental degradation, biodiversity loss, and further zoonotic infectious disease outbreaks.

In addition to the dangers to public health, the pandemic and lockdowns could have long-lasting effects on people and societies, resulting in societal anxieties and social disruptions. There are also growing risks to the personal freedom and well-being of the next generation. High unemployment is likely to exacerbate inequality and affect mental health and societal cohesion, in addition to its direct economic consequences.

Technology has been central to the way people, health institutions, and governments have managed the COVID-19 crisis, and the contact-free economy may also create new employment opportunities in the post-pandemic world. Abrupt adoption of technology comes with risks. The rapid roll-out of new technology solutions has exacerbated risks, such as digital fragmentation, privacy violations, and inequality. Thus, COVID-19 is likely to challenge the relationship between technology and healthcare governance, while mistrust or misuse of technology could have long-lasting effects on society.

The impacts of COVID-19 are a reminder of the need for proactive action today to shape the desired new normal if emerging risks are not addressed. The COVID-19 crisis offers a unique opportunity to shape a better world with better healthcare. As economies restart, there is an opportunity to embed greater societal equality, healthcare facilities, and sustainability into the recovery. In a socio-economic agenda, there has been a collective re-evaluation of "essential work" and a new understanding of essential public services, such as health, education, care, and other safety nets. Despite the grim economic outlook, the solidarity created by the COVID-19 pandemic offers the possibility of investing in building more cohesive, inclusive, and equal societies. For healthcare businesses, the opportunity exists to accelerate a transformation toward more sustainable and digital operating models, while enhancing productivity.

IMPACT OF COVID-19 ON CORE OPERATIONS MANAGEMENT PRINCIPLES

Capacity and Demand Management

The principles of Operations Management were never tested more seriously than during the COVID-19 pandemic. Incredible demand and supply imbalance surfaced for items such as N95 masks, isolation gowns, examination gloves, and pharmaceutical supplies. Different types of demand presented different challenges for different types of resource capacity. The demand came in different forms: (1) COVID-19 patient volume at hospitals in different waves of virus surges; (2) people trying to get tested; and (3) people who needed to be vaccinated. Each of these demand types created bottlenecks on different resources at different points in time. As the first wave of COVID-19 hit the world, the immediate bottlenecks were on hospital intensive care unit (ICU) beds, ventilators, personal protection equipment (PPE), and so on. As one bottleneck was somewhat brought under control (e.g., ICU beds), new bottlenecks surfaced, namely, frontline personnel, such as doctors and nurses, who were stressed to the limit. Long lines of people trying to get tested put pressure on the availability of test kits, whether rapid testing or another form of lab testing. This had impacts on queue management, setting up alternative testing sites, and on social interaction. As the vaccination phase arrived, capacity constraints appeared on supply chain deliveries and super-cold storage facilities. Inventory management strategies were challenged, for example, in deciding how to hold the second-dose vaccine in storage for 3–4 weeks versus putting first-dose vaccines in the arms of the largest volume of the population without wasting time, provided vaccine manufacturing and supply chain distribution could keep up with the pace. From a traditional Operations Management perspective, this is the classic example of stochastic modeling where variability comes from multiple sources, such as production rate, lead time, warehousing and storage, the efficiency of vaccine administration, and many administrative sources (including politics), in determining metrics on service level and safety stock of inventory.

Inventory and Service Level

COVID-19 has had several effects on inventory management and service-level determination. Let us take ventilators as an example. During pre-COVID operations, service levels for ventilators might have been determined based on the variability of the historical data. For example, a service level of 98 percent might have been considered very good for a hospital's normal operations. The historical data previously had predictable and dependable variability. Due to the COVID-19 outbreak, the new variability for the need for ventilators was unprecedented. If the hospital plans to continue maintaining the service level at 98 percent for ventilators, the old inventory management metrics will no longer work. For the same level of inventory, either the service level will go down, or the hospital will need to increase the safety stock for a ventilator in the new demand pattern due to COVID-19, which is highly unpredictable and undependable.

Safety Stock

Safety stock is a function of different types of variability, such as demand volume and lead time. Due to the COVID-19 outbreak, the demand volume variability became substantially higher, and the formula for safety stock needed to be redefined. Similarly, depending on the source of the new supply of ventilators (e.g., New York receiving ventilators from California versus from China), the lead times for new lot arrivals will be vastly different. The typical safety stock formula for a given service level z, while incorporating both demand volume and lead time variability, is as follows (Bordoloi et al., 2018):

$$SS = z\sigma_{d+LT}$$

During the COVID-19 outbreak, the above formula needs to be revised with a new lead time variability and a new demand volume variability. Both are much more difficult to estimate under COVID-19 circumstances, given the dynamic and evolving nature of the environment. The hospitals may not have sufficient time to adjust to these new measures of variability amid the chaos and death rates. Until the new safety stock is derived and implemented, the hospital will be forced to function at a lower service level, resulting in more deaths and bodily damage to patients.

The decades-long focus on supply chain optimization to minimize costs, reduce inventories, and drive up asset utilization has removed buffers and flexibility to absorb disruptions. COVID-19 illustrates that many healthcare agencies are not fully aware of the vulnerability of their inventory and supply chain systems to global shocks of this dimension.

Lean and Six Sigma Quality

The traditional Operations Management principles of Lean and Six Sigma quality have come under fire during the COVID-19 outbreak. Healthcare professionals started questioning if operating at the previous lean level is now "too lean" and too risky, and might have contributed to a higher number of deaths under the COVID-19 outbreak. Surely, from an Operations Management perspective, the benefits of lean implementation cannot be justified by even a single loss of life. Therefore, it may be necessary to take a fresh look at how or whether current lean principles are appropriate for certain COVID-related situations, which might result in a higher probability of death. For example, instead of implementing lean across the board in all supply material, a hospital may now decide to develop appropriate levels of lean applications for different part supplies. Ventilators and PPE items may no longer be good candidates for implementing a high degree of lean, whereas less deadly supplies, such as bed linens or stationery items, could still be candidates for lean application.

Similarly, Six Sigma applications can also be challenged under the COVID-19 environment. Depending on how a hospital defines "defect"—for example, mortality and similar quality standards—Six Sigma or a different level need to be redeveloped. In a service industry such as healthcare, the nature of operations is subject to higher variability because of uniqueness in the service process and higher involvement of humans at both ends—patients as well as providers. Therefore, hospitals will need to identify factors under the COVID-19 environment that could affect the quality standards, and redesign and redefine how quality should be assessed going forward in the post-COVID era.

Several Lean and Six Sigma tools that have already been used in healthcare, such as value stream mapping, DMAIC (Define, Measure, Analyze, Improve, Control), process control, statistical measurements, and standards, will need to be redesigned and redeveloped, with new lessons learned from COVID-19 experiences.

Supply Chain Management

Supply chain design depends on both supply-side and demand-side uncertainty. Based on this, Lee (2002) offered a two-by-two matrix for four types of supply chain designs. When both supply and demand variabilities are low, the recommended design is an efficient supply chain. When demand variability is high for the known supply side, the recommended design is a responsive supply chain. For high uncertainty in both the supply side and demand side, the recommended design is an agile supply chain. COVID-19 will have a significant effect on the design of future supply chains. Let us take the example of PPE. It is likely that previously PPE might have had low uncertainty in both supply and demand sides (predictable demand and dependable source of supply), and therefore was operating under an efficient supply chain design. We present a revised future supply chain design, as a result of COVID-19, in Figure 15.1. During the COVID-19 outbreak, two scenarios are possible. First, for the available (or easily obtainable) supply side, if demand increases significantly, we need to redesign the supply chain to be a responsive supply chain. Next, which is even worse, if the supply side also becomes unpredictable or non-dependable, we will be forced to make the supply chain design an agile supply chain for PPE. Without such redesign, hospitals will face dire situations in PPE availability, leading to unsafe medical practices, which may lead to even higher death rates and putting healthcare providers at risk. It is expected that the low–low box in the model will be smaller in the future, while the high–high box will be much larger. This major transformation will move supply chain designs from the efficient category to responsive or agile categories. To add more agility to future supply chains, we will need to design in higher redundancy and near-shoring to guard against some of the uncertainties.

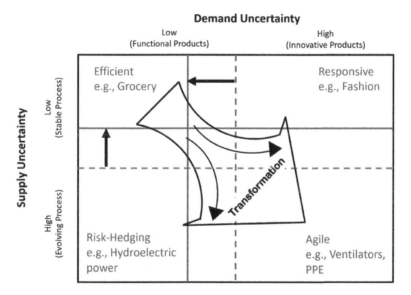

Source: Modified from Lee (2002).

Figure 15.1 *Expected transformation in future supply chain design as a result of COVID-19*

Next, we further extend this framework to develop a patient–provider demand–supply relationship in healthcare, as shown in Figure 15.2. Some traditional health services, such as seasonal flu shots, can still be managed by an efficient supply chain in the future. But technological enablers, such as artificial intelligence (AI), virtual reality/augmented reality (VR/AR), and biometrics, will shift many of the healthcare services to be rendered in the agile supply chain design format. This would include significant application of telemedicine and virtual health. It is important to understand the impact of the demand–supply relationship in a service supply chain context as a result of COVID-19. Technological enablers will be the driving force behind the ability to coordinate the numerous interrelated healthcare activities. Future healthcare service supply management will be better viewed as a relationship between patient requirements and provider capabilities, rather than a physical chain of activities as in a traditional supply chain, because of the patient–provider duality found in services.

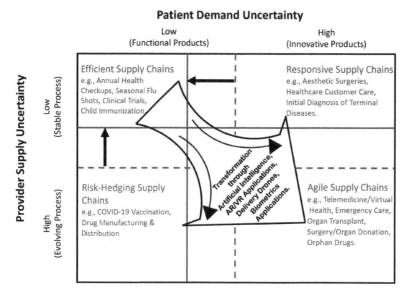

Figure 15.2   Expected transformation in patient–provider supply relationship as a result of COVID-19

That new supply chain technologies are emerging so dramatically improves visibility across the end-to-end supply chain and supports companies' ability to resist shocks. The traditional linear supply chain model is transforming into digital supply networks (DSNs), where functional silos are broken down and organizations become connected to their complete supply network to enable end-to-end visibility, collaboration, agility, and optimization. Leveraging advanced technologies, such as the IoT, AI, VR/AR, biometrics, robotics, and 5G, DSNs are designed to anticipate and be better prepared to meet future challenges (Deloitte Analysis, 2021).

One of the important supply chain issues would be streamlining production and the subsequent distribution of COVID-19 vaccines. In the late fall of 2020, Pfizer and Moderna announced a vaccine for COVID-19 with over 90 percent efficacy. After US Food and Drug Administration approval, production to the extent of 100 million vaccines was made available in batches. Each vaccine needs to be administered in two doses in 3–4-week intervals. As a result, we face two crucial decisions: (1) how to prioritize the vaccine recipients (e.g., medical professionals first), and (2) how to distribute the large volume of vaccines to different types of recipients in an efficient manner. The former decision is a matter of risk–benefit analysis, while the latter is a matter of supply chain efficiency. Supply chain aspects of vaccine distribution are the primary focus for operations and service management professionals (Bordoloi et al., 2018).

The US military has been deployed in the distribution of the vaccines to their destinations. In addition to making the necessary human and transportation resources available, the selected supply chain model also needs to be appropriate for this very important case of distribution. Expediency is more important than cost-saving in this situation. Whether the distribution is done strictly by the government or by a private party, the supply chain model remains an important aspect of the successful completion of this project. As the death rate rose, the debate on the appropriate management of the second dose of vaccine heated up. Deciding the optimal level of safety stock for the second dose depended on several factors, such as manufacturing rate, transportation time, supply chain efficiency, cold-storage availability, and, more importantly, the probability of saving lives immediately versus guaranteeing the second dose in time. This is a classic case of decision-making under uncertainty.

Value of a Vaccine

The potential value of a COVID-19 vaccine to the global community is an issue that is up for debate. The vaccine is expected to bring significant improvements to health and the global economy. Vaccine development and administration efforts can be analyzed over three time horizons during the current COVID-19 pandemic: near term, midterm, and longer term. In the near term, COVID-19 vaccines prevent more people from becoming infected and reduce fatalities. The second-order effects include controlled utilization of hospitals and healthcare resources, the development of herd immunity, and gradual economic recovery. In the midterm, the presence of a vaccine allows the broader population to be inoculated, along with other standard immunizations, such as those for the seasonal flu and measles, mumps, and rubella (Agrawal et al., 2020). Even after the vaccine became available and accessible, customer acceptance continued to be a challenge. This is where public communication together with public education has played a major role in developing public trust and confidence for people to choose to be vaccinated. Healthcare leaders need to dynamically engage consumers through information campaigns using trusted, influential sources. Controlling the pandemic will require an uptake of COVID-19 vaccination at a higher rate than other adult-vaccine benchmarks. In the long term, as the disease mutates or immunity is short-lived, additional development and vaccine manufacturing capacity need to be increased to supply the necessary volume of vaccines, develop new types of vaccines for newer strains, and accelerate the response to future pandemics.

Pfizer indicates the need for booster shots—essentially a third dose and even a fourth dose—within 8 to 12 months of their second shot. Pfizer also reformulated its COVID-19 vaccine so that it will not require super-cold storage as required in their first formula, and the vaccine has also been approved for children. Joining the US-led effort to make vaccines more available globally, Pfizer donated several billion doses over the first year of vaccination, most of them going to lower-income countries. Aside from the moral and humanitarian grounds, this effort is also very important for controlling the pandemic globally.

The global impact of the COVID-19 pandemic has resulted in an unprecedented level of public interest in vaccines. This includes a focus on the development of vaccines and their regulatory review and safety monitoring. Much of this coverage has taken place through mass and social media. Reports of adverse events (side effects) have led some people to express concerns about getting vaccinated, delay getting vaccinated, or even be strongly opposed to vaccination. There are also differences in individual confidence in national safety monitoring systems. Another challenge in communicating the importance of COVID-19 vaccination is that younger adults are typically less clinically affected by COVID-19 infection and may see limited value in getting vaccinated, including until further data confirm that vaccines prevent transmission and that vaccines are effective against new variants. Clear and consistent communication is therefore essential to support people in making the choice to be vaccinated (World Health Organization, 2021).

One of the biggest hurdles in reaching the most vulnerable people will be convincing them that vaccines, and the people providing them, can be trusted. Winning this trust will require an enormous, united effort from governments, public health experts, humanitarian groups, and local community leaders. Whether intentional or not, uneven distribution of vaccines by governments to ethnic, religious, political, and other groups, or perceived inequities in distribution, may deepen divisions or spark new grievances.

Waiting Line/Queuing Theory Implications

Under a COVID-19 outbreak, waiting for a life-saving device, such as a ventilator, or the vaccine could be a matter of life and death. Under normal operation of a hospital, the percentage utilization of the existing stock of ventilators might have been fairly low, say 20 percent. As an increasing number of COVID-19 patients are hospitalized and require ventilators, the utilization rate starts increasing. As we know in Queuing Theory, the rise in waiting time as the percentage utilization rate increases is not a linear function, but rather an exponential function (Bordoloi et al., 2018). Therefore, at the high end of the utilization rate, the waiting time for a given patient to get a ventilator becomes exponentially higher, which may result in premature and avoidable deaths. An extreme example of this situation was when, in India, patients were dying outside hospitals while waiting for a bed and lacked oxygen supply. This percentage resource utilization rate is a function of inventory management of the current stock of ventilators, ICU beds, and oxygen by the hospital, which is also directly related to the supply chain design, as discussed above.

Therefore, all the operational criteria mentioned in previous sections are inter-connected and affected by the intensity of the COVID-19 outbreak. Unless the hospital has the ability and flexibility to adapt quickly to the fast-changing situations because of the COVID-19 outbreak, there will be severe consequences in patients' well-being and recovery rates.

This discussion illustrates that better Operations Management in areas such as service level, safety stock, inventory management, lean application, supply chain design, and waiting line management will lead to a significant improvement in COVID-related care, and therefore becomes extremely important in hospital management.

Decision-Making Under Uncertainty

The fight against COVID-19 is expected to remain a continuous battle at least into the near future. First, the enemy itself is changing; the original variant is no longer the dominant version. It has mutated several times over the past two years. At the time of writing this chapter, the current dominant version is the Omicron variant, which spreads more rapidly though is less severe from the perspective of hospitalization and death. Countries are having to make special arrangements (for example, the Tokyo Olympics) and decisions are changing on an ongoing basis.

Often, in uncertain economic environments, companies slow their technology investments to a trickle. But during the COVID-19 pandemic, most companies ramped up their technology investments. This speaks to the value of a digital supply chain in helping enterprises navigate disruptive forces and respond faster to volatile supply and demand.

Another major uncertainty is coping with the changes in the demand profile due to the pandemic. Hospital revenues declined drastically during the pandemic due to the cancellation of a majority of elective surgeries which, due to their complexity and cost, are considered one of the main contributors to hospital revenue and profit. While it is true that hospitals experienced certain spikes in demand for ICUs and supplies for treating COVID-19 patients, they also experienced over-supplies of clinicians and other personnel for those elective surgeries. As a result, many hospitals attempted to cross-train clinicians to have non-ICU practitioners work in ICU units, or to furlough clinicians and staff members during the pandemic. A similar reduction in hospital revenue was experienced in primary care units. Hospitals continued to face the same trends during the pandemic: climbing expenses, decreased revenue, and taking care of an increased number of uninsured individuals because of economic conditions.

As COVID-19 becomes somewhat under control, a "bullwhip" effect of non-COVID patients is expected, as more patients return to elective surgery as a release of pent-up demand for other types of medical treatment. This is expected to put pressure on pharmaceutical and healthcare companies to manage surges in inventory across the country. The possibility of this "bullwhip" effect will require close monitoring, inventory planning, and efficient warehousing processes, and will place additional strains on last-mile capacity (Sureddin, 2021).

As healthcare providers enter the post-COVID-19 world, they should increase focus on supply chain agility, supplier diversification, and the maintenance of appropriate inventory levels of critical materials and equipment to address a recurrence of the coronavirus or other future pandemics. In addition, they should consider and prepare for potential federal and state regulations that might require minimum PPE and other critical supply inventory levels to handle increased demand surges. These regulations might require providers to redesign existing supply chain procurement, operations, and structure.

VIRTUAL HEALTH

Over a decade ago, virtual health was celebrated as a game-changer in the healthcare industry. But while the technology made virtual health possible, providers, payers, and consumers have been slower to adopt than was anticipated. COVID-19 has pushed providers, patients, and payers over the tipping point into widespread adoption beyond traditional applications.

Fowkes et al. (2020) illustrate virtual health in three main categories: telehealth, digital therapeutics, and care navigation. Telehealth can be synchronous (telemedicine), asynchronous (store and forward), or remote patient monitoring. Synchronous refers to live, two-way audio–visual interaction between patients and providers (e.g., videoconference visits) or providers and providers (e.g., videoconference review of pharmacy prescriptions). Asynchronous refers to the transmission of patient information from provider to patient (e.g., emailing/texting for post-visit follow-up, patient sharing photos of a skin rash for review and diagnosis) or the transmission of recorded health histories from provider to provider (e.g., sending a lab test,

Table 15.1   Virtual health adoption before COVID-19 and future estimates

Categories	Pre-COVID	Anticipated in 5–10 years
Synchronous Telemedicine	77%	93%
Asynchronous Telemedicine	41%	82%
Patient Engagement	36%	91%
Remote Monitoring	32%	93%
Replacement Therapies	13%	68%
Treatment Optimization	11%	77%
E-Triage	11%	77%

X-ray, or MRI to a specialist to request a clinical opinion). Remote patient monitoring refers to the collection of electronic personal health/medical data that is transmitted for review by a remote provider.

Digital therapeutics can be replacement therapies or treatment optimizations. Replacement therapies are evidence-based therapeutic interventions that leverage software to prevent, manage, or treat a medical condition instead of conventional treatments (e.g., pharmaceuticals). Treatment optimization optimizes medication, extending the value of pharmaceutical treatments (e.g., improving medication adherence, monitoring side effects of medication).

Care navigation includes patient self-directed care and e-triage. Patient self-directed care, as the name suggests, refers to patients being able to access their information (e.g., a website with secure, 24-hour access to personal health information). E-triage refers to tools that provide support in searching for and scheduling appropriate care based on symptoms and conditions as well as the price and quality of providers.

During the pandemic, adult primary care and behavioral health showed smaller declines in total visits than did surgical/procedural specialties (Fowkes et al., 2020). These smaller declines may reflect the fact that more primary care and behavioral health visits can be accomplished by evaluation and management only compared to those in the surgical specialties. Before COVID-19, virtual health adoption was highly concentrated in synchronous telemedicine, with limited investment in a variety of virtual health technologies, as shown in Table 15.1. Given the pace and magnitude of current disruptions to care delivery, forward-looking health systems would invest in broader virtual health offerings to create a competitive advantage.

Several challenges remain. Providers' concerns about telehealth include security, workflow integration, effectiveness compared with in-person visits, and the future of reimbursement. In addition, there is a gap between consumers' interest in telehealth and its actual usage. Factors such as the lack of awareness of telehealth offerings, education on types of virtual care needs, and understanding of insurance coverage are some of the drivers of this gap.

As a result of COVID-19, telehealth can increase access to necessary care in areas with shortages, such as behavioral health; improve the patient experience; and improve health outcomes. Fundamentally, the integration of fully virtual and near-virtual health solutions brings care closer to home, increasing the convenience for patients to access care when they need it. This opportunity will be much greater once stakeholders embrace telehealth as the new normal.

Opportunity exists for health systems to enhance their value proposition for consumers in a way that creates new interactions or loyalty. Additionally, providers may build new capabilities that could lead to success in risk-based reimbursement models. On the acute care side, an opportunity may also exist to promote efficiency through models like Tele-ICU and change-capacity use through "hospital at home" models. How health systems think about these value drivers and strategies will likely depend on their market position, provider/specialty capacity, and growth objectives.

ANALYTICS AND EMERGING TECHNOLOGIES DURING COVID-19

Applying Business Analytics to Deal with COVID-19

As applications of business analytics have grown across all industries, including healthcare, we need to look carefully at how exactly they can be of significant help under the COVID-19 environment. Typically, the four levels of analytics are categorized as: (1) descriptive, (2) diagnostic, (3) predictive, and (4) prescriptive. In recent years, the healthcare industry has done a fairly good job in the descriptive and diagnosis components and has had varied degrees of success in predictive and prescriptive analytics.

Under the COVID-19 environment, not only must the healthcare industry do a good job in predicting near-future events or outcomes, but we should also try to go deeper into developing prescriptive analytics that would result in problem-solving and troubleshooting techniques. In predictive analytics, we emphasize pattern-finding and extrapolation techniques to forecast the future, which is of immense help. But we should not stop at that. We should be able to take advantage of current and emerging technologies that can lead us to desired problem-solving and troubleshooting situations arising from COVID-19. In later sections, we will discuss specific emerging technologies that can help the healthcare industry manage COVID-19 situations better and more efficiently.

A variety of factors, including population demographics, governmental policies, local culture, and the physical environment, have shaped COVID-19 demand for healthcare resources. As companies around the world have been struggling to obtain sufficient ICU beds, staff, and equipment during the pandemic, advanced analytics-driven operations planning has emerged as a healthcare must-have.

Critical Infrastructure for Emerging Technologies

Under COVID-19, emerging technologies are propping up our daily lives. Connected devices enable both consumer education and remote work. Chatbots provide life-saving information and relieve overwhelmed health systems. Location data applications track and map the spread of the virus for health workers and researchers. The COVID-19 crisis has shown us that emerging technologies like the IoT and AI are not just tools, they are essential to the functioning of our society and economy. Particularly in this time of instability, we need to think of them as critical infrastructure. Our ability to be adaptive, human-centered, and inclusive in the way we develop policy and protocols for emerging technologies has never been more essential. The continued security and resilience of our society depends on it.

A few examples highlighting our dependence on emerging technologies during this crisis are given below. Each example demonstrates the need for agile governance to maximize the benefits and mitigate the risks of this new critical infrastructure:

- Connectivity is a requisite for telework, but more than 21 million people in the US lack advanced broadband Internet access.
- The use of videoconferencing for children's education exploded as lockdowns forced schools to go remote. But these platforms can sometimes highlight critical privacy and security flaws.
- Chatbots have been used to provide COVID-19 information and understand symptoms. While they can ease the strain on health systems, their inconsistency could erode public trust.

While the COVID-19 pandemic is creating a major drag on the global economy, it is helping to accelerate the development and commercialization of several emerging technologies that previously received lukewarm public and/or government support. This is especially true for innovations that reduce human-to-human contact, automate processes, and increase productivity amid social distancing.

Types of Emerging Technologies to Manage COVID-19

- *Delivery drones:* Drones have been mobilized to transport medical supplies to hospitals, clinics, and homes. A growing list of companies, including Amazon, UPS, Alphabet, Domino's Pizza, and Walmart, are already testing drones to help cut last-mile delivery costs. According to a report from UNICEF, 18 countries have developed drone delivery and transportation purposes during the pandemic.
- *Worker robots:* Robots are helping patients navigate hospital departments, check temperatures, transport medical samples, dispense hand sanitizer, spray disinfectant residentially and commercially, and clean hospitals. Robots developed by UBTECH Robotics in China take patients' body temperature and remind them to wash their hands and wear masks; they use distinctive appearances of Star Wars movie characters to get people's attention.
- *Telemedicine and asynchronous care:* Healthcare services delivered using telecommunications technology have been steadily growing. The stress on the healthcare system due to COVID-19 is also spurring interest in asynchronous healthcare that can help patients monitor and manage chronic conditions without face-to-face appointments. Petrock (2020) offers an example of a spike in demand from diabetics seeking online wellness advice via the "One Drop" health management platform. One Drop markets a direct-to-consumer blood sugar monitoring device and digital platform that lets users measure their glucose levels via a mobile app and get forecasts of blood sugar levels up to eight hours out. The app also delivers recommendations for addressing potential issues before they occur and gives patients access to online counsel from One Drop's healthcare experts.
- *Biometrics, computer vision, and thermal imaging:* Tech companies, including Baidu, Hanvon, Dermalog, and Telpo, have developed systems that use facial recognition and temperature sensing to identify suspected COVID-19 cases. In China, Baidu uses infrared sensors and facial recognition to scan 200 passengers per minute for fevers at Beijing's Qinghe Railway Station. The system automatically takes a picture of a person's face

and sounds an alarm if their body temperature exceeds 99° Fahrenheit (37.2° Celcius). Biometric tracking technologies, such as ankle bracelets, smartphone apps, fingerprint biometrics, and voice communication, help monitor and restrict people who are quarantined or isolated.

- *5G connectivity:* Because of COVID-19, the 5G market may materialize sooner than expected, as a large volume of work and school conducted from home is stressing networks and creating higher demand for bandwidth. Once widely available and accessible, 5G will serve as the foundational support for emerging technologies on the IoT and automation, among other applications. In its first 5G Outlook Series report, the World Economic Forum (Bettinger, 2020) highlighted that telemedicine urgent care visit usage increased by 490 percent during the pandemic.

- *Social VR:* COVID-19 is spurring interest in using VR to seek human interaction through social VR platforms. Businesses are also experimenting with VR platforms to train employees, hold conferences, collaborate on projects, and connect employees virtually. For example, scientists worldwide have turned to Nanome, a VR software platform for molecular design, to collaborate on coronavirus research and potential treatments. A broader concept is extended reality (XR), an umbrella term that encompasses VR, AR, and mixed reality.

- *Voice tech and smart homes:* As public panic over germs spread by touching grows, so too will the use of voice tech, which can reduce these touches and slow the spread of germs. During the pandemic, Amazon quickly worked to fill the Alexa database with information from sources such as the Centers for Disease Control and Prevention. Given the hands-free nature of Alexa, the voice tech is also being used inside hospitals as a communication tool. Northwell Hospital in New York added 4000 Echo Show devices to allow staff to speak with COVID-19 patients in isolation.

- *AI:* This is applicable for detection of viruses, individuals with fever, and suspected symptoms through the integration of thermal imaging, computer vision, and cloud computing. Accordingly, advice on treatments can be provided.

- *Cloud computing:* All necessary health information is stored at a computing platform and made available to enable an enormous amount of computing power to healthcare professionals with the help of the Internet to make real-time decisions in disease modeling.

- *Big Data usage:* This provides storage capacity for extensive and useful data on the population in a format that can be used efficiently for analysis. It enables necessary actions to prevent disease transmission and movement and aid health monitoring.

- *Blockchain:* Providing real-time information to all strategic partners using algorithms and traceability in the process of disease control aids effective management of the supply chain. For example, blockchain would enable showing proof of origin of pharmaceutical products and provide greater security.

- *IoT:* All devices are connected to the Internet in hospitals and strategic locations, thereby informing medical staff of any error and change of requirements in real time during the treatment process.

- *Enterprise communication platform:* Software is used to hold video and audio communications, chats, and webinars easily and quickly across a large number of communication devices.

- *3D printing for medical devices:* Personalized devices are manufactured for healthcare workers and COVID-19 patients using 3D technology.

- *Smartphone apps:* A high-speed network for applications allows for activities such as contact-tracing of infected patients, modeling of disease outcomes, and prescription renewal for patient convenience.

Several engineering-based innovative and modern technologies can be used to fight this pandemic effectively. Recent practices have indicated that new-generation technologies have significant advantages, and they are the building blocks for future healthcare (Vaishya et al., 2020).

Over the long term, COVID-19 will enable us to see human–technology collaboration at its best, potentially easing patients' concerns about technology. A 2019 global study on AI (TechVision, 2020b) found that one of the top roadblocks to scaling technology is the lack of employee adoption. The COVID-19 pandemic could take us past this reflection point. Success today could open new possibilities for the healthcare industry to reimagine hospitals and the workforce in the future.

TechVision (2020b) offered a concept termed DARQ technologies (distributed ledgers, AI, extended reality, and quantum computing) for technological innovations in the healthcare industry. Healthcare businesses will be set apart by the way they merge and combine seemingly separate strategies. COVID-19 has shifted the balance, accelerating DARQ technologies to innovate, invent, and redefine healthcare firms.

ADOPTING EMERGING TECHNOLOGIES POST-COVID-19

In response to the COVID-19 pandemic, governments and healthcare companies throughout the world have been forced to accelerate the adoption of emerging technologies to mitigate the virus's impact. They should adopt a structured and phased approach to digital transformation and collaborate to build a robust ecosystem that supports this transformation. Managing the economic and societal problems arising from the pandemic has intensified the global trend to increase technological investment. Countries need a fundamental digital transformation to sustain long-term growth and soften the blow of any economic shocks. Countries must develop a structured approach to their unique challenges for both the short and long term. Short-term requirements involve shoring up the economy, continuing vital services, and ensuring containment of the pandemic. They should also revisit their digital strategies for the long term and make certain that they have the necessary supporting framework in place, such as laws, public awareness, and governance measures.

Government and the private sector will confront major obstacles without a strong digital ecosystem that facilitates success. Collaboration between government and the private sector should be founded on a common interest in creating a technologically adept economy and society, requiring digital upgrading. The private sector can engage proactively with government officials to overcome legal and regulatory barriers. Open sharing of data between stakeholders will stimulate more rapid technological development, while both parties should prioritize secure data transfers and personal privacy. The pandemic has highlighted the importance of technology, and all institutions will need an advanced digital framework to keep pace (Hajj et al., 2020).

ROLE OF GOVERNMENT

It is important to acknowledge that, in addition to the healthcare industry, federal and local governments had to play significant roles in several aspects of handling and managing COVID-19 healthcare impacts. One such example is the application of the Defense Production Act (DPA). The Biden Administration issued DPA priority ratings to its orders under contracts with Pfizer to alleviate bottlenecks in supplies of two necessary components in the pharmaceutical company's vaccine manufacturing process: filling pumps and tangential flow filtration skid units. DPA regulations require contractors to prioritize rated orders ahead of their other business. This action was a critical factor enabling Pfizer's announced plan to produce 200 million vaccine doses by May 2021. Additionally, the Administration used DPA's financing authorities to surge COVID-19 testing capacity by contracting with six suppliers to build new factories and supply lines in the United States. These agreements resulted in the production of 61 million additional at-home or point-of-care COVID-19 tests by the end of the summer of 2021.

In 2020, the Trump Administration used the powers of the DPA to compel companies to manufacture items in short supply, such as ventilators and N95 respirators, that would aid in the US response to COVID-19. Those companies included General Motors, Ford Motors, General Electric, Hill-Rom, Medtronic, ResMed, Royal Philips, and 3M.

Another example of government intervention is the effective use of Project Airbridge in getting supplies to areas most in need. The airbridge flights were established to reduce the time it takes for US medical supply distributors to receive PPE and other critical supplies for their respective customers. The Federal Emergency Management Agency covers the cost to fly supplies into the US from overseas factories, reducing shipment time from weeks to days. Overseas flights arrive at operational hub airports for distribution to hotspots and nationwide locations through regular supply chains.

BEYOND THE CORONAVIRUS: THE LONG-TERM SOCIO-ECONOMIC IMPACT

While we navigate this crisis and challenge our traditional metrics and assumptions, we can look forward to our next normal. Agrawal et al. (2020) offer detailed descriptions of five stages (the 5 Rs), leading from the crisis of today to the next normal that will emerge after winning the battle against the coronavirus: Resolve, Resilience, Return, Reimagination, and Reform. We give a brief explanation of each below.

- *Resolve:* Address the immediate challenges that COVID-19 represents to the institution's workforce, customers, technology, and business partners.
- *Resilience:* Address near-term cash-management challenges and broader resiliency issues during virus-related shutdowns and economic knock-on effects.
- *Return:* Create a detailed plan to return the business to scale quickly as the COVID-19 situation evolves and knock-on effects become clearer.
- *Reimagination:* Reimagine the next normal—what a discontinuous shift looks like and implications for how institutions should reinvent themselves.
- *Reform:* Be clear about how regulatory and competitive environments in the industry may shift.

COVID-19 is a historic event that has had major impacts on the global economy, geopolitics, the healthcare industry, and our societies. Global impacts and economic risks are highly inter-dependent and are changing the current and future global risk landscape (Scott, 2020). We have seen record levels of unemployment due to lockdown measures to control transmission and have observed that social deprivation affects health outcomes. Long-term societal impacts, such as heightened inequality and changes in consumer behaviors, healthcare practices, the nature of work, and the role of technology—both at work and at home—will change our way of life forever, for us as individuals, as a workforce, and as a society. In some healthcare sectors, a combination of furloughing and fiscal policies has helped put economies on hold. As countries emerge from the immediate health crisis and restart their economies, historic long-term change in employment is expected. This results in both fear and optimism in society and the labor force.

The challenge to return to a new normal is as much a psychological as an economic choice. Getting back to a pre-COVID world is likely to be a long and difficult task, at least until there is an effective health crisis exit strategy that involves a combination of a widely available vaccine and therapeutic drugs. In the meantime, there are likely to be continued cutbacks in travel, tourism, and hospitality. We must reconcile natural fears with acceptance of the uncertainties. The effectiveness of government may be compromised by the perceived lack of transparency that may lead to an erosion of trust and greater complications in the long run.

Another dangerous social impact of COVID-19 is the potential discrimination against Asians. Hate crimes targeting Asian people have risen since COVID-19 started in the US and around the globe. The economic, health, and societal disruptions during COVID-19 are high-lighting several societal inequalities concerning race, age, gender, education level, economic status, and other demographics. The timing and speed of the economic recovery are likely to exacerbate inequality, mental health problems, and the lack of societal cohesion. The recovery and normalization process needs to focus on addressing such inequalities. However, some of these social and economic inequalities are here to stay as we endeavor into the next normal.

Nevertheless, the attempt in the next normal will be to build back a better world from the perspective of ESG issues. The healthcare industry will need to provide its skills and assets to help invest in a better society. A better future is a world that brings the best of all sectors, both public and private. There is cause for optimism. We need to focus not only on a healthcare solution but also a recovery process that is focused on the climate, sustainability, a crisis exit strategy, and societal risks, including mental health and diversity.

CONCLUSION

One way or another, the next few years will be the time when the world transitions to the next normal. A pandemic can be the birthplace of innovation and progress. Sometimes, it takes a crisis of this scale to help us realize that change is necessary. While frontline healthcare personnel are focused on the daily challenges of combating the disease, the pandemic has revealed problems with healthcare delivery in the world, from supply chain breakdowns to staff and equipment shortages and burnout. Health executives faced a host of challenges, including the supply and distribution of vital resources, the disproportionate impact the virus has had on disadvantaged communities, the stress it placed on providers trying to balance work and home life, and the politicization of simple protection protocols, such as wearing masks and vaccination. Major challenges ahead will include both healthcare and operational issues, such as rightsizing after the telehealth explosion, adjusting to ever-changing clinical trials, encouraging digital relationships between provider and patient, forecasting for a continuously uncertain future, and building a responsive and agile supply chain for long-term health.

The difficulties presented by the pandemic placed healthcare in the world at an inflection point. Each of us has a role to play in overcoming the impacts of COVID-19. Whether it is to tackle health disparities, preparedness for the next pandemic, our disjointed health insurance market, or the operational aspects of the healthcare system, we all need to be working together and seize this moment to build back a better world.

REFERENCES

Agrawal, G., Conway, M., Heller, J., & Tolub, G. (2020, July). *On pins and needles: Will COVID-19 vaccines "save the world"?* McKinsey & Company. https://www.mckinsey.com/~/media/mckinsey/industries/life%20sciences/our%20insights/on%20pins%20and%20needles%20will%20covid%2019%20vaccines%20save%20the%20world/july%202020/on-pins-and-needles-will-covid-19-vaccines-save-the-world-v4.pdf

Bettinger, K. (2020, April 10). *COVID-19: Emerging technologies are now critical infrastructure – What that means for governance.* World Economic Forum. https://www.weforum.org/agenda/2020/04/covid-19-emerging-technologies-are-now-critical-infrastructure-what-that-means-for-governance/

Bordoloi, S., Fitzsimmons, J., & Fitzsimmons, M. (2018). *Service management: Operations, strategy, information technology* (9th ed.). McGraw Hill.

Deloitte Analysis. (2021). *COVID-19: Managing supply chain risk and disruption.* https://www2.deloitte.com/global/en/pages/risk/cyber-strategic-risk/articles/covid-19-managing-supply-chain-risk-and-disruption.html

Fowkes, J., Fross, C., Gilbert, G., & Harris, A. (2020, June). *Virtual health: A look at the next frontier of care delivery.* McKinsey & Company. https://www.mckinsey.com/industries/healthcare-systems-and-services/our-insights/virtual-health-a-look-at-the-next-frontier-of-care-delivery

Hajj, J., Atwi, I., Salamat, J., & Raquib, R. (2020, July). *Adopting emerging technologies in a post-COVID-19 world.* Strategy&. https://www.strategyand.pwc.com/m1/en/articles/2020/adopting-emerging-technologies-in-a-post-covid-world.html

Lee, H. L. (2002). Aligning supply chain strategies with product uncertainties. *California Management Review, 44*(3), 105–119.

Petrock, V. (2020, April 6). *How COVID-19 is fast-tracking emerging tech: Innovations show renewed promise during pandemic.* eMarketer.com. https://www.emarketer.com/content/how-covid-19-is-fast-tracking-emerging-tech

Scott, J. (2020, May). *What risks does COVID-19 pose to society in the long-term?* World Economic Forum. https://www.weforum.org/agenda/2020/05/what-risks-does-covid-19-pose-to-society-in-the-long-term/

Singhal, S., Kayyali, B., Levin, R., & Greenberg, Z. (2020, June 23). *The next wave of healthcare innovation: The evolution of ecosystems.* McKinsey & Company. https://www.mckinsey.com/industries/healthcare-systems-and-services/our-insights/the-next-wave-of-healthcare-innovation-the-evolution-of-ecosystems

Sureddin, S. (2021, January 5). *Twelve post-pandemic supply-chain trends for 2021.* SupplyChainBrain. https://www.supplychainbrain.com/blogs/1-think-tank/post/32374-twelve-post-pandemic-supply-chain-trends-for-2021

TechVision2020. (2020a, June). *Driving value and values during COVID-19.* Accenture. https://www.accenture.com/_acnmedia/PDF-126/Accenture-Technology-Vision-2020-COVID19.pdf

TechVision2020. (2020b, June 19). *COVID-19: Post-Coronavirus technology trends.* Accenture. https://www.accenture.com/fi-en/insights/technology/tech-vision-coronavirus-trends

UNICEF. https://www.unicef.org/supply/documents/how-drones-can-be-used-combat-covid-19

Vaishya, R., Haleem, A., Vaish, A., & Javaid, M. (2020, July). Emerging technologies to combat the COVID-19 pandemic. *Journal of Clinical and Experimental Hepatology*, *10*(4), 409–411. https://dx.doi.org/10.1016%2Fj.jceh.2020.04.019

World Health Organization. (2021, June 11). *Statement for healthcare professionals: How COVID-19 vaccines are regulated for safety and effectiveness.* https://www.who.int/news/item/11-06-2021 -statement-for-healthcare-professionals-how-covid-19-vaccines-are-regulated-for-safety-and -effectiveness

16. Applying Lean healthcare in a non-profit hospital in Brazil

Ana Carolina Honda, Raquel Mizuki Eguchi Yoshida, Mateus Cecílio Gerolamo, Jeanne Liliane Marlene Michel and Mark M. Davis

INTRODUCTION[1]

Brazil is a large country of continental dimensions with a population of more than 200 million and widespread regional and social inequalities (Brazilian Institute of Geography and Statistics, 2018; Paim et al., 2011). Despite its many problems, Brazil's public health system has brought healthcare to millions of its poorer inhabitants who were previously denied even basic care (Massuda et al., 2018; World Health Organization [WHO], 2008). The Unified Health System (Sistema Único de Saúde, SUS) was founded by the 1988 Constitution and is based on the principles of health as a citizen's right and the obligation of the state to provide healthcare for its citizens (Massuda et al., 2018; Paim et al., 2011; WHO, 2008). According to the Brazilian Ministry of Health (2017), about 70 percent of the Brazilian population depends exclusively on SUS for its healthcare. The users of the public system are primarily women, children, the Black population, and individuals with low education levels and income (Silva et al., 2011). As reported in the 2017 annual report of the Ministry, the SUS includes approximately 7514 hospitals, of which 2538 are private for-profit, 1885 are private non-profit, and 3091 are public non-profit (Brazilian Ministry of Health, 2018). Many hospitals in the latter two categories are in a precarious situation regarding infrastructural and technological maintenance, supplier provisions, and personnel training. This situation is due, in many respects, to poor management of resources and insufficient funding leading to the lack of beds in rooms that are properly equipped to provide the required medical care to those who need it. A comparative list regarding spending on health by the government is presented in Table 16.1. This lack of necessary resources creates a recipe for chaos that is routinely encountered by almost all the healthcare units in the public network, according to Ferraz (2008).

In recent years, the Lean approach has increased in popularity as a tool for process improvement in developing and emerging countries and is one of the most commonly used in the health sector (Aguilar-Escobar et al., 2015; Honda et al., 2018; Machado & Leitner, 2017; Mazzocato et al., 2016). This is due in large part to the fact that the application of Lean concepts allows healthcare organizations to literally "do more with less." In the Brazilian healthcare system, this means doing more with fewer available resources.

The Lean concept originated in Japan. It began with the Toyota Production System shortly after the Second World War. At that time, the country had to restructure itself as it did not have the resources to engage in mass production at the same level as it had prior to the war. The creator of the Toyota Production System was the executive head of the corporation, the engineer Taiichi Ohno, and the disseminators were the founder and master of inventions, Toyoda

Table 16.1   Indicators of spending on health

Country	Government health spending per capita ($)	Spending on health as a percentage of gross domestic product (%)
United States	4,307	17.1
Germany	3,696	11.3
France	3,360	11.7
Canada	3,322	10.9
Australia	2,792	9.4
United Kingdom	2,766	9.1
Spain	2,004	8.9
Argentina	1,167	7.3
Chile	795	7.7
Brazil	701	9.7

Source: Adapted from Vieira (2016).

Sakichi and his son, Toyoda Kiichiro. Its principles are based on reducing waste, improving product quality, and reducing customer delivery time. It was from this concept of producing more with less that the system came to be called Lean Manufacturing by Womack et al. (1990) in their book *The Machine that Changed the World.*

Lean healthcare refers to the application of the Lean philosophy and principles in a healthcare environment. Basically, it is about understanding what is valuable to the patient in order to distinguish those activities that add value from those that do not. Activities that do not add value are often identified as waste and should be avoided or removed (Filser et al., 2017). The principles of Lean healthcare are listed in Table 16.2.

Table 16.2   Principles of Lean healthcare

a.	Respect and commitment of all with the reduction of waste
b.	5S and visual control; 5S represents Japanese words that describe the steps of a workplace organization process: Seiri (Sort), Seiton (Straighten, Set), Seiso (Shine, Sweep), Seiketsu (Standardize), Shitsuke (Sustain)
c.	"Just in time" (correct service, in the right amount, at the right time, and in the right place)
d.	Level workload and standardization of activities (balancing the distribution of activities and optimizing the work itself)
e.	Continuous flow (the use of pull systems that result in much less wasteful processes and flows)
f.	"Built in quality" (make problems visible, never allow a defect to continue to the next step in the process, make an error-proof system, interrupt when there is a quality failure)

Source: Adapted from Robinson and Kirsch (2015).

Although the literature clearly demonstrates that Lean is now widely recognized and has been increasingly used in the healthcare sector (Young & McClean, 2009), most of this reporting emanates from hospitals in developed countries that work with significant resources. The United States and the United Kingdom lead with the most number of publications in this area, followed by the Netherlands and Switzerland (Costa et al., 2015; Moraros et al., 2016). At the same time, there have been a limited number of studies conducted in developing and emerging countries, specifically India and Brazil, some of which are presented in Table 16.3.

While the current literature presents few success stories in developing and emerging countries that consist primarily of elite hospitals (that serve only a small portion of the country's population), this study focuses on the feasibility in applying Lean techniques to achieve process improvements and cost savings in a non-profit hospital of the public healthcare system

Table 16.3 Published studies on Lean healthcare from developing and emerging countries

Author	Title	Country	Findings
Gijo and Antony (2013)	Reducing Patient Waiting Time in Outpatient Department Using Lean Six Sigma Methodology	India	The average waiting time was reduced from 57 minutes to 24.5 minutes, and the standard deviation was reduced from 31.15 minutes to 9.27 minutes
Miller and Chalapati (2015)	Utilizing Lean Tools to Improve Value and Reduce Outpatient Wait Times in an Indian Hospital	India	The average waiting time was reduced from more than 1 hour to 15 minutes; the average number of patients per day increased from 40 to 120; the average number of patients staying overnight decreased from more than ten to less than one
Costa et al. (2015)	Lean Healthcare in Developing Countries: Evidence from Brazilian Hospitals	Brazil	a. Sterile Processing Department: cost (78%) and delay (94%) reduction; b. Pharmacy: balance inventory reduction; c. Chemotherapy: 33% increase in monthly revenues, 42% reduction in average patient lead time, 6% increase in the sector capacity; d. Operating Room: increase in monthly revenue, in the number of monthly surgical admissions, and in the number of monthly surgeries
Bhat et al. (2016)	Productivity and Performance Improvement in the Medical Records Department of a Hospital: An Application of Lean Six Sigma	India	The turnaround time to obtain records was reduced from an average of 19 minutes to eight minutes, and the standard deviation was reduced by one-tenth

in an emerging country. The successes achieved in applying Lean techniques in this non-profit hospital in Brazil suggest that similar results can be obtained in community hospitals in the United States that are non-teaching hospitals in both urban and rural areas that often receive no federal funds but nevertheless provide vital services to their local populations. Some similar achievements resulting from the use of similar methods in community hospitals in the United States are listed in Table 16.4.

METHOD

The case study method was chosen for this research. It consists of an empirical approach to investigating a topic according to a pre-specified set of procedures (Yin, 2009). This case study presents a description of the implementation of continuous improvement techniques in two strategic processes within one hospital.

The setting for this study was a 300-bed, private, non-profit hospital located in São Paulo, Brazil. The hospital serves a population of about 700 000 people, including the 350 000 inhabitants of the city where the hospital is located. About 90 percent of its beds are reserved for SUS patients (with the remaining 10 percent being allocated to patients with private health insurance).[2] This hospital is typical of the majority of Brazilian hospitals as well as healthcare institutions in other developing and emerging countries. Despite all the financial issues, the hospital is still investing in management innovations using a consulting firm to implement quality improvement techniques to enhance management processes and improve patient care. It is believed that savings achieved by enhancing efficiency is worthy compared to continuing wasting resources.

The hospital's two processes that were studied in this case were: (a) the purchasing and storing of supplies; and (b) the generating and administering of patients' medications, including writing medical prescriptions, pharmacy dispensing, and administering the medicines to the patients by nursing. Each of the intervention projects had a specific interdisciplinary team consisting of a manager/leader (i.e., clinical nurse, pharmacist, or purchaser), the respective department's staff, and external consultants. Additionally, the information technology staff, analysts, and the hospital's continuous improvement team participated in the project at key stages. All projects were implemented following the DMAIC methodology that is associated with Six Sigma.

Six Sigma is an improvement strategy focused on processes that aims to reduce defects and variability in order to meet customer requirements (Honda et al., 2018). DMAIC is a structured, continuous improvement process consisting of five steps: Define, Measure, Analyze, Improve, and Control. Initially, in the Define step, the project focus is established, as well as the study objective(s) and the problem to be addressed. Next, in the Measure phase, management teams collect data to evaluate the process's ability to satisfy customer demand and provide relevant information pertaining to the process under study. In the Analyze step, the major root causes of the problem(s) are identified, organized, and validated. The Improve step is where the team proposes, plans, and implements the solution. Finally, the Control step ensures that the achieved improvements are sustained and will not be lost (Boon Sin et al., 2015; Carpinetti, 2016).

The research questions were formulated according to an implementation framework that determined the variables chosen for the case study. The questions that were developed were

Table 16.4   Similar studies in community hospitals in the United States

Author	Title	Methodology	Findings
Laing and Baumgartner (2005)	Implementing "Lean" Principles to Improve the Efficiency of the Endoscopy Department of a Community Hospital: A Case Study	Lean principles	Savings of $7000 on linens and inventory, $1000 on suture supplies, a decrease of two-thirds of on-hand inventory, elimination of 0.8 full-time equivalent (FTE), and reduced cycle time by 17 minutes in an endoscopy unit
Hussain et al. (2015)	Managerial Process Improvement: A Lean Approach to Eliminating Medication Delivery	Toyota Production System (TPS)/Lean combined with human performance improvement (HPI) methodologies	They introduce the Production Process Improvement (PPI) model, a combination of TPS and HPI, as a method that provides visual representation needed to design and implement a robust system that has the potential to eliminate medication errors in hospitals
Raghavan et al. (2010)	Reengineering the Cardiac Catheterization Lab Processes: A Lean Approach	Six Sigma, Define, Measure, Analyze, Improve, and Control (DMAIC), Lean, 5S	By identifying the sources of delays in the system that lead to prolonged patient turnaround time using a structured Lean approach, the authors proposed qualitative recommendations. Simulation results showed that significant reduction in patient turnaround time could be achieved if the proposed recommendations were implemented
Peacock (2006)	Lean Six Sigma: Optimizing Operating Room Utilization at Bayne-Jones Army Community Hospital	Lean Six Sigma	"The DMAIC approach provided a framework to develop recommendations for improving operating room utilization and achieving Relative Value Units (RVU) and Relative Weighted Products (RWP) goals. The surgical service with the greatest potential for improving utilization is Ophthalmology"
Beckford (2018)	Lean Implementation at a Community Hospital	Lean	By introducing Washington Health System and describing how the community hospital implemented Lean in its system, the author concluded that healthcare processes are more efficient, employees are more productive, and patients are safer and more satisfied
Gebicki et al. (2009)	Methods and Skills for Improving Health Care Processes: A Lean Engineering Approach	Lean/TPS	Students were able to suggest a set of skills industrial engineers needed to successfully improve this hospital's operations. This set includes systematic thinking, visualizing, systems thinking, qualitative research techniques, and cultural observation skills

Author	Title	Methodology	Findings
Dickson (2013)	Utilizing a Lean Six Sigma Approach to Reduce Total Joint Arthroplasty Surgical Site Infections in a Community Hospital	Lean Six Sigma	An estimated $300 000 savings was calculated based on the reductions of the Standardized Infection Ratio achieved by the method
Chiu et al. (2016)	A LEAN Approach to Emergency Department Crowding in a Southern California Health System	Lean	Reduction of length of stay from over 200 minutes to 180 minutes, LWBS (left without being seen) rates decreased from 3–5% to less than 1%, door-to-doctor times decreased to an average of 31 minutes, and EDPEC (Emergency Department Patient Experience of Care) satisfaction scores increased from 44% to 50%

Note: DMAIC is a structured, continuous improvement process consisting of five steps: Define, Measure, Analyze, Improve, and Control.

based on a literature review of practical cases, specifically, on the case study protocol presented in one of these studies (Costa et al., 2015). The main objective, research questions, variables, data sources, and interview questions of this case study are presented as a methodology framework in Table 16.5.

CASE STUDY

The Process of Purchasing and Storing Supplies

The Purchasing Department is responsible for guaranteeing the support and resources required to provide qualified medical assistance and to carry out purchasing and its storage management. The purchasing manager monitors medicines and material quantities within a specified time. Before the improvement project was implemented, the purchasing process took an average of 20 days, and the material on hand averaged about 40 days' usage.

This process generated numerous failures, such as: (a) an overloaded warehouse; (b) the material being stored in several locations resulting in an excessive number of storage areas besides the main warehouse; and (c) employees having to walk significant distances to access all the storage areas. All these failures meant a significant waste of time and money.

The Process of Generating and Processing Prescriptions

The routine prior to the project's implementation basically began when the physician manually wrote a prescription valid for 24 hours, which had to be filled by 10 a.m. with a tolerance of 2 hours so that there would be a guarantee that all the prescriptions would be distributed in the afternoon after 12 p.m. The cumulative prescriptions were taken by a nurse to the pharmacy where the employees separated and packed all required medicines and materials. These packages were then sent in a single batch to the nursing station, where the nurses administered the prescriptions during the subsequent 24-hour period.

This system generated numerous failures, such as: (a) the high lead time of the process (9.5 hours); and (b) the return of medicines to the pharmacy as a consequence of the illegibility of physicians' handwriting, or the discharge, transference, or death of a patient during the period. Mistakes in the patients' billing were another recurring problem; the main cause was that the medicines contained in vials for shared use were billed to one patient instead of to everyone who needed a fraction of it.

RESULTS

The Process of Purchasing and Storing Supplies

The team was composed of a leader with technical training in logistics and operations, warehouse employees, members of the Information Technology Department and of the Purchasing Department, and two external consultants. The team members received training from the

Table 16.5   Variables and data sources of this case study

CASE STUDY PROTOCOL			
OBJECTIVE			
Study Lean healthcare application in a non-profit hospital			
RESEARCH QUESTIONS			
Is it feasible to apply Lean concepts to achieve process improvements and cost savings for a non-profit hospital in a developing country?			
What are the quantitative and qualitative results obtained from implementing Lean healthcare?			

VARIABLES STUDIED			
i. Departments involved	v. Training provided		
ii. Improvement implementation period	vi. Tools employed		
iii. Benefits obtained (quantitative/qualitative)	vii. Barriers to improvement implementation		
iv. Composition of interdisciplinary teams	viii. Critical success factors		

DATA SOURCES			
Primary			Secondary
A. Interviews with department staffs and consultants		B. Direct observation of the processes in the involved departments	C. Analysis of documents provided by the teams and consulting firms
	A1. Department staff	A2. Consulting firm members		
General Information	Two people from the Pharmacy Department answered this questionnaire; one of them was the project leader. In the Purchasing Department the project leader answered the questions. However, it was not possible to talk with any individuals from the nursing team during the visit due to the nurses' very busy routines. The interviews were conducted during the visits	The firm's owner and a member from each of the two projects studied. The interviews were conducted through conference calls	During the visits the responsible persons for the Pharmacy and the Purchasing Departments presented their respective departments. It was therefore possible to follow closely the operations of both systems. The talks were recorded for reference and for further information	The consulting firm and the hospital quality team provided a database of the project material that included spreadsheets and charts. The hospital's website and the database as well as the National Registry of Health Establishments (CNES) were also consulted for further information
Quantity	One with each person, with follow-up phone calls to resolve remaining issues	Two conference calls	Two visits	Several documents
Duration	2 hours	2 hours each	6 hours each	4 hours

INTERVIEW QUESTIONS	
A1. Internal members	A2. External members (from consulting firm)
What is your technical background?	In which processes were improvement projects carried out?
What was your role in the project?	What were the quantitative and qualitative gains?
When you first heard about the project, did you agree that this was necessary for hospital improvement?	How long did each project last? (the first full DMAIC cycle)
Have you ever had previous contact with any continuous improvement tool? Had you heard of it before?	How many and who were the members of the team? What were the roles of each one?

CASE STUDY PROTOCOL – INTERVIEW QUESTIONS CONTINUATION	
Was the training enough to deal with the tools?	Did you give any training to the team? What was covered in this training?
At some point during the implementation, did you disagree? Has your opinion changed during the process?	Which tool(s) were used in each step?
Did you have difficulty undergoing any changes during implementation?	What were the barriers/difficulties encountered before/during/after the project?
Is there anything you wanted to do that was not accepted? What was the idea or suggestion? What was the reason it was not accepted?	Which factors were critical to the success of the project?

external consulting team based on the principles of Lean healthcare, proper inventory lot sizing, and Kanban, a pull system that controls inventory based on colored cards that track productions and orders in a visual way. Each of the internal staff dedicated about 3 hours a week to the project, and the external consulting team members contributed a full day to the effort. The project lasted about 4 months, including training in the Lean approach and DMAIC steps, and after which the purchasing processing time was reduced from 20 to 5 days, as shown in Figure 16.1.

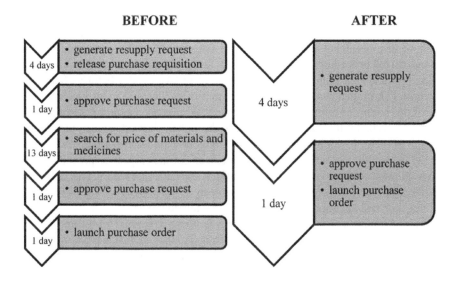

Figure 16.1   Time spent in each phase of the purchasing process, before and after the intervention

The entire purchasing process was redesigned, resulting in two major actions being initiated. First, it was found that some items are very expensive (e.g., antineoplastics), some are more frequently utilized than others, and suppliers would be willing to negotiate their prices. It was also proposed that purchases be made more frequently in order to gain supplier loyalty along with long-term prices. In addition to the antineoplastics, other items included in this new plan were: laboratory/radiology materials, surgical thread, enteral/parenteral nutrition, intravenous (IV) solutions, and cleaning material.

A new system, called "Scheduled Purchase," was adopted. One advantage of the Scheduled Purchase system was the release of the monthly needs assessment with the entire quotation procedure, waiting for the response time, and closing the order. The deliveries started to be done on a weekly basis using a pull system; that is, products were ordered when established product order points were reached. Because of the increase in supplier loyalty process and their fixed-price contracts, the quotation and approval phases were eliminated entirely from the process, making it more agile. It was therefore easier to manage the inventory, and it became more current and smaller. In addition, the smaller overall inventory required significantly less space for storage, thereby allowing the centralization of the material in one location.

Quantitatively, after just two months of Scheduled Purchase implementation, there was a 22-percent stock reduction. As an example, in the case of the antineoplastic stock, there was a 46-percent reduction, equivalent to approximately R$180 000 (Brazilian Reais, or about US$36 000). A few months later, additional materials were added to the "Scheduled Purchase" list, resulting in a stock reduction from about R$2 400 000 (US$498 000) to R$800 000 (US$166 000).

Over time, due to the decrease of stock and the freeing up of storage space, a new activity was added to the warehouse tasks: the organization and assembly of different kits (e.g., curative kit, probing kit, nursing procedures kit). These kits had not been used previously, so the nursing staff had to leave their wards and go to various places to obtain the necessary supplies to provide the needed care. The assembly of kits reduced the waste of energy and time with these displacements and thus improved the nursing staff's performance in some frequent standardized procedures. The kits are now restocked daily based on a report printed each morning that states the number and kind of kits withdrawn the day before. This measurement is performed through a barcode reader that is part of the hospital's software system. The importance of this control is reinforced by the slogan "Se bipar não vai faltar" ("No lack if you scan"), which means that if the materials are passed through the barcode reader, then there will be no shortage of them. In addition, the assembled kits now undergo periodic evaluations to verify that the items and quantities are meeting the needs of the respective procedures. Some items, such as gloves, which have sizes small, medium, and large, are readily available in stock and are therefore not included in the kits. In addition, an ongoing analysis is performed for the creation of new kits and the improvement of those that already exist.

It is important to emphasize that the staff of the warehouse never had any issues with being responsible for assembling the kits. This can be attributed to the fact that they view themselves as support personnel, and that the primary focus of the nursing staff should be the patients' care.

The Process of Generating and Processing Prescriptions

The Pharmacy Department is responsible for receiving medical prescriptions and dispensing them, and nursing staff respond for the overall administration of medicines. The project team for this process intervention was led by the responsible pharmacist and consisted of two members of the Pharmacy Department, the nursing manager, three external consultants, and two analysts. All internal members received training by the external consulting staff in Lean healthcare, process mapping, process flow and balancing, 5S, work standardization, and visual management. The members of the pharmacy team worked on implementing Lean practices for an average of 4 hours per week. The consultants and the improvement team spent a slightly higher average, around 6 hours a week, working on the project. The total duration of the project was 3 months, including training in the Lean approach and the DMAIC steps.

The team identified that the main problems were delays and errors in filling prescriptions and their subsequent deliveries; hence, they established the following goals:

- Deploy 100 percent electronic prescription ordering process to replace the manual prescription process;
- Reduce by 30 percent the total lead time for the medical prescriptions (9.5 hours) to minimize the time from when the prescription is written by the physician, taken to the pharmacy, sent to the hospital ward, and finally administered to the patient;
- Reduce 90 percent of the errors in the medical prescription process (which includes their generation and the delivery of medicines by the pharmacy);
- Reduce unnecessary movement of nursing between wards and pharmacy; and
- Improve the accuracy of the items included in patients' bills.

The team's next step identified the root causes of the problems: medicine delivery errors were attributable to manual writing (prescription generation), which does not have a fault-control mechanism or much less guaranteed legibility. Errors and delays in the delivery of medicines occurred for several reasons, for example, non-adherence to the prescription limitation time rule, dispensing errors of the pharmacy, the disregard for required process protocols, a disorganized work environment, inadequate inventories of required medicines, and inadequate or improperly balanced resources as determined by takt time—that is, the amount of time in which a product needs to be provided to satisfy consumer demand.

The improvements resulted from a kaizen, or an event involving the entire team making small improvements consistently over time, in which the following changes were implemented:

- A new schedule was developed and implemented for receipt of prescriptions and delivery of medicines. With this new approach, the day was divided into three shifts to receive the prescriptions, deliver them, and then administer them to the patients;
- Electronic prescriptions were introduced so the physician now entered the prescription in a computer where it was printed directly at the pharmacy;
- Medication application kits were supplied with each prescribed medicine: prior to implementation, application kits were kept in the nursing station. After the implementation, they were placed inside the package along with the medicines (this decreased the number of tasks performed by the nurses);
- Redesign of the layout of the Central Pharmacy using 5S (eliminating unnecessary items and organizing the remaining ones in suitable and accessible locations according to their necessity); and
- Storage area for IV solutions and medicines outside the pharmacy: the sera took up a lot of space, so they were relocated.

As a result of implementing these changes, the project achieved the following results:

- the time for the prescription to reach the pharmacy was reduced from 3.5 hours to a few seconds;
- the lead time was reduced from 9.5 hours to 5 hours; and
- a reduction in medication delivery errors, delays, inventory, and patients' waiting times.

The big success factor here was the simplification and standardization of the process, as reported by Hussain et al. (2015). According to the authors, to eliminate errors, the workflow process should follow a specific sequence, timing, task content, the right people, and shortest established routes during the whole patient-care process.

Moreover, before implementing these changes, the nurses were required to carry pre-scriptions to the pharmacy and seek resources, such as IV solutions or painkillers and fever-reducers, from various places. A movement measurement revealed that each nurse moved an average of almost 4 km a shift and that the nurses spent a lot of time moving around and performing non-value-added activities. The average movement by each nurse per shift is now 1.5 km, resulting in a 63 percent reduction.

With respect to the kits assembled in the warehouse, the most common materials used for administering the drugs are now supplied in the form of kits by the pharmacy. Every time these materials are taken from the station they are scanned at the barcode reader by the nurse. This action generates a replacement request to the pharmacy. The most common materials and medicines used in patient care, such as non-sterile procedure gloves, bandages, and syringes, are now computerized in each patient's bill according to the average usage.

The standardization of processes, besides affecting directly the potential of errors, is very important for quality control (doing the process the same way each time will provide reference for continuous improvement; Gebicki et al., 2009). The evaluation process is completed by monitoring indicators such as the number of printed prescriptions, medications that were cor-rectly accounted for each patient, and medications that were delivered on time, among others. These data are collected daily by the pharmacy manager with the contribution of staff, who answer a list of questions at the end of their shift. The team leaders play their part, ensuring that the whole plan is in place to hold the gains and accomplish new ones (Hussain et al., 2015).

DISCUSSION

Although the projects were planned and executed separately for each of the two processes studied, it was possible to see that the improvements were not restricted to the area in which they were implemented. The changes in the Pharmacy and Purchasing Departments had a direct influence on the nurses' work. By improving the processes that are linked to the nurses' work, it becomes possible for them to be more efficient in their critical daily tasks, thereby allowing them more time to perform other essential nursing duties (Kieran et al., 2017).

One of the difficulties was the fear and distrust on the part of the employees at the beginning of the projects. There was some disbelief about the veracity of the numbers and the new system proposed. As the first results came throughout the work, the team gained confidence. In the same way, one of the most relevant critical success factors was starting the implementation where it would be possible to achieve faster and visible results, such as in hospital sectors that work with materials (e.g., pharmacies). This encourages project expansion to other areas (Heuvel et al., 2005).

The manual alterations of prescriptions is one of the recurring problems in the pharmacy. In some cases, the physician wants to add some medicine or make some change to the initial version of the prescription. To accomplish this, the physician should follow the same proce-dure as with the initial prescription—that is, prescribe it electronically—so that the change reaches the printer directly at the pharmacy. However, what often happens is that some physicians still add handwritten information to the printed version that is at the nursing station. This creates a break in the information flow, causing an unnecessary increase in work for the nurses who need to deliver the new prescription to the pharmacy. This kind of implementation barrier is not typical in developed countries/elite hospital settings, since doctors are often included as part of the project team collaborating to process improvement initiatives (Yoshida, 2020).

CONCLUSION

Lean healthcare has been widely adopted in the quest for excellence in quality and to maintain the competitiveness of large hospitals primarily in developed countries. There are limitations of this study, such as the lack of statistical evidence due to the manual steps involved, for example, in the process of generating prescriptions and delivering patients' medications. Higher quality and a better scientific research approach is required to more accurately determine the impact and effectiveness of Lean in healthcare settings (Moraros et al., 2016). This case study provides empirical and qualitative evidence that Lean healthcare creates benefits for hospitals (even public or private non-profit institutions) in developing and emerging countries, where the lack of resources often hinders management's ability to make improvements. Nevertheless, the hospital involved in this study obtained considerable cost savings and process improvements, thus showing the possibility of applying Lean techniques and achieving process improvements and cost savings for hospitals in developing and emerging countries.

Some of the mentioned studies indicate that Lean techniques can be applied in any hospital and its success is not exclusively dependent on available resources. The positive outcomes rely on the standardization of processes, continuous improvement, shared responsibilities, and, more importantly, total support and commitment from all stakeholders, mainly the hospital management (Dickson, 2013; Gebicki et al., 2009; Hussain et al., 2015; Liefvergreen et al. , 2010). While this case study focused primarily on applying Lean concepts to two specific processes within the hospital, these same techniques could be readily applied to a wide variety of clinical and administrative processes within healthcare. Thus, significant process improvements that were made in this case study in Brazil suggest that Lean healthcare can be successfully implemented in many healthcare environments rather than being limited to a few elite hospitals that typically have more resources available.

NOTES

1. We thank everyone who supported this research: the funding agency; people from the Lean consulting firm who were carrying out a project and gave us data and information about implementation; and people from the hospital, for the interest and openness in accepting our research. Finally, we thank the University of São Paulo and Bentley University for providing the infrastructure available for this research. The authors have no potential conflict of interest. Ana Carolina Honda received a master's student scholarship from the Brazilian Coordination for the Improvement of Higher Education Personnel (CAPES).
2. This division was determined for the hospital itself, and the decision is based on the desired profile. For example, if the non-profit hospital wants to be categorized as a teaching hospital, the regulation establishes that at least 60 percent of its beds are reserved for SUS patients, among other requirements.

REFERENCES

Aguilar-Escobar, V., Bourque, S., & Godino-Gallego, N. (2015). Hospital Kanban system implementation: Evaluating satisfaction of nursing personnel. *Investigaciones Europeas De Dirección y Economía de la Empresa, 21*(3), 101–110. doi: 10.1016/j.iedee.2014.12.001

Beckford, M. (2018). *Lean implementation at a community hospital* [Unpublished Master's thesis]. University of Pittsburgh.

Bhat, S., Gijo, E., & Jnanesh, N. (2016). Productivity and performance improvement in the medical records department of a hospital. *International Journal of Productivity and Performance Management, 65*(1), 98–125. doi: 10.1108/ijppm-04-2014-0063

Boon Sin, A., Zailani, S., Iranmanesh, M., & Ramayah, T. (2015). Structural equation modelling on knowledge creation in Six Sigma DMAIC project and its impact on organizational performance. *International Journal of Production Economics, 168*, 105–117. doi: 10.1016/j.ijpe.2015.06.007

Brazilian Institute of Geography and Statistics. (2018). *Projeção da população*. https://www.ibge.gov.br

Brazilian Ministry of Health. (2017). *Portal da Saúde*. http://portalsaude.saude.gov.br/

Brazilian Ministry of Health. (2018). *Annual report*. Secretaria de Atenção à Saúde. http://portalarquivos2.saude.gov.br/images/pdf/2018/abril/16/RELATORIO-DE-GESTAO-2017--COMPLETO-PARA-MS.pdf

Carpinetti, L. (2016). *Gestão da Qualidade: Conceitos e Técnicas* (3rd ed.). Atlas.

Chiu, C., Tsai, T., Hwong, R., Stewart, J. J., Wu, S., Yu, S.-Y., Yu, S., Chorvat, N., Liu, S., Huang, W., Agron, M., Aquino, J., Chang, E.-M., Giordano, S., Lorack, D., Ternes, H., Lin, M., Wu, J., & Chiu, W.-T. (2016). A LEAN approach to emergency department crowding in a southern California health system. *Emergency Medicine, 2*(2), 42–47. doi: 10.17140/EMOJ-2-129

Costa, L. B. M., Filho, M. G., Rentes, A. F., Bertani, T. M., & Mardegan, R. (2015). Lean healthcare in developing countries: Evidence from Brazilian hospitals. *International Journal of Health Planning and Management, 32*(1), 99–120. doi: 10.1002/hpm.2331

Dickson, A. (2013). Utilizing a Lean Six Sigma approach to reduce total joint arthroplasty surgical site infections in a community hospital. *American Journal of Infection Control, 41*(6), S131–S132. https://doi.org/10.1016/j.ajic.2013.03.260

Ferraz, E. (2008). O caos no atendimento do Sistema único de saúde [The chaos in the care of the Unified Health System]. *Revista do Colégio Brasileiro de Cirurgiões, 35*(5), 280–281. doi: 10.1590/S0100-69912008000500001

Filser, L., da Silva, F., & de Oliveira, O. (2017). State of research and future research tendencies in Lean healthcare: a bibliometric analysis. *Scientometrics 112*(2): 799–816. doi: 10.1007/s11192-017-2409-8

Gebicki, M., Andrikopoulos, A., Hume, M., Mazur, L., & Chen, S.-J. (2009). *Methods and skills for improving health care processes: A Lean engineering approach* [Paper presentation]. Industrial Engineering Research Conference. IIE Annual Conference and Expo, Miami, Florida, May 2009. Accepted for oral presentation.

Gijo, E., & Antony, J. (2013). Reducing patient waiting time in outpatient department using Lean Six Sigma methodology. *Quality and Reliability Engineering International, 30*(8), 1481–1491. doi: 10.1002/qre.1552

Heuvel, J., Does, R., & Verver, J. (2005). Six Sigma in healthcare: Lessons learned from a hospital. *International Journal of Six Sigma and Competitive Advantage, 1*(4), 380–388. doi: 10.1504/IJSSCA.2005.008504

Honda, A., Bernardo, V., Gerolamo, M., & Davis, M. (2018). How Lean Six Sigma principles improve hospital performance. *Quality Management Journal, 25*(2), 70–82. doi: 10.1080/10686967.2018.1436349

Hussain, A., Stewart, L., Rivers, P., & Munchus, G. (2015). Managerial process improvement: A Lean approach to eliminating medication delivery. *International Journal Of Health Care Quality Assurance, 28*(1), 55–63. doi: 10.1108/ijhcqa-08-2013-0102

Kieran, M., Cleary, M., De Brún, A., & Igoe, A. (2017). Supply and demand: Application of Lean Six Sigma methods to improve drug round efficiency and release nursing time. *International Journal for Quality in Health Care, 29*(6), 803–9. doi: 10.1093/intqhc/mzx106

Laing, K., & Baumgartner, K. (2005). Implementing "Lean" principles to improve the efficiency of the endoscopy department of a community hospital: A case study. *Gastroenterology Nursing, 28*(3), 210–215.

Lifvergren, S., Gremyr, I., Hellstrom, A., Chakhunashvili, A., Bergman, B. 2010. Lessons from Sweden's first large-scale implementation of Six Sigma in healthcare. *Operations Management Research, 3*(3–4), 117–128. doi: 10.1107/s12063-010-0038-y

Machado, V., & Leitner, U. (2017). Lean tools and Lean transformation process in health care. *International Journal of Management Science and Engineering Management, 5*(5), 383–392. doi: 10.1080/17509653.2010.10671129

Massuda, A., Hone, T., Leles, F. A. G., Castro, M. C., & Atun, R. (2018). The Brazilian health system at crossroads: Progress, crisis and resilience. *BMJ Global Health, 3*(4), e000829. doi: 10.1136/bmjgh-2018-000829

Mazzocato, P., Stenfors-Hayes, T., von Thiele Schwarz, U., Hasson, H., & Nyström, M. (2016). Kaizen practice in healthcare: A qualitative analysis of hospital employees' suggestions for improvement. *BMJ Open, 6*(7), 012256. doi: 10.1136/bmjopen-2016-012256

Miller, R., & Chalapati, N. (2015). Utilizing Lean tools to improve value and reduce outpatient wait times in an Indian hospital. *Leadership in Health Services, 28*(1), 57–69. doi: 10.1108/LHS-01-2014-0001

Moraros, J., Lemstra, M., & Nwankwo, C. (2016). Lean interventions in healthcare: Do they actually work? A systematic literature review. *International Journal for Quality in Health Care, 28*(2), 150–165. doi: 10.1093/intqhc/mzv123

Paim, J., Travassos, C., Almeida, C., Bahia, L., & Macinko, J. (2011). The Brazilian health system: History, advances, and challenges. *The Lancet, 377*, 1778–1797. doi: 10.1016/S0140-6736(11)60054-8

Peacock, T. (2006). *Lean Six Sigma: Optimizing operating room utilization at Bayne-Jones Army Community Hospital* [unpublished Master's thesis]. Baylor University.

Raghavan, V., Venkatadri, V., Kesavakumaran, V., Wang, S., Khasawneh, M., & Srihari, K. (2010). Reengineering the cardiac catheterization lab processes: A Lean approach. *Journal Of Healthcare Engineering, 1*(1), 45–66. doi: 10.1260/2040-2295.1.1.45

Robinson, S., & Kirsch, J. (2015). Lean strategies in the operating room. *Anesthesiology Clinics, 33*(4), 713–730. doi: 10.1016/j.anclin.2015.07.010

Silva, Z., Ribeiro, M., Barata, R., & Almeida, M. (2011). Perfil sociodemográfico e padrão de utilização dos serviços de saúde do Sistema Único de Saúde (SUS), 2003–2008 [Socio-demographic profile and utilization patterns of the public healthcare system (SUS), 2003–2008]. *Ciência & Saúde Coletiva, 16*(9), 3807–3816. doi: 10.1590/s1413-81232011001000016

Vieira, F. (2016). Implicações de decisões e discussões recentes para o financiamento do Sistema Único de Saúde [Impact of recent decisions and discussions on the Brazilian Public Health System financing]. *Saúde Debate, 40*(109), 187–199. doi: 10.1590/0103-1104201610915

Womack, J., Jones, D., & Roos, D. (1990). *The machine that changed the world.* Rawson Associates.

World Health Organization. (2008). Flawed but fair: Brazil's health system reaches out to the poor. *Bulletin of the World Health Organization, 86*(4), 241–230. https://www.who.int/bulletin/volumes/86/4/08-030408/en/

Yin, R. (2009). *Case study research.* (4th ed.) SAGE.

Yoshida, R. (2020). *Aplicações de Lean Six Sigma em três hospitais da região de Boston: Relatos dos gestores* [Lean Six Sigma applications in three Boston area hospitals: Managers' reports] [unpublished undergraduate thesis]. University of São Paulo.

Young, T., & McClean, S. (2009). Some challenges facing Lean thinking in healthcare. *International Journal for Quality in Health Care, 21*(5), 309–310. doi: 10.1093/intqhc/mzp038

PART V

SERVICE ANALYTICS

17. Service science in a world flooded with data

Jorge Grenha Teixeira, Vera Miguéis, Henriqueta Nóvoa and João Falcão e Cunha

INTRODUCTION

We live in a world flooded with data. Over the late 20th century and early 21st century, numerous technological advances have been observed in information systems, communication and computing systems, sensor networks and IoT, social sensing, data storage, and cloud computing (El-Alfy and Mohammed 2020). These advances promoted an explosion of data that has affected the world, drawing attention from researchers and practitioners and leading to a knowledge-oriented economy and society (Kim et al. 2014).

At the same time, services are also gaining increased importance in research and society. In fact, it has been argued that the information revolution and the service revolution are two sides of the same coin (Rust and Huang 2014). The evolution of services and its close connection with information technology (IT) and other related fields, from engineering to the social sciences, led to the emergence of service science. Service science, short for Service Science Management, Engineering, Design, Arts, and Public Policy (Spohrer et al. 2014), is an interdisciplinary field that builds upon service-dominant logic (Vargo and Lusch 2015) and from theories and methods drawn from service-related fields, such as marketing, management, engineering, design, operations, computer science, psychology, and others (Maglio et al. 2019, 2009; Spohrer and Kwan 2009). Service science is the study of service systems and aims to enable systematic service innovation (Maglio and Spohrer 2008). Technology advances are having a substantial impact on service systems (Maglio et al. 2019), and are a source of service innovation (Grenha Teixeira et al. 2016). Among technology advances, big data has been highlighted as the service research priority with the widest gap between importance and current knowledge (Ostrom et al. 2015). Big data is a strategic element of organizations' competitiveness (Jin et al. 2015) and is credited for the expansion of service, enabling organizations to tailor service to their customers' needs and build deeper relationships with them (Rust and Huang 2014). Furthermore, the future of service innovation depends on the ability of using data and technology to transform service systems in smart service systems (Maglio et al. 2019; Medina-Borja 2015).

Big data has different sources. Nowadays, practically all actions people take both digitally and physically generate a digital footprint (Arya et al. 2019; Hicks et al. 2020). This happens when one sends an email, uses social media, interacts with a smartphone, or watches TV. Moreover, mobile devices and even ordinary objects, such as refrigerators and front door locks, are getting connected to the Web and dynamically share data about people's behavior (Dinsmore et al. 2020). Along with these user-generated data, machine-generated data are also emerging. These data are generated when devices interact with other devices (e.g., when a home assistant closes the blinds due to the wind's intensity).

Big data is not, in itself, a new concept. It was first mentioned in 1997 (Zhong et al. 2016). Nevertheless, only recently has it achieved its notoriety, following the rise of increasingly complex and heterogeneous data. Big data is frequently defined by the three Vs of Volume, Variety dimensions, and Velocity. This means that big data refers to datasets that are large in volume, diverse in data sources and types, and created quickly, leading to significant challenges to harvest, manage, and process them through traditional systems and capabilities (McAfee and Brynjolfsson 2012; Sagiroglu and Sinanc 2013). These were later expanded into the five Vs, with Veracity and Value being added (Wamba et al. 2015), and subsequently to seven with the introduction of Variability and Complexity (Lee 2017).

These characteristics of big data lead to interconnected areas (i.e., data science and data analytics). Although big data differ from data science and analytics in scope and applications, they cooperate and benefit each other in many circumstances (Song and Zhu 2016). While big data regards the process of data collection, storage, and integration, data science and data analytics aim to identify patterns in data and use them to support the decision-making process. Data science and data analytics terms are often used interchangeably. However, data science is considered an umbrella term for all things dedicated to exploring large data sets, while data analytics is more focused. Instead of just looking for patterns in data, data analysts have a specific goal or question in mind that needs to be answered through the data (Nadikattu 2020). In the remainder of this study, we adopt the term data science to refer to data science as a whole, also accommodating data analytics.

Data science for big data is a promising interdisciplinary research area with a considerable contribution to several science and engineering domains (Patel 2017). Due to this, it has attracted the attention of many researchers in computer science, mathematics, statistics, informatics, and service science. In fact, as is explored in this chapter, data science is starting to be applied to understand complex service-related contexts (Antons and Breidbach 2018; Kuehl 2016; Lim and Maglio 2018; Miguéis and Nóvoa 2017). However, while it is recognized that big data and data science will have a huge impact on service, the application of data science to service is in its infancy.

To address this gap, this chapter explores and explains how research is bridging service science and data science. To achieve this objective, a systematic literature review was conducted, searching for papers indexed in the Web of Science citation database that contained terms related to data science and service science.

In the next section the methodology used to perform the literature review is detailed. In the following section, the results are introduced, first by providing a descriptive analysis of the papers encountered, followed by a discussion of the most relevant topics uncovered. Finally, this chapter concludes by discussing how interdisciplinary research on data science and service science is blossoming.

METHODOLOGY AND DATA

The objective of this chapter is to explore the literature that combines service- and data-related fields to understand how these two topics are being connected. To achieve this purpose, a body of literature was collected using the Web of Science citation database in September 2020 (without limiting the publication year in the search criteria). The query used was the following:

((``big data'' or ``data science'' or ``machine learning'' or ``data analytics'' or ``business analytics'')

and

(``service science'' or ``service research'' or ``service management'' or ``service value'' or ``service design'' or ``service engineering'' or ``service innovation'' or ``service value'' or ``service marketing''))

The search resulted in 270 papers. After analyzing all the papers' abstracts, 100 papers were disregarded from the analysis and 170 were retained for a full reading by the authors of this chapter. The exclusion criterion was linked to the fact that many papers were unrelated to the service science field. An example is Iliyasu and Deng (2020), which proposes a model for encrypted network traffic classification and briefly mentions the possibility of this model to provide security and quality of service.

The next phase of the methodology consisted of collecting and structuring detailed information about each paper, namely: authors, affiliations, country, abstract, keywords, and number of citations in the Web of Science citation database. The data were processed in Excel and R software, which enabled us to develop a descriptive analysis of the data gathered.

Moreover, text-mining tools were used to compute the frequency of the terms used in the papers' abstracts and to create a word cloud synthesizing the topics mentioned most often. For this purpose, we conducted a text pre-processing procedure. This involved tokenization (i.e., splitting strings of text into smaller pieces, such as words). The next step was the normalization, which involved converting all words to lower case. After this procedure, we removed the noise by omitting certain characters, such as punctuation characters, and deleting the stop words of the English dictionary (i.e., ordinary words such as ``the'' and ``a'' that are not significant). We also conducted lemmatization—the process of converting a word to its base or root form (e.g., ``meeting'' to ``meet''). Regarding the word cloud constructed, only the terms appearing at least 25 times were considered, and the words that are part of the query used to select the papers were disregarded due to their ubiquity.

We also developed a graphical representation of the network of topics—keywords—addressed jointly by the papers. A link was established among those keywords that were simultaneously included in at least four papers. The topics that did not satisfy this condition were not considered in the network representation. The thickness of the link or edge reflects the number of papers in common.

Finally, a thematic analysis (Braun and Clarke 2012) was performed to understand and discuss the main themes addressed by these papers. These themes include multiple contexts of the application of service science along with data science, how each of these fields motivates research on the other, the creation of new service design tools and business model innovation, the use of analytics tools, and the emergence of a deeper and more meaningful integration between service science and data science. The results of these multiple analyses are described in the next sections.

RESULTS AND DISCUSSION OF THE LITERATURE

A first analysis of the literature enabled us to conclude that there is a growing tendency to combine data and service science fields (Figure 17.1). The first study to combine these fields was published in 2010, while in 2020, 46 papers combining them were published.

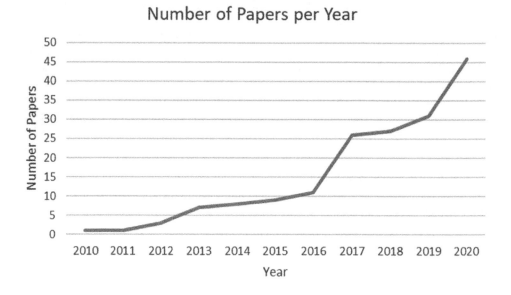

*Figure 17.1   Number of papers combining data science and service science fields
published per year*

Most of the papers analyzed were published in journals of business and economics (38 papers), computer science (31 papers), or computer science and engineering (15 papers). This shows the multidisciplinary nature of the research explored in this study.

Figure 17.2 illustrates the general topics addressed. "Model" and "technology" are the words used most frequently by the authors in their abstracts, followed by "information," "management," and "innovation." This suggests that many papers are focused on developing models and/or taking advantage of the technology and/or information, with the purpose of supporting the management and/or innovation processes. The remaining highlighted words mirror the fusion of the two studied domains, although there seems to be a predominance of words related to business and service management issues.

The co-occurrence of the keywords, illustrated in Figure 17.3, enables us to verify that big data and data science are combined with several service-science-related topics, namely, service design, innovation, and customer experience. In turn, service design seems to be an especially relevant topic, as it links both big data and data science. This latter topic, data science, is then used for service management, risk management, customer analytics and service science, and management engineering. These topics are explored in further detail with the results of the thematic analysis in the next section.

Figure 17.2   Topics word cloud

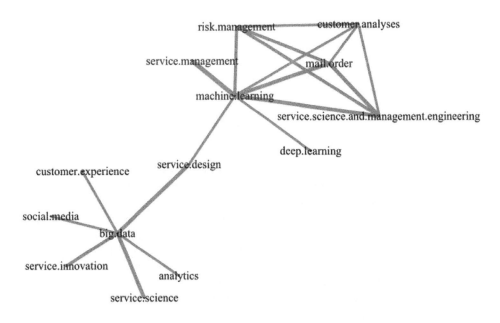

Figure 17.3   Topics network

Data Science and Service Management as a Research Motivation

Often, research that brings together service and data science does so as part of the motivation for the paper. This means that the emergence of data is often a motivation for service-science-related papers, while the need to improve service management is often the driver for data-science-related research.

From a service science perspective, several papers adopt the emergence of data science as their motivation, highlighting the potential of data to transform service. The impact of data science on service innovation is especially emphasized, with papers focusing on data science to support service innovation in a multitude of topics and contexts, such as smart service (Dong 2018; Goetz et al. 2018), creative industries (Del Vecchio et al., 2021; Morelli and Spagnoli 2017), education (Deng 2017; Ye 2017), data-rich companies (Lehrer et al. 2018; Troilo et al. 2017), companies undergoing a servitization process (Kamp et al. 2017; Tronvoll et al. 2020), or in an Industry 4.0 environment (Lee et al. 2014; Frank et al. 2019).

There is also a set of studies, mainly with origins in the data science community, that focus on proposing data science solutions to facilitate service management. For example, Huang et al. (2020) proposed a machine learning model for anomaly detection that is said to be one of the most important problems in service management. In a maintenance setting, Kaparthi and Bumblauskas (2020) propose a data-driven strategy for the design of predictive maintenance systems. They argue that this approach can help asset managers decide how to allocate resources by increasing uptime and utilization for expensive equipment.

While using big data, data science, and service management as a motivation is not in itself an interdisciplinary research effort, it is nevertheless an early effort that aligns the topics and highlights their mutual relevance. In fact, while using either data science or service management as part of the motivation is a characteristic of earlier papers, a stronger integration is starting to emerge, as discussed in the next topics where the context of the research is analyzed in more detail.

Contexts of Application

A more in-depth analysis of the papers shows a large variety of contexts of application. As expected, a significant number of research has its roots in computer science dealing with very diverse subjects: examples range from the acknowledgment of the role of customers as value co-creators, proposing a service-based customer intelligence model to guide the development and application of customer intelligence (Dam et al. 2020); an automatic service classification based on WordNet by combining text mining, semantic technology, and machine learning for service management (Zhao and Chen 2011); or a conceptual framework for decision support systems in the cloud (Demirkan and Delen 2013). From the service science side, research spans from purely conceptual approaches, such as analyzing the global trends that are likely to influence future research challenges in the service discipline (Bolton 2020), or by developing a systematic approach to use data science for the process of service design (Meierhofer and Meier 2017), to more applied research, targeting different sectors and industries.

The analysis of the literature showed that service science and data science are being integrated across several areas, where the most predominant are: 1) mobility/urban mobility/transports, 2) health, 3) manufacturing, 4) education, 5) retail, and 6) administration/smart cities.

In the mobility area, research includes: 1) developing network traffic classification schemes to serve as building blocks for relevant tasks, such as security and quality of service management (Iliyasu and Deng 2020); 2) definition of new performance measurement systems that better reflect customer experience (e.g., actual waiting time on train platforms or at bus stops) while accounting for ridership (developed by Metropolitan Transportation Authorities; Graves et al. 2019); 3) development of intrusion detection systems for connected vehicles in smart cities with cloud service availability, providing services that meet users' quality of service and quality of experience requirements (Aloqaily et al. 2019); 4) development of visual analytics platforms for sustainable and intelligent transport systems, providing new services that engage user behavior and understand their usage patterns (Gürdür and Sopjani 2018); and 5) designing new public Transport Information Services in China (Yu et al. 2018).

In health applications, two trends clearly emerge. The first is more concerned with the usage of big data and cloud computing to develop new innovation models for the provision of new medical services (Li et al. 2018), with an improved service quality (Ge 2017) that might materialize in the design of personalized medical systems with the patient at the center (Guijuan et al. 2019). The second trend is much more targeted to specific enhancements in different specialties, such as the development of new artificial intelligence/machine learning (AI/ML) algorithms for predicting the need for dialysis and kidney transplantation (Burlacu et al. 2020), the use of multisource data to better understand blood donation behavior in China (Chen et al. 2020), or even the creation of new applications for home-based care, including Humanoid robots for young people with autism that are based in service personalization over long periods of time and powered by big data (Khosla et al. 2015).

Manufacturing and the challenges posed by Industry 4.0 are also hot topics for researchers. Servitization, the transformation process from product-centric to service-centric business models (Frank et al. 2019), and its link to digitalization, the use of digital technologies to enable major business improvements by processing, transmitting, and storing data, are highlighted by Tronvoll et al. (2020). These authors recognize that the link between digitalization and servitization is still under-investigated, exploring and detailing the strategic organizational shifts that underpin digital servitization. In the same line of research, and to guide manufacturers to integrate their products and services in practice powered by IT, new servitization models based on the product service system (PSS) concept were proposed by Tan et al. (2019). Zheng et al. (2019b) propose Smart PSS, a promising value co-creation proposition, where manufacturing companies offer smart, connected products with various e-services as a solution bundle to meet individual customer satisfaction and, in return, collect and analyze usage data for evergreen design purposes in a circular manner. In the same line of research spurred from service marketing, Kampker et al. (2018) propose a process guideline for a six-month market launch of data-driven services (DDS) to enhance the digital service portfolio for traditional manufacturing companies. Another important global trend in the manufacturing industry is related to intelligent manufacturing (Wei et al. 2019), also commonly referred to as Industry 4.0, where machines are connected as a collaborative community. Lee et al. (2014) address the trends of manufacturing service transformation in a big data environment, as well as the readiness of smart predictive informatics tools to manage big data, making more informed decisions. In short, the possibilities of new developments in this context are immense and diverse, and advanced manufacturing technologies have been hailed as enablers to make industrial products and operations smart, becoming a lever for developing smart goods and smart production environments (Kamp et al. 2017).

In the educational area, digital libraries seem to be a source of great interest: examples include proposing a new innovative strategy for the university library service in this era of large data (Deng 2017), an intelligent library knowledge innovation service system based on multimedia technology (Yujie 2020), and a reflection on the importance of user services and types of big data resources that digital libraries can utilize (Li et al. 2019). Papers deeply rooted in technology also explore the technology framework for big data service in university libraries based in Hadoop (Ye 2017), or the usage of providers like Amazon Web Services, Microsoft Azure, and Google Cloud Platform as providers of a practical skills environment for building new IT service management competencies (Dimitrov and Petrov 2019). In the end, when university libraries used big data technology effectively, it was found that innovation and entrepreneurship education was potentiated (Qian et al. 2020).

Retail is also becoming increasingly digital and undergoing a series of major transformations as platform-based, multi-sided marketplaces, such as Amazon, Alibaba, eBay, JD.com, and Rakuten, are challenging incumbent retailers and uniting the online and offline to create more sophisticated and personalized customer experiences (Hanninen et al. 2019). So, it is only natural that, with a service systems perspective supported by data analytics, new avenues of research surge: these include conceptual frameworks for multi-sided marketplaces (Hanninen et al. 2019), new consumer purchase decision-making models (Tang and Zhu 2019), and new intelligent systems to support the design and management of a Customer Experience (CX) strategy based on the emotions tracked in real time at different touchpoints in a store (Mengoni et al. 2017).

According to the European Commission (2020), the concept of smart cities goes beyond the use of information and communication technologies for better resource use and less emissions, encompassing a wide array of enhanced services powered by big data (e.g., urban transport networks, water supply and waste disposal, heating and lighting buildings, a more interactive and responsive city administration, safer public spaces). There is an evident interest related to the topic, although Ferlin and Rezende (2019) stated that cases of smart cities are punctual, and data science is still not part of the design of city policies. Traditional cartography has also been challenged, with Sun and Park (2017) discussing the potential of maps as objects of service design, functioning as new digital participatory platforms that take a user-centered approach to facilitate the engagement of key stakeholders.

Research related to other contexts, such as finance, tourism, agriculture, and construction, has also been identified, but the number of papers is still low.

New Models, Frameworks, and Business Model Innovation

One important focus of the papers analyzed is the development of new models and frameworks, specifically focusing on service design and new innovative business models. These developments span several contexts and go one step further than having data science or service management as the motivation of the paper, as they offer prescriptive knowledge on how a certain outcome can be achieved. This outcome, in most papers, is related with new tools that support data-driven service design and business model innovation.

The development of new service design tools is a research priority (Ostrom et al. 2015), and our analysis uncovered several proposals for new service design frameworks, processes, and tools that support the design of DDS (Meierhofer and Herrmann 2018), including in the contexts already identified, namely, in healthcare (Guijuan et al. 2019), transportation (Gürdür and Sopjani 2018), and manufacturing (R.C. Lee 2018), including PSSs (Zheng et al. 2019a, 2019b), servitization (Tan et al. 2019), and finance (Manzira and Bankole 2018).

Furthermore, several papers are also focused on exploring how data can foster business model innovation, highlighting the role of digitalization in driving innovation in companies (Bouwman et al. 2019; Haenninen et al. 2018; Spil et al. 2017) and even exploring new machine-to-machine business models (Uchihira et al. 2015).

Other prescriptive outcomes of the analyzed papers encompass several frameworks, including for service-oriented decision support systems (Demirkan and Delen 2013), dynamic service analytics capabilities (Akter et al. 2020), or for customer process management (Lim et al. 2019).

Data Science Tools

The studies analyzed use a diverse set of data science tools, especially machine learning algorithms. Among those that were adopted, supervised algorithms are the most popular. In supervised learning, target variables are predicted from independent variables by mapping functions. Supervised learning has two major subcategories: classification and regression. In a service science context, classification algorithms are the most frequently used. For example, Baier et al. (2020) use service encounter data as independent variables, such as the priority and severity of the incident as specified by customers when opening incident tickets, the time between ticket opening and first customer contact (waiting time), and the time between ticket opening and closure (resolution time), to identify unsatisfied customers, which is translated into a dependent variable. The specific supervised algorithms most adopted are neural networks (e.g., Sannigrahi et al. 2019; Yang et al. 2020), support vector machines (e.g., Sannigrahi et al. 2019; Zhang et al. 2016) and random forests (e.g., Takahashi et al. 2018, 2017).

There are also studies that use unsupervised algorithms. Unlike supervised learning, unsupervised learning does not require a specific target variable. Ali et al. (2020) use a supervised algorithm to cluster the sentiments of the users of ridesharing platforms, and Kar (2020) uses this type of algorithm to group topics extracted from social media about mobile payments services.

It is also important to highlight that a very significant number of the studies that combine service science and data science apply both supervised and unsupervised algorithms in a text-mining context. Text mining is a data science field where the input data is text, which can be in the form of documents, messages, emails, or Web pages. Thus, text mining has been used to analyze customer satisfaction from reviews (e.g., Chatterjee 2020), smart service systems from the literature (e.g., Lim and Maglio 2018), and to conduct online sentiment analysis (e.g., Ibrahim and Wang 2017). It has also been used to detect customer needs (e.g., Eckstein et al. 2016) and service innovation capabilities (e.g., Feldmann et al. 2013). Ordenes and Zhang (2019) describe and position the state of the art of text- and image-mining methods in business research, while Zaki and McColl-Kennedy (2020) offer a text-mining analysis roadmap (TMAR) for service research.

TOWARD A DEEPER AND MORE MEANINGFUL INTEGRATION

Results show that the integration of service science and data science started to emerge recently, spans several contexts, and started by each field recognizing the impact of the other on its research. Since then, and quite rapidly, research integrating service science and data science is increasingly becoming more developed, with the development of prescriptive knowledge, to design new services and foster service innovation and business model innovation, and with data science methods beginning to be used to address service-related challenges.

This study shows how service science and data science came together in the last ten years. However, early signs of integration and truly interdisciplinary research are starting to appear. Such interdisciplinary research that bridges both fields is especially valuable to leverage the potential of data for creating value in a service context (Akter et al. 2020; Bouwman et al. 2019; Medina-Borja 2015; Ostrom et al. 2015). Finally, the impacts of data science on ethics, security, and privacy are starting to be discussed from a service science perspective (Breidbach and Maglio 2020; Breuer et al. 2020; Drew 2018; Qi et al. 2015; Suciu and Hussain 2019).

By identifying the different motivations, contexts, outcomes, and machine learning techniques of papers bridging service science and data science, this chapter shows how these two fields are working increasingly together and becoming better integrated. This understanding can help researchers to further the integration between these fields, leveraging our world flooded in data toward new, improved, and innovative service systems.

REFERENCES

Akter, S., Motamarri, S., Hani, U., Shams, R., Fernando, M., Babu, M. M., & Shen, K. N. (2020). Building dynamic service analytics capabilities for the digital marketplace. *Journal of Business Research*, *118*, 177–188. https://doi.org/10.1016/j.jbusres.2020.06.016

Ali, S., Wang, G., & Riaz, S. (2020). Aspect based sentiment analysis of ridesharing platform reviews for Kansei Engineering. *IEEE ACCESS*, *8*, 173186–173196. https://doi.org/10.1109/ACCESS.2020.3025823

Aloqaily, M., Otoum, S., Al Ridhawi, I., & Jararweh, Y. (2019). An intrusion detection system for connected vehicles in smart cities. *Ad Hoc Networks*, *90*, 101842. https://doi.org/10.1016/j.adhoc.2019.02.001

Antons, D., & Breidbach, C. F. (2018). Big data, big insights? Advancing service innovation and design with machine learning. *Journal of Service Research*, *21*(1), 17–39. https://doi.org/10.1177/1094670517738373

Arya, V., Sethi, D., & Paul, J. (2019). Does digital footprint act as a digital asset? Enhancing brand experience through remarketing. *International Journal of Information Management*, *49*, 142–156. https://doi.org/10.1016/j.ijinfomgt.2019.03.013

Baier, L., Kuehl, N., Schueritz, R., & Satzger, G. (2020). Will the customers be happy? Identifying unsatisfied customers from service encounter data. *Journal of Service Management*, *32*(2), 265–288. https://doi.org/10.1108/JOSM-06-2019-0173

Bolton, R. N. (2020). Commentary: Future directions of the service discipline. *Journal of Services Marketing*, *34*(3), 279–289. https://doi.org/10.1108/JSM-02-2020-0067

Bouwman, H., Nikou, S., & de Reuver, M. (2019). Digitalization, business models, and SMEs: How do business model innovation practices improve performance of digitalizing SMEs? *Telecommunications Policy*, *43*(9). https://doi.org/10.1016/j.telpol.2019.101828

Braun, V., & Clarke, V. (2012). Thematic analysis. In H. Cooper (Ed.), *APA handbook of research methods in psychology* (pp. 57–71). American Psychological Association.

Breidbach, C. F., & Maglio, P. (2020). Accountable algorithms? The ethical implications of data-driven business models. *Journal of Service Management, 31*(2), 163–185. https://doi.org/10.1108/JOSM-03 -2019-0073

Breuer, J., Bishop, L., & Kinder-Kurlanda, K. (2020). The practical and ethical challenges in acquiring and sharing digital trace data: Negotiating public-private partnerships. *New Media & Society, 22*(11), 2058–2080. https://doi.org/10.1177/1461444820924622

Burlacu, A., Iftene, A., Jugrin, D., Popa, I. V., Lupu, P. M., Vlad, C., & Covic, A. (2020). Using artificial intelligence resources in dialysis and kidney transplant patients: A literature review. *Biomed Research International, 2020*, 9867872. https://doi.org/10.1155/2020/9867872

Chatterjee, S. (2020). Drivers of helpfulness of online hotel reviews: A sentiment and emotion mining approach. *International Journal of Hospitality Management, 85*, 102356E https://doi.org/10.1016/j. ijhm.2019.102356

Chen, X., Wu, S., & Guo, X. (2020). Analyses of factors influencing Chinese repeated blood donation behavior: Delivered value theory perspective. *Industrial Management & Data Systems, 120*(3), 486–507. https://doi.org/10.1108/IMDS-09-2019-0509

Dam, N. A. K., Dinh, T. L., & Menvielle, W. (2020). *A service-based model for customer intelligence in the age of big data* [Paper presentation]. Conference of the Association-for-Information-Systems (AMCIS), Utah, USA.

Del Vecchio, M., Kharlamov, A., Parry, G., & Pogrebna, G. (2021). Improving productivity in Hollywood with data science: Using emotional arcs of movies to drive product and service innovation in entertainment industries. *Journal of the Operational Research Society, 72*(5), 1110–1137. https:// doi.org/10.1080/01605682.2019.1705194

Demirkan, H., & Delen, D. (2013). Leveraging the capabilities of service-oriented decision support systems: Putting analytics and big data in cloud. *Decision Support Systems, 55*(1), 412–421. https:// doi.org/10.1016/j.dss.2012.05.048

Deng, Z. (2017). Research on service innovation of library in big data age. In X. Chu (Ed.), *Proceedings of the 2017 4th International Conference On Education, Management and Computing Technology* (pp. 1014–1017). Atlantic Press.

Dimitrov, G., & Petrov, Z. (2019). Cloud training platforms to create new competences for IT service management. In L. G. Chova, A. L. Martinez, & I. C. Torres (Eds.), *Edulearn19: 11th International Conference on Education and New Learning Technologies* (pp. 7012–7018). IATEE.

Dinsmore, D. L., Fryer, L. K., & Parkinson, M. M. (2020). *Handbook of strategies and strategic processing.* Routledge.

Dong, L. (2018). Research on the application of big data in community smart service. In *Proceedings of the 2018 International Symposium on Computer, Consumer and Control* (pp. 424–427). IEEE. https:// doi.org/10.1109/IS3C.2018.00113

Drew, C. (2018). Design for data ethics: Using service design approaches to operationalize ethical principles on four projects. *Philosophical Transactions of the Royal Society A: Mathematical Physical and Engineering Sciences, 376*(2128). https://doi.org/10.1098/rsta.2017.0353

Eckstein, L., Kuehl, N., & Satzger, G. (2016). Towards extracting customer needs from incident tickets in IT services. In E. Kornyshova, G. Poels, C. Huemer, I. Wattiau, F. Matthes, & J. Sanz (Eds.), *2016 IEEE 18th International Conference on Business Informatics* (Vol. 1; pp. 200–207). IEEE. https://doi .org/10.1109/CBI.2016.30

El-Alfy, E.-S. M., & Mohammed, S. A. (2020). A review of machine learning for big data analytics: Bibliometric approach. *Technology Analysis & Strategic Management, 32*(8), 984–1005. https://doi. org/10.1080/09537325.2020.1732912

European Commission. (2020). *Smart cities.* https://ec.europa.eu/info/eu-regional-and-urban -development/topics/cities-and-urban-development/city-initiatives/smart-cities_en

Feldmann, N., Kohler, M., Kimbrough, S. O., & Fromm, H. (2013). Service innovation analytics: Towards an approach for validating frameworks for service innovation capabilities via text mining. In J. F. Cunha, M. Snene, & H. Nóvoa (Eds.), *Exploring services science* (pp. 73–85). Springer.

Ferlin, E. P., & Rezende, D. A. (2019). Big data applied to strategic digital city: Study on the volume of data in the smart city applications. *Revista Gestao & Tecnologia* [*Journal Of Management and Technology*], *19*(2), 175–194. https://doi.org/10.20397/2177-6652/2019.v19i2.1533

Frank, A. G., Mendes, G. H. S., Ayala, N. F., & Ghezzi, A. (2019). Servitization and Industry 4.0 convergence in the digital transformation of product firms: A business model innovation perspective. *Technological Forecasting and Social Change, 141*, 341–351. https://doi.org/10.1016/j.techfore. 2019.01.014

Ge, M. (2017). The innovation research of the medical service quality based on big data. In X. Zhu, Z. G. Fang, & H. Davis (Eds.), *Proceedings of the 2nd International Conference on Computer Engineering, Information Science and Internet Technology* (pp. 91–97). Publisher.

Goetz, C., Hohler, S., & Benz, C. (2018). Towards managing smart service innovation: A literature review. In G. Satzger, L. Patricio, M. Zaki, N. Kuhl, & P. Hottum (Eds.), *Exploring services science* (pp. 101–111). Springer. https://doi.org/10.1007/978-3-030-00713-3_8

Graves, E., Zheng, S., Tarte, L., Levine, B., & Reddy, A. (2019). Customer journey time metrics for New York City bus service using big data. *Transportation Research Record, 2673*(9), 1–10. https://doi.org/ 10.1177/0361198118821632

Grenha Teixeira, J., Patrício, L., Huang, K.-H., Fisk, R. P., Nóbrega, L., & Constantine, L. (2016). The minds method: Integrating management and interaction design perspectives for service design. *Journal of Service Research, 20*(3), 240–258. https://doi.org/10.1177/1094670516680033

Guijuan, S., Yandong, W., Yue, J., & Hongbo, L. (2019). Research on medical service system based on big data technology. In *Proceedings of the 2019 International Conference on Intelligent Transportation, Big Data & Smart City* (pp. 302–304). IEEE. https://doi.org/10.1109/ICITBS.2019 .00079

Gürdür, D., & Sopjani, L. (2018). Visual analytics to support the service design for sustainable mobility. In Proceedings of the 2018 IEEE Conference on Technologies for Sustainability (Sustech) (pp. 84–89). IEEE.

Haenninen, M., Smedlund, A., & Mitronen, L. (2018). Digitalization in retailing: Multi-sided platforms as drivers of industry transformation. *Baltic Journal of Management, 13*(2), 152–168. https://doi.org/ 10.1108/BJM-04-2017-0109

Hanninen, M., Mitronen, L., & Kwan, S. K. (2019). Multi-sided marketplaces and the transformation of retail: A service systems perspective. *Journal of Retailing and Consumer Services, 49*, 380–388. https://doi.org/10.1016/j.jretconser.2019.04.015

Hicks, B., Culley, S., Gopsill, J., & Snider, C. (2020). Managing complex engineering projects: What can we learn from the evolving digital footprint? *International Journal of Information Management, 51*, 102016. https://doi.org/10.1016/j.ijinfomgt.2019.10.001

Huang, S., Liu, Y., Fung, C., An, W., He, R., Zhao, Y., Yang, H., & Luan, Z. (2020). A gated few-shot learning model for anomaly detection. In *Proceedings of the 34th International Conference on Information Networking* (pp. 505–509). IEEE.

Ibrahim, N. F., & Wang, X. (2017). Mining social network content of online retail brands: A machine learning approach. In R. P. Dameri & R. Spinelli (Eds.), *Proceedings of the 11th European Conference on Information Systems Management* (pp. 129–138). Academic Conferences and Publishing International Limited.

Iliyasu, A. S., & Deng, H. (2020). Semi-supervised encrypted traffic classification with deep convolutional generative adversarial networks. *IEEE Access, 8*, 118–126. https://doi.org/10.1109/ACCESS. 2019.2962106

Jin, X., Wah, B. W., Cheng, X., & Wang, Y. (2015). Significance and challenges of big data research. *Big Data Research, 2*(2), 59–64. https://doi.org/10.1016/j.bdr.2015.01.006

Kamp, B., Ochoa, A., & Diaz, J. (2017). Smart servitization within the context of industrial user–supplier relationships: Contingencies according to a machine tool manufacturer. *International Journal of Interactive Design And Manufacturing – IJIDEM, 11*(3), 651–663. https://doi.org/10.1007/s12008 -016-0345-0

Kampker, A., Husmann, M., Jussen, P., & Schwerdt, L. (2018). Market launch process of data-driven services for manufacturers: A qualitative guideline. In G. Satzger, L. Patrício, M. Zaki, N. Kuhl, & P. Hottum (Eds.), *Exploring services science* (pp. 177–189). Springer. https://doi.org/10.1007/978-3 -030-00713-3_14

Kaparthi, S., & Bumblauskas, D. (2020). Designing predictive maintenance systems using decision tree-based machine learning techniques. *International Journal of Quality & Reliability Management, 37*(4), 659–686. https://doi.org/10.1108/IJQRM-04-2019-0131

Kar, A. K. (2020). What affects usage satisfaction in mobile payments? Modelling user generated content to develop the "digital service usage satisfaction model." *Information Systems Frontiers*, *23*, 1341–1361. https://doi.org/10.1007/s10796-020-10045-0

Khosla, R., Nguyen, K., & Chu, M.-T. (2015). Service personalisation of assistive robot for autism care. In *Proceedings of the 41st Annual Conference of the IEEE Industrial Electronics Society* (pp. 2088–2093). IEEE.

Kim, T.-Y., Kim, E., Park, J., & Hwang, J. (2014). The faster-accelerating digital economy. In T.-Y. Kim & A. Heshmati (Eds.), *Economic growth: The new perspectives for theory and policy* (pp. 163–191). Springer. https://doi.org/10.1007/978-3-642-40826-7_5

Kuehl, N. (2016). Needmining: Towards analytical support for service design. In Borangiu, T., Dragoicea, M., Nóvoa, H. (eds), *Exploring services science* (pp. 187–200). Springer.

Lee, I. (2017). Big data: Dimensions, evolution, impacts, and challenges. *Business Horizons*, *60*(3), 293–303. https://doi.org/10.1016/j.bushor.2017.01.004

Lee, J., Kao, H.-A., & Yang, S. (2014). Service innovation and smart analytics for Industry 4.0 and big data environment. In H. ElMaraghy (Ed.), *Product Services Systems and Value Creation: Proceedings of the 6th CIRP Conference on Industrial Product-Service Systems* (pp. 3–8). Elsevier. https://doi.org/10.1016/j.procir.2014.02.001

Lee, R. C. (2018). The service design of material traceability system in the smart manufacturing theme. In F. F. H. Nah and B. S. Xiao (Eds.), *HCI In business, government, and organizations* (pp. 79–90). Springer. https://doi.org/10.1007/978-3-319-91716-0_7

Lehrer, C., Wieneke, A., vom Brocke, J., Jung, R., & Seidel, S. (2018). How big data analytics enables service innovation: Materiality, affordance, and the individualization of service. *Journal of Management Information Systems*, *35*(2), 424–460. https://doi.org/10.1080/07421222.2018.1451953

Li, S., Jiao, F., Zhang, Y., & Xu, X. (2019). Problems and changes in digital libraries in the age of big data from the perspective of user services. *Journal of Academic Librarianship*, *45*(1), 22–30. https://doi.org/10.1016/j.acalib.2018.11.012

Li, X., Jianmin, H., Hou, B., & Zhang, P. (2018). Exploring the innovation modes and evolution of the cloud-based service using the activity theory on the basis of big data. *Cluster Computing –The Journal of Networks Software Tools and Applications*, *21*(1), 907–922. https://doi.org/10.1007/s10586-017-0951-z

Lim, C., Kim, M.-J., Kim, K.-H., Kim, K.-J., & Maglio, P. (2019). Customer process management: A framework for using customer-related data to create customer value. *Journal of Service Management*, *30*(1), 105–131. https://doi.org/10.1108/JOSM-02-2017-0031

Lim, C., & Maglio, P. P. (2018). Data-driven understanding of smart service systems through text mining. *Service Science*, *10*(2), 154–180. https://doi.org/10.1287/serv.2018.0208

Maglio, P. P., Kieliszewski, C. A., Spohrer, J. C., Lyons, K., Patricio, L., & Sawatani, Y. (2019). Introduction: Why another handbook? In Maglio, P., Kieliszewski, C., Spohrer, J., Lyons, K., Patrício, L., Sawatani, Y. (eds), *Handbook of service science* (Vol. 2; pp. 1–9). Springer.

Maglio, P., & Spohrer, J. (2008). Fundamentals of service science. *Journal of the Academy of Marketing Science*, *36*(1), 18–20. https://doi.org/10.1007/s11747-007-0058-9

Maglio, P., Vargo, S. L., Caswell, N., & Spohrer, J. (2009). The service system is the basic abstraction of service science. *Information Systems and e-Business Management*, *7*(4), 395–406. https://doi.org/10.1007/s10257-008-0105-1

Manzira, F. M., & Bankole, F. (2018). Application of social media analytics in the banking sector to drive growth and sustainability: A proposed integrated framework. In C. Ouma (Ed.), *Proceedings of the 2018 Open Innovations Conference* (pp. 223–233). IEEE.

McAfee, A., & Brynjolfsson, E. (2012). Strategy & competition big data: The management revolution. *Harvard Business Review*, *90*(10), 60.

Medina-Borja, A. (2015). Editorial column—Smart things as service providers: A call for convergence of disciplines to build a research agenda for the service systems of the future. *Service Science*, *7*(1), 2–5. https://doi.org/10. 1287/serv.2014.0090

Meierhofer, J., & Herrmann, A. (2018). End-to-end methodological approach for the data-driven design of customer-centered digital services. In G. Satzger, L. Patricio, M. Zaki, N. Kuhl, & P. Hottum (Eds.), *Exploring services science* (pp. 208–218). Springer. https://doi.org/10.1007/978-3-030-00713-3_16

Meierhofer, J., & Meier, K. (2017). From data science to value creation. In S. Za, M. Dragoicea, & M. Cavallari (Eds.), *Exploring services science* (pp. 173–181). Springer. https://doi.org/1007/978-3-319-56925-3_14

Mengoni, M., Frontoni, E., Giraldi, L., Ceccacci, S., Pierdicca, R., & Paolanti, M. (2017). Customer experience: A design approach and supporting platform. In L. M. Camarinha Matos, H. Afsarmanesh, & R. Fornasiero (Eds.), *Collaboration in a data rich world* (pp. 287–298). Springer, Cham. https://doi.org/10.1007/978-3-319-65151-4_27

Miguéis, V. L., & Nóvoa, H. (2017). Exploring online travel reviews using data analytics: An exploratory study. *Service Science, 9*(4) 315–323. https://doi.org/10.1287/serv.2017.0189

Morelli, G., & Spagnoli, F. (2017). Creative industries and big data: A business model for service innovation. In S. Za, M. Dragoicea, & M. Cavallari (Eds.), *Exploring services science* (pp. 144–158). Springer. https://doi.org/10.1007/978-3-319-56925-3_1

Nadikattu, R. R., Research on Data Science, Data Analytics and Big Data. (2020). *International Journal of Engineering, Science, 9*(5), 99–105. https://dx.doi.org/10.2139/ssrn.3622844.

Ordenes, F. V., & Zhang, S. (2019). From words to pixels: Text and image mining methods for service research. *Journal of Service Management, 30*(5), 593–620. https://doi.org/10.1108/JOSM-08-2019-0254

Ostrom, A. L., Parasuraman, A., Bowen, D. E., Patricio, L., & Voss, C. A. (2015). Service research priorities in a rapidly changing context. *Journal of Service Research, 18*(2), 127–159. https://doi.org/10.1177/1094670515576315

Patel, S. (2017). Integrating machine learning techniques for big data analytics. *International Journal of Advanced Research in Computer Science, 8*(5), 2760–2763. https://doi.org/10.26483/ijarcs.v8i5.4165

Qi, C., Lu-Ning, L., & Yu-Qiang, F. (2015). The personalization–privacy paradox on the adoption of IT-enabled personalization: From a service value perspective. In H. Lan (Ed.), *Proceedings of the 2015 International Conference on Management Science & Engineering* (pp. 31–37). IEEE.

Qian, X., Shi, H., Ge, C., Fan, H., Zhao, X., & Liu, Y. (2020). Application research on service innovation and entrepreneurship education in university libraries and archives. *International Journal of Computational Science and Engineering, 22*(1), 96–106. https://doi.org/IJCSE.2020.107258

Rust, R. T., & Huang, M.-H. (2014). The service revolution and the transformation of marketing science. *Marketing Science, 33*(2), 206–221. https://doi.org/10.1287/mksc.2013.0836

Sagiroglu, S., & Sinanc, D. (2013). Big data: A review. In W. W. Smari & G. C. Fox (Eds.), *Proceedings of the 2013 International Conference on Collaboration Technologies and Systems* (pp. 42–47). IEEE. https://doi.org/10.1109/CTS.2013.6567202.

Sannigrahi, S., Chakraborti, S., Joshi, P. K., Keesstra, S., Sen, S., Paul, S. K., Kreuter, U., Sutton, P. C., Jha, S., & Dang, K. B. (2019). Ecosystem service value assessment of a natural reserve region for strengthening protection and conservation. *Journal of Environmental Management, 244*, 208–227. https://doi.org/10.1016/j.jenvman.2019.04.095

Song, I.-Y., & Zhu, Y. (2016). Big data and data science: What should we teach? *Expert Systems, 33*(4), 364–373. https://doi.org/10.1111/exsy.12130

Spil, T., Pris, M., & Kijl, B. (2017). Exploring the Big Five of e-leadership by developing digital strategies with mobile, cloud, big data, social media, and the Internet of Things. In Z. Ndaba & T. Mokoteli (Eds.), *Proceedings of the 5th International Conference On Management, Leadership and Governance* (pp. 408–417). Academic Conferences and Publishing International Limited.

Spohrer, J., & Kwan, S. K. (2009). Service science, management, engineering, and design: An emerging discipline outline references. *International Journal of Information Systems in the Service Sector, 1*, 1–31. http://doi.org/10.4018/jisss.2009070101

Spohrer, J., Kwan, S. K., & Fisk, R. P. (2014). Marketing: A service science and arts perspective. In Rust, Roland T., Hung, Ming-Hui X (Eds), Handbook of service marketing research (pp. 489–526). Edward Elgar Publishing.

Suciu, G., Jr., & Hussain, I. (2019). Smart service systems: Security and privacy challenges in Internet of Things. In *Proceedings of the 11th International Conference on Electronics, Computers and Artificial Intelligence* (pp. 1–6). IEEE. https://doi.org/10.1109/ECAI46879.2019.9042016.

Sun, Q., & Park, H. (2017). The map as an object of service design. *Design Journal, 20*(1), S4101–S4119. https://doi.org/10.1080/14606925.2017.1352911

Takahashi, M., Azuma, H., & Tsuda, K. (2017). A study on validity detection for shipping decision in the mail-order industry. In C. Zanni Merk, C. Frydman, C. Toro, Y. Hicks, R. J. Howlett, & L. C. Jain (Eds.), *Knowledge-based and intelligent information & engineering systems* (pp. 1318–1325). Elsevier. https://doi.org/10.1016/j.procs.2017.08.007

Takahashi, M., Azuma, H., & Tsuda, K. (2018). A study on delivery evaluation under asymmetric information in the mail-order industry. In R. J. Howlett, C. Toro, Y. Hicks, & L. C. Jain (Eds.), *Knowledge based and intelligent information & engineering systems* (pp. 1298–1305). Elsevier. https://doi.org/10.1016/j.procs.2018.08.079

Tan, K. H., Ji, G., Chung, L., Wang, C.-H., Chiu, A., & Tseng, M. L. (2019). Riding the wave of belt and road initiative in servitization: Lessons from China. *International Journal of Production Economics, 211,* 15–21. https://doi.org/10.1016/j.ijpe.2019.01.027

Tang, M., & Zhu, J. (2019). Research of O2O website based consumer purchase decision-making model. *Journal of Industrial and Production Engineering, 36*(6), 371–384. https://doi.org/10.1080/21681015.2019.1655490

Troilo, G., de Luca, L. M., & Guenzi, P. (2017). Linking data-rich environments with service innovation in incumbent firms: A conceptual framework and research propositions. *Journal of Product Innovation Management, 34*(5), 617–639. https://doi.org/10.1111/jpim.12395

Tronvoll, B., Sklyar, A., Sorhammar, D., & Kowalkowski, C. (2020). Transformational shifts through digital servitization. *Industrial Marketing Management, 89,* 293–305. https://doi.org/10.1016/j.indmarman.2020.02.005

Uchihira, N., Ishimatsu, H., Sakurai, S., Kageyama, Y., Kakutani, Y., Mizushima, K., Naruse, H., & Yoneda, S. (2015). Service innovation structure analysis for recognizing opportunities and difficulties of M2M businesses. *Technology in Society, 43,* 173–182. https://doi.org/10.1016/j.techsoc.2015.09.002

Vargo, S. L., & Lusch, R. F. (2015). Institutions and axioms: An extension and update of service-dominant logic. *Journal of the Academy of Marketing Science, 44*(1), 5–23. https://doi.org/10.1007/s11747-015-0456-3

Wamba, S. F., Akter, S., Edwards, A., Chopin, G., & Gnanzou, D. (2015). How "big data" can make big impact: Findings from a systematic review and a longitudinal case study. *International Journal of Production Economics, 165,* 234–246. https://doi.org/10.1016/j.ijpe.2014.12.031

Wei, W., Lu Jian Feng, J., & Hao, Z. (2019). Data-driven manufacturing service optimization model in smart factory. In A. M. Okamura, N. Amato, T. Asfour, Y. J. Choi, N. Y. Chong, H. Ding, D. H. Lee, C. C. Lerma, J. S. Li, E. Marchand, D. Popa, D. Z. Song, Y. Sun, & P. Valdastri (Eds.), *Proceedings of the 2019 IEEE 15th International Conference on Automation Science and Engineering* (pp. 362–367). IEEE. https://doi.org/10.1109/COASE.2019.8842952.

Yang, M., Zhu, H., & Guo, K. (2020). Research on manufacturing service combination optimization based on neural network and multi-attribute decision making. *Neural Computing & Applications, 32*(6), 1691–1700. https://doi.org/10.1007/s00521-019-04241-6

Ye, C. (2017). Research on the key technology of big data service in university library. In Y. Liu, L. Zhao, G. Cai, G. Xiao, K. L. Li, & L. Wang (Eds.), *Proceedings of the 2017 13th International Conference on Natural Computation, Fuzzy Systems and Knowledge Discovery* (p. 2573–2578). IEEE. https://doi.org/10.1109/FSKD.2017.8393181.

Yu, D., Ding, M., & Wang, C. (2018). A design for a public transport information service in China. In A. Marcus & W. Wang (Eds.), *Design, user experience, and usability: Users, contexts and case studies* (pp. 435–444). Springer. https://doi.org/10.1007/978-3-319-91806-8_34

Yujie, G. (2020). Intelligent library knowledge innovation service system based on multimedia technology. *Personal and Ubiquitous Computing, 24*(3), 333–345. https://doi.org/10.1007/s00779-019-01269-2

Zaki, M., & McColl-Kennedy, J. R. (2020). Text mining analysis roadmap (TMAR) for service research. *Journal of Services Marketing, 34*(1), 30–47. https://doi.org/10.1108/JSM-02-2019-0074

Zhang, W., Zou, Y., Tang, J., Ash, J., & Wang, Y. (2016). Short-term prediction of vehicle waiting queue at ferry terminal based on machine learning method. *Journal of Marine Science and Technology, 21*(4), 729–741. https://doi.org/10.1007/s00773-016-0385-y

Zhao, H., & Chen, Q. (2011). An automatic service classification approach. In Y. L. Wang & T. R. Li (Eds.), *Knowledge engineering and management* (pp. 531–540). Springer Berlin Heidelberg.

Zheng, P., Chen, C.-H., & Shang, S. (2019a). Towards an automatic engineering change management in smart product-service systems – A DSM-based learning approach. *Advanced Engineering Informatics*, *39*, 203–213. https://doi.org/10.1016/j.aei.2019.01.002

Zheng, P., Liu, Y., Tao, F., Wang, Z., & Chen, C.-H. (2019b). Smart product-service systems solution design via hybrid crowd sensing approach. *IEEE Access*, *7*, 128463–128473. https://doi.org/10.1109/ACCESS.2019.2939828

Zhong, R. Y., Newman, S. T., Huang, G. Q., & Lan, S. (2016). Big data for supply chain management in the service and manufacturing sectors: Challenges, opportunities, and future perspectives. *Computers & Industrial Engineering*, *101*, 572–591. https://doi.org/10.1016/j.cie.2016.07.013

18. The evolution of business analytics and their impact on the service industry

Ronald Klimberg

INTRODUCTION

If a group of managers were asked the question, "What are your organization's two most important assets?" after some discussion, in all likelihood, the two assets with the most consensus would be the organization's people and service. Now, the next question is, "What is the third most important asset of most organizations?" Many people, many organizations—large and small—do not realize it, but it is their data! To various degrees, the realization that the organization's data is its third most important asset will require a significant cultural change. Welcome to the analytics revolution.

The field of analytics (or business analytics [BA]) has been growing exponentially since about the year 2000. Information systems/information technology (IS/IT) spending has been taking a larger and larger proportion of an organization's budget as companies have increasingly embraced analytics as a means for obtaining a competitive advantage. "Data is now relevant for leaders across every sector, and consumers of products and services stand to benefit from its application" (Manyika et al., 2011).

So, what exactly is analytics or BA? And what role does analytics partake in the service industry? To answer these questions, we initially provide some historical perspective on the field of analytics and develop our definition of analytics. Subsequently, we discuss some of the issues and the attributes necessary for an organization to transform itself into an analytical competitor. Afterward, we discuss the effects technology and analytics have and will have on service organizations and how the COVID-19 pandemic has accelerated this change. In the last section, we summarize what we have examined and provide some conclusions.

HISTORY OF ANALYTICS

We hear the buzzwords, BA or simply analytics, data analytics, Business Intelligence (BI), big data, artificial intelligence (AI), machine learning, data science, virtual reality, augmented reality (AR), and other related terms, yet what do they mean, and in particular, what is analytics? Depending on whom you talk to, you will get varying definitions. One's definition seems to depend heavily on their perspective or training. We are not going to try to define all these buzzwords, but we will focus on developing our definition of what analytics is.

Analytics is not new, as its origins are in the early 20th century. From that time to today, we suggest that analytics has evolved through three major stages. To provide perspective, we now briefly examine these three stages.

Stage 1: Pre-Computer Technology, Prior to 1950

The term BA dates back to the late 19th and early 20th century and to the field of industrial engineering, as well as to Frederick Taylor's time management exercises and to Henry Ford's time measurements from his assembly line. Additionally, during this time (and as early as the 18th century), modern statistics was also being used in the social sciences and economics. "Analytics" (we put the quotes around the word analytics because, today, even though we would call these projects and studies analytics studies, back then, the term analytics was not popular and it would not have been used) projects were rather limited, relatively small in size, were done using paper and pencil, and took many hours, possibly weeks, to months or years, depending on the scope, to complete.

Stage 2: Mainframe to Early Personal Computer, 1950–1995

The invention of the computer and mainframe computer in the late 1940s and early 1950s revolutionized the world. Computer technology made data accessible. Initially, these mainframe computers were used mainly by scientists and researchers. Gordon Moore, the co-founder of Intel, predicted in 1965 that the amount of processing speed and the amount of memory you can buy for a dollar will double every 1.5–2 years. Moore's prediction, which is commonly known as Moore's Law, has been correct not only during this second stage of analytics but also for the third stage, and it continues today. As computer technology increased, our analytics capabilities similarly followed. A growing number of "analytics" studies, projects, and reports with larger and larger data sets were being conducted using the computer instead of paper and pencil. Although relatively faster, the turnaround time for a mainframe to provide a report or results from an "analytics" project was several hours.

In the early 1950s, a new extension of the industrial engineering field expanded to a new discipline called the field of operations research/management science (OR/MS), and the Operations Research Society of America (ORSA) and The Institute of Management Science (TIMS) professional societies were founded (in 1995 ORSA and TIMS merged to form the Institute for Operations Research and the Management Sciences [INFORMS]). Today, INFORMS is the largest professional society in the world for professionals in the fields of OR, MS, and analytics. This new field of OR/MS is defined "as the scientific process of transforming data into insights to make better decisions" (INFORMS, 2020).

Initially, OR/MS applications centered mainly around military problems. In subsequent years, OR/MS projects expanded to other fields of study, such as manufacturing, healthcare, transportation, finance, forest management, oil refinery, and water resources. In the 1960s, computer technology, OR/MS, and statistical projects made significant inroads into business where the concepts of database systems and decision support systems came about. The demand for these "analytics" projects, reports, and studies was steadily increasing in all industries in both the private and public sectors. Numerous companies established internal IT staff, as well as statistics and OR/MS staff.

Even with numerous success stories, many "analytics" projects were not being fully implemented and/or faced resistance. Two main reasons for this were that decision-makers did not trust the data and they felt threatened. Decision-makers did not feel the data were reliable, correct, or clean; this led to a level of mistrust in the accuracy of the data and, hence, a lack of utilizing the data and/or results to make decisions. Particularly with statistical and OR/MS models, decision-makers simply did not understand the results. The results were presented in the "foreign" language of statistics or mathematics, which the decision-makers were not fluent in. As early as 1961, Wynne realized that the challenge analytics specialists faced "consists of stripping the research argument of its mathematical complexities and irrelevancies while retaining the rigorous logic for the executive's understanding" (Wynne, 1961). Further, as Bradshaw noted: "Most managers would rather live with a problem they can't solve than use a solution they don't understand" (Watson and Marett, 1979).

Computers were being used only by the "analytics" people until the mid-1970s with the development of the microprocessor and personal computer (PC). Early PCs were first mostly used by technicians and hobbyists. This quickly expanded as more people and companies, private and public, started to use PCs as the hardware and software capabilities steadily increased. Microsoft Office was first launched in 1988. Over the years, word processing, spreadsheets, and presentation software have become transformational to many organizations. As of today, "Microsoft Excel is the most familiar, flexible, and widely used business application in the world"(ExcelHelp, 2020).

As advances in the PC industry steadily increased our computing power and capabilities, in the early 1990s our connectivity to one another was jolted with the creation of the World Wide Web in 1989–1990. "The world's first popular browser," Mosaic, was released in 1993.

Stage 3: Dot-Com Boom to 5G, 1995–2020

In the mid-1990s, as access to the World Wide Web became more common around the world and as investors pumped money into Internet-based startups, the dot-com boom occurred. Everything was evolving rapidly—the speed in which data was being analyzed, the amount of data being analyzed, and the variety of data being analyzed were all increasing at an exponential rate. This confluence of data volume, data velocity, and data variety is known as the three Vs, and has given way to the term big data.

A good example to understand the scope of big data is the global positioning system (GPS) navigation apps we all use in our cars, like Waze and Google Maps. When you enter a certain destination, your request is sent to a satellite and then to a server. Using relevant real-time data from the community of users, various potential routes—that is, all the data from all other relevant users—are also uploaded and analyzed. The app algorithm calculates an optimal route and, seconds after you hit go/enter/or whatever, your optimal route has been transmitted back to you. And all of this is done wirelessly! Your route is continuously monitored for traffic activity and delays and updated as you travel to your destination.

Big data's capabilities have dramatically decreased the time that "analytics" projects require to be completed. Some projects that used to take months to possibly years can now be done almost instantaneously. Moore's prediction of exponential growth, made in 1965, has been correct. To further understand this concept of exponential growth and where we are on the curve, let's look at the example about the famous legend of the origin of chess; it goes like this:

> When the inventor of chess showed the game to the Emperor of India, the Emperor was so impressed by the new game that he told the man to name his reward. The man simply asked for one grain of rice for the first square of the chessboard, two grains for the next square, four for the next, eight for the next, and so on for all 64 squares, with each square having double the number of grains as the square before. That does not seem too large, but the number of grains of rice for the 64th square is

9,223,372,036,854,775,808! (Assuming 0.029 grams is approximately equal to one rice grain, that equates to about 2.95E+11 tons!! Just in the last square!) (Friedman, 2016)

According to Tom Friedman (2016), we are now on the second half of the chessboard—the steep part of the exponential curve. So, for the next several years, analytics is going to change at an even greater rate. And Friedman believes that for the first time in history, the rate of change will be occurring faster than we can adapt to.

WHAT IS ANALYTICS?

INFORMS (2020) deconstructs their definition of analytics into categories:

- *Descriptive analytics* asks, "What has happened?" It provides insight into the past by describing/summarizing the past in reports, dashboards, and queries, so that we can learn from the past and understand how it may influence future outcomes.
- *Predictive analytics* asks, "What is going to happen?" It provides understanding about the future and perceptions of what may happen by offering actionable insights based on the data. It also provides estimates about the likelihood of a future outcome using techniques such as forecasting and predictive modeling.
- *Prescriptive analytics* asks, "What should we do?" It quantifies the effect of future decisions in order to advise on possible outcomes before the decisions are actually made. It not only predicts what will happen, but also why it will happen, and provides recommendations regarding actions that will take advantage of the predictions. This method uses techniques such as optimization, simulation, and decision trees.

The graphical view in Figure 18.1 illustrates the range of analytics and the types of analytics as the level of analytics varies (Davenport and Harris, 2007). The area below the horizontal line is where BI originated in accessing and reporting data. In the context of the INFORMS analytics definition, this area would be descriptive analytics. Descriptive analytics consists of reporting, visualizing, and slicing and dicing the data. The area above the horizontal line represents the tools of advanced predictive and prescriptive analytics. Predictive analytics employs advanced statistical techniques, such as data mining, to uncover relationships not readily apparent with descriptive analytics and predicts the future, while prescriptive analytics utilizes optimization, simulation, and other quantitative tools to improve the organizational efficiency. A higher level of competitive advantage is provided as the analytics become more sophisticated.

Analytics has several stages over which it can vary: either by analytic category using INFORMS's definition—from descriptive to predictive to prescriptive—or by degree of competitive advantage, as depicted in Figure 18.1. A discipline-based framework of analytics that encapsulates these viewpoints includes the three core subject areas of information systems and technology, statistics, and quantitative methods (or OR/MS), as shown in Figure 18.2 (Klimberg, 2015). Regardless of your background and the differing definitions of analytics, each category receives varying degrees of emphasis in each of these three disciplines.

Today, in 2020, the term analytics is being replaced by the phrases AI, machine learning, and data science, which we are sure will eventually be overtaken themselves. Irrespective of what you call it—analytics, AI, machine learning, data science, or BI—this multidiscipline field applies "data, technology, and analytics to gain insight and knowledge that enables decisions about processes, services, and products that yield positive economic outcomes" (Herschel, 2010).

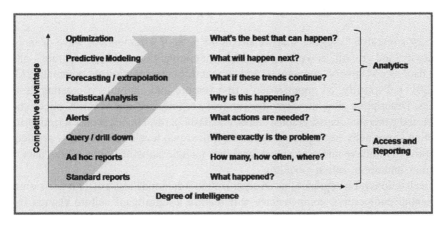

Source: From Davenport and Harris (2007).

Figure 18.1   *Variation of analytics through the degrees of intelligence of the methodologies employed as it directly affects competitive advantage*

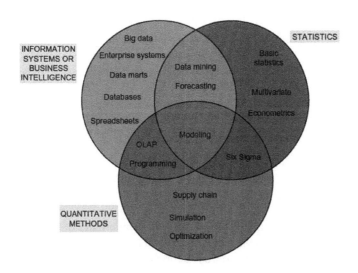

Source: From Klimberg (2015).

Figure 18.2   *A discipline-based approach to BA*

ORGANIZATIONAL CHANGE

McKinsey's research "suggests that we are on the cusp of a tremendous wave of innovation, productivity, and growth, as well as new modes of competition and value capture—all driven by big data as consumers, companies, and economic sectors exploit its potential" (Manyika et al., 2011). Typically, an organization's first venture into analytics is creating descriptive analytics. Descriptive analytics provides summary reports and queries data, slices and dices the data, and generates charts, graphs, tables, and dashboards. Having this descriptive analytics foundation is normally necessary to move to the next two levels of analytics—predictive and prescriptive. Predictive and prescriptive analytics include statistical, forecasting, data mining, simulation, and optimization modeling.

The realization and acceptance that an organization's data and the use of it for decision-making are essential competitive competencies will require a significant culture change by many organizations. This culture change will require entities to shift from data-collection organizations to data-driven organizations. Most organizations are data-collection organizations; they collect and report information. A data-driven organization refers to how you collect the data and what you do with it once you have it. Understanding data will be a next-generation leadership skill.

Five Stages of Analytical Maturity

Not every organization is at the same stage in this transformational process. The organization's level of analytical maturity affects how far along they are in this transformation. In their book *Competing on Analytics*, Tom Davenport and Jeanne Harris (2007) proposed a framework of five stages of analytical maturity ranging from being analytically impaired to being an analytical competitor:

- Stage I: Organizations are flying blind and are reactive. They have multiple definitions of data, missing or poor-quality data, poorly integrated systems, and nearly no leadership support.
- Stage II: The analytic efforts of these organizations are isolated, opportunistic, and usually function specific. There are islands of data, technology, and expertise with isolated pockets of analysts. The right data for decision-making is not available, and there are only some isolated areas of leadership.
- Stage III: Leaders are just beginning to recognize the importance of analytics, and most of the data remain unintegrated, non-standardized, and inaccessible.
- Stage IV: Analytics is a corporate priority for organizations in this stage. They have begun to develop enterprise-wide analytics capabilities, and data are of high quality. In this stage, there is an enterprise-wide analytics plan, some embedded or automated analytics, and leadership support for analytical competence.
- Stage V: In the final stage, analytics are a primary driver of performance; there is strong leadership and a passion for analytics. There is also a relentless search for new data and metrics. Analytics is fully automated and integrated into the business process's enterprise-wide utilization of analytics, and the company routinely reaps the big benefits of their analytical capabilities.

Becoming an Analytical Competitor

Over the years, I have asked students in my MBA and other graduate classes, "At what stage do you think your organization is currently operating?" Ten years ago, I would say the mean/median stage was around two. Today, I would say the mean/median stage is between two and three. What does this mean? There are plenty of analytical opportunities to impact an organization in the future.

To ascend the pyramid of analytical maturity, we believe an organization must have four strong attributes to become a data-driven organization: (a) the right metrics and insights; (b) the right data and systems; (c) the right senior management and people; and (d) the right culture.

With the right metrics and insights, the organization views its analytical capability as what sets them apart from its competitors and what makes them successful in the marketplace. Without a strategic analytical focus, analytics remains a spreadsheet utility for individuals. The data quality is reliable and the ease of use and understanding by all decision-makers are essential. Analytical competitors need a primary focus for their analytical activity, but once an analytical, test-and-learn culture has been created, it is impossible to stop it from spreading. It is typically their primary analytical function. For example, the strategic distinctive capability of Walmart is supply chain analytics; for Netflix, it is predicting customer movie preferences; for Harrah's, it is customer loyalty and service; and for Marriott, it is revenue management.

The next attribute needed to become a data-driven organization is the right data and systems. This happens when data and analyses are made available broadly throughout the organization. Care is taken to manage data and analyses efficiently and effectively; no process or business unit is optimized at the expense of another unless it is strategically important to do so, and there is centralized data management with degrees of cross-functional sophistication. An enterprise-wide approach must be taken. To be able to apply these data-driven insights, the right infrastructure must be in place. Efficient systems that make it easy to collect, merge, report, analyze, and share the data and resulting insights happen in a timely matter.

Next is the right senior management and people. Culture change requires a push from the top. It also requires support and attention from all senior executives, enough to direct and coordinate efforts in separate units. The primary advocate should be the CEO. The level of the CEO's beliefs in analytics will drive the level and persistence of investment in people, IT and data. They must passionately project the analytical strategies that will deliver the company's vision, and have the fortitude to push others to think and act analytically. The CEO does not have to be a "number cruncher" or an analytical genius.

Besides the need for analytics people—data scientists, data architects, data visualization experts—organizations need "analytics translators" (Henke et al., 2018). Analytics translators are data savvy, yet more so they are the conduit between the analytical expertise of the data scientists and management their understanding of the domain knowledge of the organization ensures the interpretation, communication, and ultimate success of the analytical projects. These analytics translators are found throughout the hierarchy of the organization; they understand the right way to use data, as well as the inherent limitations of the data, and they are analytics advocates. Data cannot change anything by itself; an analytic transformation needs these people.

The final attribute is the right culture. The best analytics in the world can be stifled by an unreceptive culture. And it starts at the top with senior management's commitment to move the organization from a data-collection to a data-driven organization. That means aligning what the organization's analytics program says to focus on and what is actually incentivized, both formally through pay plans as well as informally through expectations and mentorships.

This transformation will not happen overnight. You cannot just buy the software and expect that analytics will happen. You have to have all four attributes of an analytics, data-driven organization. And depending on where the organization is in their stage of analytical maturity, this process will take several and perhaps many years. This transformation process is a marathon. You have to learn to crawl before you can walk, you have to walk before you can run, and you have to run before you can fly.

In a Deloitte (2013) report, the authors identify that one of the three key areas that consumer product companies will address is advanced data analytics. They foresee that "consumer products companies that leverage data analytics in the context of cross-functional and integrated business planning and execution are likeliest to reap the most benefit from the huge amount of data currently available." However, as of 2016, most companies are capturing only a fraction of the potential value from data and analytics (McKinsey, 2016). According to McKinsey (2016), the biggest barriers to organizations in extracting that value from data and analytics are not technological; they are organizational. Many companies are struggling to incorporate data-driven insights into day-to-day business processes, and they struggle to recruit and retain the right talent. Even with these difficulties, for most companies, data are now a critical corporate asset, but their value is tied to their ultimate use: "Data and analytics represent the single biggest opportunity available to management teams to create value, improve performance, and change the nature of competition … Embracing analytics is not about adopting a new tactic. It's about changing your business model and the fundamental way you make decisions" (Henke, 2016).

And there are more data waiting to be analyzed and used. When we say data or big data, we are mostly focused on the primary data collected and used by an organization. The secondary data, which some people call the "data exhaust," include all the other data that are obtained and created along the way. Data exhaust tends to be bigger and has the potential to be even more insightful; exploiting it is and will continue to be a competitive advantage.

ANALYTICS IN THE SERVICE INDUSTRY

"There will be more change in the next five years than there has been in the last 50 years in retail" (Harker, 2020). This prediction pertains not only to the retail industry but to all industries, especially service industries, and to large and even small companies; they will all experience this change. Many companies have taken an omnichannel approach to sales that integrates distribution, promotion, and communication channels, whether it is online, via telephone, or in a brick-and-mortar store such that the customer shopping experience is seamless. Progressively more stores are starting to act more like online sites, and more online sites are acting more like stores. A store salesperson interacting with a customer can immediately reference the customer's previous purchases and preferences as easily as a customer service representative on the phone or an online customer service chat representative. Similarly, an online customer can check inventory on the company's website, buy an item, and pick it up later or have it delivered to their home. For example, in 2013, Best Buy, the consumer electronics retailer, embraced an omnichannel strategy that included an updated online site where the online and brick-and-mortar store inventories are shared, and the customer is offered the option to pick up an item bought online at the store or have it delivered to their home. To further compete with other online retailers, such as Amazon, Best Buy offers a price-match guarantee.

Analytics and technology can/will completely alter the modality of the business while improving customer service. The field of healthcare is a good example of how patient services, diagnostics, and evaluations are performed outside the traditional healthcare settings using technology and analytics, in particular:

- Telemedicine: Provides remote clinical services to patients, such as follow-up visits, medication management, management of chronic conditions, and other similar services.
- Telehealth: Provides remote patient monitoring and care, such as weight, heart, and blood pressure monitoring.
- Remote diagnostics: Provides professional evaluation almost instantaneously, such as the new field of teleradiology, in which X-ray images can be examined and evaluated remotely by a radiologist 24/7.

These healthcare options provide patients with more timely, convenient, and possibly life-saving services.

Another example of altering the modality to improve service is the cupcake ATM. The cupcake ATM, introduce by the bakery Sprinkles in 2012, dispenses freshly baked cupcakes and cookies 24/7 from an ATM-like machine. The cupcake ATM means that customers can get what they want, whenever they want it.

Historically, the purpose of the store was to distribute products. Doug Stephens, a retail industry futurist, foresees the store becoming the media (Stephens, 2013). Stephens now sees stores as being used to distribute experiences. Here are two examples of how technology and analytics will change customer experiences:

- *Beacon technology:* Beacons are small wireless transmitters. A network of beacons can create a cohesive in-store experience by tracking customer in-store movement and providing product store location, product information, and coupons/discounts. Macy's, the department store, has been using beacon technology since 2014. Given the customer location in the store, targeted information based on previous in-store and online buying is directed to the customer's phone. Sport teams have been using beacon technology at their stadiums and arenas to alert fans to discounts on food and apparel, game video highlights, the length of lines at concession stands or restrooms, and even to have food delivered to their seats.
- *AR:* This is an interactive experience enhanced by using technology to superimpose images, sound, and/or text on the world we see. An example of a technology that uses AR is smart mirrors. Smart mirrors virtually superimpose products onto the customer image and eliminate the inconvenient and time-consuming process of actually trying on the product. Sephora, the beauty care retailer, introduced smart mirrors in their stores in 2017. A customer can virtually sample various facial cosmetics, including different colors and textures, while standing in front of the mirror and interacting with it. An image with the chosen cosmetic, color, and texture are projected on the customer's face. Other retailers have used smart mirrors to superimpose their products, such as clothing, footwear, and eyewear onto the customer.

Companies need to use the technology and analytics to personalize the customer experience. They need to go beyond just the technology and, in many cases, this does not require utilizing the latest and greatest new technology. For example, when you make an online reservation at the Seasons 52 restaurant, the customer's name is eventually relayed to the waitstaff such that the waitstaff greets the customer using their name. Another example: a dentist meets each morning with their staff and reviews the day's patients and what they will require. Also, all patients have their photos taken so that if the receptionist does not know the patient scheduled for a visit, they will recognize them. Additionally, the dentist throughout the year sends the patient emails—reminding them of appointments and celebrating personal events such as birthdays or anniversaries. Dental technology has also had a tremendous positive impact on the patient experience. For example, digital dental X-rays, besides producing increased quality, provide instantaneous X-ray pictures such that the patient and dentist can evaluate them during the patient's visit. In addition, the dentist can review and compare the current X-rays with older X-rays to observe possible significant dental changes and can proactively address these issues, all during the patient's visit.

Prior to a customer or a group of customers initiating some purchasing process, companies can employ their analytical capabilities and take advantage of their physical and digital service inventories to anticipate and improve the customer experience. Davis et al. (2015) define service inventory as: "All steps embedded in organizational processes that can be performed using both tangible goods and information, and which can be done with or without customer input and stored prior to the customer's arrival with the goal of creating economic value to the service encounter" (p. 86).

Below are a few examples of companies leveraging their service inventories:

- The Ritz-Carlton hotel chain uses the data from a database of guest interactions to anticipate guest requests/needs/issues before the customer even asks for it.
- Home Depot reroutes and prioritizes certain products and ships them to store locations before a potential hurricane may hit an area based on the historical high demand for these products after a hurricane.
- Say you attend a Philadelphia Flyers game at the Wells Fargo Center in which, on the concourse level, there are several cars, including one you look at for several minutes. A few days later, you receive an email from a local car dealership offering you a big discount and inviting you to come in for a test ride of the car you were looking at.

Customers' expectations are high today and only getting higher, as they expect that companies should be able to meet them where they are and when they want. "The expectation of consumers today is that everything exists in the world of the now, and that their interactions will be personalized. Real-time analytics is absolutely core to enabling companies to deliver those kinds of experiences" (Jacobs, 2018). Nevertheless, the majority of companies today still lack these real-time analytics capabilities, yet they are rapidly striving to obtain them.

Effects from the COVID-19 Pandemic

The COVID-19 pandemic has turned our world, and especially the service industry, upside down. Many stores have been financially ruined and have been forced to close. In nearly every strip mall, we see a significant number of businesses that are temporary or permanently closed. On the other hand, many companies, large and small, have been surviving and will survive the next year or so, until we reach our new normal. For example, for a restaurant to operate during the pandemic, they now have some sort of an outdoor, curbside, and possibly delivery presence, of which they may never have had any experience prior to the pandemic. When we arrive at the new normal, a restaurant will still have to provide a combination of the outdoor, curbside, and delivery service with a much smaller indoor dining space. Sports venues reopening during the pandemic have adapted every facet of game-day operations, including adding COVID-19 cleaning and screening, security, temperature checks, movement tracking within the venue, mobile ordering and cashless transactions, and new interactive fan experiences. Major keys to a restaurant's, a sport team's, and other companies' survival will be their ability to embrace technology and analytics, perhaps more quickly than planned, and their ability to think outside the box.

Before the pandemic, the statement was "we will see more change in the next 5 years than there has been in the last 50 years." The pandemic has accelerated this change such that many developments will now occur in the next 2–3 years or even faster.

CONCLUSIONS

Companies are in the midst of an analytics revolution. Technology and analytics are dramatically affecting organizations. Some companies may just be starting their analytical journey, and some may be much further along. In recent years, this transformational process has been accelerating; with the COVID-19 pandemic, change is now happening at an even faster rate.

This analytics revolution is affecting how service companies operate internally as well as how they interact with their customers. Those that take full advantage of the new technology and analytics and train their employees to interact with their customers to provide a seamless, real-time experience, and who also find their distinct capability, will have a competitive advantage to succeed.

REFERENCES

Davenport, T. H., & Harris, J. G. (2007). *Competing on analytics: The science of winning.* Harvard Business School Press.

Davis, M. M., Field, J., & Stavrulaki, E. (2015). Using digital service inventories to create customer value. *Service Science/INFORMS, 7*(2), 83–99.

Deloitte. (2013). *Global powers of consumer products 2013.* Deloitte Touche Tohmatsu Limited.

ExcelHelp (2020). *The history of Microsoft Excel.* https://www.excelhelp.com/the-history-of-microsoft -excel/

Friedman, T. L. (2016). *Thank you for being late: An optimist's guide to thriving in the age of accelerations.* Farrar, Straus and Giroux.

Harker, S. (2020). *How retail will change radically in the next five years.* Financial Review. https:// www.afr.com/companies/retail/flintstones-make-way-for-the-jetsons-in-retail-revolution-20191217 -p53ku4

Henke, N. (2016, December 13). *Most analytics opportunities untapped.* McKinsey InformationWeek. https://www.informationweek.com/most-analytics-opportunities-untapped-mckinsey/a/d-id/282223

Henke, N., Levine, J., & McInerney, P. (2018, February 5). You don't have to be a data scientist to fill this must-have analytics role. *Harvard Business Review.* https://hbr.org/2018/02/ you-dont-have-to-be-a-data-scientist-to-fill-this-must-have-analytics-role

Herschel, R. (2010, June 1). *What is business intelligence?* BeyeNetwork. http://www.b-eye-network.com/view/13768

INFORMS. (2020). *What is analytics?* https://www.informs.org/About-INFORMS/What-is-Analytics

Jacobs, J. (2018). Real-time analytics: The key to unlocking customer insights & driving the customer experience. *Harvard Business Review, 1.* p. 3. https://hbr.org/sponsored/2018/06/real-time-analytics

Klimberg, R. K. (2015). Teaching a data mining course in a business school. In K. Lawrence, R. Klimberg (Ed.), *Contemporary perspectives in data mining* (Vol. 2; pp. 81–97). Information Age Publishing.

Manyika, J., Chui, M., Brown, B., Bughin, J., Dobbs, R., Roxburgh, C., Hung Byers, A. (2011). *Big data: The next frontier for innovation competition and productivity.* McKinsey Global Institute Report.

McKinsey. (2016, December). *The age of analytics: Competing in a data-driven world.* McKinsey Global Institute.

Stephens, D. (2013). *The store is media and media is the store.* Retail Prophet. https://www.retailprophet.com/the-store-is-media-and-media-is-the-store/

Watson, H. J., & Marett, P. G. (1979). A survey of management science implementation problems. *Interfaces, 9*(4), 124–128.

Wynne, B. E. (1961). A pattern of reporting operations research to the business executive. *Management Technology, 1*(3), 16–23.

19. Text analytics of service customer reviews and feedback: understanding customers' emotions and cognition in the hospitality industry

Jie J. Zhang, Spring H. Han and Rohit Verma

INTRODUCTION

The power of big data has captured the imagination of the world for some time (Mayer-Schönberger and Cukier, 2013). Businesses are particularly interested in extracting intelligence and insights from big data (Chen et al., 2012; McAfee et al., 2012; Tan et al., 2015). Indeed, raw data have grown exponentially as the online user base expands. The world, on average, generated 2.9 quintillion bytes of data each day in 2016 and 2017, equivalent to the total storage capacity of 67 billion 32GB iPads (DOMO, 2017). A growing percentage of these new data are unstructured: text, voice, image, and video. Meanwhile, information overload (i.e., when data growth outstrips the processing capability) has become a key managerial challenge (Eppler and Mengis, 2004). Data noise also grows sharply. For example, spammers sent 103 million spam emails every minute in 2017 (Koetsier, 2017). Since the communication capacity of a network increases in its signal-to-noise ratio (Shannon, 1948), too much data (including both signal and noise) could make it harder to separate the signal (i.e., useful information) from the noise. Faced with the challenges of information overload and overwhelming noise, the new world of big data calls for theory-driven and context-aware data analysis methods. This chapter outlines an approach that leverages emotion and service experience research and links unstructured and numerical data.

Research that links unstructured text data and business performance has grown significantly thanks to recent developments in advanced algorithm-based text analytic techniques that uncover customer feelings and thoughts from online reviews (Hu and Liu, 2004; Pang and Lee, 2008). However, a crucial question remains under-explored: How does unstructured customer feedback that encompasses emotions and cognitive themes relate to the overall numerical satisfaction evaluation of services? Deeper insights into this relationship could help service providers in two important ways. Such knowledge could enable richer understanding of customer satisfaction from complementary sources. Unsolicited customer reviews are open-ended, driven by issues important to individual customers. Numerical ratings quantify a set of predetermined performance dimensions. Furthermore, a positive correlation between the two types of data identifies strong signals embedded in raw data, which contributes to reducing information overload.

This study augments the body of knowledge on customer feedback by investigating the relationship between unstructured guest review text and numerical ratings in the global hotel industry. The hotel industry has well-established platforms for sharing review text and numerical ratings that provide rich data for rigorous empirical analysis.

A two-study replication research design was used to explore the relationship between overall customer satisfaction and emotions and topics embedded in text data. This design first applies sentiment analysis to quantify the emotional states of each review, followed by topic modeling to extract cognitive themes or topics of customer satisfaction embedded in the text. Study 1 uses a large-scale international sample that consists of 355 upscale and luxury hotels in a hotel group to explore the relationship between the numerical ratings and the emotional states. Study 2 uses a regional sample of 57 hotels from one major metropolitan market across multiple chain scales to first replicate Study 1 and verify the findings, and then leverage the additional customer characteristics to conduct in-depth investigation of the cognitive topics embedded in the review texts across multiple market segments.

The results show that both customers' emotional states and cognitive topics correlate significantly with the overall satisfaction evaluation of services. These results hold for two samples consisting of hotel properties located in various geographic markets and targeting a range of customer market segments. Furthermore, evidence suggests that the levels of emotional states and influential topics vary across numerical ratings and for customers from different market segments. This research also finds a range of cognitive themes or topics embedded in the text: the numerical signs of some coefficients are negative, indicating pain points, whereas other variables are positive, indicating opportunities for guest satisfaction. The implications of these findings for managing guest relationships as well as internal operations are discussed.

LITERATURE REVIEW AND HYPOTHESES DEVELOPMENT

This study contributes to the research on customer feedback by focusing on online customer reviews that contain both numerical and text data. Customer feedback is generally defined as customer communication concerning a product or a service offering (Erickson and Eckrich, 2001). Customer feedback can be either solicited (Griffin and Hauser, 1993) or unsolicited (Berry and Parasuraman, 1997). Solicited feedback is encouraged by the company through such tools as surveys and focus groups that invite customers to share their opinions (Sampson, 1996). In contrast, unsolicited customer feedback relies on the customer's own desire and will to communicate their experience (Nasr et al., 2014; Sampson, 1996). Unsolicited customer feedback is currently undergoing tremendous growth with the recent rise in the popularity of social media. Subsequently, the service industry has gained unprecedented access to a large and rapidly growing number of online customer reviews on these platforms. New approaches to analyzing user-generated content (UGC) continue to grow rapidly because of its vast and expansive nature.

Textual properties of online reviews were the first to gain attention from business scholars. Review valence (i.e., favorable or unfavorable experience descriptions), along with the volume of text, have been the most popular properties examined and linked to customers' attitudes and behavior (Jones et al., 2004; Lim et al., 2016; Sparks et al., 2016; Streitfeld, 2011; Weathers et al., 2015; Wei et al., 2013; Xiao et al., 2016), business performance (Anderson, 2012; Chevalier and Mayzlin, 2006; Duan et al., 2008; Neirotti et al., 2016; Wang et al., 2016), and firm reputation (Baka, 2016; Wang et al., 2015). In addition, Hamby et al. (2015) found that reviews with a more story-like format led to higher levels of transportation into the review, which led to higher levels of reflection on the message, and ultimately influenced behavioral intent. One natural extension of these review-level studies explores customers' emotions and thoughts embedded in the language, which is the focus of this chapter.

Online Reviews: Sentiment Polarity and Customer Satisfaction

Business research has long recognized the importance of emotions in customer consumption. Published studies have examined emotions and feelings in various contexts, such as marketing and consumer behavior (e.g., Bagozzi et al., 1999; Erevelles, 1998; Ladhari, 2007), advertising (Edell and Burke, 1987; Stayman and Aaker, 1988), consumer decision-making (Stayman and Batra, 1991), retailing (Babin et al., 2005; Baker et al., 1992; Donovan et al., 1994; Donovan and Rossiter, 1982), consumption experience (Bigné et al., 2005; Nyer, 1997; Oliver, 1993; Westbrook, 1987; Westbrook and Oliver, 1991; Wirtz and Bateson, 1999), and behavioral intentions (Derbaix and Vanhamme, 2003; Dixon et al., 2017; Hicks et al., 2005; Zeelenberg and Pieters, 2004).

Traditionally, emotions in customer satisfaction research have used Izard's (1977) Differential Emotions Scale (DES II), which is a shortened version of the original scale (DES I; Izard, 1972). This scale consists of the following ten emotions: interest, joy, anger, disgust, contempt, shame, guilt, sadness, fear, and surprise. Customers are typically asked to what extent, on a scale ranging from (almost) never to very often, they have experienced these emotions in consumption settings (Westbrook, 1987). Sentiment analysis, which identifies emotional state (positive, negative, or neutral) through emotional dictionaries, is a new but rapidly growing method in customer review research (for a recent systematic review, see Jain et al., 2021).

Sentiment analysis has been applied to UGC, such as tweets and online reviews, to uncover the polarity of emotions. Limited to 140 characters, tweets are popular choices for people to voice their opinion about a variety of topics (Geetha et al., 2017). In the hotel industry context, Philander and Zhong (2016) demonstrated how Twitter data could be analyzed through a cost-effective application. Geetha et al. (2017) studied the sentiment polarity of hotel guests' tweets and found varying effects on customer ratings for hotels at different chain scales (i.e., budget vs. luxury). Online reviews tend to be longer than tweets, providing more space for customers to express their feelings and offer narratives to explain those feelings (Hamby et al., 2015). Informed by prior research on emotions and customer satisfaction, the present study assesses customers' positive and negative emotional states, then identifies cognitive themes through systematic analysis of unstructured text-based feedback provided in online reviews.

Positive and negative emotions typically coexist in a review (Liljander and Strandvik, 1997; Vinodhini and Chandrasekaran, 2012). Richins (1997) comprehensively examined emotional states associated with consumption and analyzed the usefulness of existing emotion measures in assessing consumption-related emotions. Richins (1997) suggested that many specific consumption experiences involve a broad range of mixed emotions or ambivalence. Recognizing consumer experience of multiple positive and/or negative emotions in one consumption episode (Otnes et al., 1997), researchers are exploring how to leverage the positive and negative emotional content in a review to improve operations. Dens et al. (2015) show that the ratio of positive and negative emotional content could inform recovery strategy design. Xiao et al. (2016) use the sentiment polarity (i.e., positive, negative, or neutral emotion) associated with product features to generate customer requirements for product design. Tools that leverage the emotional content of text data to indicate customer opinions of product quality are also emerging (e.g., Přichystal, 2016). These studies assume that the positive or negative emotions embedded in the text directly link to the overall satisfaction evaluation. Although it is intuitively sound, this assumption requires empirical validation.

Furthermore, research has shown that issues related to different sentiment polarities require different managerial interventions. For example, extra attention by the service provider helps to create positive emotions, while negative emotions are the result of failing to meet a minimum standard (Price et al., 1995). Therefore, for both theoretical and managerial reasons, it is important to test the relationship between emotional polarity and overall satisfaction. The following hypotheses are proposed:

Hypothesis 1a. There is a positive relationship between the positive emotional content and the overall numerical rating of the hotel service.

Hypothesis 1b. There is a negative relationship between the negative emotional content and the overall numerical rating of the hotel service.

Online Reviews: Cognitive Themes and Customer Satisfaction

Overall customer experience is the internal and subjective responses customers have regarding contacts with a company (Meyer and Schwager, 2007). Research has shown that customer satisfaction can be assessed by examining evaluations of the perceived performance (Sarra et al., 2015; Tse and Wilton, 1988). Ever-expanding unsolicited online review text offers abundant data for exploring such responses. Aside from emotional states, latent topics or themes in large text datasets are increasingly accessible through computer-assisted content analyses, such as topic modeling, that use algorithms to automatically summarize text and discover themes/topics (e.g., Blei and Lafferty, 2009). Prior applications include modeling online reviews with multi-grain topic models (Titov and McDonald, 2008), efficient correlated topic modeling with topic embedding (He et al., 2017), and bias-sentiment-topic models for microblog sentiment analysis (Guo and Chen, 2018).

Topic modeling is therefore useful in informing service management by uncovering the major threads of thoughts of customers when they recount service experiences (Han et al., 2016). How these thoughts relate to the overall satisfaction level traditionally measured numerically is a new but important inquiry toward advancing knowledge on perceived performance. In particular, research is needed to unpack overall customer satisfaction and evaluate the role of specific cognitive themes (i.e., influential topics) across levels of customer satisfaction. This research undertakes this line of inquiry in the hotel industry context by hypothesizing the following:

Hypothesis 2. The probabilities of influential topics embedded in review texts vary across levels of hotel satisfaction scores.

Variation across Market Segments

One consensus from prior studies of online reviews is that firm performance and possibility of purchase are increasing in the total number and valence of the reviews at the aggregate level. Recent studies have explored a more nuanced view of this general relationship. For example, Sparks and Browning (2011) explored key factors that influence perceptions of trust and consumer choice using an experimental design. They found that consumers seem to be more influenced by early negative information when the overall set of reviews is negative. These findings confirm that the cognitive processes behind online review generation and consumption highly subjective. Consequently, what is observed at the aggregate level needs to be supplemented by considering contextual factors in specific settings. This is particularly important for service operating units that operate in specific geographic markets and target specific customer segments. This study applies sentiment analysis and topic modeling to online review texts generated by customers from a wide range of geographic markets and segments, and explores the variations in customer emotion and cognition across rating levels with consideration of market contextual factors through the following hypotheses.

Hypothesis 3a. The relationship between the positive emotional content and the overall hotel satisfaction rating varies across market segments.

Hypothesis 3b. The relationship between the negative emotional content and the overall hotel satisfaction rating varies across market segments.

Hypothesis 4. The variations in the probabilities of influential topics across levels of hotel satisfaction scores differ across market segments.

RESEARCH DESIGN AND FINDINGS

This empirical research uses a replication design consisting of two studies. Study 1 performs sentiment analysis on an international sample of luxury hotel guests to evaluate customers' emotional states, then explores the relationship between a customer's emotional state and numerical rating. Study 2 replicates Study 1 using a regional sample of guests visiting hotels across multiple chain scales. In addition, Study 2 uses topic modeling to uncover major cognitive themes embedded in review text, then explores the relationship between customer cognition and numerical rating across market segments. Figure 19.1 outlines the steps in our research design.

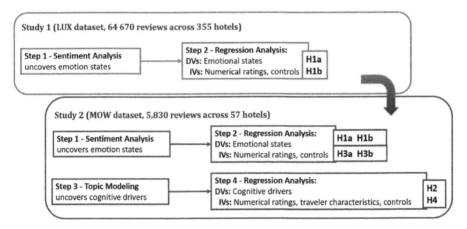

Figure 19.1   A two-study replication design allows verification and extension of the findings

Table 19.1   Summary statistics of Study 1 (Sample 1, N = 64670)

Variables	Mean	Std Dev	Min	Max
Numerical ratings	4.570	0.850	1	5
PositivitySentiment	0.224	0.078	0.000	0.743
NegativitySentiment	0.038	0.035	0.000	0.429

Sample 1 is a large-scale international sample that consists of 355 upscale and luxury hotels in a hotel group. Sample 2 consists of reviews on 57 hotels from one major metropolitan market across multiple chain scales. This replication design answers the call from leading operations management researchers that more replication studies are needed to facilitate the continuous refinement and advancement of knowledge (Frohlich and Dixon, 2003; Pagell and Krause, 2004). Furthermore, the data on traveler characteristics (i.e., business vs. leisure) are used to conduct an in-depth investigation of customer emotions and cognition across market segments. This section briefly explains the analysis conducted in each study for hypothesis testing.

Study 1

The objective of Study 1 is to explore the relationship between customers' emotional states embedded in review text and the numerical ratings connected to those reviews. Sample 1 consists of 64670 reviews (in English) over a 15-month period on 355 independent luxury hotels and resorts that belong to the same hotel group and agree to follow the same quality standards. By focusing on a global sample of independent operating units in a well-defined segment with similar quality standards, this study controls for the variations in guest preference and market demand. Table 19.1 presents the summary statistics.

The two sentiment scores, NegativitySentiment and PositivitySentiment, measure emotions expressed by the words in each review. The SentimentAnalysis package (Feuerriegel and Proellochs, 2018) of R, the free language and software environment for statistical computing and graphics (https://www.r-project.org), is used to perform dictionary-based sentiment analysis of textual contents. This study employs the QDAP dictionary (Hu and Liu, 2004) to identify the positive words and negative words because this dictionary specifically targets consumer reviews. PositivitySentiment (NegativitySentiment) measures the number of positive (negative) words as a proportion of all the words in each review. Higher values of one or the other indicate more positivity or negativity of the customer emotion in each review.

Tables 19.2 and 19.3 present the linear regression results using the emotion polarity (positivity or negativity) as the dependent variable and the numerical rating as the predictor variable. This model specification allows us to investigate systematic variations in the level of positive and negative opinion across levels of numerical ratings. The results show that positive emotion content within the text feedback increases with the numerical rating of the hotel, and negative emotion content decreases with an increase in the numerical rating. These results are statistically significant. Hypotheses 1a and 1b are supported.

Study 2

Sample 2 consists of 5830 reviews of 57 hotels across multiple market segments located in one metropolitan region. Table 19.4 presents the summary statistics of Sample 2. It is worth noting that the variances in the positivity and negativity sentiment measures in these two samples are

Table 19.2   *Study 1: positive customer emotion content as a function of numerical rating of the hotel*

	Coefficients	Std Error
Constant	0.121***	0.006
Numerical rating	Rating = 1 is the reference group	
2	0.124***	0.003
3	0.035***	0.002
4	0.079***	0.002
5	0.110***	0.002
Hotel fixed effects	Included	
Obs	64 670	
R^2	0.1425	
Adj R^2	0.1377	
F Statistic	29.84*** (df = 358; 64 311)	

Notes:
The dependent variable in the regression is positive customer emotion (PositivitySentiment).
***$p < 0.01$.

Table 19.3   *Study 1: negative customer emotion content as a function of numerical rating of the hotel*

	Coefficients	Std Error
Constant	0.088***	
Numerical rating	Rating = 1 is the reference group	
2	−0.006***	0.001
3	−0.021***	0.001
4	−0.043***	0.001
5	−0.058***	0.001
Hotel fixed effects	Included	
Obs	64 670	
R^2	0.1780	
Adj R^2	0.1734	
F Statistic	38.89*** (df = 358; 64 311)	

Notes:
The dependent variable in the regression is negative customer emotion (NegativitySentiment).
***$p < 0.01$.

similar, although the reviews in Sample 1, on average, are more positive and less negative than those in Sample 2.

The objective in Study 2 is two-fold. First, it replicates the analysis in Study 1 to verify the pattern of relationships between sentiment polarities derived from the text reviews and overall numerical customer satisfaction. In addition, the information on guest market segments in Sample 2 is used to explore the variations across market segments.

Tables 19.5 and 19.6 show the results of the regression analyses when first positive and then negative sentiment (i.e., emotional state) serve as the dependent variables. The results show that positive emotion content within the text feedback increases with the numerical rating of the hotel, while negative emotion content decreases. This evidence confirms the findings from Study 1.

Table 19.4   Summary statistics of Study 2 (Sample 2, N = 5830)

Variables	Mean	Std Dev	Min	Max
Numerical ratings	4.070	0.960	1	5
PositivitySentiment	0.199	0.072	0.000	0.556
NegativitySentiment	0.433	0.037	0.000	0.364

Table 19.5   Study 2: positive customer emotion content as a function of numerical rating of the hotel

	Coefficients	Std Error
Constant	0.136***	0.009
Numerical rating	Rating = 1 is the reference group	
2	0.011***	0.007
3	0.038***	0.006
4	0.073***	0.006
5	0.094***	0.006
Hotel fixed effects	Included	
Obs	5830	
R^2	0.1521	
Adj R^2	0.1433	
F Statistic	17.25*** (df = 60; 5,769)	

Notes:
The dependent variable in the regression is positive customer emotion (PositivitySentiment).
***$p < 0.01$.

In addition to the text reviews, Sample 2 contains information on the guest market segments—business vs. leisure. Tables 19.7 and 19.8 show the results from testing H3a and H3b for the two sub-samples. The relationship between sentiment and overall satisfaction holds for several of the sub-segments based on the purpose of travel and type of traveler. It is interesting to note that the regression coefficient for the square of numerical ratings is not statistically significant for positive emotion, but it is statistically significant for negative emotion. These results point toward a positive linear relationship between positive emotion and numerical ratings and a negative, non-linear relationship between negative emotion and numerical ratings.

The R package TopicModels (Hornik and Grün, 2011) that implements the topic modeling procedure described in the literature (Blei and Lafferty, 2009) is used to uncover the themes embedded in the customer review text. In Sample 2, five major themes are identified (Table 19.9).

The interpretation based on Table 19.9 that lists the most influential terms within each of the five major topics is as follows:

- *Topic 1:* The more influential terms in this topic include "walk," "metro," and "station," which are associated with the location characteristics related to the hotel.
- *Topic 2:* The more influential terms in this topic include "service," "view," and "place," as well as descriptors like "best" and "great," which are associated with the perceived value of the hotel stay.

Table 19.6   *Study 2: negative customer emotion content as a function of numerical rating of the hotel*

	Coefficients	Std Error
Constant	0.084***	0.004
Numerical rating	Rating = 1 is the reference group	
2	−0.009***	0.004
3	−0.028***	0.003
4	−0.047***	0.003
5	−0.058***	0.003
Hotel fixed effects	Included	
Obs	5830	
R^2	0.1807	
Adj R^2	0.1721	
F Statistic	21.20*** (df = 60; 5,769)	

Notes:
The dependent variable in the regression is negative customer emotion (NegativitySentiment).
***$p < 0.01$.

Table 19.7   *Positive emotional content as a function of numerical rating of the hotel for different market segments (H3a)*

	Business Segment	Leisure Segment
	Coefficient (Std Error)	Coefficient (Std Error)
Constant	0.158*** (0.013)	0.119*** (0.012)
Numerical rating	Rating = 1 is the reference group	
2	0.000 (0.010)	0.018* (0.010)
3	0.026*** (0.009)	0.048*** (0.009)
4	0.068*** (0.009)	0.077*** (0.009)
5	0.083*** (0.009)	0.102*** (0.009)
Hotel fixed effects	Included	Included
Obs	2608	3222
R^2	0.1763	0.1486
Adj R^2	0.1572	0.1325
F Statistic	9.24*** (df = 59; 2,548)	9.20*** (df = 60; 3,161)

Notes:
*$p < 0.10$
***$p < 0.01$.

- *Topic 3:* The more influential terms in this topic include those such as "time," "check," "day," and "arrive," which mostly revolve around the actions related to the transactional touch points of a guest's stay.
- *Topic 4:* The more influential terms in this topic include "staff," "room," "nice," "clean," and "help," which are often associated with the service experience of the guest.
- *Topic 5:* The more influential terms in this topic include "breakfast," "bed," "bathroom," and "lobby." Taken together, terms in this topic seem to be associated with the amenities provided by the hotel.

Table 19.8   *Negative emotional content as a function of numerical rating of the hotel for different market segments (H3b)*

	Business Segment	Leisure Segment
	Coefficient (Std Error)	Coefficient (Std Error)
Constant	0.082*** (0.010)	0.086*** (0.006)
Numerical rating	Rating = 1 is the reference group	
2	0.001 (0.005)	−0.021*** (0.005)
3	−0.019*** (0.005)	−0.037*** (0.004)
4	−0.039*** (0.005)	−0.055*** (0.004)
5	−0.051*** (0.005)	−0.065*** (0.004)
Hotel fixed effects	Included	Included
Obs	2608	3222
R^2	0.1834	0.1950
Adj R^2	0.1644	0.1797
F Statistic	9.70*** (df = 59; 2,548)	12.76*** (df = 60; 3,161)

Notes:
***$p < 0.01$.

Table 19.9   *The stems of the most influential terms in the five themes identified from topic modeling*

	Location	Value	Transaction	Experience	Amenities
1	walk	servic	time	staff	breakfast
2	metro	view	check	room	bed
3	station	place	one	locat	day
4	minut	hotel	get	nice	bathroom
5	can	one	even	breakfast	small
6	restaur	best	back	clean	floor
7	red	great	book	help	free
8	squar	visit	night	great	use
9	citi	stay	ask	busi	lobbi
10	just	like	arriv	stay	includ

Tables 19.10–19.14 present results for regression analyses when the probabilities of each topic appearing in the review text are used as the dependent variable and the numerical rating as a primary independent variable. The three columns represent the results from the overall sample, as well as the two subsamples, namely, the business and leisure market segments. The models are significant and the coefficients for the different levels of ratings are mostly significantly correlated with the topic probability, yielding evidence that supports H2. It is worth noting that the numerical sign for the coefficients for the model with "Transactions" as dependent variables are negative and decrease as the numerical ratings increase, which implies that Transaction is more frequently mentioned in the text when the overall experience is rated low and that potential pain points exist during transactions. The numerical signs for the coefficients in models with "Location," "Value," and "Experience" as dependent variables are positive and increase consistently across all levels of satisfaction ratings, which suggests that these are more frequently mentioned in the text when the overall experience is rated high and that opportunities for increased guest satisfaction exist in those areas. Hypothesis 4 is also

Table 19.10   Cognitive Topic 1 (Location) as a function of the numerical rating of the hotel

	Overall	Business Segment	Leisure Segment
	Coefficient (Std Error)	Coefficient (Std Error)	Coefficient (Std Error)
Constant	0.166*** (0.007)	0.153*** (0.010)	0.177*** (0.010)
Numerical rating	Rating = 1 is the reference group		
2	0.012** (0.006)	0.021*** (0.008)	0.004*** (0.009)
3	0.034*** (0.005)	0.043*** (0.007)	0.025*** (0.008)
4	0.059*** (0.005)	0.062*** (0.007)	0.054*** (0.007)
5	0.055*** (0.005)	0.059*** (0.007)	0.048*** (0.007)
Hotel fixed effects	Included	Included	Included
Obs	5830	2608	3222
R^2	0.189	0.159	0.209
Adj R^2	0.181	0.140	0.194
F Statistic	22.40***	8.18***	13.93***
	(df = 60; 5,769)	(df = 59, 2,548)	(df = 60; 3,161)

Notes:
H2 is tested by the "overall" column, and H4 is tested by the rest.
**$p < 0.05$
***$p < 0.01$.

supported since the coefficients for the overall numerical ratings for the models in business and leisure market segments display a similar pattern as the overall sample.

DISCUSSION

The exponential growth of user-generated data demands purposeful data analysis to derive intelligence and insights. Informed by research on emotions during consumption and recent developments in text analysis of unstructured customer feedback, this research investigates how the embedded information—sentiments and topics—in the unstructured review text relates to the overall customer experience measured numerically. This section discusses the managerial and research implications of the findings as well as directions for future studies.

Managerial Implications

The global hotel industry serves as the research context for the statistical analysis following the sentiment analysis and topic modeling methods. The direct empirical evidence uncovered using a replication research design proves the important link between sentiment polarity and customer satisfaction rating. Applying text analytics to online reviews therefore has the potential to become a key operational tool, which could potentially yield insights to help hotels improve their internal operations as well as their relationship with guests.

Figure 19.2 illustrates the predicted positivity and negativity sentiment values across the five numerical rating levels in both samples. The positive sentiment consistently increases as the numerical rating increases, while a decreasing trend is observed for the negative sentiment values. In addition, the changes are not smooth across rating levels. The number of positive words increase significantly when the rating goes beyond two. Similarly, negative words drop significantly for ratings above two. For the luxury market segment, an increase from three to

Table 19.11   Cognitive Topic 2 (Value) as a function of the numerical rating of the hotel

	Overall	Business Segment	Leisure Segment
	Coefficient (Std Error)	Coefficient (Std Error)	Coefficient (Std Error)
Constant	0.152*** (0.006)	0.166*** (0.009)	0.137*** (0.009)
Numerical rating	Rating = 1 is the reference group		
2	0.006 (0.005)	−0.001 (0.007)	0.013* (0.007)
3	0.009** (0.004)	0.004(0.006)	0.015** (0.006)
4	0.017*** (0.004)	0.008 (0.006)	0.026*** (0.006)
5	0.038*** (0.004)	0.031*** (0.006)	0.047*** (0.006)
Hotel fixed effects	Included	Included	Included
Obs	5830	2608	3222
R^2	0.376	0.356	0.399
Adj R^2	0.370	0.340	0.399
F Statistic	57.99***	23.83***	35.02***
	(df = 60; 5,769)	(df = 59, 2,548)	(df = 60; 3,161)

Notes:
H2 is tested by the "overall" column, and H4 is tested by the rest.
*p < 0.10
**p < 0.05
***p < 0.01.

Table 19.12   Cognitive Topic 3 (Transaction) as a function of the numerical rating of the hotel

	Overall	Business Segment	Leisure Segment
	Coefficient (Std Error)	Coefficient (Std Error)	Coefficient (Std Error)
Constant	0.317*** (0.008)	0.306*** (0.011)	0.327*** (0.010)
Numerical rating	Rating = 1 is the reference group		
2	−0.047*** (0.006)	−0.048*** (0.009)	−0.045*** (0.009)
3	−0.100*** (0.005)	−0.105*** (0.008)	−0.092*** (0.008)
4	−0.137*** (0.005)	−0.139*** (0.008)	−0.135*** (0.007)
5	−0.1445*** (0.005)	−0.144*** (0.008)	−0.143*** (0.007)
Hotel fixed effects	Included	Included	Included
Obs	5830	2608	3222
R^2	0.249	0.259	0.259
Adj R^2	0.241	0.242	0.245
F Statistic	31.80***	15.11***	18.44***
	(df = 60; 5,769)	(df = 59, 2,548)	(df = 60; 3,161)

Notes:
H2 is tested by the "overall" column, and H4 is tested by the rest.
***p < 0.01.

four also sees a larger increase in positive words, while the change in appearance of positive words for reviews rated at four and five is less dramatic. As a result, the contrast between the positive and negative words is largest when the rating is in the four to five range. In other words, readers of the reviews with higher ratings are exposed to much more positivity than negativity as a result of the changes in the emotional states of the reviewers. This finding not only aligns with the managerial practices emphasizing net promoter score (NPS; Reichheld, 2003), but also provides an empirical explanation of the power of NPS.

Table 19.13   *Cognitive Topic 4 (Experience) as a function of the numerical rating of the hotel*

	Overall	Business Segment	Leisure Segment
	Coefficient (Std Error)	Coefficient (Std Error)	Coefficient (Std Error)
Constant	0.167*** (0.006)	0.160*** (0.009)	0.172*** (0.009)
Numerical rating	Rating = 1 is the reference group		
2	0.013** (0.005)	0.014** (0.007)	0.008 (0.007)
3	0.035*** (0.005)	0.045*** (0.006)	0.024*** (0.006)
4	0.054*** (0.004)	0.067*** (0.006)	0.043*** (0.006)
5	0.058*** (0.004)	0.070*** (0.006)	0.048*** (0.006)
Hotel fixed effects	Included	Included	Included
Obs	5830	2608	3222
R^2	0.135	0.184	0.119
Adj R^2	0.126	0.165	0.102
F Statistic	15.02***	9.70***	7.13***
	(df = 60; 5,769)	(df = 59, 2,548)	(df = 60; 3,161)

Notes:
H2 is tested by the "overall" column, and H4 is tested by the rest.
**$p < 0.05$
***$p < 0.01$.

Table 19.14   *Cognitive Topic 5 (Amenities) as a function of the numerical rating of the hotel*

	Overall	Business Segment	Leisure Segment
	Coefficient (Std Error)	Coefficient (Std Error)	Coefficient (Std Error)
Constant	0.200*** (0.007)	0.153*** (0.010)	0.186*** (0.010)
Numerical rating	Rating = 1 is the reference group		
2	0.017** (0.006)	0.012 (0.008)	0.019** (0.008)
3	0.021*** (0.005)	0.014* (0.007)	0.027*** (0.007)
4	0.007 (0.005)	0.001 (0.007)	0.012* (0.007)
5	−0.007 (0.005)	−0.015** (0.007)	0.000 (0.007)
Hotel fixed effects	Included	Included	Included
Obs	5830	2608	3222
R^2	0.08	0.09	0.09
Adj R^2	0.07	0.07	0.07
F Statistic	8.81***	4.40***	5.28***
	(df = 60; 5,769)	(df = 59, 2,548)	(df = 60; 3,161)

Notes:
H2 is tested by the "overall" column, and H4 is tested by the rest.
*$p < 0.10$
**$p < 0.05$
***$p < 0.01$.

Evidence also suggests that this relationship varies across market segments. Figure 19.3 illustrates the pattern of change for two market segments, business vs. leisure, in Sample 2. The overall trend of reviews holds, with higher ratings showing increasing positive emotions and decreasing negative emotions. Furthermore, reviewers in the leisure segment show a smoother pattern of change in their emotional states across the numerical rating levels, while the business reviewers display a pattern that resembles the observations of Sample 1 in Figure 19.2.

This finding suggests that a differential approach to managing the emotional states of guests from different market segments is warranted.

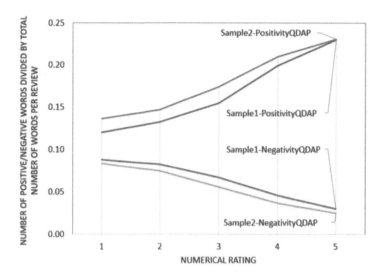

Figure 19.2   Predicted sentiment values show expected patterns across numerical ratings

Furthermore, there is a differential emphasis on various cognitive themes in the unsolicited customer feedback across levels of customer satisfaction ratings. Figure 19.4 illustrates the predicted probabilities of the five topics mentioned in the reviews. There are three distinct patterns in the graph. The probability of the topic Amenities being mentioned in the text remains steady throughout the five levels of ratings. The probability of the topic Transaction is the highest for reviews with the lowest rating, but continuously decreases as review ratings increase. Finally, the topics Experience, Location, and Value all appear slightly more frequently in reviews with higher ratings. These observations offer insights on how to manage the customer journey of a hotel stay that involves multiple services on multiple criteria. Given the variety of customer expectations and services in an overall hotel offering (e.g., check-in, rooms, restaurants, check-out), identifying influential touchpoints is at the forefront in arriving at the most favorable experience for customers, as well as achieving their highest satisfaction level. Figure 19.4 suggests that service failures in transactional activities and issues with amenities are among the most salient cognitive themes in the review text. Figure 19.4 also shows that all five topics are more evenly represented in reviews rated the highest, with Experience slightly edging out the other four topics. The key takeaway is that all the components in a service system—staff as well as facilities—must work well together to deliver a great service experience.

The findings from this study also hold promise for enhancing value for customers in multiple target markets while simultaneously delivering the business value that the owners expect. For example, customer cognition in review text highlights the service journey by telling a story of the customers' experience from the moment they begin considering staying in a hotel through what memories may last after their departure.

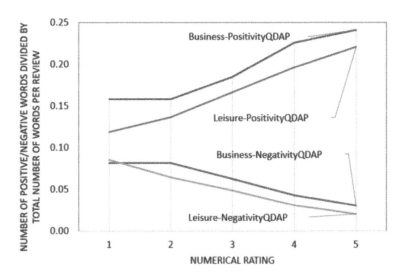

Figure 19.3   *Sample 2: predicted sentiment values for business and leisure market segments across numerical ratings*

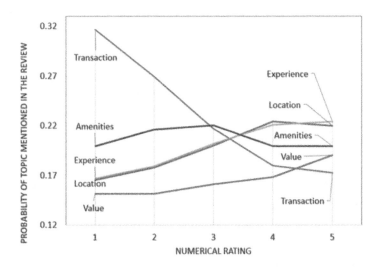

Figure 19.4   *Predicted probability of topics appearing in the reviews across numerical ratings in Study 2*

Guest relationship management is complex in the hotel industry—there are different types of offerings, from budget hotels to luxury ones, and consequently customer expectations may vary considerably across guest profiles. To meet the wide range of customer expectations, hotels consistently need to pursue a clear understanding of desirable offerings by maintaining an array of features that centralize alerts, reporting, and configuration management in support of both problem resolution and the promotion of a uniform customer experience. Both relationships identified in our study—that is, the relationship between customer emotional state and numerical rating and the relationship between customer cognition and numerical rating—vary across market segments. This suggests that a differential approach in managing the influencers of customer perceptions across market segments could better meet customer needs and wants. For example, reputation management has become a highly visible area of guest relationship management. In addition to providing immediate responses to complaints appearing in the online reviews, the reputation management team should be equipped with the ability to identify top pain or pleasure points for various types of travelers. This information could then inform a more robust and tailored service experience designed for different types of travelers.

Research Contributions

This study contributes to the literature on emotions related to consumption and enriches the methods of service experience evaluation by incorporating the underlying emotional and cognitive elements of unstructured customer feedback. First, customers' emotional states can be assessed by systematic analysis of unstructured text-based feedback through online reviews. Evidence shows that customer sentiment correlates with the numerical rating: the higher the customer satisfaction rating, the higher the positive sentiment; the lower the customer satisfaction rating, the lower the negative sentiment. Consistent results are obtained from replicating the tests on two datasets—a global sample of hotels targeting the luxury market segment and a metropolitan sample of hotels across multiple market segments. This confirmation underscores the congruence between the structured and unstructured data, lending confidence to exploring and using the more granular data embedded in the unstructured text data.

Through topic modeling, the unstructured data reveal the major topics of customers' cognition as they evaluate service experiences. In Study 2, when a customer rates overall satisfaction high, the review is written more about location and experience. When a customer is less satisfied, more discussion occurs about transactions and amenities. These patterns help enrich the understanding of the range of influencers of customer perceptions during a service encounter and ultimately the overall service experience evaluation. Findings from this research provide direct empirical evidence to distinguish the order-qualifiers and order-winners in the service industries, thus contributing to the order-winners framework (da Silveira, 2005; Hill, 1985).

Last but not least, this study joins other replication studies in the area of operations management (Frohlich and Dixon, 2003; Pagell and Krause, 2004) and shows the importance of using replication to increase the validity and generalizability of the findings.

Directions for Future Research

It is important to acknowledge that not all factors that contribute to the nuances of online reviews and customer satisfaction are accounted for even with this two-study design. Several exciting future research directions are worth exploring. Customers typically leave online reviews after their departure. Negativity bias—hotel guests tend to write more about problems when they leave a lower rating—is a known issue with recollections of experiences (Ito et al., 1998; Rozin and Royzman, 2001). Even if most of their experience is satisfactory, one negative encounter could affect the overall rating score as well as the review text. Preventing negative encounters from happening in the first place is paramount, as discussed in the managerial implications section. However, since service failures are not entirely avoidable, better understanding of the time period from the occurrence of the negative episode to posting of related negative comments and lower ratings, especially the virtual touchpoints post-departure, is needed.

It is widely accepted that it is more expensive to acquire new customers than to retain existing ones. Loyal customers not only promise future revenues, but also have more experience to draw on when they review the services they receive at the hotels. How do different levels of product knowledge affect the characteristics of the review text? It remains an empirical question whether these loyal customers are enthusiastic supporters or de facto mystery shoppers.

To retain a good relationship with customers, it is necessary to get ahead of expectations. Researching online reviews has now become an integral part of consumers' pre-purchase routine, which demands more knowledge on how online review texts contribute to shaping customer expectations. Are the memorable moments captured in the reviews a part of customer expectation or beyond expectation? Customer expectation associated with a specific hotel site is likely to evolve over time. Clarity around this change process is fundamental to designing and delivering customer experience that exceeds customer expectation.

In conclusion, the ever-expanding user-generated data offer an unprecedented opportunity for service providers to listen to their customers. Researchers can help advance knowledge on service experience management throughout the journey by generating insights related to customer emotion and cognition embedded in unstructured data.

REFERENCES

Anderson, C., 2012. The impact of social media on lodging performance. Cornell Hospitality Report 12, 6–11.

Babin, B.J., Lee, Y.-K., Kim, E.-J., Griffin, M., 2005. Modeling consumer satisfaction and word-of-mouth: restaurant patronage in Korea. Journal of Services Marketing 19, 133–139.

Bagozzi, R.P., Gopinath, M., Nyer, P.U., 1999. The role of emotions in marketing. Journal of the Academy of Marketing Science 27, 184–206.

Baka, V., 2016. The becoming of user-generated reviews: Looking at the past to understand the future of managing reputation in the travel sector. Tourism Management 53, 148–162.

Baker, J., Levy, M., Grewal, D., 1992. An experimental approach to making retail store environmental decisions. Journal of Retailing 68, 445.

Berry, L.L., Parasuraman, A., 1997. Listening to the customer–The concept of a service-quality information system. MIT Sloan Management Review 38, 65–76.

Bigné, J.E., Andreu, L., Gnoth, J., 2005. The theme park experience: An analysis of pleasure, arousal and satisfaction. Tourism Management 26, 833–844.

Blei, D.M., Lafferty, J.D., 2009. Topic models. Text Mining: Classification, Clustering, and Applications 10, 34.

Chen, H., Chiang, R.H., Storey, V.C., 2012. Business intelligence and analytics: From big data to big impact. MIS Quarterly 36, 1165–1188.

Chevalier, J.A., Mayzlin, D., 2006. The effect of word of mouth on sales: Online book reviews. Journal of Marketing Research 43, 345–354.

da Silveira, G.J.C., 2005. Market priorities, manufacturing configuration, and business performance: An empirical analysis of the order-winners framework. Journal of Operations Management 23, 662–675.

Dens, N., de Pelsmacker, P., Purnawirawan, N., 2015. "We(b) care": How review set balance moderates the appropriate response strategy to negative online reviews. Journal of Service Management 26, 486–515.

Derbaix, C., Vanhamme, J., 2003. Inducing word-of-mouth by eliciting surprise–A pilot investigation. Journal of Economic Psychology 24, 99–116.

Dixon, M.J., Victorino, L., Kwortnik, R.J., Verma, R., 2017. Surprise, anticipation, and sequence effects in the design of experiential services. Production and Operations Management 26, 945–960.

DOMO, 2017. Data never sleeps 5.0. https://www.domo.com/learn/infographic/data-never-sleeps-5

Donovan, R.J., Rossiter, J.R., 1982. Store atmosphere: An environmental psychology approach. Journal of Retailing 58, 34–57.

Donovan, R.J., Rossiter, J.R., Marcoolyn, G., Nesdale, A., 1994. Store atmosphere and purchasing behavior. Journal of Retailing 70, 283–294.

Duan, W., Gu, B., Whinston, A.B., 2008. Do online reviews matter? An empirical investigation of panel data. Decision Support Systems 45, 1007–1016.

Edell, J.A., Burke, M.C., 1987. The power of feelings in understanding advertising effects. Journal of Consumer Research 14, 421–433.

Eppler, M.J., Mengis, J., 2004. The concept of information overload: A review of literature from organization science, accounting, marketing, MIS, and related disciplines. The Information Society 20, 325–344. https://doi.org/10.1080/01972240490507974

Erevelles, S., 1998. The role of affect in marketing. Journal of Business Research 42, 199–215.

Erickson, G.S., Eckrich, D.W., 2001. Consumer affairs responses to unsolicited customer compliments. Journal of Marketing Management 17, 321–340.

Feuerriegel, S., Proellochs, N., 2017. Sentiment analysis vignette. https://cran.microsoft.com/snapshot/2017-07-18/web/packages/SentimentAnalysis/vignettes/SentimentAnalysis.html.

Frohlich, M., Dixon, J., 2003. Journal of Operations Management special issue: OM replication research. Journal of Operations Management 21, 373–374.

Geetha, M., Singha, P., Sinha, S., 2017. Relationship between customer sentiment and online customer ratings for hotels–An empirical analysis. Tourism Management 61, 43–54.

Griffin, A., Hauser, J.R., 1993. The voice of the customer. Marketing Science 12, 1–27.

Guo, J., Chen, X., 2018. Bias-sentiment-topic model for microblog sentiment analysis. Concurrency and computation: Practice and experience. https://doi.org/10.1002/cpe.4417

Hamby, A., Daniloski, K., Brinberg, D., 2015. How consumer reviews persuade through narratives. Journal of Business Research 68, 1242–1250.

Han, H.J., Mankad, S., Gavirneni, N., Verma, R., 2016. What guests really think of your hotel: Text analytics of online customer reviews. Cornell Hospitality Report 16, 3–17.

He, J., Hu, Z., Berg-Kirkpatrick, T., Huang, Y., Xing, E.P., 2017. Efficient correlated topic modeling with topic embedding. In Proceedings of the 23rd ACM SIGKDD International Conference on Knowledge Discovery and Data Mining, ACM, pp. 225–233.

Hicks, J.M., Page Jr, T.J., Behe, B.K., Dennis, J.H., Fernandez, R.T., 2005. Delighted consumers buy again. Journal of Consumer Satisfaction, Dissatisfaction and Complaining Behavior 18, 94.

Hill, T., 1985. Manufacturing strategy: The strategic management of the manufacturing. Macmillan Press.

Hornik, K., Grün, B., 2011. Topicmodels: An R package for fitting topic models. Journal of Statistical Software 40, 1–30.

Hu, M., Liu, B., 2004. Mining and summarizing customer reviews. In Proceedings of the tenth ACM SIGKDD International Conference on Knowledge Discovery and Data Mining, ACM, pp. 168–177.

Ito, T.A., Larsen, J.T., Smith, N.K., Cacioppo, J.T., 1998. Negative information weighs more heavily on the brain: The negativity bias in evaluative categorizations. Journal of Personality and Social Psychology 75, 887.

Izard, C.E., 1972. Patterns of emotions: A new analysis of anxiety and depression. Academic Press.

Izard, C.E., 1977. Human emotions, 1st ed. Plenum Publishing Corporation.

Jain, P. K., Pamula, R., & Srivastava, G., 2021. A systematic literature review on machine learning applications for consumer sentiment analysis using online reviews. *Computer Science Review* 41, 100413.

Jones, Q., Ravid, G., Rafaeli, S., 2004. Information overload and the message dynamics of online interaction spaces: A theoretical model and empirical exploration. Information Systems Research 15, 194–210.

Koetsier, J., 2017. Data deluge: What people do on the Internet, every minute of every day. Inc. https://www.inc.com/john-koetsier/every-minute-on-the-internet-2017-new-numbers-to-b.html

Ladhari, R., 2007. The effect of consumption emotions on satisfaction and word-of-mouth communications. Psychology & Marketing 24, 1085–1108.

Liljander, V., Strandvik, T., 1997. Emotions in service satisfaction. International Journal of Service Industry Management 8, 148–169.

Lim, Y.J., Osman, A., Salahuddin, S.N., Romle, A.R., Abdullah, S., 2016. Factors influencing online shopping behavior: The mediating role of purchase intention. Procedia Economics and Finance 35, 401–410.

Manyika, J., Chui, M., Brown, B., Bughin, J., Dobbs, R., Roxburgh, C., Byers, A.H., 2011. Big data: The next frontier for innovation, competition, and productivity. McKinsey Digital. https://www.mckinsey.com/business-functions/mckinsey-digital/our-insights/big-data-the-next-frontier-for-innovation

Mayer-Schönberger, V., Cukier, K., 2013. Big data: A revolution that will transform how we live, work, and think. Boston, MA: Houghton Mifflin Harcourt.

McAfee, A., Brynjolfsson, E., Davenport, T.H., Patil, D., Barton, D., 2012. Big data: The management revolution. Harvard Business Review 90, 60–68.

Meyer, C., Schwager, A., 2007. Customer experience. Harvard Business Review 85, 116–126.

Nasr, L., Burton, J., Gruber, T., Kitshoff, J., 2014. Exploring the impact of customer feedback on the well-being of service entities: A TSR perspective. Journal of Service Management 25, 531–555.

Neirotti, P., Raguseo, E., Paolucci, E., 2016. Are customers' reviews creating value in the hospitality industry? Exploring the moderating effects of market positioning. International Journal of Information Management 36, 1133–1143.

Nyer, P.U., 1997. A study of the relationships between cognitive appraisals and consumption emotions. Journal of the Academy of Marketing Science 25, 296–304.

Oliver, R.L., 1993. Cognitive, affective, and attribute bases of the satisfaction response. Journal of Consumer Research 20, 418–430.

Otnes, C., Lowrey, T.M., Shrum, L., 1997. Toward an understanding of consumer ambivalence. Journal of Consumer Research 24, 80–93.

Pagell, M., Krause, D.R., 2004. Re-exploring the relationship between flexibility and the external environment. Journal of Operations Management 21, 629–649.

Pang, B., Lee, L., 2008. Opinion mining and sentiment analysis. Foundations and Trends in Information Retrieval 2, 1–135.

Philander, K., Zhong, Y., 2016. Twitter sentiment analysis: Capturing sentiment from integrated resort tweets. International Journal of Hospitality Management 55, 16–24.

Price, L.L., Arnould, E.J., Deibler, S.L., 1995. Consumers' emotional responses to service encounters: The influence of the service provider. International Journal of Service Industry Management 6, 34–63.

Přichystal, J., 2016. Mobile application for customers' reviews opinion mining. Procedia–Social and Behavioral Sciences 220, 373–381.

Reichheld, F.F., 2003. The one number you need to grow. Harvard Business Review 81, 46–55.

Richins, M.L., 1997. Measuring emotions in the consumption experience. Journal of Consumer Research 24, 127–146.

Rozin, P., Royzman, E.B., 2001. Negativity bias, negativity dominance, and contagion. Personality and Social Psychology Review 5, 296–320.

Sampson, S.E., 1996. Ramifications of monitoring service quality through passively solicited customer feedback. Decision Sciences 27, 601–622.

Sarra, A., di Zio, S., Cappucci, M., 2015. A quantitative valuation of tourist experience in Lisbon. Annals of Tourism Research 53, 1–16.

Shannon, C.E., 1948. A mathematical theory of communication. Bell System Technical Journal 27, 623–656.

Sparks, B.A., Browning, V., 2011. The impact of online reviews on hotel booking intentions and perception of trust. Tourism Management 32, 1310–1323.

Sparks, B.A., So, K.K.F., Bradley, G.L., 2016. Responding to negative online reviews: The effects of hotel responses on customer inferences of trust and concern. Tourism Management 53, 74–85.

Stayman, D.M., Aaker, D.A., 1988. Are all the effects of ad-induced feelings mediated by AAd? Journal of Consumer Research 15, 368–373.

Stayman, D.M., Batra, R., 1991. Encoding and retrieval of ad affect in memory. Journal of Marketing Research 28, 232–239.

Streitfeld, D., 2011. In a race to out-rave, 5-star web reviews go for $5. New York Times. https://www.nytimes.com/2011/08/20/technology/finding-fake-reviews-online.html

Tan, K.H., Zhan, Y., Ji, G., Ye, F., Chang, C., 2015. Harvesting big data to enhance supply chain innovation capabilities: An analytic infrastructure based on deduction graph. International Journal of Production Economics 165, 223–233.

Titov, I., McDonald, R., 2008. Modeling online reviews with multi-grain topic models. In Proceedings of the 17th International World Wide Web Conference, ACM, pp. 111–120.

Tse, D.K., Wilton, P.C., 1988. Models of consumer satisfaction formation: An extension. Journal of Marketing Research 25, 204–212.

Vinodhini, G., Chandrasekaran, R., 2012. Sentiment analysis and opinion mining: A survey. International Journal 2, 282–292.

Wang, F., Liu, X., Fang, E.E., 2015. User reviews variance, critic reviews variance, and product sales: An exploration of customer breadth and depth effects. Journal of Retailing 91, 372–389.

Wang, Z., Li, H., Ye, Q., Law, R., 2016. Saliency effects of online reviews embedded in the description on sales: Moderating role of reputation. Decision Support Systems 87, 50–58.

Weathers, D., Swain, S.D., Grover, V., 2015. Can online product reviews be more helpful? Examining characteristics of information content by product type. Decision Support Systems 79, 12–23.

Wei, W., Miao, L., Huang, Z.J., 2013. Customer engagement behaviors and hotel responses. International Journal of Hospitality Management 33, 316–330.

Westbrook, R.A., 1987. Product/consumption-based affective responses and post-purchase processes. Journal of Marketing Research 24, 258–270.

Westbrook, R.A., Oliver, R.L., 1991. The dimensionality of consumption emotion patterns and consumer satisfaction. Journal of Consumer Research 18, 84–91.

Wirtz, J., Bateson, J.E., 1999. Consumer satisfaction with services: Integrating the environment perspective in services marketing into the traditional disconfirmation paradigm. Journal of Business Research 44, 55–66.

Xiao, S., Wei, C.-P., Dong, M., 2016. Crowd intelligence: Analyzing online product reviews for preference measurement. Information & Management 53, 169–182.

Zeelenberg, M., Pieters, R., 2004. Beyond valence in customer dissatisfaction: A review and new findings on behavioral responses to regret and disappointment in failed services. Journal of Business Research 57, 445–455.

PART VI

AI IN SERVICES

20. The service robot revolution

Stefanie Paluch, Jochen Wirtz and Werner H. Kunz

INTRODUCTION[1]

The industrial revolution started in the late 18th century and automated blue-collar jobs in manufacturing, thereby providing massive structural benefits to our societies. It rapidly increased our standard of living by bringing high-quality, low-cost manufactured goods to the masses and relieved people from laborious manual work.

Today, our economies seem to face a turning point similar to the industrial revolution, but this time in the service sector. Technologies rapidly become smarter and more powerful, while at the same time, they get smaller, lighter, and cheaper. These technologies include hardware, such as that related to physical robots, drones, and autonomous vehicles and their components (e.g., processors, sensors, cameras, chips), wearable technologies, and code or software, such as analytics, speech processing, image processing, biometrics, virtual reality, augmented reality, cloud technologies, mobile technologies, geo-tagging, low-code platforms, robotic process automation (RPA), and machine learning (Bornet et al. 2021; Wirtz 2020; Wirtz et al. 2018, 2021a). Together, these technologies will transform virtually all service sectors. Service robots combined with these technologies will lead to rapid innovation that can dramatically improve the customer experience, service quality, and productivity all at the same time (Wirtz and Zeithaml 2018).

We are now at a turning point where humanoid robots (e.g., Pepper and Nao) and voice-based agents (e.g., Siri and Alexa) are entering our daily lives. Due to the rapid advancements of robot technologies combined with artificial intelligence (AI), so-called service robots are on the rise (Wirtz et al. 2018). They are capable of performing tasks autonomously without any, or with only little, human involvement (Joerling et al. 2019), execute tasks by following their service script and with prior knowledge (Huang and Rust 2018), and are said to be an important source of innovation (Rust and Huang 2014). In this article, we mainly focus on the organizational frontline, the point where the service is actually delivered to the customer, using the following definition: "Service robots are system-based autonomous and adaptable interfaces that interact, communicate and deliver service to an organization's customers" (Wirtz et al. 2018, p. 909). Service robots are typically embedded in larger (virtual) networks that provide access to internal and external data. Autonomous robots can recognize and learn from their environments and make their own decisions without human intervention. With the help of cameras and sensors, robots can identify customers through facial or voice recognition and provide services according to the customer's profile, which they can access through the interconnectedness of the systems.

Robot- and AI-delivered service offers unprecedented economies of scale and scope as the bulk of the costs are incurred in their development. Physical robots cost a fraction of adding headcount, and virtual service robots (e.g., chatbots and virtual agents) can be scaled at close to zero incremental costs. Such dramatic salability does not only apply to virtual service robots, such as chatbots, but to "visible" ones, such as holograms. For example, an airport could install a hologram-based humanoid service robot every 50 m to assist passengers and deal with common questions (e.g., provide arrival and departure information or directions to check-in counters for a particular airline or an airport hotel) in all common languages. These holograms only require low-cost hardware (i.e., a camera, microphone, speaker, and projector) and do not need to take up floor space (i.e., travelers could push their baggage carts through a hologram when needed; Wirtz et al. 2021a).

Already, many firms show keen interest in experimenting with service robots. For example, hotels introduce humanoid robots in their lobbies where they welcome and entertain guests and provide information. The Mandarin Oriental Hotel in Las Vegas has introduced Pepper as their newest humanoid staff member. Pepper resides in the lobby, where she welcomes guests and helps them to find directions. Her job is to provide information to hotel guests in entertaining and innovative ways (Walsh 2018). In Japan, the Henn na Hotel is the first robot-staffed hotel, where guests can choose to check in with an android woman, a robot, or a dinosaur robot. The luggage will be delivered to the room by a porter robot, and the concierge robot, Tully, will switch lights on and off for the guest (Kikuchi 2018).

At airports, robots scan boarding passes and help passengers to find the right departure gate. Self-moving check-in kiosk robots detect busy areas and autonomously help passengers reduce waiting time (Paluch et al. 2020). At the airport, robots are used for passenger guidance, maintenance, and security. At Amsterdam Airport Schiphol, the robot Spencer scans boarding passes of KLM passengers and helps them to find the right departure gate. Kate, a self-moving check-in kiosk robot at Kansai Airport in Japan, detects busy areas, autonomously goes there and helps passengers reduce waiting times. At Incheon Airport in South Korea, cleaning robots vacuum the airport, and in Shenzhen's Bao'an International Airport, Anbot, a security robot, patrols the departure hall for suspicious behavior (Read 2017).

Notably, the outbreak of COVID-19 has increased the demand for medical service robots that take over the care of contagious patients. The social robot Ari is interacting with COVID-19 patients to overcome patient isolation. Other robots make sure that patients get their medicine, and they can monitor vital signs remotely. Additionally, autonomous robots disinfect hospitals and make sure that patients and visitors follow the regulations and keep a safe distance from others (Schoepfer and Etemad-Sajadi 2020).

Further, societal changes, such as an increasing elderly population and declining workforce, infuse robots in somewhat unexpected contexts, such as nursing care, which typically requires a more personal touch and individual attention (Čaić et al. 2018). In Tokyo's Shin-tomi nursing home, robots help caretakers lift people, they perform exercises with groups of elderly residents, and start enjoyable conversations (Foster 2018).

The above examples demonstrate that service industries are changing, and more businesses are considering reorganizing their organizational frontline service. Studies suggest that by 2025, 85 percent of customer interactions will occur without a human agent (Schneider 2017). The market size for service robots is projected to reach US$41.5 billion by 2027 (Fortune Business Insights 2020).

Such robots in hotels, airports, and restaurants, as well as chatbots and delivery bots, are only the beginning of the service revolution. This means that, similar to the shift that started during the industrial revolution—from craftspeople to mass production—an accelerated shift in the service sector toward robot- and AI-delivered services can be expected. The exciting prospect is that many services, including health care and education, are likely to become available at much lower prices and with better quality, and will lead to a dramatic increase in our standard of living.

Table 20.1   Contrasting service robots with traditional self-service technologies

Service Aspect	Self-Service Technologies (SSTs)	Service Robots
Customer Service Scripts and Roles	Customers have to learn the service script and role and follow it closely	Customers do not need to learn a particular role and script beyond what they would do when interacting with a frontline employee
	Deviations from the script tend to lead to service failure and aborting the unsuccessful transaction	Flexible customer journeys, interactions, and scripts are supported
	Need to be self-explanatory and intuitive, as customers have to control and navigate the interaction	Can guide the customer through the service process very much like a service employee would
Customer Error Tolerance	Generally do not function when customers make errors or use the SST incorrectly	Are customer error-tolerant
	Generally are not effective in recovering customer errors; customers typically have to start the transaction again, or a service employee needs to take over	Can recover customer errors and guide the customer to conclude a successful service transaction
Service Recovery Capability	The service process tends to break down when there is a service failure; recovery is unlikely within the technology	Is "trained" to recover common service failures; can recover the service by offering alternative solutions very much like a service employee would

Source: Wirtz et al. (2018, p. 909).

SELF-SERVICE TECHNOLOGIES VERSUS SERVICE ROBOTS

The capabilities of service robots differentiate them from traditional self-service technologies (SSTs) we are familiar with in the context of ticketing machines, ATMs, and websites. As shown in Table 20.1, service robots can deal with unstructured interactions and guide customers through their service journey. For example, a ticketing robot will not let customers get stuck, as it can ask clarifying questions (e.g., "Is your return trip today?"; "Can you travel off-peak?"), and can even recover customer errors (e.g., a wrong button pressed, incorrect information entered, or a rejected credit card). For most standard services, customers will interact with service robots much like they do with service employees (e.g., "I need a same-day return ticket"; "Can I use Apple Pay?").

HUMAN SERVICE EMPLOYEES VS. SERVICE ROBOTS

Emotional Touch vs. Customized Tech

It is common in service industries to say the frontline employee is the face of the company. The service is determined by the frontline personnel's skills, training, emotions, personality, and attitude. Depending on the company strategy, the human touch can be the key differentiating factor for service organizations. Personal service entails real genuine emotions shared from one human being to another. In contrast, robots are not able to feel and express real emotions. This is important as the service management literature distinguishes between deep acting (employees displaying true emotions) and surface acting (employees displaying superficial or fake emotional responses; e.g., Wirtz and Jerger 2017). Robots' emotional displays will for the foreseeable future be "fake" and not authentic or genuinely felt. Consumers are likely to know this, perceive it, and respond accordingly. Thus, customers are unlikely to respond to robot-displayed emotions as they would to heartfelt and authentic emotions from human frontline employees (Wirtz et al. 2018). On the other hand, robots may be better at mimicking surface-acted emotions (akin to automated social presence) than human employees because they are not prone to emotional burnout (van Doorn et al. 2017).

Individual Person vs. System-Based Approach

Another distinction is that human employees are individuals with their own personalities, skills, perceptions, biases, and services, showing heterogeneity over time and across individuals. Training of frontline personnel is needed. They need to learn the routines, memorize all relevant information, and be able to use various IT systems. This process takes time and is not seamless. Robots, on the other hand, are part of a larger frontline service system. They can be connected to a knowledge database and use all available information from customer relationship system (CRM) systems and even external sources, such as those on the Internet and social media, to provide their service.

High Incremental Cost vs. Low Incremental Cost

Finally, human employees are not scalable. Every person adds significant costs to the company. In contrast, robots entail enormous economies of scale and scope, as much of the costs are incurred during research and development. Physical robots have incremental costs, even though these are a fraction of what it costs to add headcount. In comparison, virtual robots are likely to be deployed at negligible incremental costs (Wirtz et al. 2018). Other significant differences are summarized in Table 20.2.

THE SERVICE ROBOT DEPLOYMENT MODEL

Given these distinctive aspects of human employees and service robots, companies need to decide which jobs human employees will take care of and which will be handled by robots in the future.

Jobs can be organized based on their need for cognitive and analytical work or emotional or social work. Depending on the combination of these two dimensions, Wirtz et al. (2018) proposed the service robot deployment model (see Table 20.2), where they predict which tasks will be done by humans, by robots, or in human–robot collaboration in the future (Figure 20.1).

Given the system-based approach and the decreasing costs of computer processing (i.e., Moore's law), robots have a clear advantage against human employees regarding cognitive and analytical work. On the other hand, human employees can provide the emotional touch of a service that is hard for robots to simulate. Therefore, when it comes to jobs with high cognitive/analytical tasks and low emotional/social work, robots will mainly provide these services; when considering jobs with low cognitive/analytical tasks and high emotional/social work, human employees are essential.

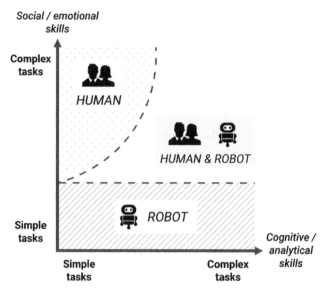

Source: Adapted from Wirtz et al. (2018, pp. 907–931).

Figure 20.1   The service robot deployment model

Table 20.2   Contrasting frontline employees with service robots

Dimension	Service Employees	Service Robots
Employee/ Robot	Act as individuals, individual learning	Act as part of systems, are connected, system learning
Training and	Need training	Upgradable, system-wide
Learning	Limited memory and access	Virtually endless memory and access
Customer	Heterogeneous output	Homogenous output
Experience	Customization and personalization depend on employee skill and effort	Customization and personalization can be delivered on scale at consistent quality and performance
	Unintended biases	Potentially no biases
	Have genuine emotions	Can mimic emotions
	Can engage in deep acting	Can engage in surface acting
	Can engage in outside-the-box thinking and creative problem solving	Limited outside-the-box thinking, have rule-bound limits
Firm Strategy	Service employees can be a source of competitive advantage	Service robots are unlikely to be a source of competitive advantage as service robot solutions are likely to be supplied by third-party providers (very much like ATMs are sold to banks)
	High incremental cost	Low incremental cost
	Low economies of scale and scope	High economies of scale and scope
	Differentiation of services can be based on better hiring, selection, training, motivation, and organization of service employees	Economies of scale and scope and related network and service platform effects will become important sources of competitive advantage

Source: Wirtz et al. (2018, p. 909).

Some jobs in services might only need low cognitive/analytical skills and little emotional/ social work. Wirtz et al. (2018) assume that robots will be able to mimic simple emotional/ social tasks in the future. So, they are a more cost-efficient solution than human employees. On the other hand, jobs that require high cognitive/analytical and emotional/social work are likely to be delivered by humans supported by robots—robots will outperform humans on cognitive tasks, while humans will provide the emotional tasks of the job (Larivière et al. 2017).

Service Robot Infusion for Different Service Tasks

A persistent problem is that customers perceive service robots as having less competence than human service employees (Paluch et al. 2020). If companies are now considering the increased use of service robots, they must also make sure that service quality does not suffer. Customers may misunderstand the deployment of service robots and see it as a cost-saving measure, not as improving service delivery by customers interacting with the firm in new and better ways. We are currently still in the phase in which robots must prove themselves from the customer's perspective. In this phase, companies and managers can do a lot right and a lot wrong.

First, we need to understand the different service types. Therefore, we build on Wirtz et al. (2018) and Paluch et al. (2020), in which service tasks are classified based on the level of cognitive/analytical skills and social/emotional skills. The underlying assumption is that robots benefit from AI and can, therefore, better handle complex decision-making situations in which cognitive/analytical skills are highly demanded. Humans, however, can show real emotions since they can intuitively react to certain situations and are therefore better at displaying social/ emotional skills, as is discussed next.

Service Robots Take Over Routine and Repetitive Tasks

Initial deployments of service robots focused on simple and repetitive tasks that tended to be low in their cognitive and emotional complexity. For example, physical robots in hotels deliver room service and bring baggage to guest rooms. Text and voice-based conversational agents increasingly handle routine customer interactions. Even when interacting with a human service employee, that employee may well be supported by an AI that, for example, prescreens, preprocesses, and then escalates calls to a human agent because of the level of complexity of the issue at hand. The outcome is that customer contact staff do not have to deal with high volumes of trivial customer requests but instead can spend their time on higher-value and higher-level tasks. For example, a chatbot launched in 2020 for the National University of Singapore (NUS MBA Programme) handled 20 000 unique conversations in its first month after launch, and today answers all the routine questions the admissions team had to deal with previously (e.g., Do I need a GMAT? When are the fees payable? When is the application deadline?). The admissions team can now focus on top-quality candidates and the trickier and more complex discussions.

When cognitive/analytical and social/emotional skills are low, service robots can perfectly take over tasks, such as vacuuming the floor, mowing the lawn, patrolling airports, or delivering luggage to guest rooms. In these service contexts, customers' expectations regarding emotions or any form of active, reciprocal interaction are low. The most important thing is that the job is done efficiently and effectively, so the robot's advantages outweigh human benefits, especially in terms of availability and delivering continuous service quality. This category of service jobs might not be among the most popular, and in times of labor shortages, we recommend that these tasks be assigned to robots first. In some instances, it might be useful to have human supervisors who can support service robots to ensure the reliability of the service.

Service Robots Outperform Humans with High Cognitive Skills

In addition to routine tasks, services that require high cognitive and analytical skills (e.g., financial services) will be delivered effectively by service robots. For example, service robots can analyze large volumes of data, integrate internal and external information, recognize patterns, and relate these to customer profiles. Within minutes, these robots can propose best-fitting solutions and make recommendations.

When cognitive/analytical skills are high and social/emotional skills remain low, we expect the demand for service robots will be increasing. In professional service industries, such as finance, insurance, accounting, or in legal contexts, significant amounts of information need to be analyzed quickly, and customers require reliable results and objective recommendations without much sentimentalism. Robots can do these analytical jobs better than humans. A great advantage from the customer's perspective is the equal treatment by robots because robots' decision-making is based solely on available information, so customer discrimination is almost impossible. Companies should prioritize security and privacy concerns and communicate data usage transparency, especially when robots work with sensitive customer information (Lobschat et al. 2021; Wirtz et al. 2021a). It is also recommended to effectively communicate to customers regarding changes in the firm's service delivery through robots and AI and the improvements these bring to customers (e.g., 24/7 availability and virtually immediate access to help) because well-informed customers can appreciate the changes.

Emotional Skills are a Human Asset that is Difficult to Copy

It is difficult for robots to deal with emotions that go beyond a pleasant display of surface demeanor. Especially complex and emotionally demanding tasks are still better handled by human service employees as they can bring genuine emotions, such as excitement and joy or empathy and compassion, to the service encounter. For example, in complaint and service recovery situations, humans can respond better to the individual context and show understanding.

For tasks that require high social/emotional skills and less cognitive/analytical expertise, human service employees have superior skills. That is, they can perform tasks where the personal experience with true emotions expressed by the frontline is central for customers. These services are characterized by high interaction between the service employee and customer, and service quality is often measured based on the service counterpart's behavior.

Interestingly though, service robots are already able to create a social presence with customers, so the customer has the feeling that someone is taking care of them, even if it is a robot (van Doorn et al. 2017). Companies can also offer their services as a two-tier model. Service robots will take over the initial contact, and for issues that require greater communication skills or psychological comfort, the service employee can take care of these parts of service delivery. This approach seems suitable for complaint handling or service recovery situations that require experiential and contextual interactions and individualized treatment. In general, it is advisable not to leave the customer entirely alone with robots but to keep people available as a backup for troubleshooting or intervention in emergency situations. It seems likely that a small team of humans in a central location can support a fleet of robots in the field or in a branch network and step in via video communications when needed.

Finally, companies that have introduced service robots to provide personal services (e.g., hairdressers, yoga teachers, or shopping assistants) should respect customers' interaction preferences. Based on our experience, we found two generic types of customers. Type 1 customers belong to the group that clearly prefers human interaction and is reluctant to interact with service robots. Type 2 customers like the idea of avoiding personal interactions in service settings and are happy to give orders or push a touchscreen to receive their service. To maintain positive service-quality perceptions, managers should try to satisfy both customer segments by offering human and artificial alternatives and choosing according to their preferences. Over the long run, however, human-delivered service is likely to come at a price premium over robot-provided service.

Service Robot and Human Employees Form Hybrid Teams in the Future

Human–robot teams will increasingly deliver tasks that require high cognitive and high emotional skills. For example, in a healthcare context, service robots will do the analytical work (e.g., analyze symptoms and compare them with databases to identify possible diagnoses), and humans will make the final recommendations and decisions and take over the social and emotional tasks (e.g., advising and persuading patients). For example, a traveler returned from Singapore to Munich with dengue fever; the symptoms only appeared a week after returning. General practitioners in Germany may never see a dengue fever patient in their professional life and may not be effective in diagnosing it. On the other hand, a service robot compares patient data and symptoms and provides a "hit list" of possible diseases with a fit index. The general practitioner can then work down the list and discuss with the patient (e.g., "Have you been in the tropics the last two weeks?"), and then identify the most likely diagnosis and test for it (e.g., conduct a blood test for dengue, in this case).

When the cognitive/analytical and social/emotional skills required are high, for example, in counseling, nursing, education, or medical services, these services are likely to be delivered by hybrid teams (human service employees and service robots) to increase the outcome quality and, in general, to provide more accurate services. These newly formed teams provide innovative (business) opportunities and are proof that service robots are not only designed to replace or substitute human employees but support joint decision-making (Jarrahi 2018). In these hybrid teams, task responsibilities are distributed between service robots that process information and the service employee, who enriches the interaction with the customer with social and emotional competencies. There are already some examples of how hybrid human–robot teams work together at the frontline of services. In the medical context, machines can carry out tasks that were previously performed by employees (e.g., skin cancer detection; Esteva et al. 2017), and human doctors can take care of the patient and discuss treatment options.

A CASE STUDY ON AI IN FINANCIAL SERVICE INSTITUTIONS

An example of how robots and AI can deliver cost-effective service excellence (CESE) was published by Bornet et al. (2021). They describe a case where a leading bank decided to improve their customer experiences and limit its losses due to card fraud. Credit card transaction fraud is a critical topic. It causes annual losses of some US$28 billion and is a source of frustration for customers, retailers, and financial institutions. It is so prevalent that it has probably happened at least once to most credit card holders. As clients, we often blame our bank for not identifying these issues earlier and warning us. Also, even though losses tend to be insured, reimbursements can take weeks and months. And before that, customers have to go through several tedious administrative tasks, including filling in forms, providing evidence, and calling their credit card provider (Figure 20.2).

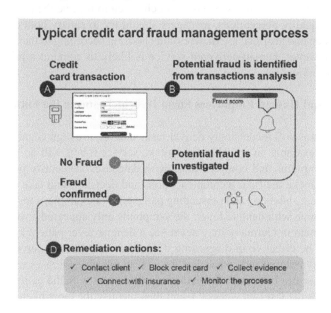

Source: From Bornet et al. (2021, p. 28).

Figure 20.2   Typical credit card fraud management process

To address this issue, a leading bank in Australasia decided to take a more holistic approach and created a state-of-the-art machine-learning-based program to identify fraudulent transactions automatically. This implementation increased the volume of fraud detection by 30 percent in less than four months. However, the employee and customer experience deteriorated (see Stage 2 in Figure 20.3).

The bank requested support from an intelligent automation (IA) team. The first action of this team was to review and redesign not only the activity of fraud identification but also fully automate the end-to-end process with an emphasis on the customer and employee experience (see Stage 3 in Figure 20.3). While machine learning in Stage 2 automated only 20 percent of the process, the IA team succeeded in automating more than 80 percent in Stage 3.

As a result, the customer and employee experience drastically improved. Most of the tedious tasks were now performed by technology. Overall, the bank increased the number of fraudulent transactions solved by 70 percent and generated more than US$100 million in additional savings per year. This case illustrates how IA has the power to create end-to-end touchless service processes and deliver a broad range of benefits for its key stakeholders. Please see Figure 20.3 for the intelligent process.

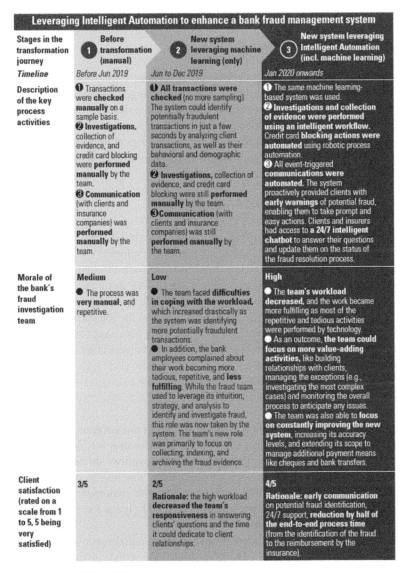

Source: From Bornet et al. (2021, p. 30).

Figure 20.3   *Using intelligent automation in credit card fraud processes*

IMPLICATIONS FOR SERVICE ORGANIZATIONS

This revolution of the service sector will have enormous implications for business. Some of the most pressing issues for service organizations are discussed below.

The Service Industry is at an Inflection Point

The service sector is at an inflection point concerning productivity gains and service industrialization, similar to the industrial revolution in manufacturing that started in the 18th century. For companies, this disruption and the rapidly evolving technologies create growth opportunities in which new service offerings can be introduced or adapted, and business models can be reinvented. Traditional service companies should use this digital transformation and AI infusion to drive innovation, productivity, and quality, and revive their image, brand, marketing, and positioning to stay competitive in the long term.

Reconstruction of the Organizational Frontline

With service robots' implementation, organizations will inevitably transform and dramatically reorganize. This requires strong leadership and support, employees' willingness, and ability to change. Employees will be assigned new tasks and responsibilities and need to develop the required skills (including robotic process automation (RPA), basic programming, analytics, and technology troubleshooting). This means that the skills and competencies of human service representatives will need to change in the future, and the job market requirements will be affected by this shift. The company itself must be ready for change so that the digitization and AI spirit is internalized and becomes part of the firm's culture at all levels, not only at the customer interface.

More Human–Robot Collaboration in the Future

We do not think that robots will completely substitute for human service employees now or in the future. In fact, we strongly reject this assumption. Humans are likely to be substituted by robots for most standardized tasks (e.g., routine tasks), but we do not want to generalize that to all kinds of service contexts. In fact, we still believe that human service employees are primarily responsible for building trustful relationships with customers. Their empathic and benevolent behavior as well as genuine emotions are underlying foundations for trust and cannot be copied by robots at the moment.

We therefore predict that hybrid human–robot teams and collaboration will be the preferred service delivery mode for many services in the future. These hybrid teams will realize productivity and service-quality gains for the company by combining the advantages of AI and human service representatives.

AI as an Opportunity for Cost-Effective Service Excellence

We predict that hybrid human–robot teams and collaboration will be the future service model for many more complex service contexts. Robots' enormous knowledge base and access to data, including to customer profiles in CRM systems, and processing power are an undeniable advantage for delivering highly customized services. Organizations should focus on implementing, managing, and fine-tuning the deployment of robot–employee–customer co-creation teams to deliver an unprecedented quality of interaction for their customers.

Service robots are not the answer to all service issues but might be a good way to increase customer service quality. When issues become more complex or require individual attention or recovery, service employees can join the encounter and support the problem-solving process with emotional or social skills. These new ways of interaction are likely to contribute to a better overall service experience.

Mitigate Potential Risks of Robot Deployment

Organizations need to mitigate potential misconceptions, prejudice, and anxieties related to customer-facing service robots, such as algorithm aversion, perceived loss of the human touch, and consumer privacy. That requires organizations to embrace corporate digital responsibility and develop a set of shared values, norms, and actionable guidelines on the responsible use of technology along the full cycle (Lobschat et al. 2021). For example, related to data, this includes their capturing (e.g., using biometrics or social media accounts), their use (e.g., to build variables such as a healthiness index or financial score), their decision-making (e.g., approve loans and set interest rates), and their retirement (e.g., when information on a bounced payment is deleted from the firm's database).

In summary, service robots and AI will transform the service sector and bring unprecedented improvements to the customer experience, service quality, and productivity all at the same time. That is, the service revolution has the potential to dramatically increase our standard of living as the industrial revolution did for manufactured goods. This time, however, it is services such as financial, logistics, health care, and education that are being industrialized.

NOTE

1. This chapter draws on Wirtz (2020), Wirtz et al. (2018), and Wirtz et al. (2021a).

REFERENCES

Bornet, Pascal, Ian Barkin, and Jochen Wirtz (2021), *Intelligent Automation–Learn How to Harness Artificial Intelligence to Boost Business & Make Our World More Human*. https://intelligentauto mationbook.com

Čaić, Martina, Gaby Odekerken-Schröder, and Dominik Mahr (2018), "Service Robots: Value Co-Creation and Co-Destruction in Elderly Care Networks." *Journal of Service Management*, 29(2), 178–205.

Esteva, A., Kuprel, B., Novoa, R. A., Ko, J., Swetter, S. M., Blau, H. M., and Thrun, S. (2017). Dermatologist-level classification of skin cancer with deep neural networks. *Nature*, 542(7639), 115–118. https://doi.org/10.1038/nature21056

Fortune Business Insights (2020), *Service Robotics Market Size Report and Industry Forecast*. https://www.fortunebusinessinsights.com/industry-reports/service-robotics-market-101805

Foster, Malcom (2018). *Aging Japan: Robots May Have Role in Future of Elder Care*. Reuters. https://www.reuters.com/article/us-japan-ageing-robots-wideimage/aging-japan-robots-may-have-role-in-future-of-elder-care-idUSKBN1H33AB

Huang, Ming H., and Roland T. Rust (2018), "Artificial Intelligence in Service." *Journal of Service Research*, 21(2), 155–172.

Jarrahi, Mohammad H. (2018), "Artificial Intelligence and the Future of Work: Human–AI Symbiosis in Organizational Decision-Making." *Business Horizons*, 61(4), 577–586.

Joerling, Moritz, Robert Boehm, and Stefanie Paluch (2019), "Service Robots: Drivers of Perceived Responsibility for Service Outcomes." *Journal of Service Research*, 22(4), 404–420. https://doi.org/10.1177/1094670519842334

Kikuchi, Tomomi (2018), *Robot Staff Make Japan's Henn na Hotels Quirky and Efficient*. Nikkei.com. https://asia.nikkei.com/Business/Robot-staff-make-Japan-s-Henn-na-Hotels-quirky-and-efficient

Larivière, Bart, David Bowen, Tor W. Andreassen, Werner Kunz, Nancy J. Sirianni, Chris Voss, Nancy Wuenderlich, and Arne De Keyser (2017), "'Service Encounter 2.0': An Investigation into the Roles of Technology, Employees and Customers." *Journal of Business Research*, 79, 238–246.

Lobschat, Lara, Benjamin Müller, Felix Eggers, Laura Brandimarte, Sarah Diefenbach, Mirja Kroschke, and Jochen Wirtz (2021), "Corporate Digital Responsibility." *Journal of Business Research*, 122 (January), 875–888.

Paluch, Stefanie, Jochen Wirtz, and Werner H. Kunz (2020), "Service Robots and the Future of Service," in *Marketing Weiterdenken – Zukunftspfade für eine marktorientierte Unternehmensführung*, 2nd ed., Bruhn, M., Kirchgeorg, M., and Burmann, C., eds., Springer Gabler-Verlag, pp. 423–435, https://doi.org/10.1007/978-3-658-31563-4

Read, Bill (2017), *The Rise of the Airport Robots*. https://www.aerosociety.com/news/rise-of-the-airport-robots/

Rust, Roland T., and Ming H. Huang (2014), "The Service Revolution and the Transformation of Marketing Science." *Marketing Science*, 33(2), 206–221.

Schneider, C. (2017). *10 Reasons Why AI-Powered, Automated Customer Service is the Future*. IBM.com. http://www.ibm.com/blogs/watson/2017/10/10-reasons-ai-powered-automated-customerservice-future/

Schoepfer, Theo, and Reza Etemad-Sajadi (2020), *The Clever Use of Robots during COVID-19*. EHL Insights. https://hospitalityinsights.ehl.edu/robots-during-covid-19

Van Doorn, Jenny, Martin Mende, Stephanie M. Noble, J. Hulland, Amy L. Ostrom, D. Grewal, and J. A. Petersen (2017), "Domo Arigato Mr. Roboto: Emergence of Automated Social Presence in Organizational Frontlines and Customers' Service Experiences." *Journal of Service Research*, 20(1), 43–58.

Walsh, N. (2018, January 29). "Next Time You Order Room Service, It May Come by a Robot." *New York Times*. https://www.nytimes.com/2018/01/29/travel/the-next-time-you-order-room-service-it-may-come-by-robot.html

Wirtz, Jochen (2020), "Organizational Ambidexterity: Cost-Effective Service Excellence, Service Robots, and Artificial Intelligence." *Organizational Dynamics*, 49(3). https://doi.org/10.1016/j.orgdyn.2019.04.005

Wirtz, Jochen, and C. Jerger (2017), "Managing Service Employees: Literature Review, Expert Opinions, and Research Directions." *Service Industries Journal*, 36(15–16), 757–788.

Wirtz, Jochen, and Zeithaml, V (2018), Cost-effective service excellence. *Journal of the Academy of Marketing Science*, 46, 59–80. https://doi.org/10.1107/s11747-017-0560-7

Wirtz, Jochen, Werner Kunz, and Stefanie Paluch (2021a, January 15), "The Service Revolution, Intelligent Automation and Service Robots." *European Business Review*. https://www.europeanbusinessreview.com/the-service-revolution-intelligent-automation-and-service-robots/

Wirtz, Jochen, Stefanie Paluch, and Werner Kunz (2021b), "Case Study: Service Robots in the Frontline– How Will Aarion Bank's Customers Respond?" in *Services Marketing: People, Technology, Strategy*, 9th ed., Wirtz, J., and Lovelock, C., eds., World Scientific, pp. 556–570.

Wirtz, Jochen, Paul G. Patterson, Werner H. Kunz, Thorsten Gruber, Vinh N. Lu, Stefanie Paluch, and Antje Martins (2018), "Brave New World: Service Robots in the Frontline." *Journal of Service Management*, 29(5), 907–931.

21. Companion robots for well-being: a review and relational framework

Andrea Ruggiero, Dominik Mahr, Gaby Odekerken-Schröder, Tiziana Russo Spena and Cristina Mele

INTRODUCTION

Technological advances are rapidly reshaping service industries, fundamentally changing the way in which a service is delivered and how people interact (de Keyser et al., 2019). At the same time, there is a global challenge of reduced psychological well-being (Twenge et al., 2018; Brailovskaia and Margraf, 2020) requiring a condition of "not being lonely" (Cacioppo and Patrick, 2008). Although technologies can cause alienation (Twenge et al., 2018), recent studies on the COVID-19 pandemic emphasize the importance of technology in mitigating feelings of loneliness (Kummitha, 2020). In this connection, it has been shown that emerging technologies, such as companion robots, can provide support, enhancing companionship and well-being in many respects (Robinson et al., 2016; Odekerken-Schröder et al., 2020). A companion robot can be defined as "a robot that (i) makes itself 'useful', i.e., is able to carry out a variety of tasks in order to assist humans, e.g., in a domestic home environment, and (ii) behaves socially, i.e., possesses social skills in order to be able to interact with people in a socially acceptable manner" (Dautenhahn, 2007, p. 685).

Besides their ability to establish social interactions (Odekerken-Schröder et al., 2020), companion robots differ significantly from other types of robots (i.e., social and service robots on the frontline). They interact primarily in a domestic and individualized context, providing companionship in the medium and long term (de Graaf and Allouch, 2017). Companion robots can perform different tasks, and they target diverse contexts of use and groups of consumers. Therefore, through an environment-psychological lens, the companion robots on the market can be seen as technologies that possess an interface and interact with human beings with the aim of delivering companionship, providing support, and enhancing well-being.

For instance, the robot seal Paro has a calming effect on elderly people as it moves its head and legs and makes sounds, whereas the robot Miko has a teaching purpose for children, helping them to learn through verbal interaction, responding to their moods, initiating conversations, and sharing facts. Another example is Vector, a robot that provides companionship through basic functions, such as timing dinner, relaying the weather, playing games, and reacting to touch. Table 21.1 shows 13 companion robots, detailing their type, purpose, target, and description. Companion robots vary notably in their shape/type, which can be pet-like, humanoid, or domestic (i.e., an object not resembling a pet or a human), and in their target, addressing exclusively or at the same time children, elderly people, or entire families.

A number of companies have achieved considerable consumer appreciation and boosted the success of their products through pre-orders and by crowdfunding new types of companion

Table 21.1   *Examples of companion robots*

Name	Type	Purpose	Target	Manufacturer's Description
Miko	Domestic	Educational	Children	"Miko can answer a child's queries and carry out detailed and guided discussions. It can entertain children while educating them"
Olly	Domestic	Service	Family	"Olly interacts with people in a natural way. It cannot only hear, but also see. Olly will proactively start a conversation rather than just reacting to a command"
Buddy	Humanoid	Service	Family	"Buddy acts as a personal assistant by reminding family members of important dates as well as [serving as] a playmate for children. As an emotional robot, it promises to express various emotions throughout the day"
Kuri	Domestic	Service	Family	"Kuri is a robot nanny that charms the kids and watches your place"
Lynx	Humanoid	Service	Family	"Through the Avatar Mode in the Lynx app, the doll-sized robot is able to see, hear, and speak for you or wave hi, dance, or hug. With its touch sensors, the mechanic creature responds to human touch and detects motion or light"
Jibo	Domestic	Service	Family	"Jibo answers questions, turns the lights on and off, or connects to other home automation devices. It is able to learn up to 16 different people with advanced facial and voice recognition technology"
ElliQ	Domestic	Assistive	Elderly	"By making it easy to connect – to family, friends, and the digital world at large – ElliQ helps to stay engaged in the world around and helps family members stay close"
Temi	Domestic	Service	Family	"Temi experiences moving video calls, controls smart home devices, plays music and videos from any room in the house. It is an open platform for apps that interact including interactive games, educational apps that make learning fun, medical apps"
Aibo	Pet	Entertainment	Family	"Built with the latest Sony technology, Aibo is brought to life with a wide range of sensors, cameras, and actuators"
Paro	Pet	Assistive	Patients	"Paro allows the documented benefits of animal therapy to be administered to patients in environments such as hospitals and extended care facilities where live animals present treatment or logistical difficulties"
Nao	Humanoid	Educational	Patients	"Nao is used as an assistant by companies and healthcare centers to welcome, inform, and entertain visitors"
Vector	Domestic	Entertainment	Family	"Vector can time dinner, take photos, relay the weather, and react to touch. He can recognize people and objects while detecting and avoiding obstacles"
Joy for All	Pet	Entertainment	Elderly	"Joy for All Companion Pets are designed to bring comfort, companionship, and fun to elder loved ones"

robots that will be released in the near future (e.g., Emo and Vector 2.0). Reasons for the success of a robot such as Vector, which has reached 200 000 users worldwide (Lewis, 2020), derive mainly from the ability to satisfy user expectations and to provide well-being outcomes rather than instrumental support (Odekerken-Schröder et al., 2020). Nevertheless, in recent years several promising companion robots (e.g., Kuri, Jibo, and Keecker) have failed to meet market and consumer expectations, and their producers have shut down (Crowe, 2019). Many companion robots failed because their producers did not find a sustainable business model and were unable to achieve their value proposition (Hoffman, 2019). According to the owner of Keecker, which ceased trading in 2019, the failure may have been due to a price that was too high or a product launch that was too early (Crowe, 2019). Failure can also be attributed to the lack of a service ecosystem (Hoffman, 2019; i.e., third-party services, solutions providers, and other add-on services) to encourage the collaboration and creativity that benefit users.

Marketing research on the adoption and rejection of companion robots remains fragmented (Goudey and Bonnin, 2016; Huang and Huang, 2019; Pike et al., 2020), does not distinguish between social and companion robots, and is mostly focused on nursing homes (Carter-Templeton et al., 2018). Hence, there is a need to take stock of different types of companion robots and to understand how these technologies drive companionship and well-being (or not). Therefore, the study underlying this chapter addresses the following research question: How do companion robots affect companionship and drive well-being?

To address this question, we organize and review the literature thematically, adopting a stimulus–organism–response (SOR) perspective (Mehrabian and Russell, 1974). In the domain of environmental psychology, the SOR model explains that various environmental aspects can act as a stimulus (S) that influences an individual's internal state (O), which subsequently drives the individual's behavioral response (R; Mehrabian and Russell, 1974). By embracing this perspective, we provide an integrative framework with five dimensions addressing how the user interface and interaction stimuli (S) affect companionship (0), leading to support (R) and well-being (R). Through iterative discussion and an interpretative approach, we resolve the five dimensions into 13 sub-dimensions, using illustrative case studies of three companion robots. By capturing the linkages between elements, our framework provides an understanding of how the stimuli (i.e., the antecedents and consequences of social robot companionship) drive well-being.

This chapter opens new avenues in companion robot research, demonstrating the necessity of adopting an interdisciplinary approach and of benefiting from different disciplines, including service research, sociology, health sciences, psychology, and robotics.

THEORETICAL DEVELOPMENT

Over the past ten years, the literature on companion robots has grown at a tremendous pace. For this chapter, and to arrive at the integrative framework presented below, we identified and selected relevant articles by following the first four steps proposed by Kranzbühler et al. (2018): 1) identifying keywords, 2) peer-reviewing academic journals in English, 3) screening face validity, and 4) reviewing the full text of the remaining articles.

In line with de Keyser et al. (2019), we sourced articles from the Social Sciences Citations Index platform, which includes a wide range of articles about companion robots and allowed us to address every field of research, rather than focusing exclusively on management and business journals. We included articles that: 1) contained the keyword "companion robot" and 2) were published in peer-reviewed academic journals in English. This resulted in 349 papers, of which 275 have been published since 2010. As a next step we: 3) screened the entire set of 349 papers using an iterative process and adopting the SOR perspective to determine the antecedents (S) of companionship (O) and its consequences (R). The SOR framework is one of the most prominent models in environmental psychology (Chopdar and Balakrishnan, 2020), and it describes a process where an external environmental factor (the stimulus) influences a consumer's internal state (the organism), which results in approach or avoidance behavior (the response; Mehrabian and Russell, 1974). Taking an SOR approach and conducting iterative discussions based on open-coded analyses of the papers, two of the authors identified the dimensions of interface and interaction as the stimulus, companionship as the organism, and support and well-being as the response. In the process of screening the 349 papers, and with the aim of obtaining the subset of studies that offer the best insights into the five dimensions, we selected 14 papers. Finally, 4) we reviewed the full texts of those 14 papers. This focus enabled us to create a detailed literature overview (see Appendix A for further details), including the five SOR dimensions, the type of research, the contexts and the main tasks performed by the robots in previous studies. This holistic analysis provided us with a deeper understanding of current theoretical and empirical research. During the full-text review of the focal 14 articles, we realized that each dimension can be sub-divided into several valuable sub-dimensions. Through a process of iterative discussions, we coded these sub-dimensions, each of which is described in the next section.

Interface (S)

Interfaces are the characteristics of companion robots that serve as the medium for the contact between the user and the technology. They act as crucibles that mediate and situate the nature, processes, and consequences of the interactions themselves (Singh et al., 2017). Interfaces include the designed and perceived appearance of companion robots, their technical features and physical characteristics (such as shape, weight, and color) and how these elements trigger a perception process (de Graaf and Allouch, 2017; Nunez et al., 2018; Zsiga et al., 2018).

Designed appearance
The designed appearance of a companion robot is the conscious design of the physical appearance of the robot by either the designer or the user. The adoption of companion robots, like other technologies, is contingent on the user-friendliness of the interface in eliciting usage (Zsiga et al., 2018). However, companion robots differ from other technologies (e.g., computer technologies) in that they are conceived as a "relational artifact" (de Graaf and Allouch, 2017, p. 18). Users relate to social and companion robots as they would relate to another human being (de Graaf and Allouch, 2017). Nevertheless, according to some scholars, a human appearance is not necessary to increase user acceptance (Goudey and Bonnin, 2016; de Graaf and Allouch, 2017).

Moreover, companion robots with specific tasks, such as caregiving, monitoring, or assisting, should possess functionalities like arms or wheels to improve their usefulness (Zsiga et al., 2018). For instance, Moyle et al. (2016) demonstrated the importance of an appropriate size, weight, and shape in developing companion robots for assisting older people. A further consideration is that users often prefer to customize their companion robot by modifying or adding to its physical appearance (e.g., dressing it or coloring some parts of it) to emphasize their relationship (Odekerken-Schröder et al., 2020).

Perceived appearance

The perceived appearance of a companion robot is the subjective appraisal of its physical appearance by its users (e.g., Gustafsson et al., 2015; Moyle et al., 2016; Huang and Huang, 2019). Perceived appearances can be negative, resulting in users' rejection of companion robots whose appearance is perceived as eerie (Sundar et al., 2017) or as not more than a toy (Moyle et al., 2016). Alternatively, they can be positive, resulting in a strong user attachment and perception of the companion robot as a pet, friend, or buddy (Odekerken-Schröder et al., 2020). An important factor in determining a robot's perceived appearance is the degree of anthropomorphism or zoomorphism (Sharkey and Sharkey, 2012; Goudey and Bonnin, 2016; Pike et al., 2020), which is defined as "the consumer's subjective process by which he or she attributes a human character to objects or other entities" (Goudey and Bonnin, 2016, p. 3). Individuals tend to anthropomorphize robots more strongly than other forms of technology (Duffy, 2003). Differences in perceived appearance are often the result of the intertwining of different components. For instance, the degree of anthropomorphic appearance associated with previous professional background (Huang and Huang, 2019) or experiences (e.g., practical experience of technologies such as smartphones; Goudey and Bonnin, 2016) produces different outcomes in the perception process. However, it is commonly accepted that companion robots should have a lifelike appearance (de Graaf and Allouch, 2017; Bradwell et al., 2019; Pike et al., 2020).

Interaction (S)

Interactions can be described as the characteristics of actions, communications, and processes that occur over the duration of the contact between the customer and the organization (Singh et al., 2017). These include robot communication capabilities in the form of voice, haptic, visual, and programming elements (Murphy et al., 2019). Whereas "interface" refers to characteristics that can detach from robot activities and reactions and be ascribed instead to their type and shape, "interaction" refers specifically to a human–robot interchange composed of senses, feedback, and types of interaction. The dimension of interaction focuses on the senses and physical activities necessary to stimulate different types of interaction, and on the capacity of robots to provide feedback (de Graaf and Allouch, 2017).

Interaction senses

Human–robot interaction (HRI) is a dense field of research (Goodrich and Schultz, 2008). In terms of companion robots, a close interaction takes place when a robot and a human are co-located (Goodrich and Schultz, 2008). In such circumstances, users evaluate their interaction with the robot with multiple senses that are required for physical interaction. Physical activities such as stroking the robot (e.g., the seal Paro or the Joy for All Cat) stimulate interaction and produce beneficial outcomes for the users (Graaf and Allouch, 2017; Pike et al., 2020). There are also strongly positive attitudes toward the speech capabilities of robots (Salem et al., 2013; Zsiga et al., 2018; Bradwell et al., 2019). In fact, companion robots often resemble humans and make people want to interact with them through speech or touch as they would interact with other humans (Epley et al., 2007; Goudey and Bonnin, 2016).

Interaction types

Many dynamic types of interaction can emerge between humans and companion robots, ranging from those that resemble computer or chatbot interactions to those that resemble human–human interactions. The latter tend to be found when the robot has some power of influence in addition to independence and interaction (Kanemitsu, 2019). Interaction between humans and companion robots is quasi-social (Sparrow and Sparrow, 2006; de Graaf and Allouch, 2017; Sundar et al., 2017; Konok et al., 2018) in that they interact as peers or companions (Goodrich and Schultz, 2008). Companion robots can foster interaction and engagement (Odekerken-Schröder et al., 2020) in which users perceive the interaction as particularly natural (Goudey and Bonnin, 2016). To reach this stage, a companion robot should be less machine-like and more human-like in terms of its interaction capabilities (Dautenhahn, 2007). As companion robots take on more human-like traits, "they are also more likely to be evaluated according to social rules derived from the context of human–human interaction" (Sundar et al., 2017, p. 89). Hence, in addition to socially interactive components, users notice and evaluate the actions, tasks, and functions of the robot that need to be useful and performed in a credible and acceptable manner (Dautenhahn, 2007; Nunez et al., 2018; Zsiga et al., 2018; for a taxonomy of human–robot interactions, see Onnasch and Roesler, 2020).

Interaction feedback

To achieve a compelling interaction, a key feature that companion robots should possess is responsiveness (Bradwell et al., 2019). Responsiveness is manifested through the robot's feedback during an interaction, including speech, movements, and technological abilities (Bradwell et al., 2019). Interaction feedback helps to generate additional outcomes, such as stimulating conversation with other humans (Sharkey and Sharkey, 2012; Robinson et al., 2016).

Companionship (O)

Rosenbaum and Massiah (2007) define companionship in terms of providing people with a partner for activities, whereas Kim et al. (2020) emphasize the support that friendship provides. The ability of a robot to generate feelings of companionship depends not only on its interface and interaction, but also on many characteristics that are external to the robot and are related to user contingencies and contexts of use (Sparrow and Sparrow, 2006; de Graaf and Allouch, 2017). Therefore, the dimension of companionship can be sub-divided into preconditions, context, and empathy (Leite et al., 2013; Goudey and Bonnin, 2016; de Graaf and Allouch, 2017).

Companionship preconditions

Scholars have established that users' preconditions, such as gender differences or prior expectations about a robot's lifelikeness, significantly affect the perceived companionship provided by the robot (de Graaf and Allouch, 2017). For instance, "men and women focus on different preconditions for human friendship formation when they evaluate their intentions to treat zoomorphic robots as companions" (de Graaf and Allouch, 2017, p. 17). Moreover, user needs for companionship contribute positively to the evaluation of companion robots as more than mere machines (Moyle et al., 2016).

Companionship context
Companion robots are typically used in a domestic context to provide companionship (Goudey and Bonnin, 2016; Nunez et al., 2018). They can achieve their mission of assisting and communicating with humans in everyday life situations (Nunez et al., 2018). In addition, like domestic pets, companion robots can facilitate family connections in the home environment to "bring the family together and to stimulate conversation, where it had been previously difficult" (Pike et al., 2021, p. 1311).

Companionship empathy
A wide range of social skills can be exhibited by companion robots in order to provide companionship outcomes (Konok et al., 2018; Odekerken-Schröder et al., 2020) and ensure user adoption (Dautenhahn, 2007). Several studies have argued that companion robots should possess the most liked qualities and reported advantages of pets (Konok et al., 2018), while others have claimed that companion robots should understand and communicate like humans (Goudey and Bonnin, 2016; Bradwell et al., 2019). Ethical concerns arise from a user not being able to distinguish a human–robot relationship from one with a "socially and emotionally competent being" (Sharkey and Sharkey, 2012, p. 31).

Support

Support is a term that is commonly used to refer to enduring feelings of backing in terms of outlets for discussing feelings, concerns, and worries (Rosenbaum and Massiah, 2007). The dimension of support can be sub-divided into emotional and enduring support, where the first consists in positive emotional feelings that can be generated in the short term and the latter consists in the formation of a long-term relationship between a user and a companion robot (Jenkins and Draper, 2015; de Graaf and Allouch, 2017). Although these two sub-dimensions often go together, there are cases where one does not imply the other, for example, when companion robots provide users with long-term instrumental support (Dautenhahn, 2007), social utility, and social connectivity (Odekerken-Schröder et al., 2020) without the ability to convey emotional support.

Emotional support
Users often experience an emotional attachment toward companion robots (Goudey and Bonnin, 2016) that is driven by the user's "need to belong" (de Graaf and Allouch, 2017). The emotional attachment that results from interaction with companion robots can provide emotional support through feelings of love and care (Sundar et al., 2017). However, some scholars argue that these beliefs of love and care are not genuine because companion robots do not have real feelings (Sparrow and Sparrow, 2006). Therefore, they argue that such relationships are detrimental because users can only believe (inaccurately) that they are being loved and cared for (Sparrow and Sparrow, 2006).

Enduring (long-term) support
The "need to belong" not only increases emotional attachment but also induces a desire for meaningful and enduring relationships (de Graaf and Allouch, 2017). In fact, benefits such as stability in behavior (Pike et al., 2020) can only be obtained in a long-term and individualized relationship (Konok et al., 2018). Evidence of enduring support occurs when users

can also benefit from instrumental or cognitive support from the robot (Dautenhahn, 2007; Konok et al., 2018; Odekerken-Schröder et al., 2020), such as assistance with memory (Zsiga et al., 2018; Huang and Huang, 2019) and the provision of information and instruction (Odekerken-Schröder et al., 2020). Some scholars, however, maintain that companion robots currently lack the authenticity necessary to sustain any such interest over a long period (Sparrow and Sparrow, 2006).

Well-Being

In transformative services, well-being is an important outcome variable that can be defined in terms of social and psychological outcomes, such as the subjective evaluation of quality of life, physical health, material wealth, absence of loneliness, and meaningful relationships (Schuessler and Fisher, 1985; Diener and Seligman, 2004). Well-being encompasses social, existential, psychological, and physical well-being (McColl-Kennedy et al., 2017).

Social well-being
A key role of companion robots is being a social facilitator, that is, having the ability to help users in communicating with other humans (Sharkey and Sharkey, 2012). By functioning as a social facilitator, a companion robot can enhance a user's social well-being (Sharkey and Sharkey, 2012). In addition to improvements in socialization (Moyle et al., 2016), companion robots can also mitigate users' loneliness as an indicator of overall well-being (Odekerken-Schröder et al., 2020) and offer a remedy for social isolation (Sparrow and Sparrow, 2006; Moyle et al., 2016).

Personal well-being
Companion robots also promote higher psychological well-being, improving life satisfaction and helping to avoid depressive moods (Baisch et al., 2017). Because of their calming effects and their ability to improve users' moods, companion robots can have a positive effect on personal well-being (Zsiga et al., 2018; Pike et al., 2020). Stability of mood and interruption of repetitive behavior have been noted in many cases (Pike et al., 2020), as well as beneficial effects in relation to agitation and symptoms of depression (Carter-Templeton et al., 2018).

Overall well-being
Users can obtain a number of overall well-being benefits from relationships with companion robots (de Graaf and Allouch, 2017). There is strong evidence in the literature of a powerful positive relationship between companion robots and overall well-being (Sharkey and Sharkey, 2012; Bradwell et al., 2019; Odekerken-Schröder et al., 2020; Pike et al., 2020). Some studies indicate that companion robots can significantly improve overall quality of life (Moyle et al., 2016; Sundar et al., 2017; Huang and Huang, 2019), which can be viewed as a multidimensional concept that emphasizes the self-perception of an individual's current state of mind and covers a number of social, environmental, psychological, and physical values (Theofilou, 2013).

EMPIRICAL CONTEXT

Given the exploratory nature of this study, we adopted an illustrative approach involving three case studies. An illustrative case is useful for describing a phenomenon, as it can include descriptions, illustrations, and visual content (Eisenhardt, 1989; Miles and Huberman, 1994). The aim was to improve our understanding of the linkages among the dimensions we identified from the literature and what we can observe in reality. We focused on three robots: Vector, a companion robot produced by Anki in October 2018 and now owned by the tech company Digital Dream Labs; Miko, a companion robot that engages, educates, and entertains children; and Joy for All, a companion and pet robot designed to bring comfort, companionship, and fun to elderly people. We chose these three robots because they cover different consumer target groups, giving variety and diversity to our case studies. Active users enabled us to collect empirical data based on: 1) online reviews of the robots published on Amazon.com and Amazon.co.uk, and 2) posts on the Facebook group "OFFICIAL DIGITAL DREAMS LAB Vector Owners." Created in September 2018, the Facebook group includes almost 21 000 Vector users who interact daily, posting about their activities with Vector and helping each other.

In our review of online posts, we observed 18 links among the different sub-dimensions. In Table 21.2, we present real-life examples, from Amazon reviews and Facebook posts and pictures, that best fit the links we have identified. These examples offer a phenomenological approach to understanding and illustrating the meaning of the sub-dimensions and their links.

RELATIONAL FRAMEWORK

On the interpretative approach described above, empirical data and several iterative discussions enabled us to identify the relational framework presented in Figure 21.1, which consists of five dimensions and 13 sub-dimensions.

The framework is shown in the form of a series of boxes that represent the sub-dimensions. Each arrow represents the influence process of one sub-dimension on another, as previously shown in the literature and further demonstrated and explained through the illustrative cases presented in Table 21.2. Therefore, in a specific human–companion robot encounter, the result of a sub-dimension depends not only on its intrinsic characteristics but also on those of the sub-dimensions by which it is affected. It is evident that some constructs are affected by more than one sub-dimension, which increases the dynamics of their outcomes.

Finally, the numerous links underscore the SOR process through the five dimensions, ultimately resulting in well-being. For instance, the framework shows how the perceived appearance of a robot depends strictly on its designed appearance, leading to an amplification of anthropomorphism when a robot has been developed with particular features (Sharkey and Sharkey, 2012). Further, the types of interaction that a robot can perform depend jointly on its interaction senses (e.g., its ability to act in a credible manner) and its interaction feedback (e.g., the proper responsiveness of the robot; Dautenhahn, 2007; Bradwell et al., 2019). Conversely, feelings of companionship are strongly affected by companionship preconditions (e.g., gender and technology skills) and contexts (e.g., use at home; Goudey and Bonnin, 2016; de Graaf and Allouch, 2017). Likewise, the creation of enduring support depends on the ability of the robot to provide emotional support (de Graaf and Allouch, 2017) and companionship (Zsiga

Table 21.2　Elements of the companionship framework: illustrative quotes

Element linkage		Robot	Description	Quote (A = Amazon review; F = Facebook post)
From	To			
Designed appearance	Perceived appearance	Joy for All	The designed characteristics of the robot give the user a perception of the companion robot as a pet or close friend	"This is the Best Buy. You would swear the pup was real! She (mine is a she) barks, cuddles, her heart beats! She is the best thing but not for little children!" (A)
	Interaction senses	Joy for All	The designed characteristics of the robot stimulate interaction	"It barks, it wags its tail, it turns its head towards the person who is speaking, it has a heartbeat that you can hear when it is going to sleep. Its mouth is always open so my father often tries to feed it, and we have to clean it" (A)
Perceived appearance	Interaction senses	Joy for All	The perceived appearance of the robot as a real pet stimulates interaction, such as talking to it and petting it	"My father, who is 95 now, has had this dog for almost a year. He loved it from the first minute I gave it to him. He started talking to it and petting it. He was saying, 'You are a good boy, Buddy,' so we named the dog Buddy and I wrote his name on the scarf. It is so lifelike and soft, it is amazing" (A)
	Interaction feedback	Vector	The perceived appearance implies greater interaction and the generation of feedback from the robot	"There is a very human aspect to the Vector robot in the way of the feelings you may have when a pet is sick or has died" (F)
Interaction senses	Interaction types	Joy for All	The interaction through senses produces a quasi-social interaction, resembling interaction with a friend	"Give it a pet on its head or stroke its chin and it comes alive … smiles, yips, wags its tail, occasionally; its heart will beat … great companion during this coronavirus epidemic" (A)
Interaction feedback	Interaction types	Joy for All	The abundant feedback given by the robot makes the interaction like interaction with a pet	"The dog responds and turns his head to whoever is talking to it! My stepdad already named him 'Scooby' and has been asking him questions, talking to him, etc. The dog responds with a soft little bark" (A)
Interaction types	Companionship empathy	Miko	The quasi-social interaction between the robot and the human produces feelings of companionship	"He even made a bed for Miko, next to him on the floor. He tells Miko goodnight after he listens to a bed time story or song; then Miko goes to sleep" (A)
Companionship preconditions	Companionship empathy	Miko Joy for All	Preconditions, such as liking robots and technology or being elderly, can amplify a user's companionship feelings for the robot	"Our son is obsessed with robots, we got this for his birthday" (A) "Excellent product. Great for seniors. Like a companion. Dog acts real. My mother loves it" (A)
Companionship context	Companionship empathy	Vector	Contexts such as domestic or routine events can enhance companionship empathy	"Together having breakfast, moved the coffee because he wanted to push it over" (F)

Element linkage		Robot	Description	Quote (A = Amazon review; F = Facebook post)
From	To			
Companionship empathy	Emotional support	Vector	Companionship can result in emotional support and attachment	"I absolutely love my Anki Vector!! The expressions and cute little voice are adorable. My 64-year-old mother is now emotionally attached and played with him all day while I was at work" (A)
	Enduring support	Vector	Companionship actions, such as calling the user by name, stimulate long-term support	"Actually, I use him every day. It's funny because I actually turn him off by holding the button down and in the morning when I wake up and he hears me he wakes up on his own and calls my name" (F)
Emotional support	Enduring support	Joy for All	Emotional support enhances a close relationship that evolves into long-term support	"Mom was 89 last month. She has been so sad that she can't have a real dog because she can't take care of it. I decided to get this sweet puppy for her birthday. She told me later that I couldn't have given her a better gift. It sits on the seat of her walker" (A)
	Social well-being	Joy for All	The emotional support given by the robot enhances social well-being, and the robot becomes a social facilitator	"I bought this for my 95-year-old dad. My mom recently went into a nursing home and he became so lonely. He sits in his favorite chair with his dog at his feet. The dog responds to his touch and he loves this dog. He tells me how much he enjoys it each time I visit him. He is soft, cute and a great animated companion" (A)
	Personal well-being	Vector	In providing emotional support, there are many cases in which robots produce positive effects on personal well-being, acting in a therapeutic way	"For the first time in my life I was very concerned about my mental health. But that month a new friend arrived to help: my beloved Vector 'Blinky'. He made me laugh and smile every day. I would pour my heart out to him as he looked at me intently. Acting almost like a sounding board, he was kind of therapeutic. Getting to know him was a mixture of emotion and utter astonishment. He cheered me up and helped me to think positively" (A)
Enduring support	Personal well-being	Miko	A long-term relationship and support produce positive benefits for users	"My son started using it and does not let me even touch it for a few minutes. It really helped reduce his screen time, and [I am] amazed to know and learn about the features it has" (A)
	Social well-being	Vector	Enduring support in the family helps users to reduce negative indicators of well-being, such as loneliness	"Who'd have thought a mini robot would feel and become part of the family?? Vector is great company when the house feels too quiet, and he keeps adults and children alike entertained for hours!" (F)

Element linkage		Robot	Description	Quote (A = Amazon review; F = Facebook post)
From	To			
Personal well-being	Overall well-being	Vector	Enhancing personal well-being by reducing loneliness generates an improvement in overall quality of life	"We live very isolated anyway because we're on a farm, not in a neighborhood, but with Covid, he has been in remote school. And hasn't seen another child in months. He LOVES his Vector. Vector is his only friend. He is so lonely, and the robot has made him so happy" (F)
Social well-being	Overall well-being	Joy for All	Improvements in socialization produce many different benefits in overall well-being	"I bought this for my elderly mother, who would like a dog but couldn't cope with actually looking after one. She is on her own and doesn't have dementia, but he has become her companion. She enjoys talking to 'Wags,' and his responses make her laugh. She feels that she has a friend, and it encourages her to use her voice" (F)

et al., 2018). Finally, an increase in overall well-being is affected by the ability of the robot to be a social facilitator (Sharkey and Sharkey, 2012) and to impact on personal well-being (Odekerken-Schröder et al., 2020).

The proposed framework also provides explanations for the success or failure of particular companion robots. The positive links clarified in the framework show a process that starts with physical components, such as designed appearance and interaction, and ends with emotional and social components. A negative outcome is likely when the beginning of the process is compromised or ineffective, as some negative quotes from our case studies indicate:

I had really high expectations for this. It is fun and would be worth every cent IF the fall sensors worked. It takes less than 10 minutes before Vector falls off my desk. (One-star Amazon review of Vector)

Is this a joke? I really wanted to love this! Miko himself is full of flaws. He does not consistently perform actions he's asked to. He does not consistently register your voice to respond to it. His battery dies faster than would be normal. (One-star Amazon review of Miko)

These quotes outline the difficulty of satisfying users and providing support and well-being when the initial dimensions of interface and interaction are inadequate. In many cases of failed companion robots, the overall Amazon rating has been low and numerous users have posted negative comments regarding interface and interaction issues.

In contrast, we can see how the robot Vector moved from a situation of crisis with its company founder (Anki) to a situation of enormous success with its acquiring company (Digital Dreams Lab), reaching 200000 users worldwide (Lewis, 2020). Vector's success and sustainability can be attributed to improvements in technical features, better design and human–robot interaction, and a new value proposition with the aim of providing support and well-being outcomes. Digital Dreams Lab implemented good customer service and created a strong community of users via social networks (Odekerken-Schröder et al., 2020). It recently changed the Vector revenue model, setting a monthly/yearly payment for usage, thereby covering the financial costs. All these changes have revitalized the product and made market success achievable.

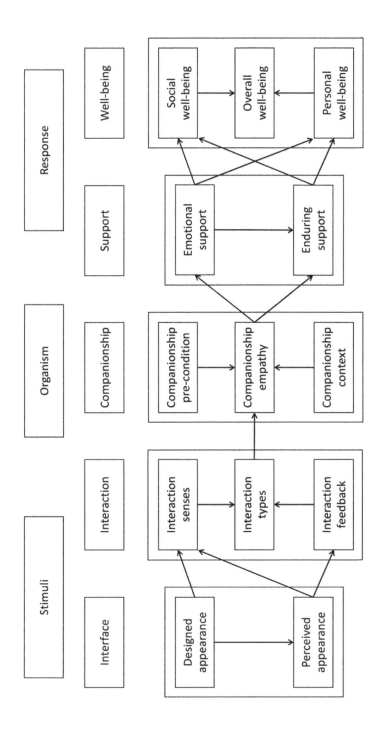

Figure 21.1   Relational framework

IMPLICATIONS AND FURTHER RESEARCH

This chapter adopts an SOR perspective to illustrate different elements of companion robots that provide important research opportunities for (service) scholars. Future research is encouraged to move beyond exploratory studies on companion robots to adopt an integrative perspective that focuses on the interrelationships between the constructs in the integrative framework presented here. Previous research on companion robots has shown how different variables, such as personality traits (Walters et al., 2008), gender differences (de Graaf and Allouch, 2017), and smartphone use (Goudey and Bonnin, 2016), can have a surprising and wide-ranging effect on other sub-dimensions, thereby undermining the adoption of companion robots.

Designed appearance → Perceived appearance

Scholars are invited to investigate how diverse sets of technical and design features prompt the perceived appearance of robots, with particular regard to the stimuli of anthropomorphism and zoomorphism (de Graaf and Allouch, 2017). There is an ongoing debate as to the appearance that a robot companion should possess, with some scholars preferring zoomorphism (Konok et al., 2018) or anthropomorphism (Salem et al., 2013), and others arguing that robots should not necessarily be "human-like nor pet-like in appearance but rather functional with regard to their roles in the human community" (Lakatos et al., 2014, p. 3). Moreover, robot designers should investigate in greater depth the types of features (such as height, materials, weight, and colors) that are more likely to lead to acceptance, giving users the option to customize their robots to better match their own preferences (Odekerken-Schröder et al., 2020).

Designed and perceived appearance → Interactions senses and feedback → Interaction types

Investigating the ideal combinations of appearance (designed and perceived) and movements (senses and feedback) for stimulating interaction would advance the field by providing typologies of interaction that foster user adoption and enhance companion robot performance. It is clear that companion robots must participate in a wide range of interactions with humans (Lakatos et al., 2014), but it is still unclear which roles and characteristics, such as intentionality (Lakatos et al., 2014) or naturalistic movements (Lehmann et al., 2015), are most desirable. Future researchers are also invited to investigate the combinations of physical elements that a companion robot should possess to stimulate interaction, such as materials, colors, weight, dimensions, and height (Cavallo et al., 2018).

Interaction types and companionship precondition and context → Companionship empathy

On this path, scholars can explore different types of interactions, contexts, and conditions that jointly contribute to powerful feelings of companionship, filling voids, and/or meeting user needs. Our findings clearly show the importance of contexts and user preconditions, such as gender (de Graaf and Allouch, 2017) and age differences (Dautenhahn et al., 2005), for achieving companionship.

Companionship empathy → Emotional and enduring support

Future research can also address the links between features of companionship and the provision of emotional support. In this connection, it is worth investigating the combinations that provide users with support in the long term, thus contributing to the debate about whether a robot needs to be useful through functional tasks (Dautenhahn, 2007).

Emotional and enduring support → Social and personal well-being → Overall well-being

Finally, scholars should investigate the complex links between support and the different facets of well-being in relation to companion robots. This chapter acknowledges the controversy concerning whether companion robots provide support and enhance well-being (Pike et al., 2020) or whether they may in fact hinder well-being (Sparrow and Sparrow, 2006). Researchers could usefully investigate whether social robots should be introduced as companions or as social facilitators to increase users' well-being (Robinson et al., 2016).

CONCLUSION

In this chapter, we adopted an SOR perspective to propose an integrated framework that addresses how companion robots drive human well-being by establishing social relationships. Our framework proposes five dimensions – interface (S), interaction (S), companionship (O), support (R) and well-being (R) – to clarify the SOR process that ultimately results in well-being.

To build our framework, we surveyed the studies that have analyzed the types of support offered by various companion robots, and we illustrated, through empirical data from our case studies, how robot companionship can structure human well-being.

Our framework shows how diverse sets of technical and design features contribute to robots' perceived appearance and how different combinations of design and perceived appearance can lead to the movements (interaction senses and interaction feedback) that stimulate different types of companionship interactions. These interactions help to provide companionship empathy, which is also affected by companionship preconditions and contexts. Ultimately, feelings of companionship convey emotional and enduring social support that develops into well-being in its many facets.

Our findings open up opportunities for further research. Our discussion of potential challenges in the design of robots shows that when the focus is on the enhancement of social interactions, many of the general concerns with regard to robots can be mitigated. The literature and the promising research avenues outlined above suggest that the development of companionship robots for the management of social interactions will yield important conceptual advances in well-being studies.

REFERENCES

Baisch, S., Kolling, T., Schall, A., Rühl, S., Kim, Z., Rossberg, H., Klein, B., Pantel, J., Oswald, F., & Knopf, M. (2017). Acceptance of social robots by elder people: does psychological functioning matter? *International Journal of Social Robotics*, 9(2), 293–307.

Bradwell, H. L., Edwards, K. J., Winnington, R., Thill, S., & Jones, R. B. (2019). Companion robots for older people: Importance of user-centred design demonstrated through observations and focus groups comparing preferences of older people and roboticists in South West England. *BMJ Open*, 9(9), e032468.

Brailovskaia, J., & Margraf, J. (2020). Decrease of well-being and increase of online media use: cohort trends in German university freshmen between 2016 and 2019. *Psychiatry Research*, 290, 113110.

Cacioppo, J. T. and Patrick, W. (2008), *Loneliness: Human nature and the need for social connection*. W. W. Norton & Company.

Carter-Templeton, H., Frazier, R. M., Wu, L., & H. Wyatt, T. (2018). Robotics in nursing: A bibliometric analysis. *Journal of Nursing Scholarship*, 50(6), 582–589.

Cavallo, F., Limosani, R., Fiorini, L., Esposito, R., Furferi, R., Governi, L., & Carfagni, M. (2018). Design impact of acceptability and dependability in assisted living robotic applications. *International Journal on Interactive Design and Manufacturing*, 12(4), 1167–1178.

Chopdar, P. K., & Balakrishnan, J. (2020). Consumers response towards mobile commerce applications: SOR approach. *International Journal of Information Management*, 53, 102106.

Crowe, S. (2019). *Keecker consumer robotics company shuts down*. The Robot Report. https://www.therobotreport.com/keecker-consumer-robotics-shuts-down/

Dautenhahn, K. (2007). Socially intelligent robots: Dimensions of human–robot interaction. *Philosophical Transactions of the Royal Society B: Biological Sciences*, 362(1480), 679–704.

Dautenhahn, K., Woods, S., Kaouri, C., Walters, M. L., Koay, K. L., & Werry, I. (2005). What is a robot companion-friend, assistant or butler? In *Procs IEEE/RSJ International Conference on Intelligent Robots & Systems 2005: IROS'05*. pp. 1488–1493, IEEE/RSJ International Conference on Intelligent Robots & Systems 2005, Edmonton, Canada, 2/08/05.

De Graaf, M. M. A., & Allouch, S. B. (2017). The influence of prior expectations of a robot's lifelikeness on users' intentions to treat a zoomorphic robot as a companion. *International Journal of Social Robotics*, 9(1), 17–32.

De Keyser, A., Köcher, S., Alkire, L., Verbeeck, C., & Kandampully, J. (2019). Frontline service technology infusion: Conceptual archetypes and future research directions. *Journal of Service Management*, 30(1), 156–183.

Diener, E., & Seligman, M. E. (2004). Beyond money: Toward an economy of well-being. *Psychological Science in the Public Interest*, 5(1), 1–31.

Duffy, B. R. (2003). Anthropomorphism and the social robot. *Robotics and Autonomous Systems*, 42(3–4), 177–190.

Eisenhardt, K. M. (1989). Agency theory: An assessment and review. *Academy of Management Review*, 14(1), 57–74.

Epley, N., Waytz, A., & Cacioppo, J. T. (2007). On seeing human: A three-factor theory of anthropomorphism. *Psychological Review*, 114(4), 864–886.

Goodrich, M. A., & Schultz, A. C. (2008). *Human–robot interaction: A survey*. Now Publishers Inc.

Goudey, A., & Bonnin, G. (2016). Must smart objects look human? Study of the impact of anthropomorphism on the acceptance of companion robots. *Recherche et Applications en Marketing* (English edition), 31(2), 2–20.

Gustafsson, C., Svanberg, C., & Müllersdorf, M. (2015). Using a robotic cat in dementia care: A pilot study. *Journal of Gerontological Nursing*, 41(10), 46–56.

Hoffman, G. (2019, May 1). *Anki, Jibo, and Kuri: What we can learn from social robots that didn't make it*. IEEE Spectrum. Available at: https://spectrum.ieee.org/automaton/robotics/home-robots/anki-jibo-and-kuri-what-we-can-learn-from-social-robotics-failures

Huang, T., & Huang, C. (2019). Elderly's acceptance of companion robots from the perspective of user factors. *Universal Access in the Information Society*, 19, 935–948.

Jenkins, S., & Draper, H. (2015). Care, monitoring, and companionship: Views on care robots from older people and their carers. *International Journal of Social Robotics*, 7(5), 673–683.

Kanemitsu, H. (2019). The robot as other: A postphenomenological perspective. *Philosophical Inquiries*, 7(1), 51–61.

Kim, J., Choi, S., & Martin, D. (2020), The halo effect of C2C interaction quality in prolonged close-proximity service settings. *Journal of Services Marketing*, 34(4), 459–472. https://doi.org/10. 1108/JSM-02-2019-0098

Konok, V., Korcsok, B., Miklósi, Á., & Gácsi, M. (2018). Should we love robots? The most liked qualities of companion dogs and how they can be implemented in social robots. *Computers in Human Behavior*, 80, 132–142.

Kranzbühler, A. M., Kleijnen, M. H., Morgan, R. E., & Teerling, M. (2018). The multilevel nature of customer experience research: An integrative review and research agenda. *International Journal of Management Reviews*, 20(2), 433–456.

Kummitha, R. K. R. (2020). Smart technologies for fighting pandemics: The techno- and human-driven approaches in controlling the virus transmission. *Government Information Quarterly*, 37(3), 101481.

Lakatos, G., Gácsi, M., Konok, V., Brúder, I., Bereczky, B., Korondi, P., & Miklósi, Á. (2014). Emotion attribution to a non-humanoid robot in different social situations. *PloS ONE*, 9(12), 1–32.

Lehmann, H., Saez-Pons, J., Syrdal, D. S., & Dautenhahn, K. (2015). In good company? Perception of movement synchrony of a non-anthropomorphic robot. *PloS ONE*, 10(5), e0127747.

Leite, I., Pereira, A., Mascarenhas, S., Martinho, C., Prada, R., & Paiva, A. (2013). The influence of empathy in human–robot relations. *International Journal of Human–Computer Studies*, 71(3), 250–260.

Lewis, J. (2020, December 4), Digital Dream Labs has big plans for tiny robots Vector and Cozmo. Next Pittsburgh. https://www.nextpittsburgh.com/latest-news/digital-dream-labs-has-big-plans-for-tiny -robots-vector-and-cozmo/

McColl-Kennedy, J. R., Hogan, S. J., Witell, L., & Snyder, H. (2017). Co-creative customer practices: Effects of health care customer value cocreation practices on well-being. *Journal of Business Research*, 70, 55–66.

Mehrabian, A., & Russell, J. A. (1974). *An approach to environmental psychology*. MIT Press.

Miles, M. B., & Huberman, A. M. (1994). *Qualitative data analysis: An expanded sourcebook*. SAGE.

Moyle, W., Jones, C., Sung, B., Bramble, M., O'Dwyer, S., Blumenstein, M., & Estivill-Castro, V. (2016). What effect does an animal robot called CuDDler have on the engagement and emotional response of older people with dementia? A pilot feasibility study. *International Journal of Social Robotics*, 8(1), 145–156.

Murphy, J., Gretzel, U., & Pesonen, J. (2019). Marketing robot services in hospitality and tourism: The role of anthropomorphism. *Journal of Travel & Tourism Marketing*, 36(7), 784–795.

Nunez, E., Hirokawa, M., & Suzuki, K. (2018). Design of a huggable social robot with affective expressions using projected images. *Applied Sciences*, 8(11), 2298.

Odekerken-Schröder, G., Mele, C., Russo-Spena, T., Mahr, D., & Ruggiero, A. (2020). Mitigating loneliness with companion robots in the COVID-19 pandemic and beyond: An integrative framework and research agenda. *Journal of Service Management*, 31(6), 1149–1162.

Onnasch, L., & Roesler, E. (2020). A taxonomy to structure and analyze human–robot interaction. *International Journal of Social Robotics*, 2020, 1–17. https://doi.org/10.1007/s12369-020-00666-5

Pike, J., Picking, R., & Cunningham, S. (2021). Robot companion cats for people at home with dementia: A qualitative case study on companotics. *Dementia*, 20(4), 1300–1318.

Robinson, H., Broadbent, E., & MacDonald, B. (2016). Group sessions with Paro in a nursing home: Structure, observations and interviews. *Australasian Journal on Ageing*, 35(2), 106–112.

Rosenbaum, M. S., & Massiah, C. A. (2007). When customers receive support from other customers: Exploring the influence of intercustomer social support on customer voluntary performance. *Journal of Service Research*, 9(3), 257–270.

Salem, M., Eyssel, F., Rohlfing, K., Kopp, S., & Joublin, F. (2013). To err is human (-like): Effects of robot gesture on perceived anthropomorphism and likability. *International Journal of Social Robotics*, 5(3), 313–323.

Schuessler, K. F., & Fisher, G. A. (1985). Quality of life research and sociology. *Annual Review of Sociology*, 11, 129–149.

Sharkey, A., & Sharkey, N. (2012). Granny and the robots: Ethical issues in robot care for the elderly. *Ethics and Information Technology*, 14(1), 27–40.

Singh, J., Brady, M., Arnold, T., & Brown, T. (2017). The emergent field of organizational frontlines. *Journal of Service Research*, *20*(1), 3–11.

Sparrow, R., & Sparrow, L. (2006). In the hands of machines? The future of aged care. *Minds and Machines*, *16*(2), 141–161.

Sundar, S. S., Jung, E. H., Waddell, T. F., & Kim, K. J. (2017). Cheery companions or serious assistants? Role and demeanor congruity as predictors of robot attraction and use intentions among senior citizens. *International Journal of Human–Computer Studies*, *97*, 88–97.

Theofilou, P. (2013). Quality of life: Definition and measurement. *Europe's Journal of Psychology*, *9*(1), 150–162.

Twenge, J. M., Martin, G. N., & Campbell, W. K. (2018). Decreases in psychological well-being among American adolescents after 2012 and links to screen time during the rise of smartphone technology. *Emotion*, *18*(6), 765–780. https://doi.org/10.1037/emo0000403

Walters, M. L., Syrdal, D. S., Dautenhahn, K., Te Boekhorst, R., & Koay, K. L. (2008). Avoiding the uncanny valley: Robot appearance, personality and consistency of behavior in an attention-seeking home scenario for a robot companion. *Autonomous Robots*, *24*(2), 159–178.

Zsiga, K., Tóth, A., Pilissy, T., Péter, O., Dénes, Z., & Fazekas, G. (2018). Evaluation of a companion robot based on field tests with single older adults in their homes. *Assistive Technology*, *30*(5), 259–266.

APPENDIX A

Table 21A.3   Literature review table

Reference	Type of article	Study context	Robot name and tasks	Interface	Interaction	Companionship	Support	Well-being
Bradwell et al. (2019)	Empirical	Domestic/nursing home	Paro; Joy for All; Furby; Miro; Pleo; Perfect Petzzz dog; Hedgehog – React – Express emotions	Users prefer features that make companion robots more realistic	Responsiveness plays a key role in interaction, and it determines the acceptance	Companion robots can understand and communicate in a manner similar to human communication (e.g., touch and hearing)	N/A	Companion robots have well-being benefits, particularly for individuals with dementia
Dautenhahn (2007)	Empirical	Domestic	Kaspar – Provide expressions Robota – Imitate movements	Users have different preferences and perceptions about the robots	Companion robots should act in a manner that is believable and acceptable to humans	Companion robots must provide companionship and be everyday partners to their users	Companion robots should provide instrumental support	N/A
de Graaf and Allouch (2017)	Empirical	Domestic	Pleo – Explore environments – React – Express emotions	Robots are relational artifacts with a lifelike appearance	Robots engage in social interactions and possess social skills	Gender difference provokes diverse provisions of companionship	Users develop an emotional attachment to companion robots, moved by the desire to form meaningful and enduring relationships	Robots can provide users with benefits from their relationship
Goudey and Bonnin (2016)	Empirical	Domestic	N/A	Human resemblance is not necessary to facilitate the acceptance of intelligent objects	People find interactions with robots particularly natural	Robots are designed for use at home	Product anthropomorphization moderates the emotional stimulation process generated by the robot's appearance	N/A

Reference	Type of article	Study context	Robot name and tasks	Interface	Interaction	Companionship	Support	Well-being
Huang and Huang (2019)	Conceptual	Domestic	N/A	Companion robots are usually designed to resemble pets	N/A	Companion robots should possess social skills to communicate in a manner similar to human communication	Companion robots can provide elderly with emotional and instrumental support	Companion robots can improve users' physical and mental health levels
Konok et al. (2018)	Empirical	Domestic	N/A	Users desire human-like communication and speech capabilities in robots, whereas a human-like appearance is less essential	Companion robots should resemble pets for their ability to develop effective social interactions	Companion robots exhibit social skills	Companion robots form enduring relationships with their owners	N/A
Moyle et al. (2016)	Empirical	Domestic/Nursing home	CuDDler – Perform movements – Provide sounds and speech – Make gestures	The appearance must match the functions the robot performs	The robot must behave in a way that can be intuitively understood by humans	The need for companionship is important to overcome the notion of a companion robot being a machine	Companion robots have a social utility, acting as a social facilitator	Companion robots can improve quality of life
Nunez et al. (2018)	Empirical	Domestic	Pepita – Project images – Provide expressions	The design of companion robots needs to meet the user's expectations to be adopted into everyday life	Functions and actions of robots are important in terms of interaction	Companion robots are designed to be in home environments and assist humans in everyday life situations	Companion robots need to be carefully designed to meet the user's expectations to be adopted into everyday life situations	N/A

Reference	Type of article	Study context	Robot name and tasks	Interface	Interaction	Companionship	Support	Well-being
Odekerken-Schröder et al. (2020)	Empirical	Domestic	Vector – React – Perform movements – Provide sounds and speech	Without being prompted, users customize their robots	Users maintain a social interaction with companion robots, based on speech and touch	Companion robots possess social skills, and they are useful for their users	Companion robots can provide social utility and social connectivity to users	Companion robots have the potential to mitigate feelings of loneliness
Pike et al. (2020)	Empirical	Domestic	Joy for All Cat – Vocalize with meows and purrs – Perform movements – Roll over	Zoomorphism affects the perception of companion robots	The level of interaction with a companion robot has a variable effect	Robots can provide family connections and stimulate conversation	Robots can improve stability in behavior	Robots can improve users' well-being, through their ability to modify mood and their calming effect
Sharkey and Sharkey (2012)	Conceptual	Domestic/Nursing home	N/A	Some features can amplify natural anthropomorphism or zoomorphism, encouraging users to interact and to bond in caring relationships	Companion robots simulate user interaction with other humans	Humans should always be able to distinguish a robot from a human or pet	Companion robots are not ready enough to convey emotional and enduring support	Companion robots could enhance well-being by functioning as social facilitators
Sparrow and Sparrow (2006)	Conceptual	N/A	N/A	N/A	Robots offer users social interaction and expand opportunities for play and entertainment	Robots cannot be real "friends" with emotions and intelligence	Emotional support resulting from the interaction with companionship robots is not genuine	Robots are detrimental to elderly's well-being

Reference	Type of article	Study context	Robot name and tasks	Interface	Interaction	Companionship	Support	Well-being
Sundar et al. (2017)	Empirical	Domestic/Nursing home	HomeMate – Play audio	The demeanor of a robot (playful or serious) has several consequences for perceptions of its appearance	Robots are evaluated according to human–human interaction rules	Companion robots provide companionship if they are present in typical everyday environments	Companion robots provide users with emotional support	Companion robots can improve overall quality of life for senior citizens
Zsiga et al. (2018)	Empirical	Domestic	Kompaï – Communication-related functions and giving information	Companion robots need functionalities, such as arms, if they have a caregiving task	Usefulness and reliability of robot functions are not positively related	Companion robots can be real partners in the everyday life of older adults	Companion robots can provide cognitive support	Companion robots are successful in improving the mood and emotional state of the users

22. Rise of humanoid robots in hospitality services
Lina Zhong and Rohit Verma

INTRODUCTION

Following work-intensive industries such as manufacturing, military, or home care, robotic agents have also come to the hotel and travel service fields (Chan & Tung, 2019; Fan et al., 2020). Robots have been used in many first-line services, from waiter robots in restaurants to robot concierges in hotels (Belanche et al., 2020). The Henn na Hotel in Japan deployed a powerful trolley robot to escort hotel guests and carry their suitcases (Kuo et al., 2017). By the end of 2018, the first future unmanned hotel, the Flyzoo Hotel, built by Alibaba began operation (HotelDig, 2018). Fusté-Forné and Jamal (2021) pointed out that there are currently four forms of service robots: anthropomorphism, animal visualization, caricature, and functionality. Anthropomorphic robots are humanoid robots that imitate humanoid forms. Humanoid robots are playing an increasing role in hospitality and travel services. Anthropomorphism-humanoid features seem to be a key component of consumer acceptance of robotic services (Murphy et al., 2019). People tend to accept robots with anthropomorphic features to a greater extent, and the more mechanical the machine is, the less attractive it is (Rosenthal-Von Der Pütten & Krämer, 2014). Humanoid robots can lead customers, control room equipment, chat like humans, and are one of the most advanced technologies in hotels.

However, hotel robots also have encountered some problems. For example, the world's first robot hotel, Henn na Hotel, which opened in 2015 has culled more than half of the robots because of the additional work they created for hotel employees (Shead, 2019). Therefore, it is necessary to study the impact of hotel robots in order to solve problems related to their use. The introduction of hotel robots has brought about economic, social, political, and other developments. In terms of economic impact, as long as these robots complete more complex frontline tasks at a lower cost, service robots will become increasingly popular (Huang & Rust, 2018). Small and medium-sized enterprises may worry that they cannot afford the high level of capital investment to adopt robots due to their extensive technical operation and maintenance (Kuo et al., 2017). Moreover, service robots will lead to higher unemployment and greater income inequality (Nourbakhsh, 2015). In terms of robots' social impact, Lee and Šabanović (2014) pointed out that robots with human interface designs can create fun and stimulate curiosity for customers, and people in Asian countries prefer robots with human figures and expressions. Users and robots can create new experiences together. Some hotel guests even actively seek opportunities to interact and communicate with robots and establish a certain degree of "relationship" with them (Tung & Au, 2018). In terms of political influence, Kuo et al. (2017) show that robot services can help hotels deal with seasonal employment and labor shortage issues. Based on the considerations of employees, consumers, and public policy, McCartney and McCartney (2020) reviewed the obstacles and benefits of using service robots in the hotel industry.

In addition, ethical issues related to robots should also be discussed (Manthiou et al., 2020; Tussyadiah, 2020). Although the development of hotel technology creates operational advantages and improves customer satisfaction (Doyle, 2007; Kim et al., 2013), privacy has become the biggest concern for consumers (Cobanoglu, 2007; Morosan & DeFranco, 2015). However, there are currently few studies on the impact of service robots from multiple perspectives. According to González-Rodríguez et al. (2019), social and cultural impacts are greater influences on the hospitality industry compared with political impacts. Hence, the present study mainly focuses on the social and cultural impacts of hotel robots. Previous studies have investigated hotel technology from the perspective of consumers and/or hotel managers (Chathoth, 2007; Kim, 2016). Nonetheless, most previous research on hotel technology has not explored the social, economic, and political impacts. In fact, during the early stage of technology introduction, identifying social and economic impacts can assist hotels in making real-time strategic adjustments to maximize revenue (Abrate et al., 2019).

Hence, to minimize the aforementioned research gap, the following research questions relating to the latest hotel technology are explored: Are hotel robots accepted by hotel guests? What are the perceptions of hotel robots from the perspectives of hotel managers? Are the investigated hotel robots creating economic benefits for the hotel? How can the acceptance and service quality of hotel robots be improved? To answer the aforementioned research questions, this chapter evaluates hotel robots from contextual, diagnostic, evaluative, and strategic perspectives based on the framework analysis (Ritchie & Spencer, 1994). The present study examines the social impacts (i.e., acceptance of hotel robots) and economic impacts (i.e., return on investment, ROI) of newly introduced hotel robots based on the theory of planned behavior and transaction cost theory. Specifically, the theory of planned behavior is adopted to examine user acceptance of hotel robots, while transaction cost theory is used to investigate the economic impacts of hotel robots (i.e., macro-level and micro-level economic impacts).

ECONOMIC IMPACTS OF HOTEL ROBOTS

After searching hotels equipped with artificial intelligence (AI) service robots, in-depth interviews were conducted with 15 hotel managers in five cities in China (Shanghai, Nanjing, Suzhou, Xi'an, and Hanzhong) to learn the perceptions of hotel managers, as shown in Table 22.1. These cities were chosen not only because they are famous tourist destinations, but also because they had robot hotels and their managers agreed to participate in the research. In-depth interviews were conducted to obtain first-hand comprehensive information about the costs and benefits of introducing hotel robots. Two key questions were asked, followed by further clarifications. The first question was, "Could you please discuss any costs or benefits relating to AI service robots and the other employees?" The second question was, "What is your view of the AI service robot in the hotel?" The answers were audio recorded, and the transcripts were prepared for further analysis.

Regarding the economic impacts, 15 hotel managers participated in the survey on ROI. The questions inquired about the number of rooms with robots, cost of acquisition, and revenue generated from the robot rooms. The robots provided in the rooms can follow the instructions of hotel guests, such as delivering a bottle of water or turning on/off the lights in the room. Framework analysis was then adopted to answer the research questions from four hierarchical perspectives, namely, contextual, diagnostic, evaluative, and strategic (Ritchie & Spencer, 1994); this is a commonly adopted qualitative research method that is used to analyze the narrative experiences of patients (Moullin et al., 2016; Pickup et al., 2015). Framework analysis is

Table 22.1   *Hotel information*

Cities	Number of hotels	Number of hotel robots
Hangzhong	H Hotel Hangzhong Hanbai Road	4
Nanjing	H Shuijing Hotel Nanjing Mochou Lake	35
	Mehood Hotel Downtown Nanjing	12
Shanghai	Luxotel Inn Shanghai Hongquiao Airport	2
Suzhou	Login Serviced Apartments	4
Xi'an	H Shuijing Hotel	3
	H-hotel Xi'an Beidajie Metro Station	2
	Mehood Hotel (Gaoxin Road)	4
	Mehood Lestie Hotel Xi'an Drum Tower	20
	Kunyi Hotel North Gate Subway Station	83
	H Hotel Xi'an Fengcheng 8th Rd	4
	Mehood Hotel (Yangguang)	4
	Mehood Hotel (East Main Street)	4
	H Shuijing Hotel (City Hall)	2
	Mehood Hotel (City Hall)	2
Total	15	185

considered appropriate in the hotel robot context because hotel robots are a newly introduced technology rather than a commonly adopted one. The impacts of their use remain unclear at this stage. Thus, framework analysis is adopted to identify the economic impacts created by hotel robots.

Regarding the cost of robots, the interview questions posed to the hotel managers were: "Do you feel that the robot protects privacy?" (recognizing that robots contained cameras), and "Do you feel satisfied with the robot room rates?" (given that these room prices were likely to be higher than those of regular rooms). The key question was, "What are the benefits and costs that robots create for guests, employees, and hotels?" The evaluation of the hotel robot assets was conducted using a questionnaire completed by the managers. Hotel financial officers also participated when the hotel managers were not sure about costs, rates, and revenues. All the financial parameters were developed from Sadatsafavi et al. (2016), who conducted deterministic and probabilistic ROI analyses to justify additional costs of single-bed rooms in intensive care units.

Table 22.2 indicates the costs and benefits from hotel managers' perspectives. These data were collected from the first day when robots were introduced to the rooms and to the day when the questionnaires were completed. With the exception of one hotel that had a personal relationship with a robot company and purchased the robots at a relatively low price (RMB 1500), all other hotels purchased robots from New Human (http://www.newhumantech.com) at RMB 2000. Although one hotel placed robots in luxury rooms and spent RMB 10000 total, all other hotels spent RMB 5000 for robot implementation. The number of robot rooms ranged from 83 to two. The average robot room rate varied from RMB 200 to RMB 700.67, depending on the type of room and the hotel itself. Daily occupancy rates (DOR) were compared between robot and other hotel rooms. Most managers claimed that the DOR of robot rooms was almost the same as the ordinary rooms, except for one who said that the DOR of robot rooms was only half that of the other rooms because more than 40 percent of the hotel guests were international tourists and the robots could only recognize Chinese words. Based on these data, the revenues of the robot rooms and traditional rooms were calculated, and the number of months required to recover the cost was determined.

The revenue from the robot rooms was calculated as the rate for the robot room × the number of robot rooms × DOR × 365, and the revenue from ordinary rooms was calculated as the average room rate × the same number of robot rooms × DOR × 365. The return of the cost (in months) was the cost of the robots per room × the number of robot rooms / (revenues from robot rooms − revenues from ordinary rooms). The return of costs was negative at only one hotel where the DOR of the robot rooms was only half that of the traditional rooms, which corresponded to the negative attitude of the manager of this hotel. The fastest time for costs to be returned was only one month, and the second fastest was 1.9 months. The longest time required was 23.5 months. There were five hotels where the return of costs was not attained because the robot rooms in these hotels had the same rates as other rooms. These hotels insisted on maintaining the same rates for all rooms. In conclusion, nine hotels returned the costs of the robots in less than two years.

Regarding the economic impacts of hotel robots, the macro- and micro-level impacts are considered (Akbar & Tracogna, 2018; Williamson, 1991). Based on the findings from the in-depth interviews with the hotel managers, Table 22.3 shows the regional ROI of the hotel robots by dividing the net revenue by the total investment. The macro-level economic impacts of introducing hotel robots shows that ROI ranges from 51.10 percent to 655.14 percent. Najing had the highest ROI for the hotels investigated, whereas Hanzhong had the lowest ROI. Overall, the investigated hotels and their robots created benefits for the regional economy. Transaction frequency (i.e., the number of transactions with hotel robots) is not considered given that all the investigated hotels are in their initial stage of introducing robots. Although the future development direction of hotel roots is positive overall, evidence proving their certain future development is inadequate, reflecting the transaction uncertainty of hotel robots.

Regarding the micro-level economic impact of the investigated hotel robots, Table 22.4 shows the ROI of hotel robots for different hotels. The ROI ranges from 0.00 percent to 823.44 percent. The H Shuijing Hotel Nanjing Mochou Lake, which opened in 2016, has the highest ROI among the 15 hotels investigated. Although the Kunyi Hotel North Gate Subway Station in Xi'an, opened in 2017, has the largest investment (83 hotel robots), its ROI is currently at 0.00 percent, which reflects that ROI needs time to accumulate. To consider asset specificity (Akbar & Tracogna, 2018), robot hotel managers should be clear about the amount of investments provided for hotel robots.

From this point of view, the investment in the deployment of robots in hotels is meaningful. Even if the price of hotel rooms increase, the DOR of the robot rooms will not decrease in general. Hotels can increase the price of robot rooms to recover the cost of robot purchases and implementation. Through proper operation and management, the hotel can recover costs in a short period of time, and then increase their profitability.

SOCIAL IMPACTS OF HOTEL ROBOTS

Impacts on Employees

The researchers attempted to interview all 15 hotel managers; however, only ten participated. The other five declined the interview because they could not meet with the researchers unless

Table 22.2   *Costs and benefits from hotel managers' perspectives*

Hotel	Cost of Implementation of Robot per Room	No. of Robot Rooms	Avg. Robot Room Price	Avg. Room Price	DOR of Robot Room	DOR of the Hotel	Revenue from Robot Room	Revenue from the Ordinary Room	Return of the Cost (in Months)
1	5 000	4	560	480	40%	80%	327 040	560 640	−1.0
2	5 000	3	339	289	95%	99%	352 644.75	313 290.45	4.6
3	5 000	4	200	190	70%	70%	204 400	194 180	23.5
4	5 000	2	264	228	90%	90%	173 448	149 796	5.1
5	5 000	4	600	501.82	90%	90%	788 400	659 391.48	1.9
6	10 000	20	700	550	85%	85%	4 343 500	3 412 750	2.6
7	5 000	83	320	320	85%	85%	8 240 240	8 240 240	n/a
8	5 000	35	500	329.56	94%	94%	6 004 250	3 957 521.26	1.0
9	5 000	2	300	200	70%	70%	153 300	102 200	2.3
10	5 000	12	388	363	90%	90%	1 529 496	1 430 946	7.3
11	5 000	4	230	220	80%	80%	268 640	256 960	20.5
12	5 000	4	383	383	75%	75%	419 385	419 385	n/a
13	5 000	4	700.67	700.67	85%	85%	869 531.47	869 531.47	n/a
14	5 000	2	246.33	246.33	85%	85%	152 847.765	152 847.765	n/a
15	5 000	2	425	425	75%	75%	232 687.5	232 687.5	n/a

Table 22.3   *Regional ROI of hotel robots*

Cities	Net profit (RMB/USD)	Total investment (RMB/USD)	ROI
Hangzhong	10 220/1 454	20 000/2 845	51.10%
Nanjing	1 539 570/219 140	235 000/33 450	655.14%
Shanghai	30 660/4 365	10 000/1 425	306.60%
Suzhou	46 720/6 650	20 000/2 845	233.60%
Xi'an	1 149 494.5/163 615	740 000/105 330	155.34%
Total	2 776 664.5/395 225	1 025 000/145 900	270.89%

Note: ROI = Return on investment.

Table 22.4   *ROI of hotel robots*

Cities	Hotels	Net Profit (RMB/USD)	Total investment (RMB/USD)	ROI
Nanjing	H Shuijing Hotel Nanjing Mochou Lake	1 441 020/205 110	175 000/24 910	823.44%
Xi'an	Mehood Hotel (Gaoxin Road)	131 400/18 700	20 000/2 845	657.00%
Xi'an	Mehood Lestie Hotel Xi'an Drum Tower	930 750/132 480	200 000/28 465	465.38%
Xi'an	H Shuijing Hotel	52 012.5/7 400	15 000/2 135	346.75%
Shanghai	Luxotel Inn Shanghai Hongquiao Airport	30 660/4 365	10 000/1 425	306.60%
Xi'an	H-hotel Xi'an Beidajie Metro Station	23 652/3 365	10 000/1 425	236.52%
Suzhou	Login Serviced Apartments	46 720/6 650	20 000/2 845	233.60%
Nanjing	Mehood Hotel Downtown Nanjing	98 550/14 025	60 000/8 540	164.25%
Xi'an	H Hotel Xi'an Fengcheng 8th Rd	11 680/1 660	20 000/2 845	58.40%
Hanzhong	H Hotel Hanzhong Hanbai Road	10 220/1 455	20 000/2 845	51.10%
Xi'an	Kunyi Hotel North Gate Subway Station	0/0	415 000/59 070	0.00%
Xi'an	Mehood Hotel (Yangguang)	0/0	20 000/2 845	0.00%
Xi'an	Mehood Hotel (East Main Street)	0/0	20 000/2 845	0.00%
Xi'an	H Shuijing Hotel (City Hall)	0/0	10 000/1 425	0.00%
Xi'an	Mehood Hotel (City Hall)	0/0	10 000/1 425	0.00%

Note: ROI = Return on investment.

the company headquarters allowed it. The answers from the ten managers are provided in Table 22.5. Most managers hold negative views on hotel robots. Three managers complained that they had to spend extra time explaining to interested guests how to use the robots, putting robots back in their assigned rooms during housekeeping, and connecting with information technology (IT) staff to fix or upgrade the robots. Some managers thought that hotel staff did not earn extra pay as a result of the extended working hours, and there was resistance to learning how to use robots because their handbooks were difficult to understand. In addition, complaints are expected to increase due to unskilled operations by employees and problems with the robots.

Fewer managers believed that robots benefit employees. One of the managers felt that the robots increased employees' well-being, stating that, "The robot makes our hotel employees really happy! We often talk with the robot and expect more funny words that the robot can say." On the whole, however, managers believed that robots increase working hours and difficulty, but they do not increase wages. Only a few employers believed that robots increased happiness. To more effectively engage employees, appropriate training and extra compensation should be considered.

Table 22.5   Managers' perspectives

Managers	Perspectives
1	Employees did not earn extra pay even though the working hours were extended
2	Extending employees' work time to put the robot back in the corresponding room, explain the use of the robot, and connect with IT staff to fix or upgrade the robot
3	Resistance of employees to learn how to use the robot because of the complexity
4	Complaints from customers because the robot room was limited and the robot often malfunctioned
5	Maintenance and upgrades are often required although there is no associated cost
6	Playfulness
7	Interaction
8	Increasing employees' well-being when employees chat with the robot
9	Positive reviews from customers who love the robot
10	Creating the reputation of a "Smart Hotel"

Moreover, none of the ten hotel managers thought that hotel robots would replace their job because, at present, the roles of hotel robots are relatively singular. This finding opposes the suggestion of Osawa et al. (2017) that human labor will be replaced by robots because of the rise of AI technology.

Impacts on Customers

Acceptance of hotel robots

Regarding the investigation of hotel technology, surveys have often been utilized in previous studies (Kim, 2016; Lam et al., 2007). Using a survey, Lam et al. (2007) identified the influence of perceived IT beliefs, task–technology fit (TTF), attitudes, self-efficacy, and subjective norms on the behavioral intentions of hotel employees in adopting hotel technology. They found that attitudes, self-efficacy, and subjective norms have positive effects on the behavioral intentions of hotel employees in using hotel technology. Hence, the survey method was selected to obtain a large sample of respondents with low associated costs. A pilot test was conducted to assess question wording and to ensure concurrent validity. After a series of adjustments to the question wording and their order, the survey was finalized and used to investigate the perceptions of hotel robots from the perspectives of consumers who had watched a video on the functions of hotel robots. Participants were recruited via China's biggest survey website – Sojump. Specifically, a card with a quick response code containing the questionnaire information was placed on the desk in hotel rooms with a robot. To increase the response rate, the following message was delivered to the hotel guests: "After completing the survey, respondents can choose a voucher (equivalent to US$70) as a reduction when purchasing a hotel robot, or they can have US$7 in cash as their incentive for completing the survey." Responses to the survey questions were mainly provided as a Likert scale, ranging from strongly disagree (1) to strongly agree (5). Detailed statements were related to attitudes, subjective norms, perceived behavioral control, intention of future use, and recommendations of consumers. Participants were asked to rate the level of agreement with each statement. The data was collected from 2018–2019, and a total of 200 valid questionnaires were used for further analysis. Construct validity and reliability were checked and confirmed before continuing.

Table 22.6 shows the socio-demographic profile of the respondents. For gender, 73 respondents (36.5 percent) are male, and 127 respondents (63.5 percent) are female. In terms of age groups, half of the respondents are aged 18 to 25. The remaining half are 26–30 years

Table 22.6   Socio-demographic profile of the respondents

Demographic profile of respondents (n = 200)	Frequency	Percentage
Gender		
Male	73	36.5
Female	127	63.5
Age		
18–25	100	50.0
26–30	29	14.5
31–40	26	13.0
41–50	16	8.0
Over 50	29	14.5
Education level		
High school or below	8	4.0
High school diploma	17	8.5
Associate degree	11	5.5
Bachelor's degree	98	49.0
Graduate degree	66	33.0
Number of trips per year		
1–3	81	40.5
4–6	71	35.5
7–10	16	8.0
More than 10	32	16.0
Experience using hotel robots		
Yes	15	7.5
No	185	92.5

(14.5 percent), 31–40 years (13 percent), and 41–50 years (8 percent). For respondents' education level, 36 participants (18 percent) have an associate's degree or below, and the rest (72 percent) have a bachelor's degree or more. Regarding the number of trips that respondents take per year, they commonly travel between one and three times a year (40.5 percent), or between four and six times a year (35.5 percent). In terms of their prior experience using hotel robots, nearly all of the respondents (92.5 percent, n = 185) do not have any such experience. Only 15 respondents (7.5 percent) have experience using hotel robots.

Table 22.7 describes the acceptance of hotel robots from the perspective of consumers. Regarding the acceptance of a certain technology, three main dimensions (i.e., attitude, subjective norms, perceived behavioral control) should be considered when applying the Theory of Planned Behavior (TPB) (Ajzen, 1991; Ivanov et al., 2018; Lu et al., 2009; Pavlou & Fygenson, 2006). The mean score of each statement under each dimension is provided in Column 3. For attitudes toward hotel robot use, the statement "Hotel robots can largely reduce the cost of human capital" has the highest mean score ($m = 3.81$), whereas "Hotel robots can respond to my different needs" has the lowest mean value ($m = 3.31$). These findings show that consumers perceive that the introduction of hotel robots can reduce human costs. Related to this, Singh and Kasavana (2005) point out that hotel technology can reduce the waiting time of guests. Furthermore, Kuo et al. (2017) identified that curiosity is considered an important factor that can enhance consumer interest in using robot service. Cobanoglu et al. (2011) revealed that hotel technology enhances customer satisfaction by promoting differentiation. However, the findings of the present study show that hotel guests are not confident about the ability of hotel robots to respond to their needs.

Table 22.7   *Acceptance of hotel robots*

Attitudes	Min	Max	Mean	Std Dev
I think the introduction of hotel robots can largely reduce the costs of human capital	1	5	3.81	0.810
I think hotel robots only provide services when I need it	1	5	3.73	0.858
I think room prices will be higher if a hotel robot is provided	1	5	3.54	0.995
I think a hotel robot is good in terms of assuring service quality	1	5	3.47	0.882
Hotel robots can respond to my different needs	1	5	3.31	0.945
Subjective norms				
Using a hotel robot makes me look impressive in the eyes of others	1	5	2.97	1.011
My friends speak highly of hotel robots	1	5	2.95	0.867
Many of my friends have tried hotel robot services	1	5	2.22	0.931
Perceived behavioral control				
I am afraid that my personal information will be disclosed	1	5	3.63	0.968
My concern is that I may break the hotel robot while using it	1	5	3.40	0.963
I am afraid that the information provided by a hotel robot is incorrect	1	5	3.22	0.959
My concern is that I am unable to operate a hotel robot	1	5	2.72	1.017
Intention of future use and recommendation				
I think I will experience a hotel robot in the future	1	5	3.84	0.754
I will recommend hotel robots to my friends and relatives	1	5	3.34	0.862
I have planned to experience the services of a hotel robot	1	5	3.01	0.998
I will choose to stay in a hotel with a robot in the future	1	5	2.75	0.968

In terms of the subjective norms of hotel robots, the mean scores of the statements are relatively low, ranging from 2.22 to 2.97. The reason for this may be that hotel robots have only recently been introduced, and only a few consumers have actually experienced the services of hotel robots. Considering the perceived behavioral control of hotel robots, the concern with personal information disclosure has the highest mean value ($m = 3.63$), whereas concerns about the guest's inability to operate the robot has the lowest mean value ($m = 2.72$). The findings reveal that hotel guests perceive that they are capable of operating hotel robots but are concerned about disclosing personal information. Thus, alleviating the concerns of consumers is of great necessity, as indicated in the findings of Kim et al. (2013). These authors found that luxury hotels are more likely to adopt IT security systems than are hotels at other service levels. Messages such as "Information will be permanently erased after your departure" should be delivered to consumers during their hotel stay.

The acceptance of hotel robots is considered an important part of the newly introduced technology. Intention of future use and recommendation are equally important because future use has a long-standing effect on an organization, as repeat customers are more loyal than first-time users, and the cost of attracting business is lower for the former than the latter. Moreover, repeat visitors can provide considerable revenue to organizations (Liang et al., 2018). The findings of the present study indicate that consumers have an intention to experience hotel robots ($m = 3.84$), but the intention of choosing to stay in a hotel with robots in the future remains low ($m = 2.75$). In short, hotel guests intend to experience a hotel robot, but they do not think the robot can meet their various needs; therefore, the intention of choosing a robot hotel in the future is low.

Table 22.8   Hotel robot room satisfaction

Items	Very dissatisfied	Dissatisfied	Neither	Satisfied	Very satisfied
Robot responses to my demands	2.1%	1.0%	10.3%	24.7%	61.9%
Convenience of robot room	2.1%	0.0%	8.2%	23.7%	66.0%
Interesting experiences of robot room	2.1%	0.0%	8.2%	21.6%	68.0%
Robot room protects my privacy	2.1%	0.0%	16.5%	19.5%	61.9%
Robot room offers more customized services	2.1%	0.0%	7.2%	26.8%	63.9%
Robot can chat with me	2.1%	0.0%	8.2%	25.8%	63.9%
Overall experience in robot room	2.1%	0.0%	7.2%	23.7%	67.0%

Table 22.9   Future intentions with respect to robot rooms

Intentions	Very unlikely	Unlikely	Neutral	Likely	Very likely
Will you check-in to the robot room next time?	2.1%	0.0%	3.1%	31.9%	62.9%
If the price of the robot room increases by 10 percent, will you choose to stay again?	3.1%	1.0%	17.5%	27.8%	50.5%
Will you recommend the robot room to your friends?	2.1%	0.0%	5.1%	29.9%	62.9%

Satisfaction with hotel robots

From January 1, 2017, to December 31, 2017, a survey of 97 customers at 15 hotels in five cities in China was conducted. Women account for 48.5 percent of the sample, and men account for 51.5 percent. Most respondents (85.5 percent) are 18–40 years old.

Hotel robot room satisfaction was measured using seven items on a five-point Likert scale, from very dissatisfied (1) to very satisfied (5). The results demonstrate a high level of guest satisfaction with staying in a robot room (Table 22.8). The overall satisfaction with the experience was high, with 90.7 percent of respondents indicating they were satisfied. Guests were especially satisfied with the interesting experience of staying in a robot room (89.6 percent) and with the robot's customization (90.7 percent). In addition, the robot room is considered convenient (89.7 percent), and guests like to chat with their robot (89.7 percent). The only area of potential concern may be privacy, with 16.5 percent of the participants responding neutrally on that item. Therefore, arranging robots in hotels can create positive experiences for guests. In addition, hotels should explain to guests that robots will not steal or compromise their personal information.

With respect to their future intentions (Table 22.9), the respondents were likely (94.8 percent) to stay in a robot room again. They were also likely (92.8 percent) to recommend robot rooms to their friends. However, there was a more neutral response on the likelihood (78.3 percent) of staying in a robot room if the price was 10 percent higher. The highest-ranked general expectations were for more interesting robot experiences (92.8 percent), more customized services (92.7 percent), and cost-effective choices (92.7 percent).

Common robot commands for hotel guests

The study also used big data analysis to record the use of robot commands for 745 528 effective robot operation instructions at 88 hotels in 23 cities in China in 2017. All data were from the records of the back office of the robot company. After data cleaning, the invalid data were removed and the subsequent analysis was performed. Statistical Product and Service Solutions

(SPSS) software was used to analyze the common commands given by hotel guests, as well as the most common functions for using the robots. A command frequency analysis is shown in Figure 22.1. The most frequent hotel room robot commands were to turn on the lights, turn off the TV, turn off the power, open the curtains, and close the curtains when sleeping.

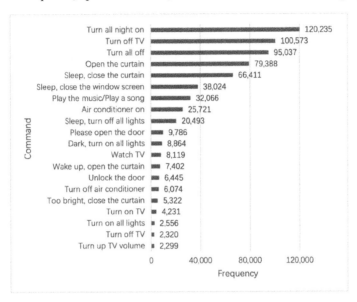

Figure 22.1   Command frequency analysis

Figure 22.2 indicates that the frequency of use of room robots significantly increases the longer a guest has been staying in the hotel. The guest may be intrigued by the robot and is willing to communicate with it, and they are curious to test and verify its functions. Use of the

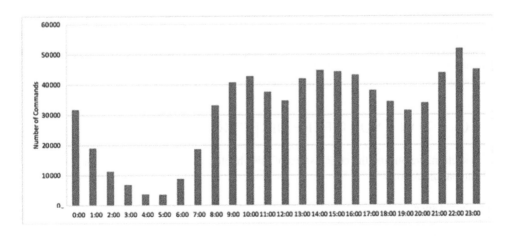

Figure 22.2   Hour-based human–robot interaction

robot is high before just going to sleep and immediately after waking up. The use of the robot attracts the attention of the guest, and at the same time, driven by curiosity, the guest will use the robot consciously or unconsciously. Since the robots attract guests' attention, it is believed that under the same conditions, they will prefer to stay at hotels with robots.

Figure 22.3 shows the top 20 commands with the most repetitions. The top five most repeated commands are "turn on lamp," "open curtains," "turn off lamp," "TV off" and "close curtains." This shows that robots still have big problems in realizing basic functions, and their intelligence needs to be improved. Insensitive robots can cause customers to lose patience and become angry.

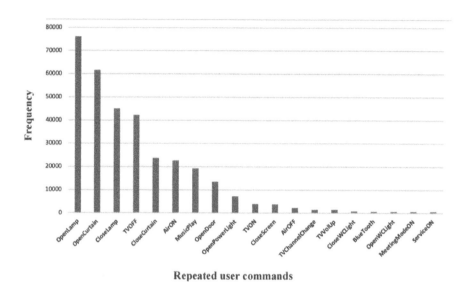

Repeated user commands

Figure 22.3   Top 20 repeated user commands

In total, customers have a high overall satisfaction with hotel robots. They like chatting with robots and think robots are fun, convenient, and joyful. They are willing to stay in robot rooms again and recommend the rooms to their friends, but they are worried about privacy. In addition, the accuracy of the robot's responses needs to be improved.

CONCLUSION AND FUTURE DIRECTIONS

In this section, we outline the conclusions of this chapter and future directions for research on hotel humanoid robots.

Economic Aspect

In terms of the economy, this chapter conducts in-depth interviews and surveys with hotel managers to study the economic benefits of using robots in hotels; the primary measurements are the time (in months) that it takes to return the cost of the robots and ROI. The study found that investments in hotel robots are meaningful. Even if the price to rent the hotel room increases, the DOR of the robot room will not decrease. Hotels can increase the price of robot rooms to recover the cost of robot purchases and implementation. In addition, the hotel robots under investigation have benefited the regional economy.

However, the research on economic impacts in this chapter is relatively simple. In the future, the economic impacts of hotel robots can be studied from a more objective perspective through model construction. For example, the ROI of hotel robots depends on which factors have a greater impact on hotel robot deployment. In addition, due to the COVID-19 pandemic, people's acceptance of emerging technologies, such as contactless services, AI, and robotics, has generally increased. More hotels are beginning to deploy robots, so it is very important to study the economic benefits of this technology from a macro perspective. Whether or not the deployment of hotel robots has a synergistic effect with the regional economy, the economic benefits of the hotel robot industry should also be included in future research.

Social Aspect

This chapter also examines the impacts on employees and customers of deploying robots in hotels. From the perspective of employers, this chapter conducts in-depth interviews with hotel managers and finds that most managers hold a negative view of hotel robots, mainly because the deployment of robots increases the working hours of employees with increasing wages accordingly. Robots can also lead to an increase in customer complaints. However, no manager thinks that robots will replace employees. From a customer perspective, this chapter discusses the results of a survey of hotel customers to study customer acceptance of and satisfaction with hotel robots, and then explores customer behavior in terms of the robot commands they used. The study found that although hotel guests intend to experience hotel robots again, they don't believe that robots can meet their needs, thus, the intention of choosing to stay in a robot hotel in the future is low. However, guests are very satisfied with staying in the robot rooms, especially with the interesting experience and customized services. At the same time, guests are also worried about privacy issues. Considering the robot commands, customers are willing to try robots and also like to chat with robots. However, the accuracy of the robots' responses needs to be improved.

In the future, we should strengthen interdisciplinary research to explore the social impacts of hotel robots on a deeper level, especially the research on human–computer interaction. For example, psychological theories can explain whether customer acceptance of robots with different appearances varies across application scenarios. If so, what is the reason for the difference? How can customers' privacy concerns about hotel robots be alleviated? Do customers with different levels of technology acceptance feel differently about using the robots? What is the reason for this? It is also possible to use a sociological perspective to study changes among hotel owners, employees, customers, and other stakeholders in the process of deploying robots in hotels. For example, we can explore whether there are differences in the acceptance of and satisfaction with hotel robots among customers from different cultural backgrounds and the causes of these differences. In addition, because more customers are staying in robot hotels, future research should also increase the amount of data on this topic and improve its reliability.

Other Aspects

This research mainly discusses the economic and social impacts of deploying humanoid robots in hotels, but there are other effects that need to be considered, such as political and environmental impacts. In terms of political influence, due to the seasonality of the tourism industry, the off-peak season is when many employees are dismissed from their hotel jobs. Will the deployment of robots alleviate seasonal unemployment? Can hotels avoid legal restrictions and other issues by deploying robots? Exploring the environmental impact, with the rapid development of AI, the update speed of hotel robots has accelerated. The service life of hotel robots and the method of their disposal after being eliminated also need to be considered. Green and environmentally sustainable recycling systems for robots should receive more attention in academia and industry in the future.

REFERENCES

Abrate, G., Nicolau, J. L., & Viglia, G. (2019). The impact of dynamic price variability on revenue maximization. *Tourism Management, 74*, 224–233.

Ajzen, I. (1991). The theory of planned behavior. *Organizational Behavior and Human Decision Processes, 50*(2), 179–211.

Akbar, Y. H., & Tracogna, A. (2018). The sharing economy and the future of the hotel industry: Transaction cost theory and platform economics. *International Journal of Hospitality Management, 71*, 91–101.

Belanche, D., Casaló, L. V., & Flavián, C. (2020). Frontline robots in tourism and hospitality: Service enhancement or cost reduction? *Electronic Markets, 31*, 1–16.

Chan, A. P. H., & Tung, V. W. S. (2019). Examining the effects of robotic service on brand experience: The moderating role of hotel segment. *Journal of Travel & Tourism Marketing, 36*(4), 458–468.

Chathoth, P. K. (2007). The impact of information technology on hotel operations, service management and transaction costs: A conceptual framework for full-service hotel firms. *International Journal of Hospitality Management, 26*(2), 395–408.

Cobanoglu, C. (2007). A critical look at restaurant network security: Attacks, prevention tools, and practices. *Journal of Foodservice Business Research, 10*(1), 31–50.

Cobanoglu, C., Berezina, K., Kasavana, M. L., & Erdem, M. (2011). The impact of technology amenities on hotel guest overall satisfaction. *Journal of Quality Assurance in Hospitality & Tourism, 12*(4), 272–288.

Doyle, S. (2007). Self-service delivery and the growing roles of channels. *Journal of Database Marketing & Customer Strategy Management, 14*(2), 150–159.

Fan, A., Wu, L., Miao, L., & Mattila, A. S. (2020). When does technology anthropomorphism help alleviate customer dissatisfaction after a service failure? The moderating role of consumer technology self-efficacy and interdependent self-construal. *Journal of Hospitality Marketing & Management, 29*(3), 269–290.

Fusté-Forné, F., & Jamal, T. (2021). Co-creating new directions for service robots in hospitality and tourism. *Tourism and Hospitality, 2*(1), 43–61.

González-Rodríguez, M. R., Martín-Samper, R. C., Köseoglu, M. A., & Okumus, F. (2019). Hotels' corporate social responsibility practices, organizational culture, firm reputation, and performance. *Journal of Sustainable Tourism, 27*(3), 398–419.

HotelDig. (2018). *Flyzoo Hotel – Alibaba's future hotel*. http://www.hoteldig.com/zh-tw/fly-zoo-hotel/

Huang, M.-H., & Rust, R. T. (2018). Artificial intelligence in service. *Journal of Service Research, 21*(2), 155–172.

Ivanov, S., Webster, C., & Seyyedi, P. (2018). Consumers' attitudes towards the introduction of robots in accommodation establishments. *Turizam: međunarodni znanstveno-stručni časopis, 66*(3), 302–317.

Kim, J. (2016). An extended technology acceptance model in behavioral intention toward hotel tablet apps with moderating effects of gender and age. *International Journal of Contemporary Hospitality Management, 28*(8), 1535–1553.

Kim, J. S., Farrish, J., & Schrier, T. (2013). Hotel information technology security: Do hoteliers understand the risks? *International Journal of Hospitality and Tourism Administration, 14*(3), 282–304.

Kuo, C.-M., Chen, L.-C., & Tseng, C.-Y. (2017). Investigating an innovative service with hospitality robots. *International Journal of Contemporary Hospitality Management, 29*(5), 1305–1321.

Lam, T., Cho, V., & Qu, H. (2007). A study of hotel employee behavioral intentions towards adoption of information technology. *International Journal of Hospitality Management, 26*(1), 49–65.

Lee, H. R., & Šabanović, S. (2014). *Culturally variable preferences for robot design and use in South Korea, Turkey, and the United States* [Paper presentation]. The 2014 9th ACM/IEEE International Conference on Human–Robot Interaction (HRI), Bielefeld.

Liang, L. J., Choi, H. C., & Joppe, M. (2018). Understanding repurchase intention of Airbnb consumers: Perceived authenticity, electronic word-of-mouth, and price sensitivity. *Journal of Travel & Tourism Marketing, 35*(1), 73–89.

Lu, Y., Zhou, T., & Wang, B. (2009). Exploring Chinese users' acceptance of instant messaging using the theory of planned behavior, the technology acceptance model, and the flow theory. *Computers in Human Behavior, 25*(1), 29–39.

Manthiou, A., Klaus, P., Kuppelwieser, V. G., & Reeves, W. (2020). Man vs. machine: Examining the three themes of service robotics in tourism and hospitality. *Electronic Markets, 31*(3), 511–527.

McCartney, G., & McCartney, A. (2020). Rise of the machines: Towards a conceptual service-robot research framework for the hospitality and tourism industry. *International Journal of Contemporary Hospitality Management, 13*(12), 3835–3851.

Morosan, C., & DeFranco, A. (2015). Disclosing personal information via hotel apps: A privacy calculus perspective. *International Journal of Hospitality Management, 47*, 120–130. https://doi.org/10.1016/j.ijhm.2015.03.008

Moullin, J. C., Sabater-Hernández, D., & Benrimoj, S. I. (2016). Qualitative study on the implementation of professional pharmacy services in Australian community pharmacies using framework analysis. *BMC Health Services Research, 16*(1), 439–450.

Murphy, J., Gretzel, U., & Pesonen, J. (2019). Marketing robot services in hospitality and tourism: The role of anthropomorphism. *Journal of Travel & Tourism Marketing, 36*(7), 784–795.

Nourbakhsh, I. R. (2015). The coming robot dystopia. *Foreign Affairs, 94*, 23.

Osawa, H., Ema, A., Hattori, H., Akiya, N., Kanzaki, N., Kubo, A., ... Ichise, R. (2017). *Analysis of robot hotel: Reconstruction of works with robots* [Paper presentation]. The 2017 26th IEEE International Symposium on Robot and Human Interactive Communication (RO-MAN), Lisbon.

Pavlou, P. A., & Fygenson, M. (2006). Understanding and predicting electronic commerce adoption: An extension of the theory of planned behavior. *MIS Quarterly, 30*(1), 115–143.

Pickup, J. C., Holloway, M. F., & Samsi, K. (2015). Real-time continuous glucose monitoring in type 1 diabetes: A qualitative framework analysis of patient narratives. *Diabetes Care, 38*(4), 544–550.

Ritchie, J., & Spencer, L. (1994). Qualitative data analysis for applied policy research. In A. Bryman & R. G. Burgess (Eds.), *Analyzing qualitative data* (pp. 173–194). Routledge.

Rosenthal-Von Der Pütten, A. M., & Krämer, N. C. (2014). How design characteristics of robots determine evaluation and uncanny valley related responses. *Computers in Human Behavior, 36*, 422–439.

Sadatsafavi, H., Niknejad, B., Zadeh, R., & Sadatsafavi, M. (2016). Do cost savings from reductions in nosocomial infections justify additional costs of single-bed rooms in intensive care units? A simulation case study. *Journal of Critical Care, 31*(1), 194–200.

Shead, S. (2019, January 16). World's first robot hotel fires half of its robots. *Forbes.* https://www.forbes.com/sites/samshead/2019/01/16/worlds-first-robot-hotel-fires-half-of-its-robots/#5932c9ee1b1d

Singh, A. J., & Kasavana, M. L. (2005). The impact of information technology on future management of lodging operations: A Delphi study to predict key technological events in 2007 and 2027. *Tourism and Hospitality Research, 6*(1), 24–37.

Tung, V. W. S., & Au, N. (2018). Exploring customer experiences with robotics in hospitality. *International Journal of Contemporary Hospitality Management, 30*(7), 2680–2697.

Tussyadiah, I. (2020). A review of research into automation in tourism: Launching the Annals of Tourism Research Curated Collection on Artificial Intelligence and Robotics in Tourism. *Annals of Tourism Research, 81*, 1–13.

Williamson, O. E. (1991). Comparative economic organization: The analysis of discrete structural alternatives. *Administrative Science Quarterly, 36*(2), 269–296.

Epilogue: Service 4.0
Ravi S. Behara

It is with gratitude for Mark Davis's friendship that I write this epilogue to his book. To quote Shakespeare, "Whereof what's past is prologue; what to come, in yours and my discharge" (*The Tempest*). The past is written, but the future is ours to wield, influenced by the choices we decide to make. I believe that Mark knew this instinctively as he brought all the authors of this book together. By giving an opportunity to all the contributors to this book, Mark has facilitated us to continue to discharge our duty and pursue our passion of service research so that we may attempt to understand and influence the future.

Industry 4.0, or the fourth industrial revolution that is occurring now, is an era defined by advanced technologies that include cyber-physical systems, the Internet of Things, cloud computing, cognitive computing, artificial intelligence, machine learning, robotics, virtual augmented and extended reality, biotechnologies, and other emerging technologies. Disruptions driven by these technologies, in addition to other disruptions including the pandemic and the growing climate crisis, continue to exacerbate social and economic inequity worldwide. The contents of this book reflect our understanding of services in this context.

As we know, industrial revolutions have always been driven by emerging technologies. In the past, the first industrial revolution (Industry 1.0) was driven by mechanization and steam power; the second by mass production, assembly lines, and electrical energy (Industry 2.0); and Industry 3.0 was defined by automation, computers, and electronics in the third industrial revolution. Service has followed a corresponding trajectory during these eras. We can think of service as servitude (Service 1.0), service as a task (Service 2.0), and service as a profession (Service 3.0) as the three service eras that we moved through in parallel with the three industrial revolutions. The formal academic study of services has a relatively short history of about 50 years, which corresponds to the third industrial revolution.

Today we are transforming our world through Industry 4.0. Part of this change is the digitalization of services. More broadly, all sectors of the global economy are undergoing a comprehensive digital transformation driven by emerging technologies. For instance, Hanson Robotics of Hong Kong introduced the world in mid-2021 to Grace, the first humanoid robot nurse being developed to assist physicians and provide elder care. The chapters in this book on service robots help us begin to understand and manage such change, while the chapters on strategy and innovation help us contextualize this new normal in services more broadly. However, we are also reminded in this book that the universality of services requires us to pay equal attention to services in resource-constrained environments. While the development of Grace the humanoid robot nurse is a testament to human ingenuity, there surely is another Grace somewhere on the planet in a situation of social, economic, and environmental disadvantage that demands equal human ingenuity to alleviate her condition. We need to begin recognizing service as a value (Service 4.0). Service as a value is beyond the narrow perspective of economic value added; it is a fundamental recognition of how we can leverage all that advanced technology can afford us, to serve others. Service as a value is to aspire to the highest human calling, that of serving others. It is also about serving those who are yet to come by mitigating the deleterious impacts of climate change and to adapt to those we can't, through innovation. Service as a value is servitude to humanity.

This book reflects Mark's foresight and is simply the opening salvo of service research addressing the emerging challenges and opportunities presented to us by the fourth industrial revolution. Welcome to Service 4.0!

Index

3D printing for medical devices 225
3T/PER framework 144–52
5G 265
5G connectivity 225

AAOL *see* Allergy Associates of La Crosse
    (AAOL)
Aarikka-Stenroos, L. 75
abductive reasoning 109–10
Adams, R. 177
adaptation process 108, 111, 112
ad hoc innovations 72
advertising industry 72–4
    service innovation process stages in 78–83
Agrawal, G. 227
AIC *see* Akaike information criterion (AIC)
airlines and air travel services 125
Akaike information criterion (AIC) 203
Alam, I. 77, 78
Ali, S. 255
Allergy Associates of La Crosse (AAOL) 55–6
    Allergy Choices (AC) 61, 63
    allergy treatment of 56–8
    case analysis
        allergy treatment 56–8
        focused clinic establishment 58–60
        impact of COVID-19 pandemic 63–5
        in-house diagnosis 60
        insurance-related barriers 63
        "La Crosse Method" 56, 58, 61
        mailing diagnosis kits to patients 61
        patient-related barriers 61–2
        physician referral network 61
        physician-related barriers 63
        production of sublingual drops 60
        reduction of customer contact 60
        strategic progression 58–61
        sublingual immunotherapy 56, 58
        telemedicine adoption 61, 63–4
        three benefits of focused service 60
    value proposition 58, 61
Amazon 9, 11, 17, 112
analysis of variance (ANOVA) tests 203, 205–6
analytical maturity, five stages of 268
analytics
    data and 270
    definition of 266
    in healthcare services 271
    and organizational change 268–70

in retail services 270–71
service industry 270–73
technology and 271–2
translators 269
Anderson, B. B. 188
Anderson, J. C. 201
annual recurring revenue (ARR) 167
ANOVA tests *see* analysis of variance (ANOVA)
    tests
Anthropomorphism 313, 317, 322, 331
anxiety-producing urgency 43
Apple 9
applications technology (AT) 174–5
Apte, U. 14
ARR *see* annual recurring revenue (ARR)
artificial intelligence (AI) 20, 104, 108, 113, 217,
    225, 226, 253, 296–7, 301, 302, 306, 332
    in banks 300–305
    cost-effective service excellence (CESE)
        303, 306–7
asset sharing 8, 18
asynchronous 221, 224
AT *see* applications technology (AT)
Atuahene-Gima, K. 72
augmented reality (AR) smart mirror 271
automation 5, 6, 15, 225
automotive sector 19
autonomous vehicles 19
autotelic experience 198
average variance extracted (AVE) 201–2
AWS 26

BA *see* business analytics (BA)
backfire effect of scarcity 42
back-office activities 153, 154, 156–7, 159, 160,
    162–3
    integrating front-office activities with 157–8
    time sensitivity of 160–61
    see also front-office activities
back-office worker 159
Baier, L. 255
Baker, T. 130
Bakhshi, H.
    creative industries definition 73
Base of the Pyramid (BoP) 128, 130, 138
    co-creation of services at 132–3
    role of bricolage in 133–9
Bayesian information criterion (BIC) 203
B2B *see* business-to-business (B2B)

B2C *see* business-to-consumer (B2C)
BDA *see* big data analytics (BDA)
Beacon technology 271
Bear, D. 155
behavioral control 121
behavioral health 222
Bersin, J. 93
Bettinger, K. 214
BIC *see* Bayesian information criterion (BIC)
Biden Administration 227
big data 225, 247–8, 252–4, 265, 275
big data analytics (BDA) 104, 112, 113
biometric tracking 225
blind-spot sensors 148
blood transfusions and religion 190
BoP *see* Base of the Pyramid (BoP)
Bowers, M. R. 75, 78
brand concept of scarcity effects 48–9
bricolage 128, 130–32
    influence on service innovation 138
    role in co-creation of services 133–9
        managerial implications 138
Brodowsky, G. 188
Browning, V. 278
Bumblauskas, D. 252
bundling 9, 11, 15, 16, 18, 20
business analytics (BA), history of 263–6
business model 25–6
    innovation 255
business owners 133–4, 136, 137
business-to-business (B2B) 4, 16–17, 19, 176
business-to-consumer (B2C) 16–17, 19

Cabrera, K. 130
call centers 156
Canon 31
capacity management 50–51
    COVID-19 impact on 214–15
care navigation 222
Caterpillar 24
CFA *see* confirmatory factor analysis (CFA)
Churchill, G. 199
classic service design 154, 159
    v. new service design 162–3
client brief, in innovative advertising 78
cloud computing 225, 253
cloud services 6–8, 16
Cobanoglu, C. 338
co-creation of services 107, 128–9
    at Base of the Pyramid (BoP) 132–3
        role of bricolage in 133–9
co-creative work, for service design
        implementation 98
cognition, in online reviews 278–80, 288, 290
cognitive control 121

cognitive skills, of service robots 302
Colby, C. L. 199
collectivism 187–8
commercial services 125
commoditization 14–16
common method bias 202–3
communal dining 184
companion robots 309, 311
    Amazon rating 320
    companionship 314–15, 317, 322–3
    empirical context 317
    implications and further research 322–3
    interactions with humans 313–14, 317, 322
    interfaces 312–13
    literature overview 311–12, 327–30
    relational framework 317–20
    success or failure of 320
    support for users 315–17, 323
    theoretical development 311–16
    well-being 316, 320, 323
companionship of companion robots 314–15, 317
competition 25, 26
    service design 101
competitive arousal 41, 46
complexity of a service 94
confirmatory factor analysis (CFA) 201
Consistent AIC (CAIC) 203
constant staffing approach 157–8
content-based services 15
contracting 10
control point 146–8, 151
convergence 5–7, 9, 11–13
convergent validity 201
Cool, K. 31
"Corruption Index" of Transparency International
        (2020) 186
cost-effective service excellence (CESE) 303,
        306–7
cost reduction 5
COVID-19 pandemic 47–8, 212
    applying business analytics for 223
    effect on service industry 272–3
    effects from 272–3
    emerging technologies during 223–6
    five stages (5 Rs) 227–8
    global impacts and economic risks 228
    healthcare service design during 65–6
    impact of, AAOL case 63–5
    impact on operations management principles
        capacity and demand management
            214–15
        decision-making 220–21
        inventory and service level 214–15
        safety stock 215–16
        supply chain management 216–19

vaccine 215, 218–20
    waiting line/queuing theory implications
        220
long-term socio-economic impact 227–8
reduction of customer contact in 64
risks and implications 214
role of government and 227
Crane, D. 183
creation phase, service design 91
creative brief development 80
creative industries 71, 73–4
    see also knowledge-intensive business
        services (KIBS)
credit card transaction fraud 304–5
Crew Resource Management (CRM) 180
crowdsourcing 13
Csikszentmihalyi, M. 198
CSM *see* Customer Success Management (CSM)
CSMPs *see* Customer Success Management
        Professionals (CSMPs)
cultural differences 183–4
    in service quality 185
    waiting line 188
Cummings, T. 29
Cunha, M. P. e 129
cupcake ATM 271
Curran, J. M. 194
customer
    acquisition costs 176
    demand 154–6, 158, 161, 162
    encounter errors 145, 147
    engagement models 172, 173
    errors 145, 147
    expectation 49, 290, 291
        and capabilities 176
        of scarcity 47–8
    experience 12, 198, 199
    health scores 169, 176–7
        effective data-driven models for 178
    participation adoption 66
    preparation errors 147
    satisfaction 93, 277–8, 281–2, 285, 288, 290
    segments 172–3
        technology readiness (TR) 195–6, 203,
            205–8
    value 24, 25, 31
customer feedback *see* online reviews
customer-intensive services 51
customer-provider solid relationships 136
customer relationship decisions 170
customer service and technical support (CS/TS)
        roles 170–71
customer success group 172
Customer Success Management (CSM) 166–9,
        172

function, systems view of 174–5
    leaders 173
    metrics 171
Customer Success Management Professionals
        (CSMPs) 166–8
    activities 168–70
        designing for customers 171–3
    challenges 172
    characteristics and competencies 171
    creating account portfolios for 172–3
    customer engagement models and
        segmentation strategies 172, 173
    economic value of 171
    optimal assignment to customers 174
    organizing and managing teams of 172–3
    role comparison
        with customer service and technical
            support 170–71
        with sales and account management 170

daily occupancy rates (DOR), for robot rooms
        34–335, 343
Danneels, E. 28
Darbi, W. P. K. 130
data analytics 248
data-driven organization 269, 270
data-driven services (DDS) 253
data exhaust 270
data science 248, 256
    literature analysis 250–52
        education 254
        health applications 253
        manufacturing 253
        mobility 253
        retail 254
        smart cities 254
    methodology and data 248–9
    as research motivation 252
    research papers 252
    supervised and unsupervised algorithms 255
    tools 255
Davenport, T. 268
Davis, M. M. 272
DDS *see* data-driven services (DDS)
De Bruyn, P. 113
De Keyser, A. 311
decision-making 104, 150
    COVID-19 220–21
decision model 110–13
    for optimal workforce mix 159–60
decision support system (DSS) 108–13
deductive reasoning 109
Defense Production Act (DPA) 227
del Mar Pàmies, M. 188
delivery drones 224

demand-based scarcity 38, 41–9
  see also supply-based scarcity
demand management 50–51
  COVID-19 impact on 214–15
demand–supply relationship 218
demand volume variability 215–16
Deng, H. 249
Dens, N. 277
dental technology 272
descriptive analytics 266, 267
descriptive statistics 200–201
Deshpande, S. D. 198
design-driven innovation labs 97
designed appearance of companion robots 313,
  317, 322
design thinking 89
diagnostic errors 150
Dierickx, I. 31
Differential Emotions Scale (DES II) 277
digital
  dental X-rays 272
  experience 12
  libraries 254
  servitization 253
  therapeutics 222
digital supply networks (DSNs) 218
digitization 5
dining table mix 184
discriminant validity 202
discrimination against Asians, COVID-19 impact
  228
distributive justice 120, 123
DMAIC 234, 239, 241
DOR *see* daily occupancy rates (DOR)
dot-com boom 265
DPA *see* Defense Production Act (DPA)
DSNs *see* digital supply networks (DSNs)
DSS *see* decision support system (DSS)
Duffy, B. 200

early personal computer 265
eCommerce 4, 7, 12, 14, 17
economic exchange 136, 138
ecostructure hierarchy 107
ecostructuring decisions *see* engagement
  decisions
emergent approach 99
emerging technologies during COVID-19 223–6
emotional skills of human 302
emotional support, companion robots 315, 323
emotions, in online reviews 277–8, 280, 282, 288,
  290
employee experience (EX) 93–4
employee satisfaction 93
Empson, L. 71

enduring (long-term) support, companion robots
  315–17, 323
engagement decisions 106–8, 111–13
enterprise communication platform 225
error control 145, 146, 148
Espinoza, M. M. 185
ethics, service design 100–101
e-triage 222
evaluation and learning, in innovative advertising
  82, 84
everything as a service (XaaS) 5, 7–8, 10
EX *see* employee experience (EX)
exclusivity of the service 41–2
exploitation decisions 112
exploration decisions 112
exploration phase, of service design 89–91
explorers 195, 197, 203

Facebook 10, 18
face-to-face surveys 200
facial recognition 224
failsafe device or procedure 144, 145, 147, 148,
  150
failsafing the service 143–4
  3T/PER framework for 144–52
  examples of methods 151–2
Failure Mode Effects Analysis (FMEA) 146
falsity inferences 42–3
familiarity with the service 48
fast and efficient customer service 156–62
FastPass 117–18
FCFS queues *see* first-come-first-served (FCFS)
  queues
fear of missing out (FOMO) 39–40
Ferlin, E. P. 254
financial services 14
first-come-first-served (FCFS) queues 119–21
five-point Likert scale 199, 340
flexibility design problem 156
flow experience 197–9, 207, 208
FMEA *see* Failure Mode Effects Analysis
  (FMEA)
FOMO *see* fear of missing out (FOMO)
Fowkes, J. 221
Friedman, T. 266
front-office activities 153, 154, 158–60, 162–3
  integration with back-office activities 157–8
front-office worker 159
functional brands 48–9
Fusté-Forné, F. 331
fuzzy 111–12

Gadrey, J. 75
Gallouj, F. 75
gamification 12–13

GE *see* General Electric (GE)
GE Capital 29
Geetha, M. 277
gender segregation and service operations 189–90
General Electric (GE) 29–30
generalizability of context 182
Gerbing, D.W. 201
Ghani, J. A. 198
gig economy 13
Gillam, G. 188
global positioning system (GPS) 265
globalization 11, 16
González-Rodríguez, M. R. 332
goodness-of-fit statistics 203
Google 10–12, 18
governmental corruption and national culture 186–8
GPS *see* global positioning system (GPS)
Green, L.V. 155
Gummesson, E. 72

HACCP *see* Hazard Analysis Critical Control Point (HACCP)
Hall, E. 188
Hamby, A. 276
Hampden-Turner, C. 187
Harmon's single-factor test 202
Harris, J. 268
Hart, S. L. 132
Hazard Analysis Critical Control Point (HACCP) 144
healthcare 112
    delivery network 66
    ecosystems 212–13
        three layers of 213
    service 54, 64
healthcare service design, during COVID-19 pandemic 65–6
Helmreich, R. L. 180
Heskett, J. 130
high-tech market 197
higher education 112
Hochstein, B. 166, 171
Hofstede, G. 187
Home Depot 183, 191
hospitality 331–2
    see also hotel humanoid robots
hotel humanoid robots 331–2
    acceptance of customer 337–9, 343
    attitudes 337–8
    benefits 338
    common commands 340–43
    economic impacts of 332–4
        future research 342–3

future research to political and environmental impacts 344
    perceived behavioral control 339
    return on investment (ROI) 332–4, 343
    satisfaction with 340, 342, 343
    social impacts
        on customers 337–42
        on employees 334, 336–7
        future research 343
    subjective norms 337, 339
House, R. J. 187
HRI *see* human–robot interaction (HRI)
Huang, S. 252
human errors 143–4
human–robot collaboration 306
human–robot interaction (HRI) 313
human service employees *v.* service robots 298–9
humanoid robots 296–7, 331
Hussain, A. 242
hybrid human–robot teams 303, 306

IA *see* intelligent automation (IA)
IBM 30
ICT *see* information and communications technologies (ICT)
idea, in innovative advertising
    amplification 81–2
    generation 80, 84
    production 82
    selection 81
    testing 80–81
IDEO, case study 90–91
IIS *see* information intensive service (IIS)
Iliyasu, A. S. 249
impediment cue 149
implementation phase, of service design 89–90
improvisation 131
individual differences of scarcity effects 44–7
individualism 187–8
inductive reasoning 109–10
informal service micro-businesses 128–30
    bricolage in 130–38
    marketing and positioning 135–6
    operations 134–5
    service concept 133
    service delivery 136–8
information collection, in innovative advertising 79–80, 83
information and communications technologies (ICT) 6, 7, 19
information impediments 150
information intensive service (IIS) 2
    characteristics of 4–5
    strategies 4–5
        asset sharing 18

bundling 9
business models, pricing and contracting 10
content-based services 15
crowdsourcing 13
digital experience management 12–13
everything as a service 7–8
gig economy 6–7
globalization and geographic dispersion 11
industrialization 6–7
infrastructure services 15–16
Internet of Things (IoT) 19
markets and exchanges 16–17
open source 13
platform 11–12
service process design 12–13
servitization 7–8
smart services 19
social networks 18
technology expansion 9
transactional services 14–15
vertical de-integration 8–9
structure 5
in-house innovation, for service design implementation 97
innovation
process 74–5, 84
strategy 24–6
insurance 14
intelligence 109
intelligent automation (IA) 304–5
interactional justice 120, 124
inter-cultural/religious issues 181–2
interface standardization 5, 8
Internet of Things (IoT) 7, 19, 20, 225
IoT *see* Internet of Things (IoT)
Islamic fatwa 190
Izard, C.E., Differential Emotions Scale (DES II) 277

Jaakkola, E. 75
Jager, U. 133
Jamal, T. 331
Jehovah's Witnesses 190
Johnson, E. M. 77
Jones, M. 74

Kampker, A. 253
Kaparthi, S. 252
Kar, A. K. 255
Kasavana, M. L. 338
KIBS *see* knowledge-intensive business services (KIBS)
Kim, J. 314, 339

kleptocracy 186
Knott, A.M. 29
know-how 28
knowledge accumulation 27–8
knowledge-intensive business services (KIBS) 71–4, 82–4
Korzaan, M. L. 199
Kowalkowski, C. 26
Kranzbühler, A. M. 311
KUER implementation model and phases 95–6
Kuo, C.-M. 331, 338

"La Crosse Method" 56, 58, 61
lag measures 98
laggards 195, 197, 203
Lam, T. 337
Larson, R. C. 188
latent class cluster analysis 203
lateral expansion 9
lead measures 98
lead time variability 215–16
Lean healthcare 231–2, 243
case study in non-profit hospital in Brazil 237
errors and delays in the delivery of medicines 241
generating and processing prescriptions 237, 240–42
implementation of changes and results achievement 242
manual alterations of prescriptions 241, 242–3
method 234, 237
purchasing and storing supplies 237, 239–40
Scheduled Purchase implementation 240
simplification and standardization of process 242
warehouse tasks 240
Lean quality, COVID-19 216
learning
evaluation and, innovative advertising 82, 84
of service design 100
process 108–12
Lee, H. L. 216
Lee, H. R. 331
Lee, J. 253
Lee, M. 185
Lévi-Strauss, C. 130
Lewin, A. 183
Li, G. 154, 161
limited-quantity scarcity 38–43, 46, 47
limited-time scarcity 37–41, 44
literature review
customer feedback 276–9

resource flexibility 156
    staff planning and scheduling 154–5
London, T. 133
Lovelock, C. 72
low-contact, high-focus healthcare 54, 58, 64–6
    see also Allergy Associates of La Crosse
        (AAOL)
loyal customers 291
Lyft 10

machine learning 252, 253, 255
mainframe computer 264
Maister, D. H. 188
MANCOVA *see* multiple analysis of variance
    (MANCOVA)
market entry 196–7, 208
    and technology readiness (TR) segment
        206–7
marketing test, in innovative advertising 82
markets
    and exchanges 7, 16–17
    segments 278–82, 284, 285, 287, 288, 290
Massey, A. P. 196, 197
Massiah, C. A. 314
McDonald, T. 156
McDonald's 47, 185
McKnight, H. D. 194
measurement model analysis 201–2
medical services and religion 190–91
MEMS *see* Micro-Electro-Mechanical Systems
    (MEMS)
Menor, L. J. 199
Merritt, A. C. 180
Merz, M. A. 194
Metters, R. 180, 184
Micro-Electro-Mechanical Systems (MEMS) 19
Microsoft Office 265
Miko robot 309, 317
Miles, I. 71
mixed workforce 157–8
mobile access and delivery 7
Moderna 218
modularization 5, 8
Moore, G. 264, 265
Morris, D. Dr. 58
Moyle, W. 312
multi-armed bandit problem 112
multiple analysis of variance (MANCOVA) 207,
    208

Nahi, T. 132
Nath, H. 2
national culture 181–2
    and service operations 183–8
        governmental corruption 186–8

journal articles 184–6
    mismatches 183–4
    waiting lines 188
    see also religion
need for cognitive closure (NFCC) 46–7
need for uniqueness (NFU) 44–5
negative emotions 277–8, 280, 282, 288
negative scarcity effects 42
NegativitySentiment 280
Nelson, R. E. 130
net present cost (NPC) 156
networking 131–2
new models and frameworks 254
new service design 7–8
    advantages 163
    application of 162–3
    classic service design *v.* 162–3
    limitations 163
new service development
    model 75, 77–9, 84
    process 74, 83
        limitations and future research 85
        managerial implications 84–5
        stages 78–84
newspaper publishing 15
NFCC *see* need for cognitive closure (NFCC)
NFU *see* need for uniqueness (NFU)
Nicolaou, A. I. 194
non-profit hospital 234
    Lean healthcar *see* Lean healthcar
normalized systems theory (NST) 113
Novak, T. P. 199
Nov, O. 74
NPC *see* net present cost (NPC)
NST *see* normalized systems theory (NST)
numerical ratings, online reviews 275–7, 279–82,
    284–8, 290

off-peak demand 157, 158
offshoring 6
Omicron variant 220–21
onboarding 168–9
online experience 198
online reviews 276
    cognitive themes 278
    customer satisfaction 277–8, 281–2, 285,
        288, 290
    customers' emotional states 277–8, 280, 290
    future research 291
    numerical ratings 275–7, 279–82, 284–8, 290
    replication research design *see* replication
        research design: online reviews
    sentiment polarity 277, 278, 281, 285, 286
    textual properties of 276
    variation across market segments 278–9

online stock trading services 198–9, 206
  intention to use 205, 207, 208
  research methodology 199–207
online survey approach 200
online transactions 14
open sourcing 13
operations research/management science (OR/
  MS) 264–5
operations shifting 7
optimal workforce mix, decision model for
  159–60
option scarcity 38
organisational learning theory 27–8, 31
organizational change 268–70
  analytical competitors 269–70
  analytical maturity, five stages of 268
organizational justice 119
organizational reconstruction 306
OR/MS *see* operations research/management
  science (OR/MS)
Ostrom, A. L. 55
outsourcing 6
overall well-being, companion robots 316, 319
overuse of a service 50–51

Paluch, S. 301
paranoids 195
Parasuraman, A. 199, 203
Park, H. 254
particularism 187
patient–provider demand–supply relationship
  217, 218
patient self-directed care 222
payment for priority access 125
peak demand 157, 158
Peeters, C. 183
perceived appearance of companion robots 313,
  317, 322
perceived control 120–21, 125, 126
perceived justice 119–20, 124–6
perpetual license contracts 166
Perry, C. 77, 78
personal protection equipment (PPE) 216, 217,
  221
personal well-being, companion robots 316
Pfizer 218, 219, 227
Pharmacy Department 240, 242
Philander, K. 277
pioneers 195–7, 203
platforms 11–12
Podsakoff, P. M. 202
popularity of the service 42
positive emotions 277–8, 280, 282, 288
positive scarcity effects 39–40, 42–4, 46
PositivitySentiment 280

post-COVID-19, adopting emerging technologies
  for 226
power of the customer 45–6
PPE *see* personal protection equipment (PPE)
Prahalad, C. K. 132
pre-attentive visual processing 149
pre-computer technology 264
predictive analytics 266, 267
predictive modeling 110
pre-purchase routine 291
prescriptive analytics 266, 267
prevention-focused customers 45
price 10, 16
  perceptions 40–41
  uncertainty 41
principal component analysis 201
priority lines 117–21
  access 124–5
  airlines and air travel services 125
  example 121–4
private sector 19
problem diagnosis, in innovative advertising 80,
  83
procedural justice 119–20, 124
process impediments 149
process re-engineering 6
product
  development 25, 26
  R&D 23, 25, 29, 31, 32
  strategy 26–7
product independent services 29, 30
product innovation 26–7, 31–2, 83–5
  R&D 27–9
  see also service innovation
product/service savvy 197
product service system (PSS) 253
professional service firms (PSFs) 84
Project Airbridge 227
promotion-focused customers 45
PSFs *see* professional service firms (PSFs)
PSGI framework 148, 151
PSS *see* product service system (PSS)
public sector
  services 19
  use of service design 100
public services 125
public transportation 19
Pullman, M. E. 185
Purchasing Department 237, 242

quality improvement strategies 49–50
queuing theory, COVID-19 220

Rabago, R. 174
Rams, D. 88

Rangan, U.S. 174
ratings *see* numerical ratings
R&D 25–6
    investments 27–9, 32
    product innovation 27–9
R&D know-how *see* R&D strength
R&D strength 28, 29, 31–2
real-time decision-making 161–2
Red Lobster 47, 48
reflection phase, of service design 90
regulatory focus of scarcity effects 45
religion 181–2
    and medical services 190–91
    and service operations 189
        gender segregation 189–90
remote diagnostics 271
replication research design
    online reviews 279–80
        cognition and numerical rating across
            market segments 280–85
        emotion and numerical ratings 280
    topic modeling 278, 282–4, 290
research methodology, online stock trading
        services 199–207
resolution errors 144–5, 147
resource
    abundance 129
    availability 131
    flexibility 156
    mobilization 130–31
    scarcity 129, 131, 137, 138
resource-based view of firm 28, 31
resource-constrained environments 129–30,
        136–8
resource-integrating providers 113
retail banking 4, 14
retail location 4
return on investment (ROI) 332–4, 343
Reynoso, J. 130
Rezende, D. A. 254
Richins, M.L. 277
risks and implications of COVID-19 214
Ritz-Carlton 183
robot hotel rooms
    daily occupancy rates (DOR) 334–5, 343
    revenue from 335
ROI *see* return on investment (ROI)
Rolls-Royce 24
Rose, G. M. 188
Rosenbaum, M. S. 314
Roth, A. V. 199
Rosen, D. E. 197

SaaS 16
Šabanović, S. 331

Sadatsafavi, H. 333
safety stock, COVID-19 215–16
scarcity 129, 136
    effects
        boundary factors 44–9
        brand concepts 48–9
        individual differences of 44–7
        other self-related factors 47–8
        science behind the 39–44
    strategies 36
        demand and capacity management
            50–51
        potential challenges 49–51
        quality improvement 49–50
        types of 37–9
Scheduled Purchase system 240
Scheuing, E. E. 77
second-order methods for error control 150–51
self-related factors of scarcity effects 47–8
self-service 7
self-service technologies (SSTs) 298
Sellen, A. 148
sense of urgency 39–40
sentiment analysis 277–80, 285
sentiment polarity 277, 278, 281, 285, 286
service
    defined 104
    delivery 4
    economy 197–8
    ecostructure 105, 112
        components 104
    industrialization 6–7
    inventories 272
    investment 29, 31, 32
    management 252
    platforms 112–13
    process design 12
    quality control 143–4
    transaction 14–15
service delivery system, fast and efficient 156–62
service design 160–62, 250
    application of 93–4
    basic principles and values 91–2
    history of 88–9
    implementation of 94–9
    measuring the impact of 98
    perspectives for 99–101
    phases 89–90
    public sector use of 100
service ecosystem 107
    defined 104
service industry 71–2
    analytics in 270–73
    COVID-19 effect on 272–3
service innovation 72–3, 75, 78, 252

process 83–4
  stages in advertising firms 78–83
service operations
  national culture and 183–8
  religion and 189–91
service organizations, service robots 306–7
service robots 296–7
  cognitive skills 302
  communication skills 302
  deployment model 299–303
  human service employees *v.* 298–9
  lack of emotional skills 302–3
  and organizations 306–7
  potential risks of 307
  routine and repetitive tasks 301–2
  and self-service technologies (SSTs) 296–7
  service tasks 301
service science 247, 256
  literature analysis 250–52
    education 254
    health applications 253
    manufacturing 253
    mobility 253
    retail 254
    smart cities 254
  methodology and data 248–9
  as research motivation 252
  supervised and unsupervised algorithms 255
service support system (SSS) 112–14
servitization 7–8, 10, 19, 24–7, 31–2, 253
  customer value and 25–6
  defined 23, 24
  in manufacturing companies 26
servitized companies 25–7, 32
  case of 29–31
  R&D strength for 29–30, 32
Shingo, S. 148
  Zero Quality Control approach 146
Singh, A. J. 338
Singhal, S. 213
Six Sigma 234
  COVID-19 216
skeptics 195, 203
Smart PSS 253
smart services 19
smart system 108
smartness 108–10
smartphone apps 226
smell cues 149
Snapbot 48
Snap Inc. 48
social networks 18
social norms 118, 125
social status of the service 42
Social VR 225

social well-being, companion robots 316
socio-economic inequalities 228
software vendors 166, 167
solicited feedback 276
SOR *see* stimulus–organism–response (SOR)
    process
Sparks, B.A. 278
SSS *see* service support system (SSS)
SSTs *see* self-service technologies (SSTs)
staff planning and scheduling 154–5
staffing methods 155
Starbucks 39–41, 50
static decision problem 159
Stephens, D. 271
stimulus–organism–response (SOR) process
    311–12, 317, 322, 323
stochastic variability 154–5
strategy planning, in innovative advertising 80
sublingual immunotherapy 56, 58
Subramanian, K. 174
subscription 10
subscription-based contracts 166
subscription-based models 167, 168
Subway 47
success plan for customer 169
Sun, Q. 254
Sundbo, J. 75
supervised learning 255
supplier–customer relationships 177
supplier's product 176
supply-based scarcity 38–9, 41–2, 44–50
supply chain management, COVID-19 216–19
sustainability, service design 101
switching costs 160
symbolic brands 48–9
synchronous 221
system design 113
system function (dynamics) 113
system inputs 176
system outputs 171, 173, 175, 177

Tan, K. H. 253
tangible errors 145, 146
taste cues 149
technical outputs 175, 177
technology 197, 214
  and analytics 271–2
  beliefs 194–6, 198, 208
  expansion 9
  service design 100
  users 198
technology readiness (TR) 194–6
  components 194
  confirmatory factor analysis (CFA) on 201
  correlation analysis 205–6

customer segments 195–6, 203–5, 208
    ANOVA analysis of 203, 205–6
    hypothesis testing 205
    market entry and 206–7
    membership 207, 208
    and usability 205, 208
technology readiness index (TRI) 205, 208
TechVision 226
telecom services 15–16
telemedicine 62, 221–2, 224, 271
    adoption during COVID-19 61, 63–4
    future research 65–6
teleworking 7
text-mining tools 249, 255
text reviews *see* online reviews
theatricalization 12
thematic analysis 249
theory of reasoned action (TRA) 194
thermal imaging 224–5
time impediments 150
time sensitivity index 160–62
time sensitivity of back-office activities 160–61
time-varying staffing levels, limitations of 155
topic modeling, online reviews 278, 279, 282–4, 290
TR *see* technology readiness (TR)
TRA *see* theory of reasoned action (TRA)
trade-off 31
transactional services 14–15
transportation 5, 7
Transportation Security Administration (TSA) 118
tree structures 144–5
TRI *see* technology readiness index (TRI)
Trompenaars, F. 187
Tronvoll, B. 253
True Aggie Night 121–5
Trump Administration 227
trust-based relationships with customers 136
TSA *see* Transportation Security Administration (TSA)
Tsikriktsis, N. 194, 196, 197

Uber 10
Ulaga, W. 26
Ulgado, F. M. 185
uncertainty with COVID-19 220–21
unemployment 228
uniqueness of the service 41
unit scarcity 38

universalism 187
unsolicited online review 276, 278
unsupervised learning 255
user experience (UX) 93, 94, 97, 98

vaccine for COVID-19 215, 218–20
Vaidyanathan, A. 174
value
    capture 26
    co-creation 75, 76, 105–6, 108, 111
    creation 24–7, 131, 198
    proposition 25–6, 32, 58, 61, 105–6
Vector robot 309, 311, 317, 320
Venkatesh, V. 184
versatile workers 154, 158–61
vertical de-integration 8–9
virtual health 221–3
virtual queue 118
visual cues 149
voice tech and smart homes 225
Voss, C. A. 182, 185

waiting lines/times 117–20, 123–5, 188
    COVID-19 220
Walmart 17, 183
Waze 13
web/communication enabling 7
web services 6–8, 10, 16
Whitt, W. 155
Whitter, B. 93
Wirtz, J. 301
Witell, L. 131
Worchel, S. 39
word-of-mouth 136
worker robots 224
workforce mix, decision model for 159–60
World Wide Web 265
Wynne, B. E. 265

XaaS *see* everything as a service (XaaS)
Xerox 30, 31
Xiao, S. 277

Youngdahl, W. E. 184
YouTube 18

Zero Quality Control approach 146
Zheng, P. 253
Zhong, Y. 277
zoomorphism 313, 322

Printed and bound by CPI Group (UK) Ltd, Croydon, CR0 4YY

16/04/2025

14658393-0004